SPEAKING OF AMERICA

Readings in U.S. History

VOLUME TWO

Since 1865

LAURA A. BELMONTE

Oklahoma State University

THOMSON

WADSWORTH

Australia • Canada • Mexico • Singapore • Spain • United Kingdom • United States

D0543971

History Editor: Clark Baxter
Acquisitions Editor: Clark Baxter
Assistant Editor: Julie Yardley
Editorial Assistant: Anne Gittinger
Technology Project Manager: Melinda Newfarmer
Marketing Manager: Caroline Croley
Marketing Assistant: Mary Ho
Advertising Project Manager: Brian Chaffee
Project Manager, Editorial Production: Ryan Heal

Print/Media Buyer: Judy Inouye
Permissions Editor: Joohee Lee
Production Service: Desktop Direct
Copy Editor: Laurel Williams
Cover Designer: Lisa Devenish
Cover Image: *Revival* by Julia Eckel, 1934,
 Smithsonian American Art Museum,
 Washington, DC / Art Resource, NY
Cover Printer:
Compositor: Desktop Direct

COPYRIGHT © 2005 Wadsworth, a division of Thomson
Learning, Inc. Thomson Learning™ is a trademark used
herein under license.

ALL RIGHTS RESERVED. No part of this work covered
by the copyright hereon may be reproduced or used in any
form or by any means—graphic, electronic, or mechanical,
including but not limited to photocopying, recording,
taping, Web distribution, information networks, or
information storage and retrieval systems—without the
written permission of the publisher.

Printed in Canada
1 2 3 4 5 6 7   08 07 06 05 04

Text and Cover Printer: Transcontinental

ISBN: 0-15-506363-4

For more information about our products,
contact us at:
Thomson Learning Academic Resource Center
1-800-423-0563

For permission to use material from this text,
contact us by:
Phone: 1-800-730-2214
Fax: 1-800-730-2215
Web: http://www.thomsonrights.com

Wadsworth—Thomson Learning, Inc.
10 Davis Drive
Belmont, CA 94002-3098
USA

Asia
Thomson Learning
5 Shenton Way #01-01
UIC Building
Singapore 068808

Australia/New Zealand
Thomson Learning
102 Dodds Street
Southbank, Victoria 3006
Australia

Canada
Nelson
1120 Birchmount Road
Toronto, Ontario M1K 5G4
Canada

Europe/Middle East/South Africa
Thomson Learning
High Holborn House
50/51 Bedford Row
London WC1R 4LR
United Kingdom

Latin America
Thomson Learning
Seneca, 53
Colonia Polanco
11560 Mexico D.F.
Mexico

Spain/Portugal
Paraninfo
Calle/Magallanes, 25
28015 Madrid, Spain

Contents

Secondary Source

CHAPTER 25: CONSERVATIVE RESURGENCE 915

Primary Sources

To the Students
Who Inspire Me

In Memory of
Karla Frances Smith
(1976-2003)

PREFACE

When I began *Speaking of America*, I had no idea how deeply it would enrich my appreciation and understanding of the American people. The voices I encountered haunted, moved, and enraged me. In returning to the words of well-known citizens, I was sometimes amazed at how historians have simplified, even distorted, the meanings and contradictions of the original writings. In discovering the perspectives of common people ignored by future generations, I was awed by their extraordinary insights on their communities.

Speaking of America is designed to expose students to a variety of sources on United States history from the colonial era to the present day. The collection includes a wide array of speeches, letters, paintings, artifacts, poems, short stories, photographs, lyrics, book excerpts, articles, and news accounts encompassing multicultural and regional perspectives. The selected readings address important episodes in politics, economics, and foreign policy, as well as social and cultural changes, and come from both famous and "ordinary" Americans.

Speaking of America uses interdisciplinary materials to expose students to the broadest perspective on American history.

- The collection combines primary and secondary sources that can stand alone or supplement a U.S. history textbook.

- Each chapter begins with an introduction providing a historical overview of a specific era.

- Biographical sketches and historical context precede the individual primary sources.

- Each reading incorporates questions prompting students to analyze multiple perspectives, change over time, and the relevance of the past to the present.

- The secondary source readings appear on the accompanying CD bound into the book and keep the book a manageable size. These secondary sources are drawn from cutting-edge writings by today's historians, as well as works that have shaped scholarly thinking for decades.

- Each chapter ends with a list of additional sources available in the web-based *American Journey On-Line* archive. This resource contains hundreds of written texts as well as audio and visual materials.

A NOTE TO THE STUDENT

PRIMARY SOURCES

Speaking of America requires students to examine a variety of historical readings and objects. Primary sources are firsthand accounts of historical events (for example, diaries, oral histories, court testimony, laws, newspapers, public records, memoirs, correspondence, official reports). Some of this evidence comes from individuals who actually witnessed or participated in an event and immediately recorded their impressions—for example, James Madison's copious notes on the Constitutional Convention. Primary sources also include cultural or material artifacts created at a certain time. Photographs, maps, films, songs, poems, furniture, clothing, toys, artwork, or literature are examples. Historians use primary sources to determine what happened in the past and to interpret an event or a person's historical significance.

In order to use primary sources appropriately, one must pay careful attention to details. First, try to focus on the particular time and place in which it was produced. Remember that historical actors are describing their era, not the contemporary world. Second, keep in mind how other people living at the same time might describe an event differently, and how events change over time. By comparing these perspectives and evaluating how the past differs from the present, students can gain a sense of the complexity and progression of history.

Here are some suggestions about issues students should consider when assessing primary source documents.

1. CONTEXT — Read the introduction of each chapter and the individual document carefully. Keep in mind the events, people, and ideas of a particular era.

2. ARGUMENTS — Identify an author's theses, and assess how well he or she develops and supports these claims. At times, I have included parenthetical definitions or modernized spelling and grammar in order to make it easier to understand an author's style.

3. PERSPECTIVE — Ask *who* is writing a specific account. Consider how an individual's background may have affected his or her beliefs. Can you detect a bias? Use the introductory paragraphs for helpful clues about the author's social or political status, race, religion, gender, class, and so on. It is also important to inquire *when* a documented was produced. For example, a soldier writing home from the battlefield might portray his or her experience differently than he or she would in a memoir written forty years later. Evaluate whether an individual may be distorting events in order to serve personal interests or to harm or benefit someone. Assess *why* this person is writing. Is he or she trying to persuade or deceive an audience? What were his or her motivations?

4. AUDIENCE — An author's style will vary greatly depending on his or her intended audience. One will use a different tone in a private letter to a loved one than in a public speech made before Congress. At the same time, keep in mind that a diary, autobiography, or letter may reflect an author's desire to be perceived in a specific way.

5. SIGNIFICANCE — Inquire why a source is *historically important*. Does it reshape our understanding of a particular event or
person? Does it offer a perspective that broadens our knowledge
about a certain time or place?

INTERPRETING VISUAL SOURCES

Artwork, artifacts, and objects are tangible forms of historical evidence. These materials may give voice to people who had an oral culture or
whose written documents may have been damaged or lost. For example,
archeologists at Jamestown have discovered earthworks, wooden foundations, weapons, and armor that are revising historians' understanding of the
settlement and its inhabitants. Consider how touching or wearing a corset
might enrich one's perception of women's lives in the Victorian era.
Comparing the furniture, kitchen utensils, and linens of different homes
enables us to assess the socio-economic background of their residents.
Artists' techniques and subjects can reveal important insights about a
certain era and individuals' perceptions of themselves.

USING *AMERICAN JOURNEY ONLINE*

Purchasing *Speaking of America* grants you access to *American
Journey Online*—an extensive Web database of written documents, audio
recordings, photographic and video images. Undoubtedly, there will be
subjects that *Speaking of America* omits or does not explore in the depth
that you desire. *American Journey Online* may fill such gaps. Each chapter
of *Speaking of America* ends with a thematic list of materials in *American
Journey Online* that are appropriate to the chapter. Simply go to
http://www.ajaccess.wadsworth.com, enter the passcode that came with

your copy of the book, choose the appropriate collection (for example, <u>The African-American Experience</u>), click Contents, choose •<u>Documents</u>, •<u>Images</u>, or •<u>Multimedia</u>, and find the Title of the item you want.

SECONDARY SOURCES

The CD bound with your book includes a longer secondary reading for each chapter. (The publisher put these on a CD to keep the book as brief—and as inexpensive—as possible.) *Secondary sources* are created by someone who did not directly observe an event or who lived in a different period. Occasionally, a secondary source may be used as a primary source. For example, medical books from the late nineteenth century reflect assumptions about gender and race that were echoed in greater society.

Historians who have completed extensive research in primary sources wrote most of the secondary sources in *Speaking of America*. Scholars use secondary sources to support interpretations of the past. Keep in mind, however, that historians can draw different conclusions based on the same materials. Therefore, a secondary source does not offer a definitive truth about an event or person. Like you, academics are products of their social and economic background and can read evidence in remarkably dissimilar ways. At times, their work will demonstrate certain biases or arguments that other scholars—and you—may reject. *Speaking of America* will ask you to make intellectual and moral judgments. Be sure to support your opinions with facts and quotes gleaned from the readings and your professor's lectures and discussions.

ACKNOWLEDGMENTS

It is my great pleasure to thank several people who helped make *Speaking of America* a reality. Susan Oliver spent countless hours scanning materials and tracking down copyright permissions. Marion Umeno, Shelly Lemons, Lisa Guinn, Stefanie Decker, and Jim Klein were gifted teaching assistants who offered wonderful feedback on readings and questions. Charlene Boyer Lewis, Rebecca B. Edwards, Mark Schultz, and Victoria Allison shared insights that immeasurably improved these volumes. During the 2002-2003 academic year, my colleagues at the Center for Humanities at Oregon State University provided encouragement and friendship during the final stages of writing. Clark and Abigail Baxter of Thomson Wadsworth championed and enriched this project in ways I cannot enumerate. At home, Catheryn Mason filled my life with more love and beauty than these pages could contain.

As I was finishing this collection, I learned that Karla Smith, one of my favorite students at Oklahoma State University, died after a long illness. Her spirit, empathy, and intelligence made her an absolute joy to teach. A few weeks before her death, she thanked me for "helping me see how my life is connected to a bigger picture, past, present, and future." I can only hope that the voices you meet in *Speaking of America* inspire you to draw the same conclusion.

RECONSTRUCTION

The end of the Civil War presented the nation with many difficult questions. How would the South be reintegrated into the Union? Would the president or Congress determine Reconstruction policies? What rights would the federal government grant former slaves? Would women also gain new political privileges? For over a decade, such contentious issues consumed national political life.

Even before the war ended, U.S. leaders considered strategies for reuniting the country. President Lincoln proposed the "10 percent plan," allowing southern states to reconstitute their governments after ten percent of their citizens affirmed their loyalty to the United States and renounced slavery. He made no provisions for black suffrage or the social and economic reconstruction of the South. After Lincoln's assassination in April 1865, President Andrew Johnson continued Lincoln's lenient policies. Taking advantage of a long congressional recess, Johnson pardoned many former Confederates and allowed them to create new state legislatures. Some southern states immediately instituted "black codes" greatly restricting the lives of former slaves.

These actions outraged many U.S. congressmen. Determined to reshape southern society dramatically, Radical Republicans passed the Fourteenth Amendment granting freed slaves U.S. citizenship and due process of law. Opposed to these efforts, President Johnson campaigned against his own party in the elections of 1866. Dismayed by Johnson's behavior and reports of southern intransigence, northern voters gave the Radical Republicans sweeping victories.

Emboldened by these events, Congress instituted stronger measures in the South. With the Reconstruction Act of 1867, Congress divided the South into military districts, guaranteed freedmen the right to vote in state elections, and stripped Confederate leaders of their political powers. Republican-dominated governments now ruled the South with coalitions of carpetbaggers (northerners who moved to the postwar South), scalawags (white southerners who cooperated with Reconstruction officials), and blacks. Passage of the Fifteenth Amendment granted black men the right to vote. The decision to limit suffrage to men infuriated women's suffrage activists. After continued clashes with Johnson, Congress impeached the president and almost removed him from office.

Most southern whites bitterly resented Reconstruction. Some resorted to violence through new groups like the Ku Klux Klan. Fraud and intimidation coupled with appeals to white supremacy enabled the Democrats to regain control of several state governments and to begin institutionalizing racial segregation.

For a brief time, African Americans benefited from Reconstruction. Many families ripped apart by slavery reunited. New black churches and schools provided unprecedented opportunities for spiritual and intellectual fulfillment. Over 600 African-American men won political offices. Yet Reconstruction also proved disappointing. Legal and economic barriers forced many freedpeople into sharecropping. Black attempts to exercise their political rights met white resistance. Freedom was only the first step on a long road to racial equality.

By the early 1870s, Reconstruction was faltering badly. Political corruption and economic instability overshadowed efforts to create a biracial democracy in the South. In 1877, after a hotly disputed election, Rutherford B. Hayes withdrew federal troops from the South and abandoned Reconstruction.

12.1

AFRICAN AMERICANS AND THE IMPACT OF FREEDOM

Although they faced obstacles like poverty and illiteracy, most slaves were thrilled at their newfound freedom. Emancipation created a vast migration throughout the South. Former slaves searched for jobs, often in urban areas. Parents looked for children who had been sold. Spouses reunited after forced separations and rushed to legalize their unions. African Americans built scores of businesses, schools, and churches. They zealously pursued economic, educational, and cultural opportunities impossible under slavery.

These readings illustrate many of these changes. The first demonstrates some of the challenges former slaves encountered when trying to rebuild their families. Philip Gray, a freedmen living in Virginia, tracked down his wife Willie Ann and their daughter Maria, both of whom had been sold to a Kentucky planter years earlier. Willie Ann's response is included below. In the other selections, Mingo White and Charles Davenport, two former slaves, recall emancipation and Reconstruction. Both were interviewed as part of the Federal Writers' Project, a New Deal program of the 1930s. Traveling throughout the country, federal officials collected hundreds of testimonies from former slaves. The original spelling, punctuation, and syntax of these documents have been preserved.

FOCUS QUESTIONS

1. How does Willie Ann Grey react to the letter from her husband Philip?
2. What has Philip asked Willie Ann to do? What has changed since she was taken to Kentucky?

3. What seem to be Willie Ann's biggest concerns?
4. What does her letter suggest about the ways that slavery affected families?
5. How did Mingo White and Charles Davenport respond to news of their emancipation?
6. What problems did White and Davenport encounter?
7. What do White and Davenport's experiences reveal about Reconstruction?

Willie Ann Grey

Salvisa, KY
April 7th 1866

Dear Husband
    I seat myself this morning to write you a few lines to let you know that I received your letter the 5 of this month and was very glad to hear from you and to hear that you was well this leaves us all well at present and I hope these lines may find you still in good health. you wish me to come to Virginia I had much rather that you would come after me but if you cannot make it convenient you will have to make some arrangements for me and family I have 3 fatherless little girls my husband went off under Burbridges command and was killed at Richmond Virginia if you can pay my passage through there I will come the first of May I have nothing much to sell as I have had my things all burnt so you know that what I would sell would not bring much you must not think my family to large and get out of heart for if you love me you will love my children and you will have to promise me that you will provide for them all as well if they were your own. I heard that you spoke of coming for Maria [their daughter] but was not coming for me. I know that I have lived with you and loved you then and I love you still every time I hear from you my love grows stronger. I was very low spirited when I heard that you was not coming for me my heart sank within me in an instant you will have to write and give me directions how to come I want when I start to come the quickest way I can come I do not want to be detained on the road if I was the expense would be high and I would rather not have much expense on the road give me directions which is the nearest way so that I will not have any trouble after I start from here Phebe wishes to know what has become of Lawrence she heard that he was married but did not know whether it was so or [not] Maria sends her love to you but seems to be low spirited for fear that you will come her and not for me. John Phebe['s] son says he would like to see his father but does not care about leaving his mother who has taken care of him up to this time he thinks that she needs help and if he loves her he will give her help I will now close by requesting you to write as soon as you receive this so no more at present but remain your true (I hope to be with you soon) wife.

Willie Ann Grey
To Philip Grey

Aunt Lucinda sends her love to you she has lost her Husband & one daughter Betsy she has left 2 little children the rest are all well at present. Phebe's Mary was

sold away from her she heard from her the other day she was well.
Direct your letter to Mrs. Mollie Roche Salvisa Ky

Ira Berlin and Leslie S. Rowland, *Families and Freedom: A Documentary History of African-American Kinship in The Civil War Era* (New York: The New Press, 1997), 173, 176.

Mingo White
Interviewed at Burleson, Alabama
Interviewed by Levi D. Shelby, Jr.
Age when interviewed: 85-90

D e day dat we got news dat we was free, Mr. White called us niggers to the house. He said, "You are all free, just as free as I am. Now go and get yourself somewhere to stick your heads."

Just as soon as he say dat, my mammy hollered out, "Dat's 'nough for a yearlin'." She struck out across de field to Mr. Lee Osborn's to get a place for me and her to stay. He paid us seventy-five cents a day, fifty cents to her and two bits for me. He gave us dinner along with de wages. After de crop was gathered for that year, me and my mammy cut and hauled wood for Mr. Osborn. Us left Mr. Osborn dat fall and went to Mr. John Rawlins. Us made a sharecrop with him. Us'd pick two rows of cotton and he'd pick two rows. Us'd pull two rows of corn and he'd pull two rows of corn. He furnished us with rations and a place to stay. Us'd sell our cotton and open corn and pay Mr. John Rawlins for feedin' us. Den we moved with Mr. Hugh Nelson and made a sharecrop with him. We kept movin' and makin' sharecrops till us saved up 'nough money to rent us a place and make a crop for ourselves.

Us did right well at dis until de Ku Klux got so bad, us had to move back with Mr. Nelson for protection. De mens that took us in was Union men. Dey lived here in the South but dey taken us part in de slave business. De Ku Klux threat to whip Mr. Nelson, 'cause he took up for de niggers. Heap of nights we would hear of de Ku Klux comin' and leave home. Sometimes us was scared not to go and scared to go away from home.

One day I borrowed a gun from Ed Davis to go squirrel huntin'. When I taken de gun back I didn't unload it like I always been doin'. Dat night de Ku Klux called on Ed to whip him. When dey told him to open de door, he heard one of 'em say, "Shoot him time he gets de door open." "Well," he says to 'em, "Wait till I can light de lamp." Den he got de gun what I had left loaded, got down on his knees and stuck it through a log and pulld de trigger. He hit Newt Dobbs in de stomach and kilt him.

He couldn't stay round Burleson any more, so he come to Mr. Nelson and got 'nough money to get to Pine Bluff, Arkansas. The Ku Klux got bad sure 'nough den and went to killin' niggers and white folks, too.

Charles Davenport
Interviewed at Natchez, Mississippi
Interviewed by Edith Wyatt Moore
Age at interview: About 100

L ike all de fool niggers o'dat time I was right smart bit by de freedom bug for awhile. It sounded powerful nice to be told: "You don't have to chop cotton no more. You can throw dat hoe down and go fishin' whensoever de notion strikes you. And you can roam 'round at night and court gals just as late as you please. Ain't no marster gwine to say to you, "Charlie, you's got to be back when de clock strikes nine."

I was fool 'nough to believe all dat kind o' stuff. But to tell de honest truth, most o' us didn't know ourselfs no better off. Freedom meant us could leave where us'd been born and bred, but it meant, too, dat us had to scratch for us ownselfs. Dem what left de old plantation seems so all fired glad to get back dat I made up my mind to stay put. I stayed right with my white folks as long as I could.

My white folks talked plain to me. Dey say real sadlike, "Charlie, you's been a dependence, but now you can go if you is so desirous. But if you wants to stay with us you can sharecrop. Dey's a house for you and wood to keep you warm and a mule to work. We ain't got much cash, but dey's de land and you can count on havin' plenty o'victuals. Do just as you please."

When I looked at my marster and knowed he needed me, I pleased to stay. My marster never forced me to do nary thing about it....

Lord! Lord! I knows about de Kloo Kluxes. I knows a-plenty. Dey was sure 'nough devils a-walkin' de earth a-seekin' what dey could devour. Dey larruped de hide off de uppity niggers an' drove de white trash back where dey belonged.

Us niggers didn't have no secret meetin's. All us had was church meeting in arbors out in de woods. De preachers would exhort us dat us was de chillen o'Israel in de wilderness an' de Lord done sent us in to take dis land o'milk and honey. But how us gwine-a take land what's already been took?

I sure ain't never heard about no plantations bein' divided up, neither. I heard a lot o'yaller niggers spountin' off how dey was gwine-a take over de white folks' land for back wages. Dem bucks just took all dey wages out in talk. 'Cause I ain't never seen no land divided up yet.

In dem days nobody but niggers and "shawlstrap" folks voted. Quality folks didn't have nothin' to do with such truck. If dey hada wanted to de Yankees wouldn'ta let 'em. My old marster didn't vote and if anybody knowed what was what he did. Sense didn't count in dem days. It was powerful ticklish times and I let votin' alone....[O]ne night a bunch o'uppity niggers went to a entertainment in Memorial Hall. Dey dressed deyselfs fit to kill and walked down de aisle and took seats in de very front. But just about time dey got good set down, de curtain dropped and de white folks rose up without a-sayin' a word. Dey marched out de buildin' with dey chins up and left dem niggers a-sittin' in a empty hall.

Dat's de way it happen every time a nigger tried to get too uppity. Dat night after de breakin' up o'dat entertainment, de Kloo Kluxes rode through de land. I heard dey grabbed every nigger what walked down dat aisle, but I ain't heard yet what dey done with 'em.

Federal Writers' Project, Slave Narratives, "A Folk History of Slavery in the United States from Interviews with Former Slaves" (Washington, D.C.: Typewritten Records Prepared by the Federal Writers' Project, 1941).

12.2

ELIZABETH HYDE BOTUME, A NORTHERN TEACHER'S VIEW OF THE FREEDMEN (1863-1865)

Early in the Civil War, Union troops occupied the islands off the coast of South Carolina. Under the "contraband" policy, all property—including land and slaves—was confiscated and placed under the jurisdiction of the U.S. government. Cognizant that soldiers could not care for war refugees and slaves, Secretary of the Treasury Salmon P. Chase authorized charitable organizations to send aide workers and teachers into the occupied territory. In October 1863, the New England Freedmen's Aid Society dispatched Elizabeth Hyde Botume to educate former slaves. She later recounted her experiences in First Days Amongst the Contrabands, *excerpted below.*

FOCUS QUESTIONS

1. How does Botume describe the condition of the freedmen she encounters?
2. Describe white attitudes toward the freedmen.
3. Describe the freedmen's attitudes toward whites and their newfound freedom.

Contrabands were coming into the Union lines, and thence to the town, not only daily, but hourly. They came alone and in families and in gangs, — slaves who had been hiding away, and were only now able to reach safety. Different members of scattered families following after freedom, as surely and safely guided as were the Wise Men by the Star of the East.

On New Year's Day I walked around amongst these people with Major Saxton. We went to their tents and other quarters. One hundred and fifty poor refugees from Georgia had been quartered all day on the wharf. A wretched and most pitiable gang, miserable beyond description. But when we spoke to them, they invariably gave a cheerful answer. Usually to our question, "How do you do?" the response would be, "Thank God, I live!"

Sometimes they would say, "Us ain't no wusser than we been."

These people had been a long time without food, excepting a little hominy and uncooked rice and a few ground-nuts. Many were entirely naked when they started, and all were most scantily clothed and had already had some extremely cold days, which we, who were fresh from the North, found hard to bear.

It was the same old story. These poor creatures were covered only with blankets, or bits of old carpeting, or pieces of bagging, "crocus," fastened with thorns and sharp sticks....

I went first to the negro quarters at the "Battery Plantation," a mile and a half away. A large number of Georgia refugees who had followed Sherman's army were quartered here. Around the old plantation house was a small army of black children, who swarmed like bees around a hive. There were six rooms in the house, occupied by thirty-one persons, big and little. In one room was a man whom I had seen before. He was very light, with straight red hair and a sandy complexion, and I mistook him for an Irishman. He had been to me at one time grieving deeply for the loss of his wife, but he had now consoled himself with a buxom girl as black as ink. His sister, a splendidly developed creature, was with them. He had also four sons. Two were as light as himself, and two were very black. These seven persons occupied this one room. A rough box bedstead, with a layer of moss and a few old rags in it, a hominy pot, two or three earthen plates, and a broken-backed chair, comprised all the furniture of the room. I had previously given one of the women a needle and some thread, and she now sat on the edge of the rough bedstead trying to sew the dress she ought, in decency, to have had on....

The winter of 1864-1865 was a sad time, for so many poor creatures in our district were wretchedly ill, begging for help, and we had so little to give them. Many of the contrabands had pneumonia. Great exposure, with scanty clothing and lack of proper food, rendered them easy victims to the encroachments of any disease. I sent to Beaufort for help. The first doctor who came was exasperatingly indifferent. He might have been a brother of a "bureau officer," who was sent down especially to take care of the contrabands, and who wished all the negroes could be put upon a ship, and floated out to sea and sunk. It would be better for them and for the world. When we expressed our surprise that he could speak so of human beings, he exclaimed, "Human beings! They are only animals, and not half as valuable as cattle."

When a doctor came, I went from room to room and talked with the poor sick people, whose entire dependence was upon us. Finally I could endure his apathy and indifference no longer.

"Leave me medicines, and I will take care of people as I can," I said....

I could not, however, excuse the doctor, a man in government employ, drawing a good salary with no heart in his work. Beaufort was reported to be a depot for officials whom government did not know what to do with....

Early in February we went to Savannah with General and Mrs. Saxton, and members of the general's staff, and other officers. How it had become known that we were to make this trip I cannot tell, but we found a crowd of our own colored people on the boat when we went aboard. To our exclamations of surprise they said with glee—

"Oh, we're goin' too, fur us has frien's there."

We found the city crowded with contrabands who were in a most pitiable condition. Nearly all the negroes who had lived there before the war had gone away. A large number went on with the army; those left were the stragglers who had come in from the "sand hills" and low lands. The people from the plantations too had rushed into the city as soon as they knew the Union troops were in possession.

A crowd of poor whites had also congregated there. All were idle and destitute. The whites regarded the negroes as still a servile race, who must always be inferior by virtue of their black skins. The negroes felt that emancipation had lifted them out of old conditions into new relations with their fellow beings. They were no longer chattels, but independent creatures with rights and privileges like their neighbors....

Nothing in the history of the world has every equaled the magnitude and thrilling importance of the events then transpiring. Here were more than four millions of human beings just born into freedom; one day held in the most abject slavery, the next, "de Lord's free men." Free to come and to go according to the best lights given them. Every movement of their white friends was to them full of significance, and often regarded with distrust. Well might they sometimes exclaim, when groping from darkness into light, "Save me from my friend, and I will look out for my enemy."

Whilst the Union people were asking, "Those negroes! what is to be done with them?" they, in their ignorance and helplessness, were crying out in agony, "What will become of us?" They were literally saying, "I believe, O Lord! help thou mine unbelief."

They were constantly coming to us to ask what peace meant for them? Would it be a peace indeed? Or oppression, hostility, and servile subjugation? This was what they feared, for they knew the temper of the baffled rebels as did no others.

Elizabeth Hyde Botume, *First Days Amongst the Contrabands* (Boston, 1893), 78-79, 82-83, 117-118, 168-169, 176-177.

12.3

THE LOUISIANA BLACK CODE (1865)

Most former Confederates bitterly resented racial integration and the emancipation of the slaves. Accordingly, every Southern state passed "black codes" designed to protect white supremacy and to replicate the slave system. While the laws granted freedmen some civil rights such as marriage and property ownership, the statutes greatly restricted the lives of ex-slaves. To ensure a servile labor force, states barred African Americans from many businesses and trades. Under broadly defined vagrancy laws, unemployed freedmen could be arrested, fined, imprisoned, and bound out as laborers. Some states instituted segregation and most prohibited interracial marriage. Former slaves were forbidden to carry firearms, travel freely, or to testify in court against whites. The black codes and white violence against ex-slaves outraged northerners and prompted more rigorous Reconstruction policies.

FOCUS QUESTIONS

1. What were some of the ways Louisiana restricted the lives of African Americans?
2. What do these laws suggest about the white response to the end of the Civil War?
3. Compare life under the black codes to life under slavery. What did African Americans gain from emancipation?

Sec. 1 *Be it ordained by the police jury of the parish of St. Landry,* That no negro shall be allowed to pass within the limits of said parish without special permit in writing from his employer. Whoever shall violate this provision shall pay a fine of two dollars and fifty cents, or in default thereof shall be forced to work four days on the public road, or suffer corporeal punishment as provided hereafter....

Sec. 3 ...No negro shall be permitted to rent or keep a house within said parish. Any negro violating this provision shall be immediately ejected and compelled to find an employer; and any person who shall rent, or give the use of any house to any negro, in violation of this section, shall pay a fine of five dollars for each offence.

Sec. 4 ...Every negro is required to be in the regular service of some white person, or former owner, who shall be held responsible for the conduct of said negro. But said employer or former owner may permit said negro to hire his own time by special permission in writing, which permission shall not extend over seven days at any one time....

Sec. 5 ...No public meeting or congregations of negroes shall be allowed within said parish after sunset; but such public meetings and congregations may be held between the hours of sunrise and sunset, by the special permission in writing of the captain of patrol, within whose beat such meetings shall take place....

Sec. 6 ...No negro shall be permitted to preach, exhort, or otherwise declaim to congregations of colored people, without a special permission in writing from the president of the police jury....

Sec. 7 ...No negro who is not in the military service shall be allowed to carry fire-arms, or any kind of weapons, within the parish, without the special written permission of his employers, approved and endorsed by the nearest and most convenient chief of patrol....

Sec. 8 ...No negro shall sell, barter, or exchange any articles of merchandise or traffic within said parish without the special written permission of his employer, specifying the article of sale, barter or traffic....

Sec. 9 ...Any negro found drunk within the said parish shall pay a fine of five dollars, or in default thereof work five days on the public road, or suffer corporeal punishment as hereinafter provided.

Sec. 11 ...It shall be the duty of every citizen to act as a police officer for the detection of offences and the apprehension of offenders, who shall be immediately handed over to the proper captain or chief of patrol.

Louisiana Black Code, 1865, Senate Executive Document No.2, 39th Cong., 1st Sess., p. 93.

12.4

AFRICAN AMERICANS SEEK PROTECTION (1865)

Although no longer enslaved, the freedmen faced significant obstacles. With limited education and economic resources, many ex-slaves found themselves at the mercy of their former masters. Cognizant of their precarious position, many African Americans attended conventions held throughout the South in order to discuss possible methods for protecting themselves. In this passage, a group of African Americans in Virginia describe their plight and request assistance from the U.S. Congress.

FOCUS QUESTIONS

1. What are the delegates' major concerns?
2. What protections do they request?
3. Why are the delegates dissatisfied with Andrew Johnson's Reconstruction policies?
4. What does this reading suggest about race relations and Reconstruction policies in the immediate aftermath of the Civil War?

e, the undersigned members of a convention of colored citizens of the State of Virginia, would respectfully represent that, although we have been held as slaves, and denied all recognition as a constituent of your nationality for almost the entire period of the duration of your government, and that by your permission we have been denied either home or country, and deprived of the dearest rights of human nature; yet when you and our immediate oppressors met in deadly conflict upon the field of battle—the one to destroy and the other to save your government and nationality, we, with scarce an exception, in our inmost souls espoused your cause, and watched, and prayed, and waited, and labored for your success....

When the contest waxed long, and the result hung doubtfully, you appealed to us for help, and how well we answered is written in the rosters of the two hundred thousand colored troops now enrolled in your service; and as to our undying devotion to your cause, let the uniform acclamation of escaped prisoners, "Whenever we saw a black face we felt sure of a friend," answer.

Well, the war is over, the rebellion is "put down," and we are declared free! Four-fifths of our enemies are paroled or amnestied, and the other fifth are being pardoned, and the President [Andrew Johnson] has, in his efforts at the reconstruction of the civil government of the States, late in rebellion, left us entirely at the mercy of these subjugated but unconverted rebels, in everything save the privilege of bringing us, our wives and little ones, to the auction block. He has, so far as we can understand the tendency and bearing of his action in the case, remitted us for all our civil rights, to men, a majority of whom regard our devotions to your cause and flag as that which decided the contest against them! This we regard as destructive of all we hold dear, and in the name of God, of justice, of humanity, of good faith, of truth and righteousness, we do most solemnly and earnestly protest. Men and brethren, in the hour of your peril you called upon us, and despite all time-honored interpretation of constitutional obligations, we came at your call and you are saved; and now we beg, we pray, we entreat you not to desert us in this the hour of our peril!

We know these men—know them well—and we assure you that, with the majority of them, loyalty is only "lip deep," and that their professions of loyalty are used as a cover to the cherished design of getting restored to their former relation with the Federal Government, and then, by all sorts of "unfriendly legislation," to render the freedom you have given us more intolerable than the slavery they intended for us.

We warn you in time that our only safety is keeping them under Governors of the military persuasion until you have so amended the Federal Constitution that it will prohibit the States from making any distinction between citizens on account of race or color. In one word, the only salvation for us besides the power of the Government, is in the possession of the ballot. Give us this, and we will protect ourselves. No class of men relatively as numerous as we were ever oppressed when armed with the ballot. But, 'tis said we are ignorant. Admit it. Yet who denies we know a traitor from a loyal man, a gentleman from a rowdy, a friend from an enemy?....

....All we ask is an equal chance with the white traitors varnished and japanned with the oath of amnesty. Can you deny us this and still keep faith with us? "But," say some, "the blacks will be overreached by the superior knowledge and cunning of the whites." Trust us for that. We will never be deceived a second time. "But," they continue, "the planters and landowners will have them in their power, and dictate the way their votes shall be cast." We did not know before that we were to be left to the tender mercies of their landed rebels for employment. Verily, we thought the Freedmen's Bureau was organized and clothed with power to protect us from this very thing, by compelling those for whom we labored to pay us, whether they liked our political opinions or not!....

We are "sheep in the midst of wolves," and nothing but the military arm of the Government prevents us and all the truly loyal white men from being driven from the land of our birth. Do not then, we beseech you, give to one of these "wayward sisters" the rights they abandoned and forfeited when they rebelled until you have secured our rights by the aforementioned amendments to the Constitution.

Let your action in our behalf be thus clear and emphatic, and our respected President, who, we feel confident, desires only to know your will, to act in harmony therewith, will give you his most earnest and cordial cooperation; and the Southern States, through your enlightened and just legislation, will speedily award us our rights. Thus not only will the arms of the rebellion be surrendered, but the ideas also.

"The Late Convention of Colored Men," *The New York Times*, 13 August 1865, 3.

12.5

THADDEUS STEVENS ATTACKS PRESIDENTIAL RECONSTRUCTION (1865)

In the wake of the Civil War, politicians sharply disagreed over the best way to rebuild the nation. Their differences sparked clashes between Congress and Presidents. Where Presidents Abraham Lincoln and Andrew Johnson offered lenient plans designed to readmit the Southern states quickly, a small group of Radical Republicans demanded a more punitive policy. In this speech, Senator Thaddeus Stevens (R-PA), a strong advocate for racial equality, calls for harsh punishment of former Confederates. He later played significant roles in drafting the Fourteenth Amendment and the military reconstruction acts of 1867.

FOCUS QUESTIONS

1. Why does Stevens believe that Congress should control Reconstruction?
2. What proposals does he offer for governing the postwar South? What is his attitude toward the former Confederates?
3. What is his attitude toward the freedmen?
4. How do you think white southerners responded to Stevens's remarks?

December 18, 1865

T he President assumes, what no one doubts, that the late rebel States have lost their constitutional relations to the Union, and are incapable of representation in Congress, except by permission of the Government. It matters but little, with this admission, whether you call them States out of the

Union, and now conquered territories, or assert that because the Constitution forbids them to do what they did do, that they are therefore only dead as to all national and political action, and will remain so until the Government shall breathe into them the breath of life anew and permit them to occupy their former position. In other words, that they are not out of the Union, but are only dead carcasses lying within the Union. In either case, it is very plain that it requires the action of Congress to enable them to form a State government and send representatives to Congress. Nobody, I believe, pretends that with their old constitutions and frames of government they can be permitted to claim their old rights under the Constitution. They have torn their constitutional States into atoms, and built on their foundations fabrics of a totally different character. Dead men cannot raise themselves. Dead States cannot restore their existence *"as it was."* Whose especial duty is it to do it? In whom does the Constitution place the power? Not in the judicial branch of Government, for it only adjudicates and does not prescribe laws. Not in the Executive, for he only executes and cannot make laws. Not in the Commander-in-Chief of the armies, for he can only hold them under military rule until the sovereign legislative power of the conqueror shall give them law....

Congress alone can do it.... Congress must create States and declare when they are entitled to be represented. Then each House must judge whether the members presenting themselves from a recognized State possess the requisite qualifications of age, residence, and citizenship; and whether the election and returns are according to law....

It is obvious from all this that the first duty of Congress is to pass a law declaring the condition of these outside or defunct States, and providing proper civil governments for them. Since the conquest they have been governed by martial law. Military rule is necessarily despotic, and ought not to exist longer than is absolutely necessary. As there are no symptoms that the people of these provinces will be prepared to participate in constitutional government for some years, I know of no arrangement so proper for them as territorial governments. There they can learn the principles of freedom and eat the fruit of foul rebellion. Under such governments, while electing members to the territorial Legislatures, they will necessarily mingle with those to whom Congress shall extend the right of suffrage. In Territories Congress fixes the qualifications of electors; and I know of no better place nor better occasion for the conquered rebels and the conqueror to practice justice to all men, and accustom themselves to make and obey equal laws.

They ought never to be recognized as capable of acting in the Union, or of being counted as valid States, until the Constitution shall have been so amended as to make it what the framers intended; and so as to secure perpetual ascendancy to the party of the Union; and so as to render our republican Government firm and stable forever. The first of those amendments is to change the basis of representation among the States from Federal numbers to actual voters.... With the basis unchanged the 83 Southern members, with the Democrats that will in the best times be elected from the North, will always give a majority in Congress and in the Electoral College.... I need not depict the ruin that would follow....

But this is not all that we ought to do before inveterate rebels are invited to participate in our legislation. We have turned, or are about to turn, loose four million slaves without a hut to shelter them or a cent in their pockets. The infernal laws of slavery have prevented them from acquiring an education, understanding the common laws of contract, or of managing the ordinary business of life. This Congress is bound to provide for them until they can take of themselves. If we do not furnish them with homesteads, and hedge them around with protective laws; if we leave them to the legislation of their late masters, we had better have left them in bondage.

"Reconstruction," *Congressional Globe*, 39th Congress, 1st Session, part 1 (18 December 1865), 72-74.

12.6

PRESIDENT ANDREW JOHNSON
OPPOSES BLACK SUFFRAGE (1867)

Thrust into presidency after the assassination of Abraham Lincoln, Andrew Johnson inherited the contentious question of how to reconstruct the Union. The only southern Senator to remain in Congress following secession, Johnson had long opposed the planter class and slavery. But as a lifelong Democrat, Johnson's political agenda differed greatly from that of the Radical Republicans.

In May 1865, while Congress was in recess, Johnson implemented a lenient Reconstruction policy. Johnson's program included few provisions for protecting the freedmen and enabled many unrepentant former Confederates to regain political power. When Congress reconvened in December 1865, outraged Radical Republicans refused to recognize newly elected southern congressional representatives. In the following months, Congress overrode Johnson's vetoes of the Civil Rights Act and the Supplementary Freedmen's Bureau Act. In March 1867, Congress passed a Reconstruction Act requiring southern states to permit black male suffrage in order to reenter the Union. In many intense debates, Johnson alienated many moderate Republicans and lost control over Reconstruction. In this message to Congress, Johnson explains why he opposes enfranchising African American men.

FOCUS QUESTIONS

1. Why is Johnson opposed to granting southern black men the right to vote?
2. Compare Johnson's racial attitudes to those of Thaddeus Stevens (Document 12.5).
3. If you had been one of the architects of federal Reconstruction policy, what would you have proposed? How would you have punished the South for secession? What provisions would you have made for the former slaves?

I t is manifestly and avowedly the object of these laws to confer upon negroes the privilege of voting and to disfranchise such a number of white citizens as will give the former a clear majority at all elections in the Southern States. This, to the minds of some persons, is so important that a violation of the Constitution is justified as a means of bringing it about. The morality is always false which excuses a wrong because it proposed to accomplish a desirable end. We are not permitted to do evil that good may come. But in this case the end itself is evil, as well as the means. The subjugation of the States to negro domination would be worse than the military despotism under which they are now suffering. It was believed beforehand that the people would endure any amount of military oppression for any length of time rather than degrade themselves by subjection to the negro race. Therefore they have been left without a choice. Negro suffrage was established by act of Congress, and the military officers were commanded to superintend the process of clothing the negro race with the political privileges torn from white men.

The blacks in the South are entitled to be well and humanely governed, and to have the protection of just laws for all their rights of person and property. If it were practicable at this time to give them a Government exclusively their own, under which they might manage their own affairs in their own way, it would become a grave question whether we ought to do so, or whether common humanity would not require us to save them from themselves. But under the circumstances this is only a speculative point. It is not proposed merely that they shall govern themselves, but they shall rule the white race, make and administer State laws, elect Presidents and members of Congress, and shape to a greater or less extent the future destiny of the whole country. Would such a trust and power be safe in such hands?

The peculiar qualities which should characterize any people who are fit to decide upon the management of public affairs for a great state have seldom been combined. It is the glory of white men to know that they have had these qualities in sufficient measure to build upon this continent a great political fabric and preserve its stability for more than ninety years, while in every other part of the world all similar experiments have failed. But if anything can be proved by known facts, if all reasoning upon evidence is not abandoned, it must be acknowledged that in the progress of nations negroes have shown less capacity for government than any other race of people. No independent government of any form has ever been successful in their hands. On the contrary, wherever they have been left to their own devices they have shown a constant tendency to relapse into barbarism. In the Southern States, however, Congress has undertaken to confer upon them the privilege of the ballot. Just released from slavery, it may be doubted whether as a class they know more than their ancestors how to organize and regulate civil society.

Andrew Johnson, "Third Annual Message," December 3, 1867, James D. Richardson, ed. *A Compilation of the Messages and Papers of the Presidents, 1789-1908* (Washington, D.C.: Bureau of National Literature and Art, 1909), Vol. VI, pp. 564-565.

12.7

WHITE PLANTER RESPONDS TO EMANCIPATION (1866)

The Civil War destroyed much of the South. Cities, factories, farms, and railroads lay in ruins. 260,000 Confederate soldiers died. Ratification of the Thirteenth Amendment ended slavery nationwide. These losses devastated the southern economy. Many whites found themselves fighting with former slaves for scarce land and resources. Unwilling to accept such humiliation, southern states passed Black Codes designed to force freed people back onto plantations and deny them basic civil liberties.

Whenever possible, former slaves resisted white subjugation. Eager to demonstrate control over their households, freedmen took their wives out of the fields and placed them at home raising children and keeping house. Black men struggled to preserve their economic independence and avoid white supervision. But, with no redistribution of southern lands, many found it impossible to rent or buy their own property.

At the same time, whites desperately searched for ways to replace slave labor. They persuaded freedmen to sign labor contracts that were often unfair. For blacks looking for alternatives to wage labor under white bosses, sharecropping seemed like a good solution. Sharecropping, however, proved a mixed blessing. Unable to absorb the production costs and living expenses between harvests, sharecroppers of both races were trapped in a vicious cycle of debt and dependency in which all family members spent long hours farming. Overproduction of cotton depleted soil and depressed prices. While wealthier southerners pursued new business opportunities in mining, lumber, and textiles, poor southerners working in agriculture battled bad weather, unstable markets, and ill health.

In this letter, M.C. Fulton, a Georgia planter, offers the Freedmen's Bureau suggestions for improving the southern economy.

FOCUS QUESTIONS

1. How does M.C. Fulton describe the lives of the freedpeople in his community?
2. What do his comments suggest about the former slaves' reactions to emancipation?
3. What does Fulton want the Freedmen's Bureau to do? Do racial and gender stereotypes inform his remarks? If so, provide examples.
4. What do Fulton's suggestions indicate about the economic impact of emancipation? How were the economic needs of whites and blacks interconnected?
5. How does Fulton seem to be responding to emancipation? Do you think his reactions were typical? Explain your answers.

Snow Hill near Thomson Georgia April 17th 1866

Dear Sir—Allow me to call your attention to the fact that most of the Freedwomen who have husbands are not at work—never having made any contract at all—Their husbands are at work, while they are nearly idle as it possible for them to be, pretending to spin—knit or something that really amounts to nothing for their husbands have to buy them clothing I find from my own hands wishing to buy of me—

Now these women have always been used to working out [in the fields] & it would be far better for them to go to work for reasonable wages & their rations—both in regard to health & furtherance of their family wellbeing—Say their husbands get 10 to 12—or 13$ a month and out that feed their wives and from 1 to 3 or 4 children—& clothe the family—It is impossible for one man to do this & maintain his wife in idleness without stealing more or less of their support, whereas if their wives (where they are able) were at work for rations & fair wages—which they can all get; the family could live in some comfort & more happily—besides their labor is a very important percent of the entire labor of the South—& if not made available, must affect to some extent the present crop—Now is a very important time in the crop—& the weather being good & to continue so for the remainder of the year, I think it would be a good thing to put the women to work and all that it is necessary to do this in most cases is an order from you directing the agents to require the women to make [labor] contracts for the balance of the year—I have several that are working well—while others and generally younger ones who have husbands & from 1 to 3 or 4 children are idle—indeed refuse to work & say their husbands must support them. Now & then there is a woman who is not able to work in the field—or who has 3 or 4 children at work & can afford to live on her children[']s labobor [labor]—with that of her husband—Generally however most of them should be in the field—

Could not this matter be referred to your agents They are generally very clever men and would do right I would suggest that you give this matter your favorable consideration & if you can do so to use your influence to make these idle women go to work. You would do them & the country a service besides gaining favor & the good opinion of the people generally—

I beg you will not consider this matter lightly for it is a very great evil & one that the Bureau ought to correct—if they wish the Freedmen & women to do well—I have 4 or 5 good women hands now idle that ought to be at work because their families cannot really be supported honestly without it This should not be so—& you will readily see how important it is to change it at once—I am very respectfully Your obt [obedient] servant

M.C. Fulton

I am very willing to carry my idle women to the Bureau agency & give them such wages as the Agent may think fair—& I will further garanty [guarantee] that they shall be treated kindly & not over worked—I find a general complaint on this subject everywhere I go—and I have seen it myself and experienced its bad effects among my own hands—These idle women are bad examples to those at work & they are often mischief makers—having no employment their brain becomes more or less the Devil's work shop as is always the case with idle people—black or white & quarrels & Musses among the colored people generally can be traced to these idle folks that are neither serving God—Man or their country—

Are they not in some sort vagrants as they are living without employment— and mainly without any visible means of support—and if so are they not amenable to vagrant act—? They certainly should be—I may be in error in this matter but I have no patience with idleness or idlers Such people are generally a nuisance—& ought to be reformed if possible or forced to work for a support—Poor white women...have to work—so should all poor people—or else stealing must be legalized—or tolerated for it is the sister of idleness—

Ira Berlin and Leslie S. Rowland, *Families and Freedom: A Documentary History of African-American Kinship in The Civil War Era* (New York: The New Press, 1997), 185-187.

12.8

HOWELL COBB, A WHITE SOUTHERN PERSPECTIVE ON RECONSTRUCTION (1868)

Congressional Reconstruction policies drastically changed Southern politics and society. Under the supervision of federal troops, existing governments were dismantled and replaced with new governments dominated by Republicans. Coalitions of African Americans, newly-arrived Northerners (carpetbaggers), and Southern whites (scalawags) passed ambitious social reforms and expensive public works programs. Horrified by these changes, many former Confederates attacked Reconstruction as intrusive and corrupt.

Howell Cobb (1815-1868) was one of the best-known opponents of Recon-struction. Born into an elite Georgia family, Cobb studied at the University of Georgia and became a lawyer. After entering politics, Cobb served in the U.S. House of Representatives, became governor of Georgia, and was secretary of the treasury under President James Buchanan. Following Abraham Lincoln's election, Cobb resigned his cabinet post and became a leading secessionist. After chairing the Confederate constitutional convention, he commanded a military regiment. Following the war, Cobb distanced himself from politics but assailed Reconstruction in private letters like the one excerpted here.

FOCUS QUESTIONS

1. Why is Howell Cobb so critical of Reconstruction policies? Which policies does he find most upsetting?

2. How does Cobb describe the postwar South?
3. Describe Cobb's attitudes toward northerners and African Americans. Do you think attitudes like Cobb's were common among white Southerners? Explain your answer.

Macon [GA] 4 Jany., 1868

e of the ill-fated South realize only the mournful present whose lesson teaches us to prepare for a still gloomier future. To participate in a national festival would be a cruel mockery, for which I frankly say to you I have no heart, however much I may honor the occasion and esteem the association with which I would be thrown.

The people of the south, conquered, ruined, impoverished, and oppressed, bear up with patient fortitude under the heavy weight of their burdens. Disarmed and reduced to poverty, they are powerless to protect themselves against wrong and injustice; and can only await with broken spirits that destiny which the future has in store for them. At the bidding of their more powerful conquerors they laid down their arms, abandoned a hopeless struggle, and returned to their quiet homes under the plighted faith of a soldier's honor that they should be protected so long as they observed the obligations imposed upon them of peaceful law-abiding citizens. Despite the bitter charges and accusations brought against our people, I hesitate not to say that since that hour their bearing and conduct have been marked by a dignified and honorable submission which should command the respect of their bitterest enemy and challenge the admiration of the civilized world. Deprived of our property and ruined in our estates by the results of the war, we have accepted the situation and given the pledge of a faith never yet broken to abide it.

Our conquerors seem to think we should accompany our acquiescence with some exhibition of gratitude for the ruin which they have brought upon us. We cannot see it in that light. Since the close of the war they have taken our property of various kinds, sometimes by seizure, and sometime by purchase, and when we asked for remuneration have been informed that the claims of rebels are never recognized by the Government. To this decision necessity compels us to submit; but our conquerors express surprise that we do not see in such ruling the evidence of their kindness and forgiving spirit. They have imposed upon us in our hour of distress and ruin a heavy and burthensome tax, peculiar and limited to our impoverished section. Against such legislation we have ventured to utter an earnest appeal, which to many of their leading spirits indicates a spirit of insubordination which calls for additional burdens. They have deprived us of the protection afforded by our state constitutions and laws, and put life, liberty and property at the disposal of absolute military power. Against this violation of plighted faith and constitutional right we have earnestly and solemnly protested, and our protests have been denounced as insolent, and our restlessness under the wrong and oppression which have followed these acts has been construed into a rebellious spirit, demanding further and more stringent restrictions of civil and constitutional rights. They have arrested the wheels of State government, paralyzed the arm of industry, engendered a spirit of bitter antagonism on the part of our negro population towards the white people with whom it is the interest of both races they should maintain kind and friendly relations, and are now struggling by all the means in their power both legal and illegal, constitutional and unconstitutional, to make our former slaves *our masters*, bringing these Southern states under the power of *negro supremacy.*

To these efforts we have opposed appeals, protests, and every other means of resistance in our power, and shall continue to do so until the bitter end. If the South is to be made a pandemonium and a howling wilderness the responsibility shall not rest upon our heads. Our conquerors regard these efforts on our part to save ourselves and posterity from the terrible results of their policy and conduct as a new rebellion against the constitution of our country, and profess to be amazed that in all this we have failed to see the evidence of their great magnanimity and exceeding generosity. Standing today in the midst of the gloom and suffering which meets the eye in every direction, we can but feel that we are the victims of cruel legislation and the harsh enforcement of unjust laws.... We regarded the close of the war as ending the relationship of enemies and the beginning of a new national brotherhood, and in the light of that conviction felt and spoke of constitutional equality.... We claimed that the result of the war left us a state in the Union, and therefore under the protection of the constitution, rendering in return cheerful obedience to its requirements and bearing in common with the other states of the Union the burdens of government, submitting even as we were compelled to do *to taxation without representation;* but they tell us that a successful war to keep us in the Union left us out of the Union and that the pretension we put up for constitutional protection evidences bad temper on our part and a want of appreciation of the generous spirit which declares that the constitution is not over us for the purposes of protection.... In such reasoning is found a justification of the policy which seeks to put the South under negro supremacy. Better, they say, to hazard the consequences of negro supremacy in the south with its sure and inevitable results upon Northern prosperity than to put faith in the people of the south who though overwhelmed and conquered have ever showed themselves a brave and generous people, true to their plighted faith in peace and in war, in adversity as in prosperity....

With an Executive who manifests a resolute purpose to defend with all his power the constitution of his country from further aggression, and a Judiciary whose unspotted record has never yet been tarnished with a base subserviency to the unholy demands of passion and hatred, let us indulge the hope that the hour of the country's redemption is at hand, and that even in the wronged and ruined South there is a fair prospect for better days and happier hours when our people can unite again in celebrating the national festivals as in the olden time.

Howell Cobb to J.D. Hoover, 4 January 1868, *Annual Report of the American Historical Association for the Year 1911: Vol. 2. The Correspondence of Robert Toombs, Alexander H. Stephens, and Howell Cobb,* ed. U. B. Phillips (Washington, DC, 1913), 690-694.

12.9

EQUAL RIGHTS ASSOCIATION PROCEEDINGS (1869)

The politics of Reconstruction strained long-standing partnerships between abolitionists and women's rights activists. Radical Republicans refused to link black suffrage and women's suffrage. In 1869, Congress passed the Fifteenth Amendment prohibiting the denial of suffrage on the basis of race, color, or previous condition of servitude. It did not, however, extend voting rights to women of any race. The decision ignited heated debates among social reformers and prompted a split in the women's movement that lasted over twenty years. In this reading, members of the American Equal Rights Association, an interracial coalition, try to reconcile African American and women's demands for voting rights.

FOCUS QUESTIONS

1. Compare the arguments of Frederick Douglass and Susan B. Anthony. With whom do you most agree? Explain your answer.
2. How does Lucy Stone attempt to reconcile Douglass and Anthony's points of view?
3. What do these proceedings suggest about 19th century America? Was Reconstruction the appropriate time to enfranchise women as well as black men? Explain your answers.

*M*r. *[Frederick] Douglass:* I must say that I do not see how any one can pretend that there is the same urgency in giving the ballot to woman as to the negro. With us, the matter is a question of life and death, at least, in fifteen States of the Union. When women, because they are women, are hunted down through the cities of New York, and New Orleans, when they are dragged from their houses and hung upon lampposts; when their children are torn from their arms, and their brains dashed out upon the pavement; when they are objects of insult and outrage at every turn; when their children are not allowed to enter schools; then they will have an urgency to obtain the ballot equal to our own. (Great applause.)

A Voice: Is that not all true about black women?

Mr. Douglass: Yes, yes, yes; it is true of the black woman, but not because she is a woman, but because she is black. (Applause.) Julia Ward Howe at the conclusion of her great speech delivered at the convention in Boston last year, said "I am willing that the negro shall get the ballot before me." (Applause.) Woman! Why, she has 10,000 modes of grappling with her difficulties. I believe that all the virtue of the world can take care of all the evil. I believe that all the intelligence can take care of all the ignorance. (Applause.) I am in favor of woman's suffrage in order that we shall have all the virtue and vice confronted. Let me tell you that when there were few houses in which the black man could have put his head, this woolly head of mine found a refuge in the house of Mrs. Elizabeth Cady Stanton, and if I had been blacker than sixteen midnights, without a single star, it would have been the same. (Applause.)

Miss [Susan B.] Anthony: The old anti-slavery school says women must stand back and wait until the negroes shall be recognized. But we say, if you will not give the whole loaf of suffrage to the entire people, give it to the most intelligent first. (Applause.) If intelligence, justice, and morality are to have precedence in the Government, let the question of woman be brought up first and that of the negro last. (Applause.) While I was canvassing the State with petitions and had them filled with names for our cause to the Legislature, a man dared to say to me that the freedom of women was all a theory and not a practical thing. (Applause.) When Mr. Douglass mentioned the black man first and the woman last, if he had noticed he would have seen that it was the men that clapped and not the women. There is not the woman born who desires to eat the bread of dependence, no matter whether it be from the hand of father, husband, or brother; for any one who does so eat her bread places herself in the power of the person from whom she takes it. (Applause.) Mr. Douglass talks about the wrongs of the negro; but with all the outrages that he to-day suffers, he would not exchange his sex and take the place of Elizabeth Cady Stanton. (Laughter and applause.)....

Mrs. Lucy Stone: Mrs. Stanton will, of course, advocate the precedence for her sex, and Mr. Douglass will strive for the first position for his, and both are perhaps right. If it be true that the government derives its authority from the consent of the governed, we are safe in trusting that principle to the uttermost. If one has a right to say that you can not read and therefore can not vote, then it may be said that you are a woman and therefore can not vote. We are lost if we turn away from the middle principle and argue for one class.... Over in New Jersey they have a law which says that *any* father—he might be the most brutal man that ever existed—*any* father, it says, whether he be under age or not, may by his last will and testament dispose of the custody of his child, born or to be born, and that such disposition shall be good against all persons, and that the mother may not recover her child; and that law modified in form exists over every State in the Union except Kansas. Woman has an ocean of wrongs too deep for any plummet, and the negro, too, has a ocean of wrongs that can not be fathomed. There are two great oceans; in one is the black man, and in the other is the woman. But I thank God for that XV Amendment, and hope that it will be adopted in every State. I will be thankful in my soul if *any* body can get out of the terrible pit. But I believe that the safety of the government would be more promoted by the admission of woman as an element of restoration and harmony than the negro. I believe that the influence of woman will save the country before every other power. (Applause.) I see the sighs of the times pointing to this consummation, and I believe that in some parts of the country women will vote for the President of the United States in 1872. (Applause.)....

Elizabeth Cady Stanton, Susan B. Anthony, and Matilda Joslyn Gage, eds. *History of Woman Suffrage* (New York: Fowler & Wells, 1882), 2:382, 391-92, 397, and Proceedings, American Equal Rights Association, New York City, 1869; *Stanton-Anthony Papers*, reel 13, frame 0504.

12.10

Susan B. Anthony on Women's Rights (1873)

Incensed when neither the Fourteenth nor Fifteenth Amendments granted women suffrage, some women's rights activists began challenging state laws barring women from voting. In November 1872, Susan B. Anthony (1820-1906) and thirteen other women persuaded officials in Rochester, New York to allow them to vote in the presidential election. After gaining national attention, the women were arrested for illegal voting, but only Anthony was put on trial. Henry R. Selden, Anthony's attorney, made a strong case for women's suffrage based on the Fourteenth Amendment. But his efforts failed. Without allowing the all-male jury to deliberate, Judge Ward Hunt directed them to find Anthony guilty. In imposing sentence, Hunt ordered Anthony to pay a $100 fine as well as court costs. Their fiery exchange follows. Anthony never paid a cent of her fine. But, in order to prevent her from appealing to the U.S. Supreme Court, Hunt refused to imprison her.

Focus Questions

1. Describe the interchange between Judge Hunt and Susan B. Anthony.
2. What are Anthony's major complaints? Do you find her arguments persuasive? Explain your answer.

udge Hunt: The prisoner will stand up. Has the prisoner anything to say why sentence shall not be pronounced?

Anthony: Yes, your honor. I have many things to say; for in your ordered verdict of guilty, you have trampled underfoot, every vital principle of our government. My natural rights, my civil rights, my political rights, are alike ignored. Robbed of the fundamental privilege of citizenship, I am degraded from the status of a citizen to that of a subject; and not only myself individually, but all of my sex, are, by your honor's verdict, doomed to political subjection under this so-called republican government.

Hunt: The Court can not listen to a rehearsal of arguments the prisoner's counsel has already consumed three hours in presenting.

Anthony: May it please your honor, I am not arguing the question, but simply stating the reasons why sentence can not, in justice, be pronounced against me. Your denial of my citizen's rights to a vote is the denial of my consent as one of the governed, the denial of my representation as one of the taxed, the denial of my right to a trial of my peers as an offender against the law, therefore, the denial of my sacred rights to life, liberty, property, and—

Hunt: The Court can not allow the prisoner to go on.

Anthony: Of all my prosecutors,...not one is my peer, but each and all are my political sovereigns; and had your honor submitted my case to the jury, as was clearly your duty, even then I should have had cause of protest, for not one of those men was my peer; but, native or foreign, white or black, rich or poor, educated or ignorant, awake or asleep, sober or drunk, each and every man of them was political superior; hence, in no sense, my peer.... Jury, judge, counsel, must all be of the superior class.

Hunt: The Court must insist—the prisoner has been tried according to the established forms of law.

Anthony: Yes, your honor, but by forms of law all made by men, interpreted by men, administered by men, in favor of men, and against women; and hence, your honor's ordered verdict of guilty, against a United States citizen for the exercise of "that citizen's right to vote," simply because that citizen was a woman and not a man. But, yesterday, the same man-made forms of law declared it a crime punishable with a $1,000 fine and six months imprisonment, for you, for me, or any of us, to give a cup of cold water, a crust of bread, or a night's shelter to a panting fugitive as he was tracking his way to Canada. And every man or woman in whose veins coursed a drop of human sympathy violated that wicked law, reckless of consequences, and was justified in so doing. As then the slaves who got their freedom [had to] take it over, or under, or through the unjust forms of law, precisely so now must women, to get their right to a voice in this Government, take; and I have taken mine, and mean to take it at every possible opportunity.

Hunt: The Court orders the prisoner to sit down. It will not allow another word.

Anthony: When I was brought before your honor for trial, I hoped for a broad and liberal interpretation of the Constitution and its recent amendments, that should declare all United States citizens under its protecting aegis—that should declare equality of rights the national guarantee to all persons born or naturalized in the United States. But failing to get this justice—failing, even to get a jury of my peers—I ask not leniency at your hands—but rather the full rigors of the law.

Hunt: The Court must insist—The prisoner will stand up. The sentence of the Court is that you pay a fine of one hundred dollars and the costs of the prosecution.

Anthony: May it please your honor, I shall never pay a dollar of your unjust penalty. All the stock in trade I possess is a $10,000 debt, incurred by publishing my paper—*The Revolution*—four years ago, the sole object of which was to educate all women to do precisely as I have done, rebel against your man-made laws, unjust, unconstitutional forms of law, that tax, fine, imprison, and hang women, while they deny them the right of representation in the Government; and I shall work on with might and main to pay every dollar of that honest debt, but not a penny shall go to this unjust claim. And I shall earnestly and persistently continue to urge all women to the practical recognition of the old revolutionary maxim, that "Resistance to tyranny is obedience to God."

Hunt: Madam, the Court will not order you committed until the fine is paid.

U.S. Circuit Court for the Northern District of New York, *United States v. Anthony* (January 1873).

12.11

KU KLUX KLAN DURING RECONSTRUCTION (1872)

Some white southerners used terrorist tactics to thwart Reconstruction. In spring 1866, a group of Confederate veterans organized the Ku Klux Klan, a social club based in Pulaski, Tennessee. The club adopted elaborate costumes and secret rituals. It soon evolved into a protest movement directed at Republicans and African Americans. Determined to preserve white supremacy and impede Reconstruction, Klansmen targeted "uppity" African Americans, Republicans, and people who cooperated with the Reconstruction governments. While Klan activity was limited to certain areas, state officials were unable to control the vigilantes and asked the federal government for assistance. In 1871, Congress investigated Klan activities and passed three Enforcement Acts that successfully suppressed the Klan. In this selection, Edward "Ned" Crosby, an African American, describes Klan actions in Mississippi.

FOCUS QUESTIONS

1. What types of Klan activities does Crosby describe?
2. How did Klansmen attempt to influence elections?
3. Why do you think someone would have joined the Klan during Reconstruction?
4. Do you think that Reconstruction was a success or failure? Support your answer.

Columbus, Mississippi, November 17, 1871

EDWARD CROSBY (colored) sworn and examined.
By the Chairman:

Question. Where do you live?
Answer. Right near Aberdeen—ten miles east of Aberdeen.

Question. State whether you were ever visited by the Ku-Klux; and, if so, under what circumstances.

Answer. I have been visited by them. They came to my house, and came into my house.... It looked like there were thirty-odd of them, and I didn't know but what they might interfere with me, and I just stepped aside, out in the yard to the smokehouse. They came up there and three of them got down and came in the house and called for me, and she told them I had gone over to Mr. Crosby's.... She didn't know but they might want something to do to me and interfere with me and they knocked around a while and off they went.

Question. Was this in the night-time?

Answer. Yes, sir.

Question. Were they disguised?

Answer. Yes, sir.

Question. Had you been attempting to get up a free-school in your neighborhood?

Answer. Yes, sir.

Question. Colored school?

Answer. Yes, sir.

Question. Do you know whether their visit to you had reference to this effort?

Answer. No, sir; I know only this; I had spoken for a school, and I had heard a little chat of that, and I didn't know but what they heard it, and that was the thing they were after.

Question. Were their horses disguised?

Answer. Yes, Sir....

Question. Did you know any of the men?

Answer. No, sir; I didn't get close enough to know them. I could have known them, I expect, if I was close up, but I was afraid to venture.

Question. Did they ever come back?

Answer. No, sir.

Question. What do you know as to the whipping of Green T. Roberts?

Answer. Only from hearsay. He told me himself. They didn't whip him. They took him out and punched him and knocked him about right smart, but didn't whip him.

Question. Was he a colored man?

Answer. He was a white man—a neighbor of mine.

Question. Who took him out?

Answer. The Ku-Klux....

Question. What if anything do you know of any colored men being afraid to vote the republican ticket and voting the democratic ticket at the election this month, in order to save their property, and to save themselves from being outraged?

Answer. Well sir, the day of the election there was, I reckon, thirty or forty; I didn't count them, but between that amount; they spoke of voting the radical [Republican] ticket. It was my intention to go for the purpose. I had went around and saw several colored friends on that business.... I know some of the party would come in and maybe they would prevent us from voting as we wanted to. I called for the republican tickets and they said there was none on the ground. I knocked around amongst them, and I called a fellow named Mr. Dowdell and asked if there would be any there; he said he didn't know; he asked me how I was going vote; I told him my opinion, but I was cramped for fear. They said if we didn't act as they wanted they would drop us at once. There is only a few of us, living amongst them like lost sheep where we can do the best; and they were voting and they stood back and got the colored population and pushed them in front and let them vote first, and told them there was no republican tickets on the ground. I didn't see but three after I voted. Shortly after I voted, Mr. James Wilson came with some, and a portion of the colored people had done voting. I met Mr. Henderson; I was going on to the other box at the Baptist church. He asked if there were any colored voters there; I told him there was thirty or forty, and there was no republican tickets there. Mr. Wilson had some in his pocket, but I didn't see them. I saw that I was beat at my own game, and I had got on my horse and dropped out.

Question. Who told you that unless the colored people voted the democratic ticket it would be worse for them?

Answer. Several in the neighborhood. Mr. Crosby said as long as I voted as he voted I could stay where I was, but he says, "Whenever Ned votes my rights away from me, I cast him down."

Question. Was he a democrat?

Answer. A dead-out democrat.

Question. Did you hear any other white men make the same declaration?

Answer. Not particular; I only heard them talking through each other about the colored population. I heard Mr. Jerome Lamb—he lived nigh Athens—tell a fellow named Aleck that lived on his place, he spoke to him and asked him if he was going to vote as he did; Aleck told him he was—he did this in fear, mind you—and Aleck went and voted, and after he voted he said, "Aleck, come to me;" says he, "Now, Aleck, you have voted?" Aleck says, "Yes sir;" he said, "Well, now, Aleck, you built some very nice houses. Now, I want you to wind your business up right carefully. I am done with you; off of my land."

Question. Had Aleck voted the republican ticket?

Answer. Yes, sir.

Question. Did all the colored men except these three vote the democratic ticket that day?

Answer. Up at Grub Springs all voted the democratic ticket. There was no republican ticket given to the colored people at all.

Question. Did they vote the democratic ticket from fear that they would be thrown out of employment or injured?

Answer. That was their intention. You see pretty nigh every one of them was the same way I was, but there was none there; and them they were all living on white people's land, and were pretty fearful. The Ku-Klux had been ranging around through them, and they were all a little fearful.

Question. Do you think they were all radical in sentiment, and would have been glad to have voted the radical ticket if uninfluenced?

Answer. They would. They had a little distinction up amongst themselves—the white and colored people. One of the said, "Ned, put in a republican ticket."

Well, there was none on the ground and I remarked, "If there is any radical tickets on the ground I will take one of them, and I will not take a democratic ticket, and I will fold them up and drop that in the box, and they will never tell the difference," and it got out that I had voted the radical ticket, and some were very harsh about it.

Question. Would the colored people of your county vote the radical ticket if left alone?

Answer. Well, sir, I suppose they would have done it.

U.S. Congress, *Testimony Taken by the Joint Select Committee to Inquire into the Condition of Affairs in the Late Insurrectionary States* (Washington, DC, 1872), 12: 1133-1134.

SECONDARY SOURCE

■

ANNE SARAH RUBIN, "EVERY 'TRUE-HEARTED' SOUTHERNER: OATHS AND SOUTHERN IDENTITY DURING RECONSTRUCTION"

Nationalism is one of humankind's most powerful forces. Ethnic, religious, cultural, and political factors drive citizens to form—or destroy—nations. But what happens when a people fail to realize their nationalistic ambitions? How do they redirect their loyalties to an externally imposed government? Following their defeat in the Civil War, Confederates faced such questions. In this article, Anne Sarah Rubin, a historian at the University of Maryland-Baltimore County, explores how Confederate men redefined themselves during Reconstruction.

Go to your *Speaking of America* CD-ROM to read "Every 'True-Hearted' Southerner: Oaths and Southern Identity during Reconstruction."

■

FOCUS QUESTIONS

1. How does Rubin use the terms "Southerner" and "Confederate"?
2. Why was taking a loyalty oath so significant for white southerners? What reasons did they provide for taking such oaths?
3. How did southern notions of honor and masculinity shape men's decisions to take loyalty oaths?
4. How did southerners reconcile pledging loyalty to the United States and preserving the memory of the Confederacy?
5. How does Rubin claim that southern identity affected the course of Reconstruction?

AMERICAN JOURNEY ONLINE

—————————■—————————

http://ajaccesss.wadsworth.com [†]

About Legislation and Legal Debates during Reconstruction
— In The Civil War
   Documents
   • Proclamation of Amnesty (1863), Abraham Lincoln
   • Excerpt of the Wade-Davis Bill (1864), U.S. Congress
   • North Carolina Proclamation (1865), Andrew Johnson
   • The 13th Amendment to the Constitution (1865)
   • Speech on Territorialization and Confiscation (1865), Thaddeus Stevens
   • Civil Rights Bill Veto (1866), Andrew Johnson
   • Fourteenth Amendment to the U.S. Constitution (1868), U.S. Congress
— In Civil Rights
   Document
   • Ex Parte Milligan (1866), U.S. Supreme Court
   Image
   • Civil Rights Act (1866)
— In The Constitution and Supreme Court
   Document
   • Congress Debates the Fourteenth Amendment (1866), U.S. Congress

About the Impeachment of Andrew Johnson
— In The Civil War
   Images
   • House of Representatives Impeachment Committee (1868), Matthew Brady
   • Last Speech on Impeachment (1868)
   • Ticket to Admission to Johnson Impeachment Trial (1868)

About the Freedmen's Bureau
— In The African-American Experience
   Document
   • Life on the Sea Islands (1864), Charlotte Forten
   Images
   • Freedmen's Bankbook (circa 1865)
   • Issuing Rations to the Old and Sick (1866), James F. Taylor
   • Industrial School, Richmond, Virginia (1866)
   • The Freedmen's Bureau! (1866)

———————————————

[†] Enter password, choose the Archive indicated above, click on Contents, choose •Documents, •Images, or •Multimedia, and click on the title of the item.

— In The Civil War
Image
- The Freedmen's Bureau (1868), Alfred R. Waud

About the Postwar South
— In The African-American Experience
Documents
- Excerpts from The South (1866), John Trowbridge
- Excerpts from *The South Since the War* (1866), Sidney Andrews
- The Freedmen's Story (1866), William Parker

About White Resistance
— In The African-American Experience
Images
- What Miscegenation Is! (1864)
- Reconstruction of a White Man's Government (1864)
- Negro Expulsion from Railway Car, Philadelphia (circa 1868)
- Chain Gang at Richmond (1868)
— In The Civil War
Documents
- Police Regulations of Saint Landry Parish (1865), Louisiana Legislature
- Address from the Committee on Education (1866), Illinois State Convention of Colored Men
- Excerpt of a Black Protest of Hamburg Riots (1867), Richard Cain
Image
- Verdict: Hang the D____ Yankee and Nigger (1867)
Multimedia
- Lucy Tibbs, Court Testimony Describing Memphis Riots (1866)

About African Americans and Civil Rights
— In Civil Rights
Document
- Appeal to Congress for Impartial Suffrage (1867), Frederick Douglass
— In The African-American Experience
Image
- Ballots (1867)
— In The Civil War
Images
- The First Vote (1867), Alfred R. Waud
- Jury of Black and Whites (1867)
- The African Race in Congress, John Willis Menard (1869)

About Women's Suffrage
— In <u>Women in America</u>
  Documents
  • Petition to the Senate and House of Representatives (1865), Elizabeth
    Cady Stanton and Susan B. Anthony
  • A Law against Women (1865), *New York Independent*
  • A Cry from The Females (1866), *New York Tribune*
  • Public Letter to the Electors of the 8th Congressional District (1866),
    Elizabeth Cady Stanton
  • Letter to *The Standard* (1866), Elizabeth Cady Stanton
  • Women Politicians (1866), *Albany* (NY) *Evening Journal*
  • Speech for Suffrage by Elizabeth Cady Stanton (1868)

THE WEST

During the nineteenth century, the American West changed dramatically. With stunning beauty and impressive natural riches, the region drew thousands of settlers from very diverse backgrounds. These migrants often clashed with the Indians and Mexicans who had long resided there. Environmental degradation and racial violence coexisted with economic development and social change. At the same time, glorified images of the West pervaded American culture.

White migration irreparably changed the lives of American Indians. Greed for land and valuable minerals intensified white demands for tribal lands. Some tribes reluctantly agreed to move to reservations. Others fought white encroachment through bloody confrontations and cultural resistance. Nomadic tribes found these events especially difficult. Accustomed to traveling with vast herds of buffalo upon which they depended for food, clothing, tools, and shelter, Plains Indians clashed with ranchers and farmers who sought to develop and enclose the open range. White destruction of the buffalo was a catastrophe for these tribes.

The federal government repeatedly attempted to resolve the "Indian Problem." Such efforts usually failed through a combination of ethnocentrism, avarice, and incompetence. While U.S. troops and different tribes battled for years, reformers searched for peaceful answers. Many claimed that Christianity and education were the best ways to assimilate Indians into white society. Through boarding schools and breaking up the reservations, they tried to undermine tribal loyalties and to foster individualism. Although the destruction of the reservation system plunged many Indians into poverty and desperation, others adapted to the changes. In both instances, Indians retained their cultural identity and traditions.

Economic development dramatically altered the western landscape. Railroads became the nation's biggest business and hired thousands of immigrants for dangerous construction jobs. Mining, ranching, and farming became lucrative industries. The federal government aided western migration through generous land grants, railroad subsidies, and military efforts against Indians. Aggressive publicity campaigns promised fertile lands and prosperity.

Life in the West was much more difficult than such promotions suggested. Large companies controlled the mining, ranching, and farming sectors and made it difficult for small producers and laborers to succeed. Although mechanical and agricultural innovations triggered great increases in farm production, these machines and materials were far too expensive for most small growers. Unpredictable weather, market fluctuations, insects, drought, and personal isolation presented additional obstacles. Federal land policies often benefited speculators, railroads, and state governments instead of individual pioneers. Not surprisingly, many settlers returned to the East. Those who remained worked collectively to build new communities and eventually western territories applied for statehood.

Like Indians, Mexicans clashed with the whites arriving in the West. While a few Mexicans forged economic partnerships with Anglo emigrants, most found themselves socially segregated and economically marginalized. While trying to preserve their culture, Mexican-Americans struggled against poverty, anti-Catholicism, and racism. At times, tensions with whites erupted into violence.

Cultural images of the West masked its complexities and contradictions. In novels, songs, and paintings, Americans celebrated the region as a land of romance, moral purity, adventure, and opportunity. Heroic images of cowboys and lawmen offered escape from the "soft" world of urbanization and industrialization. The myths of the West, however, ignored the backbreaking physical labor, economic uncertainties, violence, and racial discrimination many of its residents experienced.

13.1

JUAN CORTINA, PROCLAMATION TO TEXANS (1859)

After the Mexican War ended in 1848, Anglos and Mexicans vied for control of the Southwest. While some formed business partnerships and social ties, others fought bitterly over resources and culture. As Anglos seized Mexican-owned lands, violence often erupted. Many Mexican-Americans were forced into low-paying jobs and segregated neighborhoods. They struggled to maintain their culture and dignity.

Juan Cortina (1824-1892) was one of the most militant opponents of Anglo racism. Born into a wealthy Mexican ranching family, Cortina moved to an area claimed by both Texas and Mexico. By the late 1850s, even after losing land to the United States, Cortina was a successful rancher with important connections in the South Texas Democratic Party. Nonetheless, he detested white legal authorities that exploited Tejanos (Mexican residents of Texas).

On July 13, 1859, in Brownsville, Cortina witnessed an Anglo city marshal pistol-whipping a Mexican formerly employed by the Cortina family. In the ensuing confrontation, Cortina shot the marshal and rode off with the prisoner. Two months later, Cortina led a raid on Brownsville. Cortina and his followers killed four Anglos who had murdered Mexicans but had not faced criminal prosecution. They also stormed the jail and released Mexicans imprisoned unjustly. They did not, however, loot or destroy the city. After raising the Mexican flag, Cortina retreated to a nearby ranch and issued the proclamation excerpted below.

Following the Brownsville raid, rumors of Cortina's exploits spread throughout Texas. He and approximately 500 men conducted successful raids throughout the Rio Grande Valley. Many Tejanos supported Cortina and helped supply his army. After several battles with Texas Rangers and U.S. Army troops, Cortina disbanded his forces and moved to Mexico. He became a general in the Mexican Army and later served as acting governor of Tamaupilas. In 1876, Mexican dictator Porfirio Diaz incarcerated Cortina until 1890. He died in Tamaupilas two years later.

———————————■———————————

FOCUS QUESTIONS

1. How does Cortina describe Anglo-Mexicans relations in Brownsville?
2. How does he justify the Brownsville raid?
3. Was Juan Cortina a hero? Explain your answer.

P ROCLAMATION

Juan Nepomuceno Cortina to the inhabitants of the State of Texas, and especially to those of the city of Brownsville.

An event of grave importance, in which it has fallen to my lot to figure as the principal actor since the morning of the 28th instant; doubtless keeps you in suspense with regard to the progress of its consequences. There is no need of fear. Orderly people and honest citizens are inviolable to us in their persons and interests. Our object, as you have seen, has been to chastise the villainy of our enemies, which heretofore has gone unpunished. These have connived with each other, and form, so to speak, a perfidious inquisitorial lodge to persecute and rob us, without any cause, and for no other crime on our part than that of being of Mexican origin, considering us, doubtless, destitute of those gifts which they themselves do not possess.

To defend ourselves, and making use of the sacred right of self-preservation, we have assembled in a popular meeting with a view of discussing a means by which to put an end to our misfortunes.

Our identity of origin, our relationship, and the community of our sufferings, has been, as it appears, the cause of our embracing, directly, the proposed object which led us to enter your beautiful city, clothed with the imposing aspect of our exasperation.

The assembly organized, and headed by your humble servant, (thanks to the confidence which he inspired as one of the most aggrieved,) we have careered over the streets of the city in search of our adversaries, inasmuch as justice, being administered by their own hands, the supremacy of the law has failed to accomplish its object.

Some of them, rashly remiss in complying with our demand, have perished for having sought to carry their animosity beyond the limits allowed by their precarious position. Three of them have died—all criminal, wicked men, notorious among the people for their misdeeds. The others, still more unworthy and wretched, dragged themselves through the mire to escape our anger, and now, perhaps, with their usual bravado, pretend to be the cause of an infinity of evils, which might have been avoided but for their cowardice.

They concealed themselves, and we were loath to attack them within the dwellings of others, fearing that their cause might be confounded with that of respectable persons, as at last, to our sorrow, did happen. On the other hand, it behooves us to maintain that it was unjust to give the affair such a terrible aspect, and to represent it as of a character foreboding evil; some having carried their blindness so far as to implore the aid of Mexico, alleging as a reason that their persons and property were exposed to vandalism. Were any outrages committed by us during the time we had possession of the city, when we had it in our power to become the arbiters of its fate? Will our enemies be so blind, base, or unthinking, as to deny the evidence of facts? Will there be one to say the he was molested, or that his house was robbed or burned down?...

Innocent persons shall not suffer—no. But, if necessary, we will lead a wandering life, awaiting our opportunity to purge society of men so base that they degrade it with their opprobrium. Our families have returned as strangers to their old country to beg for an asylum. Our lands, if they are to be sacrificed to the avaricious covetousness of our enemies, will be rather so on account of our own vicissitudes. As to land, Nature will always grant us sufficient to support our frames, and we accept the consequences that may arise. Further, our personal enemies shall not possess our lands until they have fattened it with their own gore....

JUAN NEPOMUCENO CORTINA
Rancho Del Carmen,
County of Cameron, September 30, 1859

U.S. Congress, House, *Difficulties on the Southwestern Frontier*, 36th Congress; 1st Session, 1860, H. Exec. Doc. 52, pp. 70-82.

13.2

REPORT OF THE COMMISSION ON INDIAN AFFAIRS (1869)

In the 1860s, the federal government intensified its efforts to concentrate Indians on small reservations. In exchange for abandoning their nomadic lifestyle, tribes received promises of support. Local militia and federal agents controlled the reservations. Some tribes, such as the Crow and Pueblo, accepted reservation life. Many of the 100,000 Plains Indians, however, did not. Facing dwindling food supplies and enraged by fraudulent treaties, several tribes began attacking white settlers and fighting the U.S. Army.

Both sides committed horrible atrocities in these confrontations. In 1864, a militia led by Colonel John M. Chivington attacked Cheyenne and Arapahos camped at Sand Creek, Colorado. Ignoring the Indians' attempts to surrender, Chivington's men slaughtered 200 men, women, and children. "Kill and scalp all," Chivington screamed, "nits make lice." Two years later, Teton Sioux, attempting to stop construction of the Bozeman Trail linking Wyoming and the gold fields of Montana, set a trap for U.S. troops. Hours later, eighty cavalrymen lay dead beside the Powder River.

Such shocking carnage compelled the federal government to reassess its Indian policies. In 1869, in response to pleas from evangelical reformers, Ulysses S. Grant established the Board of Indian Commissioners. This reading is drawn from the commissioners' first report to the president.

FOCUS QUESTIONS

1. How do the commissioners characterize federal policies toward the Indians?
2. Whom do the commissioners hold responsible for the hardships facing many Indians?
3. What solutions do they propose? What is your opinion of these recommendations?

 hile it cannot be denied that the government of the United States, in the general terms and temper of its legislation, has evinced a desire to deal generously with the Indians, it must be admitted that the actual treatment they have received has been unjust and iniquitous beyond the power of words to express.

Taught by the government that they had rights entitled to respect; when those rights have been assailed by the rapacity of the white man, the arm which should have been raised to protect them has been ever ready to sustain the aggressor.

The history of the government connections with the Indians is a shameful record of broken treaties and unfulfilled promises.

The history of the border white man's connections with the Indians is a sickening record of murder, outrage, robbery, and wrongs committed by the former as the rule, and occasional savage outbreaks and unspeakably barbarous deeds of retaliation by the latter as the exception....

The testimony of some of the highest military officers of the United States is on record to the effect that in our Indian wars, almost without exception, the first aggressions have been made by the white man, and the assertion is supported by every civilian of reputation who has studied the subject. In addition to the class of robbers and outlaws who find impunity in their nefarious pursuits upon the frontiers, there is a large class of professedly reputable men who use every means in their power to bring on Indian wars, for the sake of the profit to be realized from the presence of troops and the expenditure of government funds in their midst.

They proclaim death to the Indians at all times, in words and publications, making no distinction between the innocent and the guilty. They incite the lowest class of men to the perpetration of the darkest deeds against their victims, and, as judges and jurymen, shield them from the justice due to their crimes. Every crime committed by a white man against an Indian is concealed or palliated; every offense committed by one Indian against a white man is borne on the wings of the post or the telegraph to the remotest corner of the land, clothed with all the horrors which the reality or imagination can throw around it.... Against the inhuman idea that the Indian is only fit to be exterminated, and the influence of the men who propagate it, the military arm of the government cannot be too strongly guarded. It is hardly to be wondered at that inexperienced officers, ambitious for distinction, when surrounded by such influences, have been incited to attack Indian bands without adequate cause, and involve the nation in an unjust war. It should, at least, be understood that in the future such blunders should cost the officer his commission, and that such destruction is infamy.

Paradoxical as it may seem, the white man has been the chief obstacle in the way of Indian civilization. The benevolent measures attempted by the government for their advancement have been almost uniformly thwarted by the agencies employed to carry them out. The soldiers, sent for their protection, too often carried demoralization and disease into their midst. The agent, appointed to be their friend and counsellor, business manager, and the almoner of the government bounties, frequently went among them only to enrich himself in the shortest possible time, at the cost of the Indians, and spend the largest available sum of the government money with the least ostensible beneficial result.... If in spite of these obstacles a tribe made some progress in agricultures, or their lands became valuable from any cause, the process of civilization was summarily ended by driving them away from their homes with fire and sword, to undergo similar experiences in some new locality....

To assert that "the Indian will not work" is as true as it would be to say that the white man will not work.... Why should the Indian be expected to plant corn, fence lands, build houses, or do anything but get food from day to day, when experience has taught him that the product of his labor will be seized by the white man tomorrow!...

The policy of collecting the Indian tribes upon small reservations contiguous to each other, and within the limits of a large reservation, eventually to become a State of the Union, and of which the small reservations will probably be the counties, seems to be the best that can be devised....

The treaty system should be abandoned, as soon as any just method can be devised to accomplish it, existing treaties should be abrogated.

The legal status of the civilized Indians should be that of wards of the government; the duty of the latter being to protect them, to educate them in industry, the arts of civilization, and the principles of Christianity; elevate them to the rights of citizenship, and to sustain and clothe them they can support themselves.

The payment of money annuities to the Indians should be abandoned, for the reason that such payments encourage idleness and vice, to the injury of those whom it is intended to benefit. Schools should be established, and teachers employed by the government to introduce the English language to every tribe. It is believed that many of the difficulties with Indian occur from misunderstandings as to the meaning and intention of either party. The teachers employed should be nominated by some religious body having a mission nearest to the location of the school. The establishment of Christian missions should be encouraged, and their schools fostered. The pupils should at least receive the rations and clothing they would get if remaining with their families. The religion of our blessed Saviour is believed to be the most effective agent for the civilization of any people.

United States, Department of Interior, Bureau of Indian Affairs, *Report of the Commission on Indian Affairs*, 41st Congress, 2nd Session, House Executive Documents, 3; 487-493.

13.3

HARPER'S WEEKLY ON THE CUSTER MASSACRE (1876)

No act of Indian resistance gained more attention than the Battle of Little Big Horn. The bloody conflict between federal troops and a band of Dakota [eastern Sioux] and Northern Cheyenne Indians stemmed from the Treaty of Fort Laramie (1868). Ending the Powder River War, the treaty granted the Sioux permanent possession of the Dakota Territory west of the Missouri River. But not all the Sioux had fought in the war or signed the treaty. Many refused to move to the newly created reservation. Oglala and Brulé bands occasionally attacked white settlers who threatened sacred tribal grounds.

These raids and the discovery of gold in the Black Hills compelled the U.S. government to act. After an attempt to purchase the Dakota Territory failed, President Ulysses S. Grant issued an order declaring that all Indians outside of the reservations after January 31, 1876 would be taken by force. A confrontation was inevitable.

In June 1876, the U.S. government dispatched troops to destroy the defiant Indians. Lieutenant Colonel George A. Custer led the 7th Cavalry to Little Big Horn River, an Indian stronghold. After encountering a large Sioux and Cheyenne encampment, Custer divided his forces and planned an attack. Underestimating the number of Indians, Custer led 209 men against 1,500 to 5,000 Indians. Within an hour, the Indians surrounded and destroyed most of Custer's army.

This editorial from Harper's Weekly *demonstrates how the Indians' surprising coup stunned the nation. Determined to avenge "Custer's Last Stand," U.S. troops flooded the West and began crushing Indian opposition.*

———————————— ■ ————————————

FOCUS QUESTIONS

1. What do the editorial writers believe caused the Custer massacre? How do they characterize federal Indian policies? How does their interpretation of the government's Indian policies differ from that found in Document 13.2?
2. How do the authors regard the Indians? What solutions do they propose to the "Indian problem"?
3. If you had been a federal Indian agent in this era, how would you have improved relations between the U.S. government and the Indians?

The Custer Massacre
5 August 1876

T he fate of the brave and gallant Custer has deeply touched the public heart, which sees only a fearless soldier leading a charge against an ambushed foe, and falling at the head of his men and in the thick of the fray. A monument is proposed, and subscriptions have been made. But a truer monument, more enduring than brass or marble, would be an Indian policy intelligent, moral, and efficient. Custer would not have fallen in vain if such a policy should be the result of his death. It is a permanent accusation against our humanity and ability that over the Canadian line the relations between the Indians and whites are so tranquil, while upon our side they are summed up in perpetual treachery, waste, and war. When he was a young lieutenant on the frontier, General [Ulysses] Grant saw this, and watching attentively, he came to the conclusion that the reason of the difference was that the English respected the rights of the Indians and kept faith with them, while we make solemn treaties with them as if they were civilized and powerful nations, and then practically regard them as vermin to be exterminated. The folly of making treaties with the Indian tribes may be as great as treating with a herd of buffalo. But the infamy of violating treaties when we have made them is undeniable, and we are guilty both of the folly and the infamy.

We make treaties—that is, we pledge our faith—and then leave swindlers and knaves of all kinds to execute them. We maintain and breed pauper colonies. The savages who know us and who will neither be pauperized nor trust our word we pursue and slay if we can at an incredible expense. The flower of our young officers is lost in inglorious forays, and one of the intelligent students of the whole subject rises in Congress and says, "The fact is that these Indians, with whom we have made a solemn treaty that their territory should not be invaded, and that they should receive supplies upon their reservations, have seen from one thousand to fifteen hundred miners during the present season entering and occupying their territory, while the Indians, owing to the failure of this and the last Congress to make adequate appropriations for their subsistence, instead of being fattened, as the gentleman says, by the support of the government, have simply been starved."...

It is plain that so long as we undertake to support the Indians as paupers, and then fail to supply the food; to respect their rights to reservations, and then permit the reservations to be overrun; to give them the best weapons and ammunition, and then furnish the pretext of their using them against us; to treat with them as men, and then hunt them like skunks—so long we shall have the most costly and bloody Indian wars, and the most tragical ambuscades, slaughters, and assassinations. The Indian is undoubtedly a savage, and a savage greatly spoiled by the kind of contact with civilization which he gets at the West. There is generally no interest whatever in him or his fate. But there should be some interest in our own good faith and humanity, in the lives of our soldiers and frontier settlers, and in the taxation to support our Indian policy. All this should certainly be enough to arouse a public demand for a thorough consideration of the subject, and the adoption of a system which should neither be puerile nor disgraceful, and which would tend to spare us the constant repetition of such sorrowful events as the slaughter of Custer and his brave men.

Harper's Weekly, 5 August 1876.

13.4

CHIEF JOSEPH'S LAMENT (1879)

In the face of increased military opposition and continued white settlement, many tribes still refused to surrender. In 1877, Chief Joseph (1840-1904) led several Nez Percé on a 1,000-mile journey in order to evade the U.S. army. The Nez Percé had been one of the most powerful tribes in the Pacific Northwest and were initially friendly to whites. Many Nez Percé, including Chief Joseph's father, converted to Christianity. Chief Joseph attended a white school. But when whites began forcing nearby Indians onto reservations in the 1850s, many Nez Percé resisted. In 1877, the U.S. government attempted to force the dissenting Nez Percé onto a reservation in Idaho.

After reluctantly agreeing, Chief Joseph changed his mind when three braves murdered a group of white settlers. Fearing retaliation, he led his people on a remarkable three-month trek toward Canada. During the retreat, the band won several battles over larger white forces. They drew admiration for their humane treatment of opponents and refusal to steal from ranchers and merchants. After traveling through Oregon, Washington, Idaho, and Montana, Chief Joseph and his followers were forced to surrender, only forty miles from the Canadian border.

They were first sent to a desolate reservation in the Indian Territory (now Oklahoma), where many grew ill and died. But two trips to Washington, D.C. and personal appeals to high government officials eventually enabled Chief Joseph and his supporters to return to their ancestral grounds. One of these petitions follows.

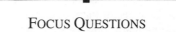

FOCUS QUESTIONS

1. What are the major themes of Chief Joseph's appeal? What does he want from the U.S. government?
2. Why do you think that the federal government acceded to Chief Joseph's wishes but disregarded those of so many other tribes?

t last I was granted permission to come to Washington and bring my friend Yellow Bull and our interpreter with me. I am glad I came. I have shaken hands with a good many friends, but there are some things I want to know which no one seems able to explain. I cannot understand how the government sends a man out to fight us, as it did General Miles, and then breaks his word. Such a government has something wrong about it....

I have heard talk and talk, but nothing is done. Good words do not last long unless they amount to something. Words do not pay for my dead people. They do not pay for my country, now overrun by white men. They do not protect my father's grave. They do not pay for my horses and cattle.

Good words do not give back my children. Good words will not make good the promise of your war chief, General Miles. Good words will not give my people good health and stop them from dying. Good words will not get my people a home where they can live in peace and take care of themselves.

I am tired of talk that comes to nothing. It makes my heart sick when I remember all the good words and all the broken promises. There has been too much talking by men who had no right to talk. Too many misinterpretations have been made; too many misunderstandings have come up between the white men and the Indians.

If the white man wants to live in peace with the Indian, he can live in peace. There need be no trouble. Treat all men alike. Give them the same laws. Give them all an even chance to live and grow.

All men are made by the same Great Spirit Chief. They are all brothers. The earth is the mother of all people, and all people should have equal rights upon it. You might as well expect all rivers to run backward as that any man who was born a free man should be contented penned up and denied liberty to go where he pleases. If you tie a horse to a stake, do you expect he will grow fat? If you pen an Indian up on a small spot of earth and compel him to stay there, he will not be contented nor will he grow and prosper.

I have asked some of the Great White Chiefs where they get their authority to say to the Indian that he shall stay in one place, while he sees white men going where they please. They cannot tell me.

I only ask of the government to be treated as all other men are treated. If I cannot go to my own home, let me have a home in a country where my people will not die so fast. I would like to go to Bitter Root Valley [western Montana]. There my people would be healthy; where they are now, they are dying. Three have died since I left my camp to come to Washington. When I think of our condition, my heart is heavy. I see men of my own race treated as outlaws and driven from country to country, or shot down like animals.

I know that my race must change. We cannot hold our own with the white men as we are. We only ask an even chance to live as other men live. We ask to be recognized as men. We ask that the same law shall work alike on all men. If an Indian breaks the law, punish him by the law. If a white man breaks the law, punish him also.

Let me be a free man—free to travel, free to stop, free to work, free to trade where I choose, free to choose my own teachers, free to follow the religion of my fathers, free to think and talk and act for myself—and I will obey every law or submit to the penalty.

Whenever the white man treats the Indian as they treat each other, then we shall have no more wars. We shall all be alike—brothers of one father and mother, with one sky above us and one country around us and one government for all. Then the Great Spirit Chief who rules above will smile upon his land and send rain to wash out the bloody spots made by brothers' hands upon the face of the earth. For this time the Indian race are waiting and praying. I hope no more groans of wounded men and women will ever go to the ear of the Great Spirit Chief above, and that all people may be one people.

North American Review, CXXVIII, (April, 1879), 431-32.

13.5

BENJAMIN "PAP" SINGLETON ON THE "EXODUSTERS" (1880)

In the 1870s, as federal troops left the South and racial conflict escalated, thousands of African-Americans headed to Kansas. These "Exodusters" saw the West as an escape from poverty and racism. Stories and rumors about Kansas intrigued southern blacks. Some believed (erroneously) that the federal government was giving forty acres, supplies, and transportation to the freedpeople. Thousands sold their possessions and made their way to Kansas.

Benjamin "Pap" Singleton (1809-1892) was known as the "Father of the Exodus." Born a slave in Tennessee, Singleton escaped to Canada. Returning to the United States after emancipation, he traveled throughout the South urging blacks to establish their own communities. In 1873, he and his Tennessee associates founded the Edgefield Real Estate and Homestead Association. Between 1877 and 1879, the group steered more than 20,000 former slaves toward its settlements in Kansas. The organization tried to control the migration process but was soon overwhelmed. By 1900, African Americans in Kansas usually enjoyed greater political freedom and economic opportunities than their southern brethren.

In this passage, Singleton testifies to a congressional panel investigating the black migration.

FOCUS QUESTIONS

1. How does Singleton describe his role in the Exoduster movement? What motivated him to urge blacks to move to Kansas?
2. How does Singleton claim that migrants' lives change after they settle in Kansas?
3. Why do you think that the U.S. Senate investigated the Exoduster movement?
4. What does the Exodusters' story tell us about the West?

Benjamin Singleton (colored) sworn and examined.
By Mr. Windom:

 uestion. Where were you born, Mr. Singleton?
Answer. I was born in the State of Tennessee, sir.

Q. Where do you now live?
A. In Kansas.

Q. What part of Kansas?
A. I have a colony sixty miles from Topeka, sir.

Q. Which way from Topeka—west?
A. Yes, sir; sixty miles from Topeka, west.

Q. What is your colony called?
A. Singleton colony is the name of it, sir.

Q. How long has it been since you have formed that colony?
A. I have two colonies in Kansas—one in Cherokee County, and one in Lyon, Morris County.

Q. When did you commence the formation of that colony—the first one?
A. It was in 1875, perhaps.

Q. That is, you first began this colonizing business in 1875?
A. No; when I first commenced working at this it was in 1869.

Q. You commenced your colony, then, in 1869?
A. No, I commenced getting the emigration up in 1875; I think it was in 1875.

Q. When did you leave Tennessee, Mr. Singleton?
A. This last time; do you mean?

Q. No; when you moved from there to Kansas?
A. It has been a year this month, just about now.

Q. You misunderstand me; you say you were born in Tennessee?
A. Yes, sir.

Q. And you now live in Kansas?
A. Yes, sir.

Q. When did you change your home from Tennessee to Kansas?
A. I have been going there for the last six or seven years, sir.

Q. Going between Tennessee and Kansas, at different times?
A. Yes, sir; several times.

Q. Well, tell us about it?
A. I have been fetching out people; I believe I fetched out 7,432 people.

Q. You have brought out 7,432 people from the South to Kansas?
A. Yes, sir; brought and sent.

Q. That is, they came out to Kansas under your influence?
A. Yes, sir; I was the cause of it.

Q. How long have you been doing that—ever since 1869?
A. Yes, sir; ever since 1869.

Q. Did you go out there yourself in 1869, before you commenced sending them out?
A. No, sir.

Q. How did you happen to send them out?
A. The first cause, do you mean, of them going?

Q. Yes; What was the cause of your going out, and in the first place how did you happen to go there, or to send these people there?
A. Well, my people, for the want of land—we needed land for our children—and their disadvantages—that caused my heart to grieve and sorrow; pity for my race, sir, that was coming down, instead of going up—that caused me to go to work for them. I sent out there perhaps in '66—perhaps so; or in '65, any way—my memory don't recollect which; and they brought back tolerable favorable reports; then I jacked up three or four hundred, and went into South- ern Kansas, and found it was a good country, and I thought Southern Kansas was congenial to our nature, sir; and I formed a colony there, and bought about a thousand acres of ground—the colony did—my people.

Q. And they went upon it and settled there?
A. Yes, sir; they went and settled there.

Q. Were they men with some means or without means?
A. I never carried none there without means.

Q. They had some means to start with?
A. Yes; I prohibited my people leaving their country and going there without they had money—some money to start with and go on with a while.

Q. You were in favor of their going there if they had some means?
A. Yes, and not staying at home.

Q. Tell us how these people are getting on in Kansas?
A. I am glad to tell you, sir.

Q. Have they any property now?
A. Yes; I have carried some people in there that when they got there they didn't have fifty cents left, and now they have got in my colony—Singleton colony—a house, nice cabins, their milch cows, and pigs, and sheep, perhaps a span of horses, and trees before their yeards, and some three or four or ten acres broken up, and all of them has got little houses that I carried there. They didn't go under no relief assistance; they went on their own resources; and when they went in there first the country was not overrun with them; you see they could get good wages; the country was not overstocked with people; they went to work, and I never helped them as soon as I put them on the land.

Q. Well, they have been coming continually, and adding from time to time to your colony these few years past, have they?
A. Yes, sir; I have spent, perhaps, nearly six hundred dollars flooding the country with circulars.

Q. You have sent the circulars yourself, have you?
A. Yes, sir; all over these United States.

Q. Did you send them into other Southern States besides Tennessee?
A. O, yes, sir.

Q. Did you do that at the instance of Governor St. John and others in Kansas?
A. O, no, sir; no white men. This was gotten up by colored men in purity and confidence; not a political negro was in it; they would want to pilfer and rob at the cents before they got the dollars. O, no, it was the muscle of the arm, the men that worked that we wanted.

Q. Well, tell us all about it.
A. These men would tell all their grievances to me in Tennessee—the sorrows of their heart. You know I was an undertaker there in Nashville, and worked in the shop. Well, actually, I would have to go and bury their fathers and mothers. You see we have the same heart and feelings as any other race and nation. (The land is free, and it is nobody's business, if there is land enough, where the people go. I put that in my people's heads.) Well, that man would die, and I would bury him; and the next morning maybe a woman would go to that man [meaning the landlord], and she would have six or seven children, and he would say to her, "Well, your husband owed me before he died" and they would say that to every last one of them, "You owe me." Suppose he would? Then he would say, "You must go to some other place; I cannot take care of you." Now, you see, that is something I would take notice of. That woman had to go out, and these little children was left running through the streets, and

the next place you would find them in a disorderly house [a brothel], and their children in the State's prison.

Well, now, sir, you will find that I have a charter here. You will find that I called on the white people in Tennessee about that time. I called conventions about it, and they sat with me in my conventions, and "Old man," they said, "you are right." The white people said, "You are right; take your people away." And let me tell you, it was the white people—the ex-governor of the State, felt like I did, and they said to me, "You have tooken a great deal on to yourself, but if these negroes, instead of deceiving one another and running for office, would take the same idea that you have in your head, you will be a people."

I then went out to Kansas, and advised them all to go to Kansas; and, sir they are going to leave the Southern country. The Southern country is out of joint. The blood of a white man runs through my veins. That is congenial, you know, to my nature. That is my choice. Right emphatically, I tell you today, I woke up the millions right through me! The great God of glory has worked in me. I have had open air interviews with the living spirit of God for my people; and we are going to leave the South. We are going to leave it if there ain't an alteration and signs of change. I am going to advise the people who left that country [Kansas] to go back.

Q. What do you mean by a change?
A. Well, I am not going to stand bulldozing and half pay and all those things. Gentlemen, allow me to tell you the truth; it seems to me that they have picked out the negroes from the Southern country to come here and testify who are in good circumstances and own their homes and not the poor ones who don't study their own interests. Let them go and pick up the men that has to walk when they goes, and not those who have money.

There is good white men in the Southern country, but it ain't the minority [majority]; they can't do nothing; the bulldozers has got possession of the country, and they have got to go in there and stop them; if they don't the last colored man will leave them. I see colored men testifying to a positive lie, for they told me out there all their interests were in Louisiana and Mississippi. Said I, "You are right to protect you own country," and they would tell me, "I am obliged to do what I am doing." Of course I have done the same, but I am clear footed.

Q. Now you say that during these years you have been getting up this colony you have spent, yourself, some six hundred dollars in circulars, and in sending them out; where did you send them, Mr. Singleton?
A. Into Mississippi, Alabama, South Carolina, Georgia, Kentucky, Virginia, North Carolina, Texas, Tennessee, and all those countries.

Q. To whom did you send them; how were they circulated?
A. Every man that would come into my country, and I could get a chance, I would put one in his hand, and the boys that started from my country on the boats, and the porters in the cars. That is the way I circulated them.

Q. Did you send any out by mail?
A. I think I sent some perhaps to North Carolina by mail—I think I did. I sent them out by people, you see.

Q. Yes; by colored people, generally?
A. Some white people, too. There was Mrs. Governor Brown, the first Governor Brown of Tennessee—Mrs. Sanders, she was a widow, and she married the governor. He had thirty on his place. I went to him, and he has given me advice. And Ex-Governor Brown, he is there too.

Q. You say your circulars were sent all over these States?
A. Yes, sir; to all of 'em.

Q. Did you ever hear from them; did anybody ever write to you about them?
A. O, yes.

Q. And you attribute this movement to the information you gave in your circulars?
A. Yes, sir; I am the whole cause of the Kansas immigration!

Q. You take all that responsibility on yourself?
A. I do, and I can prove it; and I think I have done a good deal of good, and I feel relieved!

Q. You are proud of your work?
A. Yes, sir; I am! [Uttered emphatically.]

Testimony of Benjamin Singleton, April 17, 1880, Senate Select Committee Investigating the "Negro Exodus from the Southern States."

13.6

RULES FOR INDIAN BOARDING SCHOOLS (1890)

The U.S. army's attacks on Indians horrified many Americans. While the Indian wars raged, humanitarians searched for peaceful solutions to the "Indian problem." Calling for the "Americanization" of Indians, reformers advocated ending the reservation system that encouraged tribal separation from mainstream culture. They also recommended that Indian children be educated and "civilized" so that they could join white society. While contemporaries considered these efforts progressive and humane, they also reflected a deep belief in white supremacy. By 1881, the federal government was operating 106 day and boarding schools for Indians. Many of the schools were on or near reservations, but reformers preferred boarding schools that isolated Indian children from tribal influences. Some spelling has been modernized.

FOCUS QUESTIONS

1. What were the main objectives of these rules? What traits do children need to adopt in order to succeed at the school?
2. How do you think these rules affected Indian children?
3. How did the rules treat boys and girls differently? Why do you think regulators made these distinctions?
4. Are there any similarities between the Indian schools and today's schools? Explain your answer.

 ## GENERAL RULES

39. The Sabbath must be properly observed. There shall be a Sabbath school or some other suitable service every Sunday, which pupils shall be required to attend. The superintendent may require employees to attend and participate in all the above exercises; but any employee declining as a matter of conscience shall be excused from attending and participating in any or all religious exercises....

41. All instruction must be in the English language. Pupils must be compelled to converse with each other in English, and should be properly rebuked or punished for persistent violation of this rule. Every effort should be made to encourage them to abandon their tribal language. To facilitate this work it is essential that all school employees be able to speak English fluently, and that they speak English exclusively to pupils, and also to each other in the presence of pupils.

42. Instruction in music must be given at all schools. Singing should be a part of the exercises of each school session, and wherever practicable instruction in instrumental music should be given.

43. Except in cases of emergency, pupils shall not be removed from school either by their parents or others, nor shall they be transferred from a Government to a private school without special authority from the Indian Office.

44. The school buildings should be furnished throughout with plain, inexpensive, but substantial furniture. Dormitories or lavatories should be so supplied with necessary toilet articles, such as soap, towels, mirrors, combs, hair, shoe, nail, and tooth brushes, and wisp brooms, as to enable the pupils to form exact habits of personal neatness.

45. Good and healthful provisions must be supplied in abundance; and they must be well cooked and properly placed on the table. A regular bill of fare for each day of the week should be prepared and followed. Meals must be served regularly and neatly. Pains should be taken not only to have the food healthful and the table attractive, but to have the bill of fare varied. The school farm and dairy should furnish an ample supply of vegetables, fruits, milk, butter, cottage cheese, curds, eggs, and poultry. Coffee and tea should be furnished spar-

ingly; milk is preferable to either, and children can be taught to use it. Pupils must be required to attend meals promptly after proper attention to toilet, and at least one employee must be in the dining room during each meal to supervise the table manners of the pupils and to see that all leave the table at the same time and in good order....

47. So far as practicable, a uniform style of clothing for the school should be adopted. Two plain, substantial suits, with extra pair of trousers for each boy, and three neat, well-made dresses for each girl, if kept mended, ought to suffice for week-day wear for one year. For Sunday wear each pupil should be furnished with a better suit. The pupils should also be supplied with underwear adapted to the climate, with night clothes, and with handkerchiefs, and, if the climate requires it, with overcoats and cloaks and with overshoes....

49. There should be a flag staff at each school, and the American flag should be hoisted, in suitable weather, in the morning and lowered at sunset daily.

50. Special hours should be allotted for recreation. Provision should be made for outdoor sports, and the pupils should be encouraged in daily healthful exercise under the eye of a school employee; simple games should also be devised for indoor amusement. They should be taught the sports and games enjoyed by white youth, such as baseball, hopscotch, croquet, marbles, bean bags, dominoes, checkers, logomachy, and other word and letter games, and the use of dissected maps, etc. The girls should be instructed in simple fancy work, knitting, netting, crocheting, different kinds of embroidery, etc.

51. Separate play grounds, as well as sitting rooms, must be assigned the boys and the girls. In play and in work, as far as possible, and in all places except the school room and at meals, they must be kept entirely apart. It should be so arranged, however, that at stated times, under suitable supervision, they may enjoy each other's society; and such occasions should be used to teach them to show each other due respect and consideration, to behave without restraint, but without familiarity, and to acquire habits of politeness, refinement, and self-possession....

53. Corporal punishment must be resorted to only in cases of grave violations of rules, and in no instances shall any person inflict it except under the direction of the superintendent to whom all serious questions of discipline must also be referred. Employees may correct pupils for slight misdemeanors only.

54. Any pupil twelve years of age or over, guilty of persistently using profane or obscene language; of lewd conduct; stubborn insubordination; lying; fighting; wanton destruction of property; theft; or similar misbehavior, may be punished by the superintendent either by inflicting corporal punishment or imprisonment in the guardhouse, but in no case shall unusual or cruel or degrading punishments be permitted....

INDUSTRIAL WORK

56. A regular and efficient system of industrial training must be a part of the work of each school. At least half of the time of each boy and girl should be devoted thereto—the work to be of such character that they may be able to apply the knowledge and experience gained, in the locality where they may be ex-

pected to reside after leaving school. In pushing forward the school-room training of these boys and girls, teachers, and especially superintendents, must not lose sight of the great necessity for fitting their charges for the every-day life of their after years.

57. A farm and garden, if practicable an orchard also, must be connected with each school, and especial attention must be given to instruction in farming, gardening, dairying, and fruit growing.

58. Every school should have horses, cattle, swine, and poultry, and when practicable, sheep and bees, which the pupils should be taught to care for properly. The boys should look after the stock and milk the cows, and the girls should see to the poultry and the milk.

59. The farm, garden, stock, dairy, kitchen, and shops should be so managed as to make the school as nearly self-sustaining as practicable, not only because Government resources should be as wisely and carefully utilized as private resources would be, but also because thrift and economy are among the most valuable lessons which can be taught Indians. Waste in any department must not be tolerated....

61. The girls must be systematically trained in every branch of housekeeping and in dairy work; be taught to cut, make, and mend garments for both men and women; and also be taught to nurse and care for the sick. They must be regularly detailed to assist the cook in preparing the food and the laundress in washing and ironing.

U.S. Bureau of Indian Affairs, "Rules for Indian Schools," *Annual Report of the Commissioner of Indian Affairs, 1890* (Washington, D.C., 1890), cxivi, cl-clii.

13.7

JOHN MUIR, "AMERICAN FORESTS" (1901)

As white settlement changed the West, calls arose for the protection of its beautiful landscape. By the 1860s, a small number of Americans were calling for the establishment of national parks and more cautious use of the environment. John Muir (1838-1914) was one of the nation's most eloquent naturalists. After emigrating from Scotland in 1849, Muir attended the University of Wisconsin and then worked as a mechanical inventor. After nearly losing an eye in an industrial accident, Muir abandoned his job and dedicated himself to nature. He spent over forty years exploring the West and writing about the outdoors. His demands for forest conservation contributed to the creation of Sequoia and Yosemite National Parks in 1890. Two years later, he founded the Sierra Club, one of the nation's most influential environmental organizations. In this passage, Muir calls for the preservation of the nation's woodlands.

---■---

Focus Questions

1. How does Muir describe America's forests? Why does he believe that the forests are imperiled?
2. What does Muir propose to ensure that the forests are protected? Is his solution feasible? Explain your answer.

T he forests of America, however slighted by man, must have been a great delight to God; for they were the best he ever planted. The whole continent was a garden, and from the beginning it seemed to be favored above all the other wild parks and gardens of the globe....

In the settlement and civilization of the country, bread more than timber or beauty was wanted; and in the blindness of hunger, the early settlers, claiming Heaven as their guide, regarded God's trees as only a larger kind of pernicious weeds, extremely hard to get rid of. Accordingly, with no eye to the future, these pious destroyers waged interminable forest wars; chips flew thick and fast; trees in their beauty fell crashing by millions, smashed to confusion, and the smoke of their burning has been rising to heaven more than two hundred years....

Surely, then, it should not be wondered at that lovers of their country, bewailing its baldness, are now crying aloud, "Save what is left of the forests!" Clearing has surely now gone far enough; soon timber will be scarce, and not a grove will be left to rest in or pray in. The remnant protected will yield plenty of timber, a perennial harvest for every right use, without further diminution of its area, and will continue to cover the springs of the rivers that rise in the mountains and give irrigating waters to the dry valleys at their feet, prevent wasting floods and be a blessing to everybody forever.

Notwithstanding all the waste and use which have been going on unchecked like a storm for more than two centuries, it is not yet too late—though it is high time—for the government to begin a rational administration of its forests. About seventy million acres it still owns,—enough for all the country, if wisely used. These residual forests are generally on mountain slopes, just where they are doing the most good, and where their removal would be followed by the greatest number of evils; the lands they cover are too rocky and high for agriculture, and can never be made as valuable for any other crop as for present crop of trees. It has been shown over and over again that if these mountains were to be stripped of their trees and underbrush, and kept bare and sodless by hordes of sheep and the innumerable fires the shepherds set, besides those of the millmen, prospectors, shake-makers, and all sorts of adventurers, both lowlands and mountains would speedily become little better than desert, compared with their present beneficent fertility. During heavy rainfalls and while the winter accumulations of snow were melting, the large streams would swell into destructive torrents, cutting deep, rugged-edged gullies, carrying away the fertile humus and soil as well as sand and rocks, filling up and overflowing their lower channels, and covering the lowland fields with raw detritus. Drought and barrenness would follow....

All sorts of local laws and regulations have been tried and found wanting, and the costly lessons of our own experience, as well as that of every civilized nation, show conclusively that the fate of the remnant of our forests is in the hands of the federal government, and that if the remnant is to be saved at all, it must be saved quickly.

Any fool can destroy trees. They cannot run away; and if they could, they would still be destroyed,—chased and hunted down as long as fun or a dollar could be got out of their bark hides, branching horns, or magnificent bole backbones. Few that fell trees plant them; nor would planting avail much towards getting back anything like the noble primeval forests. During a man's life only saplings can be grown, in the place of the old trees—tens of centuries old—that have been destroyed. It took more than three thousand years to make some of the trees in these Western woods,—trees that are still standing in perfect strength and beauty, waving and singing in the mighty forests of the Sierra. Through all the wonderful, eventful centuries since Christ's time—and long before that—God has cared for these trees, saved them from drought, disease, avalanches, and a thousand straining, leveling tempests and floods; but he cannot save them from fools,—only Uncle Sam can do that.

John Muir, *Our National Parks* (Boston: Houghton, Mifflin and Company, 1901).

13.8

■

JOHN GAST, *AMERICAN PROGRESS* (1872)

Throughout the nineteenth century, Americans embraced westward expansion as the key to ensuring the future prosperity and greatness of their nation. In 1839, journalist John O'Sullivan coined the term "Manifest Destiny" to encapsulate the religious, political, economic, and racial justifications for white migration to the West. John Gast's American Progress *(1872) portrayed these ideas artistically. The painting, and the text that entrepreneur George Crofutt used to market lithographs of it, offer powerful illustrations of white attitudes toward the West and its inhabitants.*

■

FOCUS QUESTIONS

1. What do Gast's painting and Crofutt's text suggest about how whites defined "progress" in the West?
2. What are some of the technological symbols used to convey the advance of "civilization" in the West?
3. Why do you think Gast chose a woman as his symbol for westward expansion?

4. What are some of the attitudes toward Indians and the environment expressed by Gast and Crofutt?

5. Compare the ideas expressed by Gast and Crofutt to perspectives on the American West expressed in other documents in this chapter.

John Gast, *American Progress*, Library of Congress, Prints and Photographs Division, Washington, D.C.

Excerpts from Croffut's text:

T his rich and wonderful country—the progress of which at the present time, is the wonder of the old world—was until recently, inhabited exclusively by the lurking savage and wild beasts of prey. If the rapid progress of the "Great West" has surprised our people, what will those of other countries think of the "Far West," which was destined at an early day, to be the vast granary [grain producing region], as it is now the treasure chamber of our country?...

In the foreground, the central and principal figure, a beautiful and charming Female, is floating westward through the air bearing on her forehead the "Star of Empire...." On the right of the picture is a city, steamships, manufactories, schools and churches over which beams of light are streaming and filling the air— indicative of civilization. The general tone of the picture on the left declares darkness, waste and confusion. From the city proceed the three great continental lines of railway.... Next to these are the transportation wagons, overland stage, hunters, gold seekers, pony express, pioneer emigrant and the warrior dance of the "noble red man." Fleeing from "Progress"…are Indians, buffaloes, wild horses, bears, and other game, moving Westward, ever Westward, the Indians with their squaws, papooses, and "pony lodges," turn their despairing faces towards, as they flee the wondrous vision. The "Star" is too much for them.

…What home, from the miner's humble cabin to the stately marble mansion of the capitalist, should be without this Great National Picture, which illustrates in the most artistic manner all the gigantic results of American Brains and Hands! Who would not have such a beautiful token to remind them of the country's grandeur and enterprise which have caused the mighty wilderness to blossom like the rose!!!

Published at http://www.bmcc.cuny.edu/acadpts/socscience/billfheim/ibindex.htm.

SECONDARY SOURCE

L.G. Moses, "Wild West Shows, Reformers, and the Image of the American Indian, 1887-1914"

In the 1860s and 1870s, romanticized images of the West appeared in scores of dime novels. These stories usually featured frontier heroes fighting for justice and stability against "savage" Indians and outlaws. William Cody (1846-1917), also known as Buffalo Bill, was one of the most famous western folk idols. His colorful careers included buffalo hunter, U.S. Army scout, and Indian fighter. His marksmanship and navigation skills were legendary. Such exploits inspired Ned Buntline (pen name of Edward Judson) to write fictionalized accounts of Cody's life. The books' success prompted Cody to organize a Wild West show in 1883. His four-hour exhibitions featured buffalo hunts, "battles" between Indians and cowboys, sharpshooting, and other scenes of frontier life. These performances reinforced mythologized images of the West as a land where "good" always defeated "evil." The shows became wildly popular in the United States and abroad.

Hundreds of Indians, including Chief Sitting Bull, toured with Buffalo Bill's extravaganza. Scholars have long debated the impact of the Wild West shows on its Indian participants and American conceptions of the West. In this article, L.G. Moses, a noted specialist on Indian history, examines how reformers and Wild West show organizers fought over the role of Indians in the exhibitions.

 Go to your *Speaking of America* CD-ROM to read "Wild West Shows, Reformers, and the Image of the American Indian, 1187-1914."

FOCUS QUESTIONS

1. What were some of most common stereotypes of Indians held by white Americans in the late nineteenth-century? How did the Wild West shows reinforce these stereotypes?
2. Why did many reformers and Indians agents object to the Wild West exhibitions? How did Wild West show organizers respond to these complaints?
3. Why do you think individual Indians joined the Wild West shows? Do you think that the shows exploited them?
4. Why do you think that the Wild West shows were so popular?

AMERICAN JOURNEY ONLINE

http://ajaccesss.wadsworth.com [†]

About Exploration
— In <u>Westward Expansion</u>
Documents
*   Joseph C. Ives, Report upon the Colorado River of the West (1861)
*   John Wesley Powell, Excerpt from *Report on the Lands of the Arid Region of the United States* (1878)
*   John Charles Fremont, Excerpt from *Memoirs of My Life* (1887)
Images
*   E.O. Beaman, First Camp of the John Wesley Powell Expedition (1871)
*   John K. Hillers, The Grand Canyon and the Colorado River (1872)

About American Indians, the Indian Wars, and Indian Policy
— In <u>The Native American Experience</u>
Documents
*   Choctaw Nation General Council, Resolutions Expressing the Feelings and Sentiments of the General Council of the Choctaw Nation in Reference to the Political Disagreement Existing Between the Northern and Southern States of the American Union (1861)
*   Chickasaw Legislature, Resolutions of the Senate and House of the Chickasaw (1861)
*   Little Crow, Speech on the Eve of the Great Sioux Uprising (1862)
*   Big Eagle, Big Eagle's Story of the Sioux Outbreak (1862)

[†] Enter password, choose the Archive indicated above, click on Contents, choose •Documents, •Images, or •Multimedia, and click on the title of the item.

- George Bent, Excerpt from *The Fighting Cheyennes*, An Eyewitness Report of the Sand Creek Massacre, November 20, 1864
- Black Kettle, Speech (1865)
- Cochise, Speech (1866)
- Choctaw Nation and Chickasaw Nation, Treaty with the Choctaw and Chickasaw (1866)
- Don Turner, Custer Surprises Sleeping Cheyenne Indians in Battle Near Washita (1966)
- U.S. Government and the Sioux and Arapaho Nations, Fort Laramie Treaty (1868)
- Ely Parker and Ulysses S. Grant, Annual Report of the Board of Indian Commissioners (1869)
- Jacob D. Cox, Annual Report of the Secretary of the Interior, November 15, 1869
- Ulysses S. Grant, Second Annual Message to Congress (1870)
- Red Cloud, Speech of Red Cloud (1870)
- White-Man-Runs-Him, An Account of One of Custer's Scouts
- Two Moons, The Battle of Little Bighorn, Narrated by an Indian Who Fought in It
- Document with Audio Commentary—Chief Joseph, Surrender Speech of Chief Joseph (1877)
- Crazy Horse, The Last Words of Crazy Words (1877)
- Chief Joseph, An Indian's View of Indian Affairs (1879)
- Standing Bear, The Account of Standing Bear (1881)
- Helen Hunt Jackson, Excerpt from *A Century of Dishonor* (1881)
- School Rules
- *Ex Parte Crow Dog* (1883)
- Geronimo, Speech (1886)
- U.S. Congress, General Allotment Act (1887)
- Wovoka, The Revelation of Wovoka
- Wovoka, Letter from Wovoka
- Thomas J. Morgan, Rules for Courts of Indian Offenses (1892)
- Orthodox Citizens of Sitka, Alaska and Orthodox Tlingit Chiefs, Alaska Native Petitions to Russian Ambassador and to President McKinley (1897)
- U.S. Congress, Curtis Act (1898)
- Don C. Talayevsa, The Reservation School (circa 1900)
- Testimony of D.W.C. Duncan before Senate Committee (1906)

Images
- Stand Watie (circa 1860)
- Little Crow
- Robert Lindeux, The Sand Creek Massacre
- John Chivington
- William J. Fetterman
- The Fetterman Engagement

- Black Kettle
- Cochise
- *Harper's Weekly*, Attack on Cheyenne at Washita (1868)
- The Black Hills
- Red Cloud (circa 1870)
- General George Crook (1873)
- George Armstrong Custer
- Custer with His Scouts
- Photograph Reputed to be Crazy Horse
- Chief Joseph
- Standing Bear (1879)
- Department of Interior, General Land Office, Indian Territory (1879)
- Crow Dog
- Bud Glunz, A Class at the Lac la Ronge Residential School
- Last Sun Dance of the Ponca (1883)
- The Execution of the Thirty-Five Sioux Indians at Mankato, Minnesota on December 26, 1862
- Geronimo
- Julius Bien & Co., Ghost Dance Shirt
- Ghost Dance in Oklahoma (circa 1889)
- George Trayor, The Day after at Wounded Knee (1890)
- James Mooney, Inspiration (circa 1891)
- Chickasaw Freedman File for Allotments (circa 1898)
- James Mooney (circa 1900)

— In Westward Expansion
   Documents
- Alfred H. Terry, Custer's Orders Prior to Little Bighorn Battle (1876)
- Alfred H. Terry, Report to General Sheridan on Little Bighorn Battle (1876)
- Massacre of Our Troops (1876)
- General Nelson Miles, Excerpt from *The Indian Problem* (1879)
- E.D. Townsend and U.S. Army, Findings of a Court of Inquiry (1879)
- Document with Audio Commentary—Sarah Winnemucca, Excerpt from *Life among the Paiutes* (1883)
- Porcupine (Cheyenne), Account of the Ghost Dance Religion (1890)
- Alice Fletcher Cunningham, Excerpt from *Indian Story and Song from North America* (1900)
- George Dorsey, Excerpt from *The Arapaho Sun Dance* (1903)
- Document with Audio Commentary—Percival Lowe, Excerpt from *Five Years a Dragoon* (1906), 2 parts
- Geronimo and S.M. Barret, Geronimo's Story of His Life (1906)
- Frances Carrington, Excerpt from *My Army Life* (1911)

Images
- J.P. Davis, The Kidder Murder (1874)
- W.H. Illingworth, A View of Custer's Camp on Black Hills Expedition (1874)
- General Crook's Field Headquarters in Dakota Territory (1876)
- Site of Custer's Last Stand with Bones of Dead Horses (circa 1877)
- Blacksmithing at an Indian Training School in Oregon (1882)
- Dress of a Ghost Dancer (circa 1885)
- Camillus S. Fly, Conference between General George Crook and Geronimo (1886)
- A.J. McDonald, Apaches and Their Soldier Guard (1886)
- Chirachua Apaches on Arrival at Carlisle Indian School (1886)
- George Trager, Bird's Eye View of Sioux Indian Camp, South Dakota (1890)
- John C.H. Grabill, Sioux Ready to Perform Religious Dance in South Dakota (1890)
- George Trayor, Frozen Body of Big Foot, Sioux Leader at Wounded Knee (1890)
- George Trayor, Dead Indians on the Battlefield of Wounded Knee (1890)
- John G.C. Grabill, Council of Sioux Chiefs to End Indian Resistance (1891)
- John C.H. Grabill, Nelson Miles and Buffalo Bill View an Indian Camp in South Dakota (1891)
- John C.H. Grabill, The Great Hostile Indian Camp near Pine Ridge, South Daokta (1891)
- Nez Percé Girls Playing with Dolls (1891)
- Mary Irvin Wright, Arapaho Ghost Dance (1892)
- Geronimo and Family at Fort Sill (1895)
- Indians Studying Art at Phoenix Indian School (1900)
— In Civil Rights in the United States
Images
- George Armstrong Custer
- Indian Wars
- Sitting Bull
- Geronimo
- North Western Photo Co., Battle of Wounded Knee (1890)
— In The African-American Experience
Images
- Negro-Seminole Scouts of the 9th Cavalry (circa 1875)
— In The Immigrant Experience
Documents
- U.S. Congress, Dawes Severalty Act (1887)

About African Americans and the West
— In <u>The African-American Experience</u>
  Documents
  • John Mercer Langston, The Exodus (1879)
— In <u>Westward Expansion</u>
  Images
  • The Shores Family Near Westerville, Custer County, Nebraska (1887)
  • Frederic Remington, A Scout with the Buffalo Soldiers (1888)
  • African Africans Picking Cotton in Oklahoma (circa 1898) in Westward Expansion

About Mexican Americans
— In <u>The Hispanic-American Experience</u>
  Documents
  • Maria Amparo Ruiz de Burton, Excerpt from *The Squatter and the Don* (1885)

About Women
— In <u>Westward Expansion</u>
  Documents
  • Territorial Government of Wyoming, An Act to Grant to the Women of the Wyoming Territory the Right of Suffrage (1869)

About the Mormons
— In <u>Westward Expansion</u>
  Images
  • Mormons Emigrating in Covered Wagon Caravan (circa 1879)
— In <u>Civil Rights in the United States</u>
  Documents
  • U.S. Supreme Court, *Reynolds v. United States* (1879)

About the Buffalo
— In <u>Westward Expansion</u>
  Images
  • Slaughter of Buffalo on the Kansas Pacific Railroad (1870s)

About Land Policies
— In <u>Westward Expansion</u>
  Documents
  • Justin S. Morrill, Morrill Land-Grant Act (1862)
  • U.S. Congress, Homestead Act of 1862
  • Albert Richardson, Excerpt from *Beyond the Mississippi* (1867)
  • U.S. Congress, An Act to Prevent Unlawful Occupancy of Public Lands (1885)
  • William Howard, The Rush to Oklahoma (1889)

Images
- A Kansas Land Office (1874)
- First Auction of Lots at Imperial, California (1904)

About Farming
— In <u>Westward Expansion</u>
  Images
- Guthrie Cotton Market (1890s)
- Cherry Picking at an Oklahoma Fruit Ranch (circa 1900)
- Children Helping Harvest Fruit (circa 1900)
- Camp of Men Invited to Invest in California Agriculture (1904)

About Water and Irrigation
— In <u>Westward Expansion</u>
  Documents
- William E. Smythe, The Secret of Mormon Power (circa 1895)
  Images
- William J. Lubkin, Inside View of Cold Springs Reservoir (1907)

About Ranching, the Cattle Industry, and Cowboys
— In <u>Westward Expansion</u>
  Documents
- Joseph McCoy, Excerpt from *Historic Sketches of the Cattle Trade* (1874
- G. Pomeroy Keese, Beef, from the Range to the Shambles (1884)
- W.S. James, Excerpt from *Cowboy Life in Texas: Or 27 Years as a Maverick* (1893)
- Asa S. Mercer, Excerpt from *Banditti of the Plains* (1894)
- Andy Adams, Excerpt from *The Log of a Cowboy: A Narrative of the Old Trail Days* (1903)
- Nat Love, Excerpt from *The Life and Adventures of Nat Love* (1907)
  Images
- Texas Cattle Being Loaded on Train in Abilene, Kansas (1871)
- Cattle Raid Gun Fight Between Cattleman and Bandits (1874)
- Generals Sheridan and Miles En Route to a Cattle War (1885)
- Bull's Eye View of Stockyards, Kansas City (1887)
- Solomon D. Butcher, Cowboys and Bronco Busters (circa 1901)

About Mining
— In <u>Westward Expansion</u>
  Images
- Crowd Watching Miners Seeking Gold at Deadwood, South Dakota (1876)
- The Coeur d'Alene Mining Troubles (1892)

About Transportation
— In <u>Westward Expansion</u>
Documents
- U.S. Congress, Excerpt from Pacific Railway Act (1862)
- Grenville M. Dodge, Excerpt from *How We Built the Union Pacific Railway* (1910)

Images
- John Carbutt, Directors of the Union Pacific Railroad on the 100th Meridian (1866)
- M.R. Longacre, Westward Ho! (1868)
- Alfred R. Waud, Workers Race to Finish Last Mile of the Transcontinental RR (1869)
- Deadwood Stagecoach (circa 1876)
- The Waiting Room of the Union Pacific RR Depot (1877)

About Communications
— In <u>Westward Expansion</u>
Documents
- The Overland Telegraph (1861)

Images
- Poster Announcing the Pony Express Schedule (1861)
- Pony Express Rider (1861)
- The Progress of the Century (1876)

About Oklahoma Land Rush
— In <u>Westward Expansion</u>
Images
- Boomers Camp, Arkansas County, Kansas (1893)
- Registration Booths for Oklahoma Land Rush (1893)
- Train and Wagons Leaving the Line, Oklahoma Land Run (1893)
- Holding Down a Lot at Guthrie, Oklahoma (circa 1889)
- Oklahoma City, Indian Territory (1889)
- In Line at the Land Office, Perry, Oklahoma Territory (1893
- Harrison Avenue, Guthrie, Oklahoma Territory (1893)
- First Waterworks at Perry, Oklahoma Territory (1893)
- Robert Kennett, Claims Bought and Sold, Round Pond, Oklahoma Territory (1894)
- Schoolhouse in Oklahoma Territory (circa 1895)

About Boomtowns and Outlaws
— In <u>Westward Expansion</u>
Documents
- Thomas J. Dimsdale, Excerpt *The Vigilantes of Montana* (1866)
- State of Missouri Executive Department, Proclamation of the Governor of Missouri Rewards for the Arrest of Express and Train Robbers (1881)

- Alejandro Segura, The Legal Paper Attesting to Death of Billy the Kid (1881)
- John Poe, The Killing of Billy the Kid (1919)

Images
- Cabins at Deadwood in Black Hills, Dakota Territory (1876)
- Lynching of Robber in Tombstone, Arizona (1884)
- Camillus S. Fly, Group Portrait of Dodge City (Kansas) Peace Officers (circa 1890)
- Dorothea Lange, Graveyard Sign at Tombstone, Arizona (1937)

About Conservation
— In Westward Expansion
Documents
- U.S. Congress, Law Creating Yellowstone National Park (1872)
- John Muir, Excerpt from *The Mountains of California* (1894)
- U.S. Government, Newlands Reclamation Act (1902)
- George Bird Grinnell, Brief History of the Boone and Crockett Club (1913)

Images
- William Henry Jackson, Lower Falls of the Yellowstone River (1871
- John Muir and John Burroughs (1909)

About Travel Accounts
— In Westward Expansion
Documents
- Horace Greeley, Excerpt from *An Overland Journey from New York to San Francisco* (1860)
- Emily Faithfull, Excerpt from *Three Visits to America* (1884)
- Document with Audio Commentary– Robert Louis Stevenson, Excerpt from *Across the Plains* (1892)

Images
- Portrait of Horace Greeley

About Cultural and Intellectual Depictions of the West
— In Westward Expansion
Documents
- Joaquin Miller, Exodus for Oregon (circa 1870)
- Bret Harte, Excerpt from *The Luck of Roaring Camp* (1870)
- Samuel Langhorne Clemens (Mark Twain), Excerpt from *Roughing It* (1872)
- George A. Custer, Excerpt from *My Life on the Plains* (1874)
- Jesse James (song) (1880s)
- Theodore Roosevelt, Excerpt from *The Winning of the West* (1889)
- Frederick Turner Jackson, The Significance of the Frontier in American History (1893)

- Calamity Jane, *The Life and Adventures of Calamity Jane* (1896)
- Owen Wister, Excerpt from *The Virginian* (1902)

Images

- Fanny Palmer, *Across the Continent: Westward the Course of Empire Takes Its Way* (1868)
- *The Scouts of the Prairie* (1872)
- Frederic Remington, Prospecting for Cattle Range (1889)
- H.R. Locke, Portrait of Calamity Jane (1896)
- Poster for Pawnee Bill's Wild West Shows (1898)
- Buffalo Bill's Wild West Show (1898)

THE RISE OF MODERN AMERICA

From 1870-1900, the United States changed dramatically. Advances in technology and business made America the world's leading industrial power. Mass production and new inventions improved the daily lives of millions. But this progress was accompanied by poverty, pollution, and worker exploitation. While explosive urban growth generated economic opportunities and cultural vitality, it also strained city infrastructures and services.

In the decades following the Civil War, industrial growth and business innovations transformed the U.S. economy. Fueled by cheap energy sources, factories boosted the nation's manufacturing output by 600% between 1870 and 1900. Large corporations began dominating entire industries. Led by the railroads, these corporations pioneered new business techniques including issuing stock, building distribution and marketing networks, maximizing efficiency in mass production, diversifying corporate holdings, and employing sophisticated management practices. Consumers enjoyed low prices on a wider variety of products. Transportation and communication improved greatly.

The rise of the "robber barons" had negative effects too. Through pools, rebates, kickbacks, and trusts, they crushed small competitors. Many factory owners paid workers poorly and allowed them to labor in dangerous and unsanitary conditions. Corporate greed contributed to overall economic volatility. In the late 1870s and early 1890s, depressions paralyzed the nation. Encouraged by pro-business Supreme Court rulings and virtually non-existent government regulation of commerce, corporations disregarded the damage they inflicted on workers, consumers, and the environment.

The South struggled to keep pace with America's industrial revolution. Physical devastation from the Civil War, limited access to financial capital, and a poorly educated populace were only a few of the factors impeding southern economic progress. Adherents of "the New South creed" began calling for the region to capitalize on its natural resources and cheap sources of labor in order to foster industrial development. Such demands persuaded southern states to use tax incentives, exhibitions, convict leasing, and mineral and lumber rights to draw businesses. Timber, coal, iron, and steel soon emerged as lucrative southern industries. Textile mills sprung up in rural areas and employed scores of poor whites. For many southerners, factory work was an attractive alternative to the economic uncertainties of sharecropping.

The growth of factories forced workers to adjust their habits and expectations. Between 1860 and 1900, America's industrial workforce rose from 885,000 to 3.2 million. Skilled artisans found themselves displaced by machines operated by unskilled workers. Instead of building an entire item alone, workers repeatedly constructed one part of the finished whole. Managers closely supervised production and enforced strict codes of discipline. Child labor, accidents, long hours, and lay-offs were common in the nation's factories.

Spectacular growth of cities accompanied the industrial transformation. By 1900, almost half of Americans lived in cities. A wave of eleven million immigrants fueled the urban explosion. While the prospect of economic opportunities drew millions to the cities, the diversity and size of the urban population created problems. Native-born Americans resented having to compete for jobs and political power with immigrants. The urban influx overwhelmed housing, transportation, education, and sanitation facilities. While some residents languished in filthy slums, others gravitated toward new suburbs. Parks, streetcars, and commercial districts altered urban landscapes. Ethnic communities blossomed and vied for influence with political bosses. Reformers searched for ways to address urban problems and assimilate new immigrants.

Industrialization and urbanization highlighted increasing class differences among Americans. Clothing, furniture, houses, leisure, culture, and education became symbols of class status. Tycoons built luxurious mansions, threw elaborate parties, and engaged in philanthropy. Middle-class Americans eased their housekeeping burdens with indoor plumbing, commercially prepared foods, and mechanical washing machines. Telephones and electric lights changed domestic life. As more Americans moved into "white-collar" jobs, they no longer needed big families in order to sustain themselves economically and began practicing contraception. Labor-saving devices and smaller families enabled women to lavish more attention on their children. Many families ascribed to a Victorian moral code that emphasized industry, sobriety, and self-restraint.

These trends varied among minorities and the working class. Families remained large and members contributed to the family income whenever possible. Working-class people eagerly sought escapes from stressful factories and squalid housing. They gathered in streets, saloons, amusement parks, vaudeville theaters, and sporting clubs. When upper and middle-class people objected to the "indecency" and violence of these activities, working-class people resented their condescension. Despite such clashes, working-class culture left a profound impact on American traditions.

14.1

SELLING TO THE MASSES (1870-1900)

In the years following the Civil War, many Americans greatly improved their standards of living. The emergence of large-scale manufacturing created millions of new jobs. Cheap energy sources, industrial competition, and technological innovation drove down prices as production levels soared. When supply exceeded demand, companies used advertising in order to reach new customers. Brand names, slogans, warranties, endorsements, and testimonials created consumer loyalty and increased sales. Advertising became a lucrative industry with the ability to shape national tastes and desires.

FOCUS QUESTIONS

1. What do these advertisements suggest about life in this era?
2. Which products are being marketed toward wealthier consumers? Explain your answer.
3. Which products are being sold to women? How did advertisers appeal to female consumers?
4. What are the major themes of these advertisements? Do advertisers use similar appeals today? Explain your answer.

"Germproof" Glass, reprinted with permission of Rare Book, Manuscript, and Special Collections Library, Duke University.

MRS. LYDIA E. PINKHAM, OF LYNN, MASS.,

Woman can Sympathize with Woman.

Health of Woman is the Hope of the Race.

Yours for Health
Lydia E. Pinkham

LYDIA E. PINKHAM'S
VEGETABLE COMPOUND.

Is a Positive Cure

for all those Painful Complaints and Weaknesses so common to our best female population.

It will cure entirely the worst form of Female Complaints, all ovarian troubles, Inflammation and Ulceration, Falling and Displacements, and the consequent Spinal Weakness, and is particularly adapted to the Change of Life.

It will dissolve and expel tumors from the uterus in an early stage of development. The tendency to cancerous humors there is checked very speedily by its use.

It removes faintness, flatulency, destroys all craving for stimulants, and relieves weakness of the stomach. It cures Bloating, Headaches, Nervous Prostration, General Debility, Sleeplessness, Depression and Indigestion.

That feeling of bearing down, causing pain, weight and backache, is always permanently cured by its use.

It will at all times and under all circumstances act in harmony with the laws that govern the female system.

For the cure of Kidney Complaints of either sex this Compound is unsurpassed.

TINGLEY'S PATENT
HORIZONTAL
ICE-CREAM FREEZER

Is recommended for FAMILIES, HOTELS, SALOONS, and WHOLESALE MANUF. TURERS

As the best Ice-Cream Freezer in the market.

It saves ICE,
Saves TIME,
Saves LABOR,

And produces the finest quality of Cream known to the Art.

Send for Descriptive Catalogue.

CHAS. G. BLATCHLEY, Manufacturer,
506 COMMERCE STREET,
Philadelphia, Pa.

TIFFANY & CO.,

UNION SQUARE, N. Y.,

SILVERSMITHS,

Manufacture and sell, at very close and fixed prices, the following articles of STERLING SILVER, 925-1000 Fine:

Table Spoons,	Nut Spoons,	Table Forks,
Dessert Spoons,	Ice-Cream Spoons,	Dessert Forks,
Tea Spoons,	Fruit Spoons,	Oyster Forks,
Coffee Spoons,	Cake Knives,	Pie Forks,
Berry Spoons,	Soup Ladles,	Dessert Knives,
Sugar Spoons,	Gravy Ladles,	Pie Knives,
Jelly Spoons,	Oyster Ladles,	Crumb Knives,
Gravy Spoons,	Cream Ladles,	Fish Knives,
Preserve Spoons,	Punch Ladles,	Butter Knives,
Egg Spoons,	Waffle Knives,	Macaroni Knives,
Cheese Scoops,	Nut Picks,	Pickle Knives,
	&c., &c.	

☞ Patterns and Estimates sent to any part of the country. ☜

WORKS, 53 AND 55 PRINCE ST., N. Y.

Lydia Pinkham ad from *Salt Lake Herald* (1881); Ice Cream Freezer and Tiffany Silver ads reprinted with permission from http://advertising.harpweek.com.

14.2

FREDERICK LAW OLMSTED ON URBAN LIFE (1870)

In the latter half of the nineteenth century, many American cities grew tremendously. Construction of residences, factories, stores, and parks transformed urban landscapes. City planners, contractors, and politicians scrambled for innovative ways to accommodate expanding urban populations. In this passage, landscape architect Frederick Law Olmsted (1822-1903) describes New York City in 1870. Most noted for planning New York's Central Park, Olmsted also designed the grounds of the U.S. Capitol, Stanford University, and several other parks.

FOCUS QUESTIONS

1. According to Olmsted, how is New York City changing? How is the city meeting the needs of its growing population?
2. What is Olmsted's opinion of urban life? Do you agree with him? Explain your answer.

W e began experimentally with street railways twenty years ago. At present, in New York, one pair of horses serves to convey one hundred people, on an average, every day at a rate of fare about one-fiftieth of the old hackney coach rates; and the total number of fares collected annually is equal to that of the population of the United States. And yet thousands walk a number of miles every day because they cannot be seated in the cars. It is impossible to fix a limit to the amount of travel which really ample, convenient, and still cheap means of transportation for short distances would develop....

See how rapidly we are really gaining and what we have to expect. Two recent inventions give us the means of reducing by a third, under favorable circumstances, the cost of good McAdam roads. There have been sixteen patents issued from one office for other new forms of perfectly smooth and nearly noiseless street pavement, some of which, after two or three years' trial, promise so well as to render it certain that some improvement will soon come by which more than one of the present special annoyances of town life will be abated. An improvement in our sewer system seems near at hand, also, which will add considerably to the comparative advantages of a residence in towns, and especially the more open town suburbs.

Experiments indicate that it is feasible to send heated air through a town in pipes like water; and that it may be drawn upon; and the heat which is taken, measured and paid for according to quantity required. Thus may come a great saving of fuel and trouble in a very difficult department of domestic economy. No one will think of applying such a system to farmhouses.

Again, it is plain that we have scarcely begun to turn to account the advantages offered to townspeople in the electric telegraph; we really have not made a beginning with those offered in the pneumatic tube, though their substantial character has been demonstrated....

As railroads are improved, all the important stations will become centers or subcenters of towns, and all the minor stations suburbs. For most ordinary, everyday purposes, especially housekeepers' purposes, these will need no very large population before they can obtain urban advantages....

The construction of good roads and walks, the laying of sewer, water, and gas pipes, and the supplying of sufficiently cheap, rapid, and comfortable conveyances to town centers is all that is necessary to give any farming land in a healthy and attractive situation the value of town lots....

It is hardly a matter of speculation, I am disposed to think, but almost of demonstration that the larger a town becomes because simply of its advantages for commercial purposes, the greater will be the convenience available to those who live in and near it for cooperation, as well with reference to the accumulation of wealth in the higher forms—as in seats of learning, of sciences, and of art—as with reference to merely domestic economy and the emancipation of both men and women from petty, confining, and narrowing cares.

It also appears to be nearly certain that the recent rapid enlargement of towns and withdrawal of people from rural conditions of living is the result mainly of circumstances of a permanent character.

Frederick Law Olmsted, "Public Parks and the Enlargement of Towns," *Journal of Social Science*, No. 3 (1871).

14.3

—————■—————

HARPER'S NEW MONTHLY, "BOWERY, SATURDAY NIGHT" (1871)

In the wake of the Civil War, 11 million immigrants moved to U.S. cities. Immigrants contributed economically and enriched American culture, but also clashed with each other and with native-born Americans pursuing jobs, housing, and political power. While many immigrants were eager to assimilate into American life, they also preserved their own cultural traditions and social mores. This excerpt from Harper's New Monthly *demonstrates the ethnic diversity, economic contrasts, and cultural diversity characteristic of many urban areas. Established in 1850,* Harper's *remains one of the nation's most influential periodicals.*

FOCUS QUESTIONS

1. How does the author describe the Bowery neighborhood? Provide specific examples.
2. What kinds of people does he encounter? What is his attitude toward them?
3. How do you think that residents of the Bowery might have reacted to this article?
4. How does this portrait of urban life differ from that presented by Frederick Law Olmsted (Document 14.2)?

April 1871

The more noticeable features of the growth of New York city, from its grotesque and singular germ in the little Dutch village on the southern end of Manhattan Island, have been to a certain extent forced upon it by topographical peculiarities, both of land and water; but social and national groupings have also exercised an important agency. Like has sought and clung to its like, and as strenuously shunned and avoided its unlike or its opposite, until now, speaking within limits, different classes and nationalities have assumed and occupied their different quarters almost as distinctively as if assigned to them by despotic edicts of the Middle Ages. Neither has the city's growth been at all subservient to the prophecies or plans of those who have sought to direct or control it. Nothing has gone as it was meant to go, nor is any thing where, according to map and calculation, it should be....

If, however, we resign the doubtful task of prophesying what and where the city will be, there is a good deal in the study of the city as it is....

Turning off to the right, or easterly, from the City Hall, is a street of varying width, irregular direction, and no great length, destitute of all pretensions to beauty, architectural or otherwise, always dirty, crowded, and busy....

Let no unlettered rustic win derision to himself by calling this great thoroughfare Bowery Street, for it is The Bowery, and nothing more....

Various lines of street railway converge from different directions toward the Bowery.... The very cars with their passengers have something special for the eyes of him who would see. If observations are begun early enough in the afternoon, it may be possible to stratify the successive loads to a certain extent, and study the uses of the Bowery as a main artery and thoroughfare. It is so on all days, but more especially on Saturday, when the hours of labor terminate somewhat earlier than usual. Let us begin our researches between three and four o'clock, and pass from car to car, as the pickpockets, who are plenty here on Saturday night, are accustomed to do....

[A]t various intervals, from four until six, with belated exceptions, lingering along till seven, or even after, come swarms of weary and grimy mechanics and other workmen, with bevies of laughing shop-girls and factory operatives, tired enough, all of them, but buoyant for the moment, at least, with the sense of relief from labor, and the certainty that the week has reached an end, and that rest is before them. This, too, is almost a universal pay-day, and it is easy to discern in the countenances of these children of toil the traces of that peculiar feeling of satisfaction which is the sure effect of money in the pocket. No matter if the sum be small, or how soon it is to vanish before the demands of the evenings necessities, for the moment the well-earned wealth is there, and they are rich....

The evening ride of a very large number, especially those of German birth, terminates in the Bowery, while, even of those who are to be carried beyond, many pause briefly here, to transact their modest shopping and marketing. But here we are at the lower terminus of the Bowery, and as yet there is nothing very brilliant about it; something rather of gloom seems to pervade the atmosphere; and so it will be later in the evening, in spite of the street lamps and the glare from the windows, as if shadows floated out from the over-crowded tenement houses that loom in the darkness on either side. Here, in the dingy beer-shops and dirtier cellars, lurk some of the worst specimens of our foreign population, and uncanny forms of varied evil stop a moment to stare at you before they dive down dimly lighted stairways or slink around the corners....

It is after six o'clock now, but the cars that pass are still densely packed. They might be likened unto human sardine-boxes, but that no living being ever yet saw the little oily fishes clinging that way on the outside of their portable sarcophagi. The workmen with their tools, of manifold shape and use, are on the front platforms, while inside are women with their arms full of finished work, or babies, while every inch of standing room, and every last hope of holding on, are utilized to the uttermost. It is hot tonight, and how that mass of over-packed humanity manages to catch its breath is a problem for the philosophers.

There are some few manufacturing establishments in and about the Bowery; but except these there are no wholesale concerns, the business carried on being for the most part strictly retail. As a consequence of this, one of the first things to strike the eye of a wanderer from Broadway is the multiplicity of small, narrow-fronted shops, none of them deep, and, as a general thing, squeezed uncomfortably into sections of the lower stories of queer, antiquated little edifices of wood or brick....

It is evident at a glance, however, that during the more active hours of the day the retail commerce is expanding, for it overflows upon the sidewalks, and furniture, boots and shoes, crockery, hardware, and unlimited notions confine to a strait and narrow way the ample space theoretically allotted to foot passengers. Here and there the merchant, male or female, paces seductively up and down among or in front of his heaps of wares; and among these may be discerned numerous representatives of the absentee landlords of Juden, to many of whom the Bowery has proved indeed a land of promise, overflowing with mercantile milk and honey.

The larger part of these shops, it is worth while to notice, are thoroughly family affairs, containing both home and warehouse, and frugally employing the time and energies of all the generations gathered under the humble roof. The father, spectacles on nose, may be plying his trade in the far corner; the mother, baby on arm, may be chaffering with hard-to-please customers within, while keen-eyed youngsters of either sex watch from the threshold over the safety of the wares on the sidewalk. Keen-eyed, indeed, for they seem to discern, with an unerring instinct, the pause of the probable customer from the mere stare of curiosity, and the field of *their* survey is a poor one for the shop-lifter. Most assuredly the business interests of the house will be well served by the coming generation....

On either side of Bowery, for its entire length, the parallel streets are given up to tenement houses, while the transverse streets to the eastward, on which side the population is more German in its character, are lined with long rows of unpretending two and three story dwellings, relics of an earlier and less crowded era in the city's history. Many of these tenement houses offer commodious and decently arranged apartments, but the greater number aim only at packing the largest possible aggregate of humanity into the smallest possible modicum of space....

It is getting along into the dusk of the evening, and on the street corners the fruit wagons and other stands are beginning to show their flaring torches of smoky kerosene, while their salesmen are shouting forth their descriptions of wares, and the wonderful cheapness of their prices. Here are the remnants of stocks of oranges, lemons, etc., left over from the days business in the down-town markets, closing out at sacrifices alarming enough, in view of the fact that few of them would keep safely till Monday; and here are eloquent peripatetic soap and patent-wonder vendors, each with his little knot of curious customers holding up their motley faces in the glare of the kerosene,....

Coffees, teas, wines, liquors, wholesale and retail. You can buy almost any thing you want there, and a good many things you ought not to want....

As for the lager-beer salons, their name is legion, with legions of names. The larger and more pretentious supply more or less of music—some of it of a very excellent character, and some of it, alas! of a character as debased and execrable as that of those who make it and the audiences who hear it; for Bowery has its free concert halls, as evil and disgusting, if possible, as those of Broadway, though not nearly so numerous....

Yes, think of the stifling tenement houses and the uninviting streets, and then look carefully around you.

Germans all, and our own exceptional nationality is promptly and good-humoredly noted by the crowd. On every side are family groups, father, mother, and children, all merry, all sociable, all well-behaved and quiet. There is not the remotest danger of insult or disturbance, or need of the presence of any policeman. The Germans are proud to keep up the respectability of the place to which they bring their female friends and relatives, and we hope they may fully succeed in maintaining it. Here and there are couples from whose appearance not even the crowd, the laughter, and the lager can drive away the sheepish romance; for this is a great place for courting.

It is doubtless true that Croton is a healthful, sociable, and stimulating beverage of a Saturday night, after a week's labor, and there are better places than the beer gardens, but also there are worse. And do not let us moralize over what we perhaps do not altogether understand....

One more brief walk on our way up town through the still crowded street, for it is yet early. Not much extravagance in dress about us, and an endless stream of oddities in face and form and apparel, but very little noise, or nonsense, or glaring vice—that is, much less than you would naturally expect.

It is wonderfully easy to collect a crowd, for every body is out to be amused, and an excitement is an especial windfall. A dog-fight or a broken window would gather a thousand in a minute; but there are no fights or broken windows, and we are compelled to admit that Bowery has a respectability of its own. Two or three hours later things may have changed for the worse, but then these throngs who are passing us now will be at home and abed; for their week's work is over, they have had their Saturday evening, and every soul of them is honestly and reasonably tired.

W.O. Stoddard, *Harper's New Monthly Magazine*, Volume 42, Issue 251 (April 1871), 670-680.

14.4

DR. JOHN B. WHITAKER ON FACTORY WORKER HEALTH (1871)

Industrialization profoundly affected American workers. As technology enabled manufacturers to cut costs, employers relied on semi-skilled and unskilled workers who were easily replaceable. Laborers endured long hours and boring, dangerous work. Having formerly produced handcrafted goods, many skilled artisans found mechanized work demoralizing. In this passage, a Massachusetts physician evaluates the health of factory laborers.

FOCUS QUESTIONS

1. What psychological and physical problems did Whitaker observe among industrial workers?
2. Compare Whitaker's remarks to those of John D. Rockefeller (Document 14.5). What do their accounts suggest about the industrial revolution in America?

 Accidents and casualties were very numerous, partly owing to the exposed machinery and partly owing to carelessness.... It is really painful to go round among the operatives and find the hands and fingers mutilated, in consequence of accidents.

2. Unnatural or monotonous working positions...in some cases [make the worker] round-shouldered, in other cases producing curvature of the spine and bow-legs.

3. Exhaustion from overwork. In consequence of the long hours of labor, the great speed the machinery is run at, the large numbers of looms the weavers tend, and the general over-tasking, so much exhaustion is produced, in most cases, that immediately after taking supper, the tired operatives drop to sleep in their chairs....

4. Work by artificial light. It is injurious to the eyes. The affections consist principally in conjunctivitis, opacity of cornea, granulations of the lids, &c.

5. The inhalation of foreign articles.... I have been called to cases where I suspected this to be the cause of trouble in the stomach. After giving an emetic, they have in some cases vomited little balls of cotton....

10. Predisposition to pelvic diseases...among the female factory operatives produces difficulty in parturition. The necessity for instrumental delivery has very much increased within a few years, owing to the females working in the mills while they are pregnant and in consequence of deformed pelvis....

11 ...Predisposition to sexual abuse. There is no doubt that this is very much increased, the passions being excited by contact and loose conversation.... They arc, also, as a general thing, ignorant—at least to the extent that they do not know how to control their passions nor to realize the consequences....

12. Predisposition to depression of spirits.... Factory life predisposes very much to depression of spirits.

Dr. John B. Whitaker to the Gentlemen of the Massachusetts Bureau of Labor Statistics, Massachusetts Bureau of Labor Statistics, *Annual Reports*, 1870-1871, pp. 504-506.

14.5

JOHN D. ROCKEFELLER ON THE SUCCESS OF STANDARD OIL (1899)

In the late nineteenth-century, fierce competition consumed many of America's leading businesses. Corporate officials searched for ways to maximize efficiency and undermine their rivals. The oil industry provides a good example of these trends. After oil was first discovered in northwestern Pennsylvania, entrepreneurs rushed to build rigs and refineries.

John D. Rockefeller (1839-1937) became one of the leaders of the new oil industry. After opening his first refinery near Cleveland, Ohio in 1863, Rockefeller recognized the tremendous potential of the oil business. In 1870, he and a few associates founded the Standard Oil Company. Rockefeller scrutinized the smallest details of production in order to cut costs. One famous example was his insistence that managers reduce from forty to thirty-nine the number of solder drops required to seal kerosene cans. In mass production, such small changes saved millions of dollars. Rockefeller also embraced vertical integration—a tactic in which businesses own all aspects of a product's manufacture from raw materials to distribution. He purchased tanker cars and pipelines to ensure widespread availability of his oil. He also worked to ensure the consistent quality of his products.

Some of Rockefeller's business practices were much less benign. He strong-armed railroads into giving him rebates on Standard Oil cargo and demanded kickbacks on his competitors' shipments. He cut prices in order to force rivals into bankruptcy. By 1879, these tactics enabled Rockefeller to control ninety percent of the oil industry. Three years later, he hoped to garner more profits by establishing a trust in which stockholders from several companies placed their holdings under the control of a board of nine trustees. The trust enabled Standard Oil to absorb many of its competitors and to expand internationally. By 1890, Rockefeller had amassed a personal fortune of more than $800 million. Inspired by Standard Oil's success, many other industries established trusts.

By that time, public opinion was turning against ruthless "robber barons" like Rockefeller. In 1890, Congress passed the Sherman Anti-Trust Act outlawing trusts and other attempts to restrain trade. Vague wording and lax government enforcement, however, made the law ineffective for several years. Alarmed by the growing power of the trusts, Congress began investigating corporate practices. In this excerpt, Rockefeller testifies before an 1898 congressional committee. In 1911, the Supreme Court declared Standard Oil an illegal monopoly.

FOCUS QUESTIONS

1. What were some of the techniques Rockefeller used to make Standard Oil successful? What is Rockefeller's opinion toward these practices? What is his opinion of "industrial combinations" in particular?
2. Why do you think that Congress outlawed some of the tactics Rockefeller used? Should monopolies be outlawed? Explain your answers.
3. Compare Rockefeller's views on business to those of Dr. John B. Whittaker (Document 14.4). What do their accounts suggest about the industrial revolution in America?
4. Compare modern business practices to those described by Rockefeller. Are today's corporations more ethical than Standard Oil?

 Did the Standard Oil Company or other affiliated interests at any time before 1887 receive from the railroads rebates on freight shipped, or other special advantages?

A. The Standard Oil Company of Ohio, of which I was president, did receive rebates from the railroads prior to 1880, but received no special advantages for which it did not give full compensation. The reason for rebates was that such was the railroad's method of business. A public rate was made and collected by the railway companies, but so far as my knowledge extends, was never really retained in full, a portion of it was repaid to the shippers as a rebate. By this method the real rate of freight which any shipper paid was not known by his competitors nor by the other railway companies, the amount being in all cases a matter of bargain with the carrying company. Each shipper made the best bargain he could, but whether he was doing better than his competitor was only a matter of conjecture. Much depended upon whether the shipper had the advantage of competition of carriers. The Standard Oil Company of Ohio, being situated at Cleveland, had the advantage of different carrying lines, as well as water transportation in the summer, and taking advantage of those facilities made the best bargains possible for its freights. All other companies did the same, their success depending largely upon whether they had the choice of more than one route. The Standard sought also to offer advantages to the railways of the purpose of lessening rates of freight. It offered freights in large quantity carloads and trainloads. It furnished loading facilities and discharging facilities. It exempted railways from liability for fire. For these services it obtained contracts for special allowances on freights. There never exceeded, to the best of my present recollections, 10 per cent. But in almost every instance it was discovered subsequently that our competitors had been obtaining as good, and, in some instances, better rates of freight than ourselves....

9. Q. To what advantages, or favors, or methods of management do you ascribe chiefly the success of the Standard Oil Company?

A. I ascribe the success of the Standard to its consistent policy to make the volume of its business large through the merits and cheapness of its products. It has spared no expense in finding, securing, and utilizing the best and cheapest methods of manufacture. It has sought for the best superintendents and workmen and paid the best wages. It has not hesitated to sacrifice old machinery and old plants for new and better ones. It has placed its manufactories as the points where they could supply markets at the least expense. It has not only sought markets for its principal products, but for all possible by-products, sparing no expense in introducing them to the public. It has not hesitated to invest millions of dollars in methods for cheapening the gathering and distribution of oils by pipe lines, special cars, tank steamers, and tank wagons. It has erected tank stations at every important railroad station to cheapen the storage and delivery of its products. It has spared no expense in forcing its products into the markets of the world among people civilized and uncivilized. It has had faith in American oil, and has brought together millions of money for the purpose of making it what it is, and holding its market against the competition of Russia and all the many countries which are producers of oil and competitors against American oil....

It is too late to argue about advantages of industrial combinations. They are a necessity. And if Americans are to have the privilege of extending their business in all the States of the Union, and into foreign countries as well, they are a necessity on a large scale, and require the agency of more than one corporation....

I speak from my experience in the business with which I have been intimately connected for about 40 years. Our first combination was a partnership and afterwards a corporation in Ohio. That was sufficient for a local refining business. But dependent solely upon local business we should have failed long ago. We were forced to extend our markets and to seek for export trade. This latter made the seaboard cities a necessary place of business, and we soon discovered that manufacturing for export could be more economically carried on at the seaboard, hence refineries at Brooklyn, at Bayonne, at Philadelphia, and necessary corporations in New York, New Jersey, and Pennsylvania.

We soon discovered as the business grew that the primary method of transporting oil in barrels could not last. The package often cost more than the contents, and the forests of the country were not sufficient to supply the necessary material for an extended length of time, hence we devoted attention to other methods of transportation, adopted the pipe-line system, and found capital for pipe-line construction equal to the necessities of the business.

To operate pipe-lines required franchises from the States in which they were located and consequently corporation in those States, just as railroads running through differed States are forced to operate under separate State charters. To perfect the pipe-line system of transportation required in the neighborhood of fifty millions of capital. This could not be obtained or maintained without industrial combination. The entire oil business is dependent upon this pipe-line system. Without it, every well would shut down and every foreign market would be closed to us....

I have given a picture rather than a detail of the growth of one industrial combination. It is a pioneer, and its work has been of incalculable value. There are other American products besides oil for which the markets of the world can be opened, and legislators will be blind to our best industrial interests if they unduly hinder by legislation the combination of persons and capital requisite for the attainment of so desirable an end.

11. Q. What are the chief disadvantages or dangers to the public arising from them?
A. The dangers are that the power conferred by combination may be abused; that combinations may be formed for speculation in stocks rather than for conducting business, and that for this purpose prices may be temporarily raised instead of being lowered. These abuses are possible to a greater or less extent in all combinations, large or small, but this fact is no more of an argument against combinations than the fact that steam may explode is an argument against steam. Steam is necessary and can be used comparatively safe. Combination is necessary and its abuses can be minimized; otherwise our legislators must acknowledge their incapacity to deal with the most important instrument of industry. Hitherto most legislative attempts have been an effort not to control but to destroy; hence their futility.

U.S. Congress, Industrial Commission, "John D. Rockefeller, Answers to Interrogatories," *Reports of the Industrial Commission:* Vol 2. *Hearings before the Industrial Commission* (Washington, D.C., 1900). 794-797.

14.6

■

HENRY W. GRADY, "THE NEW SOUTH" (1866)

Following the devastation of the Civil War, the South was in ruins. While some southerners returned to agriculture, others supported an industrialized "New South." Pointing to the region's natural resources and supplies of cheap labor, advocates of "The New South" convinced northern businesses and banks to invest in southern factories. By 1900, textiles, lumber, coal, and iron were profitable enterprises. Nonetheless, debt, limited capital, and an inadequate banking system prevented southern industrial development from reaching northern levels for several decades.

Henry W. Grady (1850-1889) was one of the foremost proponents of "The New South." Under his leadership, The Atlanta Constitution *became the most widely circulated newspaper in the South. In his writings and speeches, Grady promoted industrialization and diversified agriculture as the keys to southern economic success. In this excerpt from his most famous speech, Grady addresses a New York audience on the economic potential of the South.*

■

FOCUS QUESTIONS

1. According to Grady, how has the South changed since the Civil War?
2. How does Grady distinguish between the Old South and the New South?
3. How does Grady describe southern race relations? Do you find his remarks convincing? Explain your answer.
4. Why would some northerners find Grady's speech persuasive?

22 December 1886

I n speaking to the toast with which you have honored me, I accept the term, "The New South," as in no sense disparaging to the Old. Dear to me, sir, is the home of my childhood and the traditions of my people. I would not, if I could, dim the glory they won in peace and war, or by word or deed take aught from the splendor and grace of their civilization—never equaled and, perhaps, never to be equaled in its chivalric strength and grace. There is a New South, not through protest against the Old, but because of new conditions, new adjustments and, if you please, new ideas and aspirations. It is to this that I address myself, and to the consideration of which I hasten lest it become the Old South before I get to it....

Let me picture to you the footsore Confederate soldier, as, buttoning up in his faded gray jacket the parole which was to bear testimony to his children of his fidelity and faith, he turned his face southward from Appomattox in April, 1865.

Think of him as ragged, half-starved, heavy-hearted, enfeebled by want and wounds; having fought to exhaustion, he surrenders his gun, wrings the hands of his comrades in silence, and lifting his tear-stained and pallid face for the last time to the graves that dot the old Virginia hills, pulls his gray cap over his brow and begins the slow and painful journey. What does he find—let me ask you, who went to your homes eager to find in the welcome you had justly earned, full payment for four years' sacrifice—what does he find when, having followed the battle-stained cross against overwhelming odds, dreading death not half so much as surrender, he reaches the home he left so prosperous and beautiful? He finds his house in ruins, his farm devastated, his slaves free, his stock killed, his barns empty, his trade destroyed, his money worthless; his social system, feudal in its magnificence, swept away; his people without law or legal status, his comrades slain, and the burdens of others heavy on his shoulders. Crushed by defeat, his very traditions are gone; without money, credit, employment, material or training; and, besides all this, confronted with the gravest problem that ever met human intelligence—the establishing of a status for the vast body of his liberated slaves.

What does he do—this hero in gray with a heart of gold? Does he sit down in sullenness and despair? Not for a day. Surely God, who had stripped him of his prosperity, inspired him in his adversity. As ruin was never before so overwhelming, never was restoration swifter. The soldier stepped from the trenches into the furrow; horses that had charged Federal guns march before the plow, and fields that ran red with human blood in April were green with the harvest in June; women reared in luxury cut up their dresses and made breeches for their husbands, and, with a patience and heroism that fit women always as a garment, gave their hands to work. There was little bitterness in all this. Cheerfulness and frankness prevailed....

But in all this what have we accomplished? What is the sum of our work? We have found out that in the general summary the free Negro counts more than he did as a slave. We have planted the schoolhouse on the hilltop and made it free to white and black. We have sowed towns and cities in the place of theories and put business above politics. [Applause.] We have challenged your spinners in Massachusetts and your iron-makers in Pennsylvania. We have learned that the $400,000,000 annually received from our cotton crop will make us rich, when the supplies that make it are home-raised. We have reduced the commercial rate of interest from twenty-four to six per cent, and are floating four per cent bonds. We have learned that one Northern immigrant is worth fifty foreigners, and have smoothed the path to southward, wiped out the place where Mason and Dixon's line used to be, and hung our latch-string out to you and yours....We have established thrift in city and country. We have fallen in love with work. We have restored comfort to homes from which culture and elegance never departed. We have let economy take root and spread among us.... In the record of her social, industrial, and political illustrations we await with confidence the verdict of the world....

But what of the Negro? Have we solved the problem he presents or progressed in honor and equity towards the solution? Let the record speak to the point. No section shows a more prosperous laboring population than the Negroes of the

South; none in fuller sympathy with the employing and land-owning class. He shares our school fund, has the fullest protection of our laws and the friendship of our people. Self-interest, as well as honor, demand that he should have this. Our future, our very existence depends upon our working out this problem in full and exact justice. We understand that when Lincoln signed the Emancipation Proclamation, your victory was assured; for he then committed you to the cause of human liberty, against which the arms of man cannot prevail [Applause]; while those of our statesmen who trusted to make slavery the cornerstone of the Confederacy doomed us to defeat as far as they could, committing us to a cause that reason could not defend or the sword maintain in the sight of advancing civilization. [Renewed applause.]...

The relations of the Southern people with the Negro are close and cordial. We remember with what fidelity for four years he guarded our defenceless women and children, whose husbands and fathers were fighting against his freedom.... Ruffians have maltreated him, rascals have misled him, philanthropists established a bank for him, but the South, with the North, protects against injustice to this simple and sincere people. To liberty and enfranchisement is as far as law can carry the Negro. The rest must be left to conscience and common sense. It should be left to those among whom his lot is cast, with whom he is indissolubly connected and whose prosperity depends upon their possessing his intelligent sympathy and confidence. Faith has been kept with him in spite of calumnious assertions to the contrary by those who assume to speak for us or by frank opponents. Faith will be kept with him in the future, if the South holds her reason and integrity.... .

Under the old regime the Negroes were slaves to the South, the South was a slave to the system. The old plantation, with its simple police regulation and its feudal habit, was the only type possible under slavery. Thus we gathered in the hands of a splendid and chivalric oligarchy the substance that should have been diffused among the people.... The Old South rested everything on slavery and agriculture, unconscious that these could neither give nor maintain healthy growth. The New South presents a perfect democracy, the oligarchs leading in the popular movements social system compact and closely knitted, less splendid on the surface but stronger at the core—a hundred farms for every plantation, fifty homes for every palace, and a diversified industry that meets the complex needs of this complex age....

This is said in no spirit of time-serving or apology. The South has nothing for which to apologize. She believes that the late struggle between the States was war and not rebellion, revolution and not conspiracy, and that her convictions were as honest as yours. I should be unjust to the dauntless spirit of the South and to my own convictions if I did not make this plain in this presence. The South has nothing to take back....

Every foot of the soil about the city in which I live is sacred as a battleground of the Republic. Every hill that invests it is hallowed to you by the blood of your brothers, who died for your victory, and doubly hallowed to us by the blood of those who died hopeless, but undaunted, in defeat—sacred soil to all of us rich with memories that make us purer and stronger and better, silent but stanch witnesses in its red desolation of the matchless valor of American hearts and the deathless glory of American arms—speaking an eloquent witness in its white peace and prosperity to the indissoluble union of American States and the imperishable brotherhood of the American people. [Immense cheering.]

Now, what answer has New England to this message? Will she permit the prejudices of war to remain in the hearts of the conquerors, when it has died in the hearts of the conquered? [Cries of "No! No!"] Will she transmit this prejudice to the next generation, that in their hearts, which never felt the generous ardor of conflict, it may perpetuate itself? ["No! No!"] ...Standing hand to hand and clasping hands, we should remain united as we have been for sixty years, citizens of the same country, members of the same government, united, all united now and united forever....

Joel Chandler Harris, *Henry W. Grady: His Life, Writings, and Speeches* (New York: Cassell Publishing Co., 1890), pp. 15-16.

14.7

ANDREW CARNEGIE, "THE GOSPEL OF WEALTH" (1889)

Visionary if controversial businessmen led America to industrial prominence. Aided by technological innovations, these men maximized profits through cost reduction and efficient production. Most were ruthless competitors who drove many smaller rivals out of business. Determined to keep overhead low, many industrialists paid their workers abysmal wages. At the same time, they amassed unprecedented fortunes and created the nation's most successful corporations.

The career of Andrew Carnegie (1835-1919) exemplifies these contrasts. Scottish by birth, Carnegie and his family moved to the United States in 1848. At the age of twelve, he began working as a bobbin boy in a textile mill. Determined to succeed, Carnegie attended night school and read voraciously. He eventually became a successful railroad executive. In the 1870s, he entered the steel industry. With Bessemer technology, vertical integration, and cost accounting, he made Carnegie Steel the world's largest corporation. In 1901, Carnegie sold his company to J.P. Morgan's United States Steel.

Carnegie pursued philanthropy with equal vigor. He established foundations and donated more than $300 million for libraries, schools, universities, and the arts. He wrote widely on social and political issues. In this famous essay, Carnegie explains his philanthropic philosophy.

Focus Questions

1. How does Carnegie believe that wealth changes societies in both positive and negative ways?
2. What are the ways of administering wealth? Which method does Carnegie prefer? Why?
3. What is Carnegie's opinion of estate taxes? Do you agree with him? Explain your answer.
4. Whom does Carnegie believe the wealthy should assist?
5. Is Carnegie's "gospel of wealth" philosophy a good solution to the problem of poverty? Explain your answer.

June 1889

The problem of our age is the proper administration of wealth, so that the ties of brotherhood may still bind together the rich and poor in harmonious relationship. The conditions of human life have not only been changed, but revolutionized, within the past few hundred years. In former days there was little difference between the dwelling, dress, food, and environment of the chief and those of his retainers....

This change, however, is not to be deplored, but welcomed as highly beneficial. It is well, nay, essential for the progress of the race, that the houses of some should be homes for all that is highest and best in literature and the arts, and for all the refinements of civilization, rather than that none should be so. Much better this great irregularity than universal squalor....

The price we pay for this salutary change is, no doubt, great. We assemble thousands of operatives in the factory, in the mine, and in the counting-house, of whom the employer can know little or nothing, and to whom the employer is little better than a myth. All intercourse between them is at an end. Rigid Castes are formed, and, as usual, mutual ignorance breeds mutual distrust. Each Caste is without sympathy for the other, and ready to credit anything disparaging in regard to it. Under the law of competition, the employer of thousands is forced into the strictest economies, among which the rates paid to labor figure prominently, and often there is friction between the employer and the employed, between capital and labor, between rich and poor. Human society loses homogeneity.

The price which society pays for the law of competition, like the price it pays for cheap comforts and luxuries, is also great; but the advantages of this law are also greater still, for it is to this law that we owe our wonderful material development, which brings improved conditions in its train. But, whether the law be benign or not, we must say of it, as we say of the change in the conditions of men to which we have referred: It is here; we cannot evade it; no substitutes for it have been found; and while the law may be sometimes hard for the individual, it is best for the race, because it insures the survival of the fittest in every department. We accept and welcome, therefore, as conditions to which we must accommodate ourselves, great inequality of environment, the concentration of business, industrial and commercial, in the hands of a few, and the law of competition between these, as being not only beneficial, but essential for the future progress of the race....

We start, then, with a condition of affairs under which the best interests of the race are promoted, but which inevitably gives wealth to the few. Thus far, accepting conditions as they exist, the situation can be surveyed and pronounced good. The question then arises...What is the proper mode of administering wealth after the laws upon which civilization is founded have thrown it into the hands of the few?...

There are but three modes in which surplus wealth can be disposed of. It can be left to the families of the decedents; or it can be bequeathed for public purposes; or, finally, it can be administered during their lives by its possessors. Under the first and second modes most of the wealth of the world that has reached the few has hitherto been applied. Let us in turn consider each of these modes. The first is the most injudicious. In monarchical countries, the estates and the greatest portion of the wealth are left to the first son, that the vanity of the parent may be gratified by the thought that his name and title are to descend to succeeding generations unimpaired. The condition of this class in Europe to-day teaches the futility of such hopes or ambitions. The successors have become impoverished through their follies or from the fall in the value of land.... Beyond providing for the wife and daughters moderate sources of income, and very moderate allowances indeed, if any, for the sons, men may well hesitate, for it is no longer questionable that great sums bequeathed oftener work more for the injury than for the good of the recipients....

As to the second mode, that of leaving wealth at death for public uses, it may be said that this is only a means for the disposal of wealth, provided a man is content to wait until he is dead before it becomes of much good in the world. Knowledge of the results of legacies bequeathed is not calculated to inspire the brightest hopes of much posthumous good being accomplished. The cases are not few in which the real object sought by the testator is not attained, nor are they few in which his real wishes are thwarted. In many cases the bequests are so used as to become only monuments of his folly.... Men who leave vast sums in this way may fairly be thought men who would not have left it at all, had they been able to take it with them....

The growing disposition to tax more and more heavily large estates left at death is a cheering indication of the growth of a salutary change in public opinion.... Of all forms of taxation, this seems the wisest. Men who continue hoarding great sums all their lives, the proper use of which for public ends would work good to the community, should be made to feel that the community, in the form of the state, cannot thus be deprived of its proper share. By taxing estates heavily at death the state marks its condemnation of the selfish millionaire's unworthy life...

There remains, then, only one mode of using great fortunes; but in this we have the true antidote for the temporary unequal distribution of wealth, the reconciliation of the rich and the poor a reign of harmony—another ideal, differing, indeed, from that of the Communist in requiring only the further evolution of existing conditions, not the total overthrow of our civilization. It is founded upon the present most intense individualism...Under its sway we shall have an ideal state, in which the surplus wealth of the few will become, in the best sense, the property of the many, because administered for the common good, and this wealth, passing through the hands of the few, can be made a much more potent force for the elevation of our race than if it had been distributed in small sums to the people themselves....

This, then, is held to be the duty of the man of Wealth: First, to set an example of modest, unostentatious living, shunning display or extravagance; to provide moderately for the legitimate wants of those dependent upon him; and after doing so to consider all surplus revenues which come to him simply as trust funds, which he is called upon to administer, and strictly bound as a matter of duty to administer in the manner which, in his judgment, is best calculated to produce the most beneficial results for the community— the man of wealth thus becoming the mere agent and trustee for his poorer brethren, bringing to their service his superior wisdom, experience, and ability to administer, doing for them better than they would or could do for themselves....

Those who would administer wisely must, indeed, be wise, for one of the serious obstacles to the improvement of our race is indiscriminate charity. It were better for mankind that the millions of the rich were thrown into the sea than so spent as to encourage the slothful, the drunken, the unworthy.....

In bestowing charity, the main consideration should be to help those who will help themselves; to provide part of the means by which those who desire to improve may do so; to give those who desire to rise the aids by which they may rise; to assist, but rarely or never to do all. Neither the individual nor the race is improved by alms-giving.... He is the only true reformer who is as careful and as anxious not to aid the unworthy as he is to aid the worthy, and, perhaps, even more so, for in alms-giving more injury is probably done by rewarding vice than by relieving virtue....

Thus is the problem of Rich and Poor to be solved. The laws of accumulation will be left free; the laws of distribution free. Individualism will continue, but the millionaire will be but a trustee for the poor; entrusted for a season with a great part of the increased wealth of the community, but administering it for the community far better than it could or would have done for itself. The best minds will thus have reached a stage in the development of the race in which it is clearly seen that there is no mode of disposing of surplus wealth creditable to thoughtful and earnest men into whose hands it flows save by using it year by year for the general good. This day already dawns. But a little while, and although, without incurring the pity of their fellows, men may die sharers in great business enterprises from which their capital cannot be or has not been withdrawn, and is left chiefly at death for public uses, yet the man who dies leaving behind him millions of available wealth, which was his to administer during life, will pass away unwept, unhonored, and unsung, no matter to what uses he leaves the dross which he cannot take with him. Of such as these the public verdict will then be: "The man who dies thus rich dies disgraced."

Such, in my opinion, is the true Gospel concerning Wealth, obedience to which is destined some day to solve the problem of the Rich and the Poor, and to bring Peace on earth, among men Good-Will.

Andrew Carnegie, "Wealth," *North American Review*, Vol. CXLVIII, No. 391 (June 1889), 653-64.

14.8

JACOB RIIS DESCRIBES LIFE IN THE TENEMENTS (1890)

During the massive urban migration of the late nineteenth century, slums developed in virtually every major city. Although many cities instituted housing codes and built sanitation facilities, many impoverished neighborhoods remained crowded and dirty. Epidemics of typhoid, smallpox, tuberculosis, and other diseases were routine. In his writings and photographs of New York's Lower East Side Jacob Riis (1849-1914) alerted millions of Americans to the problems of urban poverty. His book, How the Other Half Lives *(1890), prompted legislation to improve tenement living conditions.*

FOCUS QUESTIONS

1. How does Riis describe life in the tenements?
2. What is his attitude toward the poor? How do his views compare to modern views of poor people and the causes of poverty?
3. What solutions does Riis propose for helping the poor? Would Andrew Carnegie (Document 14.7) help the people whom Riis describes?

The statement once made a sensation that between seventy and eighty children had been found in one tenement. It no longer excites even passing attention, when the sanitary police report counting 101 adults and 91 children in a Crosby Street house, one of twins, built together. The children in the other, if I am not mistaken, numbered 89, a total of 180 for two tenements!...

New York's wage-earners have no other place to live, more is the pity. They are truly poor for having no better homes; waxing poorer in purse as the exorbitant rents to which they are tied, as ever was serf to soil, keep rising. The wonder is that they are not all corrupted, and speedily, by their surroundings....

The poorest immigrant comes here with the purpose and ambition to better himself and, given half a chance, might be reasonably expected to make the most of it. To the false plea that he prefers the squalid houses in which his kind are housed there could be no better answer. The truth is, his half chance has too long been wanting, and for the bad result he has been unjustly blamed....

As we stroll from one narrow street to another the odd contrast between the low, old-looking houses in front and the towering tenements in the back yards grows even more striking, perhaps because we expect and are looking for it....

Suppose we look into one?... Be a little careful, please! The hall is dark and you might stumble over the children pitching pennies back there. Not that it would hurt them; kicks and cuffs are their daily diet. They have little else. Here where the hall turns and dives into utter darkness is a step, and another, another. A flight of stairs. You can feel your way, if you cannot see it. Close? Yes! What would you have? All the fresh air that ever enters these stairs comes from the hall-door that is forever slamming, and from the windows of dark bedrooms that in turn receive from the stairs their sole supply of the elements God meant to be free, but man deals out with such niggardly hand. That was a woman filling her pail by the hydrant you just bumped against. The sinks are in the hallway, that all the tenants may have access—and all be poisoned alike by their summer stenches. Hear the pump squeak! It is the lullaby of tenement-house babes. In summer, when a thousand thirsty throats pant for a cooling drink in this block, it is worked in vain. But the saloon, whose open door you passed in the hall, is always there. The smell of it has followed you up....

Come over here. Step carefully over this baby—it is a baby, spite of its rags and dirt—under these iron bridges called fire-escapes, but loaded down, despite the incessant watchfulness of the firemen, with broken household goods, with wash-tubs and barrels, over which no man could climb from a fire. This gap between dingy brick-walls is the yard. That strip of smoke-colored sky up there is the heaven of these people. Do you wonder the name does not attract them to the churches? That baby's parents live in the rear tenement here. She is at least as clean as the steps we are now climbing. There are plenty of houses with half a hundred such in. The tenement is much like the one in front we just left, only fouler, closer, darker—we will not say more cheerless. The word is a mockery....

I tried to count the children that swarmed there, but could not. Sometimes I have doubted that anybody knows just how many there are about. Bodies of drowned children turn up in the rivers right along sin summer whom no one seems to know anything about. When last spring some workmen, while moving a pile of lumber on a North River pier, found under the last plank the body of a little lad crushed to death, no one had missed a boy, though his parents afterward turned up. The truant officer assuredly does not know, though he spends his life trying to find out, somewhat illogically, perhaps, since the department that employs him admits that thousands of poor children are crowded out of the schools year by year for want of room....

The old question, what to do with the boy, assumes a new and serious phase in the tenements. Under the best conditions found there, it is not easily answered. In nine cases out of ten he would make an excellent mechanic, if trained early to work at a trade, for he is neither dull nor slow, but the short-sighted despotism of the trades unions has practically closed that avenue to him. Trade-schools, however excellent, cannot supply the opportunity thus denied him, and at the outset the boy stands condemned by his own to low and ill-paid drudgery, held down by the hand that of all should labor to raise him. Home, the greatest factor of all in the training of the young, means nothing to him but a pigeon-hole in a coop along with so many other human animals. Its influence is scarcely of the elevating kind, if it have any....

The causes that operate to obstruct efforts to better the lot of the tenement population are, in our day, largely found among the tenants themselves. This is true particularly of the poorest. They are shiftless, destructive, and stupid; in a word, they are what the tenements have made them. It is a dreary old truth that those who would fight for the poor must fight the poor to do it. It must be confessed that there is little enough in their past experience to inspire confidence in the sincerity of the effort to help them. I recall the discomfiture of a certain well-known philanthropist, since deceased, whose heart beat responsive to other suffering than that of human kind. He was a large owner of tenement property, and once undertook to outfit his houses with stationary tubs, sanitary plumbing, wood-closets, and all the latest improvements. He introduced his rough tenants to all this magnificence without taking the precaution of providing a competent housekeeper, to see that the new acquaintances got on together. He felt that his tenants ought to be grateful for the interest he took in them. They were. They found the boards in the wood-closets fine kindling wood, while the pipes and faucets were as good as cash at the junk shop. In three months the owner had to remove what was left of his improvements. The pipes were cut and the houses running full of water, the stationary tubs were put to all sorts of uses except washing, and of the wood-closets not a trace was left. The philanthropist was ever after a firm believer in the total depravity of tenement-house people....

That the education comes slowly need excite no surprise. The forces on the other side are ever active. The faculty of the tenement for appropriating to itself every foul thing that comes within its reach, and piling up and intensifying its corruption until out of all proportion to the beginning, is something marvelous. Drop a case of scarlet fever, of measles, or of diphtheria into one of these barracks, and, unless it is caught at the very start and stamped out, the contagion of the one case will sweep block after block, and half people a graveyard....

It has since been fully demonstrated that a competent agent on the premises, a man of the best and the highest stamp, who knows how to instruct and guide with a firm band, is a prerequisite to the success of any reform tenement scheme....

The readiness with which the tenants respond to intelligent efforts in their behalf, when made under fair conditions, is as surprising as it is gratifying, and fully proves the claim that tenants are only satisfied in filthy and unwholesome surroundings because nothing better is offered. The moral effect is as great as the improvement of their physical health. It is clearly discernible in the better class of tenement dwellers to-day.... The Italian himself is the strongest argument of all. With his fatal contentment in the filthiest surroundings, he gives undoubted evidence of having in him the instinct of cleanliness that, properly cultivated, would work his rescue in a very little while....

Jacob Riis, *How the Other Half Lives* (New York: Charles Scribner's Sons, 1890).

14.9

A DAY AT CONEY ISLAND (1874)

Urbanization and industrialization sparked new forms of recreation. After long hours in factories and stores, working-class Americans were eager to relax. Saloons, streets, dance halls, amusement parks, sporting events, and vaudeville halls offered inexpensive escapes from boring work and crowded living conditions. While these forms of leisure sometimes clashed with middle-class standards of morality, they permanently changed the ways Americans socialized and played.

Coney Island was a favorite leisure destination for New Yorkers. Located about five miles south of Brooklyn, Coney Island was easily accessible by boat or rail and attracted thousands of city dwellers during the summer months. People enjoyed the beaches, restaurants, hotels, and varied diversions. One portion of the island, Gravesend Point, became notorious for gambling, prostitution, drinking, and fighting. More respectable visitors flocked to West Brighton, Brighton Beach, and Manhattan Beach. By 1900, Coney Island was a flourishing resort filled with amusement parks, dance halls, saloons, sideshows, restaurants, and hotels. In this article, a magazine writer describes a day at Coney Island.

FOCUS QUESTIONS

1. How does the author describe Coney Island?
2. What types of people does he encounter? What is his attitude toward them?
3. Why do you that many middle and upper-class Americans of the Victorian era objected to places like Coney Island? How do you think that people who went to Coney Island might have responded?

NEW YORK, although not yet the largest city in the world, has the largest suburb in the world; Long Island, the name by which that suburb is appropriately called, being about one hundred and twenty miles in length by twenty in breadth..... . Viewed as a suburb; Long Island offers greater inducements to all sorts of comers, perhaps, than any other city outlet in the world..... .

And among the least aristocratic features of the great suburb, none, perhaps, is more characteristic than Coney Island, the popular watering place of New York city, to the people of which, the tradesmen, mechanics, and workers generally, it stands in the same relation that Long Branch does to the wealthier and more exclusive classes. The fact that it is within one hour's journey from New York by steamboat, and but little more than that by the horse cars from Brooklyn, renders Coney Island unfashionable, since its advantages are attainable by all. Twelve years ago the facilities for reaching it were fewer than at present, as were the accommodations on the beach, and it is only within seven or eight years past that it has assumed the appearance of a great bathing place now presented by it....

At the lower end of the island there is a wharf to which the steamboats come, and when one of them disgorges its contents, very motley is the crowd that winds its way from it along the rush-laid path that leads to the beach. The women and children usually outnumber the men, and, as is generally the case in New York assemblages that do not rally round the standard of fashion, the German element is largely represented in the throng. Family groups are always a feature here, the thrifty mothers carrying provision baskets, the jars that protrude from which, having probably been emptied during the voyage, are taken by the happy fathers to the bar of some beach hostelry, thereto be replenished with lager beer or something stronger, according to order. Holiday attire, not gay, but of the picnic kind, is the rule here that is, among the respectable women, who are in the majority, though certain flaunting exceptions generally occur. The younger women usually have their beaux with them, which is judicious, seeing that beach flirtation is not only compatible with learning to swim, but absolutely indispensable to the perfect acquisition of that useful accomplishment. Children of all sizes are here, from the baby whose bath is to be a bucket of seawater, to the bigger ones who can flounder about in the surf or swim upon the crested waves. Several flashy men are usually to be seen in the crowd; men with velvet coats, and having Alaska diamond pins stuck in the breasts of their filigree shirts; men curled and oiled within an inch of their wild lives. These are gamblers from New York, though they usually describe themselves as sports, and they do a stroke of business at the island in more ways than one. Small speculators with various wares for sale are usually among the passengers that come by the boat; and here is one of them who has posted himself at a turn of the path, offering to the passers a variety of styles in very short bathing drawers carried in a card box....

Starting from the lower end of the island, and walking along the beach, one of the first things observable by the visitor is a series of small groups of men, gathered at intervals upon the shelving sand. On approaching one of these circles, the explorer will see in the center of it a man provided with a bit of plank propped upon a crutch or leg stuck into the sand. This fellow is one of the beach gamblers by whom the place is infested during the bathing season, and for whose suppression movements have been made year after year, but hitherto without success. He is manipulating three cards, which he shifts about with great rapidity, pattering volubly all the time about his game, which he offers to back for any amount the spectators may see fit to "plank down." He keeps jingling heavy gold pieces to allure the unwary, and his display of greenbacks of all denominations is absolutely profuse. Presently the circle is joined by one of the flashy gentlemen in velvet and diamonds who came down by the boat, and this person, producing a sheaf of greenbacks, at once enters into a dispute with the dealer, whose proffered stake he covers, and of course wins. It appears strange that the hollowness of this old trick of collusion does not put people on their guard, but the parting of the fool from his money seems to be a law of nature, illustrations of which are daily to be seen upon Coney Island beach. Young men who come down here to bathe frequently lose all the money they have about them to these thimble-rigging rascals, led away by the sight of the gold or greenbacks pocketed by some tawdry fellow who has the word confederate branded everywhere on his brazen face.

During the three summer months vast numbers of people are daily to be seen bathing all along the stretches of this beach. Out from the bathing houses come tumbling, indiscriminately, men, women, and children, all of them disguised beyond any possibility of recognition in their wild attire. The scene enables one to realize the notion of a lunatic asylum let loose, its inmates chasing each other with mad gesticulations about the shore and into the lapping surf. The women flap about in the water and scream like the fowls to which that element is natural; and some of them are strong swimmers, too, striking out boldly to a good distance from the beach. Numbers of the men lie wallowing for hours in the sand, in which they roll like wild beasts, rubbing it madly into their hair, and plastering themselves all over with it. Some of the bathers wear fancy dresses which they have brought with them. Here comes one in a striped black and white shirt with scanty drawers to match, and he is immediately hailed as a "zebray" by one of the grovelers in the sand. The word spreads from mouth to mouth along the shore, until the striped gentleman is fain to seek an asylum beneath the friendly waves. The scene upon the beach and in the water alike is a very rough one, having nothing about it of the reserve that regulates manners at the more aristocratic summer resorts.

Not infrequently some of the small Arabs of New York and Brooklyn streets are to be seen here, paddling in the pools left by the tide in the sandy hollows of the beach. It is certain that none of these urchins could have comedown either by horse car or boat, as that kind of traveling would be quite beyond their means. They are pedestrians through necessity, and have padded it all the way down upon their little bare feet. Absolutely independent of the sea-beaten gentlemen who furnish bathing dresses are these energetic pigwidgins, whose only costume generally consists of a fragmentary shirt and piecemeal trousers, the two garments, in some cases, being mysteriously combined into one. In this guise they splash into the pools or surf at some secluded point of the island, afterwards running about under the scorching sun until they are dry. Here, driven up sternforemost on the beach, is the hull of a wrecked vessel, lettered on her stern as the Polly Price, of Great Egg Harbor. Into this the seawater flows, affording a safe and commodious bath for a troop of these waifs from the city, who are plunging and flapping about in it like young ducks in a shower of rain....

The journey between Coney Island and Brooklyn by horse car offers disadvantages, one experience of which would be sufficient to deter many persons from trying it again. Except at very early morning these cars are crowded to excess, and, especially on the way back to the city, roughs of the worst New York type, and what can be worse than that? not infrequently force their way into these vehicles. The wonder is how little the passengers generally, many of them women of respectable appearance, seem to be incommoded by, or even disgusted at, the presence of these pernicious brutes. Here, now, soon after leaving the terminus at Coney Island, the conductor of the car stops it to take up three young men who have hailed him in terms that did not sound like blandishment. None of them are sober, and one, a powerfully built young fellow of twenty or thereabouts, is so drunk that, as he is supported to the car by his two companions, his feet trail upon the ground. He is in his shirtsleeves and has been fighting, for his features are battered out of drawing, and his clothes are saturated with blood. In the breast of his shirt is stuck the diamond pin, without which no New York rough ever considers himself presentable to decent society, and his fingers, which are all bruised and excoriated, are loaded with cheap, tawdry rings. There is no opposition whatever made to the entrance of this fascinating trio into the car. The fighting rough is hustled into it by his companions and laid out upon a seat, every object touched by him in the car being immediately smeared with his blood. No person among the passengers and they are by no means a rough-looking set appears to consider the circumstance an unusual one, or one to which exception should be taken. It seems from the testimony of the companions of the battered young man, whom one of them with pride avers to be a first-class bully of the Fourth Ward, that, while he was yet sober or partially so, he got into a roadside quarrel with one of a gang of negroes from the city, who were seeking for employment about the hotels on the island, and was badly thrashed by his opponent. Mortification at this drove him to drink, and hence his pleasing addition to the company in the car.

It will be seen from this brief account of a peculiar place, that Coney Island is more conspicuous for a rough side than for a smooth one. Its natural advantages as a sea bathing place for New York city are numerous, but they are counterbalanced by many circumstances at present inseparable from it. Few things could be more shocking to the sensibilities of a fashionable New York family than to inquire whether they intended going to Coney Island for the season. Occasionally, indeed, a "heavy swell" of the fashionable avenue will take a turn down there, with his team, "by way of a lark," but he does this in the confidence that he is not likely to be brought face to face with any of his set, and his account of things when he returns to the city includes nothing of Coney Island with its vulgar associations and motley crowd.

Charles Dawson Shanly, "Coney Island." *The Atlantic Monthly.* Volume 34, Issue 203 (September 1874), pp. 306-311.

SECONDARY SOURCE

EDWARD L. AYERS, "STORE AND MILL"

As the South integrated into the national economy, the region changed greatly. New products reached consumers via trains, salesmen, and mail-order catalogs. Stores opened in great numbers, even in isolated places. Advertisers tailored their messages for southern audiences. At the same time, new textile mills, lumber camps, and mines created economic opportunities for workers. Manufac-turing jobs, however, proved a mixed blessing for many southern families. Edward Ayers, a professor of southern history at the University of Virginia, explores these developments in the following excerpt from his Southern Crossing: A History of the American South, 1877-1906 *(1995).*

Go to your *Speaking of America* CD-ROM to read "Store and Mill."

FOCUS QUESTIONS

1. What techniques did firms use to reach southern consumers? Provide several examples.
2. How and why did consumers' buying patterns vary?
3. Why did many southern stores charge high prices and interest rates? How did customers react?
4. How did modern products and merchandising change southern life? What were some of the ways that the South lagged behind national trends?
5. What types of industries flourished in the South? What was distinctive about southern industrial development?
6. How did employment in these industries affect workers in both positive and negative ways?

AMERICAN JOURNEY ONLINE

http://ajaccesss.wadsworth.com [†]

About Consumption
—   In Women in America
    Images
    •   American Woman's Home (1869)

About Urbanization
—   In World War I and the Jazz Age
    Documents
    •   Urban Growth, 1870-1920 in
    Images
    •   Jacob Riis in Civil Rights in the United States
    •   Jacob Riis, Photographing Poverty (1889)
    •   Jacob Riis, Tenement Housing (1889)
    •   Jacob Riis, Excerpt from *How the Other Half Lives* (1890)

[†]   Enter password, choose the Archive indicated above, click on Contents, choose •Documents, •Images, or •Multimedia, and click on the title of the item.

— In <u>Civil Rights in the United States</u>
  • Jacob Riis

About Business and Industry
— In <u>World War I and the Jazz Age</u>
  Documents
  • John D. Rockefeller, Sr., Excerpt from *The Difficult Art of Giving* (1908)
  Images
  • Bessemer Converter
  • John D. Rockefeller Sr.
  • Matthew Brady, Andrew Carnegie (circa 1890)
— In <u>Civil Rights in the United States</u>
  Images
  • Female Labor
— In <u>The Constitution and Supreme Court</u>
  Images
  • Andrew Carnegie (circa 1901)

About Law
— In <u>The Constitution and Supreme Court</u>
  Documents
  • Samuel F. Miller, The Slaughter-House Cases (1873)
  • Morrison R. Waite, *Munn v. Illinois* (1877)
  • Melville Weston Fuller, *United States v. E.C. Knight Company* (1895)

About Economics
— In <u>World War I and the Jazz Age</u>
  Documents
  • Richard T. Ely, Excerpt from Statement of Principles of the American Economic Association (1885)

About the New South
— In <u>World War I and the Jazz Age</u>
  Images
  • Henry Grady

About Education
— In <u>World War I and the Jazz Age</u>
  Documents
  • Charles W. Dabney, Educational Limits to Reform in the South (1901)
— In <u>Women in America</u>
  Images
  • Alumnae Parade at Vassar (1903)

About Culture
— In <u>World War I and the Jazz Age</u>
  Images
  • Chicago's White City (1893)

OLD AMERICANS, NEW AMERICANS

Between 1865 and 1914, 25 million immigrants arrived in the United States. While many found economic opportunities and excitement, the emigrants also discovered that America could be a lonely and difficult place. Many native-born Americans considered the new arrivals racially inferior, culturally backward, and economically threatening. Intellectuals offered pseudoscientific justifications for white supremacy. Labor unions and politicians demanded restrictions on immigration. At the same time, African Americans watched in horror as disfranchisement, segregation, and racial violence swept the South. In this volatile climate, activists challenged America to abandon racism and fulfill its democratic promise.

Immigrants' experiences could vary a great deal depending on their economic aspirations, national origins, and place of residence. Prior to 1890, most immigrants came from northern and western European nations such as Great Britain, Ireland, Germany, and Sweden. These "old" immigrants were usually white, Protestant, and used to living under constitutional forms of government. These factors made assimilation into American society easier. After 1890, the majority of immigrants came from southern and eastern Europe. The "new" immigrants were often olive-skinned, Catholic or Jewish, and fleeing from political instability or religious persecution. These differences made native-born Americans especially suspicious of these emigrants.

The journey to the United States could be quite an ordeal. Most immigrants traveled steerage on crowded, unsanitary ships. Many fell ill during the voyage. Upon arrival, U.S. officials examined them for contagious illnesses, physical defects, and mental instability. If they discovered any of these conditions, they could order quarantine or deportation. Most immigrants, however, made it through the process without incident.

Since few emigrants could afford to buy land in the United States, most settled in urban areas. Certain ethnic groups came to dominate some cities. Boston, for example, developed a large and politically influential Irish community. St. Louis and Milwaukee attracted significant numbers of Germans. By 1900, eighty percent of New York City residents were immigrants or children of immigrants. Immigrants tended to live among members of their own ethnic group. Living conditions were often overcrowded and unhealthy, but ethnic neighborhoods also offered the foods, languages, festivals, and religions of the Old World.

Immigrants' rates of assimilation varied. Young people usually embraced American culture and English much faster than their parents. Some ethnic groups found the process easier than others. Large ethnic communities sometimes helped new arrivals in finding employment and housing. But not all immigrants wanted to remain in America. Thousands of single men came to work in the United States for short periods of time. Since they had no plans to settle permanently, they usually took the least desirable jobs and housing. After earning enough money, they returned to their homelands.

As the immigrant population increased, so did native-born Americans' animosity. Some blamed the immigrants for the filth and epidemics in urban slums. Because factories relied heavily on immigrants for unskilled labor, workers accused the emigrants of depressing wages and "stealing" jobs from U.S. citizens. In reality, immigrants often had low-paying and dangerous positions that native-born laborers rejected. Nonetheless, unions and politicians began demanding limits on immigration. Their efforts gathered support as belief in the genetic superiority of white Anglo-Saxons permeated American culture and intellectual life. At times, these factors erupted in violent confrontations between immigrants and native-born Americans.

Throughout the era, African Americans faced increasing difficulties. Those living outside the South endured *de facto* segregation, limited economic opportunities, and substandard housing. At the same time, southern blacks witnessed the rise of Jim Crow laws, lynching, and disfranchisement. Federal authorities did little to stop white supremacy from dominating southern life. In 1896, the Supreme Court ruled in *Plessy v. Ferguson* that "separate but equal" facilities were legal. Separate, however, was rarely equal in the following decades.

African Americans did not passively accept these conditions. Booker T. Washington advised blacks to make themselves economically indispensable to whites before pressing for political inclusion. Many built banks, insurance companies, churches, and other institutions in order to serve their communities. Others employed stronger tactics. W.E.B. DuBois demanded for immediate political equality and racial integration. New groups like the National Association for the Advancement of Colored People (NAACP) arose and pushed Americans to make all of her citizens political and social equals.

15.1

—————————■—————————

ON THE "EVILS" OF CHINESE IMMIGRATION (1878)

During the Gold Rush, about 24,000 Chinese immigrants came to California. Racial discrimination forced most to leave the gold fields. Some became launders, cooks, gardeners, farmers, and domestic servants. Others gravitated to dangerous jobs in railroad construction and mining. Although the Chinese immigrants proved tireless workers, many white laborers resented their willingness to work for low wages and refusal to abandon their language or cultural traditions. When an economic depression hit in the 1870s, white displays of nativism escalated. In 1877, a labor rally in San Francisco degenerated into anti-Chinese riot. In the wake of this violence, a committee of California legislators examined the impact of Chinese immigration. Their report is excerpted below.

FOCUS QUESTIONS

1. How do the legislators believe that the Chinese are affecting the culture and economy of California? How might a Chinese immigrant have responded to these characterizations?
2. Why do the legislators believe that the Chinese cannot be Americanized? Was this a fair generalization? Explain your answer.
3. Compare this report to Yan Phou Lee's "The Chinese Must Stay" (Document 15.2). Which reading do you find most persuasive? Why?

he Chinese have now lived among us, in considerable numbers*, for a quarter of a century, and yet they remain separate, distinct from, and antagonistic to our people in thinking, mode of life, in tastes and principles, and are as far from assimilation as when they first arrived.

They fail to comprehend our system of government; they perform no duties of citizenship; they are not available as jurymen; cannot be called upon as a *posse comitatus* to preserve order, nor be relied upon as soldiers.

They do not comprehend or appreciate our social ideas, and they contribute but little to the support of any of our institutions, public or private.

They bring no children with them, and there is, therefore, no possibility of influencing them by our ordinary educational appliances.

There is, indeed, no point of contact between the Chinese and our people through which we can Americanize them. The rigidity which characterizes these people forbids the hope of any essential change in their relations to our own people or our government.

We respectfully submit admitted proposition that no nation, much less a republic, can safely permit the presence of a large and increasing element among its people which cannot be assimilated or made to comprehend the responsibilities of citizenship.

The great mass of the Chinese residents of California are not amenable to our laws. It is almost impossible to procure the conviction of Chinese criminals, and we are never sure that a conviction, even when obtained, is in accordance with justice.

This difficulty arises out of our ignorance of the Chinese language and the fact that their moral ideas are wholly distinct from our own. They do not recognize the sanctity of an oath, and utterly fail to comprehend the crime of perjury. Bribery,

---

* In 1878, the Chinese comprised 1 percent of the California population, and a miniscule 0.002 percent of the nation's population.

intimidation, and other methods of baffling judicial action, are considered by them as perfectly legitimate. It is an established fact that the administration of justice among the Chinese is almost impossible, and we are, therefore, unable to protect offenses against our own people. This anomalous condition, in which the authority of law is so generally vacated, imperils the existence of our republican institutions to a degree hitherto unknown among us....

We now come to an aspect of the question more revolting still. We would shrink from the disgusting details did not a sense of duty demand that they be presented. Their lewd women induce, by the cheapness of their offers, thousands of boys and young men to enter their dens, very many of whom are inoculated with venereal disease, and some of our physicians treat a half dozen cases daily. The fact that these diseases have their origin chiefly among the Chinese is well established....

But we desire to call your attention to the sanitary aspect of the subject. The Chinese herd together in one spot, whether in a city or village, until they transform the vicinage into a perfect hive—there they live packed together, a hundred living in a space that would be insufficient for an average American family.

Their place of domicile is filthy in the extreme, and to a degree that cleansing is impossible except by the absolute destruction of the dwellings they occupy. But for the healthfulness of our climate, our city populations would have long since been decimated by pestilence from these causes. And we do not know how long this natural protection will suffice us.

In almost every house is found a room devoted to opium smoking, and these places are visited by white boys and women, so that the deadly opium habit is being introduced among our people....

We now call attention to an aspect of the subject of such huge proportions, and such practical and pressing importance, that we almost dread to enter upon its consideration, namely, the effect of Chinese labor upon our industrial classes. We admit that the Chinese were, in the earlier history of the State, when white labor was not attainable, very useful in the development of our peculiar industries; that they were of great service in railroad building, in mining, gardening, general agriculture, and as domestic servants.

We admit that the Chinese are exceedingly expert in all kinds of labor and manufacturing; that they are easily and inexpensively handled in large numbers.

We recognize the right of all men to better their condition when they can, and deeply sympathize with the overcrowded population of China....

Our laborers cannot be induced to live like vermin, as the Chinese and these habits of individual and family life have ever been encouraged by our statesmen as essential to good morals.

Our laborers require meat and bread, which have been considered by us as necessary to that mental and bodily strength which is thought to be important in the citizens of a Republic which depends upon the strength of its people, while the Chinese require only rice, dried fish, tea, and a few simple vegetables. The cost of sustenance to the whites if four-fold greater than that of the Chinese, and the wages of the whites must of necessity be greater than the wages required by the Chinese. The Chinese are, therefore, able to underbid the whites in every kind of labor. They can be hired in masses; they can be managed and controlled like unthinking slaves. But our laborer has an individual life, cannot be controlled as a slave by brutal masters, and this individuality has been required of him by the genius of our institutions, and upon these elements of character the State depends for defense and growth....

As a natural consequence the white laborer is out of employment, and misery and want are fast taking the places of comfort and plenty.

Now, to consider and weigh the benefits returned to us by the Chinese for these privileges and for these wrongs to our laboring class. They buy little or nothing from our own people, but import both their food and clothing from China; they send their wages home; they have not introduced a single industry peculiar to their own country; they contribute nothing to the support of our institutions; can never be relied upon as defenders of the State; they have no intention of becoming citizens; they acquire no homes, and are a constant tax upon the public treasury....

California, Senate, Special Committee on Chinese Immigration, "An Address to the American People of the United States upon the Evils of Chinese Immigration," *Report of the Special Committee on Chinese Immigration to the California State Senate, 1878*, 8-9, 25, 35, 46-47.

15.2

YAN PHOU LEE, "THE CHINESE MUST STAY" (1889)

In 1882, popular demands for limits on immigration convinced Congress to pass the Chinese Exclusion Act. The law greatly restricted Chinese immigration for ten years, but exempted merchants, teachers, students, and other visitors. Congress closed these loopholes with the Geary Act of 1892. The prohibition on Chinese emigration to the United States remained in effect until 1943.

In this passage, Yan Phou Lee protests anti-Chinese discrimination. Born in China in 1861, Yan won a scholarship to study in the United States. After graduating from Yale, he wrote When I Was a Boy in China *(1887).*

FOCUS QUESTIONS

1. According to Yan, what are the major stereotypes about the Chinese immigrants? How does Yan challenge these characterizations?
2. What does Yan believe that the Chinese contribute to American society? How does he describe those who oppose the Chinese?
3. What kind of tone does Yan use? Why do you think he chose to write in this style?

4. Compare Yan Phou Lee's "The Chinese Must Stay" to "On the 'Evils' of Chinese Immigration. "(Document 15.1). Which reading do you find most persuasive? Why?

N o nation can afford to let go its high ideals. The founders of the American Republic asserted the principle that all men are created equal, and made this fair land a refuge for the whole world. Its manifest destiny, therefore, is to be the teacher and leader of nations in liberty. Its supremacy should be maintained by good faith and righteous dealing, and not by the display of selfishness and greed. But now, looking at the actions of this generation of Americans in their treatment of other races, who can get rid of the idea that that Nation, which Abraham Lincoln said was conceived in liberty, waxed great through oppression, and was really dedicated to the proposition that all men are created to prey on one another?...

Chinese immigrants never claimed to be any better than farmers, traders, and artisans. If, on the one hand, they are not princes and nobles, on the other hand, they are not coolies and slaves. They all came voluntarily, as their consular papers certified, and their purpose in leaving their home and friends was to get honest work. They were told that they could obtain higher wages in America than elsewhere, and that Americans were friendly to the Chinese and invited them to come....

So long as the Chinese served their purposes and did not come into collision with the hoodlum element afterwards imported to California, the people of that State had nothing to complain of regarding them. Why should they, when, at one time, half the revenue of the State was raised out of the Chinese miners? But the time came when wages fell with the cost of living. The loafers became strong enough to have their votes sought after. Their wants were attended to. Their complaints became the motive power of political activity. So many took up the cry against the Chinese that it was declared that no party could succeed on the Pacific coast which did not adopt the hoodlums' cause as its own....

Those who remember events of some thirty-five years ago will see nothing strange in the antagonism of one class of laborers to another. Opposition to the Chinese is identical with the opposition to the free immigration of Europeans, and especially of the Irish; for it was once urged against the trans-Atlantic immigrants that their cheap labor "would degrade, demoralize, and pauperize American labor, and displace intelligent Americans in many branches of employment." There was a bitter conflict, but the sensible view prevailed. For it was found that a greater supply of unskilled labor made it possible for skilled laborers to command higher wages and more regular employment.

Why is it that the American laborer was soon raised to a higher social and industrial plane, and ceased to fear Irish competition, while the Irish still dread the competition of the Chinese? It is simply because the Irish are industrially inferior to their competitors. They have not the ability to get above competition, like the Americans, and so, perforce, they must dispute with the Chinese for the chance to be hewers of wood and drawers of water....

But you say...the Chinese stand charged with too many things to make them desirable. Ah, yes! I see. But it is only fair to look into these charges before we pass our judgment. It has been urged:

I.   *That the influx of Chinese is a standing menace to Republican institutions upon the Pacific coast and the existence there of Christian civilization.*

That is what I call a severe reflection on Republican institutions and Christian civilization. Republican institutions have withstood the strain of 13,000,000 of the lower classes of Europe, among whom may be found Anarchists, Socialists, Communists, Nihilists, political assassins, and cut-throats; but they cannot endure the assaults of a few hundred thousands of the most peaceable and most easily-governed people in the world!

Christianity must have lost its pristine power, for, having subdued and civilized one-half the world, it is now powerless before the resistance of a handful of Chinese! Surely the Chinese must be angels or devils! If angels, they would go without your bidding. If devils, you would not be able to drive them out...

III.   *That the Chinese race seems to have no desire for progress.*

In the last fifteen years the Chinese Government has educated upwards of two hundred students in Europe and America, has built arsenals and navy-yards, established schools and colleges on Western models, disciplined an army that whipped the Russians, created a navy that would put the American navy to shame, put up thousands of miles of telegraph wires; and it is now busily opening up mines, building railroads, and availing itself of American capital and experience to put up telephones and establish a national bank. The Chinese are not ashamed to own that they appreciate the Americans.

IV.   *That the Chinese have displaced white laborers by low wages and cheap living, and that their presence discourages and retards white immigration to the Pacific States.*

This charge displays so little regard for truth and the principles of political economy that it seems like folly to attempt an answer. But please to remember that it was by the application of Chinese "cheap labor" to the building of railroads, the reclamation of swamp-lands, to mining, fruit-culture, and manufacturing, that an immense vista of employment was opened up for Caucasians, and that millions now are enabled to live in comfort and luxury where formerly adventurers and desperadoes disputed with wild beasts and wilder men for the possession of the land. Even when the Chinaman's work is menial (and he does it because he must live, and is too honest to steal and too proud to go to the almshouse), he is employed because of the scarcity of such laborers. It is proved that his work enables many to turn their whole attention to something else, so that even the hoodlum may don a clean shirt at least once a month. You may as well run down machinery as to sneer at Chinese cheap labor. Machines live on nothing at all; they have displaced millions of laborers; why not do away with machines?...

V. *That the Chinese do not desire to become citizens of this country.*

Why should they? Where is the inducement? Let me recite briefly a few of the laws and ordinances which, though couched in general terms, were made for their special benefit.

The Foreign-Miners' License Law, which forced every Chinese miner, during a period of twenty years, to pay from $4 to $20 per month for the privilege of working claims which others had abandoned.

An act of the California Legislature, 1885, laid a tax of $55 on each Chinese immigrant.

Another, 1862, provided (with a few exceptions) that every Chinaman over eighteen years of age should pay a capitation-tax of $2.50.

A San Francisco city ordinance, passed March 15, 1876, provided that all laundries should pay licenses as follows: those using a one-horse vehicle, $2 per quarter; two horses, $4; no vehicle, $15. This is discrimination with a vengeance!

I maintain that a sober, industrious, and peaceable people, like the Chinese, who mind their own business and let others do the same, are as fit to be voters as the quarrelsome, ignorant, besotted, and priest-ridden hordes of Europe....

VII. *The Chinese neither have intercourse with the Caucasians nor will assimilate with them.*

Yes, just think of it! As soon as the ship comes into harbor, a committee of the citizens get on board to present the Chinaman with the freedom of the city (valued at $5). A big crowd gathers at the wharf to receive him with shouts of joy (and showers of stones). The aristocrats of the place flock to his hotel to pay their respects (and to take away things to remember him by). He is so feted and caressed by Caucasian society that it is a wonder his head is not turned (or twisted off)....

IX. *That the Chinese immigrants are mostly criminals.*

It is not true. I admit that we have a criminal class in China, but the few that got over here came through the neglect of the officers of the Custom-House to enforce the laws...

Every fair-minded man can testify that the Chinese are the most law-abiding people in the community, that they are not easily provoked, but are patient (oh, too patient!) under insult and injury. They seldom appear in court-rooms in the character of prisoners. You have never seen one drunk in your life. But, you say, he smokes opium. That, I answer, is his own affair. The law provides no penalties against private vices. You have never heard of Chinamen who organized strikes, stuffed ballot-boxes, and corrupted legislation at the fountain-head. Why, then, are they not as desirable as other immigrants? Is it a crime to be industrious, faithful, law-abiding? Wrong to coin one's honest toil into gold, and, instead of wasting one's earnings in drink and debauchery, to support wife and children therewith?...

XI. *That the Chinese bring women of bad character to San Francisco, and that their vices are corrupting the morals of the city.*

How serious a charge this is we cannot realize until we get at all the facts. Just imagine California, the most virtuous of States, and San Francisco, the most immaculate of cities, lying helpless under...Chinese immorality! Have you ever been to San Francisco? Unless you can endure paradise and Eden-like purity, you would better not go there. Why, the Sabbath stillness in that city is simply appalling. The people all go to church, and if you suggest whiskey toddy or a base-ball game on Sunday, they will turn up their eyes, throw up their hands, and pray the Lord to have mercy on you. There are no drunken brawls at any time (except in Chinatown), and it is the policeman's picnic-ground (except in Chinatown)…. Californians are pure, moral, and religious, in all that they do. As for having disreputable houses, or women with loose morals about them, I tell you they are as innocent as lambs. Indeed, Satan could not have made a greater commotion in Eden than the Chinese in California. One would suppose that such a model community would "clean out" those bad Chinese women. But it did not. It deputed a number of special policemen to watch them and arrest them, but it seems that these specials had the marvelous power of transmuting their brass into pure gold, and that, in the exercise of that power, they were as blind as bats. If the virtuous community of San Francisco permitted their morals to be corrupted, it is their own fault….

Yan Phou Lee, "The Chinese Must Stay," *North American Review* Vol. 48, No. 389 (April 1889), pp. 476-83.

15.3

GRANT HAMILTON, "WHERE IS THE BLAME?" (1891)

Throughout the late nineteenth century, many native-born Americans opposed immigrants for religious, political, economic, and cultural reasons. This disdain for immigrants, known as nativism, pervaded American life. Political cartoons provided a powerful medium for expressing nativist attitudes. Publications like Puck Magazine *and* The Judge *were primarily humor magazines, but many of their artists had pointed political views. Each reached several thousand readers every week. While* Puck *closed in 1918,* The Judge *flourished until the 1930s. In 1891, cartoonist Grant Hamilton of* The Judge *expresses his view of immigration.*

FOCUS QUESTIONS

1. How does this cartoon characterize immigration? What social problems does it ascribe to immigrants?

2. Why do you think that Grant Hamilton drew this cartoon? Who do you think was his intended audience?
3. Compare modern attitudes toward immigrants to those expressed by Hamilton.

T he caption read: "If immigration were properly restricted you would no longer be troubled with anarchy, socialism, the Mafia, and such kindred evils." The sign in the background proclaims: "Entry for emigrants, baggage the only requisite." Various immigrants are labeled: Polish vagabond, Italian brigand, English convict, Russian anarchist, and Irish pauper.

The Judge, 1891.

15.4

■

FRANCIS A. WALKER CALLS FOR
RESTRICTION OF IMMIGRATION (1896)

By the early 1890s, calls for the restriction of immigration were markedly escalating. Many native-born Americans viewed "new" immigrants from Southern and Eastern Europe as a racial, political, and economic threat to the United States. In 1894, a group of Boston elites formed the Immigration Restriction League (IRL). Within three years, the organization persuaded Congress to pass a law requiring that immigrants be literate in some language. Although President Grover Cleveland vetoed the literacy bill, President Woodrow Wilson signed similar legislation in 1917. In this selection, a member of the IRL explains his support for limits on immigration.

FOCUS QUESTIONS

1. Why does Walker believe that additional immigration restrictions are necessary? Do you find his arguments persuasive? Explain your answer.
2. How does Walker describe the newest immigrants arriving in the United States? Compare Walker's attitudes to those expressed in Grant Hamilton's cartoon (Document 15.3).

W hen we speak of the restriction of immigration, at the present time, we have not in mind measures undertaken for the purpose of straining out from the vast throngs of foreigners arriving at our ports a few hundreds, or possibly thousands of persons, deaf, dumb, blind, idiotic, insane, pauper, or criminal, who might otherwise become a hopeless burden upon the country, perhaps even an active source of mischief. The propriety, and even the necessity of adopting such measures is now conceded by men of all shades of opinion concerning the larger subject.... We already have laws which cover a considerable part of this ground.... There is a serious effort on the part of our immigration officers to enforce the regulations prescribed, though when it is said that more than five thousand persons have passed through the gates at Ellis Island, in New York harbor, during the course of a single day, it will be seen that no very careful scrutiny is practicable.

...The question of the restriction of immigration to-day does not deal with that phase of the subject. What is proposed is, not to keep out some hundreds, or possibly thousands of persons, against whom lie specific objections like those above indicated, but to exclude perhaps hundreds of thousands, the great majority of whom would be subject to no individual objections; who, on the contrary, might fairly be expected to earn their living here in this new country, at least up to the standard known to them at home, and probably much more. The question to-day is, not of preventing the wards of our almshouses, our insane asylums, and our jails from being stuffed to repletion by new arrivals from Europe; but of protecting the American rate of wages, the American standard of living, and the quality of American citizenship from degradation through the tumultuous access of vast throngs of ignorant and brutalized peasantry from the countries of eastern and southern Europe....

Let us now inquire what are the changes in our general conditions which seem to demand a revision of the opinion and policy heretofore held regarding immigration....

First, we have the important fact of the complete exhaustion of the free public lands of the United States. Fifty years ago, thirty years ago, vast tracts of arable land were open to every person arriving on our shores.... Under these circumstances it was a very simple matter to dispose of a large immigration. To-day there is not a good farm within the limits of the United States which is to be had under either of these acts.... This is not to say that more people cannot and will not, sooner or later, with more or less of care and pains and effort, be placed upon the land of the United States; but it does of itself alone show how vastly the difficulty of providing for immigration has increased....

A second change in our national condition, which importantly affects our capability of taking care of large numbers of ignorant and unskilled foreigners, is the fall of agricultural prices which has gone on steadily since 1873.... It is a necessary consequence of this that the ability to employ a large number of uneducated and unskilled hands in agriculture has greatly diminished.

Still a third cause which may be indicated, perhaps more important than either of those thus far mentioned, is found in the fact that we have now a labor problem.... There is no country of Europe which has not for a long time had a labor problem; that is, which has not so largely exploited its own natural resources, and which has not a labor supply so nearly meeting the demands of the market at their fullest, that hard times and periods of industrial depression have brought a serious strain through extensive non-employment of labor.

From this evil condition we have, until recently, happily been free. During the last few years, however, we have ourselves come under the shadow of this evil, in spite of our magnificent natural resources. We know what it is to have even intelligent and skilled labor unemployed through considerable periods of time.... No longer is it a matter of course that every industrious and temperate man can find work in the United States. And it is to be remembered that, of all nations, we are the one which is least qualified to deal with a labor problem. We have not the machinery, we have not the army, we have not the police, we have not the traditions and instincts, for dealing with such a matter, as the great railroad and other strikes of the last few years have shown.

I have spoken of three changes in the national condition, all subjective, which greatly affect our capability of dealing with a large and tumultuous immigration. There is a fourth, which is objective. It concerns the character of the foreigners now resorting to our shores. Fifty, even thirty years ago, there was a rightful presumption regarding the average immigrant that he was among the most enterprising, thrifty, alert, adventurous, and courageous of the community from which he came. It required no small energy, prudence, forethought, and pains to conduct the inquiries relating to his migration, to accumulate the necessary means, and to find his way across the Atlantic. To-day the presumption is completely reversed. So thoroughly has the continent of Europe been crossed by railways, so effectively has the business of emigration there been exploited, so much have the rates of railroad fares and ocean passage been reduced, that it is now among the least thrifty and prosperous members of any European community that the emigration agent finds his best recruiting-ground.... Illustrations of the ease and facility with which this Pipe Line Immigration is now carried on might be given in profusion. So broad and smooth is the channel, there is no reason why every foul and stagnant pool of population in Europe, which no breath of intellectual or industrial life has stirred for ages, should not be decanted upon our soil....

But it is not alone that the presumption regarding the immigrant of today is so widely different from that which existed regarding the immigrant of thirty or fifty years ago. The immigrant of the former time came almost exclusively from western and northern Europe. We have now tapped great reservoirs of population then almost unknown to the passenger lists of our arriving vessels. Only a short time ago, the immigrants from southern Italy, Hungary, Austria, and Russia together made up hardly more than one per cent of our immigration. Today the proportion has risen to something like forty per cent, and threatens soon to become fifty or sixty per cent, or even more. The entrance into our political, social, and industrial life of such vast masses of peasantry, degraded below our utmost conceptions, is a matter which no intelligent patriot can look upon without the gravest apprehension and alarm. These people have no history behind them which is of a nature to give encouragement. They have none of the inherited instincts and tendencies which made it comparatively easy to deal with the immigration of the olden time. They are beaten men from beaten races; representing the worst failures in the struggle for existence. Centuries are against them, as centuries were on the side of those who formerly came to us. They have none of the ideas and aptitudes which fit men to take up readily and easily the problem of self-care and self-government, such as belong to those who are descended from the tribes that met under the oak-trees of old Germany to make laws and choose chieftains.

Their habits of life, again, are of the most revolting kind. Read the description given by Mr. [Jacob] Riis of the police driving from the garbage dumps the miserable beings who try to burrow in those depths of unutterable filth and slime in order that they may eat and sleep there! Was it in cement like this that the foundations of our republic were laid? What effects must be produced upon our social standards, and upon the ambitions and aspirations of our people, by a contact so foul and loathsome? The influence upon the American rate of wages of a competition like this cannot fail to be injurious and even disastrous. Already it has been seriously felt in the tobacco manufacture, in the clothing trade, and in many forms of mining industry; and unless this access of vast numbers of unskilled workmen of the lowest type, in a market already fully supplied with labor, shall be checked, it cannot fail to go on from bad to worse, in breaking down the standard which has been maintained with so much care and at so much cost....

Finally, the present situation is most menacing to our peace and political safety. In all the social and industrial disorders of this country since 1877, the foreign elements have proved themselves the ready tools of demagogues in defying the law, in destroying property, and in working violence. A learned clergyman who mingled with the socialistic mob which, two years ago, threatened the State House and the governor of Massachusetts, told me that during the entire disturbance he heard no word spoken in any language which he knew,—either in English, in German, or in French. There may be those who can contemplate the addition to our population of vast numbers of persons having no inherited instincts of self-government and respect for law; knowing no restraint upon their own passions but the club of the policeman or the bayonet of the soldier; forming communities, by the tens of thousands, in which only foreign tongues are spoken, and into which can steal no influence from our free institutions and from popular discussion. But I confess to being far less optimistic....

For it is never to be forgotten that self-defense is the first law of nature and of nations. If that man who careth not for his own household is worse than an infidel, the nation which permits its institutions to be endangered by any cause which can fairly be removed is guilty not less in Christian than in natural law. Charity begins at home; and while the people of the United States have gladly offered an asylum to millions upon millions of the distressed and unfortunate of other lands and climes, they have no right to carry their hospitality one step beyond the line where American institutions, the American rate of wages, the American standard of living, are brought into serious peril.... Our highest duty to charity and to humanity is to make this great experiment, here, of free laws and educated labor, the most triumphant success that can possibly be attained. In this way we shall do far more for Europe than by allowing its city slums and its vast stagnant reservoirs of degraded peasantry to be drained off upon our soil....

Francis A. Walker, "Restriction of Immigration," *The Atlantic Monthly*, Vol. 77, No. 464 (June, 1896), pp. 822-29.

15.5

SADIE FROWNE, A POLISH SWEATSHOP GIRL (1906)

Hoping to escape political unrest, religious persecution, and poverty, millions of immigrants from eastern and southern Europe arrived in the United States in the years following the Civil War. Most emigrants settled in cities where they could find industrial employment. Many chose to live in crowded ethnic neighborhoods. Such places enabled immigrants to speak their own languages and retain their traditions. But most were also eager to assimilate into American culture and to improve their daily lives. In this reading, Sadie Frowne, a sixteen-year-old Polish immigrant, tells her life story.

FOCUS QUESTIONS

1. Why did Sadie and her mother move to America?
2. Describe Sadie's life in America. Does she attempt to assimilate into mainstream society?

3. Why does Sadie join a union? What does her explanation suggest about contemporary attitudes toward organized labor?
4. Do you think that Francis Walker (Document 15.4) would have wanted someone like Sadie Frowne to come to the United States? Explain your answer.

T he grocer's shop was only one story high, and had one window, with very small panes of glass. We had two rooms behind it, and were happy while my father lived, although we had to work very hard. By the time I was six years of age I was able to wash dishes and scrub floors, and by the time I was eight I attended to the shop while my mother was away driving her wagon or working in the fields with my father. She was strong and could work like a man.

When I was a little more than ten years of age my father died. He was a good man and a steady worker, and we never knew what it was to be hungry while he lived. After he died troubles began, for the rent of our shop was about $6 a month and then there were food and clothes to provide. We needed little, it is true, but even soup, black bread and onions we could not always get.

We struggled along till I was nearly thirteen years of age and quite handy at housework and shop keeping, so far as I could learn them there. But we fell behind in the rent and mother kept thinking more and more that we should have to leave Poland and go across the sea to America where we heard it was much easier to make money. Mother wrote to Aunt Fanny, who lived in New York, and told her how hard it was to live in Poland, and Aunt Fanny advised her to come and bring me. I was out at service at this time and mother thought she would leave me—as I had a good place—and come to this country alone, sending for me afterward. But Aunt Fanny would not hear of this. She said we should both come at once, and she went around among our relatives in New York and took up a subscription for our passage.

We came by steerage on a steamship in a very dark place that smelt dreadfully. There were hundreds of other people packed in with us, men, women and children, and almost all of them were sick. It took us twelve days to cross the sea, and we thought we should die, but at last the voyage was over, and we came up and saw the beautiful bay and the big woman with the spikes on her head and the lamp that is lighted at night in her hand (Goddess of Liberty).

Aunt Fanny and her husband met us at us gate of this country and were very good to us, and soon I had a place to live out (domestic servant), while my mother got work in a factory making white goods.

I was only a little over thirteen years of age and a greenhorn, so I received $9 a month and board and lodging, which I thought was doing well. Mother...made $9 a week on white goods, which means all sorts of underclothing, and is high class work.

But mother had a very happy disposition. She liked to go around and see everything, and friends took her about New York at night and she caught a bad cold and coughed and coughed. She really had nasty consumption [tuberculosis], but she didn't know it, and I didn't know it, and she tried to keep on working, but it was no use. She had not the strength. Two doctors attended her, but they could was no use. She had not the strength. Two doctors attended her, but they could do nothing, and at last she died and I was left alone....

Aunt Fanny had always been anxious for me to get an education as I did not know how to read or write, and she thought that was wrong. Schools are different in Poland from what they are in this country, and I was always too busy to learn to read and write. So when mother died I thought I would try to learn a trade and then I could go to school at night and learn to speak the English language well.

So I went to work in Allen Street (Manhattan) in what they call a sweatshop, making shirts by machine. I was new at the work and the foreman scolded me a great deal....

I did not know at first that you must not look around and talk, and I made many mistakes in the sewing, so that I was often called a "stupid animal." But I made $4 a week by working six days a week. For there are two Sabbaths here—our own Sabbath [the Jewish Sabbath] comes on a Saturday, and the Christian Sabbath that comes on Sunday. It is against our law to work on our Sabbath, so we would on their Sabbath....

I lived at this time with a girl named Ella, who worked in the same factory and made $5 a week. We had the room all to ourselves, paying $1.50 a week for it, and doing light housekeeping.... Of course, we could have lived cheaper, but we are both fond of good things and felt that we could afford them.

We paid 18 cents for a half pound of tea so as to get it good, and it lasted us three weeks, because we had cocoa for breakfast. We paid 5 cents for six rolls and 5 cents a loaf for bread, which was the best quality. Oatmeal cost us 10 cents for three and one half pounds, and we often had it in the morning, or Indian meal porridge in the place of it, costing about the same. Half a dozen eggs cost about 13 cents on an average, and we could get all the meat we wanted for a good hearty meal for 20 cents—two pounds of chops, or a steak, or a bit of veal, or a neck of lamb—something like that. Fish included butter fish, porgies, codfish and smelts.

Some people who buy at the last of the market, when the men with the carts want to go home, can get things very cheap, but they are likely to be stale, and we did not often do that with fish, fresh vegetables, fruit, milk or meat. Things that kept well we did buy that way and got good bargains. I got thirty potatoes for 10 cents one time, though generally I could not get more than fifteen of them for that amount. Tomatoes, onions and cabbages, too, we bought that way and did well, and we found a factory where we could buy the finest broken crackers for 3 cents a pound, and an other place where we got broken candy for 10 cents a pound. Our cooking was done on an oil stove, and the oil for the stove and the lamp cost us 10 cents a week

It cost me $2 a week to live, and I had a dollar a week to spend on clothing and pleasure, and saved the other dollar. I went to night school, but it was hard work learning at first as I did not know much English. I came to Brownsville, where so many of my people are, and where I have friends. I got work in a factory making underskirts—all sorts of cheap underskirts, like cotton and calico for the summer and woolen for the winter, but never the silk, satin or velvet underskirts. I earned 4.50 a week and lived on $2 a week, the same as before.

I got a room in the house of some friends who lived near the factory. I pay $1 a week for the room and am allowed to do light housekeeping—that is, cook my meals in it. I get my own breakfast in the morning, just a cup of coffee and a roll, and at noon time I come to dinner and take a plate of soup and a slice of bread with the lady of the house. My food for a week costs a dollar, just as it did in Allen Street, and I have the rest of my money to do as I like with. I am earning $5.50 a week now, and will probably get another increase soon.

It isn't piecework in our factory, but one is paid by the amount of work done just the same. So it is like piecework. All the hands get different amounts, some as low as $3.50 and some of the men as high as $16 a week. The factory is in the third story of a brick building. It is in a room twenty feet long and fourteen broad. There are fourteen machines in it. I and the daughter of the people with whom I live work two of these machines. The other operators are all men, some young and some old.

At first a few of the young men were rude. When they passed me they would touch my hair and talk about my eyes and my red cheeks, and make jokes. I cried and said that if they did not stop I would leave the place. The boss said that that should not be, that no one must annoy me. Some of the other men stood up for me, too, especially Henry, who said two or three times that he wanted to fight. Now the men all treat me very nicely. Some of them did not know better, not being educated.

Henry is tall and dark, and he has a small mustache. His eyes are brown and large. He is pale and much educated, having been to school. He knows a great many things and has some money saved. I think nearly $400. He is not going to be in a sweatshop all the time, but will soon be in the real estate business, for a lawyer that knows him well has promised to open an office and pay him.

Henry has seen me home every night for a long time and makes love to me. He wants me to marry him, but I am not seventeen yet, and I think that is too young. He is only nineteen, so we can wait....

I get up at half-past five o clock every morning and make myself a cup of coffee on the oil stove. I eat a bit of bread and perhaps some fruit and then go to work. Often I get there soon after six o'clock so as to be in good time, though the factory does not open till seven. I have heard that there is a sort of clock that calls you at the very time you want to get up, but I can't believe that because I don't see how the clock would know.

At seven o'clock we all sit down to our machines and the boss brings to each one the pile of work that he or she is to finish during the day, what they call in English their "stint." This pile is put down beside the machine and as soon as a skirt is done it is laid on the other side of the machine. Sometimes the work is not all finished by six o'clock and then the one who is behind must work overtime. Sometimes one is finished ahead of time and gets away at four or five o'clock, but generally we are not done till six o'clock.

The machines go like mad all day, because the faster you work the more money you get. Sometimes in my haste I get my finger caught and the needle goes right through it. It goes so quick, though, that it does not hurt much. I bind the finger up with a piece of cotton and go on working. We all have accidents like that. Where the needle goes through the nail it makes a sore finger, or where it splinters a bone it does much harm. Sometimes a finger has to come off. Generally, though, one can be cured by a salve.

All the time we are working the boss walks about examining the finished garments and making us do them over again if they are not just right. So we have to be careful as well as swift. But I am getting so good at the work that within a year I will be making $7 a week, and then I can save at least $3.50 a week. I have over $200 saved now.

The machines are all run by foot-power, and at the end of the day one feels so weak that there is a great temptation to lie right down and sleep. But you must go out and get air, and have some pleasure. So instead of lying down I go out, generally with Henry. Sometimes we go to Coney Island, where there are good dancing places, and sometimes we go to Ulmer Park to picnics. I am very fond of dancing, and, in fact, all sorts of pleasure. I go to the theater quite often, and like those plays that make you cry a great deal. "The Two Orphans" is good. Last time I saw it I cried all night because of the hard times that the children had in the play. I am going to see it again when it comes here.

For the last two winters I have been going to night school. I have learned reading, writing and arithmetic. I can read quite well in English now and I look at the newspapers every day. I read English books, too, sometimes. The last one that I read was "A Mad Marriage," by Charlotte Braeme. She's a grand writer and makes things just like real to you. You feel as if you were the poor girl yourself going to get married to a rich duke.

I am going back to night school again this winter. Plenty of my friends go there. Some of the women in my class are more than forty years of age. Like me, they did not have a chance to learn anything in the old country. It is good to have an education; it makes you feel higher. Ignorant people are all low. People say now that I am clever and fine in conversation.

We recently finished a strike in our business. It spread all over and the United Brotherhood of Garment Workers was in it. That takes in the cloakmakers, coatmakers, and all the others. We struck for shorter hours, and after being out four weeks won the fight. We only have to work nine and a half hours a day and we get the same pay as before. So the union does good after all in spite of what some people say against it—that it just takes our money and does nothing.

I pay 25 cents a month to the union, but I do not begrudge that because it is for our benefit. The next strike is going to be for a raise of wages, which we all ought to have. But though I belong to the Union I am not a Socialist or an Anarchist. I don't know exactly what those things mean. There is a little expense for charity, too. If any worker is injured or sick we all give money to help.

Some of the women blame me very much because I spend so much money on clothes. They say that instead of a dollar a week I ought not to spend more than twenty-five cents a week on clothes, and that I should save the rest. But a girl must have clothes if she is to go into good society at Ulmer Park or Coney Island or the theater. Those who blame me are the old country people who have old-fashioned notions, but the people who have been here a long time know better. A girl who does not dress well here is stuck in a corner, even if she is pretty, and Aunt Fanny says that I do just right to put on plenty of style.

I have many friends and we often have jolly parties. Many of the young men like to talk to me, but I don't go out with any except Henry.

Lately he has been urging me more and more to get married— but I think I'll wait.

"The Life Story of a Polish Sweatshop Girl," Hamilton Holt, ed., *The Life Stories of Undistinguished Americans, as Told by Themselves* (New York: James Pott and Co., 1906): pp. 34-46.

15.6

FLORIDA JIM CROW LAWS (1885-1913)

During Reconstruction, race relations in the South were somewhat fluid. Laws accorded African Americans limited civil rights protections and voting privileges. In many areas of public life, blacks and whites interacted peacefully. But the racial climate changed dramatically after federal troops left the South in 1877. White supremacist politicians instituted racial segregation and disfranchisement. Named after a popular minstrel show character, "Jim Crow" laws governed virtually every aspect of daily life. In 1896, the Supreme Court supported segregation in the Plessy v. Ferguson *decision, declaring that "separate but equal" facilities were constitutional. Some examples of Jim Crow laws passed by the Florida Legislature follow.*

FOCUS QUESTIONS

1. How did these laws regulate intimate contact between the sexes?
2. How did these laws determine an individual's racial identity?
3. How did these laws change over time?
4. Why do you think Florida politicians believed such laws were necessary? What is your opinion of the Jim Crow system?

1881

he People of the State of Florida, represented in Senate and Assembly, do enact as follows:

Section 1. Any colored man and white woman, who are not married to each other, who shall habitually live in and occupy in the night the same room, no other person over fifteen years of age being present, shall be deemed guilty of a misdemeanor....

1881

The People of the State of Florida, represented in Senate and Assembly, do enact as follows:

Section 1. That if any white man shall intermarry with a negro, mulatto or any person who has one-eighth of negro blood in her, or if any white woman shall intermarry with a negro, mulatto or any person who has one-eighth negro blood in him, such persons who so intermarry shall be fined not more than one thousand dollars nor less than fifty dollars, or imprisoned in the State Prison not more than ten years nor less than six months....

1887

Be it enacted by the Legislature of the State of Florida:

Section 1. That all railroad companies doing business in this State shall sell to all respectable persons of color first-class tickets, on application, at the same rates that white persons are charged: and shall furnish and set apart for the use of persons of color who purchased such first-class tickets a car or cars in each passenger train as may be necessary to convey passengers equally as good, and provided with the same facilities of comfort, as shall or may be provided with the same facilities for white persons using and traveling as passengers on first-class tickets.

Section 2. That no conductor or person in charge of any passenger train on any railroad in this State shall suffer or permit any white person to ride, sit or travel, or to do any act of thing, to insult of annoy any person of color, while sitting, riding and traveling in said car so set apart for the use of colored persons, as mentioned in section one of this act, nor shall he or they, while so in charge of such train, suffer or permit any person of color, nor shall such person attempt to ride, sit or travel in the car or cars set aside for the use of white persons traveling as first-class passengers; Provided, That nothing in this act shall be construes to prevent female colored nurses having the care of children or sick persons from riding or traveling in such car.

1895

Be it enacted by the Legislature of the State of Florida.

Section 1. It shall be a penal offense for any individual, body of individuals, corporation or association to conduct within this State any school of any grade, public, private or parochial wherein white persons and negroes shall be instructed or boarded within the same building, or taught in the same class, or at the same time by the same teachers.

1905

Section 1. That is shall be unlawful for any sheriff, constable, bailiff, guard or other officer having prisoners in their custody, to chain, handcuff, or in any manner fasten white female or male prisoners to colored persons in their charge.

1907

Section 1. That all persons, associations or persons, firms or corporations operating urban and suburban (or either) electric cars as common carriers of passengers in this State, shall furnish equal but separate accommodations for white and negro passengers on all cars so operated.

Section 2. That the separate accommodations for white and negro passengers directed in Section one of this act shall be separate cars, fixed divisions, movable screens, or other method of division in the cars....

Section 6. That any passenger belonging to one race who willfully occupies or attempts to occupy a car or division provided for passengers of the other race, or who occupying such car or division, refuses to leave the same when requested to do so by the conductor or other person in charge of such car, shall be deemed guilty of a misdemeanor....

Section 7. That on the car or division provided for white passengers shall be marked in plain letters in a conspicuous place, "For White," and on the car or division provided for negro passengers shall be marked in plain letter in a conspicuous place, "For Colored."

1907

Section 1. That all railroad companies and terminal companies in this State are required, within six months after the passage of this act, to provide separate waiting rooms and ticket windows of equal accommodation for white and colored passengers at all depots along lines of railway owned, controlled or operated by them, and at terminal passenger stations controlled and operated by them.

1909

Section 1. The County Commissioners of the respective counties of this State are hereby required, within twelve months from the passage of this Act, to so arrange the jails of their respective counties that it shall be unnecessary to confine in said jails in the same room, cell or apartment white and negro prisoners, or male and female prisoners

Section 2. ...It shall be unlawful for white and negro prisoners to be confined in the county jails of this State in the same cell, room or apartment, or be so confined as to be permitted to commingle together;...and it shall be the duty of the Sheriffs of this State to confine and separate all prisoners in their custody or charge in the accordance with this act.

1913

Section 1. From and after the passage of this Act it shall be unlawful in this State, for white teachers to teach negroes in negro schools, and for negro teachers to teach in white schools.

The Acts and Resolutions Adopted by the Legislature of Florida, Florida State Archives, Tallahassee, FL.

15.7

◼

BOOKER T. WASHINGTON,
THE ATLANTA EXPOSITION ADDRESS (1895)

Booker T. Washington (1856-1915) was the most influential spokesman for African Americans in the early twentieth century. Born a slave, Washington graduated from the Hampton Normal and Agricultural Institute in 1875. In 1881, he became the first president of the Tuskegee Normal and Industrial Institution, a newly established normal school for African Americans. Washington spent the remainder of his life building Tuskegee into a very successful vocational school. Convinced that African Americans should focus on attaining industrial and agricultural skills, Washington urged blacks to temporarily abandon demands for political equality. He believed that once African Americans possessed wealth and culture, racial divisions would disappear and blacks would gain full citizenship. In 1895, white southern business leaders invited Washington to make a speech at the Cotton States Exposition in Atlanta. Washington's address, featured here, generated national attention.

◼

FOCUS QUESTIONS

1. What are the major themes of Washington's speech? What does he believe is essential for southern blacks to succeed? How does he appeal to southern whites?
2. What is Washington's view of racial segregation?
3. Compare Washington's views to those of W.E.B. DuBois (Document 15.8)? Who do you think had the best solutions to the problems facing African Americans? Why?

r. President and Gentlemen of the Board of Directors and Citizens. One-third of the population of the South is of the Negro race. No enterprise seeking the material, civil, or moral welfare of this section can disregard this element of our population and reach the highest success. I but convey to you, Mr. President and Directors, the sentiment of the masses of my race when I say that in no way have the value and manhood of the American Negro been more fittingly and generously recognized than by the managers of this magnificent Exposition at every stage of its progress. It is a recognition that will do more to cement the friendship of the two races than any occurrence since the dawn of our freedom.

Not only this, but the opportunity here afforded will awaken among us a new era of industrial progress. Ignorant and inexperienced, it is not strange that in the first years of our new life we began at the top instead of at the bottom; that a seat in Congress or the state legislature was more sought than real estate of industrial skill; that the political convention of stump speaking had more attractions than starting a dairy farm or truck garden.

...To those of my race who depend on bettering their condition in a foreign land or who underestimate the importance of cultivating friendly relations with the Southern white man, who is their next door neighbor, I would say: "Cast down your bucket where you are"—cast it down in making friends in every manly way of the people of all races by whom we are surrounded.

Cast it down in agriculture, mechanics, in commerce, in domestic service, and in the professions. And in this connection it is well to bear in mind that whatever other sins the South may be called to bear, when it comes to business, pure and simple, it is in the South that the Negro is given a man's chance in the commercial world, and in nothing is this exposition more eloquent than in emphasizing this chance. Our greatest danger is that in the great leap from slavery to freedom we may overlook the fact that the masses of us are to live by the productions of our hands, and fail to keep in mind that we shall prosper in proportion as we learn to dignify and glorify common labor and put brains and skill into the common occupations of life; shall prosper in proportion as we learn to draw the line between the superficial and the substantial, the ornamental gewgaws of life and the useful. No race can prosper till it learns that there is as much dignity in tilling a field as in writing a poem. It is at the bottom of life we must begin, and not at the top. Nor should we permit our grievances to overshadow our opportunities.

To those of the white race who look to the incoming of those of foreign birth and strange tongue and habits for the prosperity of the South, were I permitted I would repeat what I say to my own race, "Cast down your bucket where you are." Cast it down among the eight millions of Negroes whose habits you know, whose fidelity and love you have tested in days when to have proved treacherous meant the ruin of your firesides. Cast down your bucket among these people who have, without strikes and labor wars, tilled your fields, cleared your forests, builded your railroads and cities, and brought forth treasures from the bowels of the earth, and helped make possible this magnificent representation of the progress of the South. Casting down your bucket among my people, helping and encouraging them as you are doing on these grounds, and to education of head, hand and heart, you will find that they will buy your surplus land, make blossom the waste places in your fields, and run your factories. While doing this, you can be sure in the future, as in the past, that you and your families will be surrounded by the most patient, faithful, law-abiding, and unresentful people that the world has seen.... In all things that are purely social we can be as separate as the fingers, yet one as the hand in all things essential to mutual progress....

The wisest among my race understand that the agitation of questions of social equality is the extremist folly, and that progress in the enjoyment of all the privileges that will come to us must be the result of severe and constant struggle rather than of artificial forcing. No race that has anything to contribute to the markets of the world is long in any degree ostracized. It is important and right that all privileges of the law be ours, but it is vastly more important that we be prepared for the exercises of these privileges. The opportunity to earn a dollar in a factory just now is worth infinitely more than the opportunity to spend a dollar in an opera-house.

In conclusion, may I repeat that nothing in thirty years has given us more hope and encouragement, and drawn us so near to you of the white race, as this opportunity offered by the exposition; and here bending, as it were, over the altar that represents the results of the struggles of your race and mine, both starting practically empty-handed three decades ago, I pledge that in your effort to work out the great and intricate problem with God has laid at the doors of the South, you shall have at all times the patient, sympathetic help of my race; only let this be constantly in mind, that, while the representations in these buildings of the product of field, of forest, of mine, of factory, letters, and art, much good will come, yet far above and beyond material benefits will be that higher good, that, let us pray God, will come, in a blotting out of sectional differences and racial animosities and suspicions, in a determination to administer absolute justice, in a willing obedience among all classes to the mandates of law. This, coupled with our material prosperity, will bring into our beloved South a new heaven and a new earth.

Booker T. Washington, *Up from Slavery: The Autobiography of Booker T. Washington* (New York, 1901), 218-225.

15.8

W.E.B. DuBois, *The Souls of Black Folk* (1903)

W.E.B. DuBois (1868-1963) rejected Booker T. Washington's emphasis on vocational training and racial accommodation. A Harvard University Ph.D., DuBois taught at Atlanta University and wrote several books on African Americans, including The Souls of Black Folk *(1903), extracted here. Although DuBois initially believed that academic studies could solve racial problems, he modified this view after exposure to Jim Crow laws and racial violence convinced him of the necessity for social protest. In 1905, he helped to found the Niagara Movement, a group dedicated to civil rights. After the organization disbanded, DuBois and others established the National Association for the Advancement of Colored People (NAACP). For over twenty years, DuBois played an integral role in the NAACP and edited its magazine,* The Crisis. *After leaving the NAACP in 1934, DuBois returned to teaching and writing. Throughout his career, DuBois advocated Pan-Africanism, the belief that all people of African descent should band together against racism and economic oppression. In his later years, DuBois embraced Marxism and moved to Ghana.*

Focus Questions

1. Why is DuBois critical of Washington's ideas?
2. What does DuBois identify as the most pressing needs of African Americans?
3. Compare DuBois's views to those of Booker T. Washington (Document 15.7). Who do you think had the best solutions to the problems facing African Americans? Why?

ne hesitates…to criticise a life which, beginning with so little, has done so much. And yet the time is come when one may speak in all sincerity and utter courtesy of the mistakes and shortcomings of Mr. Washington's career, as well as of his triumphs, without being thought captious or envious, and without forgetting that it is easier to do ill than well in the world….

Mr. Washington represents in Negro thought the old attitude of adjustment and submission; but adjustment at such a peculiar time as to make his programme unique. This is an age of unusual economic development, and Mr. Washington's programme naturally takes an economic cast, becoming a gospel of Work and Money to such an extent as apparently almost completely to overshadow the higher aims of life. Moreover, this is an age when the more advanced races are coming in closer contact with the less developed races, and the race-feeling is therefore intensified; and Mr. Washington's programme practically accepts the alleged inferiority of the Negro races. Again, in our own land, the reaction from the sentiment of war time has given impetus to race-prejudice against Negroes, and Mr. Washington withdraws many of the high demands of Negroes as men and American citizens. In other periods of intensified prejudice all the Negro's tendency to self-assertion has been called forth; at this period a policy of submission is advocated. In the history of nearly all other races and peoples the doctrine preached at such crises has been that manly self-respect is worth more than lands and houses, and that a people who voluntarily surrender such respect, or cease striving for it, are not worth civilizing.

In answer to this, it has been claimed that the Negro can survive only through submission. Mr. Washington distinctly asks that black people give up, at least for the present, three things,—

First, political power,

Second, insistence on civil rights,

Third, higher education of Negro youth,—

and concentrate all their energies on industrial education, the accumulation of wealth, and the conciliation of the South. This policy has been courageously and insistently advocated for over fifteen years, and has been triumphant for perhaps ten years. As a result of this tender of the palm-branch, what has been the return? In these years there have occurred:

1. The disfranchisement of the Negro.
2. The legal creation of a distinct status of civil inferiority for the Negro.

3. The steady withdrawal of aid from institutions for the higher training of the Negro.

These movements are not, to be sure, direct results of Mr. Washington's teachings; but his propaganda has, without a shadow of doubt, helped their speedier accomplishment. The question then comes: Is it possible, and probable, that nine millions of men can make effective progress in economic lines if they are deprived of political rights, made a servile caste, and allowed only the most meager chance for developing their exceptional men? If history and reason give any distinct answer to these questions, it is an emphatic No. And Mr. Washington thus faces the triple paradox of his career:

1. He is striving nobly to make Negro artisans business men and property-owners; but it is utterly impossible, under modern competitive methods, for workingmen and property-owners to defend their rights and exist without the right of suffrage.
2. He insists on thrift and self-respect, but at the same time counsels a silent submission to civic inferiority such as is bound to sap the manhood of any race in the long run.
3. He advocates common-school and industrial training, and depreciates institutions of higher learning; but neither the Negro common-schools, nor Tuskegee itself, could remain open a day were it not for teachers trained in Negro colleges, or trained by their graduates....

...Negroes must insist continually, in season and out of season, that voting is necessary to modern manhood, that color discrimination is barbarism, and that black boys need education as well as white boys.

In failing thus to state plainly and unequivocally the legitimate demands of their people, even at the cost of opposing an honored leader, the thinking classes of American Negroes would shirk a heavy responsibility,—a responsibility to themselves, a responsibility to the struggling masses, a responsibility to the darker races of men whose future depends so largely on this American experiment, but especially a responsibility to this nation,—this common Fatherland. It is wrong to encourage a man or a people in evil-doing; it is wrong to aid and abet a national crime simply because it is unpopular not to do so. The growing spirit of kindliness and reconciliation between the North and South after the frightful differences of a generation ago ought to be a source of deep congratulation to all, and especially to those whose mistreatment caused the war; but if that reconciliation is to be marked by the industrial slavery and civic death of those same black men, with permanent legislation into a position of inferiority, then those black men, if they are really men, are called upon by every consideration of patriotism and loyalty to oppose such a course by all civilized methods, even though such opposition involves disagreement with Mr. Booker T. Washington. We have no right to sit silently by while the inevitable seeds are sown for a harvest of disaster to our children, black and white....

The black men of America have a duty to perform, a duty stern and deli-cate,—a forward movement to oppose a part of the work of their greatest leader. So far as Mr. Washington preaches Thrift, Patience, and Industrial Training for the masses, we must hold up his hands and strive with him, rejoicing in his honors and glorying in the strength of this Joshua called of God and of man to lead the headless host. But so far as Mr. Washington apologizes for injustice, North or South, does not rightly value the privilege and duty of voting, belittles the emasculating effects of caste distinctions, and opposes the higher training and ambition of our brighter minds,—so far as he, the South, or the Nation, does this,—we must unceasingly and firmly oppose them. By every civilized and peaceful method we must strive for the rights which the world accords to men, clinging unwaveringly to those great words which the sons of the Fathers would fain forget: "We hold these truths to be self-evident: That all men are created equal; that they are endowed by their Creator with certain unalienable rights; that among these are life, liberty, and the pursuit of happiness."

W.E.B. DuBois, "Of Booker T. Washington and Others," *The Souls of Black Folk* (Chicago: A.C. McClurg & Co., 1903).

SECONDARY SOURCE

—————————————■—————————————

MARTHA HODES, "MURDER: BLACK MEN, WHITE WOMEN, AND LYNCHING"

As segregation and disfranchisement swept the post-Reconstruction South, whites of all classes joined in upholding white supremacy. Lynching illustrates this trend at its most vicious. Relatively uncommon prior to the Civil War, lynching rapidly escalated in the 1880s. By 1900, whites had murdered more than 1,000 people. Lynchings drew hundreds of spectators, many of whom took home grisly souvenirs. In this selection from White Women, Black Men: Illicit Sex in the Nineteenth-Century South *(1997), historian Martha Hodes examines lynching and its complicated relationship to social relations and politics in the South.*

Go to your *Speaking of America* CD-ROM to read "Murder: Black Men, White Women, and Lynching."

—————————————■—————————————

FOCUS QUESTIONS

1. How did whites usually justify lynching black men? How did the realties of intimate relations between the races complicate these allegations?

2. Describe the scene of a typical lynching. Why do you think that someone would attend?
3. What were some of the tactics whites used to deny that black men and white women could have consensual sexual relations?
4. How did African Americans criticize lynching? How did whites react?
5. What was the "one-drop rule"? How did it affect gender relations and race relations in the post-Reconstruction South?
6. How did whites define "rape" when justifying lynching?
7. How does this article revise your understanding of southern history and the history of American race relations?

AMERICAN JOURNEY ONLINE

■

http://ajaccesss.wadsworth.com [†]

About Immigration
— In The Immigrant Experience
Documents
  • George Templeton Strong, Excerpt from the Diary of George Templeton Strong (1871)
  • U.S. Supreme Court, *Henderson et al v. Mayor of New York City et al* (1875)
  • U.S. Congress, Immigration Act of 1891
  • Images
  • Erica Lee, Angel Island Immigration Station (1996)
  • Erica Lee, Approaching Angel Island (1996)

— In Civil Rights in the United States
Documents
  • Emma Lazarus, The New Colossus (1886)
  • Ellis Island
Images
  • Irish Immigration (1877)
  • Statue of Liberty in Civil Rights in the United States
  • Emma Lazarus
— In Westward Expansion
Images
  • Thomas Nast, Every Dog (No Distinction of Color) Has His Day (1879)

[†] Enter password, choose the Archive indicated above, click on Contents, choose •Documents, •Images, or •Multimedia, and click on the title of the item.

— In <u>World War I and the Jazz Age</u>
Images
- Eastern European Shelter
- Immigrant Workers
- World of Our Fathers and Mothers
- Immigrants Arriving in America

About Social Darwinism
— In <u>World War I and the Jazz Age</u>
Documents
- William Graham Sumner, Excerpt from *Sociology* (1881)

About Asian-Americans and Asian Immigrants
— In <u>Civil Rights in the United States</u>
Documents
- U.S. Supreme Court, *Yick Wo v. Hopkins* (1886)
Images
- *Frank Leslie's Illustrated Newspaper*, Anti-Chinese Workingmen's Meeting
— In <u>The Asian-American Experience</u>
Documents
- U.S. Congress, An Act to Execute Certain Treaty Stipulations Relating to Chinese, or the Chinese Exclusion Act (1882)
- U.S. Congress, Amendment to the Chinese Exclusion Act (1884)
- U.S. Congress, An Act to Prohibit the Coming of Chinese Laborers to the United States (1888)
- U.S. Congress, An Act to Prohibit the Coming of Chinese Persons into the United States, or the Geary Act (1892)
- U.S. Congress, An Act to Prohibit the Coming into and to Regulate the Residence within the United States, Its Territories, and All Territory under its Jurisdiction, and the District of Columbia, of Chinese and Persons of Chinese Descent (1902)
- Asiatic Exclusion League of North America, Preamble and Constitution (1905)
- Theodore Roosevelt, Excerpt of Message to Congress Concerning the Japanese Question (1906)
- Theodore Roosevelt, Gentlemen's Agreement (1908)
Images
- Anti-Chinese Riot in Denver (circa 1880)

About African-Americans
— In <u>The African-American Experience</u>
Documents
- Joel Chandler Harris, Excerpt from *Uncle Remus: His Songs and Sayings* (1880)
- J.B. Harrison, Excerpt from *Studies in the South* (1882)

- Catherine Gordon, A Letter from Catherine Gordon to Her Niece, Catherine Felix Webb (1889)
- Ida B. Wells, Excerpt from *A Red Record* (1895)
- *Plessy v. Ferguson* (1896)
- Paul Laurence Dunbar, When Malindy Sings (1896)
- George H. White, A Defense of the Negro Race (1901)
- Document with Audio Commentary—Booker T. Washington, Excerpt from *Up from Slavery*, 2 selections, (1901)
- W.E.B. DuBois, Excerpt from *The Negro Skilled Laborer* (1902)
- W.E.B. DuBois, Excerpt from *The Souls of Black Folk*, 4 selections (1903)
- Resolutions of the National Association of Colored Women (1904)
- R.H. Boyd, A Letter to the *Nashville Banner* (1906)

Images
- Frances Benjamin Johnson, The Chemistry Laboratory at Tuskegee Institute (circa 1900)
- The Booker T. Washington Agricultural School on Wheels (circa 1910)
— In The Civil War
Documents
- Henry McNeal Turner, Excerpt of A Plea for African Emigration (1883)
- Charles Chesnutt, "The Goophered Grapevine" (1887)
— In World War I and the Jazz Age
Documents
- W.E.B. DuBois, The Niagara Movement (1906)
Images
- Jim Crow in the South
— In Women in America
Images
- Ida B. Wells (1917)
— In Civil Rights in the United States
Documents
- Paul Laurence Dunbar, Rights Security (1896)
Images
- Paul Laurence Dunbar
- Russell Lee, Segregated Drinking Facilities
- Chain Gangs (circa 1901)
- Booker T. Washington
- W.E.B. DuBois

About Culture
— In Civil Rights in the United States
Documents
- Mark Twain, *The Adventures of Huckleberry Finn*, Chapter 17 (1884)

PROTESTORS AND IMPERIALISTS

The nation's industrial growth and increasing diversity unleashed a dizzying array of forces. While some Americans challenged Victorian standards of morality, others fought to preserve traditional mores. While business leaders and politicians pursued capital and power, activists and workers decried social and economic inequalities. Such volatility also characterized American imperialism. Eager to expand U.S. markets and to increase the country's international prestige, politicians, industrialists, and journalists called for territorial expansion and the "civilization" of foreign peoples. These demands sparked heated debate over America's role in global affairs and the character of democratic capitalism.

As the factory system grew, unions campaigned for workers' rights. Labor activists advocated a number of reforms including an eight-hour workday, banking and currency reforms, and the abolition of child labor and convict leasing. Their efforts met little success. Racial, ethnic, and religious differences impeded organizing efforts. Skilled artisans clashed with unskilled laborers. Employers harassed union leaders. State militias and local police crushed strikes. Courts ruled repeatedly ruled for management. By 1900, less than 5 percent of U.S. workers belonged to unions.

These obstacles and a volatile economy created great frustration among workers. In the late nineteenth century, over 7 million laborers participated in 77,000 strikes in hopes of improving pay and working conditions. Although the majority of these demonstrations were peaceful, some degenerated into violence. In several cases, federal troops and state authorities broke up strikes. Frequently, workers and law enforcement officials died in these clashes. Most Americans, however, expressed little sympathy for strikers and associated unions with class war and political radicalism. Exploiting these sentiments, employers and government officials escalated their efforts to hobble organized labor.

American culture reflected the explosive tensions of the era. Clinging to Victorian mores, elites pushed for national standards of artistic expression and combated "immorality." Others resisted these efforts. Artists and writers challenged genteel conceptions of culture and explored darker elements of daily life. New publications targeted the masses instead of focusing only on sophisticated readers. As the Victorian code began to crumble, a more diverse and complicated cultural portrait of the American people emerged.

New political actors echoed this willingness to challenge orthodoxy. Using skills honed in colleges and clubs, women pushed for a broader role in public life. Farmers protested economic inequities and political exclusion. A new political party, the Populists, scored impressive gains with a reform agenda.

Established politicians responded slowly to these changes. Republicans and Democrats battled over issues like tariffs, veterans' petitions, and monetary policy but enacted few substantive policies. As a series of undistinguished candidates won the Presidency, popular respect for the office declined precipitously. Nonetheless, political affairs were spirited, especially at the state and local levels. Family, religious, and ethnic ties usually determined party loyalty. Parades and pageantry drew large numbers of voters to the polls. Elections were extremely close and often corrupt. Few public officials believed that government should address social and economic problems. But, as violent strikes, political scandals, protest movements, and economic depressions generated widespread demands for reform, politicians could no longer be passive. By 1900, they stood poised to enact the sweeping changes of the Progressive era.

At the same time, the United States became a stronger presence on the international stage. As European nations infiltrated Africa and Asia, U.S. business leaders, politicians, and journalists clamored for an overseas empire. In pursuit of foreign markets and the opportunity to spread the American way of life, these expansionists called for a larger navy and territorial acquisitions. By 1905, the United States had acquired several colonies and won wars against Spain and Filipino insurgents. While many Americans applauded the nation's emergence as a global power, others condemned imperialism as a threat to the nation's political ideals. In years to come, U.S. foreign policy would remain a topic of passionate debate.

16.1

·

ANTHONY COMSTOCK, "THE SUPPRESSION OF VICE" (1882)

By the mid-nineteenth century, saloons, brothels, gambling halls, and theaters flourished in many American cities. Innovations in printing made inexpensive penny newspapers and dime novels readily available. In many parts of the United States, abortion was legal prior to the point of "quickening," when the mother could feel her baby move. Subtle advertisements and discreet storeowners sold methods of contraception.

Such developments greatly disturbed moral reformers like Anthony Comstock (1844-1915). A dry goods clerk in New York City, Comstock felt besieged by immoral influences. In the 1860s, he began working with the New York Y.M.C.A. in opposing sellers of "obscene" literature and gambling facilities. In 1873, Comstock and his organization, the New York Society for the Suppression of Vice, persuaded Congress, with less than an hour of debate, to pass a federal law calling for the "Suppression of Trade In, and Circulation of, Obscene Literature

and Articles of Immoral Use." The "Comstock Law" banned "indecent" litera-
ture, contraceptives, and abortifacients from the U.S. mails and other forms of
distribution. Individuals convicted of violating the statute faced up to five years of
prison and fines up to $5,000. Over the next forty years, Comstock wielded
enormous influence on American culture and determined what medical informa-
tion reached the general public. As a special agent of the United States Postal
Service, he and his aides prosecuted 3,500 people (only 10% of whom were found
guilty) and destroyed over 120 tons of printed matter. In this passage, Comstock
explains his crusade against vice.

---■---

FOCUS QUESTIONS

1. What motivated Comstock to begin attacking "immoral" social influences?
2. What methods did Comstock and his agents use to find violators of obscenity law? How does Comstock define obscenity?
3. Do you think Comstock would have objected to Thomas Eakins's *The Gross Clinic* (Document 16.2)? If so, why?
4. What is your opinion of Comstock's efforts to suppress "obscenity"? To what extent should the government engage in anti-vice activities? Explain your answers.

November 1882

I n the year 1872, being then a salesman in a mercantile house, I found that many of my former associates had been morally ruined by demoralizing publications, while others of them had been arrested for peculation [embezzlement] from their employers, in order to indulge their passion for gambling. On investigation, the fact was developed that there was a very large and systematic business, of the most nefarious character, carried on to corrupt and destroy the morals of the young. With the first arrests which I caused to be made came strenuous opposition. I soon learned that there were one hundred and sixty-five different books of the vilest kind published in New York and Brooklyn, and four thousand dealers engaged in disseminating this matter all over the country. I had neither money nor influential friends, yet I resolved that something must be done to save the youth, and, knowing that the Young Men's Christian Association was founded for the purpose of helping and saving young men, I invoked the powerful aid of that organization. Providentially, as I believe, my letter fell under the eye of Morris K. Jesup, Esq., who personally sought out the writer, and, having acquainted himself with the facts, not only furnished means with which to carry on the work I already had commenced, but also called a meeting of prominent citizens to deliberate upon the questions involved. At this meeting a committee was appointed to direct and supervise the work; but soon it became apparent that the evils to be warred against were of such a magnitude as to demand a more effective organization, and accordingly in the ensuing year the Society for the Suppression of Vice was founded.... Since its organization about two hundred and fifty gentlemen of equal respectability have been added as members.

The title of the society shows its object the Suppression of Vice the enforcement of the laws for the suppression of the trade in, and circulation of, obscene literature and illustrations, advertisements, and articles of indecent and immoral use, as may be forbidden by the laws of the State of New York, or of the United States.

About one-half of all the crimes which it is the province of this society to suppress are perpetrated through the agency of the mails, and consequently, since March, 1873, the chief agent of the society has been commissioned a special agent, or inspector of the Post-office Department (without compensation), charged with the enforcement of all laws prohibiting the transmission of obscene matter, and the conduct of the business of lotteries and fraudulent schemes, through the mail....

The first element in a case under these statutes is information that a crime is being committed. This is found most frequently in the public advertisements in the newspapers, or in printed or written circulars. Often the information is supplied by a citizen, who makes a complaint that some youth has been ruined. Again, a parent or teacher finds some of these obscene publications or other objectionable articles in the possession of his child or pupil, and demands that the vender be prosecuted. It is not enough that a complaint is lodged against a party that he offers, for a consideration, to supply these illicit wares. The point we have to ascertain is whether the party complained of is actually engaged in conducting any of the schemes which it is our province to suppress. His advertisement says that he is, and we take him at his word; and having ascertained that a party is thus regularly engaged, we seek to obtain legal evidence of the fact. This is done by purchasing the articles which the party advertises to sell (if he does advertise), and in the manner proposed by himself. To illustrate. When we began operations, hundreds of individuals were advertising Rich, Rare, and Racy Books, and often the titles of these books were given, always in the printed circulars. The advertisement, or the circular, would direct the intending buyer to send the price named, or to call at such a place. This was an invitation to the public to come and buy, and we, or our agents, as a part of the public so invited, did buy these wares, thus procuring for the ministers of the law conclusive evidence that the statutes were being violated....

Now for the United States laws, and the course of procedure we follow in securing their enforcement. What have we to say of the mode of securing evidence here? How about decoys, "inducing men to commit crimes," and "tampering with the malls," of which we hear so much? The offenses which we seek to suppress are brought to our notice either by advertisements in the newspapers, or by written or printed circulars containing the titles and prices of obscene books or other illicit articles, or by getting hold of objectionable material, sent perhaps to some child through the mail. There is no such thing as tampering with the mails practiced by this society or its agents, nor has there ever been....

The necessity for the existence of this and like societies is found in the hundreds of gambling halls, the defilement of evil reading, and the thousands of influences which threaten the morals of the young. Public sentiment must be aroused against the publication, in the newspapers, of the sickening details of hideous crimes; against the contagion, worse than yellow fever, coming from the weekly illustrated criminal papers; against the low and debasing theaters; against the indecencies of the concert dives; against the crime-breeding pestilence of the "half-dime" novel and boys story-paper; against the blasphemies of infidel publications; against all schemes for corrupting the rising generation, ere the community can call on this society to disband.

What has the society achieved? The plates for printing and illustrating one hundred and sixty-three out of the one hundred and sixty-five obscene books published ten years ago, have been seized and destroyed. The other two works were destroyed by the owner, through fear, as we have ample evidence to believe. More than twenty-five tons of contraband matter have also been seized and destroyed. Every photograph gallery and other establishment where obscene pictures or indecent articles were manufactured has been closed and their stock confiscated. Upward of six hundred and fifty persons have been arrested. Nine lotteries, claiming an aggregate income of ten million dollars per year, have been forced to close their offices in New York City. More than one hundred policy and gambling places have been raided, and their properties seized. Scores of men and boys, who formerly thronged the streets selling obscene and indecent matter, have been driven out of business, while shop-windows have been cleared of many of their objectionable features. Several of the more indecent papers have been suppressed, while nearly all publications have been purged of indecent advertisements. Over sixty abortionists have been arrested, and all but a few convicted and sentenced. We have secured for the public treasury $63,931 in fines, while bail bonds to the amount of $50,900 have been forfeited, up to January 1, 1882. Since January 1st of the present year we have made eighty-seven arrests. All this, and more, has been done, at an expense of only about $7,000 per year, all raised by voluntary contributions. There yet remains much to be done. This society has earned for itself a name, and has made an honorable record. It has shown what can be done, by patient, persistent effort, toward saving the young from contamination. Can philanthropists withhold aid and sympathy from so worthy a cause?

Anthony Comstock, "The Suppression of Vice," *The North American Review*, Volume 135, Issue 312 (November 1882): 484-489.

16.2

—————■—————

THOMAS EAKINS, *THE GROSS CLINIC* (1875)

In an age when most artists sentimentalized daily life, Thomas Eakins (1844-1916) was highly controversial. Born in Philadelphia, Eakins studied at the Pennsylvania Academy of Fine Arts. Keenly interested in science and medicine, he also attended anatomy lectures and participated in dissections at the Jefferson Medical College. In 1866, he traveled to Paris for additional artistic training under Jean-León Gérôme. Three years later, a trip to Spain exposed Eakins to the works of Diego Velázquez and José de Ribera, two 17th-century masters. When Eakins returned to Philadelphia in 1870, he devoted himself to his family and outdoor activities—both topics of many of his paintings. An avid realist, Eakins combined accurate physical representation of his subjects with poignant reflections of their inner character. His images of rowing, sailing, fishing, hunting, and swimming captured the muscularity of sportsmen and athletes. Although such scenes appeared informal and natural, Eakins actually used intricate sketches and grids in assembling his final compositions. He became a master of portraying motion and physical space.

In 1875, Eakins decided to submit works to the Centennial Exposition, an international fair to be held in Philadelphia the next year. Returning to Jefferson Medical College, he painted Dr. Samuel Gross, a renowned surgeon, performing an operation in a crowded amphitheater. The portrait shows Gross's assistants slicing open the thigh of a young man suffering from osteomyelitis—a bacterial infection of bone and bone marrow in which the resulting inflammation can lead to a reduction of blood supply to the bone. The objective was to remove the diseased bone so that the remaining bone could regenerate. The patient's mother sits nearby. Eakins himself is in the audience, seated near the curved railing. Although the selection committee accepted five of Eakins's paintings, it rejected The Gross Clinic. *In response, some of Eakins's supporters successfully campaigned for its inclusion in a display about Civil War medicine at the U.S. Army Post Hospital Building. While a few critics lavishly praised* The Gross Clinic, *most found it revolting.*

Eakins encountered similar criticism throughout his career. In 1886, the Pennsylvania Academy of Fine Arts forced him to resign from his teaching post after he used a live nude male model in a coed class. Despite these difficulties, Eakins pursued a variety of interests including sports, photography, locomotion, and sculpture. While his peers and students respected his abilities, he remained an outcast in artistic circles and sold few pictures. Able to survive on a modest income from his father, he continued to paint what and whom he wished. Now considered one of America's foremost artists, Eakins greatly influenced realist painters, particularly those of the Ashcan School.

Focus Questions

1. How would you describe the patient's mother? What do you think that she symbolizes?
2. How would you characterize Dr. Gross?
3. Why do you think *The Gross Clinic* shocked many Americans? What does its negative reception suggest about society in this era?

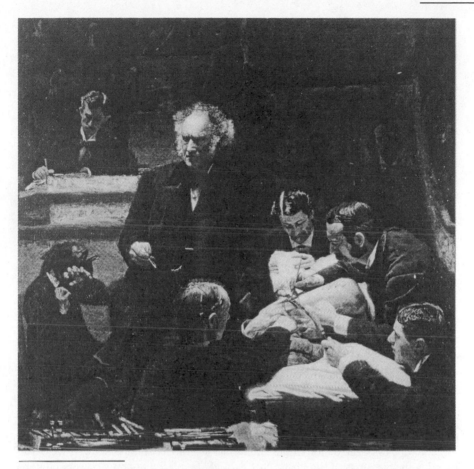

The Gross Clinic, 1875; Thomas Eakins (American, 1844-1916); Oil on canvas; 96 x 78 1/2 in. (243.8 x 199.4 cm); Jefferson Medical College of Thomas Jefferson University, Philadelphia, Pennsylvania.

16.3

TERENCE POWDERLY ON THE KNIGHTS OF LABOR (1878, 1889)

Alarmed by declining wages and dangerous working conditions, many American workers turned to collective action. But unions faced formidable obstacles. Ethnic, racial, and gender differences impeded labor organizers. Skilled and unskilled laborers quarreled. Employers fired unionists and undermined strikes by hiring scabs.

The Knights of Labor hoped to transcend these problems. Formed as a secret society by a group of Philadelphia tailors in 1869, the Knights aimed to build a national movement of "producers." They welcomed most wage earners including women and African Americans. While the Knights grew slowly at first, Terence Powderly (1849-1924) expanded the union's membership to over 700,000. Convinced that the Knights would lead the workers of America out of wage slavery, Powderly favored arbitration and boycotts over strikes. Under his leadership, the Knights won passage of laws prohibiting convict labor and restricting immigration. But this success was short-lived. By the early 1890s, internal squabbling, unauthorized strikes, and negative public images of unions forced the Knights' dissolution. This excerpt from the Knights' 1878 constitution outlines their objectives.

———————————◼———————————

FOCUS QUESTIONS

1. Why do the Knights believe that workers need to unionize?
2. What were the major goals of the Knights of Labor? What do these goals suggest about working conditions and the economy in the late nineteenth-century?
3. If you had been a worker in 1878, would you have joined the Knights of Labor? Explain your answer.
4. Do American workers still face the problems fought by the Knights of Labor? Are unions important today? Explain your answers.

T he recent alarming development and aggression of aggregated wealth, which, unless checked, will invariably lead to the pauperization and hopeless degradation of the toiling masses, render it imperative, if we desire to enjoy the blessings of life, that a check should be placed upon its power and upon unjust accumulation, and a system adopted which will secure to the laborer the fruits of his toil; and as this much-desired object can only be accomplished by the thorough unification of labor, and the united efforts of those who obey the divine injunction that "In the sweat of thy brow shalt thou eat bread," we have formed the ***** with a view of securing the organization and direction, by co-operative effort, of the power of the industrial classes; and we submit to the world the object sought to be accomplished by our organization, calling upon all who believe in securing "the greatest good to the greatest number" to aid and assist us:

I.   To bring within the folds of organization every department of productive industry, making knowledge a standpoint for action, and industrial and moral worth, not wealth, the true standard of individual and national greatness.

II.   To secure to the toilers a proper share of the wealth that they create; more of the leisure that rightfully belongs to them; more societary advantages; more of the benefits, privileges, and emoluments of the world; in a word, all those rights and privileges necessary to make them capable of enjoying, appreciating, defending, and perpetuating the blessings of good government.

III.   To arrive at the true condition of the producing masses in their educational, moral, and financial condition, by demanding from the various governments the establishment of bureaus of Labor Statistics.

IV.   The establishment of co-operative institutions, productive and distributive.

V.   The reserving of the public lands—the heritage of the people—for the actual settler;—not another acre for railroads or speculators.

VI.   The abrogation of all laws that do not bear equally upon capital and labor, the removal of unjust techniques, delays, and discriminations in the administration of justice, and the adopting of measures providing for the health and safety of those engaged in mining, manufacturing, or building pursuits.

VII.   The enactment of laws to compel chartered corporations to pay their employees weekly, in full, for labor performed during the preceding week, in the lawful money of the country.

VIII.   The enactment of laws giving mechanics and laborers a first lien on their work for their full wages.

IX.   The abolishment of the contract system of national, State, and municipal work.

X.   The substitution of arbitration for strikes, whenever and wherever employers and employees are willing to meet on equitable grounds.

XI.   The prohibition of the employment of children in workshops, mines, and factories before attaining their fourteenth year.

XII.   To abolish the system of letting out by contract the labor of convicts in our prisons and reformatory institutions.

XIII.   To secure for both sexes equal pay for equal work.

XIV.   The reduction of the hours of labor to eight per day, so that the laborers may have more time for social enjoyment and intellectual improvement, and be enable to reap the advantages conferred by the labor saving machinery which their brains have created.

XV.   To prevail upon governments to establish a purely national circulating medium based upon the faith and resources of the nation, and issued directly to the people, without the intervention of any system of banking corporations, which money shall be a legal tender in payment of all debts, public or private.

Terrence V. Powderly, *Thirty Years of Labor* (Columbus, OH, 1889), 243-245.

16.4

PERSPECTIVES ON THE HAYMARKET AFFAIR (1886-1887)

Following the Panic of 1873, an economic depression created tremendous hardship and anxiety among American workers. Thousands lost their jobs or had their wages slashed as employers cut costs in order to preserve profits. Many turned to collective action. While most strikes were peaceful, others, such as the 1877 Railway Strike, sparked violent clashes between law enforcement officials and protestors.

The labor movement was an international phenomenon. Workers in several countries collectivized. Some embraced anarchism—a radical political doctrine centered on the belief that government is unnecessary and impedes individualism. In extreme cases, anarchists assassinated public officials in order to expose the state's vulnerability and to inspire the masses. Most Americans, however, had a difficult time distinguishing between nonviolent labor activists and violent anarchists. They saw unions as a profound threat to democratic capitalism.

The Haymarket Affair demonstrates how deeply these fears pervaded American culture. It began on May 1, 1886 when 340,000 workers across the country walked off their jobs to demand an eight-hour workday. In Chicago alone, 80,000 laborers participated. The demonstrations were relatively calm and quite productive. Approximately 185,000 workers won shorter hours. But some employers, including the McCormick Harvesting Machine Company in Chicago, refused to comply with the workers' demands. McCormick fired the strikers and hired replacement laborers, denounced by protestors as "scabs." On May 3rd, when strikers swarmed strikebreakers leaving the McCormick facility, police intervened. One person died and several others were injured.

In response, Chicago anarchists—many of them German immigrants— organized a mass meeting in Haymarket Square the following evening. August Spies and Albert R. Parsons, two political radicals, addressed the audience. Serving as an observer, Mayor Carter Harrison declared the demonstration peaceful and departed. Nonetheless, police arrived and demanded that the crowd disperse. All hell broke loose when an unknown individual threw a bomb. In the ensuing riot, seven policemen and four protestors died. Dozens were injured.

The incident stunned the nation and generated widespread hysteria about labor activists and immigrants. Although the identity of the bomber was never determined, police charged eight anarchists with conspiracy and murder. On November 11, 1887, Spies, Parsons, and two others were hanged. Another defendant killed himself by putting a dynamite cap in his mouth. In 1893, Illinois Governor John Altgeld fully pardoned all eight defendants and denounced the trial as unjust. The three surviving defendants were released from jail.

The Haymarket Affair drew worldwide attention to the U.S. labor movement. Many Americans blamed the Knights of Labor for the incident despite a lack of evidence. Popular distrust of unions prompted many Knights to join the less radical American Federation of Labor (AFL). The vast majority of workers, however, shunned organized labor altogether.

These readings illustrate two different perspectives on the Haymarket Affair. In the first, the Chicago Tribune *responds to the riot. The second is an excerpt from the autobiography of Albert R. Parsons in which he explains his political views and his role in the Haymarket Square rally.*

FOCUS QUESTIONS

1. What is the *Tribune*'s view of organized labor? Whom do the editors hold responsible for the Haymarket riot?
2. How do you think that Terence Powderly (Document 16.3) reacted to the Haymarket riot?
3. How would you characterize Albert Parsons's political views?
4. Why did Parsons get involved with the eight-hour workday campaign? How did he end up at the Haymarket Square rally? Was he involved in the riot?
5. How does Parsons's interpretation of the riot differ from that of the *Chicago Tribune*?
6. Whom does Parsons hold responsible for his imprisonment and impending death? Do you think there is any validity to his claims?

Chicago Tribune, May 7, 1886

obbing, murder, and dynamite assassination were probably necessary to arouse the Americans and the Americanized foreigners of Chicago to the danger tolerating any longer the public teaching of imported Nihilism and Communism. For years this city has been made a hotbed for the propagation of anarchical doctrines. Under the leadership of Spies, Fielden, Parsons, and Schwab the bloody-minded Anarchists congregated in this city have been urging the destruction of American ideas of government and sending out their disciples to spread seditious doctrines and encourage social and political revolution. Not an effort has been made to drive out, chain, or suppress these political mad-dogs, but they have been allowed to pursue their frenzied course without the slightest interference from municipal authorities. In accordance with certain popular but delusive and misplaced notions about the sacredness of free speech and free print the Anarchists have been permitted to advocate murder, arson, and pillage as the means for the overthrow of American government and destruction of American society. The general idea seemed to be that the madness would run its course and that there might be a seed-sowing of anarchical doctrine without a harvest of riot and bloodshed. The events of the last week prove such expectations unfounded and demonstrate that the people cannot expect to escape the effects if they tolerate the cause. They must put their heel on the Anarchists and crush them out....

Let the Anarchists learn that, while the American people may be slow to wrath, they are fully able to protect themselves, their families, their institutions, and their property. While Spies, Parsons, Fielden, and Schwab are punished according to law, care should be taken that no more such social desperadoes are harbored in Chicago. Incendiary anarchical sheets should be suppressed by the police. Nihilistic meetings on the public parks ought to be broken up and the leaders sent home if need be with broken heads. No more red flags or black flags should be flaunted in the streets of Chicago. Let the Anarchists understand that they must seek some other place to preach and practice their hellish doctrines, and while they remain here they must show at least an outward respect for American laws and institutions. The sooner dynamite conspirators understand that matters have at last reached this complexion the better for all concerned.

Chicago Tribune, May 7, 1886.

Albert R. Parson's autobiography as published in a Knights of Labor newspaper:

Government is compulsory; no one freely consents to be governed by another, therefore there can be no just power of government. Anarchy is perfect liberty, is absolute freedom of the individual.... Anarchism nor anarchists either advises, abets, nor encourages the working people to the use of force or a resort to violence. We do not say to the wage-slaves; "you ought, you should use force." No. Why say this when we know they must; they will be driven to use it in self-defense in self-preservation against those who are degrading, enslaving and destroying them?

Already the millions of workers are unconsciously anarchists. Impelled by a cause the effects of which they feel but do not wholly understand, they move unconsciously, irresistibly forward to the Social revolution. Mental freedom—political equality—industrial liberty.

This is the natural order of things; the logic of events. Who is so foolish as to quarrel with it, obstruct it or attempt to stay its progress?...

An examination of the class struggle demonstrates that the Eight-Hour movement was doomed by the very nature of things to defeat. But the International gave its support to it for two reasons, viz: first because it was a class movement against class domination, therefore historical & evolutionary and necessary; & secondly, because we did not choose to stand aloof & be misunderstood by our fellow workers. We therefore gave to it all the aid & comfort in our power. I was regularly accredited under the official seal of the Trade & Labor Unions, of the Central Labor Union representing twenty thousand organized workingmen in Chicago to assist them in the organization of Trades and Labor Unions & do all in my power for the Eight-Hour movement. The Central Labor Union in conjunction with the International publishes six newspapers in Chicago to wit: one English weekly, two German weeklies, one Bohemian weekly, one Scandinavian weekly, and one German daily newspaper.

The Trades & Labor Unions of the United States & Canada having set apart the first day of May 1886 to inaugurate the 8-hour system, I did all in my power to assist the movement. I feared conflict & trouble would arise between the authorities representing the employers of labor & the wage-workers who only represented themselves. I knew that defenseless men, women & children must finally succumb to the power of the discharge, black-list & lock-out & its consequent misery & hunger enforced by the militiaman's bayonet & the policeman's club. I did not advocate the use of force. But I denounced the capitalists for employing it to hold the laborers in subjection to them & declared that such treatment would of necessity drive the workingmen to employ the same means in self-defense.

The Labor organizations of Cincinnati Ohio decided to make a grand Eight-Hour demonstration & street parade & picnic on Sunday May 2nd in commemoration of the 8-hour work-day. On their invitation I went there to address them & left Chicago on Saturday, May 1st for that purpose. Returning on Monday night I reached Chicago on the morning of Tuesday May 4th, the day of the Haymarket meeting. On arriving home, Mrs. Parsons, who had theretofore attended & assisted in several large mass-meetings of the sewing girls of the city to organize them on the eight hour workday, suggested to me to call a meeting of the American Group of the International for that evening in order to make arrangements, i.e. appropriate money for hall rent, printing hand-bills, provide speakers, etc, to help organize the sewing women for 8-hours....

Late in the afternoon I learned for the first time that a mass meeting had been called at the Haymarket for that evening, the object being to help on the 8-hour boom, & to protest against the Police atrocities upon 8-hour strikers at McCormick's factory the day before, where it was claimed six workmen had been shot down by the police & many others wounded. I did not fancy the idea of holding the meeting at that time, & said so, stating that I believed the manufacturers and corporations were so incensed at the 8-hour movement that they would defend the police in coming to the meeting to break it up and slaughtering the work people. I was invited to speak there, but declined on the ground that I had to attend another meeting that night....

Reaching the place of meeting of the American group of the International, it was at-once called to order & the objects of the meeting were stated to be how best to organize the sewing women of the city in the speediest manner.... About 9 o'clock a committee entered the meeting & said that there was a large mass-meeting at the Haymarket but no speakers except Mr. Spies, & they were sent over to request Mr. Fielden & myself to come over at once & address the crowd.

We adjourned in a few moments afterwards & went over to the Haymarket in a body where I was introduced at once & spoke for about an hour to the 3,000 persons present urging them to support the 8-hour movement & stick to their unions. There was little said about the police brutalities of the previous day, other than to complain of the use of the military on every slight occasion. I said it was a shame that the moderate & just claims of the wage-workers should be met with police clubs, pistols & bayonets, or that the murmurs of discontented laborers should be drowned in their own blood.

When I had finished speaking & Mr. Fielden began, I got down from the wagon we were using as a speaker's stand & stepping over to another wagon near by on which sat the ladies (among them my wife & children) and it soon appearing as though it would rain & the crowd beginning to disperse and the speaker having announced that he would finish in a few moments, I assisted the ladies down from the wagon and accompanied them to Zepf's Hall one block away where we intended to wait for the adjournment & the company of other friends on our walk home. I had been in this hall about 5 minutes & was looking towards the meeting expecting it to close every moment, & standing near by where the ladies sat, when there appeared a white sheet of light at the place of meeting, followed instantly by a loud roar. This was at once followed by a fusillade of pistol shots (in full view of my sight) which appeared as though 50 or more men had emptied their self-acting revolvers as rapidly as possible. Several shots whizzed by & struck beside the door of the hall from which I was looking and soon men came rushing wildly into the building. I escorted the ladies to a place of safety in the rear where we remained about 20 minutes. Leaving the place to take the ladies home, we met a man named Brown, (who was well-known to us) at the corner of Milwaukee Ave. & Desplaines St., & asking him to loan me a dollar he replied that he didn't have the change whereupon I borrowed a five dollar gold piece from him. We then parted, he went his way & we started towards home. (This man Brown told of the circumstance the next day; that he had met & loaned me $5. He was at once arrested, and afterwards indicted for conspiracy & unlawful assembly, thrown into prison where he has lain ever since!)

The next day observing that many innocent people who were not even present at the meeting were being dragooned & imprisoned by the authorities, & not courting such indignities for myself, I left the city intending to return in a few days (and publishing a letter in the newspapers to that effect). I stopped at Elgin, 2 days at a boarding house when I went from there to Waukeshaw Wisconsin, a place noted for its beautiful spring & health-giving waters, pure air, etc. At this summer resort I soon obtained employment first at carpentering & then as a painter, which occupations I pursued for seven weeks or until my return and voluntary surrender to the court for trial. I procured the Chicago newspapers every day & from them I learned that I with a great many others had been indicted for murder, conspiracy, and unlawful assembly at the Haymarket. From the editorials of the capitalist papers each day for two months during my seclusion I could see that the ruling class were wild with rage & fear against the labor organizations. Ample means were offered me to carry me safely to distant parts of the earth if I chose to go. I knew that the beastly howls against the Anarchists the demand for their bloody extermination made by the press and pulpit was merely a pretext of the ruling class to intimidate the growing power of organized labor in the United States. And I knew that if we were sacrificed by the money maloch it would be with the sole view to making examples of us from which workingmen could take warning by our fates. I also, perfectly understood the relentless hate & power of the ruling class. Nevertheless, knowing that I was innocent & that my comrades were innocent of the charge against them, I resolved to return, & share whatever persecution labor's enemies could impose upon them. Consequently on the night of June 20, I left Waukeshaw. At 4:30 a.m. June 21, I boarded a St. Paul train at the union depot in Milwaukee & arrived in Chicago at 7:30 or 8 o'clock a.m.

I repaired to the house of Mrs. Ames at No. 14 S. Morgan St. I sent for my wife who came to me and a few moments later, I conveyed word to Capt. Black (our attorney) that I was prepared to surrender. After an affectionate parting with my noble, brave and loving wife and several devoted friends who were present—I at a little past 2 o'clock p.m. June 21st accompanied by Mrs. Ames & Mr. A. H. Simpson to the court house entrance was there joined by my attorney (Capt. Black) we walked up the broad stair-way, entered the court then in session, and standing before the bar of the court announced my presence and my voluntary surrender for trial and entering the plea "Not guilty". After this ceremony was over I approached the prisoner's dock where sat my arraigned comrades Fielden, Spies, Engel, Fischer, Lingg, Neebe & Schwab, & shaking hands with each of them I took a seat among them. After the adjournment of the Court I was conveyed with the others to a cell in the Cook Co. Bastile, and securely locked-up....

My own belief, based on careful examination of all the conditions surrounding this Haymarket affair, is that the bomb was thrown by a man in the employ of certain monopolists who was sent from New York City to Chicago for that purpose, to break up the 8-hour movement, thrust the active men into prison, and scare and terrify the workingmen into submission. Such a course was advocated by all the leading mouth-pieces (newspapers) of monopoly in America just prior to May 1st....

Six of the condemned men were not present at the meeting, at the time of the tragedy two of them were not present at any time. One of the latter was addressing a mass-meeting of 2,000 workmen at Deering Harvester Works in Lakeview 5 miles away; the other one was at home abed & knew not of the affair till the next day. His verdict is 15 years in the Penitentiary. These facts stand unquestioned & undenied before the Court. There was no proof of our complicity with or knowledge of the person who threw the Bomb, nor is there any proof as to who did throw it.

The rapid growth of whole labor movement had by May first given the monopolists of the country much cause for alarm. The organized power of labor was beginning to exhibit unexpected strength & boldness. This alarmed King Money-Bags who saw in the Haymarket affair their golden opportunity to make a horrible example of the Anarchists, & by "the deep damnation of their taking off" give the discontented American workingmen a terrible warning.

Their verdict is the suppression of free speech, free press, & the assemblage of the people to discuss their grievances. More than that the verdict is the denial of the right of self-defense, it is a condemnation of the law of self-preservation in America.

The execution of this verdict will demonstrate to the working people of the United States that whoever writes, speaks, or works to help organize the working class to obtain their rights is liable to imprisonment & death, but whoever uses a ten (10) cent bomb in self-defense & destroys those who would have destroyed them, or uses it in the interests of a monopolist conspiracy to put down the labor movement is in no danger at all, if they go about their business and say nothing to anyone. This fact was clearly set forth in the address of the State's Attorney & his assistants to the jury when they said "These eight men were picked out by the grand jury because they were the leaders. They are no more guilty than the thousands of their associates in Chicago. They are leaders and we ask you to convict them & make examples of them to others." These were the words, almost the precise words, of the prosecution. The bomb-thrower goes free; the judge decides that his identity or our connection with him is immaterial if it can be shown we ever said that workingmen ought to defend themselves against the attacks & assaults of the police & militia.

As to the responsibility for the Haymarket tragedy? You have heard the side of the ruling class. I now speak for the people—the ruled. The Haymarket tragedy was the immediate result of the blood-thirsty officiousness of Police Inspector Bonfield. Mayor Harrison (commander of the Chicago Police) was present at this meeting, & testified before the court that he heard the speeches & left just before it—adjournment & went to the police station & advised Bonfield that everything at the meeting was peaceable & orderly. The Mayor left for his home. Soon thereafter, Bonfield thirsting for promotion & the blood-money which he knew that monopolists were eager to bestow, gathered his army and marched them down upon a peaceable, orderly meeting of workingmen where he expected to immortalize himself by deeds of carnage & slaughter that would put to shame a horde of Apache Indians. Had he not done such brutal things before with the striking street-car Knights of Labor, Trades Unionists & other workingmen? Why not repeat it that night also? He had received the plaudits of the capitalist press for such acts done on other occasions. Why not again? But Police Inspector Bonfield was only a willing agent not the dastardly principal in this outrage. He held plenary power & he obeyed what he knew to be the express desires of his masters—the Money Kings—who want to suppress free speech, free press, & the right of workingmen to assemble & discuss their grievances. Let the responsibility for the Haymarket tragedy rest where it belongs, to-wit: Upon the monopolists, corporations & privileged class who rule & rob the working people, and when they complain about it discharge, lock-out and black-list them or arrest, imprison and execute them....

Albert R. Parsons Autobiography (1887), Haymarket Affair Digital Collection, ICHi-31358. Courtesy of Chicago Historical Society.

16.5

ELIZABETH CADY STANTON, "SOLITUDE OF SELF" (1892)

Almost 50 years after the Seneca Falls Convention, women's rights advocates continued to fight for suffrage. Despite their exclusion from the voting process, women were finding ways to assert themselves and to challenge rigid Victorian notions of gender. Increasing numbers of women were pursuing higher education and work outside the home. Women's clubs provided opportunities for public speaking and social activism. Bicycling and other sports enabled women to free themselves from restrictive corsets and to enjoy exercise. Courts more frequently granted women divorces when husbands acted irresponsibly or were abusive. Nonetheless, society still defined women primarily as wives and mothers.

Elizabeth Cady Stanton (1815-1902) wanted women to be fully recognized as individuals. Having authored the Declaration of Sentiments in 1848, Stanton had spent decades working for women's rights. In 1878, she wrote a federal suffrage amendment that was introduced in every Congress until its adoption in 1920.

Collaborating with Matilda Jocelyn Gage and Susan B. Anthony, Stanton helped to compile a multi-volume history of the women's suffrage movement. She also published The Women's Bible *(1895-1898) and an autobiography.*

In 1892, the Senate Judiciary Committee invited Stanton and others to testify on behalf of women's voting rights. Her response became one of her most famous speeches.

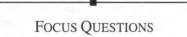

FOCUS QUESTIONS

1. What are Stanton's major goals for women? Why does she believe that these objectives are so important?
2. How does Stanton believe that women's lives have improved?
3. Does Stanton make a compelling case for women's rights? Why might someone have disagreed with her arguments? Explain your answers.

T he point I wish plainly to bring before you on this occasion is the individuality of each human soul; our Protestant idea, the right of individual conscience and judgment—our republican idea, individual citizenship. In discussing the rights of woman, we are to consider, first, what belongs to her as an individual, in a world of her own, the arbiter of her own destiny, an imaginary Robinson Crusoe with her woman Friday on a solitary island. Her rights under such circumstances are to use all her faculties for her own safety and happiness.

Secondly, if we consider her as a citizen, as a member of a great nation, she must have the same rights as all other members, according to the fundamental principles of our Government.

Thirdly, viewed as a woman, an equal factor in civilization, her rights and duties are still the same—individual happiness and development.

Fourthly, it is only the incidental relations of life, such as mother, wife, sister, daughter, that may involve some special duties and training. In the usual discussion in regard to woman's sphere, such a man as Herbert Spencer, Frederic Harrison, and Grant Allen uniformly subordinate her rights and duties as an individual, as a citizen, as a woman, to the necessities of these incidental relations, some of which a large class of woman may never assume. In discussing the sphere of man, we do not decide his rights as an individual, as a citizen, as a man by his duties as a father, a husband, a brother, or a son, relations some of which he may never fill. Moreover he would be better fitted for these very relations and whatever special work he might choose to do to earn his bread by the complete development of all his faculties as an individual.

Just so with woman. The education that will fit her to discharge the duties in the largest sphere of human usefulness will best fit her for whatever special work she may be compelled to do.

The isolation of every human soul and the necessity of self-dependence must give each individual the right to choose his own surroundings. The strongest reason for giving woman all the opportunities for higher education, for the full development of her faculties, forces of mind and body; for giving her the most enlarged freedom of thought and action; a complete emancipation from all forms of bondage, of custom, dependence, superstition; from all the crippling influences of fear, is the solitude and personal responsibility of her own individual life. The strongest reason why we ask for woman a voice in the government under which she lives; in the religion she is asked to believe; equality in social life, where she is the chief factor; a place in the trades and professions, where she may earn her bread, is because of her birthright to self-sovereignty; because, as an individual, she must rely on herself. No matter how much women prefer to lean, to be protected and supported, nor how much men desire to have them do so, they must make the voyage of life alone, and for safety in an emergency they must know something of the laws of navigation. To guide our own craft, we must be captain, pilot, engineer; with chart and compass to stand at the wheel; to match the wind and waves and know when to take in the sail, and to read the signs in the firmament over all. It matters not whether the solitary voyager is man or woman....

To throw obstacle in the way of a complete education is like putting out the eyes; to deny the rights of property, like cutting off the hands. To deny political equality is to rob the ostracized of all self-respect; of credit in the market place; of recompense in the world of work; of a voice among those who make and administer the law; a choice in the jury before whom they are tried, and in the judge who decides their punishment....

Nothing strengthens the judgment and quickens the conscience like individual responsibility. Nothing adds such dignity to character as the recognition of one's self-sovereignty; the right to an equal place, everywhere conceded; a place earned by personal merit, not an artificial attainment, by inheritance, wealth, family, and position. Seeing, then that the responsibilities of life rest equally on man and woman, that their destiny is the same, they need the same preparation for time and eternity. The talk of sheltering woman from the fierce sterns of life is the sheerest mockery, for they beat on her from every point of the compass, just as they do on man, and with more fatal results, for he has been trained to protect himself, to resist, to conquer. Such are the facts in human experience, the responsibilities of individual. Rich and poor, intelligent and ignorant, wise and foolish, virtuous and vicious, man and woman, it is ever the same, each soul must depend wholly on itself....

We may have many friends, love, kindness, sympathy and charity to smooth our pathway in everyday life, but in the tragedies and triumphs of human experience each mortal stands alone....

...Women are already the equals of men in the whole of dream of thought, in art, science, literature, and government. With telescope vision they explore the starry firmament, and bring back the history of the planetary world. With chart and compass they pilot ships across the mighty deep, and with skillful finger send electric messages around the globe. In galleries of art the beauties of nature and the virtues of humanity are immortalized by them on their canvas and by their inspired touch dull blocks of marble are transformed into angels of light.

In music they speak again the language of Mendelssohn, Beethoven, Chopin, Schumann, and are worthy interpreters of their great thoughts. The poetry and novels of the century are theirs, and they have touched the keynote of reform in religion, politics, and social life. They fill the editor's and professor's chair, and plead at the bar of justice, walk the wards of the hospital, and speak from the pulpit and the platform; such is the type of womanhood that an enlightened public sentiment welcomes today, and such the triumph of the facts of life over the false theories of the past.

Is it, then, consistent to hold the developed woman of this day within the same narrow political limits as the dame with the spinning wheel and knitting needle occupied in the past? No! No! Machinery has taken the labors of woman as well as man on its tireless shoulders; the loom and the spinning wheel are but dreams of the past; the pen, the brush, the easel, the chisel, have taken their places, while the hopes and ambitions of women are essentially changed. We see reason sufficient in the outer conditions of human being for individual liberty and development, but when we consider the self dependence of every human soul we see the need of courage, judgment, and the exercise of every faculty of mind and body, strengthened and developed by use, in woman as well as man....

Elizabeth Cady Stanton, Susan B. Anthony, and Matilda Joslyn Gage, *History of Woman Suffrage* (New York: Fowler & Wells, 1902), Vol. IV, pp. 189-191.

16.6

THE OMAHA PLATFORM OF THE POPULIST PARTY (1892)

During the late 1880s, many Americans were dissatisfied with the nation's political parties and business leaders. Although voter turnouts were high, complaints about political corruption and unresponsive public officials were widespread. Many small producers felt cheated because federal subsidies and tariff policies favored large corporations. Such inequities sparked popular demands for sweeping economic and political reforms.

Farmers were among those most eager for change. Declining crop prices, bad weather, and economic instability had forced many farmers into bankruptcy. Hoping to protect agricultural interests nationally, a coalition of agrarian groups formed the People's Party of the United States, better known as the Populist Party. On July 4, 1892, the Populists met in Omaha, Nebraska and adopted a broad platform designed to appeal to common men across the country.

---■---

FOCUS QUESTIONS

1. What do the Populists identify as the biggest problems in American society? What are some of the Populists' proposed solutions to these problems?
2. What groups would be attracted to the Populist platform? Who would find the Populist agenda uninviting?
3. Why do you think that the Populists were considered radical in the 1890s? Were the Populists successful? Explain your answers.

P REAMBLE
The conditions which surround us best justify our cooperation; we meet in the midst of a nation brought to the verge of moral, political, and material ruin. Corruption dominates the ballot-box, the Legislatures, the Congress, and touches even the ermine of the bench. The people are demoralized; most of the States have been compelled to isolate the voters at the polling places to prevent universal intimidation and bribery. The newspapers are largely subsidized or muzzled, public opinion silenced, business prostrated, homes covered with mortgages, labor impoverished, and the land concentrating in the hands of capitalists. The urban workmen are denied the right to organize for self-protection, imported pauperized labor beats down their wages, a hireling standing army, unrecognized by our laws, is established to shoot them down, and they are rapidly degenerating into European conditions. The fruits of the toil of millions are boldly stolen to build up colossal fortunes for a few, unprecedented in the history of mankind and the possessors of these, in turn, despise the Republic and endanger liberty. From the same prolific womb of governmental injustice we breed the two great classes—tramps and millionaires....

[B]elieving that the forces of reform this day organized will never cease to move forward until every wrong is remedied, and equal rights and equal privileges securely established for all the men and women of this country.

We declare, therefore—

First—That the union of the labor forces of the United States this day con-summated shall be permanent and perpetual; may its spirit enter into all hearts for the salvation of the Republic and the uplifting of mankind.

Second—Wealth belongs to him who creates it, and every dollar taken from industry without an equivalent is robbery. "If any will not work, neither shall he eat." The interests of rural and civil labor are the same; their enemies are identical.

Third—We believe that the time has come when the railroad corporations will either own the people or the people must own the railroads; and should the government enter upon the work of owning and managing any and all railroads, we should favor an amendment to the constitution by which all persons engaged in the government service shall be placed under a civil service regulation of the most rigid character, so as to prevent the increase of power of the national administration by the use of such additional government employees.

We demand that national currency, safe, sound, and flexible, issued by the general government only, a full legal tender for all debts, public and private, and that without the use of banking corporations, a just, equitable, and efficient means of distribution direct to the people, at a tax not to exceed 2 per cent per annum, be provided, as set forth in the sub-treasury plan of the farmers' alliance, or some better system; also by payments in discharge of its obligations for public improvements.

We demand free and unlimited coinage of silver and gold at the present legal ratio of 16 to 1.

We demand that the amount of the circulating medium be speedily increased to not less than $50 per capita.

We demand a graduated income tax.

We believe that the money of the country should be kept as much as possible in the hands of the people, and hence we demand that all state and national revenues shall be limited to the necessary expenses of the government, economically and honestly administered.

We demand that postal savings banks be established by the government for the safe deposit of the earnings of the people and to facilitate exchange.

Transportation being a means of exchange and a public necessity, the government should own and operate the railroads in the interest of the people.

The telegraph and telephone, like the post office system, being a necessity for the transmission of news, should be owned and operated by the government in the interest of the people.

The land, including all the natural sources of wealth, is the heritage of the people, and should not be monopolized for speculative purposes, and alien ownership of land should be prohibited. All land now held by railroads and other corporations in excess of their actual needs, and all lands now owned by aliens should be reclaimed by the government and held for actual settlers only....

Whereas, other questions have been presented for our consideration, we hereby submit the following, not as a part of the platform of the people's party but as resolutions expressive of the sentiment of this convention.

First—Resolved, That we demand a free ballot and a fair count in all elections, and pledge ourselves to secure it to every legal voter without federal intervention, through the adoption by the states of the unperverted Australian or secret ballot system.

Second—Resolved, That the revenue derived from a graduated income tax should be applied to the reduction of the burden of taxation now levied upon the domestic industries of this country.

Third—Resolved, That we pledge our support to fair and liberal pensions to ex-union soldiers and sailors.

Fourth—Resolved, That we condemn the fallacy of protecting American labor under the present system, which opens our ports to the pauper and criminal classes of the world and crowds out our wage earners; and we denounce the present ineffective laws against contract labor, and demand the further restriction of undesirable emigration.

Fifth—Resolved, That we cordially sympathize with the efforts of organized workingmen to shorten the hours of labor, and demand a rigid enforcement of existing eight-hour law on government work, and ask that a penalty clause be added to the said law.

Sixth—Resolved, That we regard the maintenance of a large standing army of mercenaries, known as the Pinkerton system, as a menace to our liberties, and we demand its abolition....

Resolved, That we commend to the favorable consideration of the people, and the reform press the legislative system known as the initiative and referendum.

Resolved, That we favor a constitutional provision limiting the office of president and vice-president to one term, and providing for the election of senators of the United States by a direct vote of the people.

Resolved, That we oppose any subsidy or national aid to any private corporation for any purpose.

"People's Party Platform," Omaha *Morning World-Herald,* 5 July 1892, 6.

16.7

THEODORE DREISER, *SISTER CARRIE* (1900)

As the nineteenth century neared its end, American culture echoed the turbulence engulfing the nation. Rejecting sentimental novels and garish art, some writers and artists tried to teach the middle classes to appreciate high culture. "Quality" publications like The Atlantic Monthly *and* The Nation *refused to publish "vulgar" and "blasphemous" stories. Such narrow notions of taste met opposition. New magazines like* Ladies Home Journal *and* McClure's *published younger writers who described ordinary people in real situations.*

Theodore Dreiser (1871-1945) was one such author. The leading figure in the naturalist literary movement, Dreiser challenged Victorian notions of propriety by exploring the darker elements of industrial America and human nature. Drawing on personal experience and intellectual influences, he concluded that heredity and environment controlled individuals. People therefore acted according to their instincts. After working as a journalist for several years, Dreiser began writing his first novel, Sister Carrie. *The book tells the story of Carrie Meeber, an innocent girl who moves from Wisconsin to Chicago. After being seduced by a traveling salesman and living with a married saloonkeeper, Carrie pursues a career in the theatre. Dreiser's gritty depictions of urban life and sexuality were so shocking that his publisher printed only 1,000 copies of the novel and limited the book's advertising. A commercial failure in its day,* Sister Carrie *is now considered a landmark in American literature. In this extract, Carrie meets an intriguing stranger during a train trip.*

■

FOCUS QUESTIONS

1. What happens to Carrie Meeber in this excerpt? Does her behavior challenge traditional ideals of womanhood? Explain your answer.
2. How does Dreiser respond to Victorian ideals of self-restraint and frugality?
3. How does the passage reflect realities of modern American life?

THE MAGNET ATTRACTING—A WAIF AMID FORCES

W hen Caroline Meeber boarded the afternoon train for Chicago, her total outfit consisted of a small trunk, a cheap imitation alligator-skin satchel, a small lunch in a paper box, and yellow leather snap purse, containing her ticket, a scrap of paper with her sister's address in Van Buren Street, and four dollars in money. It was in August 1889. She was eighteen years of age, bright, timid, and full of the illusions of ignorance and youth. Whatever touch of regret at parting characterised her thoughts, it was certainly not for advantages now being given up. A gush of tears at her mother's farewell kiss, a touch in her throat when the cars clacked by the flour mill where her father worked by the day, a pathetic sigh as the familiar green environs of the village passed in review, and the threads which bound her so lightly to girlhood and home were irretrievably broken....

When a girl leaves her home at eighteen, she does one of two things. Either she falls into saving hands and becomes better, or she rapidly assumes the cosmopolitan standard of virtue and becomes worse. Of an intermediate balance, under the circumstances, there is no possibility. The city has its cunning wiles, no less than the infinitely smaller and more human tempter. There are large forces which allure with all the soulfulness of expression possible in the most cultured human....

Caroline, or Sister Carrie, as she had been half affectionately termed by the family, was possessed of a mind rudimentary in its power of observation and analysis. Self-interest with her was high, but not strong. It was, nevertheless, her guiding characteristic. Warm with the fancies of youth, pretty with the insipid prettiness of the formative period, possessed of a figure promising eventual shapeliness and an eye alight with certain native intelligence, she was a fair example of the middle American class—two generations removed from the emigrant. Books were beyond her interest—knowledge a sealed book. In the intuitive graces she was still crude. She could scarcely toss her head gracefully. Her hands were almost ineffectual. The feet, though small, were set flatly. And yet she was interested in her charms, quick to understand the keener pleasures of life, ambitious to gain in material things....

"That," said a voice in her ear, "is one of the prettiest little resorts in Wisconsin."

"Is it?" she answered nervously.

The train was just pulling out of Waukesha. For some time she had been conscious of a man behind. She felt him observing her mass of hair. He had been fidgeting, and with natural intuition she felt a certain interest growing in that quarter. Her maidenly reserve, and a certain sense of what was conventional under the circumstances, called her to forestall and deny this familiarity, but the daring and magnetism of the individual, born of past experiences and triumphs, prevailed. She answered.

He leaned forward to put his elbows upon the back of her seat and proceeded to make himself volubly agreeable.

"Yes, that is a great resort for Chicago people. The hotels are swell. You are not familiar with this part of the country, are you?"

"Oh, yes, I am," answered Carrie. "That is, I live at Columbi City. I have never been through here, though."

"And so this is your first visit to Chicago," he observed.

All the time she was conscious of certain features out of the side of her eye. Flush, colourful cheeks, a light moustache, grey fedora hat. She now turned and looked upon him in full, the instincts of self-protection and coquetry mingling confusedly in her brain.

"I didn't say that," she said.

"Oh," he answered, in a very pleasing way and with an assumed air of mistake, "I thought you did."

Here was a type of the travelling canvasser for a manufacturing house—a class which at that time was first being dubbed by the slang of the day "drummers." He came within the meaning of still newer term, which had sprung into general use among Americans in 1880, and which concisely expressed the thought of one whose dress or manners are calculated to elicit the admiration of susceptible young women—a "masher." His suit was of a striped and crossed pattern of brown wool, new at that time, but since become familiar as a business suit. The low crotch of the vest revealed a stiff shirt bosom of white and pink stripes. From his coat sleeves protruded a pair of linen cuffs of the same pattern, fastened with large, gold plate buttons, set with the common yellow agates known as "cat's-eyes." His fingers bore several rings—one, the ever-enduring heavy seal—and from his vest dangled a neat gold watch chain, from which was suspended the secret insignia of the Order of Elks. The whole suit was rather tight-fitting, and was finished off with heavy-soled tan shoes, highly polished, and the grey fedora hat. He was, for the order of intellect represented, attractive, and whatever he had to recommend him, you may be sure was not lost upon Carrie, in this, her first glance.

Lest this order of individual should permanently pass, let me put down some of the most striking characteristics of his most successful manner and method. Good clothes, of course, were the first essential, the things without which he was nothing. Strong physical nature, actuated by a keen desire for the feminine, was the next. A mind free of any consideration of the problems or forces of the world and actuated not by greed, but an insatiable love of variable pleasure. His method was always simple. Its principal element was daring, backed, of course, by an intense desire and admiration for the sex. Let him meet with a young woman once and he would approach her with an air of kindly familiarity, not unmixed with pleading, which would result in most cases in a tolerant acceptance. If she showed any tendency to coquetry he would be apt to straighten her tie, or if she "took up" with him at all, to call her by her first name. If he visited a department store it was to lounge familiarly over the counter and ask some leading questions. In more exclusive circles, on the train or in waiting stations, he went slower. If some seemingly vulnerable object appeared he was all attention—to pass the compliments of the day, to lead the way to the parlor car, carrying her grip, or, failing that, to take a seat next her with the hope of being able to court her to her destination. Pillows, books, a footstool, the shade lowered all these figured in the things which he could do. If, when she reached her destination he did not alight and attend her baggage for her, it was because, in his own estimation, he had signally failed.

A woman should some day write the complete philosophy of clothes. No matter how young, it is one of the things she wholly comprehends. There is an indescribably faint line in the matter of man's apparel which somehow divides for her those who are worth glancing at and those who are not. Once an individual has passed this faint line on the way downward he will get no glance from her. There is another line at which the dress of a man will cause her to study her own. This line the individual at her elbow now marked for Carrie. She became conscious of an inequality. Her own plain blue dress, with its black cotton tape trimmings, now seemed to her shabby. She felt the worn state of her shoes.

"Let's see," he went on, "I know quite a number of people in your town. Morgenroth the clothier and Gibson the dry goods man."

"Oh, do you?" she interrupted, aroused by memories of longings their show windows had cost her.

At last he had a clew to her interest, and followed it deftly. In a few minutes he had come about into her seat. He talked of sales of clothing, his travels, Chicago, and the amusements of that city.

"If you are going there, you will enjoy it immensely. Have you relatives?"

"I am going to visit my sister," she explained.

"You want to see Lincoln Park," he said, "and Michigan Boulevard. They are putting up great buildings there. It's a second New York—great. So much to see—theatres, crowds, fine houses—oh, you'll like that."

There was a little ache in her fancy of all he described. Her insignificance in the presence of so much magnificence faintly affected her. She realised that hers was not to be a round of pleasure, and yet there was something promising in all the material prospect he set forth. There was something satisfactory in the attention of this individual with his good clothes. She could not help smiling as he told her of some popular actress of whom she reminded him. She was not silly, and yet attention of this sort had its weight....

Theodore Dreiser, "The Magnet Attracting the Waif," *Sister Carrie* (New York: Doubleday and Co., 1900), Chapter One.

16.8

■

ALBERT J. BEVERIDGE CALLS FOR AN AMERICAN EMPIRE (1900)

Fueled by capitalism, nationalism, white supremacy, and sensationalized journalism, a drive for territorial expansion consumed the United States in the decades following the Civil War. Imperialists set their sights on potential U.S. colonies in Latin America and Asia.

After the United States won the Spanish-Cuban-American War in 1898, Americans were bitterly divided over whether or not to annex the Philippines. The debates escalated after a vicious guerilla war erupted between Filipino rebels and U.S. soldiers. Albert J Beveridge (1862-1927), a first-term Republican senator from Indiana, was one of the most ardent advocates of imperialism. Noted for his speaking abilities and fervent nationalism, Beveridge traveled to the Philippines in order to gather information. The voyage only intensified his belief that the United States should acquire a colonial empire. After serving two terms in the Senate, Beveridge became a distinguished historian and won the Pulitzer Prize for the four-volume The Life of John Marshall. *This extract highlights one of Beveridge's speeches supporting annexation of the Philippines.*

■

FOCUS QUESTIONS

1. Why does Beveridge think that the United States should annex the Philippines? Do you find his arguments convincing? Explain your answer.
2. How does Beveridge describe Asian people? What is the meaning and significance of his use of terms like "civilization," "Anglo-Saxon," and "our race"?
3. What legal justification does Beveridge use to justify imperialism?
4. Compare Beveridge's arguments to those of Mark Twain (Document 16.9) How do their interpretations of imperialism differ? Whose arguments most closely resemble your views of imperialism? Why?

Mr. President, the times call for candor. The Philippines are ours forever, "territory belonging to the United States," as the Constitution calls them. And just beyond the Philippines are China's illimitable markets. We will not retreat from either. We will not repudiate our duty in the archipelago. We will not abandon our opportunity in the Orient. We will not renounce our part in the mission of our race, trustee, under God, of the civilization of the world. And we will move forward to our work, not howling out regrets like slaves whipped to their burdens, but with gratitude for a task worthy of our strength, and thanksgiving to Almighty God that He has marked us as His chosen people, hence forth to lead in the regeneration of the world.

This island empire is the last land left in all the oceans. If it should prove a mistake to abandon it, the blunder once made would be irretrievable. If it proves a mistake to hold it, the error can be corrected when we will. Every other progressive nation stands ready to relieve us.

But to hold it will be no mistake. Our largest trade henceforth must be with Asia. The Pacific is our ocean. More and more Europe will manufacture the most it needs, secure from its colonies the most it consumes. Where shall we turn for consumers of our surplus? Geography answers the question. China is our natural customer. She is nearer to us than to England, Germany, or Russia, the commercial powers of the present and the future. They have moved nearer to China by securing permanent bases on her borders. The Philippines give us a base at the door of all the East.

Lines of navigation from our ports to the Orient and Australia; from the Isthmian Canal to Asia; from all Oriental ports to Australia, converge at and separate from the Philippines. They are a self-supporting, dividend-paying fleet, permanently anchored at a spot selected by the strategy of Providence, commanding the Pacific. And the Pacific is the ocean of the commerce of the future. Most future wars will be conflicts for commerce. The power that rules the Pacific, therefore, is the power that rules the world. And, with the Philippines, that power is and will forever be the American Republic....

Here, then, Senators, is the situation. Two years ago there was no land in all this world which we could occupy for any purpose. Our commerce was daily turning toward the Orient and geography and trade developments made necessary our commercial empire over the Pacific. And in that ocean we had no commercial, naval, or military base. To-day we have one of the three great ocean possessions on the globe, located at the most commanding commercial, naval, and military points in the eastern seas, within hail of India, shoulder to shoulder with China, richer in its own resources than any equal body of land on the entire globe, and peopled by a race which civilization demands shall be improved. Shall we abandon it? That man little knows the common people of the Republic, little understands the instincts of our race, who thinks we will not hold it fast and hold it forever, administering just government by simplest methods....

But Senators, it would be better to abandon this combined garden and Gibraltar of the Pacific, and count our blood and treasure already spent a profitable loss, than to apply any academic arrangement of self-government to these children. They are not capable of self-government. How could they be? They are not of a self-governing race. They are Orientals, Malays, instructed by Spaniards in the latter's worst estate.

They know nothing of practical self-government except as they have witnessed the weak, corrupt, cruel, and capricious rule of Spain. What magic will anyone employ to dissolve in their minds and characters those impressions of governors and governed which three centuries of misrule has created? What alchemy will change the oriental quality of their blood and set the self-government currents of the American pouring through their Malay veins? How shall they, in the twinkling of an eye, be exalted to the heights of self-governing peoples which required a thousand years, Anglo-Saxon though we are?...

No one need fear their competition with our labor. No reward could beguile, no force compel, these children of indolence to leave their trifling lives for the fierce and fervid industry of high wrought America. The very reverse is the fact. One great problem is the necessary labor to develop these islands—to build the roads, open the mines, clear the wilderness, drain the swamps, dredge the harbors. The natives will not supply it....

Senators in opposition are estopped from denying our constitutional power to govern the Philippines as circumstances may demand, for such power is admitted in the case of Florida, Louisiana, Alaska. How, then, is it denied in the Philippines? Is there a geographical interpretation to the Constitution? Do degrees of longitude fix constitutional limitations? Does a thousand miles of ocean diminish constitutional power more than a thousand miles of land?...

Mr. President, this question is deeper than any question of party politics; deeper than any question of the isolated policy of our country even; deeper even than any question of constitutional power. It is elemental. It is racial. God has not been preparing the English-speaking and Teutonic peoples for a thousand years for nothing but vain and idle self-contemplation and self-admiration. No! He has made us the master organizers of the world to establish a system where chaos reigns. He has given us the spirit of progress to overwhelm the forces of reaction throughout the earth. He has made us adept in government that we may administer government among savage and senile peoples. Were it not for such a force as this the world would relapse into barbarism and night. And of all our race He has marked the American people as His chosen nation to finally lead in the regeneration of the world. This is the divine mission of America, and it holds for us all the profit, all the glory, all the happiness possible to man. We are the trustees of the world's programs, guardians of its righteous peace. The judgment of the Master is upon us: "Ye have been faithful over a few things; I will make you ruler over many things."

What shall history say of us? Shall it say that we renounced that holy trust, left the savage to his base condition, the wilderness to the reign of waste, deserted duty, abandoned glory, forget our sordid profits even, because we feared our strength and read the charter of our powers with the doubter's eye and the quibbler's mind? Shall it say that, called by events to captain and command the proudest, ablest, purest race of history in history's noblest work, we declined that great commission? Our fathers would not have had it so. No! They founded no paralytic government, no sluggard people, passive while the world's work calls them. They established no reactionary nation. They unfurled no retreating flag....

Mr. President and Senators, adopt the resolution offered, that peace may quickly come and that we may begin our saving, regenerating, and uplifting work.... Reject it, and the world, history, and the American people will know where to forever fix the awful responsibility for the consequences that will surely follow such failure to do our manifest duty. How dare we delay when our soldiers' blood is flowing?

"Policy Regarding the Philippines," *Congressional Record*, 56th Congress, 1st Session, (9 January 1900), 704-712.

16.9

MARK TWAIN, "TO THE PERSON SITTING IN DARKNESS" (1901)

In 1896, Filipino rebels led by Emilio Aguinaldo (1869-1964) began fighting to expel the Spanish. Aided by U.S. arms, Aguinaldo's troops won several battles and issued a declaration of independence in June 1898. But within months, Spain ceded the Philippines, Puerto Rico, and Guam to the United States in exchange for $20 million. Unwilling to disband their provisional government or agree to U.S. control, Filipino forces attacked U.S. soldiers. Four years of fierce guerilla warfare ensued. Dispatching 125,000 troops, the United States lost 4,000 men in the struggle. At the same time, over 20,000 Filipino soldiers and perhaps 200,000 civilians perished. In 1902, Congress reached a compromise in which a presidential appointee governed the islands in conjunction with a Filipino assembly. In 1946, the Philippines were granted independence.

Many Americans opposed U.S. imperialism. Prominent citizens including William Jennings Bryan, Jane Addams, and Andrew Carnegie argued that acquisition of foreign territories violated national ideals. Some anti-imperialists also claimed that U.S. colonies would jeopardize white supremacy and undermine capitalism.

Mark Twain (1835-1910) was a vociferous critic of imperialism. Twain's writings including The Adventures of Tom Sawyer *(1876) and* The Adventures of Huckleberry Finn *(1884) brought him international acclaim. He traveled widely and encountered indigenous peoples in several countries. In much of his work, Twain used satire combined with facts to comment on international relations. He was also an active member of the American Friends of Russia and the Anti-Imperialist League. In this essay, Twain attacks the imperialistic ambitions of President William McKinley and other world leaders.*

FOCUS QUESTIONS

1. Why does Twain oppose imperialism?
2. How would you describe the tone of Twain's writing? Do you think it is effective?
3. How does Twain characterize U.S. involvement in the Philippines?

4. Compare Twain's essay to Albert Beveridge's speech (Document 16.8). How do their interpretations of imperialism differ? Whose arguments most closely resemble your views of imperialism? Why?

...S hall we? That is, shall we go on conferring our Civilization upon the peoples that sit in darkness, or shall we give those poor things a rest? Shall we bang right ahead in our old-time, loud, pious way, and commit the new century to the game; or shall we sober up and sit down and think it over first? Would it not be prudent to get our Civilization-tools together, and see how much stock is left on hand in the way of Glass Beads and Theology, and Maxim Guns and Hymn Books, and Trade-Gin and Torches of Progress and Enlightenment (patent adjustable ones, good to fire villages with, upon occasion), and balance the books, and arrive at the profit and loss, so that we may intelligently decide whether to continue the business or sell out the property and start a new Civilization Scheme on the proceeds?...

The Blessings-of-Civilization Trust, wisely and cautiously administered, is a Daisy. There is more money in it, more territory, more sovereignty, and other kinds of emolument, than there is in any other game that is played. But Christendom has been playing it badly of late years, and must certainly suffer by it, in my opinion. She has been so eager to get every stake that appeared on the green cloth, that the People who Sit in Darkness have noticed it—they have noticed it, and have begun to show alarm. They have become suspicious of the Blessings of Civilization. More—they have begun to examine them. This is not well. The Blessings of Civilization are all right, and a good commercial property; there could not be a better, in a dim light. In the right kind of a light, and at a proper distance, with the goods a little out of focus, they furnish this desirable exhibit to the Gentlemen who Sit in Darkness:

LOVE,	LAW AND ORDER,
JUSTICE,	LIBERTY,
GENTLENESS,	EQUALITY,
CHRISTIANITY,	HONORABLE DEALING,
PROTECTION TO THE WEAK,	MERCY,
TEMPERANCE,	EDUCATION,

—and so on.

There. Is it good? Sir, it is pie. It will bring into camp any idiot that sits in darkness anywhere. But not if we adulterate it. It is proper to be emphatic upon that point. This brand is strictly for Export—apparently. *Apparently*. Privately and confidentially, it is nothing of the kind. Privately and confidentially, it is merely an outside cover, gay and pretty and attractive, displaying the special patterns of our Civilization which we reserve for Home Consumption, while *inside* the bale is the Actual Thing that the Customer Sitting in Darkness buys with his blood and tears and land and liberty. That Actual Thing is, indeed, Civilization, but it is only for Export. Is there a difference between the two brands? In some of the details, yes.

We all know that the Business is being ruined. The reason is not far to seek. It is because our Mr. McKinley, and Mr. Chamberlain [British prime minister], and the Kaiser, and the Czar and the French have been exporting the Actual Thing *with the outside cover left off*. This is bad for the Game. It shows that these new players of it are not sufficiently acquainted with it....

[B]y and by comes America, and our Master of the Game plays it badly— plays it as Mr. Chamberlain was playing it in South Africa. It was a mistake to do that; also, it was one which was quite unlooked for in a Master who was playing it so well in Cuba. In Cuba, he was playing the usual and regular *American* game, and it was winning, for there is no way to beat it. The Master, contemplating Cuba, said: "Here is an oppressed and friendless little nation which is willing to fight to be free; we go partners, and put up the strength of seventy million sympathizers and the resources of the United States: play!" Nothing but Europe combined could call that hand: and Europe cannot combine on anything. There, in Cuba, he was following our great traditions in a way which made us very proud of him, and proud of the deep dissatisfaction which his play was provoking in Continental Europe. Moved by a high inspiration, he threw out those stirring words which proclaimed that forcible annexation would be "criminal aggression;" and in that utterance fired another "shot heard round the world." The memory of that fine saying will be outlived by the remembrance of no act of his but one—that he forgot it within the twelvemonth, and its honorable gospel along with it.

For, presently, came the Philippine temptation. It was strong; it was too strong, and he made that bad mistake: he played the European game, the Chamberlain game. It was a pity; it was a great pity, that error; that one grievous error, that irrevocable error. For it was the very place and time to play the American game again. And at no cost. Rich winnings to be gathered in, too; rich and permanent; indestructible; a fortune transmissible forever to the children of the flag. Not land, not money, not dominion—no, something worth many times more than that dross: our share, the spectacle of a nation of long harassed and persecuted slaves set free through our influence; our posterity's share, the golden memory of that fair deed. The game was in our hands. If it had been played according to the American rules, [Admiral George] Dewey would have sailed away from Manila as soon as he had destroyed the Spanish fleet—after putting up a sign on shore guaranteeing foreign property and life against damage by the Filipinos, and warning the Powers that interference with the emancipated patriots would be regarded as an act unfriendly to the United States. The Powers cannot combine, in even a bad cause, and the sign would not have been molested.

Dewey could have gone about his affairs elsewhere, and left the competent Filipino army to starve out the little Spanish garrison and send it home, and the Filipino citizens to set up the form of government they might prefer, and deal with the friars and their doubtful acquisitions according to Filipino ideas of fairness and justice—ideas which have since been tested and found to be of as high an order as any that prevail in Europe or America.

But we played the Chamberlain game, and lost the chance to add another Cuba and another honorable deed to our good record.

The more we examine the mistake, the more clearly we perceive that it is going to be bad for the Business. The Person Sitting in Darkness is almost sure to say: "There is something curious about this—curious and unaccountable. There must be two Americas: one that sets the captive free, and one that takes a once-captive's new freedom away from him, and picks a quarrel with him with nothing to found it on; then kills him to get his land."

The truth is, the Person Sitting in Darkness *is* saying things like that; and for the sake of the Business we must persuade him to look at the Philippine matter in another and healthier way. We must arrange his opinions for him....

At this point in our frank statement of fact to the Person Sitting in Darkness, we should throw in a little trade-taffy about the Blessings of Civilization—for a change, and for the refreshment of his spirit—then go on with our tale: "We and the patriots having captured Manila, Spain's ownership of the Archipelago and her sovereignty over it were at an end—obliterated—annihilated—not a rag or shred of either remaining behind." It was then that we conceived the divinely humorous idea of *buying* both of these spectres from Spain! [It is quite safe to confess this to the Person Sitting in Darkness, since neither he nor any other sane person will believe it.] In buying those ghosts for twenty millions, we also contracted to take care of the friars and their accumulations. I think we also agreed to propagate leprosy and smallpox, but as to this there is doubt. But it is not important; persons afflicted with the friars do not mind other diseases.

"With our Treaty ratified, Manila subdued, and our Ghosts secured, we had no further use for Aguinaldo and the owners of the Archipelago. We forced a war, and we have been hunting America' guest and ally through the woods and swamps ever since."...

Having now laid all the historical facts before the Person Sitting in Darkness, we should bring him to again, and explain them to him. We should say to him:

"They look doubtful, but in reality they are not. There have been lies; yes, but they were told in a good cause. We have been treacherous; but that was only in order that real good might come out of apparent evil. True, we have crushed a deceived and confiding people; we have turned against the weak and the friendless who trusted us; we have stamped out a just and intelligent and well-ordered republic; we have stabbed an ally in the back and slapped the face of a guest; we have bought a Shadow from an enemy that hadn't it to sell; we have robbed a trusting friend of his land and his liberty; we have invited our clean young men to shoulder a discredited musket and do bandit's work under a flag which bandits have been accustomed to fear, not to follow; we have debauched America's honor and blackened her face before the world; but each detail was for the best. We know this. The Head of every State and Sovereignty in Christendom and ninety per cent of every legislative body in Christendom, including our Congress and our fifty State Legislatures, are members not only of the church, but also of the Blessings-of-Civilization Trust. This world-girdling accumulation of trained morals, high principles, and justice, cannot do an unright thing, an unfair thing, an ungenerous thing, an unclean thing. It knows what it is about. Give yourself no uneasiness; it is all right."

Now then, that will convince the Person....

Everything is prosperous, now; everything is just as we should wish it. We have got the Archipelago, and we shall never give it up.... And as for a flag for the Philippine Province, it is easily managed. We can have a special one—our States do it: we can have just our usual flag, with the white stripes painted black and the stars replaced by the skull and cross-bones....

Mark Twain, "To the Person Sitting in Darkness," *North American Review*, Vol.172, No. 531 (February 1901), pp. 11, 162-176.

SECONDARY SOURCE

◼

REBECCA EDWARDS, "THE REPUBLICAN PARTY AND DOMESTIC IDEOLOGY"

Throughout the nineteenth century, much of the middle- and upper-classes ascribed to a domestic ideology based on the assumption that women were more pious and morally pure than men. Accordingly, they expected women to use their roles as Christians, wives, and mothers to influence others. At the same time, men were to be hard working, dutiful, and self-controlled.

These ideas played an important role in American politics. Republicans and Democrats used gender to distinguish themselves from their rivals. Officials instituted policies reflecting certain notions of the family and the roles of men and women. In this selection, historian Rebecca Edwards demonstrates how domestic ideology influenced the political agenda and campaigning techniques of the Republican Party.

Go to your *Speaking of America* CD-ROM to read "The Republican Party and Domestic Ideology."

◼

FOCUS QUESTIONS

1. What first drew female evangelicals and reformers to the Republican Party? How did the Republicans demonstrate support for these women during The Civil War and Reconstruction?
2. How did Republicans and Democrats use gender in political campaigns?
3. How and why did the role of First Ladies begin to change?
4. How did domestic ideology affect the tariff debates of the 1880s and 1890s?
5. Do modern politicians use tactics similar to those described in this reading?

AMERICAN JOURNEY ONLINE

———————————— ■ ————————————

http://ajaccesss.wadsworth.com [†]

About Labor
— In <u>World War I and the Jazz Age</u>
Documents
- Homestead Strike (1892)
- U.S. Senate Strike Commission, Excerpt from Report of the U.S. Strike Commission (1894)
- Help for the Unemployed (1894)
- Excerpt from The Protest Coxey Didn't Read (1894)

Images
- Terence Powderly
- Assembly Meeting of the Knights of Labor (1886)
- G.J. Nebinger, The Great Upheaval (1886)
- Haymarket Square Riot in
- J. Edgar Thomson Steel Works
- Henry Clay Frick
- W.P. Snyder, Cover of *Frank Leslie's Illustrated Weekly*, July 14, 1892
- The Eye That Never Sleeps
- George M. Pullman
- Industrial Unemployment
- Coxey's Army on the March (1894)
- Jacob S. Coxey

— In <u>The Immigrant Experience</u>
Documents
- R.A. West, The Case of the Commonwealth vs. John Kehoe (1876)
- U.S. Congress, Foran Act of 1885

— In <u>Civil Rights in the United States</u>
Images
- Railroads and Unions (1877)
- Knights of Labor (1886)
- Child Labor in Factory
- W.P. Snyder, Homestead Strike (1892)
- Pullman Strike (1894)
- Coxey's Army (1894)
- Jacob Coxey
- Samuel Gompers

———————————————

[†] Enter password, choose the Archive indicated above, click on Contents, choose •Documents, •Images, or •Multimedia, and click on the title of the item.

— In <u>Westward Expansion</u>
Images
- G.W. Peters, The Great Railway: The Pullman Strike of 1894

About Military Affairs
— In <u>World War I and the Jazz Age</u>
Documents
- Alfred Thayer Mahan, Excerpt from *The Influence of Sea Power upon History, 1660-1783* (1890)
- Emory Upton, Excerpt from *The Military Policy of the United States from 1775* (1904)

Images
- William Tecumseh Sherman
- Emory Upton
- The New Navy of the 1880s
- U.S. Naval War College
- Steven B. Luce
- Alfred Thayer Mahan

About Politics
— In <u>Civil Rights in the United States</u>
Images
- Thomas Nast, Boss Tweed
— In <u>World War I and the Jazz Age</u>
Documents
- Document with Audio Commentary—R. Hal Williams, The Election of 1896 (1978)

Images
- Tom Watson
- Sockless Jerry Simpson
- Mary Elizabeth Lease

— In <u>Westward Expansion</u>
Documents
- William Jennings Bryan, Cross of Gold speech (1896)
Images
- Portrait of William Jennings Bryan

About Law
— In <u>Civil Rights in the United States</u>
Documents
- Samuel Warren and Louis Brandeis, The Right to Privacy (1890)

About Social Criticism
— In <u>Civil Rights in the United States</u>
Images
• Andrew Comstock

— In <u>World War I and the Jazz Age</u>
Documents
• Edward Bellamy, Excerpt from *Looking Backward: 2000-1887* (1888)
• Lester Frank Ward, Excerpt from *The Psychic Factors of Civilization* (1893)
• Henry Lloyd Demarest, Excerpt from *Wealth Against Commonwealth* (1894)
Images
• Edward Bellamy

About Women
— In <u>Westward Expansion</u>
Documents
• Mary Elizabeth Lease, Women in the Farmers' Alliance (1891)

— In <u>Women in America</u>
Documents
• Amelia Bloomer, Excerpt from *Life and Writings of Amelia Bloomer* (1895)
• Martha Carey Thomas, Monograph on the Education of Women in the 19th Century (1900)
Images
• Susan B. Anthony

— In <u>World War I and the Jazz Age</u>
Documents
• Charlotte Perkins Gilman, Excerpt from *Women and Economics* (1898)
Images
• Elizabeth Cady Stanton

About Yellow Journalism
— In <u>World War I and the Jazz Age</u>
Images
• William Randolph Hearst
• Joseph Pulitzer
• Yellow Journalism
— In <u>Civil Rights in the United States</u>
Images
• J.E. Purdy, William Randolph Hearst (1906)

About Expansion/Imperialism
— In <u>The Native American Experience</u>
  Images
  • The Alaska Purchase
— In <u>The Asian-American Experience</u>
  Documents
  • U.S. Congress, Burlingame Treaty (1868)
  • U.S. Congress, Reciprocity Treaty (1875)
  • U.S. Congress, Joint Resolution to Provide for Annexing the Hawaiian Islands to the United States (1898)
  • U.S. Congress, Excerpt of the Organic Act (1900)
  • Alfred J. Beveridge, Excerpt of *Our Philippine Policy* (1900)
— In <u>World War I and the Jazz Age</u>
  Documents
  • U.S. Congress, Teller Amendment (1898)
  • William McKinley, President McKinley's War Message, April 11, 1898
  • Herschel V. Cashin et al, Excerpt from *Under Fire with the 10th U.S. Cavalry* (1899)
  • Theodore Roosevelt, Excerpt from *The Rough Riders* (1899)
  • Emilio Aguinaldo Calls for Rebellion (1899)
  • John M. Hay et al, Open Door Policy in China (1899)
  • Document with Audio Commentary—Albert J. Beveridge, An American Empire (1900)
  • Andrew K. Weir, Army Atrocities in the Philippines (1902)
  • U.S. Government, Panama Canal Treaty (1903)
  • Theodore Roosevelt, The Roosevelt Corollary (1904)
  Images
  • General Valeriano Weyler y Nicolau
  • Image with Audio Commentary, Remember the Maine!
  • Capture of San Juan Hill
  • Commodore George Dewey
  • Emilio Aguinaldo
  • Major General Arthur MacArthur
  • Theodore Roosevelt
  • Building the Panama Canal (1906)
— In <u>Civil Rights in the United States</u>
  Document
  • U.S. Supreme Court, *Weems v. United States* (1910)
  Images
  • Sinking of the Battleship Maine (1898)

— In <u>The Hispanic-American Experience</u>
Documents
- The Treaty of Paris (1898)
- U.S. Congress, The Platt Amendment (1903)

Images
- The Maine (1911)

About Anti-Imperialism
— In <u>World War I and the Jazz Age</u>
Documents
- Anti-Imperialist League Platform (1899)
— In <u>Civil Rights in the United States</u>
Images
- Matthew Brady, Samuel Clemens (Mark Twain)

THE PROGRESSIVE ERA

Several problems accompanied the nation's rise to economic power. Millions of people lived in filthy slums and worked in dangerous factories. Poverty, illness, and exhaustion plagued many laborers. U.S. corporations wielded tremendous influence. Corruption marred the political process. At the same time, a strong middle class was emerging and women were pursing new opportunities. This volatile climate inspired the Progressive movement. Tackling dozens of issues, reformers demanded a more efficient and equitable society. They established scores of institutions and altered the role of government. Although World War I prematurely ended the Progressive era, the reformers left a profound impact on American society.

In the early twentieth century, Americans continued to wrestle with the challenges posed by industrialization and urbanization. Although immigrants still accounted for the majority of urban growth, native-born Americans also relocated to cities. By 1920, over half of the U.S. population lived in urban areas. Such growth overwhelmed the schools, sanitary facilities, and fire protection services of many cities. At the same time, however, cities presented millions of Americans with unprecedented economic opportunities. Between 1900 and 1920, the urban middle class more than doubled to 10.5 million. Many of these white-collar professionals believed that they had the expertise and vision to solve social problems.

Women were among those eager to make an impact on others. Comprising 40 percent of the college population by 1910, women searched for ways to apply their educations. Although many jobs were still closed to them, over 3 million entered white-collar professions. Nonetheless, societal norms still dictated that women's primary responsibilities were home and family. Educated women often faced a difficult choice between professional fulfillment and marriage. Some chose to devote themselves to building new social institutions such as settlement houses. Others joined clubs that advocated social reforms. These developments fueled a resurgent women's movement that cumulated in the passage of a women's suffrage amendment in 1919.

African-Americans also strove to improve their economic and social status. By 1920, 1.4 million southern blacks had joined the Great Migration to northern cities. Most found manual work in shipyards, mines, laundries, and factories.

While the North did not have Jim Crow laws, informal segregation and racism still constrained black lives. In response, African Americans protested for civil rights, built their own businesses, and sustained black churches and universities. They also left an incalculable impact on American culture by pioneering new art forms such as blues and jazz.

Throughout the Progressive era, corporations still wielded tremendous power Efficiency experts and skilled managers searched for ways to cut costs and make workers more productive. Although industrial wages increased, many laborers did not earn enough to support their families adequately. Some endured workdays as long as thirteen hours. Vacations, retirement benefits, and worker's compensation were rare.

Labor activists, political radicals, and intellectuals called for more equitable economic and social order. Calling for better wages and working conditions, the American Federation of Labor (AFL) attracted over 4 million skilled workers by 1920. In 1909 and 1911, the International Ladies' Garment Workers Union led successful strikes against New York textile manufacturers. Such measures were too moderate for the International Workers of the World (IWW) who called for a revolution to end the capitalist system. Accused of violence and sabotage by their opponents, the IWW would be destroyed by hostile government and police authorities. Less radical and more successful than the IWW, the Socialist Party of America advocated the democratic election of officials devoted to centralized economic planning and collective ownership of factories, utilities, transportation facilities, and communications systems. Throughout the era, intellectuals rejected Social Darwinism and offered rational solutions to social problems. Writers and journalists brought abuses and inequalities to the attention of national audiences. Artists and photographers captured the realities of industrial America.

Progressives instituted reforms at the local, state, and national levels. Based in urban areas, they addressed a wide array of issues driven by differing motives and actors. While many were native-born, middle-class Protestants, others were racial minorities, immigrants, and members of the working class. Locally, reformers targeted political corruption and poor living conditions. Professional city managers, free kindergartens, playground, parks, and publicly owned utilities were among their innovations. States followed suit with measures including direct election of senators, initiatives, referenda, recall, worker's compensation, and prohibition. Nationally, Progressives expanded business regulation, passed consumer protection laws, mediated labor disputes, enacted new monetary and banking policies, and safeguarded natural resources.

The Progressive agenda included some less savory elements as well. Many reformers saw segregation and immigration restriction as enlightened ways to ensure that genetically "superior" people continued to dominate American society. Some Progressives gathered "scientific" evidence used to justify practices such as forced sterilizations. The Progressives' faith in their own moral rectitude and intellectual abilities at times degenerated into repressive attempts to control others' lives.

Despite these shortcomings, the Progressive movement proved that government could be a force for social good. Public officials became more attuned to social problems and more willing to use their power to aid the less fortunate. While their agenda included some coercive and ineffective elements, the Progressives also improved the lives of millions of Americans.

17.1

CHARLES MONROE SHELDON ASKS "WHAT WOULD JESUS DO" (1897)

Deep religious convictions motivated many of the Progressives. Many faiths, especially liberal Protestant ones, fused Christianity and social reform. This "Social Gospel" urged the faithful to apply the lessons of the Bible to the real world. Charles Monroe Sheldon (1857-1897) was a minister whose writings expressed this philosophy. His most successful novel, In His Steps *(1897), described the residents of a town devoted to emulating the life of Jesus Christ. For over sixty years, the book was second only to the Bible in U.S. sales.*

FOCUS QUESTIONS

1. How might this passage have motivated a Christian to join the Progressive movement?
2. What social problems does the author believe should be remedied?
3. Do you think there is a connection between religious belief and social reform today? If so, give examples. If not, explain why.

re the Christians of America ready to have their discipleship tested? How about the men who possess large wealth? Are they ready to take that wealth and use it as Jesus would? How about the men and women of great talent? Are they ready to consecrate that talent to humanity as Jesus undoubtedly would do?

Is it not true that the call has come in this age for a new exhibition of discipleship, of Christian discipleship? You who live in this great, sinful city must know that better than I do. Is it possible you can go your ways careless or thoughtless of the awful condition of men and women and children who are dying, body and soul, for need of Christian help? Is it not a matter of concern to you personally that the saloon kills its thousands more surely than war? Is it not a matter of personal suffering in some form for you, that thousands of able-bodied, willing men tramp the streets of this city, and all cities, crying for work and drifting into crime and suicide because they cannot find it? Can you say that this is none of your business? Let each man look after himself! Would it not be true, think you, that if every Christian in America did as Jesus would do, society itself, the business world, yes, the very political system under which our commercial and governmental activity is carried on, would be so changed that human suffering would be reduced to a minimum?....

What would be the result, if in this city every church member should begin to do as Jesus would do? It is not easy to go into details of the result. But we know that certain things would be impossible that are now practiced by church members. What would Jesus do in the matter of wealth? How would He spend it? What principle would regulate His use of money? Would He be likely to live in great luxury and spend ten times as much on personal adornment and entertainment as He spent to relieve the needs of suffering humanity? How would Jesus be governed in the making of money? Would He take rentals from saloons and other disreputable property, or even from tenement property that was so constructed that the inmates had no such things as a home and no such possibility as privacy or cleanliness?....

What would Jesus do in the center of a civilization that hurries so fast after money that the very girls employed in great business houses are not paid enough to keep soul and body together without fearful temptations so great that scores of them fall and are swept over the great, boiling abyss; where the demands of trade sacrifice hundreds of lads in a business that ignores all Christian duties toward them in the way of education and moral training and personal affection? Would Jesus, if He were here today, as a part of our age and commercial industry, feel nothing, do nothing, say nothing, in the face of these facts which every business man knows?....

...[I]f our definition of being a Christian is simply to enjoy the privileges of worship, be generous at no expense to ourselves, have a good, easy time surrounded by pleasant friends and by comfortable things, live respectably and at the same time avoid the world's great stress of sin and trouble because it is too much pain to bear it—if this is our definition of Christianity, surely we are a long way from following the steps of Him who trod the way with groans and tears and sobs of anguish for a lost humanity; who sweat, as it were, great drops of blood, who cried out on the up-reared cross, 'My God! My God! why hast thou forsaken me!'

Are we ready to make and live a new discipleship? Are we ready to reconsider our definition of a Christian? What is it to be a Christian? It is to imitate Jesus. It is to do as He would do. It is to walk in His steps.

Charles Monroe Sheldon, *In His Steps: "What Would Jesus Do?"* Chicago: Smith-Andrews Publishing Co., 1899 [c1897], 342-74.

17.2

LINCOLN STEFFENS ON URBAN POLITICAL CORRUPTION (1904)

Journalists and novelists played a vital role in the Progressive movement. Many used pioneering investigative tactics to expose social problems, corporate abuses, and political corruption. With the aid of new printing and photography techniques, their exposés reached millions and generated popular demands for reform. In 1906, President Theodore Roosevelt characterized these writers as "muckrakers," a pejorative term referring to a character in John Bunyan's Pilgrim's Progress. *But "muckraker" soon became a positive way to describe social crusaders.*

Lincoln Steffens (1866-1936) was one of the nation's leading muckraking journalists. After studying psychology, Steffens spent nine years working for New York City newspapers. In 1901, after becoming managing editor of McClure's Magazine, *he began publishing articles about pervasive corruption among urban politicians. These articles were collectively published as* The Shame of the Cities *(1904).*

FOCUS QUESTIONS

1. How does Steffens describe urban politics? Whom does he hold responsible for this state of affairs?
2. What does Steffens believe will improve American politics? What is your opinion of his solution?
3. Compare today's political system to the one Steffen describes.

... [I] n government we have given proofs of potential greatness, and our political failures are not complete; they are simply ridiculous. But they are ours. Not alone the triumphs and the statesmen, the defeats and the grafters also represent us, and just as truly. Why not see it so and say it?

Because, I heard, the American people won't "stand for" it. You may blame the politicians, or, indeed, any one class, but not all classes, not the people. Or you may put it on the ignorant foreign immigrant, or any one nationality, but not on all nationalities, not on the American people. But no one class is at fault, nor any one breed, nor any particular interest or group of interests. The misgovernment of the American people is misgovernment by the American people.

When I set out on my travels, an honest New Yorker told me honestly that I would find that the Irish, the Catholic Irish, were at the bottom of it all everywhere. The first city I went to was St. Louis, a German city. The next was Minneapolis, a Scandinavian city, with a leadership of New Englanders. Then came Pittsburgh, Scotch Presbyterian, and that was what my New York friend was. "Ah, but they are all foreign populations," I heard. The next city was Philadelphia, the purest American community of all, and the most hopeless. And after that came Chicago and New York, both mongrel-bred, but the one a triumph of reform, the other the best example of good government that I had seen. The "foreign element" excuse is one of the hypocritical lies that save us from the clear sight of ourselves.

Another such conceit of our egotism is that which deplores our politics and lauds our business. This is the wail of the typical American citizen. Now, the typical American citizen is the business man. The typical business man is a bad citizen; he is busy. If he is a "big business man" and very busy, he does not neglect, he is busy with politics, oh, very busy and very businesslike. I found him...defending grafters in Minneapolis, originating corruption in Pittsburgh, sharing with bosses in Philadelphia, deploring reform in Chicago, and beating good government with corruption funds in New York. He is a self-righteous fraud, this big business man. He is the chief source of corruption....

There is hardly an office from United States Senator down to Alderman in any part of the country to which the business man has not been elected; yet politics remains corrupt, government pretty bad, and the selfish citizen has to hold himself in readiness like the old volunteer firemen to rush forth at any hour, in any weather, to prevent the fire; and he goes out sometimes and he puts out the fire (after the damage is done) and he goes back to the shop sighing for the business man in politics. The business man has failed in politics as he has in citizenship. Why?

Because politics is business. That's what's the matter with it. That's what's the matter with everything—art, literature, religion, journalism, law, medicine— they're all business, and all—as you see them. Make politics a sport, as they do in England, or a profession, as they do in Germany, and we'll have—well, something else than we have now, if we want it, which is another question. But don't try to reform politics with the banker, the lawyer, and the dry-goods merchant, for these are business men and there are two great hindrances to their achievement of reform: one is that they are different from, but no better than, the politicians; the other is that politics is not "their line." There are exceptions both ways. Many politicians have gone out into business and done well (Tammany ex-mayors, and nearly all the old bosses of Philadelphia are prominent financiers in their cities), and business men have gone into politics and done well (Mark Hanna, for example). They haven't reformed their adopted trades, however, though they have sometimes sharpened them most pointedly. The politician is a business man with a specialty. When a business man of some other line learns the business of politics, he is a politician, and there is not much reform left in him. Consider the United States Senate, and believe me....

But there is hope, not alone despair, in the commercialism of our politics. If our political leaders are to be always a lot of political merchants, they will supply any demand we may create. All we have to do is to establish a steady demand for good government. The bosses have us split up into parties. To him parties are nothing but means to his corrupt ends. He "bolts" his party, but we must not; the bribe-giver changes his party, from one election to another, from one county to another, from one city to another, but the honest voter must not. Why? Because if the honest voter cared no more for his party than the politician and the grafter, then the honest vote would govern, and that would be bad-for graft. It is idiotic, this devotion to a machine that is used to take our sovereignty from us. If we would leave parties to the politicians, and would vote not for the party, not even for men, but for the city, and the State, and the nation, we should rule parties, and cities, and States, and nation. If we would vote in mass on the more promising ticket, or, if the two are equally bad, would throw out the party that is in, and wait till the next election and then throw out the other party that is in—then, I say, the commercial politician would feel a demand for good government and he would supply it. That process would take a generation or more to complete, for the politicians now really do not know what good government is. But it has taken as long to develop bad government, and the politicians know what that is....

...We are pathetically proud of our democratic institutions and our republican form of government, of our grand Constitution and our just laws. We are a free and sovereign people, we govern ourselves and the government is ours. But that is the point. We are responsible, not our leaders, since we follow them. We let them divert our loyalty from the United States to some "party"; we let them boss the party and turn our municipal democracies into autocracies and our republican nation into a plutocracy. We cheat our government and we let our leaders loot it, and we let them wheedle and bribe our sovereignty from us. True, they pass for us strict laws, but we are content to let them pass also bad laws, giving away public property in exchange; and our good, and often impossible, laws we allow to be used for oppression and blackmail. And what can we say? We break our own laws and rob our own government, the lady at the custom-house, the lyncher with his rope, and the captain of industry with his bribe and his rebate. The spirit of graft and of lawlessness is the American spirit....

..."Blame us, blame anybody, but praise the people," this, the politician's advice, is not the counsel of respect for the people, but of contempt. By just such palavering as courtiers play upon the degenerate intellects of weak kings, the bosses, political, financial, and industrial, are befuddling and befooling our sovereign American citizenship; and—likewise—they are corrupting it.

And it is corruptible, this citizenship. "I know what Parks is doing," said a New York union workman, "but what do I care. He has raised my wages. Let him have his graft!" And the Philadelphia merchant says the same thing: "The party leaders may be getting more than they should out of the city, but that doesn't hurt me. It may raise taxes a little, but I can stand that. The party keeps up the protective tariff. If that were cut down, my business would be ruined. So long as the party stands pat on that, I stand pat on the party."

The people are not innocent....

We Americans may have failed. We may be mercenary and selfish. Democracy with us may be impossible and corruption inevitable, but...we can stand the truth; that there is pride in the character of American citizenship; and that this pride may be a power in the land....

Lincoln Steffens, *Shame of the Cities* (New York: McClure, Phillips & Co., 1904), 3-26.

17.3

————————■————————

UPTON SINCLAIR, *THE JUNGLE* (1906)

Prior to the Progressive era, few laws protected Americans from unsafe or misleading products. Foods were often prepared in unsanitary factories and improperly identified. Many medicines and drugs contained high levels of alcohol or narcotics. Upton Sinclair's novel The Jungle *(1906) was instrumental in creating public support for consumer protection. While working for a socialist newspaper in Chicago, Sinclair investigated working conditions in the city's meatpacking plants. Intended as an indictment of capitalism and the mistreatment of immigrants,* The Jungle *instead inspired widespread dismay at the poor quality of meat and other foods. Within six months of its publication,* The Jungle *persuaded Congress to pass the Pure Food and Drug Act and the Meat Inspection Act. The laws required accurate listing of ingredients, sanitary codes for meatpackers, and federal inspection of meat products. Sinclair remarked, "I aimed at the public's heart and by accident hit it in the stomach."*

————————■————————

FOCUS QUESTIONS

1. How does Sinclair describe working conditions in the Chicago meat industry?
2. Why do you think *The Jungle* alarmed so many Americans?
3. How is today's food processing industry different from that portrayed here?

So Jurgis learned a few things about the great and only Durham canned goods, which had become a national institution. They were regular alchemists at Durham's; they advertised a mushroom catsup, and the men who made it did not know what a mushroom looked like. They advertised "potted chicken,"—and it was like the boarding-house soup of the comic papers, through which a chicken had walked with rubbers on. Perhaps they had a secret process for making chickens chemically—who knows? Said Jurgis's friends; the things that went into the mixture were tripe, and the fat of pork, and beef suet, and hearts of beef, and finally the waste ends of veal, when they had any. They put these up in several grades, and sold them at several prices; but the contents of the cans all came out of the same hopper. And then there was "potted game" and "potted grouse," "potted ham" and "devilled ham"—de-vyled, as the men called it. "De-vyled" ham was made out of the waste ends of smoked beef that were too small to be sliced by the machines; and also tripe, dyed with chemicals so that it would not show white; and trimmings of hams and corned beef; and potatoes, skins and all; and finally the hard cartilaginous ingenious mixture was ground up and flavoured with spices to make it taste like something. Anybody who could invent a new imitation had been sure of a fortune from old Durham....

There was another interesting set of statistics that a person might have gathered in Packingtown—those of the various afflictions of the workers. When Jurgis had first inspected the packing plants with Szedvilas, he had marvelled while he listened to the tale of all the things that were made out of the carcasses of animals, and of all the lesser industries that were maintained there; now he found that each one of these lesser industries was a separate little inferno, in its way as horrible as the killing beds, the source and fountain of them all. The workers in each of them had their own peculiar diseases. And the wandering visitor might be skeptical about all the swindles, but he could not be skeptical about these, for the worker bore the evidence of them about on his own person—generally he had only to hold out his hand.

There were the men in the pickle rooms, for instance, where old Antanas had gotten his death; scarce a one of these that had not some spot of horror on his person. Let a man so much as scrape his finger pushing a truck in the pickle rooms, and he might have a sore that would put him out of the world; all the joints in his fingers might be eaten by the acid, one by one. Of the butchers and floorsmen, the beef-goners and trimmers, and all those who used knives, you could scarcely find a person who had the use of his thumb; time and time again the base of it had been slashed, till it was a mere lump of flesh against which the man pressed the knife to hold it. The hands of these men would be criss-crossed with cuts, until you could no longer pretend to count them or to trace them. They would have no nails—they had worn them off pulling hides; their knuckles were swollen so that their fingers spread out like a fan. There were men who worked in the cooking rooms, in the midst of steam and sickening odors, by artificial light; in these rooms the germs of tuberculosis might live for two years, but the supply was renewed every hour. There were the beef-luggers, who carried two-hundred-pound quarters into the refrigerator cars—a fearful kind of work, that began at four o'clock in the morning, and that wore out the most powerful men in a few years. There were those who worked in the chilling rooms, and whose special disease was rheumatism; the time limit that a man could work in the chilling rooms was said to be five years. There were the wool-pluckers, whose hands went to pieces even sooner than the hands of the pickle men; for the pelts of the sheep had to be painted with acid to loosen the wool, and then the pluckers had to pull out this wool with their bare hands, till the acid had eaten their fingers off. There were those who made the tins for the canned meat; and their hands, too, were a maze of cuts, and each cut represented a chance for blood poisoning. Some worked at the stamping machines, and it was seldom that one could work long there at the pace that was set, and not give out and forget himself, and have a part of his hand chopped off. There were the "hoisters," as they were called, whose task it was to press the lever which lifted the dead cattle off the floor. They ran along upon a rafter, peering down through the damp and the steam; and as old Durham's architects had not built the killing room for the convenience of the hoisters, at every few feet they would have to stoop under a beam, say four feet above the one they ran on; which got them into the habit of stooping, so that in a few years they would be walking like chimpanzees. Worst of any, however, were the fertilizer-men, and those who served in the cooking rooms. These people could not be shown to the visitor, for the odour of a fertilizer-man would scare any ordinary visitor at a hundred yards; and as for the other men, who worked in tank rooms full of steams, and in some of which there were open vats near the level of the floor, their peculiar trouble was that they fell into the vats; and when they were fished out, there was never enough of them left to be worth exhibiting—sometimes they would be overlooked for days, till all but the bones of them had gone out to the world as Durham's Pure Leaf Lard!

Upton Sinclair, *The Jungle* (New York, 1906), 115-120.

17.4

MOTHER JONES ATTACKS CHILD LABOR

The economic boom of the late-nineteenth century created a huge demand for unskilled workers. Because most factory jobs paid badly, many parents needed their children to contribute to the family income. Some companies hired entire families. By 1910, 2 million children under the age of fifteen were working for wages in industrial jobs. Their small hands and bodies were well-suited for many tasks. But illiteracy, exhaustion, injuries, and diseases were common among child workers. Many Americans began calling for end to "child slavery."

Mary Harris Jones, better known as Mother Jones, was one of the most ardent critics of child labor. Born in Cork, Ireland in 1830, she moved to Canada with her family as a child. At eighteen, she moved to Chicago and worked as a dressmaker. In 1861, she married George E. Jones, an iron worker and staunch unionist. Six years later, her husband and four children died in a yellow fever epidemic. In 1871, she lost all of her possessions in the great Chicago fire. In the aftermath of these tragedies, she became a passionate labor activist. With fiery speeches and boundless energy, she traveled the country supporting unions and workers' rights. In 1905, she became one of the founders of the Industrial Workers of the World (IWW). She also organized for the Socialist Party of America as well as the United Mine Workers. She remained active in labor causes well into her nineties. She died in Silver Spring, Maryland in 1930.

In this selection from her 1925 autobiography, Jones describes her efforts to expose child labor.

FOCUS QUESTIONS

1. What types of tactics did Mother Jones use to investigate child labor?
2. How does she describe the children she encounters? Whom does she hold responsible for child labor?

3. Why might a parent have allowed his or her children to work?
4. How did the government address the problem of child labor?

hen the railroad workers' strike ended went down to Cottondale to get a job in the cotton mills. I wanted to see for myself if the gruesome stories of little children working the mills were true.

I applied for a job but the manager told me he had nothing for me unless I had a family that would work also. I told the manager I was going to move my family to Cottondale but I had come on ahead to see what chances there were of getting work.

"Have you children"

"Yes, there are six of us."

"Fine," he said. He was so enthusiastic that he went with me to find a house to rent.

"Here's a house that will do plenty," said he. The house he brought me to was a sort of two-story plank shanty. The windows were broken and the door sagged open. Its latch was broken. It had one room down stairs and a finished loft upstairs. Through the cracks in the roof the rain had come in and rotted the flooring. Downstairs there was a big old open fireplace in front of which were holes big enough to drop a brick through.

The manager was delighted with the house. "The wind and the cold will come through these holes," I said.

He laughed. "Oh, it will be summer soon and you will need all the air you can get."

"I don't know that this house is big enough for six of us."

"Not big enough?" he stared at me. "What you all want, a hotel?"

I took the house, promising to send for my family by the end of the month when they could get things wound up on the farm. I was given work in the factory, and there I saw the children, little children working, the most heart-rending spectacle in all life. Sometimes it seemed to me I could not look at those silent little figures; that I must go north, to the grim coal fields, to the Rocky Mountain camps, where the labor fight is at least fought by grown men.

Little girls and boys, barefooted, walked up and down between the endless rows of spindles, reaching thin little hands into the machinery to repair snapped threads. They crawled under machinery to oil it. They replaced spindles all day long, all day long; night through, night through. Tiny babies of six years old with faces of sixty did an eight-hour shift for ten cents a day. If they fell asleep, cold water was dashed in their faces; and the voice of the manager yelled above the ceaseless racket and whir of the machines.

Toddling chaps of four years old were brought to the mills to "help" the older sister or brother of ten years but their labor was not paid.

The machines, built in the north, were low for the hands of little children.

At five-thirty in the morning, long lines of little grey children came out of the early dawn into the factory, into the maddening noise, into the lint filled rooms. Outside the birds sang and the blue sky shone. At the lunch half-hour, children would fall to sleep over their lunch of cornbread and fat pork. They would lie on the bare floor and sleep. Sleep was their recreation, their release, as play is to the free children. The boss would come along and shake them awake. After the lunch period, the hour-in grind, the ceaseless running up and down between the whirring spindles....

My six children not arriving, the manager got suspicious of me so I left Cottondale and went to Tuscaloosa where I got work in a rope factory. This factory was run also by child labor. Here, too, were the children running up and down between spindles. The lint was heavy in the room. The machinery needed constant cleaning. The tiny, slender bodies of the little children crawled in and about under dangerous machinery, oiling and cleaning. Often their hands were crushed. A finger was snapped off....

They die of pneumonia, these little ones,—bronchitis and consumption. But the birth rate like the dividends is large and another hand is ready to tie the snapped threads when a child worker dies....

I did not stay long in one place. As soon as one showed interest in or sympathy for the children, she was suspected, and laid off. Then, too, the jobs went to grown-ups that could bring children....

And who is responsible for this appalling child slavery? Everyone. Alabama passed a child labor law, endeavoring to some extent to protect its children. And northern capitalists from Massachusetts and Rhode Island defeated the law. Whenever a southern state attempts reform, the mill owners, who are for the most part northerners, threaten to close the mills. They reach legislatures, they send lobbies to work against child labor reform, and money, northern money for the most part, secures the nullification of reform, laws through control of the courts.

The child labor reports of the period in which I made this study put the number of children under fourteen years of age working in mills as fully 25 per cent of the workers; working for a pittance, for eight, nine, ten hours a day, a night.

And mill owners declared dividends ranging from 50 per cent to 90.

"Child labor is docile," they say. "It does not strike. There are no labor troubles." Mill owners point to the lace curtains in the windows of the children's homes. To the luxuries they enjoy. "So much better than they had when as poor whites they worked on the farms!"

Cheap lace curtains are to offset the labor of children! Behind those luxuries we cannot see the little souls deadened by early labor; we cannot see the lusterless eyes in the dark circle looking out upon us. The tawdry lace curtains hang between us and the future of the child, who grows up in ignorance, body and mind and soul dwarfed, diseased....

From the south, burdened with the terrible things I had seen, I came to New York and held several meetings to make known conditions as I had found them. I met the opposition of the press and of capital. For a long time after my southern experience, I could scarcely eat. Not alone my clothes, but my food, too, at times seemed bought with the price of the toil of children....

Mother Jones, Chapter XIV, *The Autobiography of Mother Jones* (Chicago: C.H. Kerr & Company, 1925).

17.5

JANE ADDAMS ON THE FIGHT AGAINST POVERTY (1910)

By the late 1880s, a new generation of reformers was using innovative ways to combat poverty. Jane Addams (1860-1935) won international acclaim for her efforts to help the poor. A visit to a British settlement house motivated Addams and Ellen Gates Starr to build a similar facility in Chicago. Moving into a working-class immigrant neighborhood, the pair bought a vacant residence formerly owned by Charles G. Hull. Eventually, Hull House encompassed 13 buildings as well as a playground. Facilities included a day care center, a kindergarten, a laundry, a boarding house, and a soup kitchen. Courses in English, civics, cooking, music, art, and crafts were offered. By 1895, at least fifty settlement houses were operating across the country. Young reformers from all over the world flocked to Hull House to receive training and inspiration. Addams and her associates were also heavily involved in campaigns for the prohibition of child labor, sanitation, and workers' rights. In this selection from Twenty Years at Hull House *(1910), Addams recounts her fight for public sanitation.*

FOCUS QUESTIONS

1. How does Addams describe conditions in her neighborhood?
2. What tactics do Addams and her assistants use to help the poor? How do people respond to these efforts?
3. Do institutions like Hull House still exist? If so, give a few examples.

I t is easy for even the most conscientious citizen of Chicago to forget the foul smells of the stockyards and the garbage dumps, when he is living so far from them that he is only occasionally made conscious of their existence but the residents of a Settlement are perforce constantly surrounded by them. During our first three years on Halsted Street, we had established a small incinerator at Hull-House and we had many times reported the untoward conditions of the ward to the city hall. We had also arranged many talks for the immigrants, pointing out that although a woman may sweep her own doorway in her native village and allow the refuse to innocently decay in the open air and sunshine, in a crowded city quarter, if the garbage is not properly collected and destroyed, a tenement-house mother may see her children sicken and die, and that the immigrants must therefore not only keep their own houses clean, but must also help the authorities to keep the city clean.

Possibly our efforts slightly modified the worst conditions, but they still re-mained intolerable, and the fourth summer the situation became for me absolutely desperate when I realized in a moment of panic that my delicate little nephew for whom I was guardian, could not be with me at Hull-House at all unless the sickening odors were reduced. I may well be ashamed that other delicate children who were torn from their families, not into boarding school but into eternity, had not long before driven me to effective action. Under the direction of the first man who came as a resident to Hull-House we began a systematic investigation of the city system of garbage collection, both as to its efficiency in other wards and its possible connection with the death rate in the various wards of the city....

During August and September the substantiated reports of violations of the law sent in from Hull-House to the health department were one thousand and thirty-seven.... Still the death rate remained high and the condition seemed little improved throughout the next winter. In sheer desperation, the following spring when the city contracts were awarded for the removal of garbage, with the backing of two well-known business men, I put in a bid for the garbage removal of the nineteenth ward. My paper was thrown out on a technicality but the incident induced the mayor to appoint me the garbage inspector of the ward. The salary was a thousand dollars a year, and the loss of that political "plum" made a great stir among the politicians. The position was no sinecure whether regarded from the point of view of getting up at six in the morning to see that the men were early at work; or of following the loaded wagons, uneasily dropping their contents at intervals, to their dreary destination at the dump....

With the two or three residents who nobly stood by, we set up six of those doleful incinerators which are supposed to burn garbage with the fuel collected in the alley itself. The one factory in town which could utilize old tin cans was a window weight factory, and we deluged that with ten times as many tin cans as it could use—much less would pay for. We made desperate attempts to have the dead animals removed by the contractor who was paid most liberally by the city for that purpose but who, we slowly discovered, always made the police ambu-lances do the work....

Nevertheless many evils constantly arise in Chicago from congested housing which wiser cities forestall and prevent; the inevitable boarders crowded into a dark tenement already too small for the use of the immigrant family occupying it; the surprisingly large number of delinquent girls who have become criminally involved with their own fathers and uncles; the school children who cannot find a quiet spot in which to read or study and who perforce go into the streets each evening; the tuberculosis superinduced and fostered by the inadequate rooms and breathing spaces....

It is these subtle evils of wretched and inadequate housing which are often the most disastrous. In the summer of 1902 during an epidemic of typhoid fever in which our ward, although containing but one thirty-sixth of the population of the city, registered one sixth of the total number of deaths, two of the Hull-House residents made an investigation of the methods of plumbing in the houses adjacent to conspicuous groups of fever cases.... The careful information collected concerning the juxtaposition of the typhoid cases to the various systems of plumbing and nonplumbing was made the basis of a bacteriological study by another resident, Dr. Alice Hamilton, as to the possibility of the infection having been carried by flies. Her researches were so convincing that they have been incorporated into the body of scientific data supporting that theory, but there were also practical results from the investigation. It was discovered that the wretched sanitary appliances through which alone the infection could have become so widely spread, would not have been permitted to remain, unless the city inspector had either been criminally careless or open to the arguments of favored landlords.

The agitation finally resulted in a long and stirring trial before the civil service board of half of the employees in the Sanitary Bureau, with the final discharge of eleven out of the entire force of twenty-four.... We were amazed at the commercial ramifications which graft in the city hall involved and at the indignation which interference with it produced. Hull-House lost some large subscriptions as the result of this investigation, a loss which, if not easy to bear, was at least comprehensible. We also uncovered unexpected graft in connection with the plumbers' unions, and but for the fearless testimony of one of their members, could never have brought the trial to a successful issue.

Inevitable misunderstanding also developed in connection with the attempt on the part of Hull House residents to prohibit the sale of cocaine to minors, which brought us into sharp conflict with many druggists....

For many years we have administered a branch station of the federal post office at Hull-House, which we applied for in the first instance because our neighbors lost such a large percentage of the money they sent to Europe, through the commissions to middle men....

We find increasingly, however, that the best results are to be obtained in investigations as in other undertakings, by combining our researches with those of other public bodies or with the State itself....

The investigations of Hull-House thus tend to be merged with those of larger organizations, from the investigation of the social value of saloons made for the Committee of Fifty in 1896, to the one on infant mortality in relation to nationality, made for the American Academy of Science in 1909....

I have always objected to the phrase "sociological laboratory" applied to us, because Settlements should be something much more human and spontaneous than such a phrase connotes, and yet it is inevitable that the residents should know their own neighborhoods more thoroughly than any other, and that their experiences there should affect their convictions.

Jane Addams, *Twenty Years at Hull-House with Autobiographical Notes.* (New York: The MacMillan Company, 1910), pp. 281-309.

17.6

THE TRIANGLE SHIRTWAIST FACTORY FIRE (1911)

The Triangle Shirtwaist fire ranks among the most tragic industrial accidents in U.S. history. When the blaze erupted on March 25, 1911, workers, mostly young immigrant women, found exits locked and fire escapes broken. Within thirty minutes, 146 perished. Sweatshops like the Triangle factory were found through-out New York City. Workers labored long hours for low wages under hazardous conditions. In 1910, following a landmark strike among textile workers, owners promised to improve working conditions. But Triangle executives ignored the pledge. Public outrage at the Triangle fire prompted many laws mandating workplace safety.

Focus Questions

1. How does the reporter describe the scene of the fire? Why do you think that the Triangle fire shocked Americans?
2. Is an incident like this less likely to occur today? Explain your answer.

T hree stories of a ten-floor building at the corner of Greene Street and Washington Place were burned yesterday, and while the fire was going on 141 young men and women at least 125 of them mere girls were burned to death or killed by jumping to the pavement below.

The victims who are now lying at the Morgue waiting for some one to identify them by a tooth or the remains of a burned shoe were mostly girls from 16 to 23 years of age. They were employed at making shirtwaist by the Triangle Waist Company, the principal owners of which are Isaac Harris and Max Blanck. Most of them could barely speak English. Many of them came from Brooklyn. Almost all were the main support of their hard-working families.

At 4:40 o'clock, nearly five hours after the employees in the rest of the building had gone home, the fire broke out. The one little fire escape in the interior was resorted to by any of the doomed victims. Some of them escaped by running down the stairs, but in a moment or two this avenue was cut off by flame. The girls rushed to the windows and looked down at Greene Street, 100 feet below them. Then one poor, little creature jumped. There was a plate glass protection over part of the sidewalk, but she crashed through it, wrecking it and breaking her body into a thousand pieces.

Then they all began to drop. The crowd yelled "Don't jump!" but it was jump or be burned the proof of which is found in the fact that fifty burned bodies were taken from the ninth floor alone....

Messrs. Harris and Blanck were in the building, but they escaped. They carried with the Mr. Blanck's children and a governess, and they fled over the roofs. Their employees did not know the way, because they had been in the habit of using the two freight elevators, and one of these elevators was not in service when the fire broke out....

Meantime the remains of the dead it is hardly possible to call them bodies, because that would suggest something human, and there was nothing human about most of these were being taken in a steady stream to the Morgue for identification. First Avenue was lined with the usual curious east side crowd. Twenty-sixth Street was impassable. But in the Morgue they received the charred remnants with no more emotion than they ever display over anything....

How the fire started no one knows. On the three upper floors of the building were 600 employees of the waist company, 500 of whom were girls. The victims mostly Italians, Russians, Hungarians, and Germans were girls and men who had been employed by the firm of Harris & Blanck, owners of the Triangle Waist Company, after the strike in which the Jewish girls, formerly employed, had been become unionized and had demanded better working conditions. The building had experienced four recent fires and had been reported by the Fire Department to the Building Department as unsafe in account of the insufficiency of its exits.

The building itself was of the most modern construction and classed as fire-proof. What burned so quickly and disastrously for the victims were shirtwaists, hanging on lines above tiers of workers, sewing machines placed so closely together that there was hardly aisle room for the girls between them, and shirtwaist trimmings and cuttings which littered the floors above the eighth and ninth stories.

Girls had begun leaping from the eighth story windows before firemen arrived. The firemen had trouble bringing their apparatus into position because of the bodies which strewed the pavement and sidewalks. While more bodies crashed down among them, they worked with desperation to run their ladders into position and to spread firenets.

One fireman running ahead of a hose wagon, which halted to avoid running over a body spread a firenet, and two more seized hold of it. A girl's body, coming end over end, struck on the side of it, and there was hope that she would be the first one of the score who had jumped to be saved.

Thousands of people who had crushed in from Broadway and Washington Square and were screaming with horror at what they saw watched closely the work with the firenet. Three other girls who had leaped for it a moment after the first one, struck it on top of her, and all four rolled out and lay still upon the pavement.

Five girls who stood together at a window close the Greene Street corner held their place while a fire ladder was worked toward them, but which stopped at its full length two stories lower down. They leaped together, clinging to each other, with fire streaming back from their hair and dresses. They struck a glass sidewalk cover and it to the basement. There was no time to aid them. With water pouring in upon them from a dozen hose nozzles the bodies lay for two hours where they struck, as did the many others who leaped to their deaths....

Strewn about as the firemen worked, the bodies indicated clearly the preponderance of women workers. Here and there was a man, but almost always they were women. One wore furs and a muss, and had a purse hanging from her arm. Nearly all were dressed for the street. The fire had flashed through their workroom just as they were expecting the signal to leave the building. In ten minutes more all would have been out, as many had stopped work in advance of the signal and had started to put on their wraps....

New York Times, March 26, 1911, p. 1.

17.7

THE NAACP ATTACKS *THE BIRTH OF A NATION* (1915)

Throughout the Progressive era, many African Americans demanded full political and social equality. From 1905 to 1910, W.E.B. DuBois led the Niagara Movement, a group of black intellectuals working for civil rights. Poorly funded and understaffed, the organization struggled. In 1908, however, a race riot in Springfield, Illinois persuaded white liberals to join forces with DuBois. The following year, these reformers and the Niagara Movement established the National Association for the Advancement of Colored People (NAACP). Ushering in a new phase in the fight against segregation and discrimination, the NAACP worked to secure civil rights laws and to increase public awareness of racism.

D.W. Griffith's film The Birth of a Nation *(1915) outraged NAACP activists. Griffith (1875-1948) grew up in Kentucky hearing romantic stories about the Civil War. The death of his father forced Griffith to end his formal education and begin working at a young age. He eventually became an actor, playwright, and film director. He introduced or improved filmmaking techniques including the close-up, long shots, and cross-cutting. He applied these innovations in* The Birth of a Nation, *an adaptation of Thomas Dixon's novel* The Clansman. *The film, although a cinematic masterpiece, was a racist depiction of Reconstruction. It shows Radical Republicans and blacks victimizing white southerners until the Ku Klux Klan "saves" the South.*

The NAACP denounced The Birth of a Nation *as "a vicious film." Fights erupted at many screenings. After failing to gain mass support for a boycott, the NAACP urged local censors to delete objectionable scenes. Although Boston and Chicago censors made minor revisions, most audiences saw the unexpurgated version of* The Birth of a Nation. *Many whites, including President Woodrow Wilson, proclaimed the film historically accurate. Produced for $110,000, it became one of the most profitable movies of all time. In this letter, Mary Childs Nerney, the NAACP national secretary, describes the group's campaign against* The Birth of a Nation.

FOCUS QUESTIONS

1. What does Nerney find offensive about *The Birth of a Nation*?
2. How is the NAACP protesting the film? Are their efforts successful?
3. What does the popularity of *The Birth of a Nation* suggest about race relations in the Progressive era? How might the film have contributed to the resurgence of Klan membership and racial violence in the late 1910s and early 1920s?
4. Should *The Birth of a Nation* still be shown in public? Is it a valuable tool for studying American history? Explain your answers.

April 17, 1915

Mr. George Packard
1522 First National Bank Bldg.,
Chicago, Ill.

My dear Mr. Packard:
I am utterly disgusted with the situation in regard to "The Birth of a Nation." As you will read in the next number of the *Crisis*, [NAACP publication] we have fought it at every possible point. In spite of the promise of the Mayor to cut out the two objectionable scenes in the second part, which show a white girl committing suicide to escape from a Negro pursuer, and a mulatto politician trying to force marriage upon the daughter of his white benefactor, these two scenes still form the motif of the really unimportant incidents, of which I enclose a list. I have seen the thing four times and am positive that nothing more will be done about it. Jane Addams saw it when it was in its worst form in New York. I know of no one else from Chicago who saw it. I enclose Miss Addam's opinion.

When we took the thing before the Police Magistrate he told us that he could do nothing about it unless it lead to a breach of the peace. Some kind of demonstration began in the Liberty Theatre Wednesday night but the colored people took absolutely no part in it, and the only man arrested was a white man. This, of course, is exactly what Littleton, counsel for the producer, Griffith, held in the Magistrates' Court when we have our hearing and claimed that it might lead to a breach of the peace.

Frankly, I do not think you can do one single thing. It has been to me a most liberal education and I purposely am through. The harm it is doing the colored people cannot be estimated. I hear echoes of it wherever I go and have no doubt that this was in the mind of the people who are producing it. Their profits here are something like $14,000 a day and their expenses about $400. I have ceased to worry about it, and if I seem disinterested, kindly remember that we have put six weeks of constant effort of this thing and have gotten nowhere.

Sincerely yours,
Mary Childs Nerney, Secretary.

NAACP Records, Manuscript Division, Library of Congress.

17.8

———————●———————

ALICE DUER MILLER, *ARE WOMEN PEOPLE?* (1915)

By the early twentieth century, the status of many American women was changing dramatically. Almost one in five worked for wages outside the home.

Many of those laboring in retail, social work, nursing, clerical jobs, and factories enjoyed unprecedented income and freedom. Educational opportunities were also expanding. The majority of American colleges and universities began admitting women. In 1900, women comprised one-third of those pursuing higher education. Women's clubs, sports, and philanthropies provided other forums for middle- and upper-class women to assert independence. Nonetheless, formidable barriers to equality remained.

The continued exclusion of women from voting was one of the most daunting. In 1890, after a twenty-one year split, the women's suffrage movement reunited. By 1910, it secured partial voting rights for women in twenty states. Through parades, rallies, and other means, suffragists pushed for passage of a constitutional amendment guaranteeing women the right to vote. They met powerful opposition. Many Americans believed that politics was an inappropriate arena for women. Some argued that voting could damage women's physical and mental health. Suffragists challenged such notions by asserting that political life would be immeasurably improved by the influence of women. In this excerpt from Are Women People? A Book of Rhymes for Suffrage Times *(1915), Alice Duer Miller (1874-1942) satirizes anti-suffrage sentiments and gender stereotypes. Miller, a successful novelist and journalist, first published these verses as columns in* The New York Tribune.

■

FOCUS QUESTIONS

1. How does Miller attack anti-suffrage arguments and gender stereotypes? Provide several examples.
2. Does Miller make a compelling case for women's suffrage and gender equality? Explain your answer.

INTRODUCTION

F ather, what is a Legislature?
A representative body elected by the
  people of the state.
Are women people?
No, my son, criminals, lunatics and
  women are not people.
Do legislators legislate for nothing?
Oh, no; they are paid a salary.
By whom?
By the people.
Are women people?
Of course, my son, just as much
  as men are.

TREACHEROUS TEXTS

The Gallant Sex

(A woman engineer has been dismissed by the Board of Education, under their new rule that women shall not attend high pressure boilers, although her work has been satisfactory and she holds a license to attend such boilers from the Police Department.)

> Lady, dangers lurk in boilers,
> Risks I would not let you face.
> Men were meant to be the toilers,
> Home, you know, is woman's place.
> Have no home? Well, is that so?
> Still, it's not my fault, you know.
>
> Charming lady, work no more;
> Fair you are and sweet as honey;
> Work might make your fingers sore,
> And, besides, I need the money.
> Prithee rest,—or starve or rob—
> Only let me have your job!

CAMPAIGN MATERIAL (FOR BOTH SIDES)

Our Own Twelve Anti-suffragist Reasons

1. Because no woman will leave her domestic duties to vote.
2. Because no woman who may vote will attend to her domestic duties.
3. Because it will make dissension between husband and wife.
4. Because every woman will vote as her husband tells her to.
5. Because bad women will corrupt politics.
6. Because bad politics will corrupt women.
7. Because women have no power of organization.
8. Because women will form a solid party and outvote men.
9. Because men and women are so different that they must stick to different duties.
10. Because men and women are so much alike that men, with one vote each, can represent their own views and ours too.
11. Because women cannot use force.
12. Because the militants did use force.

Why We Oppose Pockets for Women

1. Because pockets are not a natural right.
2. Because the great majority of women do not want pockets. If they did they would have them.
3. Because whenever women have had pockets they have not used them.
4. Because women are required to carry enough things as it is, without the additional burden of pockets.
5. Because it would make dissension between husband and wife as to whose pockets were to be filled.
6. Because it would destroy man's chivalry toward woman, if he did not have to carry all her things in his pockets.
7. Because men are men, and women are women. We must not fly in the face of nature.
8. Because pockets have been used by men to carry tobacco, pipes, whiskey flasks, chewing gum and compromising letters. We see no reason to suppose that women would use them more wisely.

Fashion Notes: Past and Present

1880 — Anti-suffrage arguments are being worn long, calm and flowing this year, with the dominant note that of woman's intellectual inferiority.

1890 — Violence is very evident in this season's modes, and our more conservative thinkers are saying that woman suffrage threatens the home, the Church and the Republic.

1900 — A complete change of style has taken place. Everything is being worn *l'aristocrate*, with the repeated assertion that too many people are voting already.

1915 — The best line of goods shown by the leading anti-suffrage houses this spring is the statement that woman suffrage is the same thing as free love. The effect is extremely piquant and surprising.

Why We Oppose Women Travelling in Railway Trains

1. Because travelling in trains is not a natural right.
2. Because our great-grandmothers never asked to travel in trains.
3. Because woman's place is the home, not the train.
4. Because it is unnecessary; there is no point reached by a train that cannot be reached on foot.
5. Because it will double the work of conductors, engineers and brakemen who are already overburdened.
6. Because men smoke and play cards in trains. Is there any reason to believe that women will behave better?

Why We Oppose Votes for Men

1. Because man's place is the armory.
2. Because no really manly man wants to settle any question otherwise than by fighting about it.
3. Because if men should adopt peaceable methods women will no longer look up to them.
4. Because men will lose their charm if they step out of their natural sphere and interest themselves in other matters than feats of arms, uniforms and drums.
5. Because men are too emotional to vote. Their conduct at baseball games and political conventions shows this, while their innate tendency to appeal to force renders them peculiarly unfit for the task of government.

WOMEN'S SPHERE

The Universal Answer

Oh, there you go again,
Invading man's domain!
It's Nature's laws, you know, you are defying.
Don't fancy that you can
Be really like a man,
So what's the use of all this fuss and trying?
It seems to me so clear,
That women's highest sphere
Is being loving wives and patient mothers.
Oh, can't you be content
To be as you were meant?
For { souls
books belong to husbands and to
votes .... [brothers.

Alice Duer Miller, *Are Women People? A Book of Rhymes for Suffrage Times* (New York: George H. Doran, 1915), pp. 1-68.

17.9

ANZIA YEZIERSKA, "THE FREE VACATION HOUSE" FROM *HUNGRY HEARTS* (1920)

Although usually appreciative of their assistance, many immigrants and working-class people found the Progressive reformers condescending and self-righteous. Accordingly, some resisted adopting middle-class notions of morality

*and "proper" lifestyles. In this story, Anzia Yezierska (1885?-1970) portrays such
cultural differences. An emigrant from Russian Poland, she helped to support her
large family by selling newspapers. Her unconventional views often sparked
clashes with her father, a strict rabbi. In 1907, she won a scholarship to the
American Academy. While there, she began writing about her fellow immigrants
and the injustices facing women. By the 1920s, she was a successful author. Her
works include* Children of Loneliness *(1923) and* Bread Givers *(1925).*

FOCUS QUESTIONS

1. What are the major events in this story?
2. Why do you think these reformers established the free vacation program?
   What are some of the lessons they are trying to impart to the poor?
3. How does this story illustrate the class tensions within the Progressive
   movement?

 OW came it that I went to the free vacation house was like this:
One day the visiting teacher from the school comes to find out for why
don't I get the children ready for school in time; for why are they so
often late.

I let out on her my whole bitter heart. I told her my head was on wheels from
worrying. When I get up in the morning, I don't know on what to turn first:
should I nurse the baby, or make Sam's breakfast, or attend on the older children. I
only got two hands.

"My dear woman," she says, "you are about to have a nervous breakdown.
You need to get away to the country for a rest and vacation."

"Gott im Himmel!" says I. "Don't I know I need a rest? But how? On what
money can I go to the country?"

"I know of a nice country place for mothers and children that will not cost you
anything. It is free."

"Free! I never heard from it."

"Some kind people have made arrangements so no one need pay," she explains.

Later, in a few days, I just finished up with Masha and Mendel and Frieda and
Sonya to send them to school, and I was getting Aby ready for kindergarten, when
I hear a knock on the door, and a lady comes in. She had a white starched dress
like a nurse and carried a black satchel in her hand.

"I am from the Social Betterment Society," she tells me. "You want to go to
the country?"

Before I could say something, she goes over to the baby and pulls out the rubber nipple from her mouth, and to me she says, "You must not get the child used to
sucking this; it is very unsanitary."

"Gott im Himmel!" I beg the lady. "Please don't begin with that child, or
she'll holler my head off. She must have the nipple. I'm too nervous to hear her
scream like that."

When I put the nipple back again in the baby's mouth, the lady takes herself a seat, and then takes out a big black book from her satchel. Then she begins to question me. What is my first name? How old I am? From where come I? How long I'm already in this country? Do I keep any boarders? What is my husband's first name? How old he is? How long he is in this country? By what trade he works? How much wages he gets for a week? How much money do I spend out for rent? How old are the children, and everything about them.

"My goodness!" I cry out. "For why is it necessary all this to know? For why must I tell you all my business? What difference does it make already if I keep boarders, or I don't keep boarders? If Masha had the whooping-cough or Sonya had the measles? Or whether I spend out for my rent ten dollars or twenty? Or whether I come from Schnipishock or Kovner Gubernie?"

"We must make a record of all the applicants, and investigate each case," she tells me. "There are so many who apply to the charities, we can help only those who are the most worthy."

"Charities!" I scream out. "Ain't the charities those who help the beggars out? I ain't no beggar. I'm not asking for no charity. My husband, he works."

"Miss Holcomb, the visiting teacher, said that you wanted to go to the country, and I had to make out this report before investigating your case."

"Oh! Oh!" I choke and bit my lips. "Is the free country from which Miss Holcomb told me, is it from the charities? She was telling me some kind people made arrangements for any mother what needs to go there."

"If your application is approved, you will be notified," she says to me, and out she goes.

When she is gone I think to myself, I'd better knock out from my head this idea about the country. For so long I lived, I didn't know nothing about the charities. For why should I come down among the beggars now?

Then I looked around me in the kitchen. On one side was the big wash-tub with clothes, waiting for me to wash. On the table was a pile of breakfast dishes yet. In the sink was the potatoes, waiting to be peeled. The baby was beginning to cry for the bottle. Aby was hollering and pulling me to take him to kindergarten. I felt if I didn't get away from here for a little while, I would land in a crazy house, or from the window jump down. Which was worser, to land in a crazy house, jump from the window down, or go to the country from the charities?

In about two weeks later around comes the same lady with the satchel again in my house.

"You can go to the country to-morrow," she tells me. "And you must come to the charity building to-morrow at nine o'clock sharp. Here is a card with the address. Don't lose it, because you must hand it to the lady in the office."

I look on the card, and there I see my name wrote; and by it, in big printed letters, that word "CHARITY."

"Must I go to the charity office?" I ask, feeling my heart to sink. "For why must I come there?"

"It is the rule that everybody comes to the office first, and from there they are taken to the country."

I shivered to think how I would feel, suppose somebody from my friends should see me walking to the charity office with my children. They wouldn't know that it is only for the country I go there. They might think I go to beg. Have I come down so low as to be seen by the charities? But what's the use? Should I knock my head on the walls? I had to go.

When I come to the office, I already found a crowd of women and children sitting on long benches and waiting. I took myself a seat with them, and we were sitting and sitting and looking on one another, sideways and crosswise, and with lowered eyes, like guilty criminals. Each one felt like hiding herself from all the rest. Each one felt black with shame in the face.

We may have been sitting and waiting for an hour or more. But every second was seeming years to me. The children began to get restless. Mendel wanted water. The baby on my arms was falling asleep. Aby was crying for something to eat.

"For why are we sittin' here like fat cats?" says the woman next to me. "Ain't we going to the country today yet?"

At last a lady comes to the desk and begins calling us our names, one by one. I nearly dropped to the floor when over she begins to ask: Do you keep boarders? How much do you spend out for rent? How much wages does your man get for a week?

Didn't the nurse tell them all about us already? It was bitter enough to have to tell the nurse everything, but in my own house nobody was hearing my troubles, only the nurse. But in the office there was so many strangers all around me. For why should everybody have to know my business? At every question I wanted to holler out: "Stop! Stop! I don't want no vacations! I'll better run home with my children." At every question I felt like she was stabbing a knife into my heart. And she kept on stabbing me more and more, but I could not help it, and they were all looking at me. I couldn't move from her. I had to answer everything.

When she got through with me, my face was red like fire. I was burning with hurts and wounds. I felt like everything was bleeding in me.

When all the names was already called, a man doctor with a nurse comes in, and tells us to form a line, to be examined. I wish I could ease out my heart a little, and tell in words how that doctor looked on us, just because we were poor and had no money to pay. He only used the ends, from his finger-tips to examine us with. From the way he was afraid to touch us or come near us, he made us feel like we had some catching sickness that he was trying not to get on him.

The doctor got finished with us in about five minutes, so quick he worked. Then we was told to walk after the nurse, who was leading the way for us through the street to the car. Everybody what passed us in the street turned around to look on us. I kept down my eyes and held down my head and I felt like sinking into the sidewalk. All the time I was trembling for fear somebody what knows me might yet pass and see me. For why did they make us walk through the street, after the nurse, like stupid cows? Weren't all of us smart enough to find our way without the nurse? Why should the whole world have to see that we are from the charities?

When we got into the train, I opened my eyes, and lifted up my head, and straightened out my chest, and again began to breathe. It was a beautiful, sunshiny day. I knocked open the window from the train, and the fresh-smelling country air rushed upon my face and made me feel so fine! I looked out from the window and instead of seeing the iron fire-escapes with garbage-cans and bedclothes, that I always seen when from my flat I looked—instead of seeing only walls and wash-lines between walls, I saw the blue sky, and green grass, and trees and flowers.

Ah, how grand I felt, just on the sky to look! Ah, how grand I felt just to see the green grass—and the free space—and no houses!

"Get away from me, my troubles!" I said. "Leave me rest a minute. Leave me breathe and straighten out my bones. Forget the unpaid butcher's bill. Forget the rent. Forget the wash-tub and the cook-stove and the pots and pans. Forget the charities!"

"Tickets, please," calls the train conductor.

I felt knocked out from heaven all at once. I had to point to the nurse what held our tickets, and I was feeling the conductor looking on me as if to say, "Oh, you are only from the charities."

By the time we came to the vacation house I already forgot all about my knock-down. I was again filled with the beauty of the country. I never in all my life yet seen such a swell house like that vacation house. Like the grandest palace it looked. All round the front, flowers from all colors was smelling out the sweetest perfume. Here and there was shady trees with comfortable chairs under them to sit down on.

When I only came inside, my mouth opened wide and my breathing stopped still from wonder. I never yet seen such an order and such a cleanliness. From all the corners from the room, the cleanliness was shining like a looking-glass. The floor was so white scrubbed you could eat on it. You couldn't find a speck of dust on nothing, if you was looking for it with eyeglasses on.

I was beginning to feel happy and glad that I come, when, Gott im Himmel! again a lady begins to ask us out the same questions what the nurse already asked me in my home and what was asked over again in the charity office. How much wages my husband makes out for a week? How much money I spend out for rent? Do I keep boarders?

We were hungry enough to faint. So worn out was I from excitement, and from the long ride, that my knees were bending under me ready to break from tiredness. The children were pulling me to pieces, nagging me for a drink, for something to eat and such like. But still we had to stand out the whole list of questionings. When she already got through asking us out everything, she gave to each of us a tag with our name written on it. She told us to tie the tag on our hand. Then like tagged horses at a horse sale in the street, they marched us into the dining-room.

There was rows of long tables, covered with the pure-white oil-cloth. A vase with bought flowers was standing on the middle from each table. Each person got a clean napkin for himself. Laid out by the side from each person's plate was a silver knife and fork and spoon and teaspoon. When we only sat ourselves down, girls with white starched aprons was passing around the eatings.

I soon forgot again all my troubles. For the first time in ten years I sat down to a meal what I did not have to cook or worry about. For the first time in ten years I sat down to the table like a somebody. Ah, how grand it feels, to have handed you over the eatings and everything you need. Just as I was beginning to like it and let myself feel good, in comes a fat lady all in white, with a teacher's look on her face. I could tell already, right away by the way she looked on us, that she was the boss from this place.

"I want to read you the rules from this house, before you leave this room," says she to us.

Then she began like this: We dassen't stand on the front grass where the flowers are. We dassen't stay on the front porch. We dassen't sit on the chairs under the shady trees. We must stay always in back and sit on those long wooden benches there. We dassen't come in the front sitting-room or walk on the front steps what have carpet on it—we must walk on the back iron steps. Everything on the front from the house must be kept perfect for the show for visitors. We dassen't lay down on the beds in the daytime, the beds must always be made up perfect for the show for visitors.

"Gott im Himmel!" thinks I to myself; "ain't there going to be no end to the things we dassen't do in this place?"

But still she went on. The children over two years dassen't stay around by the mothers. They must stay by the nurse in the play-room. By the meal-times, they can see their mothers. The children dassen't run around the house or tear up flowers or do anything. They dassen't holler or play rough in the play-room. They must always behave and obey the nurse.

We must always listen to the bells. Bell one was for getting up. Bell two, for getting babies' bottles. Bell three, for coming to breakfast. Bell four, for bathing the babies. If we come later, after the ring from the bell, then we'll not get what we need. If the bottle bell rings and we don't come right away for the bottle, then the baby don't get no bottle. If the breakfast bell rings, and we don't come right away down to the breakfast, then there won't be no breakfast for us.

When she got through with reading the rules, I was wondering which side of the house I was to walk on. At every step was some rule what said don't more here, and don't go there, don't stand there, and don't sit there. If I tried to remember the endless rules, it would only make me dizzy in the head. I was thinking for why, with so many rules, didn't they also have already another rule, about how much air in our lungs to breathe.

On every few days there came to the house swell ladies in automobiles. It was for them that the front from the house had to be always perfect. For them was all the beautiful smelling flowers. For them the front porch, the front sitting-room, and the easy stairs with the carpet on it.

Always when the rich ladies came the fat lady, what was the boss from the vacation house, showed off to them the front. Then she took them over to the back to look on us, where we was sitting together, on long wooden benches, like prisoners. I was always feeling cheap like dirt, and mad that I had to be there, when they smiled down on us.

"How nice for these poor creatures to have a restful place like this," I heard one lady say.

The next day I already felt like going back. The children what had to stay by the nurse in the play-room didn't like it neither.

"Mamma," says Mendel to me, "I wisht I was home and out in the street. They don't let us do nothing here. It's worser than school."

"Ain't it a play-room?" asks I. "Don't they let you play?"

"Gee wiss! play-room, they call it! The nurse hollers on us all the time. She don't let us do nothing."

The reason why I stayed out the whole two weeks is this: I think to myself, so much shame in the face I suffered to come here, let me at least make the best from it already. Let me at least save up for two weeks what I got to spend out for grocery and butcher for my back bills to pay out. And then also think I to myself, if I go back on Monday, I got to do the big washing; on Tuesday waits for me the ironing; on Wednesday, the scrubbing and cleaning, and so goes it on. How bad it is already in this place, it's a change from the very sameness of what I'm having day in and day out at home. And so I stayed out this vacation to the bitter end.

But at last the day for going out from this prison came. On the way riding back, I kept thinking to myself: "This is such a beautiful vacation house. For why do they make it so hard for us? When a mother needs a vacation, why must they tear the insides out from her first, by making her come down to the charity office? Why drag us from the charity office through the streets? And when we live through the shame of the charities and when we come already to the vacation house, for why do they boss the life out of us with so many rules and bells? For why don't they let us lay down our heads on the bed when we are tired? For why must we always stick in the back, like dogs what have got to be chained in one spot? If they would let us walk around free, would we bite off something from the front part of the house?"

"If the best part of the house what is comfortable is made up for show for visitors, why ain't they keeping the whole business for a show for visitors? For why do they have to fool in worn-out mothers, to make them think they'll give them a rest? Do they need the worn-out mothers as part of the show? I guess that is it, already."

When I got back in my home, so happy and thankful I was I could cry from thankfulness. How good it was feeling for me to be able to move around my own house, like I pleased. I was always kicking that my rooms was small and narrow, but now my small rooms seemed to grow so big like the park. I looked out from my window on the fire-escapes, full with bedding and garbage-cans, and on the wash-lines full with the clothes. All these ugly things was grand in my eyes. Even the high brick walls all around made me feel like a bird what just jumped out of a cage. And I cried out, "Gott sei dank! Gott sei dank!"

Anzia Yezierska, "The Free Vacation House" in *Hungry Hearts* (Cambridge, MA: The Riverside Press, 1920), pp. 97-113.

SECONDARY SOURCE

◼

ELISABETH I. PERRY, "THE GENERAL MOTHERHOOD OF THE COMMONWEALTH: DANCE HALL REFORM IN THE PROGRESSIVE ERA"

As the United States became more urban and industrialized, commercial amusements arose. Inexpensive and easily accessible, such facilities gave workers escapes from factory routines and crowded living conditions. Dance halls, roller rinks, nickelodeons, and vaudeville houses sprang up in working-class neighborhoods and along mass transit lines. Because many elites associated these venues with vice and immorality, they urged government officials to supervise them. These efforts met mixed success as patrons of commercialized amusements resisted efforts to control their recreation. In this article on dance hall reform, historian Elisabeth Perry illustrates many of the tensions inherent in the Progressive movement.

 Go to your *Speaking of America* CD-ROM to read "The General Motherhood of the Commonwealth: Dance Hall Reform in the Progressive Era."

◼

FOCUS QUESTIONS

1. What were the origins of the dance hall reform movement? Why did reformers object to dance halls?
2. What was the Committee on Amusements? What kinds of people joined it?
3. What were the aims of the Committee on Amusements? What tactics did it use?
4. How did dance hall reform efforts reflect traditional notions of gender and sexuality?
5. How did the public react to dance hall reform?
6. Evaluate the success of the dance hall reform movement.

AMERICAN JOURNEY ONLINE

http://ajaccesss.wadsworth.com [†]

About the Social Gospel
— In World War I and the Jazz Age
  Documents
  - Walter Rauschenbusch, Excerpt from *Christianity and the Social Crisis* (1907)
  - Federal Council of Churches, The Social Creed of the Churches (1908)
  Images
  - Washington Gladden (1905)

About Labor
— In World War I and the Jazz Age
  Documents
  - Industrial Workers of the World, Preamble of the Industrial Workers of the World (1905)
  - Shopgirl Letter to the Editor (1907)
  - Working in Urban America (1908)
  - Joe Hill, The Preacher and the Slave (1911)
  - William Walling English, Class Struggle Within the Working Class (1913)
  - Isaac M. Rubinow, Excerpt from Social Insurance (1913)
  - U.S. Commission on Industrial Relations, Excerpt from Final Report (1915)
  - American Association for Labor Legislation, Excerpt from Health Insurance: Tentative Draft of an Act (1916)
  - Patrick D. Reagan, State Commissions on Health Insurance, 1915-1921 (1976)
  - Goodyear Tire and Rubber Company, Labor Department Activities (1917)
  - Ohio Health and Old Age Insurance Commission, Excerpt from Health Problems in Industry (1918)
  - Dr. Alice Hamilton, Excerpt from *Exploring the Dangerous Trades* (1943)
  Images
  - Coal Strike (1902)
  - Founding Convention of the IWW in World War I

[†] Enter password, choose the Archive indicated above, click on Contents, choose •Documents, •Images, or •Multimedia, and click on the title of the item.

- • William Balfour Ker, From the Depths (1905)
- • Victims of the Triangle Fire (1911)
- • Big Bill Hayward (1912)
- • The Lawrence Textile Strike (1912)
- • The Patterson Silk Strike (1913)
- • John H. Patterson (1913)
- • Mining Camp at Ludlow, Colorado (1914)
- • The Ludlow Massacre (1914)
- • Women in the Work Force
— In <u>Women in America</u>
Images
- • Rheta Childe Dorr, Buying and Selling, Serving and Being Served— Women (1909)
— In <u>Civil Rights in the United States</u>
Images
- • Industrial Workers of the World
— In <u>The Constitution and Supreme Court</u>
Images
- • Girls Shucking Oysters in a Louisiana Cannery (1910)
— In <u>The Immigrant Experience</u>
Images
- • Triangle Shirtwaist Fire (1911)

About Business and Economics/Business and Economic Reform
— In <u>World War I and the Jazz Age</u>
Documents
- • Thorstein Veblen, Excerpt from *The Theory of the Leisure Class* (1899)
- • Ida M. Tarbell, Excerpt from *The History of the Standard Oil Company* (1904)
- • Theodore Roosevelt, Excerpt from 1907 Annual Message on Regulating Commerce (1907)
- • Frederick W. Taylor, Excerpt from *The Principles of Scientific Management* (1911)
- • Woodrow Wilson, Excerpt from The New Freedom (1913)
- • Ida M. Tarbell, Excerpt from *All in a Day's Work: An Autobiography* (1939) in World War I and the Jazz Age
Images
- • Thorstein B. Veblen
- • Ida M. Tarbell (1904)
- • Frederick W. Taylor
- • Federal Reserve Bank of New York
- • John Pierpont Morgan
- • Magnus W. Alexander
- • Federal Trade Commission
- • Edwin F. Gay (1919)

— In <u>The Constitution and Supreme Court</u>
Documents
* Edward D. White, *Standard Oil Co. of New Jersey v. United States* (1911)

About Politics/Political Reform
— In <u>World War I and the Jazz Age</u>
Documents
* George Washington Plunkitt, Political Corruption in the City (1905)
* Herbert D. Croly, Excerpt from *The Promise of American Life* (1909
* Theodore Roosevelt, Excerpt from *The New Nationalism* (1910)
* Benjamin Parke De Witt, Excerpt from *The Progressive Movement* (1915)
Images
* William Howard Taft
* Woodrow Wilson
* Charles McCarthy
— In <u>The Constitution and the Supreme Court</u>
Documents
* U.S. Congress, The Sixteenth Amendment (1913)
* U.S. Congress, The Seventeenth Amendment (1913)

About Law/Legal Reform
— In <u>The Constitution and Supreme Court</u>
Documents
* Rufus Peckham, *Allgeyer v. Louisiana* (1897)
* Rufus Peckham, *Lochner v. New York* (1905) Court
* David J. Brewer, *Muller v. Oregon* (1908)
* William R. Day, *Hammer v. Dagenhart* (1918)
— In <u>Civil Rights in the United States</u>
Images
* Louis Brandeis

About Foreign Policy/Military Affairs
— In <u>World War I and the Jazz Age</u>
Documents
* William Howard Taft, Dollar Diplomacy (1912)
* Woodrow Wilson, The Wilson Administration's Latin America Policy (1913)
Images
* The Great White Fleet

About Socialism/The Radical Left
— In <u>World War I and the Jazz Age</u>
    Documents
    • Eugene V. Debs, Excerpt from *The Outlook for Socialism in the United States* (1900)
    • Kate Richards O'Hare, How I Became a Socialist Agitator (1908)
    • Max Eastman, *The Masses*: A New Kind of Magazine (1912)
    • Eugene V. Debs, Speech Accepting Socialist Party Nomination (1912)
    • Randolph S. Bourne, Excerpt from *Transnational America* (1916)
    • Rose Pastor Stokes, Excerpt from *I Belong to the Working Class* (1992)
    Images
    • Daniel De Leon
    • Socialists in the Heartland (1901)
    • Socialists in New York City (1907)
    • Upton Sinclair
    • John Sloan, Artwork for *The Masses* (1914)
    • John Reed
    • Floyd Dell
    • Emma Goldman
    • Crystal Eastman
    • Victor L. Berger
    • Meyer London (1916)

About Urban Reform/Urban Life
— In <u>World War I and the Jazz Age</u>
    Documents
    • Lincoln Steffens, Excerpt from *The Shame of the Cities* (1904)
    • 1910 U.S. Census, Population Composition of Major Cities (1910)
    • Frederic C. Howe, Excerpt from *The City as the Hope of Democracy* (1913)
    Images
    • Samuel M. (Golden Rule)

About Settlement Houses
— In <u>The Immigrant Experience</u>
    Documents
    • Jane Addams, Immigrants and Their Children (1910)
— In <u>World War I and the Jazz Age</u>
    Images
    • Hull House
— In <u>Women in America</u>
    Documents
    • Samuel Lowenkrohn, Henry Street and Twenty Years (1913)

About Women's Suffrage
— In <u>Women in America</u>
Documents
- Carrie Chapman Catt, Speech Upon Election as President of the National American Women Suffrage Association (1900)
- Emma Goldman, The Tragedy of Women's Emancipation (circa 1910)
- Carrie Chapman Catt, Winning Policy (1916)

Images
- Wagon in Suffrage Parade (1913) in Women in America
— In <u>World War I and the Jazz Age</u>
Documents
- Jane Addams, Why Women Should Vote (1910)

Images
- Carrie Chapman Catt
— In <u>Civil Rights in the United States</u>
Images
- Women's Suffrage Parade (1912)
- James Donahey, Women Suffragettes Poster

About Prohibition
— In <u>Women in America</u>
Images
- Cartoon of Carry Nation (circa 1900)
— In <u>World War I and the Jazz Age</u>
Images
- Thomas Sparrow, The Anti-Saloon League of America (1915)

About Birth Control
— In <u>Women in America</u>
Documents
- Margaret Sanger, Family Limitation (1916)

Images
- Margaret Sanger and Birth Control (circa 1917)
— In <u>World War I and the Jazz Age</u>
Images
- Margaret Sanger

About African-Americans
— In <u>World War I and the Jazz Age</u>
Documents
- W.E.B. DuBois, Editorial about the NAACP (1910)
- W.E.B. DuBois, Another Open Letter to the Wilson Administration (1913)
- Darlene Clark Hine and Kathleen Thompson, Excerpt from *A Bright Shining Thread of Hope* (1998)

— In <u>The African-American Experience</u>
Documents
- Document with Audio Commentary, James Weldon Johnson, Excerpt from *Autobiography of an Ex-Colored Men* (1912)
- *Guinn and Beal v. United States* (1915)
Images
- Two Chicago Urban League Fliers (1915)

About Women
— In <u>Women in America</u>
Images
- Anna Howard Shaw (circa 1900)
- Florence Kelley, American Social Worker (circa 1910)
— In <u>World War I and the Jazz Age</u>
Images
- Leonora O'Reilly
- Charlotte Perkins Gilman
- Sophonisba P. Breckenridge
- Lillian Wald
- Jane Addams (1914)
- Edith Abbott
— In <u>Civil Rights in the United States</u>
Images
- Jane Addams

About Children
— In <u>World War I and the Jazz Age</u>
Documents
- Children's Bureau, First Report of the Work of the Federal Children's Bureau (1913)

About Immigration/Immigrants
— In <u>World War I and the Jazz Age</u>
Documents
- Dillingham Commission, Excerpt from Reports of the Dillingham Commission (1911)
- Walter Lippmann, We Are All of Us Immigrants in the Industrial World (1914)

— In <u>The Immigrant Experience</u>
Documents
- Immigration Commission, Excerpt of Abstracts of Reports of the Immigration Commission (1911)
Images
- Leo Frank (1915) in The Immigrant Experience

— In <u>The African-American Experience</u>
Documents
- Canadian Ban on Negroes (1911)

Images
- W.E.B. DuBois, A Letter to the Department of Immigration of Canada (1911)

— In <u>The Asian-American Experience</u>
Documents
- California State Legislature, Alien Land Law (1913)

About the Environment
— In <u>World War I and the Jazz Age</u>
Documents
- Theodore Roosevelt, Excerpt from 1907 Annual Message on Conserving America's Resources (1907)
- Gifford Pinchot, Excerpt from *The Fight for Conservation* (1910)
- John Muir, Excerpt from *The Yosemite* (1912)

Images
- Galveston, Texas (1900)
- Gifford Pinchot (1901)
- John Muir
- Dayton, Ohio Flood of 1913

— In <u>The Great Depression and the New Deal</u>
Documents
- Theodore Roosevelt, Theodore Roosevelt on Conservation (1908)

— In <u>Westward Expansion</u>
Images
- William J. Lubkin, Dedication Ceremonies of Roosevelt Dam (1911)

About the South
— In <u>World War I and the Jazz Age</u>
Documents
- Southern Sociological Congress, The Social Program of the Congress (1914)

About Culture
— In <u>World War I and the Jazz Age</u>
Documents
- Malcolm Cowley, The Greenwich Village Ideal (1934)

Images
- *McClure's Magazine* (1900)
- Lewis W. Hine, Social-Documentary Photography (1908)
- Greenwich Village

WORLD WAR I

In the early twentieth century, America was expanding its role in international relations. Theodore Roosevelt aggressively protected U.S. interests in Latin America and challenged Japanese imperialism in Asia. William Howard Taft used U.S. financial power as a tool in foreign policy, a strategy his critics derided as "dollar diplomacy." Renouncing the coercive policies of his predecessors, Woodrow Wilson called for a world order based on democracy, free trade, and capitalism. It proved difficult to realize these aims as the nation became deeply embroiled in Latin American and European affairs.

When WWI erupted in 1914, few Americans wanted to join the conflict. The United States did not belong to any of the secret alliances that went into effect after a Serbian terrorist killed Archduke Franz Ferdinand of Austria. The ensuing war pitted the Allies (mainly France, Russia, and Britain) against the Central Powers (chiefly Germany, Austria-Hungary, and the Ottoman Empire). Americans had ethnic, commercial, and cultural ties to many of the warring nations. Cognizant of these divisions, Woodrow Wilson declared American neutrality.

Nonetheless, U.S. policies soon reflected a bias toward the Allies. U.S. financiers loaned $2.3 billon to the Allies, compared to only $27 million to the Central Powers. Although he refused to halt shipping and travel in war zones, Wilson expressed anger when German U-Boats sank several American vessels. Even after the suspension of such attacks, Wilson viewed Germany as a threat to U.S. interests. In April 1917, three months after a desperate Germany resumed unrestricted submarine warfare, Wilson asked Congress for a declaration of war.

The nation quickly mobilized for military conflict. A Selective Service Act brought three million draftees into the armed services. New agencies, income taxes, bond sales, price controls, rationing, and production quotas enabled the government to finance the war and supply the military. Federal officials, especially those working for the Committee on Public Information, generated public support for the conflict.

Despite these efforts, many Americans continued to oppose the war. Political radicals condemned capitalists who profited from war expenditures. Public displays of anti-German sentiments and federal attempts to quash dissent drew widespread condemnation. Some protestors claimed that the war "to make the world safe for democracy" was destroying it at home.

Whatever their opinions of the conflict, Americans adjusted to its social and economic effects. Banks and businesses benefited from America's new status as a creditor nation. Most workers and farmers enjoyed increased wages and productivity. Five-hundred thousand African-Americans left the South in pursuit of economic opportunities in northern cities. Women won the right to vote. Prohibitionists secured passage of a federal law banning the sale, manufacture, and transport of alcoholic beverages. The war also unleashed social tensions. From 1917 to 1921, a wave of race riots, violent strikes, and anti-radicalism rocked the country.

The tumult in America paled in comparison to events in abroad. In March 1917, the Russians overthrew their despotic Czar. After a provisional government led by Alexander Kerensky failed to withdraw from the war, popular discontent grew. In November, Bolshevik rebels deposed Kerensky and called on the workers of the world to reject capitalism and imperialism. The Bolsheviks signed a separate armistice with Germany and began building a communist state. Alarmed by the international appeal of communism and determined to put his imprint on peace negotiations, Wilson proposed the Fourteen Points—a plan for a world order based upon liberal capitalism, self-determination, disarmament, and collective security.

While Wilson formulated visions for the postwar era, American soldiers played a crucial role in the Allied war effort. Under General John J. Pershing, the American Expeditionary Force (AEF) helped to defeat the Germans in the Meuse-Argonne campaign. After the abdication of the Kaiser, Germany established a republican government and sued for peace under the terms proposed in the Fourteen Points. When World War I ended in November 1918, millions hoped that Wilson's proposals would usher in a new era in international relations.

This enthusiasm proved short-lived. When Wilson arrived at the Paris Peace Conference, he found the Allies thirsty for revenge. Although the United States incurred 112,000 casualties in the conflict, these losses were miniscule compared to those of France and Britain. Repeatedly outmaneuvered in negotiations, Wilson was unable to gain support for most of his ideas. The resulting Versailles Treaty forced the Germans to disarm, to surrender all colonies, to pay huge reparations, and to accept sole responsibility for WWI. The treaty did, however, establish an international organization called the League of Nations. The League would be a forum for the resolution of disputes in which all members were bound by a collective security agreement. Wilson considered the League essential to his strategy for reshaping global politics.

Initially, Americans supported the Paris agreement. But, as news of the Versailles Treaty's vindictive nature filtered out, opposition grew. Liberals criticized the secrecy of the proceedings and the failure to include the Germans in the discussions. Republicans worried about the implications of collective security. Henry Cabot Lodge (R-MA), chairman of the Senate Foreign Relations Committee, led a vigorous campaign against the League of Nations. Determined to get the treaty ratified, Wilson crisscrossed the country defending it until he had a massive stroke. Permanently incapacitated and shielded from his advisors, he could not prevent the defeat of the Versailles Treaty. When Republican Warren G. Harding won the 1920 presidential election, he declared the agreement "deceased." But in the aftermath of a second world war, much of the world community embraced the concepts Wilson articulated in the Fourteen Points. Although Wilson did not live to see their impact, his ideas profoundly changed international relations.

18.1

WOODROW WILSON, DECLARATION OF WAR MESSAGE (1917)

When war erupted in Europe during the summer of 1914, few Americans were eager to participate. President Woodrow Wilson declared the United States neutral "in thought as well as in action." But maintaining neutrality proved quite difficult. Powerful cultural and family ties connected many Americans to Great Britain. Financiers and industrialists viewed European trade as the key to boosting a slow economy. At the same time, millions of Americans of German or Irish descent felt no affinity for the British. Pacifists, progressives, and socialists opposed war on moral grounds and feared that U.S. entry into the conflict would end social reforms at home.

Although Americans remained divided in their opinions of the war, the desire for expanded international trade and a bias against the Central Powers soon drew the United States into the conflict. German U-Boat attacks, especially the sinking of the Lusitania, *generated popular demands for vengeance. At first, the Wilson administration persuaded the Germans to suspend unrestricted submarine warfare against ships traveling to Great Britain. In 1916, Wilson won reelection vowing to keep America out of the war. Within months, however, desperation compelled the Germans to resume unrestricted submarine attacks. Convinced that U.S. involvement in the war could ensure a "peace without victory," Wilson asked Congress for a declaration of war on April 2, 1917. Excerpts of his war message follow.*

FOCUS QUESTIONS

1. Why does Wilson believe that the United States must enter the war?
2. How does Wilson describe the Germans? Why does his distinguish between the German government and the German people?
3. According to Wilson, what are America's war aims?
4. Compare Wilson's remarks to those of George Norris (Document 18.2). Whose speech do you find more persuasive? Why?

he present German submarine warfare against commerce is a warfare against mankind. It is a war of all nations. American ships have been sunk, American lives taken, in ways which it has stirred us very deeply to learn of, but the ships and people of other neutral and friendly nations have been sunk and overwhelmed in the waters in the same way. There has been no discrimination. The challenge is to all mankind. Each nation must decide for itself how it will meet it. The choice we make for ourselves must be made with a moderation of counsel and a temperance of judgment befitting our character and our motives as a nation. We must put excited feeling away. Our motive will not be revenge or the victorious assertion of the physical might of the nation, but only the vindication of right, of human right, of which we are only a single champion....

With a profound sense of the solemn and even tragical character of the step I am taking and of the grave responsibilities which it involves, but in unhesitating obedience to what I deem my constitutional duty, I advise that the Congress declare the recent course of the Imperial German Government to be in fact nothing less than war against the government and people of the United States; that it formally accept the status of belligerent which has thus been thrust upon it; and that it take immediate steps, not only to put the country in a more thorough state of defense but also to exert all its power and employ all its resources to bring the Government of the German Empire to terms and end the war....

Our object now, as then, is to vindicate the principles of peace and justice in the life of the world as against selfish and autocratic power and to set up among the really free and self-governed peoples of the world such a concert of purpose and of action as will henceforth ensure the observance of those principles. Neutrality is no longer feasible or desirable where the peace of the world is involved and the freedom of its peoples, and the menace to that peace and freedom lies in the existence of an autocratic government backed by an organized force which is controlled wholly by their will, not the will of their people. We have seen the last of neutrality in such circumstances. We are at the beginning of an age in which it will be insisted that the same standards of conduct and of responsibility for wrong done shall be observed among nations and their governments that are observed among the individual citizens of civilized states.

We have no quarrel with the German people. We have no feeling toward them but one of sympathy and friendship. It was not upon their impulse that their government acted in entering this war. It was not with their previous knowledge or approval. It was a war determined as wars used to be determined in the old, unhappy days when peoples nowhere [were] consulted by their rulers and wars were provoked and waged in the interest of dynasties or of little groups of ambitious men who were accustomed to use their fellowmen as pawns and tools....

The world must be made safe for democracy. Its peace must be planted upon the tested foundations of political liberty. We have no selfish ends to serve. We desire no conquest, no domination. We seek no indemnities for ourselves, no material compensation for the sacrifices we shall freely make. We are but one of the champions of the rights of mankind. We shall be satisfied when those rights have been made as secure as the faith and the freedom of nations can make them....

It will be all the easier for us to conduct ourselves as belligerents in a high spirit of right and fairness because we act without animus, not in enmity toward a people or with the desire to bring any injury or disadvantage upon them, but only in armed opposition to an irresponsible government which has thrown aside all considerations of humanity and of right and is running amuck. We are, let me say again, the sincere friends of the German people, and shall desire nothing so much as the early reestablishment of intimate relations of mutual advantage between us—however hard it may be between them, for the time being, to believe that this is spoken from our hearts. We have borne with their present government through all these bitter months because of that friendship,—exercising a patience and forbearance which would otherwise have been impossible. We shall, happily, still have an opportunity to prove that friendship in our daily attitude and actions toward the millions of men and women of German birth and native sympathy who live among us and share our life, and we shall be proud to prove it toward all who are in fact loyal to their neighbors and to the Government in the hour of test. They are, most of them, as true and loyal Americans as if they had never known any other fealty or allegiance....

It is a distressing and oppressive duty, gentlemen of Congress, which I have performed in thus addressing you. There are, it may be, many months of fiery trial and sacrifice ahead of us. It is a fearful thing to lead this great peaceful nation into war, into the most terrible and disastrous of all wars, civilization itself seeming to be in the balance. But the right is more precious than peace, and we shall fight for the things which we have always carried nearest our hearts,—for democracy, for the right of those who submit to authority to have a voice in their own governments, for the rights and liberties of small nations, for a universal dominion of right by such a concert of free peoples as shall bring peace and safety to all nations and make the world itself at last free. To such a task we can dedicate our lives and our fortunes, everything that we are and everything that we have, with the pride of those who know that the day has come when America is privileged to spend her blood and her might for the principles that gave her birth and happiness and the peace which she has treasured. God helping her, she can do no other.

"Address by the President of the United States," *Congressional Record*, 65th Congress, 1st Session, (2 April 1917), 102-104.

18.2

SENATOR GEORGE NORRIS OPPOSES U.S. ENTRY INTO WORLD WAR I (1917)

George Norris (1861-1944) was a leading critic of U.S. policies in World War I. After studying law at Northern Indiana Normal School (now Valparaiso University), he moved to Nebraska to establish his practice. Elected to the U.S. House of Representatives as a Republican in 1902, he was reelected four times. After winning election to the U.S. Senate in 1912, Norris became known for his independence, bipartisanship, and advocacy of political reform. Staunchly anti-war, Norris voted against American entry into World War I and later opposed the Treaty of Versailles. In the 1930s, he introduced the legislation creating the Tennessee Valley Authority and was co-sponsor of the Norris-La Guardia Act restricting the use of injunctions in labor disputes. In this speech to the U.S. Senate, Norris reacts to Woodrow Wilson's war message.

FOCUS QUESTIONS

1. Why does Norris oppose U.S. entry into the war? Why does he believe that the U.S. neutrality policy failed?
2. What is Norris's opinion of the German government?
3. Compare Norris's remarks to those of Woodrow Wilson (Document 18.1). Whose speech do you find more persuasive? Why?
4. Should the United States have entered World War I? Explain your answer.

April 4, 1917

 I am bitterly opposed to my country entering the war, but if, not withstanding my opposition, we do enter it, all of my energy and all of my power will be behind our flag in carrying it on to victory.

The resolution now before the Senate is a declaration of war. Before taking this momentous step, and while standing on the brink of this terrible vortex, we ought to pause and calmly and judiciously consider the terrible consequences of the step we are about to take. We ought to consider likewise the route we have recently traveled and ascertain whether we have reached our present position in a way that is compatible with the neutral position which we claimed to occupy at the beginning and through the various stages of this unholy and unrighteous war.

No close student of recent history will deny that both Great Britain and Germany have, on numerous occasions since the beginning of the war, flagrantly violated in the most serious manner the rights of neutral vessels and neutral nations under existing international law as recognized up to the beginning of this war by the civilized world.

The reason given by the President in asking Congress to declare war against Germany is that the German Government has declared certain war zones, within which, by the use of submarines, she sinks, without notice American ships and destroys American lives.

Let us trace briefly the origin and history of these so-called war zones. The first war zone was declared by Great Britain. She gave us and the world notice of it on the 4th day of November, 1914. The zone became effective November 5, 1914, the next day after the notice was given. The zone so declared by Great Britain covered the whole of the North Sea. The order establishing it sought to close the north of Scotland route around the British Isles to Denmark, Holland, Norway, Sweden, and the Baltic Sea. The decree of establishment drew an arbitrary line from the Hebrides Islands along the Scottish coast to Iceland, and warned neutral shipping that it would cross those lines at its peril, and ordered that ships might go to Holland and other neutral nations by taking the English Channel through the Strait of Dover.

The first German war zone was declared on the 4th day of February, 1915, just three months after the British war zone was declared. Germany gave 15 days' notice of the establishment of her zone, which became effective on the 18th day of February, 1915. The German war zone covered the English Channel and the high sea waters around the British Isles. It sought to close the English Channel route around the British Isles to Holland, Norway, Sweden, Denmark, and the Baltic Sea. The German war zone decreed that neutral vessels would be exposed to danger in the English Channel route, but that the route around the north of Scotland and in the eastern part of the North Sea, in a strip 30 miles wide along the Dutch coast, would be free of danger.

It will thus be seen that the British Government declared the north of Scotland route into the Baltic Sea as dangerous and the English Channel route into the Baltic Sea as safe.

The German Government in its order did exactly the reverse. It declared the north of Scotland route into the Baltic Sea as safe and the English Channel route into the Baltic Sea as dangerous....

Thus we have the two declarations of the two Governments, each declaring a military zone and warning neutral shipping from going into the prohibited area. England sought to make her order effective by the use of submerged mines. Germany sought to make her order effective by the use of submarines. Both of these orders were illegal and contrary to all international law as well as the principles of humanity. Under international law no belligerent Government has the right to place submerged mines in the high seas. Neither has it any right to take human life without notice by the use of submarines. If there is any difference on the ground of humanity between these two instrumentalities, it is certainly in favor of the submarines. The submarine can exercise some degree of discretion and judgment. The submerged mine always destroys without notice, friend and foe alike, guilty and innocent the same. In carrying out these two policies both Great Britain and Germany have sunk American ships and destroyed American lives without provocation and without notice. There have been more ships sunk and more American lives lost from the action of submarines than from English mines in the North Sea; for the simple reason that we finally acquiesced in the British war zone and kept our ships out of it, while in the German war zone we have refused to recognize its legality and have not kept either our ships or our citizens out of its area. If American ships had gone into the British war zone in defiance of Great Britain's order, as they have gone into the German war zone in defiance of the German Government's order, there would have been many more American lives lost and many more American ships sunk by the instrumentality of the mines than the instrumentality of the submarines....

The only difference is that in the case of Germany we have persisted in our protest, while in the case of England we have submitted....

There are a great many American citizens who feel that we owe it as a duty to humanity to take part in this war. Many instances of cruelty and inhumanity can be found on both sides. Men are often biased in their judgment on account of their sympathy and their interests. To my mind, what we ought to have maintained from the beginning was the strictest neutrality. If we had done this I do not believe we would have been on the verge of war at the present time. We had a right as a nation, if we desired, to cease at anytime to be neutral. While many such people are moved by selfish motives and hopes of gain, I have no doubt but that in a great many instances, through what I believe to be a misunderstanding of the real condition, there are many honest, patriotic citizens who think we ought to engage in this war and who are behind the President in his demand that we should declare war against Germany. I think such people err in judgment and to a great extent have been misled as to the real history and the true facts by the almost unanimous demand of the great combination of wealth that has a direct financial interest in our participation in the war. We have loaned many hundreds of millions of dollars to the allies in this controversy. While such action was legal and countenanced by international law, there is no doubt in my mind but the enormous amount of money loaned to the allies in this country has been instrumental in bringing about a public sentiment in favor of our country taking a course that would make every bond worth a hundred cents on the dollar and making the payment of every debt certain and sure. Through this instrumentality and also through the instrumentality of others who have not only made millions out of the war in the manufacture of munitions, etc., and who would expect to make millions more if our country can be drawn into the catastrophe, a large number of the great newspapers and news agencies of the country have been controlled and enlisted in the greatest propaganda that the world has ever known, to manufacture sentiment in favor of war. It is now demanded that the American citizens shall be used as insurance policies to guarantee the safe delivery of munitions of war to belligerent nations. The enormous profits of munition manufacturers, stockbrokers, and bond dealers must be still further increased by our entrance into the war. This has brought us to the present moment, when Congress, urged by the President and backed by the artificial sentiment, is about to declare war and engulf our country in the greatest holocaust that the world has ever known....

To whom does war bring prosperity? Not to the soldier who for the munificent compensation of $16 per month shoulders his musket and goes into the trench, there to shed his blood and to die if necessary; not to the broken-hearted widow who waits for the return of the mangled body of her husband; not to the mother who weeps at the dead of her brave boy; not to the little children who shiver with cold; not to the babe who suffers from hunger; nor to the millions of mothers and daughters who carry broken hearts to their graves. War brings no prosperity to the great mass of common and patriotic citizens. It increases the cost of living of those who toil and those who already must strain every effort to keep soul and body together. War brings prosperity to the stock gambler on Wall Street—to those who are already in possession of more wealth than can be realized or enjoyed....

I know that I am powerless to stop it. I know that this war madness has taken possession of the financial and political powers of our country. I know that nothing I can say will stay the blow that is soon to fall. I feel that we are committing a sin against humanity and against our countrymen.... I charge no man here with a wrong motive, but it seems to me that this war craze has robbed us of our judgment I wish we might delay our action until reason could again be enthroned in the brain of man. I feel that we are about to put the dollar sign upon the American flag....

Congressional Record, 65th Cong., 1st Sess., Vol LV, pt. 1, pp. 212-13.

18.3

───────────■───────────

ALICE PAUL INSPIRES HER FELLOW SUFFRAGISTS
(1917-1918)

When America entered World War I, the fight for women's suffrage was almost seventy years old. Suffragists hoped that women's support of the war effort would secure passage of a federal amendment granting women the right to vote. Members of the National American Woman Suffrage Association (NAWSA) believed that the key to success was working for suffrage on a state-by-state basis. By 1916, twelve western states had granted women voting rights.

The pace of change was far too slow for Alice Paul (1885-1977). Born into a wealthy Quaker family in New Jersey, Paul graduated from Swarthmore College and pursued additional training in social work. From 1906 to 1909, she worked in British settlement houses. While in England, Paul joined the suffragette movement led by Emmeline Pankhurst. In the face of government indifference, the suffragettes used militant tactics and were repeatedly imprisoned. When Paul returned to the United States in 1910, she joined NAWSA, but found it too conservative. In 1913, Paul and several others founded the Congressional Union for Woman Suffrage. Four years later, the Congressional Union and the Women's Party merged to form the National Women's Party.

Emulating the British suffragettes, Paul organized marches and rallies. Because President Wilson remained steadfastly opposed to women's suffrage, Paul and her fellow activists began picketing outside the White House. When the U.S. entered WWI in April 1917, some Americans considered the protests unpatriotic. Onlookers harassed and physically attacked the picketers. Rather than protect the suffragists, police arrested them for obstructing traffic. While some women spent only a few days in jail, others were sentenced to seven-month terms. News of the protestors' mistreatment by prison officials intensified public demands for women's suffrage. On January 9, 1918, Wilson called for a federal suffrage amendment in recognition of women's vital contribution to the war effort. In June 1919, the Senate passed the measure by one vote and sent it to the states for ratification. On August 26, 1920, when Tennessee became the thirty-sixth state to adopt it, the 19th Amendment went into effect.

In this passage, a suffragist describes life at the Occoquan Workhouse in Virginia.

━━━━━━━━━■━━━━━━━━━

FOCUS QUESTIONS

1. How do the women respond initially to prison conditions? How and why do their reactions change over time?
2. Why is Alice Paul such an inspiration to her comrades?
3. Why do you think that news stories about the suffragists' prison experiences increased popular support for their cause?

I t was late afternoon when we arrived at the jail. There we found the suffragists who had preceded us, locked in cells.

The first thing I remember was the distress of the prisoners about the lack of fresh air. Evening was approaching, every window was closed tight. The air in which we would be obliged to sleep was foul. There were about eighty negro and white prisoners crowded together, tier upon tier, frequently two in a cell. I went to a window and tried to open it. Instantly a group of men, prison guards, appeared; picked me up bodily, threw me into a cell and locked the door. Rose Winslow and the others were treated in the same way.

Determined to preserve our health and that of the other prisoners, we began a concerted fight for fresh air. The windows were about twenty feet distant from the cells, and two sets of iron bars intervened between us and the windows, but we instituted an attack upon them as best we could. Our tin drinking cups, the electric light bulbs, every available article of the meager supply in each cell, including my treasured copy of Browning's poems which I had secretly taken in with me, was thrown through the windows. By this simultaneous attack from every cell, we succeeded in breaking one window before our supply of tiny weapons was exhausted. The fresh October air came in like an exhilarating gale. The broken window remained untouched throughout the entire stay of this group and all later groups of suffragists. Thus was won what the "regulars" in jail called the first breath of air in their time.

The next day we organized ourselves into a little group for the purpose of rebellion. We determined to make it impossible to keep us in jail. We determined, moreover, that as long as we were there we would keep up an unremitting fight for the rights of political prisoners.

One by one little points were conceded to quiet resistance. There was the practice of sweeping the corridors in such a way that the dust filled the cells. The prisoners would be choking to the gasping point, as they sat, helpless, locked in the cells, while a great cloud of dust enveloped them from tiers above and below. As soon as our tin drinking cups, which were sacrificed in our attack upon the windows, were restored to us, we instituted a campaign against the dust. Tin cup after tin cup was filled and its contents thrown out into the corridor from every cell, so that the water began to trickle down from tier to 'tier. The District Commissioners, the Board of Charities, and other officials were summoned by the prison authorities. Hurried consultations were held. Nameless officials passed by in review and looked upon the dampened floor. Thereafter the corridors were dampened and the sweeping into the cells ceased. And so another reform was won....

However gaily you start out in prison to keep up a rebellious protest, it is nevertheless a terribly difficult thing to do. in the face of the constant cold and hunger of undernourishment. Bread and water, and occasional molasses, is not a diet destined to sustain rebellion long. And soon weakness overtook us.

At the end of two weeks of solitary confinement, without any exercise, without going outside of our cells, some of the prisoners were released, having finished their terms, but five of us were left serving seven months' sentences, and two, one month sentences. With our number thus diminished to seven, the authorities felt able to cope with us. The doors were unlocked and we were permitted to take exercise. Rose Winslow fainted as soon as she got into the yard, and was carried back to her cell. I was too weak to move from my bed. Rose and I were taken on stretchers that night to the hospital.

For one brief night we occupied beds in the same ward in the hospital. Here we decided upon the hunger strike, as the ultimate form of protest left us—the strongest weapon left with which to continue within the prison our battle against the [Wilson] Administration.

Miss Paul was held absolutely incommunicado in the prison hospital. No attorney, no member of her family, no friend could see her. With Miss Burns in prison also it became imperative that I consult Miss Paul as to a matter of policy. I was peremptorily refused admission by Warden Zinkhan, so I decided to attempt to communicate with her from below her window. This was before we had established what in prison parlance is known as the "grape-vine route." The grape-vine route consists of smuggling messages oral or written via a friendly guard or prisoner who has access to the outside world.

Just before twilight, I hurried in a taxi to the far-away spot, temporarily abandoned the cab and walked past the dismal cemetery which skirts the prison grounds. I had fortified myself with a diagram of the grounds, and knew which entrance to attempt, in order to get to the hospital wing where Miss Paul lay. We had also ascertained her floor and room. I must first pick the right building, proceed to the proper corner, and finally select the proper window.

The sympathetic chauffeur loaned me a very seedy looking overcoat which I wrapped about me. Having deposited my hat inside the cab, I turned up the collar, drew in my chin and began surreptitiously to circle the devious paths leading to a side entrance of the grounds. My heart was palpitating, for the authorities had threatened arrest if any suffragists were found on the prison grounds, and aside from my personal feelings, I could not at that moment abandon headquarters.

Making a desperate effort to act like an experienced and trusted attendant of the prison, I roamed about and tried not to appear roaming. I successfully passed two guards, and reached the desired spot, which was by good luck temporarily deserted. I succeeded in calling up loudly enough to be heard by Miss Paul, but softly enough not to be heard by the guards.

I shall never forget the shock of her appearance at that window in the gathering dusk. Everything in the world seemed black-gray except her ghost-like face, so startling, so inaccessible. It drove everything else from my mind for an instant. But as usual she was in complete control of herself. She began to hurl questions at me faster than I could answer. "How were the convention plans progressing?" "Had the speakers been secured for the mass meeting?" "How many women had signed up to go out on the next picket line?" And so on.

"Conditions at Occoquan are frightful," said I. "We are planning to..."

"Get out of there, and move quickly," shouted the guard, who came abruptly around the corner of the building. I tried to finish my message. "We are planning to habeas corpus the women out of Occoquan and have them transferred up here."

"Get out of there, I tell you. Damn you!" By this time he was upon me. He grabbed me by the arm and began shaking me. "You will be arrested if you do not get off these grounds." He continued to shake me while I shouted back, "Do you approve of this plan?"

I was being forced along so rapidly that I was out of range of her faint voice and could not hear the answer. I plead with the guard to be allowed to go back quietly and speak a few more words with Miss Paul, but he was inflexible. Once out of the grounds I went unnoticed to the cemetery and sat on a tombstone to wait a little while before making another attempt, hoping the guard would not expect me to come back. The lights were beginning to twinkle in the distance and it was now almost total darkness. I consulted my watch and realized that in forty minutes Miss Paul and her comrades would again be going through the torture of forcible feeding. I waited five minutes—ten minutes—fifteen minutes. Then I went back to the grounds again. I started through another entrance, but had proceeded only a few paces when I was forcibly evicted. Again I returned to the cold tombstone. I believe that I never in my life felt more utterly miserable and impotent. There were times, as I have said, when we felt inordinately strong. This was one of the times when I felt that we were frail reeds in the hands of cruel and powerful oppressors. My thoughts were at first with Alice Paul, at that moment being forcibly fed by men jailers and men doctors....

Later we established daily communication with Miss Paul through one of the charwomen who scrubbed the hospital floors. She carried paper and pencil carefully concealed upon her. On entering Miss Paul's room she would, with very comical stealth, first elaborately push Miss Paul's bed against the door, then crawl practically under it, and pass from this point of concealment the coveted paper and pencil. Then she would linger over the floor to the last second, imploring Miss Paul to hasten her writing. Faithfully every evening this silent, dusky messenger made her long journey after her day's work, and patiently waited while I wrote an answering note to be delivered to Miss Paul the following morning. Thus it was that while in the hospital Miss Paul directed our campaign, in spite of the Administration's most painstaking plans to the contrary.

Doris Stevens, *Jailed for Freedom* (New York: Liveright Publishing Corporation, 1920), pp. 215-220.

18.4

WOODROW WILSON, THE FOURTEEN POINTS (1918)

In late 1917, as the U.S. troops began arriving in France, Woodrow Wilson was dismayed by events in Europe and Russia. On the Western Front, the Allies reported horrific casualties, starvation, and mutinies. Various peace proposals by Germany, Austria-Hungary, Britain, and Pope Benedict XV languished. At the same time, sweeping political changes hit Russia. In March 1917, rebels overthrew the monarchy and established a provisional government headed by Alexander Kerensky. Despite the poor condition of the Russian army, Kerensky refused to withdraw from the war. He soon faced a host of problems including a dispirited populace, the desertion of non-Russian peoples from the empire, and political opposition. In November 1917, Bolsheviks led by Vladimir I. Lenin ousted Kerensky and called for the creation of a workers' state. They issued a unilateral cessation of hostilities against the Central Powers and published the secret treaties that had triggered the war.

Searching for a higher purpose to the war's unprecedented carnage and a way to undermine the international appeal of communism, Wilson offered bold plans for ending the conflict and reshaping international relations. Beginning with the Fourteen Points, Wilson made numerous speeches calling for open diplomacy, free trade, resolution of territorial disputes, and disarmament. In October 1918, after the abdication of Kaiser Wilhelm II and the establishment of a republic, the German government approached Wilson with a peace proposal based on the Fourteen Points. Although Britain and France had reservations about freedom of the seas and reparations, they accepted the terms and an armistice ended World War I on November 11, 1918.

FOCUS QUESTIONS

1. What are the major elements of the Fourteen Points? Why did they represent such a major shift in foreign affairs?
2. Why do you think that the Fourteen Points inspired so many people?
3. How did the Versailles Treaty differ from the goals of the Fourteen Points?

January 8, 1918

I t will be our wish and purpose that the processes of peace, when they are begun, shall be absolutely open and that they shall involve and permit henceforth no secret understandings of any kind. The day of conquest and aggrandizement is gone by; so is also the day of secret covenants entered into in the interest of particular governments and likely at some unlooked-for moment to upset the peace of the world. It is this happy fact, now clear to the view of every public man whose thoughts do not still linger in an age that is dead and gone, which makes it possible for every nation whose purposes are consistent with justice and the peace of the world to avow now or at any other time the objects it has in view.

We entered this war because violations of right had occurred which touched us to the quick and made the life of our own people impossible unless they were corrected and the world secured once for all against their recurrence. What we demand in this war, therefore, is nothing peculiar to ourselves. It is that the world be made fit and safe to live in; and particularly that it be made safe for every peace-loving nation which, like our own, wishes to live its own life, determine its own institutions, be assured of justice and fair dealing by the other peoples of the world as against force and selfish aggression. All the peoples of the world are in effect partners in this interest, and for our own part we see very clearly that unless justice be done to others it will not be done to us. The program of the world's peace, therefore, is our program; and that program, the only possible program, as we see it, is this:

I.   Open covenants of peace, openly arrived at, after which there shall be no private international understandings of any kind but diplomacy shall proceed always frankly and in the public view.

II.   Absolute freedom of navigation upon the seas, outside territorial waters, alike in peace and in war, except as the seas may be closed in whole or in part by international action for the enforcement of international covenants.

III.   The removal, so far as possible, of all economic barriers and the establishment of an equality of trade conditions among all the nations consenting to the peace and associating themselves for its maintenance.

IV.   Adequate guarantees given and taken that national armaments will be reduced to the lowest point consistent with domestic safety.

V.   A free, open-minded, and absolutely impartial adjustment of all colonial claims, based upon a strict observance of the principle that in determining all such questions of sovereignty the interests of the populations concerned must have equal weight with the equitable claims of the government whose title is to be determined.

VI.   The evacuation of all Russian territory and such a settlement of all questions affecting Russia as will secure the best and freest cooperation of the other nations of the world in obtaining for her an unhampered and unembarrassed opportunity for the independent determination of her own political development and national policy and assure her of a sincere welcome into the society of free nations under institutions of her own choosing; and, more than a welcome, assistance also of every kind that she may need and may herself desire. The treatment accorded Russia by her sister nations in the months to come will be the acid test of their good will, of their comprehension of her needs as distinguished from their own interests, and of their intelligent and unselfish sympathy.

VII. Belgium, the whole world will agree, must be evacuated and restored, without any attempt to limit the sovereignty which she enjoys in common with all other free nations....

VIII. All French territory should be freed and the invaded portions restored, and the wrong done to France by Prussia in 1871 in the matter of Alsace-Lorraine, which has unsettled the peace of the world for nearly fifty years, should be righted, in order that peace may once more be made secure in the interest of all.

IX. A readjustment of the frontiers of Italy should be effected along clearly recognizable lines of nationality.

X. The peoples of Austria-Hungary, whose place among the nations we wish to see safeguarded and assured, should be accorded the freest opportunity of autonomous development.

XI. Rumania, Serbia, and Montenegro should be evacuated; occupied territories restored; Serbia accorded free and secure access to the sea; and the relations of the several Balkan states to one another determined by friendly counsel along historically established lines of allegiance and nationality; and international guarantees of the political and economic independence and territorial integrity of the several Balkan states should be entered into.

XII. The Turkish portions of the present Ottoman Empire should be assured a secure sovereignty, but the other nationalities which are now under Turkish rule should be assured an undoubted security of life and an absolutely unmolested opportunity of an autonomous development, and the Dardanelles should be permanently opened as a free passage to the ships and commerce of all nations under international guarantees.

XIII. An independent Polish state should be erected which should include the territories inhabited by indisputably Polish populations, which should be assured a free and secure access to the sea, and whose political and economic independence and territorial integrity should be guaranteed by international covenant.

XIV. A general association of nations must be formed under specific covenants for the purpose of affording mutual guarantees of political independence and territorial integrity to great and small states alike.

In regard to these essential rectifications of wrong and assertions of right we feel ourselves to be intimate partners of all the governments and peoples associated together against the Imperialists. We cannot be separated in interest or divided in purpose. We stand together until the end.

For such arrangements and covenants we are willing to fight and to continue to fight until they are achieved; but only because we wish the right to prevail and desire a just and stable peace such as can be secured only by removing the chief provocations to war, which this program does not remove. We have no jealousy of German greatness, and there is nothing in this program that impairs it. We grudge her no achievement or distinction of learning or of pacific enterprise such as have made her record very bright and very enviable. We do not wish to injure her or to block in any way her legitimate influence or power. We do not wish to fight her either with arms or with hostile arrangements of trade if she is willing to associate herself with us and the other peace-loving nations of the world in covenants of justice and law and fair dealing. We wish her only to accept a place of equality among the peoples of the world,—the new world in which we now live,—instead of a place of mastery....

We have spoken now, surely, in terms too concrete to admit of any further doubt or question. An evident principle runs through the whole program I have outlined. It is the principle of justice to all peoples and nationalities, and their right to live on equal terms of liberty and safety with one another, whether they be strong or weak. Unless this principle be made its foundation no part of the structure of international justice can stand. The people of the United States could act upon no other principle; and to the vindication of this principle they are ready to devote their lives, their honor, and everything that they possess. The moral climax of this the culminating and final war for human liberty has come, and they are ready to put their own strength, their own highest purpose, their own integrity and devotion to the test.

Congressional Record, LVI (January 8, 1918), Part I, 680-682.

18.5

THE ROBERT PRAGER LYNCHING (1918)

The First World War exacerbated political and ethnic divisions in American society. Encouraged by government propaganda campaigns and restrictions on free speech, some Americans harassed German-Americans and political dissidents. Animus toward things associated with Germany neared hysteria. Many libraries banned or burned books by German authors. Some orchestras refused to play music written by German composers. Towns and individuals with German names changed them. Restaurants renamed hamburgers and sauerkraut "liberty sandwiches" and "liberty cabbage." In the notorious incident recounted below, anti-German sentiment turned violent.

FOCUS QUESTIONS

1. What happened to Robert Prager? Why did the mob attack him?
2. What happened to the men who killed Prager?

3. What does this incident suggest about the political climate in the United States during World War I?

The St Louis Globe-Democrat
(April 5, 1918)

 ERMAN ENEMY OF U.S. HANGED BY MOB
ST. LOUIS COLLINSVILLE MAN KILLED FOR ABUSING WILSON
Robert P. Prager Taken from Jail and Strung Up to Tree by 300 Men and Boys after Officers are Overpowered

Robert P. Prager, 45 years old, of Collinsville, Ill., a coal miner, charged with making disloyal utterances against the United States and President Wilson, was hanged to a tree on Mauer Heights, one mile west of Collinsville on the St. Louis road, by a mob of 300 men and boys after he had twice escaped mob violence, at 12:15 o'clock this morning. Collinsville is ten miles northeast of East St. Louis. Prager was taken from the Collinsville Jail by the mob, which battered down the doors. The prisoner was found hidden under a pile of rubbish in the basement of the Jail, where he had been placed by the police when they had learned that the mob was on the way to the Jail. The police were overpowered, there being only four on the night force, and the prisoner was carried down the street, the mob cheering and waving flags. The police were not allowed to follow the mob by a guard which had been placed over them. When led to the tree upon which he was hanged Prager was asked if he had anything to say. "Yes," he replied in broken English. "I would like to pray. He then fell to his knees, clasped his hands to his breast and prayed for three minutes in German. Without another word the noose was placed about his neck and the body pulled 10 feet into the air by a hundred or more hands which grasped the rope.... Prager was an enemy alien and registered in East St. Louis.

Prager Attended Socialist Meeting Short Time Before He was Lynched

After the mob had returned to Collinsville, several residents at Collinsville who had heard of the hanging went to the scene. Two unidentified person were found guarding the body. They would let no one approach and warned whoever came close that they would meet the same fate if they attempted to cut down the body. The mob took their prisoner from the jail about 10 o'clock last night. Prager earlier in the evening had attended a Socialist meeting in Maryville, where it is alleged he made a speech in which he uttered remarks which were termed disloyal. After word had been passed around Maryville, a mob collected there and started a search for the miner. Prager had been informed about that the mob was after him and he escaped to Collinsville. They told of the remarks of Prager and finally a mob of 300 was assembled. Prager was found on the street in front of his home, 208 Vandalia Avenue. He was marched to the main street, where his shoes were removed and a large American flag was wrapped about his body. Prager was made to kiss the flag many times and march up and down the street waving two small flags which he carried in his hands. For fear that violence would result from the mob, the police took Prager from them and placed him in jail.

Mayor Induces Mob to Go Home, but It Reassembles Later

Mayor J. H. Siegel pleaded with the mob and asked them to go to their homes. He had previously closed all the saloons. "We do not want a stigma marking Collinsville," said Mayor Siegel, "and I implore you to go to your homes and discontinue this demonstration." The mob disbanded and the mayor, thinking that everything had quieted down, went to his home. But a short time later the mob again formed and stormed the jail, taking the prisoner from the police. This is the first killing for disloyalty in the United States, although many persons have been mobbed and tarred and feathered. Prager begged for mercy. He said that he was a loyal citizen, and in a signed statement, which he had previously made to the police, he said that his heart and soul were for the United States. He admitted being a native of Germany. He said that he had applied for naturalization papers and that his second papers were waiting for him. Prager had been in Maryville looking for work. He was a coal miner. He found he could not obtain employment because the union had rejected his application. On March 22, four men, including a Polish Catholic priest, were tarred and feathered at Christopher, Ill., a mining town eighty miles from St. Louis. Previous to that time two other men were tarred and feathered in the same mining district. For the past three months many loyalty demonstrations have occurred in an effort to drive disloyal persons from Southern Illinois.

Edwardsville Intelligenser
(June 18, 1918)

J URY FINDS PRAGER DEFENDANTS NOT GUILTY AND OTHERS ARE FREE

Edwardsville—Eleven residents of Collinsville walked from the court house Saturday afternoon, exonerated for the death of Robert P. Prager, German alien enemy, who was lynched in that city during the early morning hours of April 5. On the second ballot and with deliberations of only a few minutes the jury reached its verdict. On the first vote the jurors stood 11 to 1 for acquittal. The discussions, it is understood, lasted but a few minutes and then the second vote was taken. It found the defendants not guilty. The defendants who were acquitted were:

Joseph Riegel, coal miner and shoe cobbler.
Richard Dukes, Jr., coal miner.
Cecil Larremore, coal miner.
James DeMatties, coal miner.
Frank Flannery, coal miner.
Charles Cranmer, clerk.
John Hallsworth, coal miner.

Calvin Gilmore, plumber's helper.
Wesley Beaver, saloon porter.
Enid Elmore, coal miner.
William Brockmeier, coal miner.

The court room was filled with spectators when the defendants were taken back to the court room Saturday afternoon to hear their fate. A few minutes later the court was ready to receive the jury and the twelve men filed into the court room and took their places in the jury box. There was wild applauding and cheers from 'most everyone present. Relatives, friends and acquaintances rushed toward the bar to shake hands with the defendants. In a few minutes the crowd was quieted and the jury was discharged by Judge Bernreuter.... The acquittal of most of the prisoners was no great surprise to most of those who heard the evidence.

The St. Louis Globe-Democrat, April 5, 1918; *Edwardsville Intelligenser*, June 18, 1918.

18.6

ON THE WESTERN FRONT (1918)

The First World War witnessed unprecedented bloodshed. New weapons including poison gas, airplanes, and submarines made mass killing easier. Hundreds of thousands of soldiers died in ghastly trench warfare. Although it took the United States several months to recruit, train, and deploy an army, the American Expeditionary Force (AEF) played an important role in the Allies' victory. In May 1918, AEF forces helped to stop German advances at Château Thierry and Belleau Wood. Four months later, 1.2 million Americans joined Allied troops in the bloody battles of Meuse-Argonne. At the same time, the U.S. Navy aided the British in a transatlantic convoy system and mining the North Sea. Their combined efforts defeated the German submarine campaign against Allied merchant ships.

In this selection from his diary, Clarence J. Richmond, a Marine private, describes his combat experiences in France.

FOCUS QUESTIONS

1. How does Richmond portray conditions at the front? What are his duties?
2. How does Richmond seem to feel about combat? Do you think his response was common? Explain your answers.
3. In your opinion, what would be the most difficult aspect of combat? Are there any positive aspects?

October 1-6, 1918

T he shelling eased up a little, and we cleared the crest of the hill in front of us. Quite a few shrapnel shells burst just in front of us, the shrapnel raking the ground all around us. No one had yet been wounded near me, so had no one to carry back. We still held a support position, and started to dig in soon after noon. The ground was not very favorable for digging and before we had finished, received orders to change our position.

A gap existed on our left and our battalion was ordered to fill it. Our objective was the crest of a portion of Blanc Mont ridge. As soon as the Germans saw what we were attempting to do, they met us with heavy machine gun fire and trench mortars. I think they had every conceivable kind of trench mortar. Some of the shells sounded like they were lopsided as they hit all around us, many of them exploding in the air before hitting the ground. Machine gun fire became murderously heavy as we ascended the slope of the hill.

Private Hamilton of our platoon fell with a machine gun bullet through his chest. Hamilton carried a French automatic rifle. Just before coming to the front he had been given a summary for something he had done. Getting him on a stretcher, we headed for the rear to find a first aid station. We had not gone more than a hundred yards when a trench mortar hit about twenty feet from us and wounded one of the fellows. Stopping a few minutes, I bound up his wound and we proceeded. Hamilton died before we reached the dressing station. Not wishing to leave him on the field, we buried him in a shell hole, putting up a little improvised cross and fastening one of his identification tags to the cross.

It was dark when we got back to the company. The battalion had taken the crest of the ridge, but was still under heavy fire. If it had not been for the trenches that run along the crest of the ridge, I do not believe we could have held our gains. Machine gun fire was extremely fierce right on top of the ridge. I had some difficulty in getting to where the 43rd was. Company P.C. was located in an excavation previously made for a large gun, though the gun had never been put in place. It was unsafe to stand upright, as quite often some machine gunner turned the muzzle of his machine and raked the top of our "big hole". However as long as they did not come over the top down on us, we were reasonably safe.

Anything to eat, other than emergency rations, was out of the question. However I was not to go hungry, as I had brought two cans of milk with me from Courtesols. A can of milk and some hard tack was a dish the others envied. Having lost out on the breakfast that morning, and nothing at noon, milk and hard tack was something not to be rejected with contempt. It helped fill a vacant place.

The fire became less and less as the night passed. About three o'clock in the morning we moved from our position out into the open. Firing had almost ceased by this time. A deserter came over to our company and was immediately taken in charge. We laid out in the open for about an hour and a half, finally, just before day light, took up a position along a road right on the crest of the ridge. Here we formed attacking waves and waited for good daylight. The Germans located us, and began to drop shells along the road, killing and wounding several.

With absolutely no artillery support, we were off when it got light enough to see. We could see where the Germans had hastily dug in during the night. They had dug only very shallow holes. Several field pieces were captured at the very beginning. We crossed a narrow gauged railroad track, and saw several dugouts. We met strong resistance, mostly machine gun fire. We still had no artillery support. Enemy planes hovered close overhead and kept their guns turned down on us nearly all morning. Our own planes were not so numerous during the early morning, though they showed up in great numbers later on.

We soon detected that were being fired on from almost the rear on our left, indication that no advance had been made by whoever was on our left flank. There became about as much danger of being shot from the rear as front the front. We were pursuing a course almost parallel with a main highway, and as a consequence were under direct observation. As we cleared the crest of a rise, the machine gun and artillery fire became so fierce we were unable to continue our advance. The October sun was warm and as we would rest a few minutes now and then, I would lie flat on the ground and almost fall asleep due to being sleepy and from the effect of the sun's rays, even though machine gun bullets clipped the ground here and there all around me. Finding we could not safely advance beyond the crest of the hill, we fell back a ways and dug in. Artillery fire was point blank.

Then my work began. All morning I had not seen a single one of the other stretcher bearers. I had been carrying a stretcher alone, and had not yet used it. While the others were digging in, I got some other fellows to help me, and commenced to carry wounded back along the highway. Ambulances came up within a half mile of where the battalion dug in. The road, being under direct observation, was subject to heavy shelling. There were so many wounded that we were not able to evacuate near all of them. There were calls everywhere for stretcher bearers. Some were only slightly wounded, while others were pretty badly shot up. Some bore their pain in grim silence, while others, even though only slightly wounded, acted as though they were nearly killed. One fellow, who seemed to be pretty badly wounded, said: "Never mind the pain, boys, go right on". This was in contrast to those who begged to be carried easier, when we were carrying them as easy as was possible under the circumstances. Continued to carry wounded till darkness called a halt to our work. When night came, I, for one, was pretty tired. One of the ambulances received a direct hit, during the afternoon, and was burned up. Never learned if the driver was killed or not.

An ammunition dump blew up close to one of our sergeants during the afternoon. He became very near shell shocked.

During the night we were not shelled very much, though a few large shells fell near us on our left. We could hear them coming several seconds before they landed, and when they did hit, the earth fairly trembled. A counter attack was reported on our exposed left flank just at dark, but it was repulsed by battalion headquarters and medical men.

The next day, October 5th, the French connected up with our left, and we were not bothered any more from that direction. I continued to carry wounded the second day were in this position. One fellow who had an artery severed in his leg by a piece of shrapnel, I bandaged with a tourniquet just above the wound, and rushed him back to the dressing station. Saw that he had immediate attention, as the tourniquet had to be loosened quite often. Another fellow had his whole heel shot off. Another had his head severed from his body as clean as if had been done with a knife.

During the afternoon of the 5th, the Sixth Regiment leap-frogged us and took up the attack. Also our artillery began to give us support early on the 5th. From then on we had plenty of artillery support. Our dressing station was moved up closer, but received a direct hit, killing and wounding again several in the station at the time. The enemy kept up a lively fire just over our heads. Machine gun bullets and "whiz bangs" just cleared our parapets. It was a "close shave" sometimes.

Rations came up to us during the night of the 6th. I helped carry them to the company, and was surprised to note that we got some canned pork and beans. This item was up to this time a "scarce article" with us. I celebrated by keeping two cans for myself and a "buddy." Coffee was sent up in a water cart, and we were told to carry our canteens back and fill them. Gathering up about eight canteens, I went back to where the water carts were, one for each company, and filled them with cold coffee, for it was cold by the time it reached us. Just as I started back, a battery of our heavy guns began dropping shells within our lines. The first round fell about a hundred yards in rear of me. I could hear the guns when they were fired and could also hear the shells before they hit. Doing some double-time, I could tell by the sound of the second round that the shells were coming closer. A few seconds before they hit, I fell flat on the ground, and, as soon as the air was clear of flying shell fragments, did some more double-time, only this time faster. In spite of my speed the shells kept hitting closer each time. By this time signal rockets were being sent up, indicating to the battery that the range was short. Just as I thought the next ones would get me, the battery ceased firing. If they had not ceased firing when they did, there would have been one less Marine that night. The next day I saw where shells had hit, and torn up the earth. After a while the battery started firing again, but the range was still short. They soon got it adjusted and the shells fell on the Germans instead of us. I didn't go after any more coffee that night....

The War Diary of Clarence Richmond, Episode 15: In the Midst of a Fierce Battle, October 1-6, 1918, located at http://www.en.com/users/robinr/wardiary/diary15.htm.

18.7

EUGENE V. DEBS DEFENDS POLITICAL DISSENT (1918)

Americans were deeply divided on World War I. To generate popular support for the war effort, Woodrow Wilson enlisted specialists in advertising and public relations. Through speeches, publications, and films, these officials convinced many citizens to buy war bonds and to demonstrate their loyalty to the U.S. government. At times, patriotism degenerated into anti-German hysteria, nativism, and intolerance. Despite this hostile climate, anti-war protestors, political radicals, and pacifists continued to oppose the war.

To suppress this dissent, government officials instituted severe restrictions on speech. In June 1917, Congress passed the Espionage Act imposing high fines and long jail terms for broadly defined anti-war activities. In May 1918, the law was amended with a Sedition Act penalizing "disloyal, profane, scurrilous, or abusive language" about the federal government, the U.S. flag, the Constitution, or the armed services. Most states passed similar measures. Public officials imprisoned thousands of pacifists, anti-war activists, and political radicals.

Eugene V. Debs (1855-1926) was among those incarcerated. A long-time labor activist, Debs gained national attention when he was sentenced to a six-month jail sentence for his role in leading the 1894 Pullman strike. While imprisoned, Debs read many political texts and grew highly critical of capitalism. Upon his release, he converted to socialism and led the Socialist Party of America for many years.

In June 1918, Debs gave a speech in Canton, Ohio. In the address, he declared, "The master class has always declared the wars; the subject class has always fought the battles." He was immediately arrested for violating the Espionage and Sedition Acts. During his September 1918 trial, Debs presented his own case. His address to the jury is featured here. It made little impression. Debs was sentenced to ten years and stripped of his U.S. citizenship. Though imprisoned, Debs won almost one million votes in the 1920 presidential election. The following year, President Warren G. Harding ordered Debs released. In 1976, the government restored his citizenship posthumously.

────────■────────

FOCUS QUESTIONS

1. How does Debs respond to the charges levied against him?
2. Why does Debs oppose the war? How does he defend his views?
3. Was Debs' sentence just? Should freedom of speech be restricted during wartime? Explain your answers.

September 12, 1918

ay it please the Court, and Gentlemen of the Jury.
For the first time in my life I appear before a jury in a court of law to answer an indictment for a crime. I am not a lawyer. I know little about court procedure, about the rules of evidence or legal practice. I know only that you gentlemen are to hear the evidence brought against me, that the Court is to instruct you in the law, and that you are then to determine your verdict whether I should be branded with criminal guilt and be consigned, perhaps to the end of my life, in a felon's cell....

Gentlemen, you have heard the report of my speech at Canton on June 16, and I submit that that there is not a word in that speech to warrant the charges set out in the indictment. I admit having delivered the speech. I admit the accuracy of the speech in all of its main features as reported in this proceeding....

In what I had to say there my purpose was to have the people understand something about the social system in which we live and to prepare them to change this system by perfectly peaceable and orderly means into what I, as a Socialist, conceive to be real democracy.

From what you heard in the address of the counsel for the prosecution, you might naturally infer that I am an advocate of force and violence. It is not true. I have never advocated violence in any form. I have always believed in education, in intelligence, in enlightenment; and I have always made my appeal to the reason and to the conscience of the people.

I admit being opposed to the present form of government. I admit being opposed to the present social system. I am doing what little I can, and have been for many years, to bring about a change that shall do away with the rule of the great body of the people by a relatively small class and establish in this country an industrial and social democracy....

When great changes occur in history, when great principles are involved, as a rule the majority are wrong. The minority are right. In every age there have been a few heroic souls who have been in advance of their time, who have been misunderstood, maligned, persecuted—sometimes put to death. Long after their martyrdom, monuments were erected to them and garlands woven for their graves....

A century and a half ago, when the American colonists were still foreign subjects, and when there were a few men who had faith in the common people and believed that they could rule themselves without a king. In that day to speak against the king was treason. If you read Bancroft or any other standard historian, you will find that a great majority of the colonists believed in the king and actually believed that he had a divine right to rule over them.... But there were a few men in that day who said, "We don't need a king. We can govern ourselves." And they began an agitation that has been immortalized in history.

Washington, Adams, Paine—these were the rebels of their day. At first they were opposed by the people and denounced by the press. But they had the moral courage to stand erect and defy all the storms of distraction; and that is why they are in history, and that is why the great respectable majority of their day sleep in forgotten graves....

At a later time there began another mighty agitation in this country. It was against an institution that was deemed a very respectable one in this time, the institution of chattel slavery, that became all-powerful, that controlled the President, both branches of Congress, the Supreme Court, the press, to a very large extent the pulpit. All of the organized forces of society, all the powers of government, upheld chattel slavery in that day. And again there were a few lovers of liberty who appeared. One of them was Elijah Lovejoy. Elijah Lovejoy was as much despised in his day as are the leaders of the I.W.W. in our day. Elijah

Lovejoy was murdered in cold blood in Alton, Illinois in 1837 simply because he was opposed to chattel slavery—just as I am opposed to wage slavery. When you go down to the Mississippi River and look up at Alton, you see a magnificent white shaft erected there in memory of man who was true to himself and his convictions of right and duty until death....

William Lloyd Garrison, Garret Smith, Thaddeus Stevens—these leaders of the abolition movement, who were regarded as monsters of depravity, were true to the faith and stood their ground. They are all in history. You are teaching your children to revere their memories, while all of their detractors are in oblivion.

Chattel slavery disappeared. We are not yet free. We are engaged in another mighty agitation today. It is as wide as the world. It is the rise of the toiling and producing masses who are gradually becoming conscious of their interest, their power, as a class, who are organizing industrially and politically, who are slowly but surely developing the economic and political power that is to set them free. They are still a minority, but they have learned how to wait, and to bide their time. It is because I happen to be in this minority that I stand in your presence today, charged with crime....

I believe in patriotism. I have never uttered a word against the flag. I love the flag as a symbol of freedom. I object only when that flag is prostituted to base purposes, to sordid ends, by those who, in the name of patriotism, would keep the people in subjection....

I believe that nations have been pitted against nations long enough in hatred, in strife, in warfare. I believe there ought to be a bond of unity between all of these nations. I believe that the human race consists of one great family. I love the people of this country, but I don't hate the people of any country on earth—not even the Germans....

Yes, I was opposed to the war. I am perfectly willing, on that count, to be branded as a disloyalist, and if it is a crime under the American law, punishable by imprisonment, for being opposed to human bloodshed, I am perfectly willing to be clothed in the stripes of a convict and to end my days in a prison cell....

I believe in the Constitution of the United States. Isn't it strange that we Socialists stand almost alone today in defending the Constitution of the United States? The Revolutionary fathers who had been oppressed under king rule understood that free speech and free press and the right of free assemblage by the people were the fundamental principles of democratic government. The very first amendment of the Constitution reads: "Congress shall make no law respecting an establishment of religion, or prohibiting the free exercise thereof; or abridging the freedom of speech, or of the press; or the right of the peace peaceably to assemble, and to petition the government for a redress of grievances." That is perfectly plain English. It can be understood by a child....

That is the right that I exercised at Canton on the 16th day of last June; and for the exercise of that right, I now have to answer to this indictment. I believe in the right of free speech in war as well as in peace. I would not, under any circumstances, gag the lips of my biggest enemy. I would under no circumstances suppress free speech. It is far more dangerous to attempt to gag the people than to allow them to speak freely of what is in their hearts....

Now, withstanding this fundamental provision in the national law, Socialists' meetings have been broken up all over this country. Socialist speakers have been arrested by the hundreds and flung into jail, where many of them are lying now. In some cases not even a charge was lodged against them, guilty of absolutely no crime except the crime of attempting to exercise the right guaranteed to them by the Constitution of the United States.

I have told you that I am no lawyer, but it seems to me that I know enough to know that if Congress enacts any law that conflicts with this provision in the Constitution, that law is void. If the Espionage Law finally stands, then the Constitution of the United States is dead. If that law is not the negation of every fundamental principle established by the Constitution, then certainly I am unable to read or to understand the English language....

Gentlemen, I am the smallest part of this trial. I have lived long enough to appreciate my own personal insignificance in relation to a great issue that involves the welfare of the whole people. What you may choose to do to me will be of small consequence after all. I am not on trial here. There is an infinitely greater issue that is being tried in this court, though you may not be conscious of it. American institutions are on trial here before a court of American citizens. The future will tell.

And now, Your Honor, permit me to return my hearty thanks for your patient consideration. And to you Gentlemen of the Jury, for the kindness with which you have listened to me.

My fate is in your hands. I am prepared for the verdict.

David Karsner, *Debs: His Authorized Life and Letters* (New York: Boni and Liveright: 1919), pp. 21-44.

18.8

THE NAACP CALLS FOR ACTION (1919)

The war years inspired and dismayed African Americans. Eager to prove their willingness to support the crusade to "make the world safe for democracy," 260,000 African Americans volunteered or were drafted into the American Expeditionary Force (AEF). Military service disappointed many black soldiers. Sometimes racial clashes erupted with whites incensed by the prospect of armed blacks. Although African American soldiers were often assigned menial jobs, a few distinguished themselves in combat. At home, 500,000 blacks fled the South in pursuit of better economic and social opportunities elsewhere. But their financial and psychological gains were sometimes marred by conflicts with white workers and neighbors. The National Association for the Advancement of Colored People (NAACP) hoped such incidents would persuade African Americans to demand more equitable race relations. In this selection, the NAACP publication, The Crisis, *urges blacks to push for a more just society.*

---■---

FOCUS QUESTIONS

1. How does this editorial attempt to rally African-Americans?
2. Did African-Americans' contributions to war effort result in improved economic and political opportunities? How did the government's response to black activists differ from its reaction to women's suffragists? (Document 18.3) Explain your answers.

W e are returning from war! *The Crisis* and tens of thousands of black men were drafted into a great struggle. For bleeding France and what she means and has meant and will mean to us and humanity and against the threat of German race arrogance, we fought gladly and to the last drop of blood; for America and her highest ideals, we fought in far-off hope; for the dominant southern oligarchy entrenched in Washington, we fought in bitter resignation. For the American that represents and gloats in lynching, disfranchisement, caste, brutality, and devilish insult—for this, in the hateful upturning and mixing of things, we were forced by vindictive fate to fight also.

But today we return! We return from the slavery of uniform which the world's madness demanded us to don to the freedom of civil garb. We stand again to look America squarely in the face and call a spade a spade. This country of ours, despite all its better souls have done and dreamed, is yet a shameful land.

It *lynches*....

It *disfranchises* its own citizens....

It encourages *ignorance*....

It *steals* from us....

It *insults* us....

This is the country to which we Soldiers of Democracy return. This is the fatherland for which we fought. But it is *our* fatherland. It was right for us to fight. The faults of *our* country are *our* faults. Under similar circumstances, we would fight again. But by the God of Heaven, we are cowards and jackasses if now that war is over, we do not marshal every ounce of our brain and brawn to fight a sterner, longer, more unbending battle against the hell in our own land.

We *return.*

We *return from fighting.*

We *return fighting.*

Make way for Democracy! We saved it in France, and by the Great Jehovah, we will save it in the United States of America, or know the reason why.

The author wishes to thank The Crisis Publishing Co., Inc., the publisher of the magazine of the National Association for the Advancement for the Advancement of Colored People, for the use of this work that was first published in the May 1919 issue of "The Crisis Magazine."

18.9

HENRY CABOT LODGE OPPOSES THE LEAGUE OF NATIONS (1919)

As the United States mobilized for war, President Woodrow Wilson outlined a plan for reshaping international relations. Announced in a congressional speech in January 1918, The Fourteen Points (Document 18.4) called for self-determination of nations, open navigation of the seas, free trade, arms control, and an end to secret diplomacy. The centerpiece of Wilson's vision was the League of Nations, an international organization where nations could negotiate peaceful solutions to their conflicts. Hoping to achieve these goals, Wilson attended the Paris Peace Conference in early 1919. Although the vindictive Treaty of Versailles bore little resemblance to Wilson's proposed "peace without victory," it did create the League of Nations. Wilson convinced himself that the League could correct the flaws of the Versailles agreement, but he greatly overestimated popular support for his plans. When Wilson submitted the treaty for Senate ratification in June 1919, several Republicans denounced the League of Nations as a threat to national sovereignty and congressional power. They found Article X, the portion of the League charter committing all members to collective security, particularly troubling.

Henry Cabot Lodge (1850-1924), a Republican Senator from Massachusetts, used his power as chairman of the Senate Foreign Relations Committee to oppose the Versailles Treaty. He delayed the ratification process for weeks and proposed several amendments that required congressional approval of certain League decisions. Determined to save the treaty, Wilson embarked on a rigorous speaking tour that ended when he had a debilitating stroke. Unwilling to compromise, Wilson urged Democrats to reject Lodge's amendments. Ultimately, the Senate rejected the treaty entirely. In this reading, Lodge explains his opposition to the Treaty of Versailles and the League of Nations.

FOCUS QUESTIONS

1. Why does Lodge find the treaty so objectionable?
2. How does he propose to modify the agreement?
3. Is Lodge an isolationist?
4. Do you agree with Lodge's arguments? Should the United States have joined the League of Nations? Explain your answers.

I object in the strongest possible way to having the United States agree, directly or indirectly, to be controlled by a league which may at any time, and perfectly lawfully and in accordance with the terms of the covenant, be drawn in to deal with internal conflicts in other countries, no matter what those conflicts may be. We should never permit the United States to be involved in any internal conflict in another country, except by the will of her people expressed through the Congress which represents them.

With regard to wars of external aggression on a member of the league, the case is perfectly clear. There can be no genuine dispute whatever about the meaning of the first clause of article 10. In the first place, it differs from every other obligation in being individual and placed upon each nation without the intervention of the league. Each nation for itself promises to respect and preserve as against external aggression the boundaries and the political independence of every member of the league....

Any analysis of the provisions of this league covenant, however, brings out in startling relief one great fact. Whatever may be said, it is not a league of peace; it is an alliance, dominated at the present moment by five great powers, really by three, and it has all the marks of an alliance. The development of international law is neglected. The court which is to decide disputes brought before it fills but a small place. The conditions for which this league really provides with the utmost care are political conditions, not judicial questions, to be reached by the executive council and the assembly, purely political bodies without any trace of a judicial character about them. Such being its machinery, the control being in the hands of political appointees whose votes will be controlled by interest and expedience it exhibits that most marked characteristic of an alliance—that its decisions are to be carried out by force. Those articles upon which the whole structure rests are articles which provide for the use of force; that is, for war. This league to enforce peace does a great deal for enforcement and very little for peace. It makes more essential provisions looking to war than to peace for the settlement of disputes....

Taken altogether, these provisions for war present what to my mind is the gravest objection to this league in its present form. We are told that of course nothing will be done in the way of warlike acts without the assent of Congress. If that is true let us say so in the covenant. But as it stands there is no doubt whatever in my mind that American troops and American ships may be ordered to any part of the world by nations other than the United States, and that is a proposition to which I for one can never assent....

Those of us, Mr. President, who are either wholly opposed to the league, or who are trying to preserve the independence and the safety of the United States by changing the terms of the league, and who are endeavoring to make the league, if we are to be a member of it, less certain to promote war instead of peace have been reproached with selfishness in our outlook and with a desire to keep our country in a state of isolation. So far as the question of isolation goes, it is impossible to isolate the United States.... But there is a wide difference between taking a suitable part and bearing a due responsibility in world affairs and plunging the United States into every controversy and conflict on the face of the globe. By meddling in all the differences which may arise among any portion or fragment of humankind we simply fritter away our influence and injure ourselves to no good purpose....

...In the prosecution of the war we gave unstintedly American lives and American treasure. When the war closed we had 3,000,000 men under arms. We were turning the country into a vast workshop for war. We advanced ten billions to our allies. We refused no assistance that we could possibly render. All the great energy and power of the Republic were put at the service of the good cause. We have not been ungenerous. We have been devoted to the cause of freedom, humanity, and civilization everywhere. Now we are asked, in the making of peace, to sacrifice our sovereignty in important respects, to involve ourselves almost without limit in the affairs of other nations and to yield up policies and rights which we have maintained throughout our history. We are asked to incur liabilities to an unlimited extent and furnish assets at the same time which no man can measure. I think it is not only our right but our duty to determine how far we shall go....

No doubt many excellent and patriotic people see a coming fulfillment of noble ideals in the words "league for peace." We all respect and share these aspirations and desires, but some of us see no hope, but rather defeat, for them in this murky covenant. For we, too have our ideals, even if we differ from those who have tried to establish a monopoly of idealism. Our first ideal is our country, and we see her in the future, as in the past, giving service to all her people and to the world. Our ideal of the future is that she should continue to render that service of her own free will. She has great problems of her own to solve, very grim and perilous problems, and a right solution, if we can attain to it, would largely benefit mankind. We would have our country strong to resist a peril from the West, as she has flung back the German menace from the East. We would not have our politics distracted and embittered by the dissensions of other lands. We would not have our country's vigor exhausted or her moral force abated, by everlasting meddling and muddling in every quarrel, great and small, which afflicts the world. Our ideal is to make her ever stronger and better and finer, because in that way alone, as we believe, can she be of the greatest service to the world's peace and to the welfare of mankind.

"League of Nations," *Congressional Record*, 66th Congress, 1st Session, part 4, (12 August 1919), 3778-3784.

SECONDARY SOURCE

—————————————■—————————————

TONY SMITH, "WOODROW WILSON AND A WORLD SAFE FOR DEMOCRACY"

In order to understand foreign relations in today's world, one must examine the ideas of Woodrow Wilson. Articulated in the latter stages of World War I,

Wilson's program of collective security and democratic capitalism represented a departure from autocracy and imperialism. Furthermore, liberal democratic internationalism was an alternative to violent upheavals like the Bolshevik Revolution. In this essay, Tony Smith, Professor of Political Science at Tufts University, explains Wilson's ideas, their historical context, and their long-range impact on global affairs.

Go to your *Speaking of America* CD-ROM to read "Woodrow Wilson and a World Safe for Democracy."

FOCUS QUESTIONS

1. According to Tony Smith, what were the major objectives of Wilsonianism? Why did it represent a radical change in the conduct of international relations?
2. Why did Wilson believe that liberal democracy was the best system of government?
3. How did Wilson propose to change international economics?
4. How did the political realities of the post-WWI era differ from Wilson's ideas? Provide several examples.
5. Why do realist political theorists criticize Wilsonianism? How does Smith dispute these contentions?
6. What are some examples of Wilson's impact on international relations today?

AMERICAN JOURNEY ONLINE

http://ajaccesss.wadsworth.com †

About U.S.-Latin American Relations
— In The Hispanic-American Experience
Documents
• President Meléndez, A Letter to President Wilson from the President of El Salvador (1918)
Images
• Fierro, Villa, Ortega, Medina (circa 1910)

---

† Enter password, choose the Archive indicated above, click on Contents, choose •Documents, •Images, or •Multimedia, and click on the title of the item.

— In <u>World War I and the Jazz Age</u>
Images
   • The Punitive Expedition (1916)
   • Pershing and the Punitive Expedition (1916)

About WWI Military Affairs/Combat
— In <u>World War I and the Jazz Age</u>
Documents
   • Richard Harding Davis, The Great War Begins (1914)
   • General Erich von Falkenhayn, Excerpt from The German General Staff and Its Decisions, 1914-1916
   • John J. Pershing, The State of U.S. Military in 1917
   • John Dos Passos, An American Volunteer in Europe (1917)
   • John J. Pershing, The Amalgamation Controversy (1918)
   • U.S. Army, Operations Report, October 1-6, 1918
   • Organization of the AEF (1919)
   • Leonard P. Ayres, A Statistical View of the Meuse-Argonne Offensive (1919)
   • Colonel P. Ayres, Evaluation of the Battle of Saint-Mihiel (1919)
   • Colonel Leonard P. Ayres, Significance of the Meuse-Argonne Offensive (1919)
   • Colonel Leonard P. Ayres, The American Military Contribution to World War I
   • John J. Pershing, Buildup for the Battle of Saint-Mihiel (1931)
   • Brigadier General Sir J.E. Edmonds, Gas Attack! (1967)
   • Amos Niven Wilder, Doughboys Discover the Horror of War (1968)
   • Allen R. Millet, Excerpt from *Belleau Wood: One Man's Initiation* (1993)
Images
   • The Schlieffen Plan
   • Helmuth von Moltke
   • Gavrilo Princip
   • Kaiser Wilhelm II
   • Implementing the Schlieffen Plan
   • The *Lusitania* (1915)
   • Christopher R.W. Nevinson, Machine-Gun (1915)
   • Submarine Warfare in World War I and the Jazz Age
   • French Elan Meets German Machine Guns
   • Trench Warfare (1916)
   • Artillery: The Big Killer
   • Machine Gunners in Action
   • The Maxim Machine Gunners
   • The Rifle and the Bayonet
   • Gallipoli
   • Traffic Jam at Esnes, France

- Pershing Reviewing the Troops
- New Kinds of Military Technology: Airplane
- Lafayette, We Are Here (1917)
- John J. Pershing (1918)
- German Dead at the Front (1918)
- German Field of Fire
- German Machine Gunner Dead at His Post (1918)
- John MacClancy, Charging American Troops at Cantigny (1918)
- Planes of the American Air Service
- Eddie Rickenbacker (1918)
- Allied Attacks on the Western Front, September 26-November 11, 1918
- American Battle Operation in the Meuse-Argonne Region (1918)
- Rugged Terrain in the Meuse-Argonne (1918)
- U.S. Casualties in the Meuse-Argonne (1918)
- Calamity Jane Fires the Last Shot (1918)
- Armistice! (1918)
- No Man's Land (1919)
- Colonel Leonard P. Ayres, Kilometers of Front Line Held by Allied Armies (1919)
- The Meuse-Argonne American Cemetery (1919)
- Founding the American Legion (1919)
— In The African-American Experience
Images
- The 369th in Parade (1919)

About Neutrality
— In World War I and the Jazz Age
Documents
- Woodrow Wilson, Appeal for Neutrality (1914)

About War Mobilization/Propaganda
— In World War I and the Jazz Age
Documents
- Document with Audio—George M. Cohan, "Over There" (1917) in World War I and the Jazz Age
Images
- Leonard Wood
- Howard Chandler Christy, Navy Recruiting Poster (1917)
- Drafting American Men (1917)
- You're in the Army Now (1918)
- H.R. Hopps, Destroy This Mad Brute: Enlist U.S. Army (circa 1917)
- John E. Sheridan, Food is Ammunition-Don't Waste It (circa 1918)
- The Industrialization of Warfare
- Bernard Baruch
- I Summon You to Comradeship in the Red Cross (1918)

- • That Liberty Should Not Perish from the Earth (1918)
- • Wesley Clair Mitchell
- • Howard Chandler Christy, Come On! Buy More Liberty Bonds (1919)
- • George Creel
- • Four-Minute Men
- • Herbert Hoover (1919)
— In The Immigrant Experience
Documents
- • War Department, Excerpt of Army Mental Test, Group Examination Alpha (1920)
Images
- • Soldier Saying Goodbye to His Family (1917)

About Domestic Politics
— In World War I and the Jazz Age
Documents
- • Woodrow Wilson, Prophesying Political Repression (1917)
- • John Reed, Whose War? (1917)
- • Randolph Bourne, Excerpt from The State (1918)
- • Eugene V. Debs, Socialist Leader Criticizes the War (1918)
- • Jane Addams, Excerpt from *Peace and Bread in Time of War* (1922)
- • Paul L. Murphy, Examples of Wartime Repression (1979)
Images
- • Eugene V. Debs in World War I and the Jazz Age
— In Civil Rights in the United States
Images
- • Eugene V. Debs (1920)
— In The Immigrant Experience
Images
- • A.B. Walker, My Country, 'Tis of Thee (1918)

About Labor
— In World War I and the Jazz Age
Documents
- • C.E. (Stumpy) Payne, The Mainspring of Action (1919)
- • Ohio General Assembly, Ohio Criminal Syndicalism Law (1919)
Images
- • John L. Lewis
- • William Z. Foster
- • Calvin Coolidge
- • Ole Hanson
— In Civil Rights in the United States
Images
- • Police in Front of Steel Strikers' Meeting (1919)

— In <u>The African-American Experience</u>
Documents
- Philip Randolph, Blacks Need the I.W.W. (1919)

About Law
— In <u>The Constitution and the Supreme Court</u>
Images
- Louis D. Brandeis (circa 1916)
- Oliver Wendell Holmes (1921)
— In <u>Civil Rights in the United States</u>
Documents
- U.S. Supreme Court, *Abrams v. United States* (1919)
Images
- Oliver Wendell Holmes
— In <u>World War I and the Jazz Age</u>
Documents
- U.S. Congress, Sedition Act, May 16, 1918

About Immigration
— In <u>The Immigrant Experience</u>
Documents
- U.S. Congress, Immigration Act of 1917, Literacy Test
— In <u>The Asian-American Experience</u>
Documents
- U.S. Congress, Excerpt of the Immigration Act of 1917

About Prohibition
— In <u>World War I and the Jazz Age</u>
Documents
- U.S. Congress, Eighteenth Amendment to the U.S. Constitution (1919)

About Race Relations
— In <u>World War I and the Jazz Age</u>
Documents
- Document with Audio Commentary—The Great Migration (1916)
- The Reverend Richard Carroll, Wartime Migration of Black Workers (1917)
- War Labor Policies Board, Preliminary Report of Situation in East St. Louis and National City (1918)
- W.E.B. DuBois, The Arkansas Riots (1919)
— In <u>The Immigrant Experience</u>
Documents
- The Eternal Question (1916)
Images
- African American Attacked during Illinois Race Riot (1917)

— In <u>Civil Rights in the United States</u>
Images
- Race Riot in East St. Louis (1917)
— In <u>The African-American Experience</u>
Documents
- W.E.B. DuBois, Returning Soldiers (1919)
Images
- Lieutenant James Reese, Europe (1919)

About Women
— In <u>World War I and the Jazz Age</u>
Documents
- Helena Swanwick, Excerpt from The War in Its Effect upon Women (1916)
Images
- National Women's Party Headquarters (1917)
- Exercising the Basic Right of Citizenship (1920)
— In <u>Women in America</u>
Documents
- Letter to Woodrow Wilson from Carrie Chapman Catt (1917)
- Mrs. Lawrence Lewis, Reminiscence of Prison Experience (1917)
- Lucy Burns, Recollections of Imprisonment for Picketing White House (1917)
- Mary Winsor, et al., Letter to the Commissioners of the District of Columbia Claiming Political Prisoner Status for Jailed Suffragettes (1917)
- President Wilson's Letter Supporting Suffrage Bill (1917) in Women in America
- Woodrow Wilson, Appeal to the U.S. Senate to Submit the Federal Amendment for Woman Suffrage (1918)
- Herman Bilgrien, Why I Voted Against Woman Suffrage (1919)
- Harry Burns, Congressmen's Speech Defending His Vote for Suffrage (1920)
- Nineteenth Amendment to the U.S. Constitution (1920)
Images
- Lucy Burns, Burns' Banner at White House Picket (1917)
- Suffrage Parade in New York (1918)
- Jeannette Rankin, the First Woman Member of Congress (circa 1918)
- Mary von Kleeck, Director, U.S. Women in Industry Service (circa 1918)
- African-American Women Working in a Lumber Yard (1919)
- Girl Seated by Wood Testing Machine (1919)
- Women Pushing Wheelbarrows at a Gas Plant (1919)
- Woman Forest Service Lookout (1919)
- Woman Heating Rivets at the Puget Sound, Navy Yard (1919)
- Central News Photo Service, Woman Doing Laborer's Work in Railway Yard (1919)

- Women Shoveling Sand in a Foundry (1919)
- Women Railway Workers at Busch Terminal, Brooklyn, NY (1919)
- Women Learning How to Use a Voting Machine in Chicago (1920)
- Woman Voter (circa 1920)

— In <u>Civil Rights in the United States</u>
Images
- Alice Paul

Videos
- Suffragettes Marching (1920)

About Paris Peace Conference/Versailles Treaty
— In <u>World War I and the Jazz Age</u>
Documents
- Commission on the Responsibility of the Authors of the War and on the Enforcement of Penalties (1924)

Images
- Woodrow Wilson's Triumphal Tour of Europe (1919)
- The Victorious Allied Leaders Talk Peace (1919)
- Image with Audio Commentary—Henry Cabot Lodge

About the Red Scare
— In <u>World War I and the Jazz Age</u>
Documents
- Mitchell Palmer, Excerpt from The Case Against the Reds (1920)

Images
- Frederic C. Howe

Videos
- Blaming Reds for 1919 Strikes

About Secondary Accounts of the World War I Era
— In <u>World War I and the Jazz Age</u>
Documents
- Henry May, Excerpt from *The End of American Innocence* (1959)
- Nell Irvin Painter, Excerpt from *Standing at Armageddon* (1987)

THE ROARING TWENTIES

The 1920s were a decade of stunning contrasts. Close cooperation between government and business, a thriving stock market, and technological innovations propelled a highly productive economy. This prosperity, however, obscured forces that contributed to the Great Crash of 1929 and the onset of the Great Depression. U.S. society and culture reflected similar contradictions. Although many Americans enjoyed the consumerism, fashions, and fads of the day, others criticized their materialism and self-indulgence. While jazz, flappers, and automobiles symbolized the era's modernity, a resurgent Ku Klux Klan, fundamentalist Protestantism, and conservative politicians demonstrated the continuing strength of older traditions. Such conflicts make the 1920s a fascinating era of American history.

Emerging from World War I with relatively few casualties and no physical destruction, the United States was the world's strongest economic power in the 1920s. While businessmen and government officials vigorously pursued investment opportunities abroad, assembly lines and improved management techniques boosted production at home. Through more efficient distribution networks, advertising, and credit, corporations reached greater numbers of consumers and expanded sales.

Women profited from the booming economy. Newly introduced electrical appliances such as vacuum cleaners aided in housework. The growth of supermarkets and availability of refrigerators freed women from time-consuming cooking chores and enabled them to incorporate more foods into family diets. Although companies hired increasing numbers of women as secretaries, clerks, and typists, better-paying jobs were much harder to attain.

Compared to the dynamism of the Progressive Era, the politics of the 1920s were tame. Republicans controlled Congress and the presidency. Public officials shifted away from social reforms and toward pro-business measures like high tariffs and tax cuts for the wealthy. Predictions that the recently enfranchised women would drastically change political life proved incorrect. U.S. foreign policy centered on fostering an international climate conducive to American economic interests.

Cities played a crucial role in the financial and cultural life of the nation. By 1920, more Americans lived in urban areas than in rural ones. The country's most successful industries—including publishing, motion pictures, and radio—were based in cities. Urban populations were the country's most religiously and ethnically diverse.

Wherever they lived, all Americans were influenced by the rise of mass culture. As assembly lines made work repetitive and less rewarding, millions relished the escapes offered by magazines, radio shows, and movies. As culture became more homogenized, it fostered national identity in both positive and negative ways.

Despite the forces drawing them together, Americans remained divided on many issues. Disillusioned by WWI, many young people challenged traditional morality by violating Prohibition laws and engaging in sexual experimentation. Informal "dating" replaced serious courtship. Many women smoked, wore shorter skirts, and applied the cosmetics formerly associated only with prostitutes.

Millions of Americans condemned the hedonistic attitudes of the "lost generation." Instead of embracing modernity, they clung more tightly to established values. Some became fundamentalist Christians committed to a literal interpretation of the Bible. Others supported immigration restriction or joined the Ku Klux Klan in the hope of protecting white supremacy and Protestantism.

These trends provided inspiration for writers, artists, and musicians. Authors like F. Scott Fitzgerald, Sinclair Lewis, H.L. Mencken, and Ernest Hemingway attacked the conformity and materialism of the middle-class. Artists such as Thomas Hart Benton, Edward Hopper, and Georgia O'Keefe explored new styles. While Aaron Copland fused folk and classical music, African-Americans such as Duke Ellington, Louis Armstrong, Ma Rainey, and Bessie Smith made jazz a distinctive American art form. At the same time, the Harlem Renaissance nourished important black authors and poets.

Although the Great Depression and World War II soon overshadowed the events of the 1920s, the decade spawned the society most Americans would recognize today. The business techniques, consumerism, and popular entertainment of that era remain important. So do the social, religious, and political forces that clashed at the time.

19.1

MARCUS GARVEY, "AFRICA FOR THE AFRICANS" (1922)

Marcus Garvey (1887-1940) led the first large-scale black nationalist movement in U.S. history. Born in Jamaica, Garvey left school at the age of 14 and worked as a printer. He founded the United Negro Improvement Association (UNIA) as a fraternal organization. In 1916, he arrived in the United States. Enraged by the racial unrest of the World War I era, Garvey embraced racial separatism. He used his powerful oratorical skills to advocate black racial pride and economic self-sufficiency. Drawing as many as two million members, he established UNIA chapters in many U.S. cities. To finance and strengthen his movement, Garvey launched black-owned restaurants, stores, laundries, a hotel, and a toy factory that manufactured black dolls. In 1919, he incorporated the

Black Star Line, a shipping company for transporting blacks between America and Africa. The following year, Garvey hosted an international UNIA conference attended by delegates from twenty-five nations.

But Garvey's successes proved short-lived. In 1922, following allegations of mail fraud in the Black Star operation, Garvey received a five-year prison term. After serving two years, his sentence was commuted by President Calvin Coolidge. In 1927, Garvey was deported as an undesirable alien and never returned to the United States. Although established black leaders such as W.E.B. DuBois and A. Philip Randolph harshly criticized him at the time, Garvey's ideas profoundly affected future generations of black activists, including Malcolm X.

FOCUS QUESTIONS

1. What are Garvey's major objectives?
2. How does Garvey respond to his critics?
3. What is your opinion of Garvey's ideas? Would they have resolved the racial problems of this era? Explain your answers.

ellow men of the Negro Race, Greeting:

For four and a half years the Universal Negro Improvement Association has been advocating the cause of Africa for the Africans—that is, that the Negro peoples of the world should concentrate upon the object of building up for themselves a great nation in Africa.

When we started our propaganda toward this end several of the so-called intellectual Negroes who have been bamboozling the race for over half a century said that we were crazy, that the Negro peoples of the western world were not interested in Africa and could not live in Africa. One editor and leader went so far as to say at his Pan-African Congress that American Negroes could not live in Africa, because the climate was too hot. All kinds of arguments have been adduced by these Negro intellectuals against the colonization of Africa by the black race. Some said that the black man would ultimately work out his existence alongside of the white man in countries founded and established by the latter. Therefore, it was not necessary for Negroes to seek an independent nationality of their own. The old time stories of "Africa fever," "African bad climate," "African mosquitoes," "African savages," have been repeated by these "brainless intellectuals" of ours as a scare against our people in America and the West Indies taking a kindly interest in the new program of building a racial empire of our own in our Motherland.

I trust that the Negro peoples of the world are now convinced that the work of the Universal Negro Improvement Association is not a visionary one, but very practical, and that it is not so far-fetched, but can be realized in a short while if the entire race will only co-operate and work toward the desired end. Now that the work of our organization has started to bear fruit, we find that some of these "doubting Thomases" of the three and four years ago are endeavoring to mix themselves up with the popular idea of rehabilitating Africa in the interest of the

Negro. They are now advancing spurious "programs" and in a short while will endeavor to force themselves upon the public as advocates and leaders of the African idea.

It is felt that those who have followed the career of the Universals Negro Improvement Association will not allow themselves to be deceived by these Negro opportunists who have always sought to live off the ideas of other people.

It is only a question of a few more years when Africa will be completely colonized by Negroes, as Europe is by the white race.... What we want is an independent African nationality, and if America is to help the Negro peoples of the world establish such a nationality, then we welcome the assistance.

It is hoped that when the time comes for American and West Indian Negroes to settle in Africa, they will realize their responsibility and their duty. It will not be to go to the natives, but it shall be the purpose of the Universal Negro Improvement Association to have established in Africa the brotherly co-operation which will make the interest of the African native and the American and West Indies Negro one and the same, that is to say, we shall enter into a common partnership to build up Africa in the interest of our race.

Your obedient servant,
Marcus Garvey, President General
Universal Negro Improvement Association
New York, April 18, 1922

Negro World, Vol. XII, No. 10, New York, Saturday, April 22, 1922.

19.2

SINCLAIR LEWIS, *BABBITT* (1922)

Sinclair Lewis (1885-1951) was a careful observer of modern America. Born in rural Minnesota, Lewis attended Yale University and worked as an editor for several publications. Throughout the 1920s, his novels, including Main Street *(1920),* Babbitt *(1922), and* Elmer Gantry *(1927), assailed provincialism, conformity and materialism. In 1930, he became the first American to be awarded the Nobel Prize in Literature.*

FOCUS QUESTIONS

1. What are some of the most important themes in this excerpt? How does Babbitt's story reflect historical trends of the 1920s?
2. Is George Babbitt a likeable character? Why or why not?
3. How does Lewis regard life in 1920s America? Is this a fair appraisal of the decade? Explain your answers.

T HERE are but three or four old houses in Floral Heights, and in Floral Heights an old house is one which was built before 1880. The largest of these is the residence of William Washington Eathorne, president of the First State Bank.

The mist took pity on the fretted structures of earlier generations: the Post Office with its shingle-tortured mansard, the red brick minarets of hulking old houses, factories with stingy and sooted windows, wooden tenements colored like mud. The city was full of such grotesqueries, but the clean towers were thrusting them from the business center, and on the farther hills were shining new houses, homes—they seemed—for laughter and tranquility.

Over a concrete bridge fled a limousine of long sleek hood and noiseless engine. These people in evening clothes were returning from an all-night rehearsal of a Little Theater play, an artistic adventure considerably illuminated by champagne. Below the bridge curved a railroad, a maze of green and crimson lights. The New York Flyer boomed past, and twenty lines of polished steel leaped into the glare.

In one of the skyscrapers the wires of the Associated Press were closing down. The telegraph operators wearily raised their celluloid eye-shades after a night of talking with Paris and Peking. Through the building crawled the scrub-women, yawning, their old shoes slapping. The dawn mist spun away. Cues of men with lunch-boxes clumped toward the immensity of new factories, sheets of glass and hollow tile, glittering shops where five thousand men worked beneath one roof, pouring out the honest wares that would be sold up the Euphrates and across the veldt. The whistles rolled out in greeting a chorus cheerful as the April dawn; the song of labor in a city built—it seemed—for giants.

There was nothing of the giant in the aspect of the man who was beginning to awaken on the sleeping-porch of a Dutch Colonial house in that residential district of Zenith known as Floral Heights.

His name was George F. Babbitt. He was forty-six years old now, in April, 1920, and he made nothing in particular, neither butter nor shoes nor poetry, but he was nimble in the calling of selling houses for more than people could afford to pay.

His large head was pink, his brown hair thin and dry. His face was babyish in slumber, despite his wrinkles and the red spectacle-dents on the slopes of his nose. He was not fat but he was exceedingly well fed; his cheeks were pads, and the unroughened hand which lay helpless upon the khaki-colored blanket was slightly puffy. He seemed prosperous, extremely married and unromantic; and altogether unromantic appeared this sleeping-porch, which looked on one sizable elm, two respectable grass-plots, a cement driveway, and a corrugated iron garage. Yet Babbitt was again dreaming of the fairy child, a dream more romantic than scarlet pagodas by a silver sea.

For years the fairy child had come to him. Where others saw but Georgie Babbitt, she discerned gallant youth. She waited for him, in the darkness beyond mysterious groves. When at last he could slip away from the crowded house he darted to her. His wife, his clamoring friends, sought to follow, but he escaped, the girl fleet beside him, and they crouched together on a shadowy hillside. She was so slim, so white, so eager! She cried that he was gay and valiant, that she would wait for him, that they would sail—

Rumble and bang of the milk-truck.

Babbitt moaned; turned over; struggled back toward his dream. He could see only her face now, beyond misty waters. The furnace-man slammed the basement door. A dog barked in the next yard. As Babbitt sank blissfully into a dim warm tide, the paper-carrier went by whistling, and the rolled-up *Advocate* thumped the front door. Babbitt roused, his stomach constricted with alarm. As he relaxed, he was pierced by the familiar and irritating rattle of some one cranking a Ford: snap-ah-ah, snap-ah-ah, snap-ah-ah. Himself a pious motorist, Babbitt cranked with the unseen driver, with him waited through taut hours for the roar of the starting engine, with him agonized as the roar ceased and again began the infernal patient snap-ah-ah—a round, flat sound, a shivering cold-morning sound, a sound infuriating and inescapable. Not till the rising voice of the motor told him that the Ford was moving was he released from the panting tension. He glanced once at his favorite tree, elm twigs against the gold patina of sky, and fumbled for sleep as for a drug. He who had been a boy very credulous of life was no longer greatly interested in the possible and improbable adventures of each new day.

He escaped from reality till the alarm-clock rang, at seven-twenty.

It was the best of nationally advertised and quantitatively produced alarm-clocks, with all modern attachments, including cathedral chime, intermittent alarm, and a phosphorescent dial. Babbitt was proud of being awakened by such a rich device. Socially it was almost as creditable as buying expensive cord tires.

He sulkily admitted now that there was no more escape, but he lay and detested the grind of the real-estate business, and disliked his family, and disliked himself for disliking them. The evening before, he had played poker at Vergil Gunch's till midnight, and after such holidays he was irritable before breakfast. It may have been the tremendous home-brewed beer of the prohibition-era and the cigars to which that beer enticed him; it may have been resentment of return from this fine, bold man-world to a restricted region of wives and stenographers, and of suggestions not to smoke so much.

From the bedroom beside the sleeping-porch, his wife's detestably cheerful "Time to get up, Georgie boy," and the itchy sound, the brisk and scratchy sound, of combing hairs out of a stiff brush.

He grunted; he dragged his thick legs, in faded baby-blue pajamas, from under the khaki blanket; he sat on the edge of the cot, running his fingers through his wild hair, while his plump feet mechanically felt for his slippers. He looked regretfully at the blanket—forever a suggestion to him of freedom and heroism. He had bought it for a camping trip which had never come off. It symbolized gorgeous loafing, gorgeous cursing, virile flannel shirts.

He creaked to his feet, groaning at the waves of pain which passed behind his eyeballs. Though he waited for their scorching recurrence, he looked blurrily out at the yard. It delighted him, as always; it was the neat yard of a successful business man of Zenith, that is, it was perfection, and made him also perfect. He regarded the corrugated iron garage. For the three-hundred-and-sixty-fifth time in a year he reflected, "No class to that tin shack. Have to build me a frame garage.

But by golly it's the only thing on the place that isn't up-to-date!" While he stared he thought of a community garage for his acreage development, Glen Oriole. He stopped puffing and jiggling. His arms were akimbo. His petulant, sleep-swollen face was set in harder lines. He suddenly seemed capable, an official, a man to contrive, to direct, to get things done.

On the vigor of his idea he was carried down the hard, dean, unused-looking hall into the bathroom.

Though the house was not large it had, like all houses on Floral Heights, an altogether royal bathroom of porcelain and glazed tile and metal sleek as silver. The towel-rack was a rod of clear glass set in nickel. The tub was long enough for a Prussian Guard, and above the set bowl was a sensational exhibit of tooth-brush holder, shaving-brush holder, soap-dish, sponge-dish, and medicine-cabinet, so glittering and so ingenious that they resembled an electrical instrument-board. But the Babbitt whose god was Modern Appliances was not pleased. The air of the bathroom was thick with the smell of a heathen tooth-paste. "Verona been at it again! 'Stead of sticking to Lilidol, like I've re-peat-ed-ly asked her, she's gone and gotten some confounded stinkum stuff that makes you sick!"

The bath-mat was wrinkled and the floor was wet. (His daughter Verona eccentrically took baths in the morning, now and then.) He slipped on the mat, and slid against the tub. He said "Damn!" Furiously he snatched up his tube of shaving-cream, furiously he lathered, with a belligerent slapping of the unctuous brush, furiously he raked his plump cheeks with a safety-razor. It pulled. The blade was dull. He said, "Damn—oh—oh—damn it!"

He hunted through the medicine-cabinet for a packet of new razor-blades (re-flecting, as invariably, "Be cheaper to buy one of these dinguses and strop your own blades,") and when he discovered the packet, behind the round box of bicarbonate of soda, he thought ill of his wife for putting it there and very well of himself for not saying "Damn." But he did say it, immediately afterward, when with wet and soap-slippery fingers he tried to remove the horrible little envelope and crisp clinging oiled paper from the new blade.

Then there was the problem, oft-pondered, never solved, of what to do with the old blade, which might imperil the fingers of his young. As usual, he tossed it on top of the medicine-cabinet, with a mental note that some day he must remove the fifty or sixty other blades that were also temporarily, piled up there. He finished his shaving in a growing testiness increased by his spinning headache and by the emptiness in his stomach. When he was done, his round face smooth and streamy and his eyes stinging from soapy water, he reached for a towel. The family towels were wet, wet and clammy and vile, all of them wet, he found, as he blindly snatched them—his own face-towel, his wife's, Verona's, Ted's, Tinka's, and the lone bath-towel with the huge welt of initial. Then George F. Babbitt did a dismaying thing. He wiped his face on the guest-towel! It was a pansy-embroidered trifle which always hung there to indicate that the Babbitts were in the best Floral Heights society. No one had ever used it. No guest had ever dared to. Guests secretively took a corner of the nearest regular towel.

He was raging, "By golly, here they go and use up all the towels, every dog-gone one of 'em, and they use 'em and get 'em all wet and sopping, and never put out a dry one for me—of course, I'm the goat!—and then I want one and—I'm the only person in the doggone house that's got the slightest doggone bit of considera-tion for other people and thoughtfulness and consider there may be others that may want to use the doggone bathroom after me and consider—"

He was pitching the chill abominations into the bath-tub, pleased by the vin-dictiveness of that desolate flapping sound; and in the midst his wife serenely trotted in, observed serenely, "Why Georgie dear, what are you doing? Are you going to wash out the towels? Why, you needn't wash out the towels. Oh, Georgie, you didn't go and use the guest-towel, did you?"

It is not recorded that he was able to answer.

For the first time in weeks he was sufficiently roused by his wife to look at her.

Myra Babbitt—Mrs. George F. Babbitt—was definitely mature. She had creases from the corners of her mouth to the bottom of her chin, and her plump neck bagged. But the thing that marked her as having passed the line was that she no longer had reticences before her husband, and no longer worried about not having reticences. She was in a petticoat now, and corsets which bulged, and unaware of being seen in bulgy corsets. She had become so dully habituated to married life that in her full matronliness she was as sexless as an anemic nun. She was a good woman, a kind woman, a diligent woman, but no one, save perhaps Tinka her ten-year-old, was at all interested in her or entirely aware that she was alive.

After a rather thorough discussion of all the domestic and social aspects of towels she apologized to Babbitt for his having an alcoholic headache; and he recovered enough to endure the search for a B.V.D. undershirt which had, he pointed out, malevolently been concealed among his clean pajamas.

He was fairly amiable in the conference on the brown suit.

"What do you think, Myra?" He pawed at the clothes hunched on a chair in their bedroom, while she moved about mysteriously adjusting and patting her petticoat and, to his jaundiced eye, never seeming to get on with her dressing. "How about it? Shall I wear the brown suit another day?"

"Well, it looks awfully nice on you."

"I know, but gosh, it needs pressing."

"That's so. Perhaps it does."

"It certainly could stand being pressed, all right."

"Yes, perhaps it wouldn't hurt it to be pressed."

"But gee, the coat doesn't need pressing. No sense in having the whole darn suit pressed, when the coat doesn't need it."

"That's so."

"But the pants certainly need it, all right. Look at them—look at those wrin-kles—the pants certainly do need pressing."

"That's so." "But the pants certainly need it, all right. Look at them—look at those wrinkles—the pants certainly do need pressing."

"That's so. Oh, Georgie, why couldn't you wear the brown coat with the blue trousers we were wondering what we'd do with them?"

"Good Lord! Did you ever in all my life know me to wear the coat of one suit and the pants of another? What do you think I am? A busted bookkeeper?"

"Well, why don't you put on the dark gray suit to-day, and stop in at the tailor and leave the brown trousers?"

"Well, they certainly need—Now where the devil is that gray suit? Oh, yes, here we are."

He was able to get through the other crises of dressing with comparative resoluteness and calm.

His first adornment was the sleeveless dimity B.V.D. undershirt, in which he resembled a small boy humorlessly wearing a cheesecloth tabard at a civic pageant. He never put on B.V.D.'s without thanking the God of Progress that he didn't wear tight, long, old-fashioned undergarments, like his father-in-law and partner, Henry Thompson. His second embellishment was combing and slicking back his hair. It gave him a tremendous forehead, arching up two inches beyond the former hair-line. But most wonder-working of all was the donning of his spectacles.

There is character in spectacles—the pretentious tortoiseshell, the meek pince-nez of the school teacher, the twisted silver-framed glasses of the old villager. Babbitt's spectacles had huge, circular, frameless lenses of the very best glass; the ear-pieces were thin bars of gold. In them he was the modern business man; one who gave orders to clerks and drove a car and played occasional golf and was scholarly in regard to Salesmanship. His head suddenly appeared not babyish but weighty, and you noted his heavy, blunt nose, his straight mouth and thick, long upper lip, his chin overfleshy but strong; with respect you beheld him put on the rest of his uniform as a Solid Citizen.

The gray suit was well cut, well made, and completely undistinguished. It was a standard suit. White piping on the V of the vest added a flavor of law and learning. His shoes were black laced boots, good boots, honest boots, standard boots, extraordinarily uninteresting boots. The only frivolity was in his purple knitted scarf. With considerable comment on the matter to Mrs. Babbitt (who, acrobatically fastening the back of her blouse to her skirt with a safety-pin, did not hear a word he said), he chose between the purple scarf and a tapestry effect with stringless brown harps among blown palms, and into it he thrust a snake-head pin with opal eyes.

A sensational event was changing from the brown suit to the gray the contents of his pockets. He was earnest about these objects. They were of eternal importance, like baseball or the Republican Party. They included a fountain pen and a silver pencil (always lacking a supply of new leads) which belonged in the righthand upper vest pocket. Without them he would have felt naked. On his watch-chain were a gold penknife, silver cigar-cutter, seven keys (the use of two of which he had forgotten), and incidentally a good watch. Depending from the chain was a large, yellowish elk's-tooth-proclamation of his membership in the Brotherly and Protective Order of Elks. Most significant of all was his loose-leaf pocket note-book, that modern and efficient note-book which contained the addresses of people whom he had forgotten, prudent memoranda of postal money-orders which had reached their destinations months ago, stamps which had lost their mucilage, clippings of verses by T. Cholmondeley Frink and of the newspaper editorials from which Babbitt got his opinions and his polysyllables, notes to be sure and do things which he did not intend to do, and one curious inscription— D.S.S. D.M.Y.P.D.F.

But he had no cigarette-case. No one had ever happened to give him one, so he hadn't the habit, and people who carried cigarette-cases he regarded as effeminate.

Last, he stuck in his lapel the Boosters' Club button. With the conciseness of great art the button displayed two words: "Boosters-Pep!" It made Babbitt feel loyal and important. It associated him with Good Fellows, with men who were nice and human, and important in business circles. It was his V.C., his Legion of Honor ribbon, his Phi Beta Kappa key.

With the subtleties of dressing ran other complex worries. "I feel kind of punk this morning," he said. "I think I had too much dinner last evening. You oughtn't to serve those heavy banana fritters."

"But you asked me to have some."

"I know, but—I tell you, when a fellow gets past forty he has to look after his digestion. There's a lot of fellows that don't take proper care of themselves. I tell you at forty a man's a fool or his doctor—I mean, his own doctor. Folks don't give enough attention to this matter of dieting. Now I think—Course a man ought to have a good meal after the day's work, but it would be a good thing for both of us if we took lighter lunches."

"But Georgie, here at home I always do have a light lunch."

"Mean to imply I make a hog of myself, eating down-town? Yes, sure! You'd have a swell time if you had to eat the truck that new steward hands out to us at the Athletic Club! But I certainly do feel out of sorts, this morning. Funny, got a pain down here on the left side—but no, that wouldn't be appendicitis, would it? Last night, when I was driving over to Verg Gunch's, I felt a pain in my stomach, too. Right here it was—kind of a sharp shooting pain. I—Where'd that dime go to? Why don't you serve more prunes at breakfast? Of course I eat an apple every evening—an apple a day keeps the doctor away—but still, you ought to have more prunes, and not all these fancy doodads."

"The last time I had prunes you didn't eat them."

"Well, I didn't feel like eating 'em, I suppose. Matter of fact, I think I did eat some of 'em. Anyway—I tell you it's mighty important to—I was saying to Verg Gunch, just last evening, most people don't take sufficient care of their diges—"

"Shall we have the Gunches for our dinner, next week?"

"Why sure; you bet."

"Now see here, George: I want you to put on your nice dinner-jacket that evening."

"Rats! The rest of 'em won't want to dress."

"Of course they will. You remember when you didn't dress for the Littlefields' supper-party, and all the rest did, and how embarrassed you were."

"Embarrassed, hell! I wasn't embarrassed. Everybody knows I can put on as expensive a Tux. as anybody else, and I should worry if I don't happen to have it on sometimes. All a darn nuisance, anyway. All right for a woman, that stays around the house all the time, but when a fellow's worked like the dickens all day, he doesn't want to go and hustle his head off getting into the soup-and-fish for a lot of folks that he's seen in just reg'lar ordinary clothes that same day."

"You know you enjoy being seen in one. The other evening you admitted you were glad I'd insisted on your dressing. You said you felt a lot better for it. And oh, Georgie, I do wish you wouldn't say 'Tux.' It's 'dinner-jacket.'"

"Rats, what's the odds?"

"Well, it's what all the nice folks say. Suppose Lucile McKelvey heard you calling it a 'Tux.'"

"Well, that's all right now! Lucile McKelvey can't pull anything on me! Her folks are common as mud, even if her husband and her dad are millionaires! I suppose you're trying to rub in your exalted social position! Well, let me tell you that your revered paternal ancestor, Henry T., doesn't even call it a 'Tux.'! He calls it a 'bobtail jacket for a ringtail monkey,' and you couldn't get him into one unless you chloroformed him!"

"Now don't be horrid, George."

"Well, I don't want to be horrid, but Lord! you're getting as fussy as Verona. Ever since she got out of college she's been too rambunctious to live with—doesn't know what she wants—well, I know what she wants!—all she wants is to marry a millionaire, and live in Europe, and hold some preacher's hand, and simultaneously at the same time stay right here in Zenith and be some blooming kind of a socialist agitator or boss charity-worker or some damn thing! Lord, and Ted is just as bad! He wants to go to college, and he doesn't want to go to college. Only one of the three that knows her own mind is Tinka. Simply can't understand how I ever came to have a pair of shillyshallying children like Rone and Ted. I may not be any Rockefeller or James J. Shakespeare, but I certainly do know my own mind, and I do keep right on plugging along in the office and—Do you know the latest? Far as I can figure out, Ted's new bee is he'd like to be a movie actor and—And here I've told him a hundred times, if he'll go to college and law-school and make good, I'll set him up in business and—Verona just exactly as bad. Doesn't know what she wants. Well, well, come on! Aren't you ready yet? The girl rang the bell three minutes ago."

Before he followed his wife, Babbitt stood at the westernmost window of their room. This residential settlement, Floral Heights, was on a rise; and though the center of the city was three miles away—Zenith had between three and four hundred thousand inhabitants now—he could see the top of the Second National Tower, an Indiana limestone building of thirty-five stories.

Its shining walls rose against April sky to a simple cornice like a streak of white fire. Integrity was in the tower, and decision. It bore its strength lightly as a tall soldier. As Babbitt stared, the nervousness was soothed from his face, his slack chin lifted in reverence. All he articulated was "That's one lovely sight!" but he was inspired by the rhythm of the city; his love of it renewed. He beheld the tower as a temple-spire of the religion of business, a faith passionate, exalted, surpassing common men; and as he clumped down to breakfast he whistled the ballad "Oh, by gee, by gosh, by jingo" as though it were a hymn melancholy and noble.

Chapter 1 from *Babbitt* by Sinclair Lewis, copyright 1922 by Harcourt, Inc. and renewed 1950 by Sinclair Lewis, reprinted by permission of Harcourt, Inc.

19.3

LANGSTON HUGHES, "I, TOO" (1925)

Throughout the 1920s, a remarkable array of individuals profoundly changed American culture. The Harlem Renaissance was a highly influential literary movement. As thousands of southern blacks moved to New York City, most congregated in Harlem. Although many residents faced continuing poverty and racism, aspiring black artists, musicians, and writers encouraged one another's endeavors. White patrons sometimes provided financial assistance. Producing sophisticated examinations of African-American life, James Weldon Johnson, Countee Cullen, and others led the Harlem Renaissance. While they failed to draw a large contemporary black readership, they greatly affected future interpreters of African-American experiences. This poem by Langston Hughes (1902-1967) illustrates some of the artistic themes of the Harlem Renaissance. After gaining national attention in 1921 with his poem "The Negro Dreams of Rivers," Hughes became a prolific writer and respected social critic.

FOCUS QUESTIONS

1. What are the poem's themes?
2. To whom do you think Hughes is directing this poem?

, too, sing America.
I am the darker brother.
They send me to eat in the kitchen
When company comes,
But I laugh,
And eat well,
And grow strong.
Tomorrow,
I'll be at the table

When company comes.
Nobody'll dare
Say to me,
"Eat in the kitchen,"
Then.
Besides,
They'll see how beautiful I am
And be ashamed—
I, too, am America.

The Collected Poems of Langston Hughes by Langston Hughes, copyright © 1994 by The Estate of Langston Hughes. Used by permission of Alfred A. Knopf, a division of Random House, Inc.

19.4

THE SCOPES TRIAL (1925)

As the United States became a more modern and heterogeneous nation, some Americans clung tightly to their traditional views. While liberal Christians reconciled science and religion, fundamentalists believed in the literal interpretation of the Bible. Denouncing Darwin's theory of evolution as an assault on Christianity, they persuaded several southern states to outlaw the teaching of evolution in public schools. In 1925, the American Civil Liberties Union (ACLU) offered to defend any teacher willing to challenge such laws. John T. Scopes, a biology teacher in Tennessee, accepted the offer and read a passage from Darwin's writings to his class. He was arrested.

The Scopes trial became an international sensation. Scores of journalists descended on tiny Dayton, Tennessee and gave the "trial of the century" wide exposure. Hundreds of spectators jammed streets dotted with banners, lemonade stands, and even a chimpanzee show. Afraid that the courthouse floor would collapse under the weight of overflowing crowds, Judge John T. Raulston moved the proceedings outside. Clarence Darrow led the ACLU team defending Scopes while William Jennings Bryan assisted the prosecution. Although Scopes was found guilty and fined $100 (the case was later overruled on appeal), the trial was widely viewed as a victory for academic freedom. In this excerpt from the trial transcript, Darrow questions Bryan's religious beliefs and scientific knowledge.

FOCUS QUESTIONS

1. How would you describe the exchange between Darrow and Bryan?
2. Whose views do you find more persuasive? Why?
3. What does the tremendous public interest in the Scopes trial suggest about American society in the 1920s?
4. Should public school curricula include creationism in discussions of the theory of evolution? Explain your answer.

E xamination of W.J. Bryan by Clarence Darrow, of counsel for the defense:
Q—You have given considerable study to the Bible, haven't you, Mr. Bryan?

A—Yes, sir, I have tried to....

Q—You claim that everything in the Bible should be literally interpreted?

A—I believe everything in the Bible should be accepted as it is given there: some of the Bible is given illustratively. For instance: "Ye are the salt of the earth." I would not insist that man was actually salt, or that he had flesh of salt, but it is used in the sense of salt as saving God's people.

Q—But when you read that Jonah swallowed the whale—or that the whale swallowed Jonah—excuse me please—how do you literally interpret that?

A—When I read that a big fish swallowed Jonah—it does not say whale.

Q—That is my recollection of it. A big fish, and I believe it, and I believe in a God who can make a whale and can make a man and make both what He pleases.

Q—Now, you say, the big fish swallowed Jonah, and he there remained how long—three days—and then he spewed him upon the land. You believe that the big fish was made to swallow Jonah?

A—I am not prepared to say that; the Bible merely says it was done.

Q—You don't know whether it was the ordinary run of fish, or made for that purpose?

A—You may guess; you evolutionists guess.

Q—You are not prepared to say whether that fish was made especially to swallow a man or not?

A—The Bible doesn't say, so I am not prepared to say.

Q—But do you believe He made them—that He made such a fish and that it was big enough to swallow Jonah?

A—Yes, sir. Let me add: One miracle is just as easy to believe as another

Q—Just as hard?

A—It is hard to believe for you, but easy for me. A miracle is a thing performed beyond what man can perform. When you get within the realm of miracles; and it is just as easy to believe the miracle of Jonah as any other miracle in the Bible.

Q—Perfectly easy to believe that Jonah swallowed the whale?

A—If the Bible said so; the Bible doesn't make as extreme statements as evolutionists do.

Q—You believe the story of the flood to be a literal interpretation?

A—Yes, sir.

Q—When was that Flood?

A—I would not attempt to fix the date. The date is fixed, as suggested this morning.

Q—About 4004 B.C.?

A—That has been the estimate of a man that is accepted today. I would not say it is accurate.

Q—That estimate is printed in the Bible?

A—Everybody knows, at least, I think most of the people know, that was the estimate given.

Q—But what do you think that the Bible, itself says? Don't you know how it was arrived at?

A—I never made a calculation.

Q—A calculation from what?

A—I could not say.

Q—From the generations of man?

A—I would not want to say that.

Q—What do you think?

A—I do not think about things I don't think about.

Q—Do you think about things you do think about?

A—Well, sometimes.

(Laughter in the courtyard.)

Policeman—Let us have order.

Stewart—Your honor, he is perfectly able to take care of this, but we are attaining no evidence. This is not competent evidence.

Bryan—These gentlemen have not had much chance—they did not come here to try this case. They came here to try revealed religion. I am here to defend it and they can ask me any question they please.

The Court—All right.

(Applause from the courtyard.)

Darrow—Great applause from the bleachers.

Bryan—From those whom you call "Yokels."

Darrow—I have never called them yokels.

Bryan—That is the ignorance of Tennessee, the bigotry.

Darrow—You mean who are applauding you? (Applause.)

Bryan—Those are the people whom you insult.

Darrow—You insult every man of science and learning in the world because he does believe in your fool religion.

The Court—I will not stand for that.

Darrow—For what he is doing?

The Court—I am talking to both of you....

Q—Wait until you get to me. Do you know anything about how many people there were in Egypt 3,500 years ago, or how many people there were in China 5,000 years ago?

A—No.

Q—Have you ever tried to find out?

A—No, sir. You are the first man I ever heard of who has been in interested in it. (Laughter.)

Q—Mr. Bryan, am I the first man you ever heard of who has been interested in the age of human societies and primitive man?

A—You are the first man I ever heard speak of the number of people at those different periods.

Q—Where have you lived all your life?

A—Not near you. (Laughter and applause.)

Q—Nor near anybody of learning?

A—Oh, don't assume you know it all.

Q—Do you know there are thousands of books in our libraries on all those subjects I have been asking you about?

A—I couldn't say, but I will take your word for it....

Q—Would you say that the earth was only 4,000 years old?

A—Oh, no; I think it is much older than that.

Q—How much?

A—I couldn't say.

Q—Do you say whether the Bible itself says it is older than that?

A—I don't think it is older or not.

Q—Do you think the earth was made in six days?

A—Not six days of twenty-four hours.

Q—Doesn't it say so?

A—No, sir....

The Court—Are you about through, Mr. Darrow?

Darrow—I want to ask a few more questions about the creation.... Of course, I believe I will make myself clearer. Of course, it is incompetent testimony before the jury. The only reason I am allowing this to go in at all is that they may have it in the appellate court as showing what the affidavit would be.

Bryan—The reason I am answering is not for the benefit of the superior court. It is to keep these gentlemen from saying I was afraid to meet them and let them question me, and I want the Christian world to know that any atheist, agnostic, unbeliever, can question me anytime as to my belief in God, and I will answer him.

Darrow—I want to take an exception to this conduct of this witness. He may be very popular down here in the hills....

Bryan—Your honor, they have not asked a question legally and the only reason they have asked any question is for the purpose, as the question about Jonah was asked, for a chance to give this agnostic an opportunity to criticize a believer in the world of God; and I answered the question in order to shut his mouth so that he cannot go out and tell his atheistic friends that I would not answer his questions. That is the only reason, no more reason in the world....

Darrow—Mr. Bryan, do you believe that the first woman was Eve?

A—Yes.

Q—Do you believe she was literally made out of Adams's rib?

A—I do.

Q—Did you ever discover where Cain got his wife?

A—No, sir; I leave the agnostics to hunt for her....

Q—The Bible says he got one, doesn't it? Were there other people on the earth at that time?

A—I cannot say.

Q—You cannot say. Did that ever enter your consideration?

A—Never bothered me....

Q—...Does the statement, "The morning and the evening were the first day," and "The morning and the evening were the second day," mean anything to you?

A—I do not think it necessarily means a twenty-four-hour day.

Q—You do not?

A—No....

Q—Then, when the Bible said, for instance, "and God called the firmament heaven. And the evening and the morning were the second day," that does not necessarily mean twenty-four hours?

A—I do not think it necessarily does....

Q—You think those were not literal days?

A—I do not think they were twenty-four-hour days....

Q—You do not think that ?

A—No. But I think it would be just as easy for the kind of God we believe in to make the earth in six days as in six years or in 6,000,000 years or in 600,000,000 years. I do not think it important whether we believe one or the other....

Bryan—Your Honor, I think I can shorten this testimony. The only purpose Mr. Darrow has is to slur at the Bible, but I will answer his question. I will answer it all at once, and I have no objection in the world, I want the world to know that this man, who does not believe in a God, is trying to use a court in Tennesseee—

Darrow—I object to that.

Bryan—(Continuing) to slur at it, and while it will require time, I am willing to take it.

Darrow—I object to your statement. I am exempting you on your fool ideas that no intelligent Christian on earth believes.

The Court—Court is adjourned until 9 o'clock tomorrow morning.

The Scopes Trial, http://www.law.umkc.edu/faculty/projects/ftrials/scopes/day7.htm.

19.5

━━━━━━━━━━━━━━━━━━━━━━━━━━━━━

COLLEGE STUDENTS ON "PETTING" (1925)

World War I and its turbulent aftermath greatly destabilized U.S. society. Many Americans, especially younger ones, questioned traditional values and morality. Capitalizing on the era's prosperity, they threw wild parties, listened to jazz, and drank bootleg liquor. Embracing the theories of Sigmund Freud, they discussed sex publicly. Despite widespread disapproval of premarital sexual exploration, many engaged in "petting." Revising older notions of courtship indicating a commitment to marriage, young people began "dating," a less formal ritual where marriage was not always the expected outcome. Although double standards on sexual behavior still existed, women enjoyed freer erotic expression. They wore more revealing clothing and cosmetics (formerly associated with prostitutes), cut their hair, drank alcohol in public, and smoked. The "flapper" became the cultural ideal of sophisticated womanhood.

In this passage, a reporter discusses "petting" with several female college students.

Focus Questions

1. How do these young women describe "petting" to the author? Do they equate "petting" with sexual immorality? Explain your answers.
2. What is the author's opinion of "petting"?
3. Compare sexual behavior among today's college students to those of the 1920s.

L ast summer I was at a student conference of young women comprised of about eight hundred college girls from the middle western states. The subject of petting was very much on their minds, both as to what attitude they should take toward it with the younger girls, (being upperclassmen themselves) and also how much renunciation of this pleasurable pastime was required of them. If I recall correctly, two entire mornings were devoted to discussing the matter, two evenings, and another overflow meeting....

Before the conference I made it my business to talk to as many college girls as possible. I consulted as many, both in groups and privately, as I had time for at the conference. And since it is all to be repeated in another state this summer, I have been doing so, when opportunity offered, ever since....

One fact is evident, that whether or not they pet, they hesitate to have anyone believe that they do not. It is distinctly the mores of the time to be considered as ardently sought after, and as not too priggish to respond. As one girl said—I don't particularly care to be kissed by some of the fellows I know, but I'd let them do it any time rather than think I wouldn't dare. As a matter of fact, there are lots of fellows I don't kiss. It's the very young kids that never miss a chance."

That petting should lead to actual illicit relations between the petters was not advised nor countenanced among the girls with whom I discussed it. They drew the line quite sharply. That it often did so lead, they admitted, but they were not ready to allow that there were any more of such affairs than there had always been. School and college scandals, with their sudden departures and hasty marriages, have always existed to some extent, and they still do. But only accurate statistics hard to arrive at, can prove whether or not the sex carelessness of the present day extends to an increase of sex immorality....

I sat with one pleasant college Amazon, a total stranger, beside a fountain in the park, while she asked if I saw any harm in her kissing a young man whom she liked, but whom she did not want to marry. "It's terribly exciting. We get such a thrill. I think it is natural to want nice men to kiss you, so why not do what is natural'" There was no embarrassment in her manner. Her eyes and her conscience were equally untroubled. I felt as if a girl from the Parthenon frieze had stepped down to ask if she might not sport in the glade with a handsome faun. Why not indeed? Only an equally direct forcing of twentieth century science on primitive simplicity could bring us even to the same level in our conversation, and at that, the stigma of impropriety seemed to fall on me, rather than on her.

Eleanor Rowland Wembridge, "Petting and the Campus," *Survey* (July 1, 1925).

19.6

HIRAM EVANS, "THE KLAN'S FIGHT FOR AMERICANISM" (1926)

Inspired by Thomas Dixon's novel The Clansman *and D.W. Griffith's film* The Birth of a Nation *(1915), William J. Simmons resurrected the Ku Klux Klan. While his efforts languished at first, the decision to hire public relations experts led to explosive growth in Klan membership. Tailoring its messages to suit local pre-judices, the Klan attacked several groups including blacks, immigrants, political radicals, Catholics, and Jews. In an age marked by increasing ethnic diversity and political unrest, as many as eight million people joined the Klan as a way to preserve white supremacy and traditional values. Throughout the 1920s, the Klan wielded tremendous political power and dominated dozens of state and local legislative bodies. The organization also reaped huge profits from the sales of memberships, memorabilia, and costumes. But the Klan's success proved short-lived after a series of sex scandals destroyed the Klan's image. In this 1926 article from the respected* North American Review, *Hiram Evans, Simmons's successor as Imperial Wizard, explains the Klan's goals.*

FOCUS QUESTIONS

1. What are the major goals and objectives of the Ku Klux Klan?
2. Which groups does the KKK find most objectionable?
3. Who might have found the Klan's message attractive and why?
4. Was the Klan successful in implementing its agenda? Explain your answer.

The Ku Klux Klan, in short, is an organization which gives expression, direction and purpose to the most vital instincts, hopes and resentments of the old stock Americans, provides them with leadership, and is enlisting and preparing them for militant, constructive action toward fulfilling their racial and national destiny....

There are three of these great racial instincts, vital cements in both the historic and the present attempts to build an America which shall fulfill the aspirations and justify the heroism of the men who made the nation. These are the instincts of loyalty to the white race, to the traditions of America, and to the spirit of Protestantism, which has been an essential part of Americanism ever since the days of Roanoke and Plymouth Rock. They are condensed into the Klan slogan: "Native, white, Protestant supremacy."

First in the Klansman's mind is patriotism—America for Americans. He believes religiously that a betrayal of Americanism or the American race is treason to the most sacred of trusts, a trust from his fathers and a trust from God. He believes, too, that Americanism can only be achieved if the pioneer stock is kept pure....

Americanism, to the Klansman, is a thing of the spirit, a purpose and a point of view, that can only come through instinctive racial understanding. It has, to be sure, certain deemed principles, but he does not believe that many aliens understand those principles, even when they use our words in talking about them. Democracy is one, fair dealing, impartial justice, equal opportunity, religious liberty, independence, self-reliance, courage, endurance, acceptance of individual responsibility as well as individual rewards for effort, willingness to sacrifice for the good of his family, his nation and his race before anything else but God, dependence on enlightened conscience for guidance, the right to unhampered development—these are fundamental. But within the bounds they fix there must be the utmost freedom, tolerance, liberalism. In short, the Klansman believes in the greatest possible diversity and individualism within the limits of the American spirit. But he believes also that few aliens can understand that spirit, that fewer try to, and that there must be resistance, intolerance even, toward anything that threatens it, or the fundamental national unity based upon it.

The second word in the Klansman's trilogy is "white." The white race must be supreme, not only in America but in the world. This is equally undebatable, except on the ground that the races might live together, each with full regard for the rights and interests of others, and that those rights and interests would never conflict. Such an idea, of course, is absurd; the colored races today, such as Japan, are clamoring not for equality but for their supremacy.... The world has been so made that each race must fight for its life, must conquer, accept slavery or die. The Klansman believes that the whites will not become slaves, and he does not intend to die before his time.

Moreover, the future of progress and civilization depends on the continued supremacy of the white race.... Until the whites falter, or some colored civilization has a miracle of awakening, there is not a single colored stock that can claim even equality with the white; much less supremacy.

The third of the Klan principles is that Protestantism must be supreme; that Rome shall not rule America. The Klansman believes this not merely because he is a Protestant, nor even because the Colonies that are now our nation were settled for the purpose of wresting America from the control of Rome and establishing a land of free conscience. He believes it also because Protestantism is an essential part of Americanism; without it America could never have been created and without it she cannot go forward. Roman rule would kill it.

Protestantism contains more than religion. It is the expression in religion of the same spirit of independence, self-reliance and freedom which are the highest achievements of the Nordic race....

Let it be clear what is meant by "supremacy." It is nothing more than power of control, under just laws. It is not imperialism, far less is it autocracy or even aristocracy of a race or stock of men. What it does mean is that we insist on our inherited right to insure our own safety, individually and as a race, to secure the future of our children, to maintain and develop our racial heritage in our own, white, Protestant, American way, without interference....

And we deny that either bigotry or prejudice enters into our intolerance or our narrowness. We are intolerant of everything that strikes at the foundations of our race, our country or our freedom of worship. We are narrowly opposed to the use of anything alien—race, loyalty to any foreign power or to any religion whatever—as a means to win political power.... This is our intolerance; based on the sound instincts which have saved us many times from the follies of the intellectuals. We admit it. More and worse, we are proud of it....

The Negro, the Klan considers a special duty and problem of the white American. He is among us through no wish of his; we owe it him and to ourselves to give him full protection and opportunity. But his limitations are evident; we will not permit him to gain sufficient power to control our civilization. Neither will we delude him with promises of social equality which we know can never be realized. The Klan looks forward to the day when the Negro problem will have been saved on some much saner basis than miscegenation, and when every State will enforce laws making any sex relations between a white and a colored person a crime.

For the alien in general we have sympathy, opportunity, justice, but no permanent welcome unless he becomes truly American. It is our duty to see that he has every chance for this, and we shall be glad to accept him if he does. We hold no rancor against him; his race, instincts, training, mentality and whole outlook of life are usually widely different from ours. We cannot blame him if he adheres to them and attempts to convert us to them, even by force. But we must see that he can never succeed....

Hiram Wesley Evans, "The Klan's Fight for Americanism," *North American Review* 223 (March-April-May 1926): 33-61.

19.7

FIORELLO LA GUARDIA ON PROHIBITION (1926)

In 1919, the United States ratified the Eighteenth Amendment banning the sale, manufacture, and transportation of alcoholic beverages. A response to social problems stemming from alcohol abuse as well as an attempt to control ethnic and racial minorities, prohibition initially worked well. Bars, distilleries, and wineries closed. Arrests for drunkenness declined. But Americans quickly exploited loopholes that permitted the sale of alcohol for medicinal or religious purposes and the production of alcohol for private consumption. They also flocked to illicit saloons and speakeasies run by organized criminals. Gangsters like Al Capone amassed huge fortunes in the illicit alcohol trade. Poorly funded and understaffed law enforcement agencies proved unable or unwilling to enforce prohibition laws. In 1933, the nation acknowledged the policy's failure by adopting the Twenty-First

Amendment repealing federal prohibition. The regulation of alcohol returned to state and local authorities.

In this reading, Fiorello La Guardia (1882-1947), a Republican congressman from New York, testifies before the Senate Judiciary Committee. La Guardia later served three terms as the mayor of New York.

FOCUS QUESTIONS

1. What is La Guardia's opinion of prohibition?
2. What evidence does he offer to support his arguments?
3. How would an advocate of prohibition respond to La Guardia's claims?
4. What is your opinion of prohibition?
5. What are some present-day laws that are similar to prohibition? Do they work better than prohibition did? Why or why not?

I t is impossible to tell whether prohibition is a good thing or a bad thing. It has never been enforced in this county.

There may not be as much liquor in quantity consumed today as there was before prohibition, but there is just as much alcohol.

At least 1,000,000 quarts of liquor is consumed each day in the United States. In my opinion such an enormous traffic in liquor could not be carried on without the knowledge, if not the connivance, of the officials entrusted with the enforcement of the law.

I am for temperance; that is why I am for modification.

I believe that the percentage of whisky drinkers in the United States now is greater than in any other country of the world. Prohibition is responsible for that....

At least $1,000,000,000 a year is lost to the National Government and the several states and counties in excise taxes. The liquor traffic is going on just the same. This amount goes into the pockets of bootleggers and into the pockets of the public officials in the shape of graft....

I will concede that the saloon was odious, but now we have delicatessen stores, pool rooms, drug stores, millinery shops, private parlors, and 57 other varieties of speakeasies selling liquor and flourishing.

I have heard of $2,000 a year prohibition agents who run their own cars with liveried chauffeurs.

It is common talk in my part of the country that from $7.50 to $12 a case is paid in graft from the time the liquor leaves the 12-mile limit until it reaches the ultimate consumer. There seems to be a varying market price for this service created by the degree of vigilance or the degree of greed of the public officials in charge.

It is my calculation that at least $1,000,000 a day is paid in graft and corruption to Federal, state, and local officers. Such a condition is not only intolerable, but it is demoralizing and dangerous to organized government.

The Prohibition Enforcement Unit has entirely broken down. It is discredited; it has become a joke. Liquor is sold in every large city....

Only a few days ago I charged on the floor of the House that 350 cases of liquor of a seizure of 1,500 made by Federal officials and stored in the Federal building at Indianapolis, Ind., had been removed. The Department of Justice, under date of April 9, 1926, confirmed my charge. The Attorney General admits that since this liquor was in the possession of the Federal authorities in the Federal building at Indianapolis, 330 cases are missing. If bootleggers can enter Federal buildings to get liquor, the rest can be easily imagined....

I have been in public office for a great many years. I have had the opportunity to observe first the making of the present prohibition laws as a member of Congress, and later as president of the Board of Aldermen of the largest city in this country its attempted enforcement. In order to enforce prohibition in New York City I estimated at the time would require a police force of 250,000 men and a force of 200,000 men to police the police.

Hearings before the Subcommittee of the Committee on the Judiciary, United States Senate, Sixty-ninth Congress, First Session, on...Bills to Amend the National Prohibition Act, I, 649-51.

19.8

———————————◼———————————

THE SUPREME COURT AND EUGENICS (1927)

In the late nineteenth century, a number of scientists experimented with eugenics, the altering of plant or animal characteristics through controlled reproduction. Some eugenicists applied their theories to people, advocating sterilization of "unfit" groups and restriction of "inferior" immigrants. By 1914, twelve states had passed laws authorizing the involuntary sterilization of criminals, epileptics, the insane, the mentally deficient, and "socially inadequate" people, supported with public funds. Such laws gained popularity through the 1920s. Although the Holocaust widely discredited eugenics, isolated cases of involuntary sterilization continued in many states until the 1970s. By that time, an estimated 60,000 Americans had been sterilized without their consent. In 1927, Carrie Buck challenged a Virginia law permitting her sterilization. Her case reached the U.S. Supreme Court. In this selection, Justice Oliver Wendell Holmes delivers the Court's majority opinion.

———————————◼———————————

FOCUS QUESTIONS

1. Who was Carrie Buck? Why did she file this lawsuit?
2. What did the Supreme Court rule in *Buck v. Bell*?

3. What does the Court's ruling suggest about American society in the 1920s?

4. What is your opinion of this decision? Explain your answer.

 r. Justice HOLMES delivered the opinion of the Court.

This is a writ of error to review a judgment of the Supreme Court of Appeals of the State of Virginia, affirming a judgment of the Circuit Court of Amherst County, by which the defendant in error, the superintendent of the State Colony for Epileptics and Feeble Minded, was ordered to perform the operation of salpingectomy [tubal ligation] upon Carrie Buck, the plaintiff in error, for the purpose of making her sterile. The case comes here upon the contention that the statute authorizing the judgment is void under the Fourteenth Amendment as denying to the plaintiff in error due process of law and the equal protection of the laws.

Carrie Buck is a feeble-minded white woman who was committed to the State Colony above mentioned in due form. She is the daughter of a feeble-minded mother in the same institution, and the mother of an illegitimate feeble-minded child. She was eighteen years old at the time of the trial of her case in the Circuit Court in the latter part of 1924. An Act of Virginia approved March 20, 1924 recites that the health of the patient and the welfare of society may be promoted in certain cases by the sterilization of mental defectives, under careful safeguard, etc.; that the sterilization may be effected in males by vasectomy and in females by salpingectomy, without serious pain or substantial danger to life; that the Commonwealth is supporting in various institutions many defective persons who if now discharged would become a menace but if incapable of procreating might be discharged with safety and become self-supporting with benefit to themselves and to society; and that experience has shown that heredity plays an important part in the transmission of insanity, imbecility, etc. The statute then enacts that whenever the superintendent of certain institutions including the above-named State Colony shall be of opinion that it is for the best interest of the patients and of society that an inmate under his care should be sexually sterilized, he may have the operation performed upon any patient afflicted with hereditary forms of insanity, imbecility, etc., on complying with the very careful provisions by which the act protects the patients from possible abuse....

There can be no doubt that so far as procedure is concerned the rights of the patient are most carefully considered, and as every step in this case was taken in scrupulous compliance with the statute and after months of observation, there is no doubt that in that respect the plaintiff in error has had due process at law.

The attack is not upon the procedure but upon the substantive law. It seems to be contended that in no circumstances could such an order be justified. It certainly is contended that the order cannot be justified upon the existing grounds. The judgment finds the facts that have been recited and that Carrie Buck 'is the probable potential parent of socially inadequate offspring, likewise afflicted, that she may be sexually sterilized without detriment to her general health and that her welfare and that of society will be promoted by her sterilization,' and thereupon makes the order. In view of the general declarations of the Legislature and the specific findings of the Court obviously we cannot say as matter of law that the grounds do not exist, and if they exist they justify the result. We have seen more than once that the public welfare may call upon the best citizens for their lives. It would be strange if it could not call upon those who already sap the strength of the State for these lesser sacrifices, often not felt to be such by those concerned, in order to prevent our being swamped with incompetence. It is better for all the world, if instead of waiting to execute degenerate offspring for crime, or to let them starve for their imbecility, society can prevent those who are manifestly unfit from continuing their kind. The principle that sustains compulsory vaccination is broad enough to cover cutting the Fallopian tubes. Three generations of imbeciles are enough.

But, it is said, however it might be if this reasoning were applied generally, it fails when it is confined to the small number who are in the institutions named and is not applied to the multitudes outside. It is the usual last resort of constitutional arguments to point out shortcomings of this sort. But the answer is that the law does all that is needed when it does all that it can, indicates a policy, applies it to all within the lines, and seeks to bring within the lines all similarly situated so far and so fast as its means allow. Of course so far as the operations enable those who otherwise must be kept confined to be returned to the world, and thus open the asylum to others, the equality aimed at will be more nearly reached.

U.S. Supreme Court, *Buck v. Bell*, 274 U.S. 200 (1927).

SECONDARY SOURCE

——————◼——————

WARREN SUSMAN, "CULTURE HEROES: FORD, BARTON, RUTH"

Throughout the 1920s, mass production, mass communication, and mass entertainment greatly changed American life. The era witnessed shifts in work, diet, fashion, travel, and culture. Widely circulated magazines, radio programs, and motion pictures reached national audiences. Advertisers, journalists, and performers immediately recognized the power of mass media. Never before could so many people be exposed to the same products, the same news stories, and the same celebrities. In this excerpt, the late Warren Susman, a highly influential cultural historian, explores these developments. Through biographical sketches of advertising executive Bruce Barton, automaker Henry Ford, and baseball player Babe Ruth, he examines the rise of consumerism in the United States and its impact on American culture.

Go to your *Speaking of America* CD-ROM to read "Culture Heroes: Ford, Barton, Ruth."

FOCUS QUESTIONS

1. How was American society changing in the 1920s? How do the lives of Bruce Barton, Henry Ford, and Babe Ruth illustrate these trends?
2. What were some of the techniques that Barton used? Do advertisers still use these methods?
3. How did Henry Ford change the automobile industry?
4. Describe Ford's attitudes toward workers. What methods did he use to attract, retain, and monitor laborers?
5. How and why did Ford's business practices change over time?
6. According to Susman, what accounts for the increasing popularity of sports in the 1920s?
7. When Susman describes Babe Ruth as "an ideal hero for the world of consumption," what does he mean?

AMERICAN JOURNEY ONLINE

http://ajaccesss.wadsworth.com [†]

About the Sacco and Vanzetti Case
— In World War I and the Jazz Age
   Documents
   • John Dos Passos, Excerpt from Facing the Chair (1927)
   • Bartolomeo Vanzetti, Vanzetti's Last Statement (1927)
   Images
   • Sacco and Vanzetti
— In The Immigrant Experience
   Documents
   • Louis Bernheimer, The Trial of Sacco and Vanzetti (1927)
— In Civil Rights in the United States
   Videos
   • Protests of Sentencing of Sacco and Vanzetti (1927)

About the Scopes Trial
— In Civil Rights in the United States
   Images
   • Scopes Evolution Trial (1925)

[†] Enter password, choose the Archive indicated above, click on Contents, choose •Documents, •Images, or •Multimedia, and click on the title of the item.

Videos
- Scopes (Monkey) Trial (1925)
— In <u>Civil Rights in the United States</u>
Images
- Scopes Evolution Trial (1925)
Videos
- Scopes (Monkey) Trial (1925)
— In <u>World War I and the Jazz Age</u>
Documents
- William Jennings Bryan, Excerpt from Undelivered Address in the Scopes Trial (1925)
Images
- William Jennings Bryan
- Bryan and Darrow at the Scopes Trial (1925)

About the Ku Klux Klan
— In <u>World War I and the Jazz Age</u>
Images
- Klanswomen in the 1920s (1924)
- David C. Stephenson (1925)
- Klan Marchers in Washington, D.C. (1926)
Videos
- Ku Klux Klan in the 1920s (1925)
— In <u>Civil Rights in the United States</u>
Images
- Ku Klux Klan Convention in Kokomo, Indiana (1928)

About Prohibition
— In <u>World War I and the Jazz Age</u>
Images
- Enforcing Prohibition (1923)
— In <u>The Great Depression and the New Deal</u>
Images
- Repeal the 18th Amendment (circa 1927)

About Domestic Politics
— In <u>World War I and the Jazz Age</u>
Images
- Secretary of Commerce Herbert Hoover (1922)
- Robert S. Brookings
- President Calvin S. Coolidge
— In <u>The Great Depression and the New Deal</u>
Images
- Calvin Coolidge (circa 1926)

About Business and Economics
— In <u>World War I and the Jazz Age</u>
  Documents
  • Herbert Hoover, Opening Address to the President's Conference on Unemployment (1921)
  • Klein, Unemployment in the Depression of 1920-1921 (1923)
  • Edward A. Filene, Business as the Agent of Social Progress (1926)
  • Henry S. Dennison, Management (1929)
  • George Soule, The New Era Economy (1929)
  Images
  • Charles E. Merriam
  • Henry Ford
  • Edward A. Filene (1929)

About Labor
— In <u>World War I and the Jazz Age</u>
  Documents
  • Thorstein Veblen, Excerpt from *The Engineers and the Price System* (1921)
  • James Lord, Excerpt from The Open Shop (1921)
  • John L. Lewis, Excerpt from *The Miner's Fight for American Standards* (1925)
  • David J. Goldberg, Labor in the New Era (1999)
  Images
  • American Workers in the 1920s
  • American Federation of Labor Meeting
  • William Green (1926)

About Advertising and Consumption
— In <u>World War I and the Jazz Age</u>
  Documents
  • Samuel Strauss, Things are in the Saddle (1924)
  • Earnest Elmo Caulkins, Mass Advertising in the 1920s (1928)
  • Jackson Lears, The Significance of Advertising (1994)
  Images
  • Lucky Strike Ad (1928)

About Agriculture
— In <u>World War I and the Jazz Age</u>
  Documents
  • U.S. Congress, The McNary-Haugen Bill of 1927 Age
  • Calvin Coolidge, Veto of the 1927 McNary-Haugen Bill
  • David B. Danborn, Excerpt from *Born in the Country* (1995)
  Images
  • Farming in the 1920s
  • Gilbert N. Haugen (1932)

About Law
— In The Constitution and Supreme Court
   Documents
   • Oliver Wendell Holmes, *Missouri v. Holland* (1920)
   • Edward Terry Sanford, *Gitlow v. New York* (1925)
— In Civil Rights in the United States
   Documents
   • U.S. Supreme Court, *Olmstead v. United States* (1928)

About Military Affairs
— In Civil Rights in the United States
   Images
   • Billy Mitchell Appearing at Naval Investigation (1925)

About Education
— In World War I and the Jazz Age
   Documents
   • Clarence Britten, Excerpt from School and College Life (1922)
   • U.S. Bureau of the Census, High School Enrollment and Graduation, 1890-1930 (1975)
   • U.S. Bureau of the Census, College Enrollment and Degrees Conferred, 1890-1930 (1975)

About Immigration
— In The Immigrant Experience
   Documents
   • Kenneth L. Roberts, Excerpt of *Why Europe Leaves Home* (1920)
   • U.S. Supreme Court, *Takao Ozawa v. United States* (1922)
   • U.S. Congress, Reed-Johnson Immigration Act of 1924
— In World War I and the Jazz Age
   Images
   • Lewis W. Hine, Immigrant Life through the Camera Eye (1920)
   • *The Dearborn Independent*
— In Civil Rights in the United States
   Documents
   • U.S. Congress, Debate on Immigration (1921)
— In The Asian-American Experience
   Documents
   • U.S. Congress, Excerpt of the Cable Act (1922)
   • U.S. Congress, Immigration Act of 1924

About African-Americans
— In World War I and the Jazz Age
   Documents
   • Claude A. Barnett, Black Gains in Chicago in the 1920s (1929)

Images
- Marcus Garvey (1920)

Videos
- Blacks in Postwar America

— In <u>The African-American Experience</u>

Documents
- A Negro and a Mob (1920)
- Excerpt from the Universal Negro Catechism (1920)
- Images
- James Robert Pres, A Negro Enterprise (circa 1920)
- Aaron Douglas, Jr., The Crisis (1929)

— In <u>Civil Rights in the United States</u>

Images
- Image with Audio Commentary—NAACP Protests Lynching (1922)

About Asian-Americans

— In <u>The Asian-American Experience</u>

Documents
- Angeles Monrayo Raymundo, Excerpts of the Diary of Angeles Monrayo Raymundo (1924)

About Women

— In <u>World War I and the Jazz Age</u>

Documents
- Margaret Sanger, Excerpt from Women and the New Race (1920)
- Crystal Eastman, A New Woman Remembers Her Past (1927)
- Emily Newell Blair, Excerpt from *Why I am Discouraged about Women in Politics* (1931)

Images
- Florence Kelley (1925)

— In <u>Civil Rights in the United States</u>

Images
- Nellie Ross, Suffragette

— In <u>Women in America</u>

Images
- Nellie Tayloe Ross and William B. Ross (circa 1922)
- Mary Elisa McDowell (circa 1926)

About Youth

— In <u>World War I and the Jazz Age</u>

Documents
- John F. Carter, Jr., Excerpt from *These Wild Young People* (1920)
- Frederick Lewis Allen, *The Revolution in Manners and Morals* (1931)
- Lizabeth Cohen, Excerpt from *Making a New Deal* (1990)

— In <u>The Great Depression and the New Deal</u>
Images
- John Neld, Jr., Teaching Old Dogs New Tricks (1926)

About Culture
— In <u>World War I and the Jazz Age</u>
Documents
- Van Wyck Brooks, The Literary Life (1922)
- Samuel Strauss, Things Are in the Saddle (1924)
- Arthur A. Schomberg, The Negro Digs Up His Past (1925)
- Alain Locke, The New Negro (1925)
- H.L. Mencken, Excerpt from *On Being an American* (1927)
- Sinclair Lewis, The American Fear of Literature (1930)
- Malcolm Cowley, The Revolt Against Gentility (1937)
- Roderick Nash, Sports Heroes (1970)

Images
- F. Scott Fitzgerald
- Arthur A. Schomberg
- Eugene O'Neill
- Ernest Hemingway
- Langston Hughes (1931)

Videos
- The Charleston
- Jazz-Music of the People
- Lindbergh's Welcome Home in New York City (1927)

— In <u>The African-American Experience</u>
Documents
- Document with Audio—Ma Rainey (1932)

Images
- Aaron Douglas, Jr., *Power Plant, Harlem* (circa 1920)
- Joel A. Rogers, Jazz at Home (1925)

— In <u>The Great Depression and the New Deal</u>
Images
- Babe Ruth (circa 1930)
- Bessie Smith (circa 1933)

THE GREAT DEPRESSION, THE NEW DEAL

When Herbert Hoover won the presidency in 1928, he was one of the most admired men in the United States. Born in Iowa to a devout Quaker family, he graduated from Stanford University and became a fabulously successful mining engineer. His achievements as a wartime food administrator and secretary of commerce were widely praised. With his humanitarian ethic and advocacy of voluntary cooperation between business and government, he appeared poised for a successful term. Within months, however, the onset of the Great Depression would overwhelm Hoover's presidency and shatter his sterling reputation.

Throughout the 1920s, stock prices had risen steadily. But many of the nine million Americans "playing the market" were buying stocks with money borrowed from brokers. With almost no regulation of trading practices, rampant speculation ensued. The Federal Reserve Board searched in vain for a way to halt the frenzy. In October 1929, the stock market began to implode. Prices plummeted in waves of panic buying and selling. By mid-November, stocks had lost $30 billion of their value.

The Great Crash was only one cause of the depression that soon gripped the world. The prosperity of the 1920s masked major structural weaknesses in the American economy. The gap between rich and poor was expanding. Important sectors including agriculture, automobiles, mining, and textiles were struggling. Devastation from World War I, repayment of war debts, and imbalances of trade paralyzed foreign economic systems.

The crisis had sweeping ramifications for Americans. By 1933, the unemployment rate hit 25 percent. Millions lost their savings, homes, and farms. Many suffered from malnutrition and inadequate health care. Marriage and birth rates declined. Although families and neighbors aided one another, the hardships exacted an incalculable toll on the national psyche.

Hoover reacted cautiously to the Great Depression. Consistent with his philosophy of governance, he opposed public welfare programs and federal intervention in the economy. Instead, he convinced business leaders to protect jobs and wages. As the crisis intensified, these voluntary measures failed and Hoover reluctantly instituted federal relief policies. He insisted, however, that the government maintain a balanced budget and even called for a tax increase.

Many Americans mistook Hoover's prudence for indifference and blamed him for their suffering. The administration's aggressive response to the 1932 Bonus March exacerbated public disdain for Hoover. As the election neared, the Republicans only feebly endorsed the unpopular president.

The Democrats seized the opportunity to regain the White House. Nominating Franklin D. Roosevelt, the governor of New York, they offered a platform promising industrial recovery, farm relief, and public assistance to the elderly, unemployed, and disabled. When FDR won in a landslide, he used his strong personality to calm the nation and generate support for his "new deal for the American people."

The New Deal had three phases. The first, called the 100 Days, occurred between March and June 1933. Congress passed fifteen major laws redressing the banking crisis, creating public works programs, assisting farmers, and fostering collaboration among government, business, and labor. Despite this legislation, the Depression continued. In 1935, facing criticism from the right and the left, Roosevelt proposed a second series of initiatives including Social Security, the Works Progress Administration, and the National Labor Relations Act. In paying for these programs, the government incurred huge budget deficits. Although Roosevelt won an unprecedented third term, opposition to the New Deal escalated. The Supreme Court struck down the Agricultural Adjustment Act and the National Recovery Act. Congressional conservatives blocked relief programs. In response, FDR tried to resurrect the New Deal and mounted an ill-conceived effort to "pack" the Supreme Court. Although the courts and Congress retreated from their assault on Roosevelt's programs, the Depression persisted. While the New Deal helped to blunt the worst effects of the economic crisis, it would take World War II to jolt the nation into financial recovery.

The Great Depression and the New Deal had mixed effects on American society. Union membership soared as the government became more favorable to organized labor. By 1941, over eight million workers belonged to unions. However, three-quarters of non-farm laborers remained unorganized. While women and minorities benefited from some New Deal programs, they also faced continued job discrimination. African Americans and Latinos fought persistent racism and poverty. American Indians attempted to regain lost lands and to preserve tribal culture.

The cultural mood swung from sharp pessimism to joyous celebration. While radio alerted Americans to ominous developments in international relations and national economic problems, it also entertained them with dramas, skits, and soap operas. Movie audiences saw realistic examinations of social issues as well as escapist musicals, comedies, and animation. Early in the decade, authors like James Farrell, John Dos Passos, and Clifford Odets challenged the premises of capitalist society. But the later 1930s marked a shift in tone. As the rise of fascism abroad portended another world war, authors and musicians such as Thornton Wilder, William Saroyan, and Aaron Copeland celebrated American life. With grave threats facing the United States, Americans prepared to defend their values and institutions.

20.1

HERBERT HOOVER, "AMERICAN INDIVIDUALISM" (1928)

Prior to winning the Presidency in 1928, Herbert Hoover (1874-1964) en-
joyed great professional success. Born near West Branch, Iowa and raised a
Quaker, Hoover graduated from Stanford University in 1895 with a degree in
geology. His skills as a mining engineer made him a multi-millionaire. In 1914,
President Woodrow Wilson appointed Hoover the national food administrator.
Hoover's efforts in organizing relief efforts and food production drew wide
acclaim. From 1921 to 1928, Hoover served as secretary of commerce for
Presidents Warren G. Harding and Calvin Coolidge. Hoover promoted foreign
trade, collective bargaining for workers, and government regulation of new
industries such as radio and aviation. When Coolidge decided not to run for
reelection, the Republican Party selected Hoover to challenge New York Governor
Al Smith, the Democratic nominee. In this excerpt from his final campaign speech,
Hoover explains his views on government and individual character.

FOCUS QUESTIONS

1. How does Hoover distinguish between the European and American economies?
2. What does he believe makes the American economic system successful?
3. How does Hoover claim that Republicans and Democrats differ in their
   approaches to the nation's problems?
4. What does Hoover believe is the proper role of government in American
   society? Do you share Hoover's views? Explain your answer.

hen the war closed, the most vital of all issues both in our own country
and throughout the world was whether governments should continue
their wartime ownership and operation of many instrumentalities of
production and distribution. We were challenged with a peace-time choice
between the American system of rugged individualism and a European philosophy
of diametrically opposed doctrines—doctrines of paternalism and state socialism.
The acceptance of these ideas would have meant the destruction of self-
government through centralization of government: It would have meant the
undermining of the individual initiative and enterprise through which our people
have grown to unparalleled greatness.

The Republican Party from the beginning resolutely turned its face away from
these ideas and these war practices.... When the Republican Party came into full
power it went at once back to our fundamental conception of the state and the rights
and responsibilities of the individual. Thereby it restored confidence and hope in

the American people, it freed and stimulated enterprise, it restored the government to its position as an umpire instead of a player in the economic game. For these reasons the American people have gone forward in progress while the rest of the world has halted, and some of the countries have even gone backwards....

There has been revived in this campaign, however, a series of proposals which, if adopted, would be a long step toward the abandonment of our American system and a surrender to the destructive operation of governmental conduct of commercial business. Because the country is faced with difficulty and doubt over certain national problems—that is prohibition, farm relief, and electrical power—our opponents propose that we must thrust government a long way into the businesses which give rise to these problems. In effect, they abandon the tenets of their own party and turn to state socialism as a solution for the difficulties presented by all three. It is proposed that we shall change from prohibition to the state purchase and sale of liquor. If their agricultural relief program means anything, it means that the government shall directly or indirectly buy and sell and fix prices of agricultural products. And we are to go into the hydroelectric power business. In other words, we are confronted with a huge program of government in business.

There is, therefore, submitted to the American people a question of fundamental principle. That is: shall we depart from the principles of our American political and economic System, upon which we have advanced beyond all the rest of the world, in order to adopt methods based on principles destructive of its very foundations? And I wish to emphasize the seriousness of these proposals. I wish to make my position clear, for this goes to the very roots of American life and progress....

Let us first see the effect upon self-government. When the Federal government undertakes to go into commercial business, it must at once set up the organization and administration of that business, and it immediately finds itself in a labyrinth, every alley of which leads to the destruction of self-government....

Bureaucracy is ever desirous of spreading its influence and its power. You cannot extend the mastery of the government over the daily working life of a people without at the same time making it the master of the people's souls and thoughts. Every expansion of government in business means that government in order to protect itself from the political consequences of its errors and wrongs is driven irresistibly without peace to greater and greater control of the nation's press and platform. Free speech does not live many hours after free industry and free commerce die.

It is a false liberalism that interprets itself into the government operation of commercial business. Every step of bureaucratizing the business of our country poisons the very roots of liberalism—that is, political equality, free speech, free assembly, free press, and equality of opportunity. It is the road not to more liberty, but to less liberty. Liberalism should be found not striving to spread bureaucracy but striving to set bounds to it. True liberalism seeks all legitimate freedom first in the confident belief that without such freedom the pursuit of all other blessings and benefits is vain. That belief is the foundation of all American progress, political as well as economic.

Liberalism is a force truly of the spirit, a force proceeding from the deep realization that economic freedom cannot be sacrificed if political freedom is to be preserved. Even if Governmental conduct of business could give us more efficiency instead of less efficiency, the fundamental objection to it would remain unaltered and unabated. It would destroy political equality. It would increase rather than decrease abuse and corruption. It would stifle initiative and invention. It would undermine the development of leadership. It would cramp and cripple the mental and spiritual energies of our people. It would extinguish equality and opportunity. It would dry up the spirit of liberty and progress. For these reasons primarily it must be resisted. For a hundred and fifty years liberalism has found its true spirit in the American system, not in the European systems....

By adherence to the principles of decentralized self-government, ordered liberty, equal opportunity, and freedom to the individual, our American experiment in human welfare has yielded a degree of well-being unparalleled in all the world. It has come nearer to the abolition of poverty, to the abolition of fear of want, than humanity has ever reached before. Progress of the past seven years is the proof of it. This alone furnishes the answer to our opponents, who ask us to introduce destructive elements into the system by which this has been accomplished....

I have endeavored to present to you that the greatness of America has grown out of a political and social system and a method of control of economic forces distinctly its own—our American system—which has carried this great experiment in human welfare farther than ever before in all history. We are nearer today to the ideal of the abolition of poverty and fear from the lives of men and women than ever before in any land. And I again repeat that the departure from our American system by injecting principles destructive to it which our opponents propose, will jeopardize the very liberty and freedom of our people, and will destroy equality of opportunity not alone to ourselves but to our children....

"Text of Hoover's Speech on Relation of Government to Industry," *The New York Times*, 23 October 1928, 2.

20.2

THE DEPRESSION HITS PHILADELPHIA (1931)

Disproving predictions that the economy would rebound quickly, the Great Depression was prolonged and pervasive. The banking system collapsed. Factories were overburdened with unsold merchandise. Prices plummeted. These economic problems had devastating effects on individuals. Millions lost their life savings when financial institutions failed. Unemployment reached 25 percent. Urban families and those already living in poverty were particularly hard-hit by the economic crisis. As the Depression paralyzed American cities, Congress began investigating the dire conditions facing many urban families. In this passage, Dorothy Kahn, executive director of the Jewish Welfare Society of

Philadelphia, tells the Senate Subcommittee on Unemployment Relief about the difficulties facing the urban poor.

───────────■───────────

FOCUS QUESTIONS

1. How did the Depression affect many families in Philadelphia?
2. How did people respond to their economic troubles?
3. How did the New Deal attempt to resolve the problems that Kahn describes?

T *he Chairman:* What happens to these families when they are evicted?

Miss Kahn: The families in Philadelphia are doing a number of things. The dependence of families upon the landlords, who seem to have a remarkable willingness to allow people to live in their quarters, rent free, is something that has not been measured. I think the only indication of it is the mounting list of sheriff's sales where property owners are simply unable to maintain their small pieces of property because rents are not being paid. Probably most of you saw in the newspapers the account of the "organized" representation of the taxpayers recently, where they vigorously and successfully opposed a rise in local taxes, largely because of the fact that they are under a tremendous burden through nonpayment of rents. That, of course, is the least of the difficulties, although I think this is the point at which we ought to stress one of the factors that Mr. West and other speakers have brought out in their testimony, that is the effect on families of the insecurity of living rent free, and in addition to that, the effect on their attitude toward meeting their obligations. Some of us would not be surprised if rent paying became an obsolete custom in our community. There are also, of course, evictions and the evictions in Philadelphia are frequency accompanied not only by the ghastly placing of a family's furniture on the street, but the actual sale of the family's household goods by the constable. These families are, in common Philadelphia parlance, "sold out."

One of the factors that is never counted in all of the estimates of relief in this country is the factor of neighborliness. That factor of neighborliness is a point that I would like to stress here, because it seems to us who are close to this problem that this factor has been stretched not only beyond its capacity but beyond the limits of human endurance. We have no measure in Philadelphia today of the overcrowding that is a direct or indirect result of our inability to pay rent for families. Only the other day a case came to my attention in which a family of 10 had just moved in with a family of 6 in a 3-room apartment. However shocking that may be to the members of this committee, it is almost an every-day occurrence in our midst. Neighbors do take people in. They sleep on chairs, they sleep on the floor. There are conditions in Philadelphia that beggar description. There is scarcely a day that calls do not come to all of our offices to find somehow a bed or a chair. The demand for boxes on which people can sit or stretch themselves is hardly to be believed....

Only the other day a man came to our office, as hundreds do day after day, applying for a job, in order not to have to apply for relief, I think we have already stressed the reluctance of individuals to accept relief, regardless of the source from which it comes. This man said to our worker: "I know you haven't any money to give us. I know there isn't enough money in the city to take care of the needs of everybody, but I want you to give me a job." Now, we have so many applications of that kind during the day that it has gotten to the point where we can scarcely take their names as they come in, because we have no facilities for giving jobs. In this particular case this individual interested me because when he heard that we had no jobs to give him, he said: "Have you anybody you can send around to my family to tell my wife you have no job to give me! Because she doesn't believe that a man who walks the street from morning till night, day after day, actually can't get a job in this town. She thinks I don't want to work." I think it is not necessary to dramatize the results of a situation like that. And there are thousands of them. It is only one illustration.

Another thing, it seems to me to be important to stress is the effect of this situation on the work habits of the next generation. I think it has not been brought out that in the early period of this so-called "depression" one of the most outstanding features of it was the fact that young people could get jobs even when old people of 40 years and over could not get jobs, and it has become quite customary for families to expect that their young members who are just coming of working age can replace the usual breadwinner, the father of the family. It is easy to forget about these young boys and girls reaching 14, 15, 16, 17, 18 years of age, who have had no work experience, and if we think of work not as merely a means of livelihood but as an aspect of our life and a part of our life, it has a good deal of significance that these young people are having their first work experience, and experience not with employment but with unemployment; that in addition to that they are looked to as potential breadwinners in the family; that they are under the same strain, the same onus that the father of the family is under, suspected of malingering, suspected of not wanting to work—all of these things which the average individual sees not as clearly as we see them in terms of millions of unemployed....

U.S. Congress, Senate, Subcommittee on Unemployment Relief, "Statement of Miss Dorothy Kahn," *Hearings before the Senate, Subcommittee on Unemployment Relief, Senate Committee on Manufacturers*, 72nd Congress, 1st Session, (28 December 1931), 73-77.

20.3

THE GREAT DEPRESSION IN RURAL AMERICA (1932)

Throughout the 1920s, American farmers struggled as overproduction led to declining crop prices and glutted markets. The Great Depression exacerbated this situation. In 1933 alone, over five percent of the country's farmers lost their farms through mortgage default or tax delinquency. In this reading, Oscar Ameringer, a newspaper editor from Oklahoma, describes the desperation in much of rural America.

―――――――――――■―――――――――――

FOCUS QUESTIONS

1. How does Oscar Ameringer describe the conditions in rural America?
2. How are people responding to this situation?
3. What does Ameringer believe has caused this economic crisis?
4. What does he fear will occur if the poor do not receive relief? Do you think he was right? Explain your answer.

...During the last three months I have visited, as I have said, some 20 States of this wonderfully rich and beautiful country. Here are some of the things I heard and saw: In the State of Washington I was told that the forest fires raging in that region all summer and fall were caused by unemployed timber workers and bankrupt farmers in an endeavor to earn a few honest dollars as fire fighters. The last thing I saw on the night I left Seattle was numbers of women searching for scraps of food in the refuse piles of the principal market of that city. A number of Montana citizens told me of thousands of bushels of wheat left in the fields uncut on account of its low price that hardly paid for the harvesting. In Oregon I saw thousands of bushels of apples rotting in the orchards. Only absolute flawless apples were still salable, at from 40 to 50 cents a box containing 200 apples. At the same time, there are millions of children who, on account of the poverty of their parents, will not eat one apple this winter.

While I was in Oregon the Portland *Oregonian* bemoaned the fact that thousands of ewes were killed by the sheep raisers because they did not bring enough in the market to pay the freight on them. And while Oregon sheep raisers fed mutton to the buzzards, I saw men picking for meat scraps in the garbage cans in the cities of New York and Chicago. I talked to one man in a restaurant in Chicago. He told me of his experience in raising sheep. He said that he had to kill 3,000 sheep this fall and thrown them down the canyon, because it cost $1.10 to ship a sheep, and then he could not afford to feed the sheep, and he would not let them starve, so he just cut their throats and threw them down the canyon.

The roads of the West and Southwest teem with hungry hitchhikers. The camp fires of the homeless are seen along every railroad track. I saw men, women, and children walking over the hard roads. Most of them were tenant farmers who had lost their all in the late slump in wheat and cotton. Between Clarksville and Russellville, Ark., I picked up a family. The woman was hugging a dead chicken under a rugged coat. When I asked her where she had procured the fowl, first she told me she had found it dead in the road, and added in grim humor, "They promised me a chicken in the pot, and now I got mine." [A reference to one of Herbert Hoover's campaign slogans in 1928.]

In Oklahoma, Texas, Arkansas, and Louisiana I saw untold bales of cotton rotting in the fields because the cotton pickers could not keep body and soul together on 35 cents paid for picking 100 pounds. The farmers' cooperatives who loaned the money to the planters to make the crops allowed the planters $5 a bale. That means 1,500 pounds of seed cotton for the picking of it, which was in the neighborhood of 35 cents a pound. A good picker can pick about 200 pounds of cotton a day, so that the 70 cents would not provide enough pork or beans to keep the picker in the field, so that there is fine staple cotton rotting down there by the hundreds and thousands of tons.

As a result of this appalling overproduction on the one side and staggering underconsumption on the other side, 70 per cent of the farmers of Oklahoma were unable to pay the interests on their mortgages. Last week one of the largest and oldest mortgage companies in that State went into the hands of the receiver. In that and other states we have now the interesting spectacle of farmers losing their farms by foreclosure and mortgage companies losing their recouped holdings by tax sales.

The farmers are being pauperized by the poverty of industrial populations and the industrial populations are being pauperized by the poverty of farmers. Neither has the money to buy the product of the other, hence we have overproduction and underconsumption at the same time in the same country.

I have not come here to stir you in a recital of the necessity for relief for our suffering fellow citizens. However, unless something is done for them and done soon, you will have a revolution on hand. And when the revolution comes it will not come from Moscow, it will not be made by the poor communists whom our police are heading up regularly and efficiently. When the revolution comes it will bear the label "Laid in the U.S.A." and its chief promoters will be the people of American stock....

U.S. Congress, House, Committee on Labor, "Statement of Oscar Ameringer," *Hearings before the House Committee on Labor*, 72nd Congress, 1st Session, (February 1932), 97-99.

20.4

FRANKLIN D. ROOSEVELT, FIRST INAUGURAL ADDRESS (1933)

The Depression was the central issue in the 1932 presidential election. Despite Herbert Hoover's efforts to improve the national economy, many voters found him cold and insensitive. Accordingly, they gravitated to the optimism of Franklin D. Roosevelt (1882-1945) and elected him in a landslide. Born into a privileged New York family, Roosevelt was educated at Groton, Harvard, and Columbia Law School. After a brief stint in the New York state senate, he served as Assistant Secretary of the Navy during World War I. His nomination as the Democratic candidate for vice-president in 1920 only confirmed his political promise. But a year later, polio dramatically changed FDR's life. Although he never recovered the use of his legs, his determination and personality enabled him to continue his political career. In 1928, he won the governorship of New York and earned praise for his efforts on behalf of farmers, the unemployed, the elderly, and consumers. His successes helped him win the 1932 Democratic presidential nomination.

When Roosevelt took the presidential oath in March 1933, the nation was on the verge of economic disaster. The majority of banks had closed, industrial production was only half of its 1929 level, and over 13 million people were unemployed. FDR used the occasion to calm and inspire his anxious countrymen.

———————■———————

FOCUS QUESTIONS

1. How does Roosevelt attempt to reassure his fellow Americans?
2. What does he identify as the major problems facing the United States?
3. How does Roosevelt aim to resolve the national economic crisis?
4. How did the New Deal reflect the proposals Roosevelt offers in this speech? Give examples.

March 4, 1933

I am certain that my fellow Americans expect that on my induction into the Presidency I will address them with a candor and a decision which the present situation of our Nation impels. This is preeminently the time to speak the truth, the whole truth, frankly and boldly. Nor need we shrink from honestly facing conditions in our country today. This great Nation will endure as it has endured, will revive and will prosper. So, first of all, let me assert my firm belief that the only thing we have to fear is fear itself, nameless, unreasoning, unjustified terror which paralyzes needed efforts to convert retreat into advance. In every dark hour of our national life a leadership of frankness and vigor has met with that understanding and support of the people themselves which is essential to victory. I am convinced that you will again give that support to leadership in these critical days.

In such a spirit on my part and on yours we face our common difficulties. They concern, thank God, only material things. Values have shrunken to fantastic levels; taxes have risen; our ability to pay has fallen; government of all kinds is faced by serious curtailment of income; the means of exchange are frozen in the currents of trade; the withered leaves of industrial enterprise lie on every side; farmers find no markets for their produce; the savings of many years in thousands of families are gone.

More important, a host of unemployed citizens face the grim problem of existence, and an equally great number toil with little return. Only a foolish optimist can deny the dark realities of the moment.

Yet our distress comes from no failure of substance. We are stricken by no plague of locusts. Compared with the perils which our forefathers conquered because they believed and were not afraid, we have still much to be thankful for. Nature still offers her bounty and human efforts have multiplied it....

Happiness lies not in the mere possession of money; it lies in the joy of achievement, in the thrill of creative effort....

Recognition of the falsity of material wealth as the standard of success goes hand in hand with the abandonment of the false belief that public office and high political position are to be valued only by the standards of pride of place and personal profit; and there must be an end to a conduct in banking and in business which too often has given to a sacred trust the likeness of callous and selfish wrongdoing. Small wonder that confidence languishes, for it thrives only on honesty, on honor, on the sacredness of obligations, on faithful protection, on unselfish performance; without them it cannot live.

Restoration calls, however, not for changes in ethics alone. This Nation asks for action, and action now.

Our greatest primary task is to put people to work. This is no unsolvable problem if we face it wisely and courageously. It can be accomplished in part by direct recruiting by the Government itself, treating the task as we would treat the emergency of a war, but at the same time, through this employment, accomplishing greatly needed projects to stimulate and reorganize the use of our natural resources.

Hand in hand with this we must frankly recognize the overbalance of population in our industrial centers and, by engaging on a national scale in a redistribution, endeavor to provide a better use of the land for those best fitted for the land. The task can be helped by definite efforts to raise the values of agricultural products and with this the power to purchase the output of our cities. It can be helped by preventing realistically the tragedy of the growing loss through foreclosure of our small homes and our farms. It can be helped by insistence that the Federal, State, and local governments act forthwith on the demand that their cost be drastically reduced. It can be helped by the unifying of relief activities which today are often scattered, uneconomical, and unequal. It can be helped by national planning for and supervision of all forms of transportation and of communications and other utilities which have a definitely public character. There are many ways in which it can be helped, but it can never be helped merely by talking about it. We must act and act quickly.

Finally, in our progress toward a resumption of work we require two safeguards against a return of the evils of the old order; there must be a strict supervision of all banking and credits and investments; there must be an end to speculation with other people's money, and there must be provision for an adequate but sound currency.

There are the lines of attack. I shall presently urge upon a new Congress in special session detailed measures for their fulfillment, and I shall seek the immediate assistance of the several States.

Through this program of action we address ourselves to putting our own national house in order and making income balance outgo. Our international trade relations, though vastly important, are in point of time and necessarily secondary to the establishment of a sound national economy. I favor as practical policy the putting of first things first. I shall spare no effort to restore world trade by international economic readjustment, but the emergency at home cannot wait on that accomplishment....

If I read the temper of our people correctly, we now realize as we have never realized before our interdependence on each other; that we can not merely take but we must give as well; that if we are to go forward, we must move as a trained and loyal army willing to sacrifice for the good of a common discipline, because without such discipline no progress is made, no leadership becomes effective. We are, I know, ready and willing to submit our lives and property to such discipline, because it makes possible a leadership which aims at a larger good....

I assume unhesitatingly the leadership of this great army of our people dedicated to a disciplined attack upon our common problems....

I am prepared under my constitutional duty to recommend the measures that a stricken nation in the midst of a stricken world may require. These measures, or such other measures as the Congress may build out of its experience and wisdom, I shall seek, within my constitutional authority, to bring to speedy adoption.

But in the event that the Congress shall fail to take one of these two courses, and in the event that the national emergency is still critical, I shall not evade the clear course of duty that will then confront me. I shall ask the Congress for the one remaining instrument to meet the crisis, broad Executive power to wage a war against the emergency, as great as the power that would be given to me if we were in fact invaded by a foreign foe.

For the trust reposed in me I will return the courage and the devotion that befit the time. I can do no less.

We face the arduous days that lie before us in the warm courage of the national unity; with the clear consciousness of seeking old and precious moral values; with the clean satisfaction that comes from the stern performance of duty by old and young alike. We aim at the assurance of a rounded and permanent national life.

We do not distrust the future of essential democracy. The people of the United States have not failed. In their need they have registered a mandate that they want direct, vigorous action. They have asked for discipline and direction under leadership. They have made me the present instrument of their wishes. In the spirit of the gift I take it.

In this dedication of a Nation we humbly ask the blessing of God. May He protect each and every one of us. May He guide me in the days to come.

The American Experience, The Presidents, http://www.pbs.org/wgbh/amex/presidents/nf/resource/fdr/primdocs/inaugural1.html.

20.5

HUEY LONG EXPLAINS THE "SHARE OUR WEALTH" PLAN (1934)

Following his stirring inaugural address, Franklin Roosevelt sent Congress dozens of measures designed to spark economic recovery, to aid the unemployed and poor, and to reform financial institutions blamed for the crisis. The center-pieces of the initial stage of the New Deal were the Agricultural Adjustment Act and the National Industrial Recovery Act. At first, Roosevelt's programs had overwhelming public support. However, when the depression continued, some Americans began to listen to critics who attacked the New Deal from both the political right and left.

Huey Long (1893-1935) was one of FDR's most ardent opponents. Triumph-ing over poverty and limited educational opportunities, Long passed the Louisiana bar exam in 1915. After joining the state railroad commission, his criticism of large oil companies and unfair regulation of public utilities made him popular. His unconventional humor and oratorical skills helped him win the governorship in 1928. Long's ambitious public works programs and educational reforms transformed Louisiana. Although poor whites adored Long, his imposi-tion of increased taxes drew the wrath of the wealthy. After winning election to the U.S. Senate, Long tried to keep control of Louisiana politics through dictatorial measures. Capitalizing on deep popular resentment of the rich, he publicized his "Share the Wealth" plan, an impractical scheme aimed at redistributing large fortunes to ensure a guaranteed income for all. Before he was assassinated in 1935, Long claimed that seven million people had joined Share Our Wealth clubs.

FOCUS QUESTIONS

1. What are the central elements of the Share Our Wealth plan?
2. To whom would Long's ideas appeal? Why?
3. Who would oppose Long's agenda? Why?
4. Would the Share Our Plan have ended the Depression? Explain your answer.

THE CONGRESSIONAL RECORD
February 5, 1934

eople of America: In every community get together at once and organize a share-our-wealth society—Motto: Every man a king.

PRINCIPLES AND PLATFORM:

1. To limit poverty by providing that every deserving family shall share in the wealth of America for not less than one third of the average wealth, thereby to possess not less than $5,000 free of debt.
2. To limit fortunes to such a few million dollars as will allow the balance of the American people to share in the wealth and profits of the land.
3. Old-age pensions of $30 per month to persons over 60 years of age who do not earn as much as $1,000 per year or who possess less than $10,000 in cash or property, thereby to remove from the field of labor in times of unemployment those who have contributed their share to the public service.
4. To limit the hours of work to such an extent as to prevent overproduction and to give the workers of America some share in the recreations, conveniences, and luxuries of life.
5. To balance agricultural production with what can be sold and consumed according to the laws of God, which have never failed.
6. To care for the veterans of our wars.
7. Taxation to run the Government to be supported, first, by reducing big fortunes from the top, thereby to improve the country and provide employment in public works whenever agricultural surplus is such as to render unnecessary, in whole or in part, any particular crop.

SIMPLE AND CONCRETE— NOT AN EXPERIMENT

To share our wealth by providing for every deserving family to have one third of the average wealth would mean that, at the worst, such a family could have a fairly comfortable home, an automobile, and a radio, with other reasonable home conveniences, and a place to educate their children. Through sharing the work, that is, by limiting the hours of toil so that all would share in what is made and produced in the land, every family would have enough coming in every year to feed, clothe, and provide a fair share of the luxuries of life to its members. Such is the result to a family, at the worst.

From the worst to the best there would be no limit to opportunity. One might become a millionaire or more. There would be a chance for talent to make a man big, because enough would be floating in the land to give brains its chance to be used. As it is, no matter how smart a man may be, everything is tied up in so few hands that no amount of energy or talent has a chance to gain any of it.

Would it break up big concerns? No. It would simply mean that, instead of one man getting all the one concern made, that there might be 1,000 or 10,000 persons sharing in such excess fortune, any one of whom, or all of whom, might be millionaires and over.

I ask somebody in every city, town, village, and farm community of America to take this as my personal request to call a meeting of as many neighbors and friends as will come to it to start a share-our-wealth society. Elect a president and a secretary and charge no dues. The meeting can be held at a courthouse, in some town hall or public building, or in the home of someone.

It does not matter how many will come to the first meeting. Get a society organized, if it has only two members. Then let us get to work quick, quick, quick to put an end by law to people starving and going naked in this land of too much to eat and too much to wear....

We have waited long enough for these financial masters to do these things. They have promised and promised. Now we find our country $10 billion further in debt on account of the depression, and big lenders even propose to get 90 percent of that out of the hides of the common people in the form of a sales tax.

There is nothing wrong with the United States. We have more food than we can eat. We have more clothes and things out of which to make clothes than we can wear. We have more houses and lands than the whole 120 million can use if they all had good homes. So what is the trouble? Nothing except that a handful of men have everything and the balance of the people have nothing if their debts were paid. There should be every man a king in this land flowing with milk and honey instead of the lords of finance at the top and slaves and peasants at the bottom....

Huey Long's Senate Speeches, http://www.ssa.gov/history/longsen.html

20.6

■

FRANCES PERKINS ON SOCIAL SECURITY (1935)

The Social Security Act is the most enduring New Deal initiative. The product of many years of reform efforts, the legislation instituted old-age pensions, survivors' benefits, aid to dependent mothers and children, unemployment compensation, and disability insurance. Taxes levied on employers and employees subsidize the program. Congress periodically adjusts benefits and taxes in order to keep pace with inflation.

Social Security reflected a leftward shift in Roosevelt's presidency. Cognizant that critics of the New Deal were gaining popular support, FDR offered programs aimed at the poor, the disadvantaged, and the working-class. He rightly predicted that such proposals would undermine political opponents like Huey Long and Frances Townsend.

Frances Perkins (1882-1965) played a critical role in drafting the Social Security legislation. Born in Boston, Perkins graduated from Mount Holyoke College and worked as a teacher and social worker. After earning a Master's degree in social economics from Columbia University, she held several positions in which she lobbied for better wages and working conditions. In 1933, Roosevelt appointed her secretary of labor, making her the first woman to serve in a Cabinet position. Holding the post for twelve years, Perkins successfully pushed for minimum-wage and maximum-hour laws, the creation of the Civilian Conservation

Corps, and unemployment compensation. In 1934, she served as chair of the Committee on Economic Security. In this reading, Perkins presents the committee's recommendations to a national radio audience. Her address was one of the first public explanations of what later became the Social Security program.

---■---

FOCUS QUESTIONS

1. What is the Committee on Economic Security proposing? Why is it making these recommendations?
2. How is the Social Security program to be financed? What roles would the federal and state governments play in its administration?
3. How was Social Security a response to critics of the New Deal such as Huey Long (Document 20.5)?
4. Explain how the Social Security program represented a significant change in the function of the federal government.

February 25, 1935

I have been asked to speak to you tonight on the administration's program for economic security which is now, as you know, before Congress....

As I look back on the tragic years since 1929, it seems to me that we as a Nation, not unlike some individuals, have been able to pass through a bitter experience to emerge with a newfound insight and maturity....

The process of recovery is not a simple one. We cannot be satisfied merely with makeshift arrangements which will tide us over the present emergencies. We must devise plans that will not merely alleviate the ills of today, but will prevent, as far as it is humanly possible to do so, their recurrence in the future. The task of recovery is inseparable from the fundamental task of social reconstruction....

The measures we propose do not by any means provide a complete and permanent solution of our difficulties. If put into effect, however, they will provide a greater degree of security for the American citizen and his family than he has heretofore known....

We cannot hope to accomplish all in one bold stroke. To begin too ambitiously in the program of social security might very well result in errors which would entirely discredit this very necessary type of legislation. It is not amiss to note here that social legislation in European countries, begun some 25 years ago, is still in a developmental state and has been subjected to numerous changes as experience and changing conditions dictated.

It may come as a surprise to many of us that we in this country should be so far behind Europe in providing our citizens with those safeguards which assure a decent standard of living in both good times and bad, but the reasons are not far to seek. We are much younger than our European neighbors. Our abundant pioneer days are not very far behind us. With unlimited opportunities, in those days, for the individual who wished to take advantage of them, dependency seemed a reflection on the individual himself, rather than the result of social or economic conditions. There seemed little need for any systematic organized plan, such as has now become necessary.

It has taken the rapid industrialization of the last few decades, with its mass-production methods, to teach us that a man might become a victim of circumstances far beyond his control, and finally it took a depression to dramatize for us the appalling insecurity of the great mass of the population, and to stimulate interest in social insurance in the United States. We have come to learn that the large majority of our citizens must have protection against the loss of income due to unemployment, old age, death of the breadwinners and disabling accident and illness, not only on humanitarian grounds, but in the interest of our National welfare. If we are to maintain a healthy economy and thriving production, we need to maintain the standard of living of the lower income groups in our population who constitute 90 per cent of our purchasing power....

Our program deals with safeguards against unemployment, with old-age security, with maternal aid and aid to crippled and dependent children and public health services. Another major subject—health insurance—is dealt with briefly in the report of the Committee on Economic Security, but without any definite recommendations....

Let me briefly describe the other measures now under consideration which do represent something of a departure from our usual course.

Recognizing unemployment as the greatest of all hazards, the committee gave primary emphasis to provisions for unemployment—employment assurance. This measure is embodied in the $4,800,000,000 public works resolution, which is separate from, but complementary to, the economic security bill itself. Employment assurance, the stimulation of private employment and the provision of public employment for those able-bodied workers whom private industry cannot yet absorb is to be solely a responsibility of the Federal Government and its major contribution in providing safeguards against unemployment. It should be noted that this is the largest employment program ever considered in any country. As outlined by the President, it will furnish employment for able-bodied men now on relief, and enable them to earn their support in a decent and socially useful way. It will uphold morale, as well as purchasing power, and directly provide jobs for many in private industry who would otherwise have none.

For the 80 per cent of our industrial workers who are employed, we propose a system of unemployment compensation, or insurance, as it is usually called. In our concern for the unemployed, we must not overlook this much larger group who also need protection.

No one who is now employed can feel secure while so many of his fellows anxiously seek work. Unemployment compensation, while it has distinct limitations which are not always clearly understood, is particularly valuable for the ordinarily regularly employed industrial worker who is laid off for short periods because of seasonal demands or other minor industrial disturbances. He can, during this period when he has a reasonable expectation of returning to work within a short time, receive compensation for his loss of income for a limited period as a definite, contractual right. His standard of living need not be undermined, he is not forced on relief nor must he accept other work unsuited to his skill and training.

Unemployment insurance, wherever it has been tried, has demonstrated its value in maintaining purchasing power and stabilizing business conditions. It is very valuable at the onset of a depression, and even in the later stages will serve to carry a part of the burden of providing for the unemployed. For those who have exhausted their rights to unemployment benefits and for those who, in any case, must be excluded from its provisions, we suggest that they be given employment opportunities on public work projects. In these two measures, employment assurance and unemployment compensation, we have a first and second line of defense which together should form a better safeguard than either standing alone....

The bill provides for a Federal tax on pay rolls against which credit is allowed the employer for contributions to an approved State unemployment compensation fund. By this Federal tax every employer will be placed on the same competitive basis from a National standpoint, and at the same time, aside from compliance with a few minimum Federal standards, every State will be free to adopt the kind of law it wants.

One of the most important of the Federal requirements is that all unemployment compensation funds shall be deposited with the Federal Treasury in Washington, so as to assure their availability when needed and make it possible to utilize the reserves which will accumulate in conformity with the credit policy of the Nation....

I come now to the other major phase of our program. The plan for providing against need and dependency in old age is divided into three separate and distinct parts. We advocate, first, free Federally-aided pensions for those now old and in need; second, a system of compulsory contributory old-age insurance for workers in the lower income brackets, and third, a voluntary system of low-cost annuities purchasable by those who do not come under the compulsory system.

Enlightened opinion has long since discarded the old poor-house method of caring for the indigent aged, and 28 States already have old-age pension laws. Due to financial difficulties, many of these laws are now far less effective than they were intended to be. Public sentiment in this country is strongly in favor of providing these old people with a decent and dignified subsistence in their declining years. Exploiting that very creditable sentiment, impossible, hare-brained schemes for providing for the aged have sprung into existence and attracted misguided supporters. But the administration is confident that its plan for meeting the situation is both humane and practical and will receive the enthusiastic support of the people.

We propose that the Federal Government shall come to the aid of the State pension systems already in existence and stimulate the enactment of similar legislation elsewhere by grants-in-aid equal to one-half the State expenditures for such purposes but not exceeding $15 per month. This does not necessarily mean that State pensions would not anywhere exceed $30 per month. Progressive States may find it possible to grant more than $15 per month as their share. The size of the pension would, of course, be proportionate to the need of the applicant and would quite likely vary with conditions in different States....

For those now young or even middle-aged, a system of compulsory old-age insurance will enable them to build up, with matching contributions from their employers, an annuity from which they can draw as a right upon reaching old age. These workers will be able to care for themselves in their old age, not merely on a subsistence basis, which is all that gratuitous pensions have anywhere provided, but with a modest comfort and security. Such a system will greatly lessen the hazards of old age to the many workers who could not, unaided, provide for themselves and would greatly lessen the enormous burden of caring for the aged of future generations from public funds....

This, in broad outlines, is the program now before us. We feel that it is a sound and reasonable plan and framed with due regard for the present state of economic recovery....

Social Security Online, The Official Website of the Social Security Administration, http://www.ssa.gov/history/perkinsradio.html.

20.7

THE NEW DEAL AND THE ARTS (1935-1939)

During the worst stages of the Great Depression and the early years of World War II, the federal government provided unprecedented support for the arts. Scores of artists, writers, musicians, photographs, and actors participated in New Deal programs designed not only to provide economic relief but also to demonstrate and preserve American culture. The programs generated incredible artistic energy and enabled thousands of Americans to see photographic exhibits, live theatrical performances, and musical productions. But some politicians objected to these arts initiatives. They believed these endeavors wasted public funds or reflected radical political viewpoints. Intense congressional opposition eventually killed the arts programs. Nonetheless, the creativity unleashed in these projects produced remarkable cultural reflections of a difficult era.

FOCUS QUESTIONS

1. What are the themes of these images? How do their names and content reflect American life in the 1930s?
2. How do these pictures promote the New Deal?
3. Why might someone have objected some of these works? Explain and give examples.
4. Do you believe that the federal government should support the arts? Explain your answer.

C.C.C. A Young Man's Opportunity for Work Play Study & Health, 1935; Albert Bender; Silkscreen; Chicago Federal Art Project, WPA; Library of Congress, Prints and Photographs Division, B WPA Ill.B46 1.

Mine Rescue, 1939; Fletcher Martin; Tempera on panel; National Museum of American Art, Smithsonian Institution, transfer from General Services Administration, 77.1.54.

Candide, New York, NY, 1935, WPA Federal Theatre Project, New Deal Network, http://newdeal.feri.org/library/t28.htm.

Farmer and sons...dust storm, Cimarron County, Oklahoma, 1936; Arthur Rothstein; Library of Congress, Prints and Photographs Division, FSA-OWI Collection, LC-USZ62-11491

Destitute pea pickers in California (Often referred to as "Migrant Mother"), 1936; Dorothea Lange (American, 1895-1965); Library of Congress, Prints and Photographs Division, FSA-OWI Collection, LC-USZ62-95653, LOT 997.

20.8

SONGS OF AMERICAN WORKERS

The Great Depression and the New Deal strongly affected the organized labor movement in the United States. Before the 1930s, the vast majority of workers did not belong to unions. Aided by government officials and private detectives, industrialists crushed unionization efforts. Thousands of laborers suffered dangerous work environments, low pay, and squalid living conditions.

The economic crisis convinced many workers to challenge this state of affairs. Led by a new generation of militants such as John L. Lewis of the United Mine Workers and Sidney Hillman of the Amalgamated Clothing Workers, laborers used sit-down strikes, hunger marches, and pickets to pressure employers into making concessions. The unionists received a significant boost with passage of the National Labor Relations Act of 1935. For the first time, the federal government guaranteed workers the right to bargain collectively. The legislation triggered unprecedented unionization campaigns. In 1935, Lewis and Hillman helped to found the Committee of Industrial Organizations (CIO), which, unlike the American Federation of Labor (AFL), welcomed workers of all skill levels regardless of race or gender. After bitterly contested strikes, CIO-led laborers won major victories at U.S. Steel and General Motors, two corporations that had vociferously opposed unions. Through groups like the United Auto Workers' Emergency Brigade, women supported the strikers by preparing food, manning picket lines, and publicizing workers' demands. After the CIO broke away from the AFL in 1938, it became the Congress of Industrial Organizations. By 1941, unions had eight million members, up from only three million in 1933. The union movement peaked in the mid-1950s when approximately 35 percent of the U.S. workforce was organized.

Folk singers often dramatized workers' struggles. Performers such as Woody Guthrie and Pete Seeger traveled the country and used their music to inspire the disenfranchised.

FOCUS QUESTIONS

1. How do these songs portray the lives of workers and their families during the Great Depression?
2. How do these artists feel about unions?
3. Do workers today share bonds share similar bonds? Explain your answer.

I HATE THE COMPANY BOSSES
(I HATE THE CAPITALIST SYSTEM)
— *Sarah Ogan Gunning*

I hate the company bosses,
I'll tell you the reason why:
They cause me so much suffering
And my dearest friends to die.

Oh yes, I guess you wonder
What they have done to me.
I'm goin' to tell you, Mister,
My husband had TB.

Brought on by hard work and low wages,
An' not enough to eat,
Goin' naked an' hungry
No shoes on his feet.

I guess you'll say he's lazy,
An' did not want to work.
But I must say you're crazy,
For work he did not shirk.

My husband was a coal miner,
He worked an' risked his life,
To try to support three children,
Himself, his mother and wife.

I had a blue-eyed baby,
The darlin' of my heart.
But from my little darlin'
Her mother had to part.

These mighty company bosses,
They dress in jewels an' silk.
But my darlin' blue-eyed baby,
She starved to death for milk.

I had a darlin' mother,
For her I often cry.
But with them rotten conditions
My mother had to die.

Well, what killed your mother?
I hear these bosses say.
Dead of hard work an' starvation,
My mother had to pay.

Well, what killed your mother?
Oh tell us if you please.
Excuse me, it was pellagry,
That starvation disease.

They call this the land of plenty,
To them I guess it's true.
But that's to the company bosses,
Not workers like me an' you.

Well, what can I do about it
To these men of power an' might?
I tell you company bosses
I'm goin' to fight, fight, fight.

What can we do about it
To right this dreadful wrong?
We're all goin' to join the union,
For the union makes us strong.

I'D RATHER NOT BE ON RELIEF
— *Lester Hunter*

e go around all dressed in rags
While the rest of the world goes neat,
And we have to be satisfied
With half enough to eat.
We have to live in lean-tos,
Or else we live in a tent,
For when we buy our bread and beans
There's nothing left for rent.

I'd rather not be on the rolls of relief,
Or work on the W.P.A.,
We'd rather work for the farmer
If the farmer could raise the pay;
Then the farmer could plant more cotton
And he'd get more money for spuds,
Instead of wearing patches,
We'd dress up in new duds.

From the east and west and north and south
Like a swarm of bees we come;
The migratory workers
Are worse off than a bum.
We go to Mr. Farmer
And ask him what he'll pay;
He says, "You gypsy workers
Can live on a buck a day."

I'd rather not be on the rolls of relief,
Or work on the W.P.A.,
We'd rather work for the farmer
If the farmer could raise the pay;
Then the farmer could plant more cotton
And he'd get more money for spuds,
Instead of wearing patches,
We'd dress up in new duds.

We don't ask for luxuries
Or even a feather bed.
But we're bound to raise the dickens
While our families are underfed.
Now the winter is on us
And the cotton picking is done,
What are we going to live on
While we is waiting for spuds to come?

Now if you will excuse me
I'll bring my song to an end.
I've got to go and chuck a crack
Where the howling wind comes in.
The times are going to better
And I guess you'd like to know
I'll tell you all about it,
I've joined the C.I.O.

UNION MAID
— *Woody Guthrie and Millard Lampell*

There once was a union maid, she never was afraid
Of goons and ginks and company finks and the deputy sheriffs who made the raid.
She went to the union hall when a meeting it was called,
And when the Legion boys come 'round
She always stood her ground.

Chorus:
Oh, you can't scare me, I'm sticking to the union,
I'm sticking to the union, I'm sticking to the union.
Oh, you can't scare me, I'm sticking to the union,
I'm sticking to the union 'til the day I die.

This union maid was wise to the tricks of company spies,
She couldn't be fooled by a company stool, she'd always organize the guys.
She always got her way when she struck for better pay.
She'd show her card to the National Guard
And this is what she'd say:

Chorus

You gals who want to be free, just take a tip from me;
Get you a man who's a union man and join the ladies' auxiliary.
Married life ain't hard when you got a union card,
A union man has a happy life when he's got a union wife.

Chorus

WHICH SIDE ARE YOU ON?
— *Florence Reece*

ome all you good workers,
Good news to you I'll tell
Of how the good old union
Has come in here to dwell.

Chorus:
Which side are you on?
Which side are you on?
Which side are you on?
Which side are you on?

My daddy was a miner,
And I'm a miner's son,
And I'll stick with the union
'Til every battle's won.

They say in Harlan County
There are no neutrals there.
You'll either be a union man
Or a thug for J. H. Blair. [a local sheriff]

Oh workers can you stand it?
Oh tell me how you can?
Will you be a lousy scab
Or will you be a man?

Don't scab for the bosses,
Don't listen to their lies.
Us poor folks haven't got a chance
Unless we organize.

20.9

GRANT WOOD, *AMERICAN GOTHIC* (1930)

The 1930s were a vibrant era in American art history. Social Realists like Ben Shahn, Jack Levine, and Philip Evergood offered scathing depictions of poverty, political corruption, and labor strife. In contrast, Regionalists such as Thomas Hart Benton, Grant Wood, and John Steuart Curry produced simple, seemingly uncritical portraits of rural America. Time *magazine and other publications lauded the Regionalists for their celebration of "American" values.*

Grant Wood's American Gothic *suggests that Regionalism may have been more complicated. Wood (1892-1942) grew up in Iowa and trained as a craftsman and painter. During four trips to Europe, Wood was deeply influenced by the meticulous realism of sixteenth-century Flemish artists. When his* American Gothic *appeared at the Art Institute of Chicago in 1930, it provoked passionate responses. Some viewers praised its dignified portrayal of Midwestern life. Others assumed Wood was mocking rural America. Though Wood hinted at elements of sarcasm in the painting, he never fully explained his artistic intentions.*

Much of the debate stemmed from Wood's subjects. Was he depicting a farmer and his wife, or a father and his daughter? In reality, Wood used his sister Nan and B.H. McKeeby, a dentist, as his models. After dressing the pair in 1890s clothing, he had them pose in front of a house in Eldon, Iowa. Scholars vary in their interpretations of American Gothic. *Some see a preacher defending his daughter's virtue. Others claim the man is merely a farmer. Whatever its meaning,* American Gothic *is one of the most famous images in American culture.*

FOCUS QUESTIONS

1. How do you interpret *American Gothic*? In what ways can it be viewed as a response to the Great Depression?

2. Why do you think that many Midwesterners objected to Wood's painting?
3. *American Gothic* is perhaps the most frequently parodied painting in American art history. What might account for this phenomenon?

American Gothic, 1930; Grant Wood (American, 1891-1942); Oil on beaverboard, 29 ¼ x 24 5/8 in. (74.3 X 62.4 cm); The Art Institute of Chicago, Friends of American Art Collection.

20.10

JOHN STEINBECK, *THE GRAPES OF WRATH* (1939)

Perhaps no author conveyed the plight of the poor during the Great Depression better than John Steinbeck (1902-1968). Born in California, Steinbeck attended Stanford University but did not earn a degree. He spent several years working as a manual laborer before attaining notoriety as a writer. None of Steinbeck's first three novels sold well, but he achieved popularity with Tortilla Flat *(1935), a sensitive story about Mexican Americans. His next two works,* In Dubious Battle *(1936) and* Of Mice and Men *(1937), were darker and depicted the difficulties facing workers.* The Grapes of Wrath *(1939) is his most famous novel. The best-seller described the lives of Oklahomans who migrated to California in order to flee poverty and the Dust Bowl. Prior to winning the Nobel Prize for Literature in 1962, Steinbeck penned several other works including* Cannery Row *(1945),* East of Eden *(1952), and* The Winter of Our Discontent *(1961). This extract from* The Grapes of Wrath *reflects Steinbeck's interest in the dispossessed.*

FOCUS QUESTIONS

1. What occurs in this passage? How do these events relate to America in the 1930s?
2. How does Steinbeck describe the state of American agriculture?
3. How does Steinbeck appear to view capitalism? Provide examples supporting your answer.
4. What do you think happened to the tenant family described here? Was their fate common among American farmers during the Depression? Explain your answers.

The owners of the land came onto the land, or more often a spokesman for the owners came. They came in closed cars, and they felt the dry earth with their fingers, and sometimes they drove big earth augers into the ground for soil tests. The tenants, from their sun-beaten dooryards, watched uneasily when the closed cars drove along the fields. And at last the owner men drove into the dooryards and sat in their cars to talk out of the windows. The tenant men stood beside the cars for a while, and then squatted on their hams and found sticks with which to mark the dust.

In the open doors the women stood looking out, and behind them the children—corn-headed children, with wide eyes, one bare foot on top of the other bare foot, and the toes working. The women and the children watched their men talking to the owner men. They were silent.

Some of the owner men were kind because they hated what they had to do, and some of them were angry because they hated to be cruel, and some of them were cold because they had long ago found that one could not be an owner unless one were cold. And all of them were caught in something larger than themselves. Some of them hated the mathematics that drove them. And some were afraid, and some worshiped the mathematics because it provided a refuge from thought ,and from feeling. If a bank or a finance company owned the land, the owner man said, The Bank—or the Company—needs—wants—insists—must have—as though the Bank or the Company were a monster, with thought and feeling, which had ensnared them. These last would take no responsibility for the banks or the companies because they were men and slaves, while the banks were machines and masters all at the same time. Some of the owner men were a little proud to be slaves to such cold and powerful masters. The owner men sat in the cars and explained. You know the land is poor. You've scrabbled at it long enough, God knows.

The squatting tenant men nodded and wondered and drew figures in the dust, and yes, they knew, God knows. If the dust only wouldn't fly. If the top would only stay on the soil, it might not be so bad.

The owner men went on leading to their point: You know the land's getting poorer. You know what cotton does to the land; robs it, sucks all the blood out of it.

The squatters nodded—they knew, God knew. If they could only rotate the crops they might pump blood back into the land.

Well, it's too late. And the owner men explained the workings and the thinkings of the monster that was stronger than they were. A man can hold land if he can just eat and pay taxes; he can do that. Yes, he can do that until his crops fail one day and he has to borrow money from the bank. But—you see, a bank or a company can't do that, because those creatures don't breathe air, don't eat side-meat. They breathe profits; they eat the interest on money. If they don't get it, they die the way you die without air, without side-meat. It is a sad thing, but it is so. It is just so.

The squatting men raised their eyes to understand. Can't we just hang on? Maybe the next year will be a good year. God knows how much cotton next year. And with all the wars—God knows what price cotton will bring. Don't they make explosives out of cotton? And uniforms? Get enough wars and cotton'll hit the ceiling. Next year, maybe. They looked up questioningly.

We can't depend on it. The bank—the monster has to have profits all the time. It can't wait. It'll die. No, taxes go on. When the monster stops growing, it dies. It can't stay one size.

Soft fingers began to tap the sill of the car window, and hard fingers tightened on the restless drawing sticks. In the doorways of the sun-beaten tenant houses, women sighed and then shifted feet so that the one that had been down was now on top, and the toes working. Dogs came sniffing near the owner cars and wetted on all four tires one after another. And chickens lay in the sunny dust and fluffed their feathers to get the cleansing dust down to the skin. In the little sties the pigs grunted inquiringly over the muddy remnants of the slops.

The squatting men looked down again. What do you want us to do? We can't take less share of the crop—we're half starved now. The kids are hungry all the time. We got no clothes, torn an' ragged. If all the neighbors weren't the same, we'd be ashamed to go to meeting.

And at last the owner men came to the point. The tenant system won't work any more. One man on a tractor can take the place of twelve or fourteen families. Pay him a wage and take all the crop. We have to do it. We don't like to do it. But the monster's sick. Something's happened to the monster.

But you'll kill the land with cotton.

We know. We've got to take cotton quick before the land dies. Then we'll sell the land. Lots of families in the East would like to own a piece of land.

The tenant men looked up alarmed. But what'll happen to us? How'll we eat?

You'll have to get off the land. The plows'll go through the dooryard.

And now the squatting men stood up angrily. Grampa took up the land, and he had to kill the Indians and drive them away. And Pa was born here, and he killed weeds and snakes. Then a bad year came and he had to borrow a little money. An' we was born here. There in the door—our children born here. And Pa had to borrow money. The bank owned the land then, but we stayed and we got a little bit of what we raised.

We know that—all that. It's not us, it's the bank. A bank isn't like a man. Or an owner with fifty thousand acres, he isn't like a man either. That's the monster.

Sure, cried the tenant men, but it's our land. We measured it and broke it up. We were born on it, and we got killed on it, died on it. Even if it's no good, it's still ours. That's what makes it ours—being born on it, working it, dying on it. That makes ownership, not a paper with numbers on it.

We're sorry. It's not us. It's the monster. The bank isn't like a man.

Yes, but the bank is only made of men.

No, you're wrong there—quite wrong there. The bank is something else than men. It happens that every man in a bank hates what the bank does, and yet the bank does it. The bank is something more than men, I tell you. It's the monster. Men made it, but they can't control it.

The tenants cried, Grampa killed Indians, Pa killed snakes for the land. Maybe we can kill banks—they're worse than Indians and snakes. Maybe we can fight to keep our land, like Pa and Grampa did.

And now the owner men grew angry. You'll have to go.

But it's ours, the tenant men cried. We—

No. The bank, the monster owns it. You'll have to go.

We'll get our guns like Grampa when the Indians came. What then?

Well—first the sheriff, and then the troops. You'll be stealing if you try to stay, you'll be murderers if you kill to stay. The monster isn't men, but it can make men do what it wants.

But if we go, where'll we go? How'll we go? We got no money.

We're sorry, said the owner men. The bank, the fifty-thousand-acre owner can't be responsible. You're on land that isn't yours. Once over the line maybe you can pick cotton in the fall. Maybe you can go on relief. Why don't you go on west to California? There's work there, and it never gets cold. Why, you can reach out anywhere and pick an orange. Why, there's always some kind of crop to work in. Why don't you go there? And the owner men started their cars and rolled away.

The tenant men squatted down on their hams again to mark the dust with a stick, to figure, to wonder. Their sunburned faces were dark, and their sun-whipped eyes were light. The women moved cautiously out of the doorways toward their men, and the children crept behind the women, cautiously, ready to run. The bigger boys squatted beside their fathers, because that made them men. After a time the women asked, What did he want? And the men looked up for a second, and the smolder of pain was in their eyes. We got to get off. A tractor and a superintendent. Like factories.

Where'll we go? the women asked.

We don't know. We don't know.

And the women went quickly, quietly back into the houses and herded the children ahead of them. They knew that a man so hurt and so perplexed may turn in anger, even on people he loves. They left the men alone to figure and to wonder in the dust.

After a time perhaps the tenant man looked about—at the pump put in ten years ago, with a goose-neck handle and iron flowers on the spout, at the chopping block where a thousand chickens had been killed, at the hand plowing lying in the shed, and the patent crib hanging in the rafters over it.

The children crowded about the women in the houses. What are we going to do, Ma? Where we going to go?

The women said, We don't know, yet. Go out and play. But don't go near your father. He might whale you if you go near him. And the women went on with the work, but all the time they watched the men squatting in the dust—perplexed and fighting.

The tractors came over the roads and into the fields, great crawlers moving like insects, having the incredible strength of insects. They crawled over the ground, laying the track and rolling on it and picking it up. Diesel tractors, puttering while they stood idle; they thundered when they moved, and then settled down to a droning roar. Snub-nosed monsters, raising the dust and sticking their snouts into it, straight down the country, across the country, through fences, through dooryards, in and out of gullies in straight lines. They did not run on the ground, but on their own roadbeds. They ignored hills and gulches, water courses, fences, houses.

The man sitting in the iron seat did not look like a man; gloved, goggled, rubber dust mask over nose and mouth, he was a part of the monster, a robot in the seat. The thunder of the cylinders sounded through the country, became one with the air and the earth, so that earth and air muttered in sympathetic vibration. The driver could not control it—straight across country it went, cutting through a dozen farms and straight back. A twitch at the controls could swerve the cat', but the driver's hands could not twitch because the monster that built the tractor, the monster that sent the tractor out, had somehow got into the driver's hands, into his brain and muscle, had goggled him and muzzled him—goggled his mind, muzzled his speech, goggled his perception, muzzled his protest. He could not see the land as it was, he could not smell the land as it smelled; his feet did not stamp the clods or feel the warmth and power of the earth. He sat in an iron seat and stepped on iron pedals. He could not cheer or beat or curse or encourage the extension of his power, and because of this he could not cheer or whip or curse or encourage himself. He did not know or own or trust or beseech the land. If a seed dropped did not germinate, it was nothing. If the young thrusting plant withered in drought or drowned in a flood of rain, it was no more to the driver than to the tractor.

He loved the land no more than the bank loved the land. He could admire the tractor—its machined surfaces, its surge of power, the roar of its detonating cylinders; but it was not his tractor. Behind the tractor rolled the shining disks, cutting the earth with blades—not plowing but surgery, pushing the cut earth to the right where the second row of disks it and pushed it to the left; slicing blades shining, polished by the cut earth. And pulled behind the disks, the harrows combing with iron teeth so that the little clods broke up and the earth lay smooth. Behind the harrows, the long seeders—twelve curved iron penes erected in the foundry, orgasms set by gears, raping methodically, raping without passion. The driver sat in his iron seat and he was proud of the straight lines he did not will, proud of the tractor he did not own or love, proud of the power he could not control. And when that crop grew, and was harvested, no man had crumbled a hot clod in his fingers and let the earth sift past his fingertips. No man had touched the seed, or lusted for the growth. Men ate what they had not raised, had no connection with the bread. The land bore under iron, and under iron gradually died; for it was not loved or hated, it had no prayers or curses.

At noon the tractor driver stopped sometimes near a tenant house and opened his lunch: sandwiches wrapped in waxed paper, white bread, pickle, cheese, Spam, a piece of pie branded like an engine part. He ate without relish. And tenants not yet moved away came out to see him, looked curiously while the goggles were taken off, and the rubber dust mask, leaving white circles around the eyes and a large white circle around nose and mouth. The exhaust of the tractor puttered on, for fuel is so cheap it is more efficient to leave the engine running than to heat the Diesel nose for a new start. Curious children crowded close, ragged children who ate their fried dough as they watched. They watched hungrily the unwrapping of the sandwiches, and their hunger-sharpened noses smelled the pickle, cheese, and Spam. They didn't speak to the driver. They watched his hand as it carried food to his mouth. They did not watch him chewing; their eyes followed the hand that held the sandwich. After a while the tenant who could not leave the place camp out and squatted in the shade beside the tractor.

"Why, you're Joe Davis's boy!"

"Sure," the driver said.

"Well, what you doing this kind of work for—against your own people?"

"Three dollars a day. I got damn sick of creeping for my dinner—and not getting it. I got a wife and kids. We got to eat. Three dollars a day, and it comes every day."

"That's right," the tenant said. "But for your three dollars a day fifteen or twenty families can't eat at all. Nearly a hundred people have to go out and wander on the roads for your three dollars a day. Is that right?"

And the driver said, "Can't think of that. Got to think of my own kids. Three dollars a day, and it comes every day. Times are changing, mister, don't you know? Can't make living on the land unless you've got two, five, ten thousand acres and a tractor. Crop land isn't for little guys like us a' more. You don't kick up a howl because you can't make Fords, or because you're not the telephone company. Well, crops are like that now. Nothing to do about it. You try get three dollars a day someplace. That's the only way."

The tenant pondered. "Funny thing how it is. If a man owns a little property, that property is him, it's part of him and it's like him. If he owns property only so he can walk it and handle it and be sad when it isn't doing well, and fine when the rain falls on it, that property is him, and some way he's bigger because he owns it. Even if he isn't successful he's big with his property. That is so."

And the tenant pondered more. "But let a man get property he doesn't see, or can't take time to get his fingers in, or can't be there to walk on it—why, then the property is the man. He can't do what he wants, he can't think what he wants. The property is the man, stronger than he is. And he is small, not big. Only his possessions are big—and he's the servant of his property. That is so, too."

The driver munched the branded pie and threw the crust away. "Times are changed, don't you know? Thinking about stuff like that don't feed the kids. Get your three dollars a day, feed your kids. You got no call to worry about anybody's kids but your own. You get a reputation for talking like that, and you'll never get three dollars a day. Big shots won't give you three dollars a day if you worry about anything but your three dollars a day."

"Nearly a hundred people on the road for your three dollars. Where will we go?"

"And that reminds me," the driver said, "you better get out soon. I'm going through the dooryard after dinner."

"You filled in the well this morning."

"I know. Had to keep the line straight. But I'm going through the dooryard after dinner. Got to keep the lines straight. And—well, you know Joe Davis, my old man, so I'll tell you this. I got orders wherever there's a family not moved out—if I have an accident—you know, get too close and cave the house in a little—well, I might get a couple of dollars. And my youngest kid never had no shoes yet."

"I built it with my hands. Straightened old nails to put the sheathing on. Rafters are wired to the stringers with baling wire. It's mine. I built it. You bump it down—I'll be in the window with a rifle. You even come too close and I'll pot you like a rabbit."

"It's not me. There's nothing I can do. I'll lose my job if I don't do it. And look—suppose you kill me? They'll just hang you, but long before you're hung there'll be another guy on the tractor, and he'll bump the house down. You're not killing the right guy."

"That's so," the tenant said. "Who gave you orders? I'll go after him. He's the one to kill."

"You're wrong. He got his orders from the bank. The bank told him, 'Clear those people out or it's your job.'"

"Well, there's a president of the bank. There's a board of directors. I'll fill up the magazine of the rifle and go into the bank."

The driver said, "Fellow was telling me the bank gets orders from the East. The orders were, 'Make the land show profit or we'll close you up.'"

But where does it stop? Who can we shoot? I don't aim to starve to death before I kill the man that's starving me."

"I don't know. Maybe there's nobody to shoot. Maybe the thing isn't men at all. Maybe, like you said, the property's doing it. Anyway I told you my orders."

"I got to figure," the tenant said "We all got to figure. There's some way to stop this. It's not like lightning or earthquakes. We've got a bad thing made by men, and by God that's something we can change." The tenant sat in his doorway, and the river thundered his engine and started off, tracks falling and curving, harrows combing, and the phalli of the seeder slipping into the ground. Across the dooryard the tractor cut, and the hard, foot-beaten ground was seeded field, and the tractor cut through again; the uncut space was ten feet wide. And back he came. The iron guard bit into the house-corner, crumbled the wall, and wrenched the little house from its foundation so that it fell sideways, crushed like a bug. And the driver was goggled and a rubber mask covered his nose and mouth. The tractor cut a straight line on, and the air and the ground vibrated with its thunder. The tenant man stared after it, his rifle in his hand. His wife was beside him, and the quiet children behind. And all of them stared after the tractor.

"Chapter 5," from *The Grapes of Wrath* by John Steinbeck, copyright 1939, renewed © 1967 by John Steinbeck. Used by permission of Viking Penguin, a division of Penguin Group (USA) Inc.

SECONDARY SOURCE

ALAN BRINKLEY, "THE NEW DEAL EXPERIMENTS"

After winning the 1932 presidential race against Herbert Hoover, Franklin Roosevelt took immediate steps designed to end the Great Depression. Between 1932 and 1939, his New Deal programs provided economic relief and reshaped important sectors of the American economy including industry, agriculture, banking, and housing. Although not all of the programs succeeded, the New Deal fundamentally changed the role of the federal government and revised traditional ideas about social welfare. In this excerpt, Alan Brinkley, a historian at Columbia University, evaluates New Deal programs and their long-term impact on American political culture.

 Go to your *Speaking of America* CD-ROM to read "The New Deal Experiments."

FOCUS QUESTIONS

1. What were Franklin Roosevelt's major goals when he became president? Was he able to achieve these objectives?
2. Discuss the components of three New Deal programs and evaluate the overall success of each.
3. What are some of the most important legacies of the New Deal? What is your opinion of the New Deal?

AMERICAN JOURNEY ONLINE

http://ajaccesss.wadsworth.com [†]

About the Crash of 1929
— In The Great Depression and the New Deal
  Documents
  • Walter B. Pitkin, Whither America? (1929)
  Images
  • The Floor of the New York Stock Exchange (circa 1920)
  • Black Tuesday on Wall Street (1929)
— In World War I and the Jazz Age
  Videos
  • The Stock Market Crash of 1929 (1929)

About the Scottsboro Boys
— In The African-American Experience
  Documents
  • *Powell v. Alabama* (1932)
  Images
  • Trial of the Scottsboro Boys (1933)

[†] Enter password, choose the Archive indicated above, click on Contents, choose •Documents, •Images, or •Multimedia, and click on the title of the item.

About the Bonus March
— In <u>The Great Depression and the New Deal</u>
  Images
  • The Bonus Army (1932)
— In <u>Civil Rights in the United States</u>
  Images
  • The Bonus Army March (1932)
—In <u>The Great Depression and the New Deal</u>
  Images
  • Douglas MacArthur during the Bonus March (1932)

About the Great Depression
— In <u>World War I and the Jazz Age</u>
  Images
  • Breadline for the Unemployed (1930?)
— In <u>The Great Depression and the New Deal</u>
  Documents
  • An Anonymous Letter to Herbert Hoover, #1 (1930)
  • An Anonymous Letter to Herbert Hoover, #2 (1930)
  • Wilford J. Eiteman, Two Decades of Depression (1931)
  • The Bitter and the Sweet (1931)
  • Charles R. Walker, Relief and Revolution (1932)
  • An Anonymous Letter to Franklin D. Roosevelt, #1 (1933)
  • Renwick C. Kennedy, The Face of the Poor (1933)
  • Mrs. M.H.A. to Eleanor Roosevelt (1934)
  • An Anonymous Letter to Eleanor Roosevelt, #1 (1934)
  • Mr. D.A. to Franklin Roosevelt (1934)
  • Meridel Le Sueur, Cows and Horses Are Hungry (1934)
  • Mr. N.S. to Franklin Roosevelt (1934)
  • Mrs. H.E.C. to Eleanor Roosevelt (1935)
  • Mrs. J.N.T. to Eleanor Roosevelt (1935)
  • An Anonymous Letter to Eleanor Roosevelt, #2 (1935)
  • An Anonymous Letter to Franklin D. Roosevelt, #2 (1935)
  • An Anonymous Letter to Franklin D. Roosevelt, #3 (1935)
  • An Anonymous Letter to Franklin D. Roosevelt, #4 (1935)
  • An Anonymous Letter to Franklin D. Roosevelt, #5 (1935)
  • An Anonymous Letter to Eleanor Roosevelt, #3 (1936)
  • Mari Tomasi, Four Women (1939)
  • The Family of an Automobile Worker (circa 1939)
  Images
  • The Red Cross Dispenses Foodstuffs in Arkansas (1931)
  • A Soup Kitchen in Chicago (1931)
  • Men Lined Up at the Employment Bureau (1932)
  • Young Residents of a "Hooverville" (1932)
  • Clifford Berryman, Hoover's Farm Relief (1932)

- Eleanor Roosevelt Ladling Soup (circa 1932)
- The Bread Line (circa 1933)
- George W. Ackerman, Canning Peas at the Townsend Farm (1933)
- Ben Shahn, A Destitute Family in the Ozark Mountains (1935)
- Carl Mydans, A Mother and Children Living in an Abandoned Car (1936)
- Sunday Singing: Frank Tengle and His Family (1936)
- Dorothea Lange, Two Migrant Families Looking for Work (1936)
- Dorothea Lange, Waiting for Relief Checks (1937)
- Dorothea Lange, Unemployment Assistance in California (1938)

About the New Deal and Its Critics
— In The Great Depression and the New Deal
  Documents
- Franklin D. Roosevelt, Roosevelt's "Portland Speech" (1932)
- Document with Audio—Franklin D. Roosevelt, FDR's Inaugural Address (1933)
- Franklin D. Roosevelt, Fireside Chat Outlining the New Deal (1933)
- Franklin D. Roosevelt, Fireside Chat on the Bank Crisis (1933)
- Franklin D. Roosevelt, Fireside Chat on Gold and the Dollar (1933)
- Franklin D. Roosevelt, Fireside Chat on the Purposes of the Recovery Program (1933)
- Franklin D. Roosevelt, Roosevelt's Message to Congress, March 16, 1933 (1933)
- Franklin D. Roosevelt, Roosevelt's Message to Congress, March 21, 1933 (1933)
- Franklin D. Roosevelt, Roosevelt's Remarks on Signing the NIRA, June 1933 (1933)
- Franklin D. Roosevelt, Roosevelt's Speech at Vassar College, August 1933 (1933)
- Franklin D. Roosevelt, Press Conference, November 3, 1933 (1933)
- U.S. Congress, The Tennessee Valley Authority Act (1933)
- Huey P. Long, Every Man a King (1933)
- Mrs. E.L. to Eleanor Roosevelt (1934)
- Franklin D. Roosevelt, Roosevelt's State of the Union Address, January 1934 (1934)
- Franklin D. Roosevelt, Roosevelt on Government Relief Plans, February 1934 (1934)
- Lorena Hickok, Hickok to Hopkins, June 6, 1934 (1934)
- Lorena Hickok, Hickok to Hopkins, June 11, 1934 (1934)
- Louisa Wilson, FERA Report: Detroit, Michigan, November 1934 (1934)
- Martha Gellhorn, Gellhorn to Hopkins, November 1934 (1934)
- Martha Gellhorn, Gellhorn to Hopkins, November 11, 1934 (1934)
- Henry W. Francis, Francis to Hopkins, November 18, 1934 (1934)
- Wayne W. Parrish, Parrish to Hopkins, November 1934, #1 (1934)

- Wayne W. Parrish, Parrish to Hopkins, November 1934, #2 (1934)
- Franklin D. Roosevelt, Roosevelt's Press Conference, November 23, 1934 (1934)
- Henry W. Francis, Francis to Hopkins, December 1, 1934 (1934)
- Henry W. Francis, Francis to Hopkins, December 7, 1934 (1934)
- Charles E. Coughlin, The National Union for Social Justice (1935)
- Charles E. Coughlin, Coughlin's Sermon of March 24, 1935
- Huey P. Long, *My First Days in the White House* (1935)
- Martha Gellhorn, Gellhorn to Hopkins, April 25, 1935 (1935)
- Franklin D. Roosevelt, Roosevelt's Speech to a Group of Farmers, May 1935 (1935)
- Richard L. Neuberger, The Townsend Plan Exposed (1935)
- Franklin D. Roosevelt, Roosevelt's State of the Union Address, January 1936 (1936)
- Robert Fechner, Fechner to Roosevelt on the CCC, October 1936 (1936)
- Franklin D. Roosevelt, FDR at the Dedication of the Triborough Bridge (1936)
- Owen J. Roberts, *United States v. Butler* (1936)
- Franklin D. Roosevelt, Roosevelt on the Third Anniversary of the CCC (1936)
- Franklin D. Roosevelt, Roosevelt's Message to Congress, February 5, 1937 (1937)
- Document with Audio—Franklin D. Roosevelt, Fireside Chat on Reorganizing the Judiciary (1937)
- U.S. Congress, The Senate's Response to the "Court-Packing" Plan (1937)
- Frank E. Gannett, Gannett's Statement on FDR's "Court-Packing" Scheme (1937)
- Franklin Roosevelt, Fireside Chat on Unemployment (1937)
- Franklin D. Roosevelt, Fireside Chat on Proposed Legislation (1937)
- Marion Charles Hatch, Stories of an Alcoholic World War Veteran (1938)
- Franklin D. Roosevelt, Fireside Chat on Economic Conditions (1938)
- William C. Kernan, Coughlin, the Jews, and Communism (1938)
- New Jersey Writers' Project, Newark Metropolitan Airport (1939)

Images
- John Berryman, New Deal Remedies (circa 1933)
- NRA Member—We Do Our Part (1933)
- Clifford Berryman, New Deal Remedies (circa 1933)
- Clifford Berryman, The Spirit of the New Deal (1933)
- Huey Long (circa 1934)
- A CCC Enrollee Plants a Tree (circa 1934)
- CCC Enrollees Leaving Camp Roosevelt (circa 1934)
- CCC Workers Planting Trees (circa 1934)
- Charles E. Coughlin (circa 1935)

- A TVA Construction Site (circa 1935)
- A PWA Railroad Overpass (circa 1935)
- Ben Shahn, *Lest We Forget* (1937)

— In <u>World War I and the Jazz Age</u>
Documents
- President's Research Committee on Social Trends, A Greater Role for the Federal Government? (1933)
- Frances Perkins, Excerpt from The Roots of Social Security (1962)
- Ellis W. Hawley, Excerpt from *The Great War and the Search for Modern Order* (1992)

— In <u>The Constitution and Supreme Court</u>
Documents
- Franklin D. Roosevelt, Fireside Chat on the "Court-Packing" Bill (1937)

— In The African-American Experience
Images
- John Steuart Curry, *John Brown in Kansas* (circa 1938)

About Business and Economics
— In <u>World War I and the Jazz Age</u>
Documents
- Wesley Clair Mitchell, The U.S. Economy in 1929 (1929)
- Henry S. Dennison, Management (1929)
- U.S. Bureau of the Census, Percentage Share of Money Income of American Families and Unattached Individuals in 1929 (1975)

Images
- Andrew W. Mellon (1930)

— In <u>The Great Depression and the New Deal</u>
Documents
- Daniel Willard, The Challenge to Capitalism (1931)
- New Jersey Writers' Project, The Growth of RCA (1937)

About Law/Law Enforcement
— In <u>The Great Depression and the New Deal</u>
Documents
- Charles Evans Hughes, *Near v. Minnesota* (1931)
- Charles Evans Hughes, *Missouri ex rel. Gaines v. Canada* (1938)

Images
- Al Capone and Chicago's Chief of Detectives (1930)
- Charles Evans Hughes (1935)

— In <u>The Constitution and Supreme Court</u>
Document
- U.S. Congress, The Twentieth Amendment (1933)
- U.S. Congress, The Twenty-First Amendment (1933)
- Charles Evans Hughes, *Schechter Poultry Corporation v. United States* (1935)

- George Sutherland, *Humphrey's Executor v. United States* (1935)
- Charles Evans Hughes, *West Coast Hotel v. Parrish* (1937)
- Benjamin N. Cardozo, *Palko v. Connecticut* (1937)

Images
- Benjamin N. Cardozo (circa 1932)

— In World War I and the Jazz Age

Images
- J. Edgar Hoover (1932)

— In Civil Rights in the United States

Images
- Hugo Black
- Racial Segregation of Juries (1939)
- Poll Tax (1939)
- Felix Frankfurter

About Domestic Politics

— In The Great Depression and the New Deal

Documents
- Franklin D. Roosevelt, Roosevelt's Address at Hyde Park, August 1934 (1934)
- Franklin D. Roosevelt, Roosevelt's Address at Warm Springs, November 1934 (1934)
- Franklin D. Roosevelt, Fireside Chat on the Seventy-Third Congress (1934)
- The Epic of Upton Sinclair (1934)
- Upton Sinclair, I, Candidate for Governor, #1 (1935)
- Upton Sinclair, I, Candidate for Governor, #2 (1935)
- Franklin D. Roosevelt, Roosevelt's Speech at Atlanta, November 29, 1935 (1935)
- Franklin D. Roosevelt, Roosevelt's Speech, Jefferson Day Dinner, April 1936 (1936)
- Franklin D. Roosevelt, Roosevelt's Speech at Hyde Park, July 11, 1936 (1936)
- Franklin D. Roosevelt, Roosevelt's Campaign Speech, October 13, 1936 (1936)
- Franklin D. Roosevelt, Roosevelt's Speech at Niagara Falls, October 17, 1936 (1936)
- Franklin D. Roosevelt, FDR's Second Inaugural Address (1937)

Images
- Herbert Hoover with His Family (circa 1929)
- Roosevelt Campaigning for Office in Kansas (1932)
- Roosevelt and Garner Campaign License Plate (1932)
- Roosevelt's Inauguration (1933)
- James A. Farley (1933)
- John Nance Garner (1933)

- Frances Perkins with FDR (circa 1933)
- Frank L. Miller, Another Rough Rider on the Job! (circa 1933)
- W. Averell Harriman (circa 1934)
- Roosevelt Tossing Out the Season's First Baseball (1934)
- The Department of the Interior (circa 1935)
- Roosevelt Delivering a Fireside Chat (circa 1935)
- Alf Landon (1936)
- Roosevelt Speaking in Chicago (circa 1937)
- The Roosevelts at FDR's Second Inauguration (1937)
- Roosevelt Holding a Press Conference (1939)
- Jesse Jones (1939)
— In World War I and the Jazz Age
  Images
  - President Herbert Hoover (1932)
— In The Constitution and Supreme Court
  Documents
  - Franklin D. Roosevelt, Roosevelt's First Inaugural Address (1933)

About Labor
— In Civil Rights in the United States
  Images
  - John L. Lewis
  Videos
  - Protest in Washington, D.C. (1930)
  - Strikes in the South (1930)
— In The Great Depression and the New Deal
  Images
  - A Sit-Down Strike at Woolworth's (circa 1934)
  - Dorothea Lange, Turpentine Workers in Georgia (1937)
— In The African-American Experience
  Documents
  - Victor Weybright, *Pullman Porters on Parade* (1935)

About Foreign Policy
— In The Hispanic-American Experience
  Images
  - A U.S. Air Raid on Sandinistas (1930)
— In The Asian-American Experience
  Documents
  - U.S. Congress, Tydings-McDuffie Act (1934)
  - U.S. Congress, Filipino Repatriation Act (1935)

About Birth Control
— In Civil Rights in the United States
  Images
  - Margaret Sanger (1930)

About Journalism
— In The Great Depression and the United States
  Images
  • Walter Lippmann (1934)

About the Environment
— In The Great Depression and the New Deal
  Documents
  • Robert Marshall, The People's Forests (1933)
  • Franklin D. Roosevelt, Roosevelt at Boulder Dam (1935)
  • Franklin D. Roosevelt, Fireside Chat on Drought Conditions (1936)
  • Franklin D. Roosevelt, Roosevelt's Message to Congress, March 14, 1938 (1938)
  • Florida Writers' Project, Agricultural Conservation (1939)
  Images
  • A Postcard Showing a Dust Storm (1935)
  • An Oklahoma Dust Storm (circa 1935)
  Videos
  • Roosevelt's Tour of Bonneville Dam (1937)
— In World War I and the Jazz Age
  Videos
  • Yosemite National Park (1935)

About Immigration
— In The Immigrant Experience
  Images
  • Mexican-American Deportation (1931)

About African Americans
— In The African-American Experience
  Documents
  • A WPA Interview with Rebecca Jane Grant (1930)
  • A WPA Interview with Jake McLeod (1937)
  • A WPA Interview with Sam Polite (1937)
  • A WPA Interview with Sylvia Cannon(1930s)
  • A WPA Interview with Jim Taylor (1937)
  • A WPA Interview with Mrs. Hannah Davidson (1937)
  • A WPA Interview with Mary Moriah Anne Susanna James (1937)
  Images
  • Colored Drinking Fountain (circa 1935)
— In The Constitution and the Supreme Court
  Images
  • An NAACP Antilynching Banner (circa 1930)

— In <u>The Great Depression and the New Deal</u>
Images
- A Harlem Grocery (1932)
- The Nedses of Southern Pines, North Carolina (circa 1935)
- Arthur Rothstein, Evicted Sharecroppers along Hwy. 60 in Missouri (1939)

About Asian Americans
— In <u>The Asian-American Experience</u>
Images
- Filipino Farm Workers (circa 1930)
- Korean Patriotic Women's League Seventeenth Anniversary (1936)

About American Indians
— In <u>The Great Depression and the New Deal</u>
Images
- Choctaw Girls Making Crafts (1937)

About Culture
— In <u>World War I and the Jazz Age</u>
Images
- Zora Neale Hurston
- William Faulkner in World War I and the Jazz Age
— In <u>Civil Rights in the United States</u>
Images
- James Joyce (1930)
Videos
- Book Burning in the 1930s
— In <u>The Great Depression and the New Deal</u>
Documents
- Illinois Writers' Project, Baseball in Old Chicago (1939)
- Sam Ross, Jazz Music (1939)
Images
- Bobby Jones (1930)
- The New York Skyline (1931)
- Groucho Marx (circa 1931)
- Marlene Dietrich in Blonde Venus (1932)
- Mae West (circa 1933)
- Thomas Wolfe (circa 1935)
- Jesse Owens (1936)
- Mitchell Siporin, Jane Addams Memorial (1936)
- A Scene from Macbeth (1936)
- Shirley Temple (circa 1936)
- Orson Welles as Dr. Faustis (1937)
- Benny Goodman (circa 1938)
- May Swenson, Tramp Poet (1939)
- New York World's Fair (1939)

WORLD WAR II

No event affected modern America more profoundly than the Second World War. Catapulted from a devastating depression, the nation's industrial power and scientific ingenuity propelled the Allied war machine. Over 15 million Americans joined the armed services. U.S. officials fundamentally reshaped international economics and diplomacy. While most citizens seized unprecedented opportunities for economic advancement and social mobility, others encountered political oppression and racism.

In the early 1930s, no one could have predicted these momentous changes. The Depression had forced the United States to withdraw from international affairs. When fascist governments arose in Germany, Japan, and Italy, few Americans wanted to intervene. Congress adopted a strict neutrality policy. Although the Roosevelt administration introduced a "good neighbor" policy in Latin America, it did not initially confront fascist aggression in Europe.

Fascism is a system of government characterized by dictatorial leadership, stringent economic controls, and staunch nationalism. In the post-WWI era, it appealed to people seeking economic security and political stability. In 1922, Benito Mussolini and the Fascist party seized power in Italy. After years of strikes and riots, the Fascists restored order and embarked on an ambitious public works program. But these changes came at a high price. Italy became a one-party state in which unions, the free press, and free speech were prohibited. Spies and secret policemen observed the population. In 1935, Italy invaded Ethiopia as part of plan to build an African empire.

Similar events occurred in Germany. Espousing a blend of anti-Semitism, white supremacy, and extreme nationalism, Adolf Hitler and the National Socialist (Nazi) party gained broad support during the economic crises of the 1920s. In January 1933, Hitler became chancellor of Germany. He instituted a brutal dictatorship in which all non-Nazi organizations were crushed. Intent on extricating Germany from the humiliating Versailles Treaty, the Nazis began rearming and reoccupied the Rhineland. They also expelled Jews and others viewed as "inferior" to the Aryan "master race." In 1938, Hitler declared an *Anschluss* (union) between Germany and Austria. Shortly thereafter, he announced his intention to annex the Sudetenland, a heavily German area of Czechoslovakia.

At first, the international community did not respond to the Nazis' machinations. But when the Nazis threatened the Czechs, British Prime Minister Neville Chamberlain and French Premier Edouard Daladier met with Hitler in Munich. Although the Czech government was not included in the September 1938 meeting, Chamberlain and Daladier granted Hitler the Sudetenland in exchange for a Nazi pledge not to seize any additional Czech territory. Chamberlain claimed that the

Munich agreement would ensure "peace in our time." Just months later, Hitler took the rest of Czechoslovakia. After signing a pact with the Soviet Union in August 1939, the Nazis invaded Poland on September 1st. When Britain and France honored their alliances with the Poles and declared war on Germany, the Second World War began.

While Mussolini and Hitler consolidated power in Europe, militarists gained control of the Japanese government. Melding imperialist ambitions and racial ideology, the Japanese began building an Asian empire. In 1931, they invaded the Chinese province Manchuria and established a puppet regime. Six years later, they attacked the rest of China. In 1936 and 1940, Japan, Germany, and Italy signed agreements creating the Axis alliance.

Constrained by U.S. neutrality laws, Franklin Roosevelt cautiously responded to the ominous developments abroad. He asked Congress to authorize increased defense expenditures. In September 1939, he won approval for a "cash and carry" policy in which belligerent nations could buy and transport supplies from the United States. The need for stronger measures became apparent as the Nazis gained control of virtually all of Western Europe. After June 1940, Great Britain faced the Nazis alone.

Although desperate to help the British, Roosevelt was acutely aware that the American public was deeply divided about the war in Europe. Nonetheless, he pushed for a peacetime draft, increased defense expenditures, and a "destroyers for bases" swap with Britain. These moves outraged anti-interventionist groups like America First, but Roosevelt continued to escalate U.S. involvement after winning a third term in the election of 1940. In March 1941, he persuaded Congress to pass a lend-lease policy authoring up to seven billion dollars in aid to countries fighting the Nazis. U.S. ships began accompanying British vessels in the western Atlantic. After Hitler invaded the Soviet Union in June 1941, Roosevelt sent American aid to the Soviets. In August, Roosevelt and British prime minister Winston Churchill released the Atlantic Charter articulating a vision for the postwar world. By the fall of 1941, the United States was in an undeclared naval war with Germany.

But the final impetus for war came from Japan, not the Nazis. In 1937, when Japan invaded China, the United States suspended aviation and scrap metal sales to the Japanese. Years of negotiations failed to convince Japan to withdraw from China. In July 1941, after the Japanese seized Indochina, America imposed a trade embargo and froze Japan's assets in U.S. banks. Three months later, when Hideki Tojo became prime minister, he ordered his subordinates to prepare for war against the United States. Because American operatives had broken the Japanese diplomatic code, the Roosevelt administration expected an attack but did not know when or where it would occur. The answer came on December 7, 1941 with the Japanese assault on Pearl Harbor, Hawaii. Four days later, Germany declared war on the United States.

The Pearl Harbor attack shocked Americans. They overwhelmingly supported the decision to go to war with the Axis powers. Spending $250 million a day on the war effort, the federal government mobilized with impressive speed. Hundreds of new agencies were established. Businesses received generous incentives to retool for war production. Years of high unemployment ended as defense plants created millions of new jobs.

The war transformed American politics and society. The explosive growth of the federal bureaucracy triggered a conservative backlash against the New Deal. Men and women in the armed services encountered people of different races and religions. Gays and lesbians found one another. Urban populations swelled with the influx of defense workers. Unions, women, minorities, and the elderly seized economic opportunities. Marriage, birth, and divorce rates skyrocketed. This volatile climate sometimes exploded. Anti-Japanese hysteria led to the internment of 112,000 Japanese-Americans. Militant labor leaders led wildcat strikes. Racial clashes erupted. Juvenile delinquency increased.

The battles abroad overshadowed the tumultuous homefront. In early 1942, the Allies were struggling. The Nazis controlled most of Europe and were inflicting huge losses on the Soviets. The Japanese held much of Asia and the western Pacific. Although the Allies agreed to focus first on the Nazis, they differed on strategy. Over the objections of Josef Stalin, American and British officials delayed the opening of a "second front" in France. Instead, they attacked Nazi forces in North Africa and then moved into Italy. The French invasion did not occur until June 1944. As U.S. and British forces moved toward Germany, the Soviets swept into Eastern Europe. In May 1945, the Nazis surrendered.

With Germany's collapse, the Allies turned toward the Orient. After stopping Japanese expansion in mid-1942, American and British forces began an "island-hopping" campaign northward from Australia and across the central Pacific. They encountered ferocious resistance. Even after the destruction of their navy and air force, the Japanese continued to fight. The militarist government thwarted civilian peace overtures. U.S. officials predicted massive casualties in a land invasion of Japan.

During the military campaigns, Roosevelt pursued an ambitious diplomatic agenda. He hoped that the war would lead to a peaceful world order built on national self-determination and free trade. In numerous meetings with Allied leaders, FDR worked diligently to reconcile the conflicting demands of the British and the Soviets. When Roosevelt died in April 1945, important questions had not been resolved. He did not live to see the fall of Nazi Germany only three weeks later.

The task of leading the United States to victory over Japan fell to Harry S. Truman. With little foreign policy experience, Truman relied heavily on advisors who urged him to adopt a hard line against the Soviets. Although Stalin promised to enter the Pacific war, he and Truman clashed over the future of Eastern Europe. Having sustained two catastrophic invasions in the twentieth-century, the Soviets wanted a "buffer zone." With the Red Army entrenched from Bulgaria to Poland, Stalin began organizing communist governments throughout the region.

Tensions were very high by the time of the Potsdam conference in July 1945. Although the American, British, and Soviet delegates agreed to a temporary partition of Germany and war crimes trials for Nazi leaders, they deferred action on many other issues. Upon learning of the successful test of the atomic bomb, Truman ordered U.S. forces to use it if the Japanese did not unconditionally surrender by August 3, 1945.

Three days after the deadline passed, the United States dropped an atomic bomb on Hiroshima. On August 9, a second bomb was used on Nagasaki. Although American motives for using the Bomb remain hotly disputed, the most common explanation is that U.S. officials hoped to avoid a potentially disastrous invasion of Japan. While the Bomb may or may not have been the reason, the Japanese government surrendered on August 14, 1945.

Despite their joy at the war's end, Americans faced a changed world. Forty million people had perished in the global conflict. Vast stretches of Europe and Asia lay in ruins. The Holocaust exposed horrifying inhumanity. Atomic weapons revealed terrifying new consequences of warfare. Now the world's political and economic superpower, the United States entered an age of remarkable achievements and awesome responsibilities.

21.1

---■---

FRANKLIN ROOSEVELT, THE FOUR FREEDOMS (1941)

In the mid-1930s, the fascist governments of Germany, Italy, and Japan were increasing their power. Japan remained entrenched in Manchuria and was preparing to invade the rest of China. Determined to extricate Germany from the Treaty of Versailles, Adolf Hitler withdrew from the League of Nations, reoccupied the Rhineland, and rebuilt the German armed forces. In 1935, Italy invaded Ethiopia. Shortly thereafter, Hitler and Italian dictator Benito Mussolini formed an alliance. Although outraged by these events, the international community did little to stop fascist aggression.

In 1938, the political situation in Europe rapidly deteriorated. In March, the Nazis invaded Austria and declared an Anschluss (union) between the two nations. Adolf Hitler then demanded that Czechoslovakia surrender its heavily German Sudetenland region. In a September meeting in Munich, British and French leaders acquiesced to Hitler's request in exchange for a pledge not to invade the rest of Czechoslovakia. Just months later, the Nazis violated the agreement. In August 1939, despite years of mutual hostility, the Nazis and Soviets stunned the world by signing a non-aggression pact. On September 1st, when the Nazis invaded Poland, Britain and France, both Polish allies, declared war on Germany. World War II had begun.

Franklin Roosevelt responded cautiously to the conflict in Europe. Cognizant that many Americans opposed U.S. intervention in the war, he invoked the Neutrality Acts. Nonetheless, FDR recognized the dangers posed by the Nazis and convinced Congress to approve a "cash-and-carry" policy enabling the Allies to buy and transport supplies from the United States.

Renewed Nazi aggression soon forced the United States to reconsider its isolationist policies. In early 1940, the Nazi army swept through Western Europe with incredible speed. When France surrendered in June, Britain stood alone against the onslaught. Facing devastating air raids and quickly depleting its financial resources, new British prime minister Winston Churchill implored Roosevelt for assistance. In September, the news that Germany, Italy, and Japan had formed the Tripartite Pact added further gravity to the crisis.

After winning the election of 1940, FDR alerted Americans to the perils of remaining disengaged from the fight against fascism. In his January 1941 State of the Union address, he outlined strategies for preparing the nation for war. The speech inspired artist Norman Rockwell to depict the "Four Freedoms" in a series of paintings that were circulated widely during World War II.

FOCUS QUESTIONS

1. How does FDR describe the state of international affairs? Why does he think that America is endangered?
2. What actions does Roosevelt recommend? What does he believe will occur if the United States fails to prepare for war?
3. What does Roosevelt identify as the ideological aims of U.S. involvement in WWII?
4. Why was the "Four Freedoms" speech so significant? How did U.S. policies change in the months immediately following the address?

I address you, the members of this new Congress, at a moment unprecedented in the history of the union. I use the word "unprecedented" because at no previous time has American security been as seriously threatened from without as it is today....

I suppose that every realist knows that the democratic way of life is at this moment being directly assailed in every part of the world—assailed either by arms or by secret spreading of poisonous propaganda by those who seek to destroy unity and promote discord in nations that are still at peace....

Therefore, as your President, performing my constitutional duty to "give to the Congress information of the state of the union," I find it unhappily necessary to report that the future and the safety of our country and of our democracy are overwhelmingly involved in events far beyond our borders.

Armed defense of democratic existence is now being gallantly waged in four continents. If that defense fails, all the population and all the resources of Europe and Asia, Africa and Australia will be dominated by conquerors. And let us remember that the total of those populations in those four continents, the total of those populations and their resources greatly exceeds the sum total of the population and the resources of the whole of the Western Hemisphere—yes, many times over.

In times like these it is immature—and, incidentally, untrue—for anybody to brag that an unprepared America, single-handed and with one hand tied behind its back, can hold off the whole world.

No realistic American can expect from a dictator's peace international generosity, or return of true independence, or world disarmament, or freedom of expression, or freedom of religion—or even good business. Such a peace would bring no security for us or for our neighbors. Those who would give up essential liberty to purchase a little temporary safety deserve neither liberty nor safety....

There is much loose talk of our immunity from immediate and direct invasion from across the seas. Obviously, as long as the British Navy retains its power, no such danger exists. Even if there were no British Navy, it is not probable that any enemy would be stupid enough to attack us by landing troops in the United States from across thousands of miles of ocean, until it had acquired strategic bases from which to operate....

The first phase of the invasion of this hemisphere would not be the landing of regular troops. The necessary strategic points would be occupied by secret agents and by their dupes—and great numbers of them are already here and in Latin America.

As long as the aggressor nations maintain the offensive they, not we, will choose the time and the place and the method of their attack.

And that is why the future of all the American Republics is today in serious danger. That is why this annual message to the Congress is unique in our history. That is why every member of the executive branch of the government and every member of the Congress face great responsibility—great accountability.

The need of the moment is that our actions and our policy should be devoted primarily—almost exclusively—to meeting this foreign peril. For all our domestic problems are now a part of the great emergency. Just as our national policy in internal affairs has been based upon a decent respect for the rights and the dignity of all of our fellow men within our gates, so our national policy in foreign affairs has been based on a decent respect for the rights and the dignity of all nations, large and small. And the justice of morality must and will win in the end.

Our national policy is this:

First, by an impressive expression of the public will and without regard to partisanship, we are committed to all-inclusive national defense.

Second, by an impressive expression of the public will and without regard to partisanship, we are committed to full support of all those resolute people everywhere who are resisting aggression and are thereby keeping war away from our hemisphere. By this support we express our determination that the democratic cause shall prevail, and we strengthen the defense and the security of our own nation.

Third, by an impressive expression of the public will and without regard to partisanship, we are committed to the proposition that principle of morality and considerations for our own security will never permit us to acquiesce in a peace dictated by aggressors and sponsored by appeasers. We know that enduring peace cannot be bought at the cost of other people's freedom.

In the recent national election there was no substantial difference between the two great parties in respect to that national policy. No issue was fought out on the line before the American electorate. And today it is abundantly evident that American citizens everywhere are demanding and supporting speedy and complete action in recognition of obvious danger.

Therefore, the immediate need is a swift and driving increase in our armament production. Leaders of industry and labor have responded to our summons. Goals of speed have been set. In some cases these goals are being reached ahead of time. In some cases we are on schedule; in other cases there are slight but not serious delays. And in some cases—and, I am sorry to say, very important cases—we are all concerned by the slowness of the accomplishment of our plans.

The Army and Navy, however, have made substantial progress during the past year. Actual experience is improving and speeding up our methods of production with every passing day. And today's best is not good enough for tomorrow.

I am not satisfied with the progress thus far made. The men in charge of the program represent the best in training, in ability and in patriotism. They are not satisfied with the progress thus far made. None of us will be satisfied until the job is done.

No matter whether the original goal was set too high or too low, our objective is quicker and better results. To give you two illustrations: We are behind schedule in turning out finished airplanes. We are working day and night to solve the innumerable problems and to catch up.

We are ahead of schedule in building warships, but we are working to get even further ahead of that schedule. To change a whole nation from a basis of peacetime production of implements of peace to a basis of wartime production of implements of war is no small task. The greatest difficulty comes at the beginning of the program, when new tools, new plant facilities, new assembly lines, new shipways must first be constructed before the actual material begins to flow steadily and speedily from them.

The Congress of course, must rightly keep itself informed at all times of the progress of the program. However, there is certain information, as the Congress itself will readily recognize, which, in the interests of our own security and those of the nations that we are supporting, must of needs be kept in confidence. New circumstances are constantly begetting new needs for our safety. I shall ask this Congress for greatly increased new appropriations and authorizations to carry on what we have begun.

I also ask this Congress for authority and for funds sufficient to manufacture additional munitions and war supplies of many kinds, to be turned over to those nations which are now in actual war with aggressor nations. Our most useful and immediate role is to act as an arsenal for them as well as for ourselves. They do not need manpower, but they do need billions of dollars' worth of the weapons of defense.

The time is near when they will not be able to pay for them all in ready cash. We cannot, and we will not, tell them that they must surrender merely because of present inability to pay for the weapons which we know they must have.

I do not recommend that we make them a loan of dollars with which to pay for these weapons—a loan to be repaid in dollars. I recommend that we make it possible for those nations to continue to obtain war materials in the United States, fitting their orders into our own program. And nearly all of their material would, if the time ever came, be useful in our own defense....

For what we send abroad we shall be repaid, repaid within a reasonable time following the close of hostilities, repaid in similar materials, or at our option in other goods of many kinds which they can produce and which we need....

In fulfillment of this purpose we will not be intimidated by the threats of dictators that they will regard as a breach of international law or as an act of war our aid to the democracies which dare to resist their aggression. Such aid is not an act of war, even if a dictator should unilaterally proclaim it so to be....

Yes, and we must prepare, all of us prepare, to make the sacrifices that the emergency—almost as serious as war itself—demands. Whatever stands in the way of speed and efficiency in defense, in defense preparations at any time, must give way to the national need.

A free nation has the right to expect full cooperation from all groups. A free nation has the right to look to the leaders of business, of labor and of agriculture to take the lead in stimulating effort, not among other groups but within their own groups.

The best way of dealing with the few slackers or trouble-makers in our midst is, first, to shame them by patriotic example, and if that fails, to use the sovereignty of government to save government....

The nation takes great satisfaction and much strength from the things which have been done to make its people conscious of their individual stake in the preservation of democratic life in America. Those things have toughened the fiber of our people, have renewed their faith and strengthened their devotion to the institutions we make ready to protect. Certainly this is no time for any of us to stop thinking about the social and economic problems which are the root cause of the social revolution which is today a supreme factor in the world. For there is nothing mysterious about the foundations of a healthy and strong democracy.

The basic things expected by our people of their political and economic systems are simple. They are:

> Equality of opportunity for youth and for others.
> Jobs for those who can work.
> Security for those who need it.
> The ending of special privilege for the few.
> The preservation of civil liberties for all.
> The enjoyment of the fruits of scientific progress in a wider
>   and constantly rising standard of living.

These are the simple, the basic things that must never be lost sight of in the turmoil and unbelievable complexity of our modern world. The inner and abiding straight of our economic and political systems is dependent upon the degree to which they fulfill these expectations....

I have called for personal sacrifice, and I am assured of the willingness of almost all Americans to respond to that call. A part of the sacrifice means the payment of more money in taxes. In my budget message I will recommend that a greater portion of this great defense program be paid for from taxation than we are paying for today. No person should try, or be allowed to get rich out of the program, and the principle of tax payments in accordance with ability to pay should be constantly before our eyes to guide our legislation.

If the congress maintains these principles the voters, putting patriotism ahead pocketbooks, will give you their applause.

In the future days which we seek to make secure, we look forward to a world founded upon four essential human freedoms.

The first is freedom of speech and expression—everywhere in the world.

The second is freedom of every person to worship God in his own way—everywhere in the world.

The third is freedom from want, which, translated into world terms, means economic understandings which will secure to every nation a healthy peacetime life for its inhabitants—everywhere in the world.

The fourth is freedom from fear, which, translated into world terms, means a world-wide reduction of armaments to such a point and in such a thorough fashion that no nation will be in a position to commit an act of physical aggression against any neighbor—anywhere in the world.

That is no vision of a distant millennium. It is a definite basis for a kind of world attainable in our own time and generation. That kind of world is the very antithesis of the so-called "new order" of tyranny which the dictators seek to create with the crash of a bomb.

To that new order we oppose the greater conception—the moral order. A good society is able to face schemes of world domination and foreign revolutions alike without fear.... The world order which we seek is the cooperation of free countries, working together in a friendly, civilized society.

This nation has placed its destiny in the hands, heads and hearts of its millions of free men and women, and its faith in freedom under the guidance of God. Freedom means the supremacy of human rights everywhere. Our support goes to those who struggle to gain those rights and keep them. Our strength is our unity of purpose.

To that high concept there can be no end save victory.

Franklin D. Roosevelt, "State of the Union Address, January 1941," *Public Papers and Addresses of Franklin D. Roosevelt*, ed. Samuel I. Rosenman (London, 1941), 663-672.

21.2

•

CHARLES LINDBERGH OPPOSES INTERVENTION (1941)

Throughout 1941, U.S. involvement in World War II escalated rapidly. In March, Congress approved the Lend-Lease Act authorizing up to seven billion dollars in aid to the Allies. In June, after Germany invaded the Soviet Union, Franklin Roosevelt sent aid to the U.S.S.R. To ensure the continued flow of supplies across the Atlantic Ocean, he ordered the U.S. Navy to help the British track German submarines. Within a short time, U.S. convoys with the authority to destroy enemy ships were escorting British merchant vessels. American forces occupied Greenland and Iceland to prevent additional Nazi invasions. In August, Roosevelt and British prime minister Winston Churchill met for a five-day meeting aboard a ship in the North Atlantic. They issued the Atlantic Charter articulating goals for the postwar world—despite the fact that the United States was not officially at war.

These actions outraged Americans who believed that the United States should remain neutral. Non-interventionists opposed aid to the Allies for fear that it would lead to direct U.S. military involvement. In July 1940, isolationists formed the America First Committee to oppose Roosevelt's attempts to help the British. Financed largely by Henry Ford, America First claimed over 800,000 members from diverse social and ethnic backgrounds.

Charles Lindbergh (1902-1974) was America First's most popular speaker. Best known for making the first non-stop solo flight across the Atlantic in 1927, Lindbergh was an international celebrity. He and his wife, Anne Morrow Lindbergh, made innumerable goodwill flights across the globe. In 1932, their fame proved a nightmare when their two-year-old son, Charles Jr., was kidnapped from their home in Hopewell, New Jersey and murdered. The subsequent trial and execution of accused assailant Bruno Hauptmann drew unrelenting media scrutiny. The Lindberghs fled the spotlight by moving abroad. Their travels in Europe, Latin America, Asia, and Africa gave them a perspective on global affairs that differed from many Americans. After a 1936 tour of Germany, Charles Lindbergh publicly warned of the growing power of the Nazi air force. Nonetheless, he accepted a Nazi citation two years later. Upon returning to the United States in 1940, he became a controversial advocate of American neutrality. Once the U.S. entered the conflict, however, Lindbergh supported the war effort first as a consultant and then as a combat pilot in the Pacific.

In this speech, Lindbergh makes the case for non-intervention before an audience in Des Moines, Iowa.

•

FOCUS QUESTIONS

1. Why does Lindbergh oppose American intervention in World War II?

2. Whom does he hold responsible for increasing U.S. involvement in the war? How does he characterize these interventionists?
3. Compare Lindbergh's remarks to Franklin Roosevelt's "Four Freedoms" speech (Document 21.1). With whom do you most agree? Why?

September 11, 1941

I t is now two years since this latest European war began. From that day in September 1939, until the present moment, there has been an over-increasing effort to force the United States into the conflict.

That effort has been carried on by foreign interests, and by a small minority of our own people; but it has been so successful that, today, our country stands on the verge of war.

At this time, as the war is about to enter its third winter, it seems appropriate to review the circumstances that have led us to our present position. Why are we on the verge of war? Was it necessary for us to become so deeply involved? Who is responsible for changing our national policy from one of neutrality and independence to one of entanglement in European affairs?

Personally, I believe there is no better argument against our intervention than a study of the causes and developments of the present war. I have often said that if the true facts and issues were placed before the American people, there would be no danger of our involvement....

When this war started in Europe, it was clear that the American people were solidly opposed to entering it. Why shouldn't we be? We had the best defensive position in the world; we had a tradition of independence from Europe; and the one time we did take part in a European war left European problems unsolved, and debts to America unpaid.

National polls showed that when England and France declared war on Germany, in 1939, less than 10 percent of our population favored a similar course for America. But there were various groups of people, here and abroad, whose interests and beliefs necessitated the involvement of the United States in the war. I shall point out some of these groups tonight, and outline their methods of procedure. In doing this, I must speak with the utmost frankness, for in order to counteract their efforts, we must know exactly who they are.

The three most important groups who have been pressing this country toward war are the British, the Jewish and the Roosevelt administration.

Behind these groups, but of lesser importance, are a number of capitalists, Anglophiles, and intellectuals who believe that the future of mankind depends upon the domination of the British empire. Add to these the Communistic groups who were opposed to intervention until a few weeks ago, and I believe I have named the major war agitators in this country.

I am speaking here only of war agitators, not of those sincere but misguided men and women who, confused by misinformation and frightened by propaganda, follow the lead of the war agitators.

As I have said, these war agitators comprise only a small minority of our people; but they control a tremendous influence. Against the determination of the American people to stay out of war, they have marshaled the power of their propaganda, their money, their patronage.

Let us consider these groups, one at a time.

First, the British: It is obvious and perfectly understandable that Great Britain wants the United States in the war on her side. England is now in a desperate position. Her population is not large enough and her armies are not strong enough to invade the continent of Europe and win the war she declared against Germany.

Her geographical position is such that she cannot win the war by the use of aviation alone, regardless of how many planes we send her. Even if America entered the war, it is improbable that the Allied armies could invade Europe and overwhelm the Axis powers. But one thing is certain. If England can draw this country into the war, she can shift to our shoulders a large portion of the responsibility for waging it and for paying its cost.

As you all know, we were left with the debts of the last European war; and unless we are more cautious in the future than we have been in the past, we will be left with the debts of the present case. If it were not for her hope that she can make us responsible for the war financially, as well as militarily, I believe England would have negotiated a peace in Europe many months ago, and be better off for doing so.

England has devoted, and will continue to devote every effort to get us into the war. We know that she spent huge sums of money in this country during the last war in order to involve us....

We know that England is spending great sums of money for propaganda in America during the present war. If we were Englishmen, we would do the same. But our interest is first in America; and as Americans, it is essential for us to realize the effort that British interests are making to draw us into their war.

The second major group I mentioned is the Jewish.

It is not difficult to understand why Jewish people desire the overthrow of Nazi Germany. The persecution they suffered in Germany would be sufficient to make bitter enemies of any race.

No person with a sense of the dignity of mankind can condone the persecution of the Jewish race in Germany. But no person of honesty and vision can look on their pro-war policy here today without seeing the dangers involved in such a policy both for us and for them. Instead of agitating for war, the Jewish groups in this country should be opposing it in every possible way for they will be among the first to feel its consequences.

Tolerance is a virtue that depends upon peace and strength. History shows that it cannot survive war and devastations. A few far-sighted Jewish people realize this and stand opposed to intervention. But the majority still do not.

Their greatest danger to this country lies in their large ownership and influence in our motion pictures, our press, our radio and our government.

I am not attacking either the Jewish or the British people. Both races, I admire. But I am saying that the leaders of both the British and the Jewish races, for reasons which are as understandable from their viewpoint as they are inadvisable from ours, for reasons which are not American, wish to involve us in the war.

We cannot blame them for looking out for what they believe to be their own interests, but we also must look out for ours. We cannot allow the natural passions and prejudices of other peoples to lead our country to destruction.

The Roosevelt administration is the third powerful group which has been carrying this country toward war. Its members have used the war emergency to obtain a third presidential term for the first time in American history. They have used the war to add unlimited billions to a debt which was already the highest we have ever known. And they have just used the war to justify the restriction of congressional power, and the assumption of dictatorial procedures on the part of the president and his appointees.

The power of the Roosevelt administration depends upon the maintenance of a wartime emergency. The prestige of the Roosevelt administration depends upon the success of Great Britain to whom the president attached his political future at a time when most people thought that England and France would easily win the war. The danger of the Roosevelt administration lies in its subterfuge. While its members have promised us peace, they have led us to war heedless of the platform upon which they were elected.

In selecting these three groups as the major agitators for war, I have included only those whose support is essential to the war party. If any one of these groups—the British, the Jewish, or the administration—stops agitating for war, I believe there will be little danger of our involvement....

When hostilities commenced in Europe, in 1939, it was realized by these groups that the American people had no intention of entering the war. They knew it would be worse than useless to ask us for a declaration of war at that time. But they believed that this country could be entered into the war in very much the same way we were entered into the last one.

They planned: first, to prepare the United States for foreign war under the guise of American defense; second, to involve us in the war, step by step, without our realization; third, to create a series of incidents which would force us into the actual conflict. These plans were of course, to be covered and assisted by the full power of their propaganda.

Our theaters soon became filled with plays portraying the glory of war. Newsreels lost all semblance of objectivity. Newspapers and magazines began to lose advertising if they carried anti-war articles. A smear campaign was instituted against individuals who opposed intervention. The terms "fifth columnist," "traitor," "Nazi," "anti-Semitic" were thrown ceaselessly at any one who dared to suggest that it was not to the best interests of the United States to enter the war. Men lost their jobs if they were frankly anti-war. Many others dared no longer speak.

Before long, lecture halls that were open to the advocates of war were closed to speakers who opposed it. A fear campaign was inaugurated. We were told that aviation, which has held the British fleet off the continent of Europe, made America more vulnerable than ever before to invasion. Propaganda was in full swing.

There was no difficulty in obtaining billions of dollars for arms under the guise of defending America. Our people stood united on a program of defense. Congress passed appropriation after appropriation for guns and planes and battleships, with the approval of the overwhelming majority of our citizens. That a large portion of these appropriations was to be used to build arms for Europe, we did not learn until later. That was another step.... Ever since its inception, our arms program has been laid out for the purpose of carrying on the war in Europe, far more than for the purpose of building an adequate defense for America.

Now at the same time we were being prepared for a foreign war, it was necessary, as I have said, to involve us in the war. This was accomplished under that now famous phrase "steps short of war."

England and France would win if the United States would only repeal its arms embargo and sell munitions for cash, we were told. And then [illegible] began, a refrain that marked every step we took toward war for many months—"the best way to defend America and keep out of war." we were told, was "by aiding the Allies."

First, we agreed to sell arms to Europe; next, we agreed to loan arms to Europe; then we agreed to patrol the ocean for Europe; then we occupied a European island in the war zone. Now, we have reached the verge of war.

The war groups have succeeded in the first two of their three major steps into war. The greatest armament program in our history is under way.

We have become involved in the war from practically every standpoint except actual shooting. Only the creation of sufficient "incidents" yet remains; and you see the first of these already taking place, according to plan—a plan that was never laid before the American people for their approval.

Men and women of Iowa; only one thing holds this country from war today. That is the rising opposition of the American people. Our system of democracy and representative government is on test today as it has never been before. We are on the verge of a war in which the only victor would be chaos and prostration.

We are on the verge of a war for which we are still unprepared, and for which no one has offered a feasible plan for victory—a war which cannot be won without sending our soldiers across the ocean to force a landing on a hostile coast against armies stronger than our own.

We are on the verge of war, but it is not yet too late to stay out. It is not too late to show that no amount of money, or propaganda, or patronage can force a free and independent people into war against its will. It is not yet too late to retrieve and to maintain the independent American destiny that our forefathers established in this new world.

The entire future rests upon our shoulders. It depends upon our action, our courage, and our intelligence. If you oppose our intervention in the war, now is the time to make your voice heard.

Help us to organize these meetings; and write to your representatives in Washington. I tell you that the last stronghold of democracy and representative government in this country is in our house of representatives and our senate.

There, we can still make our will known. And if we, the American people, do that, independence and freedom will continue to live among us, and there will be no foreign war.

Charles Lindbergh, An American Aviator,
http://www.charleslindbergh.com/americanfirst/speech.asp.

21.3

■

FRANKLIN D. ROOSEVELT,
DECLARATION OF WAR MESSAGE (1941)

In July 1937, Japan began a brutal invasion of China proper. During the infamous Rape of Nanking alone, Japanese troops slaughtered at least 100,000 Chinese and sexually assaulted tens of thousands. In 1940, after inflicting widespread destruction, Japan installed a puppet regime in place of the Nationalist Chinese government. In September 1940, Japan signed the Tripartite Pact with Germany and Italy. Encouraged by the Nazis' victories in Western Europe, the Japanese hoped to create the Greater East Asia Co-Prosperity Sphere, an empire encompassing much of China, Southeast Asia, and the western Pacific. In July 1941, following the German invasion of the U.S.S.R., Japan invaded French Indochina.

The United States vigorously protested Japanese expansion in Asia. Anti-Japanese racism, commercial interests, and paternalistic attitudes toward the Chinese fueled popular outrage. The Roosevelt administration responded by applying economic pressure on the Japanese. In 1939, Secretary of State Cordell Hull renounced a 1911 trade agreement and prohibited the sale of aviation fuel and scrap metal to Japan. When the Japanese joined the Tripartite Pact, the U.S. stopped sales of steel and other metals. After Japan invaded Indochina, American officials froze Japanese assets and embargoed oil.

Japan faced a choice between complying with U.S. demands to withdraw from Indochina and perhaps China, or invading additional territories to obtain vital materials. In October 1941, a new Japanese government headed by Hideki Tojo, a staunch expansionist, came to power. With American-Japanese negotiations stalled, Tojo ordered his forces to prepare for war. By late November, U.S. intelligence operatives had deciphered Japan's diplomatic code and alerted Roosevelt that an attack was imminent. Assuming that the Japanese would strike Southeast Asia, U.S. commanders issued only a general warning to the American base at Pearl Harbor, home of the U.S. Pacific fleet. Taking a huge gamble, the Japanese launched a surprise attack on Pearl Harbor on December 7, 1941. In less than three hours, two waves of bombers destroyed or damaged several ships and 180 U.S. planes. More than 2,000 Americans died. The raid swept away any vestiges of non-interventionism and unified the public. On December 8th, Roosevelt showed similar resolve when he addressed a joint session of Congress. Hours later, with only one dissenting vote (Representative Jeanette Rankin of Montana, who had also opposed the U.S. entry into WWI), Congress declared war on Japan. Three days later, Hitler and Mussolini honored the Tripartite Pact by declaring war on the United States.

■

FOCUS QUESTIONS

1. How does FDR characterize the Japanese actions?
2. Some historians argue that the U.S. policies provoked the Japanese attacks. What is your response to these claims?
3. Had the Pearl Harbor raid not occurred, do you think that the United States would have fought in WWII? Explain your answer.

r. Vice President, Mr. Speaker, members of the Senate and the House of Representatives:

Yesterday, Dec. 7, 1941—a date which will live in infamy—the United States of America was suddenly and deliberately attacked by naval and air forces of the empire of Japan.

The United States was at peace with that nation, and, at the solicitation of Japan, was still in conversation with its government and its Emperor looking toward the maintenance of peace in the Pacific.

Indeed, one hour after Japanese air squadrons had commenced bombing in the American island of Oahu, the Japanese Ambassador to the United States and his colleague delivered to our Secretary of State a formal reply to a recent American message. And, while this reply stated that it seemed useless to continue the existing diplomatic negotiations, it contained no threat or hint of war or of armed attack.

It will be recorded that the distance of Hawaii from Japan makes it obvious that the attack was deliberately planned many days or even weeks ago. During the intervening time the Japanese Government has deliberately sought to deceive the United States by false statements and expressions of hope for continued peace.

The attack yesterday on the Hawaiian Islands has caused severe damage to American naval and military forces. I regret to tell you that very many American lives have been lost in addition. American ships have been reported torpedoed on the high seas between San Francisco and Honolulu.

Yesterday the Japanese Government also launched an attack against Malaya.

Last night Japanese forces attacked Hong Kong.

Last night Japanese forces attacked Guam.

Last night Japanese forces attacked the Philippine Islands.

Last night the Japanese attacked Wake Island.

And this morning the Japanese attacked Midway Island.

Japan has therefore undertaken a surprise offensive extending throughout the Pacific area. The facts of yesterday and today speak for themselves. The people of the United States have already formed their opinions and well understand the implications to the very life and safety of our nation.

As Commander in Chief of the Army and Navy, I have directed that all measures be taken for our defense, that always will our whole nation remember the character of the onslaught against us.

No matter how long it may take us to overcome this premeditated invasion, the American people, in their righteous might, will win through to absolute victory.

I believe that I interpret the will of the Congress and of the people when I assert that we will not only defend ourselves to the uttermost but will make it very certain that this form of treachery shall never again endanger us.

Hostilities exist. There is no blinking at the fact that our people, our territory and our interests are in grave danger.

With confidence in our armed forces, with the unbounding determination of our people, we will gain the inevitable triumph. So help us God.

I ask that the Congress declare that since the unprovoked and dastardly attack by Japan on Sunday, Dec. 7, 1941, a state of war has existed between the United States and the Japanese Empire.

"The President's Message," *The New York Times*, 9 December 1941, 1, 6.

21.4

PROPAGANDA ON THE HOMEFRONT (1942-1944)

Following the Pearl Harbor attack, the United States faced immense challenges in mobilizing its war effort. In December 1941, only 1.6 million Americans served in the armed forces and just 15 percent of U.S. industrial output went to war production. These figures changed with dramatic speed. Congress granted Franklin Roosevelt sweeping powers to organize the war effort. Volunteers and draftees flooded the military. By 1945, 15 million men and almost 350,000 women had enlisted. Industry generated huge quantities of supplies for the Allied war machine. At home, federal agencies such as the War Production Board, the Office of Price Administration, and the Office of War Mobilization controlled inflation and production through rationing and strict controls on rent, prices, and wages. To raise funds for the war, Congress raised income taxes on the wealthy and imposed them for the first time on the middle- and lower-classes. Millions of Americans bought war bonds.

To sustain the war effort, public and private groups used slogans and visual images directed at the masses. In June 1942, Roosevelt created the Office of War

Information (OWI) to shape public opinion. More than 4,000 writers, artists, and public relations specialists designed campaigns to maintain civilian morale and demonize the enemy. While Americans sometimes complained about wartime restrictions, most accepted them as patriotic duties. These images offer examples of the government's efforts to mobilize citizens.

FOCUS QUESTIONS

1. What are the main themes of these posters? To whom is each directed?
2. How does the government appeal to popular fears of the enemy?
3. What are some ways that people might have responded to these appeals?

"When You Ride Alone You Ride with Hitler!" by Weimer Pursell, 1943, Printed by the Government Printing Office for the Office of Price Administration, NARA Still Picture Branch (NWDNS-188-PP-42).

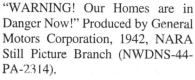

"WARNING! Our Homes are in Danger Now!" Produced by General Motors Corporation, 1942, NARA Still Picture Branch (NWDNS-44-PA-2314).

"Longing Won't Bring Him Back Sooner..." by Lawrence Wilbur, 1944, Printed by the Government Printing Office for the War Manpower Commission, NARA Still Picture Branch (NWDNS-44-PA-389).

21.5

SYBIL LEWIS AND ADELE ERENBERG
ON DEFENSE WORK (1942-1945)

Women enjoyed unprecedented economic opportunities during World War II. After discouraging women from entering the labor force in the 1930s, the federal government reversed course and appealed to women to work in defense industries. By 1945, more than six million women joined the 13 million already employed outside the home. Contrary to previous female employment trends, the new workers were often married, over age thirty-five, and mothers. Some women laborers also held jobs traditionally performed by men such as welding, construction, and shipyard work.

Nonetheless, gender discrimination persisted. Women typically earned only sixty-five percent of men's wages for the same jobs. Government campaigns repeatedly stressed that women laborers were only needed for the duration of the war. Few defense plants established child-care facilities to accommodate working mothers. Opponents of non-traditional gender roles pointed to rising divorce rates and juvenile delinquency as evidence that women belonged at home. Yet, marriage and birth rates increased as well.

However contradictory the effects of the war, women seized the chance to exercise their independence and demonstrate their patriotism. Millions volunteered for the Red Cross and the United Service Organizations (USO), and 350,000 enlisted in the armed forces. Although most women surrendered their positions at the war's end, they lamented the loss of income and autonomy. Whether or not women willingly returned to full-time marriage and motherhood, the war permanently changed traditional ideas about gender.

In these passages, Sybil Lewis, a black woman from Sapulpa, Oklahoma, and Adele Erenberg, a white woman from Los Angeles, relate their wartime experiences.

FOCUS QUESTIONS

1. What compelled these women to seek defense jobs? How do they describe their experiences with defense work?
2. What obstacles did these women encounter on the job? How did they respond?
3. How were these women changed during the war? Do you think their experiences were typical?

SYBIL LEWIS

W hen I first arrived in Los Angeles, I began to look for a job. I decided I didn't want to do maid work anymore, so I got a job as a waitress in a small black restaurant. I was making pretty good money, more than I had in Sapulpa, but I didn't like the job that much; I didn't have the knack for getting good tips. Then I saw an ad in the newspaper offering to train for defense work. I went to Lockheed Aircraft and applied. They said they'd call me, but I never got a response, so I went back and applied again. You had to be pretty persistent. Finally they accepted me. They gave me a short training program and taught me how to rivet. Then they put me to work in the plant riveting small airplane parts, mainly gasoline tanks.

The women worked in pairs. I was the riveter, and this big strong white girl from a cotton farm in Arkansas worked as the bucker. The riveter used a gun to shoot rivets through the metal and fasten it together. The bucker used a bucking bar on the other side of the metal to smooth out the rivets. Bucking was harder than shooting rivets; it required more muscle. Riveting required more skill.

I worked for a while as a riveter with this white girl, when the boss came around one day and said, "We've decided to make some changes." At this point, he assigned her to do the riveting and me to do the bucking. I wanted to know why. He said, "Well, we just interchange once in a while." But I was never given the riveting job back. That was the first encounter I had with segregation in California, and it didn't sit too well with me. It brought back some of my experiences in Sapulpa—you're a Negro, so you do the hard work. I wasn't failing as a riveter—in fact, the other girl learned to rivet from me—but I felt they gave me the job of bucker because I was black.

So I applied to Douglas Aircraft in Santa Monica and was hired as a riveter there. On that job I did not encounter the same prejudice. As a matter of fact, the foreman was congenial. But Maywood, where Lockheed was located, was a very segregated city. Going into that city, you were really going into forbidden territory. Santa Monica was not as segregated a community.

I worked in aircraft for a few years, then in '43 I saw an ad in the paper for women trainees to learn arc welding. The salary sounded good, from a dollar to a dollar twenty-five an hour. I wanted to learn that skill and I wanted to make more money, so I answered the ad and they sent me to a short course at a welding school. After I passed the trainee course, they employed me at the shipyards. That was a little different than working in aircraft, because in the shipyard you found mostly men. There I ran into another kind of discrimination: because I was a woman I was paid less than a man for doing the same job.

I was an arc welder, I'd passed both the army and navy tests, and I knew I could do the job, but I found from talking with some of the men that they made more money. You'd ask about this, but they'd say, "Well, you don't have the experience," or "The men have to lift some of the heavy pieces of steel and you don't have to," but I knew that I had to help lift steel, too....

I enjoyed working at the shipyard; it was a unique job for a woman, and I liked the challenge. But it was a dangerous job. The safety measures were very poor. Many people were injured by falling steel. Finally I was assigned to a very hazardous area and I asked to be transferred into a safer area. I was not granted that. They said, "You have to work where they assign you at all times." I thought it was getting too dangerous, so I quit.

The war years had a tremendous impact on women. I know for myself it was the first time I had a chance to get out of the kitchen and work in industry and make a few bucks. This was something I had never dreamed would happen. In Sapulpa all that women had to look forward to was keeping house and raising families. The war years offered new possibilities. You came out to California, put on your pants and took your lunch pail to a man's job. In Oklahoma, a woman's place was in the home, and men went to work and provided. This was the beginning of women's feeling that they could do something more. We were trained to do this kind of work because of the war, but there was no question that this was just an interim period. We were all told that when the war was over we would not be needed anymore.

ADELE ERENBERG

hen the war started I was twenty-six, unmarried, and working as a cosmetics clerk in a drugstore in Los Angeles. I was running the whole department, handling the inventory and all that. It seemed asinine, though, to be selling lipstick when the country was at war. I felt that I was capable of doing something more than that toward the war effort.

There was also a big difference between my salary and those in defense work. I was making something like twenty-two, twenty-four dollars a week in the drugstore. You could earn a much greater amount of money for your labor in defense plants. Also it interested me. There was a certain curiosity about meeting that kind of challenge, and here was an opportunity to do that, for there were more and more openings for women.

So I went to two or three plants and took their tests. And they all told me I had absolutely no mechanical ability. I said, "I don't believe that." So I went to another plant, A.D.E.L. I was interviewed and got the job. This particular plant made the hydraulic-valve system for the B-17. And where did they put women? In the burr room. You sat at a workbench, which was essentially like a picnic table, with a bunch of other women, and you worked grinding and sanding machine parts to make them smooth. That's what you did all day long. It was very mechanical and it was very boring. There were about thirty women in the burr room, and it was like being in a beauty shop every day. I couldn't stand the inane talk. So when they asked me if I would like to work someplace else in the shop, I said I very much would.

They started training me. I went to a blueprint class and learned how to use a micrometer and how to draw tools out of the tool crib and everything else. Then one day they said, "Okay, how would you like to go into the machine shop?"

I said, "Terrific."

And they said, "Now, Adele, it's going to be a real challenge, because you'll be the only woman in the machine shop." I thought to myself, Well that's going to be fun, all those guys and Adele in the machine shop. So the foreman took me over there. It was a big room, with a high ceiling, and fluorescent lights, and it was very noisy. I walked in there, in my overalls, and suddenly all the machines stopped and every guy in the shop just turned around and looked at me. It took, I think, two weeks before anyone even talked to me. The discrimination was indescribable. They wanted to kill me.

My attitude was, "Okay, you bastards, I'm going to prove to you I can do anything you can do, and maybe better than some of you." And that's exactly the way it turned out. I used to do the rework on the pieces that the guy on the shift before me had screwed up. I finally got assigned to nothing but rework.

Later they taught me to run an automatic screwing machine. It's a big mother, and it took a lot of strength just to throw that thing into gear. They probably thought I wasn't going to be able to do it. But I was determined to succeed. As a matter of fact, I developed the most fantastic biceps from throwing that machine into gear. Even today I have a little of that muscle left.

Anyway, eventually some of the men became very friendly, particularly the older ones, the ones in their late forties or fifties. They were journeymen tool and die makers and were so skilled that they could work anywhere at very high salaries. They were sort of fatherly, protective. They weren't threatened by me. The younger men, I think, were.

Our plant was an open shop, and the International Association of Machinists was trying to unionize the workers. I joined them and worked to get the union in the plant. I proselytized for the union during lunch hour, and I had a big altercation with the management over that. The employers and my lead man and foreman called me into the office and said, "We have a right to fire you."

I said, "On what basis? I work as well or better than anybody else in the shop except the journeymen."

They said, "No, not because of that. Because you're talking for the union on company property. You're not allowed to do that."

I said, "Well, that's just too bad, because I can't get off the grounds here. You won't allow us to leave the grounds during lunch hour. And you don't pay me for my lunch hour, so that time doesn't belong to you, so you can't tell me what to do." And they backed down.

I had one experience at the plant that really made me work for the union. One day while I was burring I had an accident and ripped some cartilage out of my hand. It wasn't serious, but it looked kind of messy. They had to take me over to the industrial hospital to get my hand sutured. I came back and couldn't work for a day or so because my hand was all bandaged.... When I got my paycheck, I saw that they had docked me for time that I was in the industrial hospital. When I saw that I was really mad.

It's ironic that when the union finally got into the plant, they had me transferred out. They were anxious to get rid of me because after we got them in I went to a few meetings and complained about it being a Jim Crow union. So they arranged for me to have a higher rating instead of a worker's rating. This allowed me to make twenty-five cents an hour more, and I got transferred to another plant. By this time I was married. When I became pregnant I worked for about three months more, then I quit.

For me defense work was the beginning of my emancipation as a woman. For the first time in my life I found out that I could do something with hands besides bake a pie. I found out that I had manual dexterity and the mentality to read blueprints and gauges, and to be inquisitive enough about things to develop skills other than the conventional roles that women had at that time. I had the consciousness-raising experience of being the only woman in this machine shop and having the mantle of challenge laid down by the men, which stimulated my competitiveness and forced me to prove myself. This, plus working in the union, gave me a lot of self-confidence.

Mark Jonathan Harris, et al. *The Homefront: America During World War II* (New York: G.P. Putnam's Sons, 1984), pp. 118-121, 126-129.

21.6

CHARLES KUKUCHI ON LIFE IN A JAPANESE INTERNMENT CAMP (1942)

During the war years, the rise of defense industries triggered a massive social migration. Millions left rural areas and moved to cities seeking defense jobs. While this population shift made Americans more cosmopolitan, it also generated social tensions as migrants competed for jobs and housing. In 1943 alone, forty-seven cities reported racial clashes. The bloodiest occurred in Detroit, where a June riot left thirty-four people dead and two million dollars in property damage. The following month, hostilities between white servicemen and Latino pachucos (youth gang members) degenerated into four days of violence in Los Angeles.

The internment of 112,000 Japanese-Americans living on the West Coast was the era's most notorious racial incident. California had a long history of intolerance toward Asians and Asian Americans. Unlike Italian Americans or German Americans, Japanese Americans were a relatively small and isolated community focused in three states. Following the Pearl Harbor attack, fears of Japanese subversion and racism fueled popular demands that "Japs" be imprisoned.

In February 1942, despite the fact that not a single Japanese-American had been found guilty of disloyalty or espionage, Franklin Roosevelt succumbed to political pressure and issued Executive Order 9066. The directive forced Japanese Americans living in California, Oregon, and Washington to live in relocation camps for the duration of the war. The decision outraged Japanese Americans, more than two-thirds of whom were U.S. citizens. Receiving only seventy-two hours notice, they were forced to sell their property and possessions at very discounted prices and then report to internment centers scattered throughout the West. Armed guards patrolled the camps and living conditions were usually poor. Ironically, the order did not apply to Hawaii, the U.S. territory with the highest percentage of Japanese Americans.

Weaknesses in the relocation policy became apparent. A shortage of agricultural workers prompted the government to release several internees almost immediately. Private humanitarian groups secured the release of hundreds of young people by offering them college scholarships or vocational training. Thousands of Japanese-American men got out of the camps by enlisting in armed services. Although the Supreme Court upheld the constitutionality of the internment policy in Hirabayashi v. United States *(1943) and* Korematsu v. United States *(1944), the government began releasing internees as wartime hysteria subsided. In 1988, the U.S. Congress issued an apology and awarded $20,000 to each of the 80,000 survivors of the relocation program.*

In these diary excerpts, Charles Kikuchi, an American-born child (Nisei) of Japanese immigrants (Issei), documents his internment at Tanforan, a relocation center in San Bruno, California. In 1943, Kikuchi was released from the camp in order to participate in a work program in Chicago.

Focus Questions

1. How does Kikuchi describe conditions prior to the evacuation of Japanese Americans?
2. What is life like at Tanforan?
3. Describe Kukuchi's attitudes toward the internment camps and his fellow Japanese Americans.
4. Where do Kikuchi's political loyalties lie?
5. Was the internment of Japanese Americans justified? Explain your answer.

April 9, 1942, Berkeley

 F. Japanese Town certainly looks like a ghost town. All the stores are closed, and the windows are bare except for a mass of "evacuation sale" signs. The junk dealers are having a roman holiday, since they can have their cake and eat it too. It works like this! They buy cheap from the Japanese leaving and sell dearly to the Okies coming in for defense work. Result, good profit....

April 30, 1942, Berkeley

Today is the day that we are going to get kicked out of Berkeley. It certainly is degrading. I am down here in the control station, and I have nothing to do so I am jotting down these notes! The Army Lieutenant over there doesn't want any of the photographers to take pictures of these miserable people waiting for the Greyhound bus because he thinks that the American public might get a sympathetic attitude towards them.

I'm supposed to see my family at Tanforan as Jack told me to give the same family number. I wonder how it is going to be living with them as I haven't done this for years and years? I should have gone over to San Francisco and evacuated with them, but I had a last final to take. [Kikuchi was studying social work at the University of California-Berkeley]. I understand that we are going to live in the horse stalls. I hope that the army has the courtesy to remove the manure first.

This morning I went over to the bank to close my account and the bank teller whom I have never seen before solemnly shook my hand and said, "Goodbye, have a nice time." I wonder if that isn't the attitude of the American people? They don't seem to be bitter against us, and I certainly don't think I am any different from them....

Mitch just came over to tell us that I was going on the last bus out of Berkeley with him. Oh, how lucky I am!...

The Church people around here seem so nice and full of consideration saying, "Can we store your things?" "Do you need clothes?" "Sank you," the Issei smile even now though they are leaving with hearts full of sorrow. But the Nisei around here seem pretty bold and their manners are brazen. They are demanding service. I guess they are taking advantage of their college educations after all. "The Japs are leaving, hurrah! Hurrah!" some little kids are yelling down the street but everybody ignores them. Well, I have to go up to the campus and get the results of my last exam and will barely be able to make it back here in time for the last bus. God, what a prospect to look forward to living among all those Japs!

May 3, 1942, Sunday

The whole family pitched in to build our new home at Tanforan. We raided the Clubhouse [Tanforan had been a horse racing park hurriedly converted into a relocation center] and tore off the linoleum from the bar table and put it on our floor....

There are still many problems to be solved such as heating, cleaner dishes, more variety of foods, recreational and other social problems but they will most likely be settled in time.

I saw a soldier in a tall guardhouse near the barbed wire fence and did not like it because it reminds me of a concentration camp. I am wondering what the effects will be on the Japanese so cut off from the world like this. Within the confines of Tanforan our radios and papers are the only touch with reality. I hardly know how the war is going now, and it is so significant that the Allied forces win even though that will not mean that democracy will by any means be perfect or even justified. The whole post war period is going to be something terrific. Sometimes I feel like a foreigner in this camp hearing so much Japanese although our family use English almost exclusively....

May 4, 1942, Monday

There are such varied reactions to the whole thing: some are content and thankful; others gush "sank you" but are full of complaints within their own circles. Still others are bolder and come right out with it. We thought we would not have any dinner tonight because the cooks went on a strike. They really are overworked—preparing 300 meals. Then there have been considerable "personality difficulties." The battle for prestige here is terrific—everyone wants to be somebody, it seems—any kind of work will do as long as they get the official badges that distinguish them....

Oh, I sure could go for a hamburger now: the big juicy kind. I've eaten so much canned food the past week that it becomes tasteless. Many of the boys are worried about being fed saltpeter because they think it will ruin their manhood.

A contrasting reaction is the number of victory gardens that are being planted: these industrious Japanese! They just don't seem to know how to take it easy— they've worked so hard all of their lives that they just can't stand idleness—or waste. They are so concerned that water is not left running or that electricity is not being wasted....

May 8, 1942, Friday

...A lot of Nisei kids come in and mix their Japanese in with their English. Now that we are cut off from the Caucasian contacts, there will be a greater tendency to speak more and more Japanese unless we carefully guard against it. Someday these Nisei will once again go out into the greater American society and it is so important that they be able to speak English well—that's why education is so important. I still think it is a big mistake to evacuate all the Japanese. Segregation is the least desirable thing that could happen and it certainly is going to increase the problem of future social adjustments. How can we expect to develop Americanization when they are all put together with the stigma of disloyalty pointed at them? I am convinced that the Nisei could become good Americans, and will be, if they are not treated with much suspicion. The presence here of all those pro-Japan Issei certainly will not help things out any....

May 10, 1942 Sunday

...As far as I am concerned, I don't like the reasons why we are put here, but I am finding it interesting so far. I don't know how I will feel a month from now though. But I haven't got so much service in years. The girls make the beds and clean house. I don't have to do my laundry; Mom darns my socks and my shirts are ironed. I don't have to wash dishes or cook; in fact I am getting all-around service without worrying about finances like I did when I went to school last term. I lived on about $25.00 a month budget and had to skimp like hell to make it; here I bet it costs the government a lot more per month for my upkeep. But then—all this still doesn't compensate for my liberty and freedom of movement from place to place…. The more Americanized Nisei are finding adjustment a bit more difficult. They are more aware of the motives behind the evacuation and they can't take it so easily as some of the others….

May 11, 1942, Monday

…There was a terrific rainstorm last night and we have had to wade through the "slush alleys" again. Everyone sink up to the ankles in mud. Some trucks came in today with lumber to build new barracks, but the earth was so soft that the truck sank over the hubs and they had a hell of a time pulling it out. The Army certainly is rushing things. About half of the Japanese have already been evacuated from the restricted areas in this state. Manzanar, Santa Anita, and Tanforan will be the three biggest centers. Now that S.F. has been almost cleared, the American Legion, the Native Sons of the Golden West, and the California Joint Immigration Committee are filing charges that the Nisei should be disfranchised because we have obtained citizenship under false pretenses, and that "we are loyal subjects of Japan" and therefore should never have been allowed to obtain citizenship. This sort of thing will gain momentum and we are not in a very advantageous position to combat it. I get fearful sometimes because this sort of hysteria will gain momentum…. I think that they are stabbing us in the back and that there should be a separate concentration camp for these so-called Americans. They are a lot more dangerous than the Japanese in the U.S. ever will or have been….

July 8, 1942

…I keep saying to myself that I must view everything intellectually and rationally, but sometimes I feel sentiments compounded of blind feelings and irrationality. Here all of my life I have identified my every act with America but when the war broke out I suddenly find that I won't be allowed to become an integral part of the whole in these times of national danger. I find I am put aside and viewed suspiciously. My set of values gets twisted; I don't know what to think. Yes, an American certainly is a queer thing. I know what I want, I think, yet it looks beyond my reach at times, but I won't accept defeat. Americanism is my only solution and I may even get frantic about it if thwarted. To retain my loyalty to my country, I must also retain my family loyalty or what else do I have to build upon? So I can't be selfish and individualistic to such a strong degree. I must view it from either angle and abide by the majority decision. If I am to be in a camp for the duration, I may as well have the stabilizing influence of the family….

August 17, 1942, Monday, 8:00

…There are so many interesting people in camp. They are Americans! Sometimes they may say things that arise out of their bewildered feelings, but they can't throw off the environmental effects of the American way of life which is ingrained in them. The injustices of evacuation will some day come to light. It is a blot upon our national life—like the Negro problem, the way labor gets kicked around, the unequal distribution of wealth, the sad plight of the farmers, the slums of our large cities, and a multitude of things. It would make me dizzy just to think about them now.

Charles Kikuchi, *The Kikuchi Diary: Chronicle from an American Concentration Camp; The Tanforan Journals of Charles Kikuchi*, ed. John Modell (Urbana, IL: University of Illinois Press, 1973), 51-55, 66, 69, 73, 170, 229.

21.7

AN AFRICAN-AMERICAN SOLDIER ATTACKS THE PARADOX OF AMERICAN DEMOCRACY (1944)

Although WWII opened opportunities for African Americans, it also high-lighted the paradox of America's segregated democracy. Accordingly, civil rights leaders enunciated a "Double V" campaign calling for the defeat of Nazism abroad and victory over racism at home. Energized by these appeals, one million African Americans enlisted in the armed forces and thousands joined civil rights organizations like the National Association for the Advancement of Colored People (NAACP). Between 1941 and 1945, NAACP membership rose from 50,000 to 500,000. The group demanded anti-lynching laws, access to voting, and racial equality in employment, education, and housing. In 1944, NAACP lawyers won the landmark Supreme Court case Smith v. Allwright, *striking down all-white primaries in Texas and eight other states.*

Other civil rights organizations also pushed for change. In 1941, A. Philip Randolph, president of the Brotherhood of Sleeping Car Porters, threatened to organize a massive march on Washington, D.C. unless the federal government ended racial bias in the military and defense industries. Unwilling to risk such an embarrassment, President Roosevelt issued Executive Order 8802. Although the directive did not address the armed services, it outlawed discrimination in the U.S. civil service and in private establishments and unions receiving federal defense contracts. The measure created the Fair Employment Practices Committee (FEPC) to enforce the policy. Although the FEPC lacked the staff or funds to ensure full compliance, FDR's order enabled two million African Americans to attain defense jobs and another 200,000 to enter the federal workforce. Black union membership doubled and African-American wages quadrupled from $457 to $1,976 a year, approximately $600 less than whites.

The military's record on racial equality was less impressive. When the war began, the army and navy rarely sent blacks into combat and relegated them to menial chores like kitchen duty and burial detail. The marines refused to admit African Americans in any capacity. The Red Cross maintained different blood supplies for white and black soldiers. Wartime demands forced revision of some of these practices. U.S. military officials deployed all-black units such as the 761st Tank Battalion and the 99th Pursuit Squadron that compiled distinguished records in combat against the Nazis. By 1944, the army and navy were experimenting with integration. Most black soldiers, however, served in segregated companies commanded by white officers. Throughout the war, African-American soldiers bitterly complained about racial harassment on and near military installations. Not surprisingly, black veterans were among the thousands of African Americans who joined the civil rights movement in the years following World War II. In these letters, an African-American soldier responds to racism in the armed services.

———————————■———————————

FOCUS QUESTIONS

1. Why does Private Wilson believe there is a paradox in the American fight against fascism? What evidence does he use to sustain his argument?
2. How and why does Wilson think that President Roosevelt should address racial discrimination in the armed forces?
3. Why do you think that World War II inspired so many African Americans to join the civil rights movement of the postwar era?

President Franklin Roosevelt
White House
Washington, D.C.

33rd AAF Base Unit (CCTS9H))
Section C
DAVIS-MONTHAN FIELD
Tucson, Arizona
9 May 1944

Dear President Roosevelt:
  It was with extreme pride that I, a soldier in the Armed Forces of our country, read the following affirmation of our war aims, produced by you at a recent press conference:
  "The United Nations are fighting to make a world in which tyranny and aggression cannot exist; a world based upon freedom, equality and justice; a world in which all persons, regardless of race, color, and creed may live in peace, honor, and dignity."
  Your use of the word "world" means that we are fighting for "freedom, equality, and justice" for "all persons, regardless of race, color, and creed" in our

own part of the world, the United States of America, as well as all other counties where such a fight is needed to be carried through. Your use of the words "all persons, regardless of race, color, and creed" means that we are fighting for "freedom, equality, and justice" for our Negro Americans, no less than for our white Americans, or our Jewish, Protestant and Catholic Americans, or for the subjugated peoples in Europe and China and all other lands....

Our driving back of the Japanese fascists in the Pacific; our driving back of the German fascists in North Africa, Sicily, and Italy, in conjunction with our British and French Allies, freeing that part of the world from "tyranny and aggression" as the prerequisite for bringing "freedom, equality and justice" to the North African and Italian peoples; the tremendous preparations and planning that we as part of the United Nations have carried out so that we now stand on the eve of the invasion, and in conjunction with Allies, the British, Russian, French and European Underground, on the eve of freeing the subjugated peoples of Europe from the German fascist tyranny; the glorious part that we played in the decision reached at Tehran, these are vivid records of the manner in which the war aims of the United Nations, as pronounced by you, are being fought for by us, throughout the world.

On the home front there are vivid examples also; your issuance of Executive Order 8802, which established the Fair Employment Practices Commission, to fight against the discriminatory employment practices of being used against Negroes and other minority groups in the war industries...the support which you have given to the fight against the flagrantly undemocratic poll tax...the production by the U.S. Army Signal Corps, as authorized by the War Department, of the film "The Negro Soldier," these are but a few of the many examples of the fight that the democratic forces in our government, with your leadership, is carrying on in our country as part of the world struggle against "tyranny"....

But the picture in our country is marred by one of the strangest paradoxes in our whole fight against world fascism. The United States Armed Forces, to fight for World Democracy, is within itself undemocratic. The undemocratic policy of Jim Crow and segregation is practiced by our Armed Forces against its Negro members. Totally inadequate opportunities are given to the Negro members of our Armed Forces, nearly one tenth of the whole, to participate with "equality"..."regardless of race and color" in the fight for our war aims. In fact it appears that the army intends to follow the very policy that the FEPC is battling against in civilian life, the pattern of assigning Negroes to the lowest types of work.

Let me give you an example of the lack of democracy in our Field, where I am now stationed. Negro soldiers are completely segregated from the white soldiers on the base. And to make doubly sure that no mistake is made about this, the barracks and other housing facilities (supply room, mess hall, etc.) of the Negro Section C are covered with black tar paper, while all other barracks and housing facilities on the base are painted white.

It is the stated policy of the Second Air Force that "every potential fighting man must be used as a fighting man. If you have such a man in a base job, you have no choice. His job must be eliminated or filled by a limited services man, WAC [Women's Army Corps], or civilian." And yet, leaving out the Negro soldiers working with the Medical Section, fully 50% of the Negro soldiers are working in base jobs such as, for example, at the Resident Officers' Mess, Bachelor Officers' Quarters, and Officers' Club, as mess personnel, BOQ orderlies, and bar tenders. Leaving out the medical men again, based on the Section C average only 4% of this 50% would not be "potential fighting men."...

Let us assume as a basis for discussion that there are no civilians or limited service men to do the menial work on the base. The democratic way based upon "equality and justice" would be to assign this work to both Negro and white. Instead the discriminatory and undemocratic method is used whereby all of this work is assigned to the Negro soldiers.

On the other hand suppose civilians were found to take over all of the base jobs and thus free the Negro soldiers for use as fighting men. They would not be given "on-the-job-training" to become members of the ground crew, such as is being done for the WAC members on the base, because there is no such program for the Negroes at Davis-Monthan Field. They would not be trained to become aerial gunners, or bombardiers, or navigators, or pilots, or bombsight mechanics, or any of the many other specialists at Davis-Monthan Field, because there is no authorization in the Second Air Force for this training to be given to Negroes....

How can we convince nearly one tenth of the Armed Forces, the Negro members, that your pronouncement of the United Nations members means what it says, when their experience with one of the United Nations, the United States of America, is just the opposite?

Are the Chinese people to believe that we are fighting to bring them "freedom, equality, and justice" when they can see that in our Armed Forces we are not even practicing what we are preaching?

However, we leave ourselves wide open for sowers of disunity. Nothing would suit Hitler, Tojo, and our own native fascists better than disunity.... We know that isn't the answer. Disunity and civil strife would only weaken our fight against the German and Japanese fascists, or more than that result in our defeat. A victory for the German and Japanese fascists would a victory for our own native fascists, who are at the bottom [of] this whole program of "white supremacy," race hatred, jim-crowism, and segregation....

The only answer is...fighting for war aims of the United Nations in our own country as well as throughout the rest of the world. That means that we must fight against the fascist shouters of "white supremacy," against the labor baiters, against segregation and jim-crowism wherever these evils show their fangs, whether in the Armed Forces, or in the civilian population....

Just as our government in civilian life, is carrying on a fight for the full integration of the Negro and all other minority groups into the war effort, with the result that Negro men and women are producing the implements of war, in jobs from the unskilled to the most highly skilled, side by side, with their white brothers and sisters, so in the Armed Forces our government must take up the same fight for the full integration of the Negro into all phases of our fighting forces from the lowest to the highest.

President Roosevelt, in the interest of the war effort you issued Executive Order 8802, which established the Fair Employment Practices Committee. Although there is still much to be done, nevertheless, this committee, against heavy opposition, has played and is playing a gallant role in fighting for democracy for the men and women behind the lines, in the industries that produce the guns, and tanks, and bombers for victory over world fascism.

With your issuance of Executive Order 8802, and the setting up of the Fair Employment Practices Committee, you established the foundation for fighting for democracy in the industrial forces of our country, in the interest of victory for the United Nations. In the interest of victory for the United Nations, another Executive Order is now needed. An Executive Order which will lay the base for fighting for democracy in the Armed Forces our country. An Executive Order which would bring about the result here at Davis-Monthan Field whereby the Negro soldiers would be integrated into all of the Sections on the base, as fighting men, instead of in the segregated Section C as housekeepers.

Then and only then can your pronouncements of the war aims of the United Nations mean to *all* that we "are fighting to make a world in which tyranny and aggression cannot exist; a world based upon freedom, equality, and justice; a world in which all persons, regardless of race, color, and creed, may live in peace, honor and dignity."

Respectfully yours,
Charles F. Wilson, 36794590
Private, Air Corps

Philip McGuire, ed. *Taps for a Jim Crow Army: Letters from Black Soldiers in World War II* (Santa Barbara, CA: ABC-Clio, 1983), pp. 134-139.

21.8

INFANTRYMAN BOB SLAUGHTER
REMEMBERS D-DAY (1944)

On June 6, 1944, the Allied invasion of Western Europe (known as D-Day or Operation Overlord) began. U.S. General Dwight D. Eisenhower coordinated a huge force of 2,000 ships, 10,000 planes, 4,126 landing craft, and hundreds of tanks and other vehicles in an attack on the shores of Normandy, France. One hundred and thirty two thousand American, British, and Canadian troops were transported across the English Channel. Another 23,500 parachuted behind enemy lines. They assaulted five beaches code-named Utah, Gold, Juno, Sword, and Omaha. While the British and Canadian contingents met little opposition, American forces encountered fierce resistance, especially at Omaha Beach.

U.S. soldiers from the 1st and 29th Infantry Divisions, along with Army Rangers and amphibious tanks, were ordered to secure Omaha Beach. They sustained heavy casualties, but succeeded in completing their mission. By late August, more than one million Allied troops had landed at Normandy and swept through France. After liberating Paris, they headed toward the German border. Although supply problems and a reorganized German army soon stopped the Allied offensive, the D-Day operation turned the tide of the war in Europe.

In this reading, Bob Slaughter, a member of the 29th Infantry Division, recalls landing at Omaha Beach.

Focus Questions

1. How does Bob Slaughter describe D-Day?
2. How do the soldiers' emotions change throughout the attack?
3. If you had been alive during World War II, would you have enlisted in the armed services? Explain your answer.

e saw the bomb explosions causing fires that illuminated clouds in the otherwise dark. We were twelve miles offshore as we climbed into our seat assignments on the LCAs and were lowered into the heavy sea from davits. The navy hadn't begun its firing because it was still dark. We couldn't see the armada but we knew it was there.

Prior to landing, friends said their so longs and good lucks. I remember finding Sgt. Jack Ingram, an old friend from Roanoke. He had suffered a back injury during training and I asked him how felt, "I'm okay. Good luck, I'll see you on the beach." Another Roanoker, a neighbor and classmate, George D. Johnson, who'd joined the army with me asked, "Are you men ready?" I couldn't imagine why he asked, but I answered yes.

Sgt. Robert Bixler of Shamokin, Pennsylvania, joked, "I'm going to land with a comb in one hand"—running his hand through his blond hair—"and a pass to Paris in the other." The feeling among most of the men was that the landing would be a "walk-in affair" but later we could expect a stiff counterattack. That didn't worry us too much, since by then the tanks, heavy artillery, and air support should bolster our defense until the beachhead grew strong enough for a breakout.

All of us had a letter signed by the Supreme Commander, Gen. Eisenhower, saying that we were about to embark upon a great crusade. A few of my cohorts autographed it and I carried it in my wallet throughout the war.

The Channel was extremely rough, and it wasn't long before we had to help the craft's pumps by bailing with our helmets. The cold spray blew in and soon we were soaking wet. I used a gas cape [a plastic sack for protection against skin irritants] as shelter. Lack of oxygen under the sack brought seasickness.

As the sky lightened, the armada became visible. The smoking and burning French shoreline also became more defined. At 0600, the huge guns of the

Allied navies opened up with what must have been one of the greatest artillery barrages ever. The diesels on board our craft failed to muffle the tornadic blasting. I could see the *Texas* firing broadside into the coastline. Boom-ba-ba-boom-ba-ba-boom! Within minutes, giant swells from the recoil of those guns nearly swamped us and added to the seasickness and misery. But one could also actually see the two-thousand-pound missiles tumbling on their targets. Twin-fuselaged P-38 fighter-bombers were also overhead protecting us from the Luftwaffe [the German air force] and giving us a false sense of security. This should be a piece of cake.

A few thousand yards from shore we rescued three or four survivors from a craft that had been swamped and sunk. Other men were left in the water bobbing in their Mae Wests [life preservers], because we did not have room for them.

About two or three hundred yards from shore we encountered artillery fire. Near misses sent water skyward and then it rained back on us. The British coxswain said he had to lower the ramp and for us to quickly disembark. Back in Weymouth these sailors had bragged they had been on several invasions and we were in capable hands. I heard Sgt. Willard Norfleet say, "These men have heavy equipment. You *will* take them all the way in."

The coxswain pleaded, "But we'll all be killed!" Norfleet unholstered his .45 Colt, put it to the sailor's head, and ordered, "*All the way in!*" The craft kept going, plowing through the choppy water.

I thought, if this boat doesn't hurry and get us in, I'll die from seasickness. Thinking I was immune to this malady, I had given my puke bag to a buddy who already had filled his. Minus the paper bag, I used my steel helmet.

About 150 yards from shore, I raised my head despite the warning "Keep your head down." I saw the boat on our right taking a terrific licking from small arms. Tracer bullets were bouncing and skipping off the ramp and sides as the enemy zeroed in on the boat which had beached a few minutes before us. Had we not delayed a few minutes to pick up the survivors of the sunken craft, we might have taken that concentration of fire.

Great plumes of water from enemy artillery and mortars sprouted close by. We knew then this was not going to be a walk-in. No one thought that the enemy would give us this kind of opposition at the water's edge. We expected A and B Companies to have the beach secured by the time we landed. In reality no one had set foot into our sector. The coxswain had missed the Vierville church steeple, our point to guide on, and the tides also helped pull us two hundred yards east.

The location didn't make much difference. We could hear the "p-r-r-r-r, p-r-r-r-r" of enemy machine guns to our right, towards the west. It was obvious someone down there was catching that hell, getting chewed up where we were supposed to come in.

The "someone catching hell" on Dog Green was Company A; more than half of the dead from Bedford, Virginia, were slain there. GIs from battalion headquarters following Company A were shocked to see their beach empty of living men.

The ramp went down while shells exploded on land and in the water. Unseen snipers were shooting down from the cliffs, but the most havoc came from automatic weapons. I was at the left side of the craft, about fifth from the front. Norfleet led the right side. The ramp was in the surf, and the front of the steel boat bucked violently up and down. Only two at a time could exit.

When my turn came, I sat on the edge of the bucking ramp, trying to time my leap on the down cycle. I sat there way too long, causing a bottleneck and endangering myself and the men to follow. But the ramp was bouncing six or seven feet, and I was afraid it would slam me in the head.

When I did get out, I was in the water. It was very difficult to shed the sixty pounds of equipment, and if one were a weak swimmer he could drown before he inflated his Mae West. Many hit in the water and drowned, good swimmers or not. There were dead men floating in the water and live men acting dead, letting the tide take them in. Initially, I tried to take cover behind one of the heavy timbers and then noticed an innocent-looking Teller mine tied to the top. I crouched down to chin deep in the water as shells fell at the water's edge. Small-arms fire kicked up sand. I noticed a G.I. running, trying to get across the beach. He was weighted down with equipment and having difficulty moving. An enemy gunner shot him. He screamed for a medic. An aidman moved quickly to help him and he was also shot. I'll never forget seeing that medic lying next to that wounded soldier, both of them screaming. They both died in minutes.

Boys were turned into men. Some would be very brave men; others would soon be dead men, but any who survived would be frightened men. Some wet their pants, others cried unashamedly. Many just had to find within themselves the strength to get the job done. Discipline and training took over.

For me it was time to get the hell away from the killing zone and across the beach. Getting across the beach became an obsession. I told Pfc. Walfred Williams, my number one gunner, to follow. He still had his fifty-one pound machine gun tripod. He once told me he developed his strength by cradling an old iron cookstove in his arms and walking around with it, daily. I felt secure with Williams on the gun. A Chicago boy of nineteen, he was dependable and loyal. He loved the army and didn't believe a German weapon could kill him. I didn't think so either. (We were both wrong. Enemy shrapnel killed him six weeks after D-Day. Part of me would die with him.)

Our rifles were encased in a plastic bag to shield them from salt water. Before disembarking, because I wanted to be ready, I had removed the covering and fixed the bayonet. I gathered my courage and started running as fast as I my long legs would carry me. I ran as low as I could to lessen the target, but since I am six-foot-five, I presented a good one. It was a long way to go, one hundred yards or more. We were loaded with gear, our shoes full of water, our impregnated woolen clothes soaked. I tripped in a tidal pool of a few inches of water, began to stumble, and accidentally fired my rifle, barely missing my foot. But I made it to the seawall.

I was joined by Pvt. Sal Augeri, and Pvt. Ernest McCanless and Williams, Augeri lost the machine gun receiver in the water. We still had one box of MG ammo and the tripod. I had gotten sand in my rifle, so I don't believe we had a weapon that could fire. I felt like a naked morsel on a giant sandy platter.

I took off my assault jacket and spread out my raincoat so I could clean my rifle. It was then I saw bullet holes in my jacket and raincoat. I lit my first cigarette; I had to rest and compose myself because I became weak in the knees.

Gerald Astor, *June 6, 1944: The Voices of D-Day* (New York: St. Martin's Press, 1994), pp. 184-189.

· 21.9

HARRY S. TRUMAN ON DECIDING TO
USE THE ATOMIC BOMB (1955)

In 1939, physicist Albert Einstein warned President Roosevelt that the Nazis were capable of producing a weapon that harnessed atomic energy. In response, the Roosevelt administration funded small studies of the military potential of fission chain reactions. When the United States entered World War II, these efforts expanded into the Manhattan Project, a top-secret program employing more than 120,000 people. American, British, and Canadian scientists—the Soviets were excluded—collaborated in laboratories in Chicago, Oak Ridge (Tennessee) and Los Alamos (New Mexico). Their challenges included collecting enough fissionable material to produce a nuclear explosion and devising a weapon that could be dropped from an airplane. The massive undertaking cost two billion dollars.

On July 16, 1945, scientists at Los Alamos exploded the first atomic bomb. At that time, the Allies had defeated Nazi Germany, but were locked in fierce combat against Imperial Japan. Earlier in the year, U.S. forces sustained heavy casualties in battles at Iwo Jima and Okinawa. Although the Japanese lost over 110,000 soldiers and 80,000 civilians in these clashes, they continued to fight. U.S. military planners predicted huge losses if American forces invaded the Japanese home islands.

News of the atomic bomb's successful test gave President Harry S. Truman an alternative. On July 25th, while he was attending the Potsdam Conference with Soviet premier Josef Stalin and British prime minister Clement Attlee, Truman issued secret orders to use the Bomb if the Japanese failed to surrender by August 3rd. British, American, and Nationalist Chinese delegates issued the Potsdam Declaration publicly warning Japan that it faced "prompt and utter destruction" if it did not capitulate. The bitterly divided Japanese government rejected the ultimatum.

In response, Truman ordered the military to use atomic weapons. On August 6, the B-29 Enola Gay *dropped a uranium bomb on Hiroshima, instantly killing at least 70,000 people and leveling five square-miles. Two days later, the Soviets kept their promise to enter the Pacific War and swept into Manchuria. On August 9th, the United States dropped a plutonium bomb on Nagasaki and 40,000 people instantly perished. On August 14th, Japan finally surrendered after receiving assurances that Emperor Hirohito could retain his throne.*

The decision to use the Bomb remains hotly disputed. Critics offer several motives including the desire to save American lives, anti-Japanese racism, and intimidation of the Soviet Union. They examine possible alternatives such as a demonstration of the Bomb's power on a deserted island. They debate the morality of nuclear war and whether or not Japan would have surrendered without atomic attacks. Although we will never know the answer to some of these questions, nuclear weapons undoubtedly changed the course of modern history. In this selection from his memoirs, Truman explains his rationale for the Hiroshima bombing.

Focus Questions

1. Prior to the successful test of the atomic bomb, how did U.S. military strategists plan to defeat Japan?
2. What recommendations did the advisory committee present to Truman? Did they offer alternatives to using the Bomb?
3. How does Truman justify his decision to drop the Bomb? Do you agree with his explanation? Why or why not?
4. How did atomic weapons change international relations following WWII?

 month before the test explosion of the atomic bomb the service Secretaries and the Joint Chiefs of Staff had laid their detailed plans for the defeat of Japan before me for approval....

The Army plan envisaged an amphibious landing in the fall of 1945 on the island of Kyusha, the southernmost of the Japanese home islands....

The first landing would then be followed approximately four months later by a second great invasion, which would be carried out by our Eighth and Tenth Armies, followed by the First Army transferred from Europe, all of which would go ashore in the Kanto plains area near Tokyo. In all, it had been estimated that it would require until the late fall of 1946 to bring Japan to her knees.

This was a formidable conception, and all of us realized fully that the fighting would be fierce and the losses heavy....

It was their [the advisory committee examining the implications of using the Bomb] recommendation that the bomb be used against the enemy as soon as it could be done. They recommended that it should be used without specific warning and against a target that would clearly show its devastating strength. I had realized, of course, that an atomic bomb explosion would inflict damage and casualties beyond imagination. On the other hand, the scientific advisers of the committee reported, "We can propose no technical demonstration likely to bring an end to the war; we see no acceptable alternative to direct military use." It was their conclusion that no technical demonstration they might propose, such as over a deserted island, would be likely to bring the war to an end. It had to be used against an enemy target.

The final decision of where and when to use the atomic bomb was up to me. Let there be no mistake about it. I regarded the bomb as a military weapon and never had any doubt that it should be used. The top military advisers to the President recommended its use, and when I talked to Churchill he unhesitatingly told me that he favored the use of the atomic bomb if it might aid to end the war.

In deciding to use this bomb I wanted to make sure that it would be used as a weapon of war in the manner prescribed by the laws of war. That meant that I wanted it dropped as nearly as possibly upon a war production center of prime military importance.

[Secretary of War Henry] Stimson's staff had prepared a list of cities in Japan that might serve as targets. Kyoto, though favored by General Arnold as a center of military activity, was eliminated when Secretary Stimson pointed out that it was a cultural and religious shrine of the Japanese.

Four cities were finally recommended as targets: Hiroshima, Kokura, Niigata, and Nagasaki. They were listed in that order as targets for the first attack. The order of selection was in accordance with the military importance of these cities, but allowance would be given for weather conditions at the time of the bombing....

General Spaatz, who commanded the Strategic Air Forces, which would deliver the bomb on the target, was given some latitude as to when and on which of the four targets the bomb would be dropped. That was necessary because of weather and other operational considerations. In order to get preparations under way, the War Department was given orders to instruct General Spaatz that the first bomb would be dropped as soon after August 3 as weather would permit....

On July 28 Radio Tokyo announced that the Japanese government would continue to fight. There was no formal reply to the joint ultimatum of the United States, the United Kingdom, and China. There was no alternative now. The bomb was scheduled to be dropped after August 3 unless Japan surrendered before that day.

On August 6, the fourth day of the journey home from Potsdam, came the historic news that shook the world. I was eating lunch with members of the *Augusta's* crew when Captain Frank Graham, White House map Room watch officer, handed me the following message:

TO THE PRESIDENT
FROM THE SECRETARY OF WAR

Big bomb dropped on Hiroshima August 5 at 7:15 P.M. Washington time. First reports indicate complete success which was even more conspicuous than earlier test.

I was greatly moved. I telephoned Byrnes aboard ship to give him the news and then said to the group of sailors around me, "This is the greatest thing I history. It's time for us to get home."

A few minutes later a second message was handed to me. It read as follows:

Following info regarding Manhattan received. "Hiroshima bombed visually with only one tenth cover at 052315A. There was no fighter opposition and no flak. Parsons reports 15 minutes after drop as follows: 'Results clear cut successful in all respects. Visible effects greater than in any test. Conditions normal in airplane following delivery.'"

When I had read this I signaled to the crew in the mess hall that I wished to say something. I then told them of the dropping of a powerful new bomb which used an explosive twenty thousand times as powerful as a ton of TNT. I went to the wardroom, where I told the officers, who were at lunch, what had happened. I could not keep back my expectation that the Pacific war might now be brought to a speedy end.

A few minutes later the ship's radio receivers began to carry news bulletins from Washington about the atomic bomb, as well as a broadcast of the statement I had authorized just before leaving Germany. Shortly afterward I called a press conference of the correspondents on board and told them something of the long program of research and development that lay behind this successful assault.

My statements on the atomic bomb, which had been released in Washington by Stimson, read in part as follows:

"...[T]he greatest marvel is not the size of the enterprise, its secrecy, nor its cost, but the achievement of scientific brains in putting together infinitely complex pieces of knowledge held by many men in different fields of science into a workable plan. And hardly less marvelous has been the capacity of industry to design, and of labor to operate, the machines and methods to do things never done before, so that the brainchild of many minds came forth in physical shape and performed as it was supposed to do. Both science and industry worked under the direction of the United States Army, which achieved a unique success in managing so diverse a problem in the advancement of knowledge in an amazingly short time. It is doubtful if such another combination could be got together in the world. What has been done is the greatest achievement of organized science in history. It was done under high pressure and without failure.

"We are now prepared to obliterate more rapidly and completely every productive enterprise the Japanese have above ground in any city. We shall destroy their docks, their factories, and their communications. Let there be no mistake; we shall completely destroy Japan's power to make war."

"It was to spare the Japanese people from utter destruction that the ultimatum of July 26th was issued at Potsdam. Their leaders promptly rejected that ultimatum. If they do not now accept our terms, they may expect a rain of ruin, the like of which has never been seen on this earth. Behind this air attack will follow sea and land forces in such numbers and power as they have not yet seen and with the fighting skill of which they are already well aware."

"...The fact that we can release atomic energy ushers in a new era in man's understanding of nature's forces. Atomic energy may in the future supplement the power that now comes from coal, oil, and falling water, but at present it cannot be produced on a basis to compete with them commercially. Before that comes there must be a long period of intensive research....

"I shall recommend that the Congress of the United States consider promptly the establishment of an appropriate commission to control the production and use of atomic power in the United States.

"I shall give further consideration and make further recommendations to the Congress as to how atomic power can become a powerful and forceful influence towards the maintenance of world peace."

Harry S. Truman, *Memoirs*, Volume One: *Year of Decisions* (Garden City, NY: Doubleday, 1955), 419-423.

SECONDARY SOURCE

—■—

GEORGE H. ROEDER, JR., "RATIONING DEATH"

Throughout U.S. history, government officials have attempted to shape public opinion. Because of the imperatives of ensuring national security and maintaining civilian morale, this process is most evident during times of war. In this excerpt from The Censored War: American Visual Experience During World War Two *(1993), George H. Roeder, Jr., Professor of Visual and Critical Studies at the Art Institute of Chicago, explores how and why U.S. officials carefully controlled the images that citizens saw during World War II.*

⊙ Go to your *Speaking of America* CD-ROM to read "Rationing Death."

—■—

FOCUS QUESTIONS

1. How did the government's approach to public information during World War II differ from its methods during World War I?
2. During World War II, what types of information did government officials censor? What methods did policy makers use to control what information reached the public?
3. How and why did official depictions of WWII change over time?

4. Compare the government's portrayal of the war to those of Hollywood and advertisers.

5. How does this reading revise your understanding of government policies during World War II?

AMERICAN JOURNEY ONLINE

◆

http://ajaccesss.wadsworth.com [†]

About Imperial Japan
— In <u>World War II</u>
   Images
- Portrait of Hirohito (1942)
- Admiral Isoruku Yamamoto in World War II
- Tojo in World War II

About Nazi Germany
— In <u>World War II</u>
   Documents
- Molotov-Ribbentrop Non-Aggression Pact (1939)
- Adolf Hitler, Proclamation by Adolf Hitler, Chancellor of the Reich, to the German People, September 3, 1939

   Images
- Do Not Buy Here (1933)
- Hitler Accepts the Ovation of the Reichstag (1938)
- Adolf Hitler in World War II

About the Axis
— In <u>World War II</u>
   Documents
- Governments of Germany, Italy, and Japan, Three-Power Pact Between Germany, Italy, and Japan, Signed at Berlin, September 27, 1940

   Images
- Adolf Hitler and Benito Mussolini

About American Politicians/Public Officials
— In <u>World War II</u>
   Images
- W. Averell Harriman (circa 1934)
- Roosevelt Delivering a Fireside Chat (circa 1935)

[†] Enter password, choose the Archive indicated above, click on Contents, choose •Documents, •Images, or •Multimedia, and click on the title of the item.

- Roosevelt's Third Inauguration (1941)
- Franklin D. Roosevelt (1942)
- Truman and Roosevelt (1944)
- Burying a President (1945)
- Tom Connally, Sam Rayburn, and John McCormick (1949)

About American Neutrality
— In <u>World War II</u>
Documents
- United States Congress, Neutrality Act of August 31, 1935, Joint Resolution
- Nye Committee, Excerpt from the Report of the Special Committee on Investigation of the Munitions Industry, U.S. Congress, Senate, 74th Congress, 2nd session, February 24, 1936
Images
- Gerald P. Nye

About Non-Interventionists
— In <u>World War II</u>
Documents
- Charles Lindbergh, Address Delivered by Charles Lindbergh at an America First Committee Meeting (1941)

About Pearl Harbor Attack/U.S. Declaration of War
— In <u>World War II</u>
Documents
- Franklin D. Roosevelt, "A Date Which Will Live in Infamy" (1941)
Images
- Japanese Aerial Photo of Pearl Harbor's "Battleship Row" on December 7, 1941
- Pearl Harbor and Military Preparedness (1941)
- *U.S.S. Shaw* Exploding During Japanese Raid on Pearl Harbor (1941)
- Damage at Pearl Harbor (1941)
- The *Baltimore News-Post*, Headline-Bombing of Pearl Harbor (1941)
- Roosevelt Before Congress, December 8, 1941
— In <u>The Great Depression and the New Deal</u>
Documents
- Franklin D. Roosevelt, Fireside Chat on the Declaration of War with Japan (1941)

About Mobilization and Propaganda
— In <u>The Great Depression and the New Deal</u>
Documents
- New York Writers' Project, Defense in the Kitchen (1941)

Images
- Drawing Numbers for the First Peacetime Draft (1940)
- Eleanor Roosevelt and Fiorello LaGuardia (1941)
- Fiorello LaGuardia, Planning for the Postwar Depression (1941)
— In World War II
Images
- Alfred T. Palmer, C-47 Transport Planes on Production Line (1942)
- Within Striking Distance (circa 1942) in World War II
- United We Win (circa 1943) in World War II
- Harold Von Schmidt, Save Gas (1944) in World War II

About Law
— In The Great Depression and the New Deal
Images
- William O. Douglas (circa 1940)
— In Civil Rights in the United States
Documents
- U.S. Supreme Court, *Minersville School District v. Gobitis* (1940)
— In The Constitution and Supreme Court
Documents
- Robert H. Jackson, *West Virginia Board of Education v. Barnette* (1943)
— In The African-American Experience
Documents
- *Smith v. Allwright* (1944)

About U.S. Foreign Policy/Military Affairs
— In World War II
Documents
- Franklin D. Roosevelt, Quarantine Address (1937)
- Secretary of State Cordell Hull, Destroyers for Bases Agreement, September 2, 1940
- Franklin D. Roosevelt, Excerpt from President Roosevelt's Radio Address, December 29, 1940
- 77th Congress of the United States of America, Lend Lease Act (1941)
- Franklin D. Roosevelt, Fireside Chat Given by President Roosevelt Announcing a National Emergency (1941)
- Secretary of State Cordell Hull, Statement on Relations with the French Republic (1941)
- Franklin D. Roosevelt and Winston S. Churchill, The Atlantic Conference: Joint Statement by President Roosevelt and Prime Minister Churchill, August 14, 1941
- Franklin D. Roosevelt, Excerpt from Radio Address Given by President Roosevelt Regarding Casablanca Conference (1943)
- U.S. State Department, World Security Organization: The Polish Question (1945)

- • Franklin D. Roosevelt, Letter to Josef Stalin on Poland, April 1, 1945 in World War II

Images
- • Telegram from Churchill to Roosevelt (1941)
- • Josef Stalin, Memo in Russian from Josef Stalin about Opening A Second Front in Europe, August 1942
— In The Great Depression and the New Deal

Documents
- • Franklin D. Roosevelt, Fireside Chat on War in Europe (1939)
- • Franklin D. Roosevelt, Fireside Chat on National Defense (1940)

Videos
- • Roosevelt Reviewing the Pacific Fleet (1938)

About the Tehran Conference
— In World War II

Documents
- • Winston Churchill, Josef Stalin, and Franklin D. Roosevelt, Declaration of the Three Powers (1943)

Images
- • The Big Three during Teheran Conference (1943)

About the Yalta Conference
— In World War II

Documents
- • Winston Churchill, Franklin D. Roosevelt, and Josef Stalin, Joint Communiqué on Crimea Conference (1945)

Images
- • Yalta Conference (1945)

About the Potsdam Conference
— In World War II

Images
- • Truman Joins the Big Three (1945)
- • Triple Handshake (1945)

About the European Theater
— In World War II

Documents
- • Franklin D. Roosevelt, Fireside Chat on War in Europe (1939)
- • Franklin D. Roosevelt, Statement Announcing Opening of Second Front in French North and West Africa (1942)

Images
- • Sudeten Woman (1939)
- • German Troops Parade Through Warsaw, Poland (1939)

- The *Baltimore News-Post*, Britain Declares War on Germany (1939)
- Damage in England from Bombs (1940)
- Adolf Hitler in Paris (1940)
- Map of Operation Barbarossa
- Operation Torch Landing (1942)
- General Bernard L. Montgomery (1942)
- General Erwin Rommel (1943)
- General George S. Patton (1943)
- Amphibious Operations in North Africa (1944)
- General Dwight D. Eisenhower (1944)
- A Note Written by General Eisenhower (1944)
- Robert F. Sargent, D-Day Landing (1944)
- De Gaulle Leads Paris in Victory Parade (1944)
- Battle of the Bulge Casualty (1944)

About V-E Day
— In World War II
   Images
   - Field Marshall Sir Harold Alexander During British Victory Parade in Berlin, Germany (1945)

About the Pacific Theater
— In World War II
   Images
   - Dive Bombers (1940)
   - Navy Fighters During the Attack on the Japanese Fleet off Midway (1942)
   - Generalisimo and Madame Chiang-Kai-Shek and Lieutenant General Joseph W. Stilwell (1942)
   - Department of the Army, Bombing of Japanese Towns (1943)
   - Admiral Chester Nimitz in Conference (1944)
   - Guadalcanal Landing (1944)
   - General Douglas MacArthur (1944)
   - Ships at the Battle of the Coral Sea (1944)
   - Joe Rosenthal, Flag Raising on Iwo Jima (1945)
   - U.S. Coast Guard, Landing at Okinawa (1945)
— In The Cold War
   Images
   - United States Navy, Japanese Surrender Aboard the *U.S.S. Missouri* (1945)
   - Mate 2nd Class F. Toedtman, *U.S.S. Intrepid* (1969)

About V-J Day
— In World War II
   Images
   - V-J Celebration (1945)

About the Atomic Bomb
— In World War II
   Documents
   • Committee on Political and Social Problems, Excerpt from The Frank Report, June 11, 1945
   Images
   • Atomic Bomb Test, Alamagordo, New Mexico, July 16, 1945
   • *Enola Gay* (1945)
   • Los Alamos Scientific Laboratory, Fat Man (1945)
   • Los Alamos Scientific Laboratory, Little Boy (1945)
   • Atomic Damage, Hiroshima (1945)
   • Bombing of Nagasaki (1945)
   • United States Air Force, Mushroom Cloud (1945)
   • Prostrate Japan (1946)
— In The Cold War
   Videos
   • Atomic Damage, Hiroshima (1945)

About Secret Codes and Code-Breaking
— In World War II
   Images
   • German Enigma Machine
   • Purple Machine

About Women
— In Women in America
   Images
   • Woman Working at Boeing Aircraft Company during World War II (circa 1943)
   • First Women Marines Reporting for Duty (1943)
   • U.S. Army, Lt. Fern Wingerd, 2nd Lt., Army Nurse Corps (1944)

About African Americans
— In The African-American Experience
   Documents
   • CORE, Statement of Purpose and Methods (1942)
   • *Smith v. Allwright* (1944)
   Images
   • Southern Migrants Leaving by Foot (circa 1940)
   • Colored Waiting Room (circa 1940)
   • Dr. Charles Drew (circa 1940)
   • Russell Lee, Negro Boys on Easter Morning on the South Side of Chicago (1941)
   • Benjamin O. Davis, Sr. (1944)
   • Tuskegee Airmen (1944)

— In <u>The Great Depression and the New Deal</u>
Images
  • An African-American Family Migrating North (1940)
— In <u>The Constitution and Supreme Court</u>
Images
  • A Colored Drinking Fountain (circa 1940)
— In <u>World War II</u>
Documents
  • Philip Randolph, Call to the March (1941)
  • Franklin Delano Roosevelt, Executive Order 8802 (1941)
Images
  • David Stone, Dorie Miller Recruiting Poster (1943)
  • Race Riot in Detroit (1943)
  • Davis: A Father and Son Reunion (1944)
— In <u>The Immigrant Experience</u>
Documents
  • Phillip McGuire, Excerpt of *Taps for a Jim Crow Army* (1943)
Images
  • White Men Attack, Detroit (1943)

About Hispanic Americans
— In <u>World War II</u>
Documents
  • Mexican Minister of Foreign Affairs, Bracero Agreement (1942)
Images
  • Zoot Suiter (1943)
— In <u>The Hispanic-American Experience</u>
Documents
  • George I. Sanchez, *Panchucos* in the Making (1943)
— In <u>The Immigrant Experience</u>
Documents
  • Carey McWilliams, The Zoot-Suit Riots (1943)
  • Sleepy Lagoon Defense Committee, The Sleepy Lagoon Case (1944)
— In <u>Civil Rights in the United States</u>
Images
  • Zoot Suit War (1943)

About Asian Americans/Internment of Japanese-Americans
— In <u>World War II</u>
Documents
  • U.S. Congress, An Act to Execute Certain Treaty Stipulations Relating to Chinese, or the Chinese Exclusion Act (1882)
  • Asiatic Exclusion League of N. America, Preamble and Constitution (1905)
  • Theodore Roosevelt, Gentlemen's Agreement (1907)
  • California State Legislature, Alien Land Law (1913)
  • U.S. Congress, Excerpt of the Cable Act (1922)

- U.S. Congress, Immigration Act of 1924
- Curtis B. Munson, The Munson Report (1941)
- Lt. Gen. John L. DeWitt, Final Recommendation, Evacuation of Japanese and Other Subversive Persons from the Pacific Coast (1942)
- Franklin D. Roosevelt, Executive Order 9066 (1942)
- Lt. Gen. John L. DeWitt, Public Proclamation No. 1, March 2, 1942
- War Relocation Authority, United States, Relocation and the Constitution (1942)
- John Okada, Excerpt of *No-No Boy* (1957)
- Jeanne Wakatsuki Houston, Excerpt from *Farewell to Manzanar* (1973)
- U.S. Congress, Commission on Wartime Relocation and Internment of Civilians Act (1980)
- Janice Mirikitani, Breaking Silence (1982)

Images
- American Farmer Sign (circa 1941)
- Instructions to All Persons of Japanese Ancestry (1942)
- Russell Lee, Closing Out Sale (1942)
- Russell Lee, Evacuees Ready to Leave (1942)
- Dorothea Lange, Manzanar Relocation Center Barracks Quarters (1942) Tokio Ueyama, The Evacuee (circa 1942)
- Dorothea Lange, Relaxing in Front of Barracks in California (1942)
- Three Soldiers (circa 1943)
- Yone Kubo, Heart Mountain Relocation Center Departure, Heart Mountain, Wyoming (1946)

— In Civil Rights in the United States
Documents
- U.S. Supreme Court, *Hirabayashi v. United States* (1943)

Videos
- Universal Pictures, Internment of Japanese Americans (1942)

— In The Constitution and Supreme Court
Documents
- Hugo L. Black, *Korematsu v. United States* (1944)

Images
- The Owens Valley Detention Center (1942)

— In The Immigrant Experience
Documents
- U.S. Supreme Court, *Ex Parte Mitsuye Endo* (1944)

Images
- Japanese-American Soldier and Interned Parents (circa 1942)

—In The Asian-American Experience
Documents
- U.S. Congress, An Act to Repeal the Chinese Exclusion Acts [and] to Establish Quotas (1943)
- U.S. Congress, Nationality Act of 1946

About the Holocaust
— In <u>The Immigrant Experience</u>
  Documents
  • Wagner/Nourse Rogers Bill (1939)
  • Cordell Hull, Maintaining Strict Limits on Immigration (1940)
  Images
  • Jewish Refugees Barred from Entering Cuba (1939)
— In <u>The Great Depression and the New Deal</u>
  Images
  • Henry Morgenthau, Jr. (1945)
— In <u>World War II</u>
  Images
  • Crematoriums at Weimar, Germany (1945)
  • Starved Prisoners From Concentration Camp (1945)

About War Crimes
— In <u>World War II</u>
  Images
  • Department of the Army, Japanese War Crimes Trial (1946)

About Culture
— In <u>The Great Depression and the New Deal</u>
  Images
  • Clark Gable (circa 1940)
— In <u>World War II</u>
  Images
  • Warner Brothers, *Casablanca* Movie Poster (1942)
  • Warner Brothers, *Casablanca*—Rick and Sam (1942)
  • Republic Pictures, *The Flying Tigers* (1942)

THE EARLY COLD WAR

Throughout WWII, the alliance between the United States and the Soviet Union was fraught with tension. Sustaining catastrophic losses, the Soviets bitterly resented the Allies' decision to delay the opening of a second front in Western Europe. Determined to protect themselves from another devastating invasion, the Soviets decided to establish a "buffer zone" in Eastern Europe. In the months following the D-Day landings, the Soviets moved a massive army into the region and began forming communist governments in Poland, Romania, and Bulgaria. When the Yalta conference convened in February 1945, the Soviets were in a position of strength. Because President Franklin Roosevelt and British Prime Minister Winston Churchill thought that Soviet assistance would be essential in defeating Japan, they made concessions to Soviet Premier Josef Stalin. In exchange for a Soviet pledge to enter the Pacific war shortly after the Nazis surrendered, they acquiesced to Stalin's demands for territory in Asia. In response, Stalin agreed to a temporary partition of Germany, future discussions of German war reparations, and the creation of a new international organization, the United Nations (UN). Most importantly, Stalin also promised to permit free elections in Poland, Czechoslovakia, Bulgaria, Hungary, and Romania. Roosevelt and Churchill trusted Stalin to keep his word.

When Roosevelt died on April 12th, American-Soviet relations changed dramatically. Harry S. Truman, FDR's successor, was inexperienced in foreign affairs and did not share Roosevelt's faith in Stalin. Taking a hard line, Truman delayed Soviet requests for economic aid and demanded that free elections in Poland be held immediately. In response, Stalin tightened his hold on Eastern Europe. During the Potsdam Conference in July and early August of 1945, the United States and Soviet Union agreed upon little other than demilitarizing Germany and ordering war crime trials for Nazi leaders. Although the Soviets kept their pledge to enter the Pacific war, the Soviet-American alliance would soon unravel.

The Soviets had ambitious plans for the postwar world. Despite incurring 27 million casualties and the destruction of their national infrastructure, they were determined to build a communist empire—whatever the cost. Stalin allowed millions to starve and live without electricity in order to divert resources to scientists working on an atomic bomb. When the Allies refused to impose huge reparations on Germany, the Soviets pillaged their zone in eastern Germany.

People with useful skills were kidnapped and taken to the U.S.S.R. Entire factories were dismantled and carried back to Russia. At the same time, Stalin ignored his Yalta promise to allow free elections in Eastern Europe and crushed political opposition to local communists.

Truman and his advisors refused to ignore Stalin's actions. They opposed the expansion of Soviet territory. Instead, they advocated self-determination of nations and a stable international order under the auspices of the United Nations. U.S. officials were deeply concerned that Soviet control of Eastern Europe would imperil American economic interests. They found the atheism and political oppression of communist states morally repugnant.

In early 1946, several events signaled that U.S.-Soviet relations were deteriorating. In February 1946, Stalin made a rare public speech in which he declared that war between communist and capitalist societies was inevitable. A month later, Churchill warned that "an iron curtain" was now dividing Eastern and Western Europe. In response, the United States adopted a containment policy designed to thwart Soviet expansionism. In 1947, the Truman Doctrine and the Marshall Plan signified the American commitment to resist communism and to assist democratic nations. Spending billions of dollars on defense and aiding war-torn countries, the United States embarked on a global crusade that became known as the Cold War.

The Soviets responded aggressively to U.S. policies. They consolidated their hold on Poland, Bulgaria, Albania, and Romania. In 1948, they installed communist governments in Hungary and Yugoslavia. They also imposed a blockade on Berlin. Unwilling to sacrifice two million East Berliners to communist oppression, the U.S. orchestrated an airlift operation to keep the city supplied. In May 1949, the Soviets ended their attempt to isolate Berlin. Shortly thereafter, Germany was divided into the democratic Federal Republic of Germany (West Germany) and the communist German Democratic Republic (East Germany). In April 1949, ten Western nations formed the North Atlantic Treaty Organization (NATO), a collective security arrangement to combat communist aggression. In 1955, communist nations entered the Warsaw Pact to counter NATO.

The Cold War also reached Asia. During their military occupation of Japan, U.S. officials instituted democratic and capitalist reforms. American policy makers helped to suppress leftist rebels in the Philippines and subsidized French efforts to defeat communist insurgents in Indochina. Not all of these efforts succeeded. In 1949, communist forces led by Mao Zedong defeated the Nationalist Chinese troops of Jiang Jeshi. Jiang fled to Taiwan. Although the U.S. had given the Nationalists more than three billion dollars, some Americans accused the Democratic Truman administration of "losing" China and being "soft on communism." In September 1949, the announcement that the Soviets had detonated an atomic bomb intensified partisan disputes about the direction of U.S. foreign policy. Shortly thereafter, Truman ordered the development of a vastly more powerful fusion-based hydrogen bomb. He also approved NSC-68, a plan for huge increases in conventional defense spending and a tremendous expansion of American military capabilities.

The Cold War in Asia turned hot when communist North Korea invaded democratic South Korea in June 1950. Aware that the Soviet Union and Communist China were supporting North Korea, the Truman administration decided to resist the North Korean attack. Without asking Congress for a declaration of war, they persuaded the United Nations Security Council (which the Soviets were temporarily boycotting for its failure to seat Red China) to adopt a resolution approving a military operation. A UN contingent comprised largely of American and South Korean troops began fighting in Korea. In September 1950, after the daring Inchon operation gave the UN the military advantage, the Truman administration approved a plan to cross the 38th Parallel in an attempt to reunify Korea as an entirely non-communist country. As UN forces neared the Yalu River along the Chinese border, Mao protested the incursion on China's territory. In November, after the UN failed to heed Mao's warnings, 300,000 Chinese troops plunged into Korea and sent the UN troops reeling in retreat. Although the military situation stabilized by March 1951, the war exposed differences between General Douglas MacArthur, the UN commander, and Truman. When MacArthur refused to stop making public statements suggesting that the UN blockade and bomb China and "unleash" Jiang on China, Truman fired him. Although the incident created a furor in the United States, it reaffirmed the principle of civilian control of the military. In June 1951, truce talks began in Korea. After two years of stalled debates on the fate of POWs and a demarcation line, the war ended in July 1953. Over 53,000 Americans died in the $54 billion conflict.

Throughout the Korean War, the United States was increasingly involved in France's struggle to retain its lucrative colony Indochina. During World War II, U.S. officials had supported Vietnamese nationalists in their resistance against the Japanese. But, in September 1945, when the Vietnamese declared their independence, American policy makers ignored overtures from Ho Chi Minh, the Vietnamese leader. Instead, the Truman administration helped France, an important U.S. ally, regain Indochina. After war erupted between the French and the Viet Minh (nationalists led by Ho), the United States contributed to the French war effort. By 1954, the U.S. was paying 75 percent of France's expenses in the conflict. Nonetheless, France was still losing. In early 1954, French generals attempted to draw the Vietnamese into a major battle in an isolated hamlet in north Vietnam called Dien Bien Phu. The tactic backfired when Viet Minh troops surrounded the French fort.

Although the French pleaded for U.S. military intervention, the Eisenhower administration was unwilling to enter another war in Asia just months after signing the Korean armistice. In May 1954, France surrendered at Dien Bien Phu. In July, an international summit at Geneva drafted an agreement halting the French-Vietnamese conflict and temporarily dividing Vietnam at the 17th Parallel. Elections were to be held in 1956 to choose the government that would rule a reunified Vietnam. Unwilling to acknowledge the communists' victory in Indochina, the United States did not participate in the Geneva meeting and did not sign the Geneva agreements.

Instead, U.S. officials established a non-communist government in South Vietnam. If Vietnam became communist, they argued, then Thailand, Burma, Indonesia, and other Asian countries would eventually too. They used this "domino theory" to justify placing Ngo Dinh Diem, an anti-communist Catholic, in the presidency of South Vietnam. When Diem refused to hold the scheduled 1956 elections, U.S. officials did not protest. They, like Diem, knew that Ho Chi Minh, now the ruler of North Vietnam, would win. Backed with U.S. aid and a secret police force, Diem crushed his political opponents, failed to institute desperately needed reforms, and enriched his corrupt family. His autocracy and Catholicism made him immensely unpopular in a deeply impoverished and predominately Buddhist nation. By December 1960, a civil war erupted between Diem's troops and the National Liberation Front, a guerilla army based in South Vietnam and supported by the Viet Minh of North Vietnam. In response, the Eisenhower administration increased U.S. aid to South Vietnam and dispatched increasing numbers of "advisors" to the Diem government. The decision to link the fate of Vietnam to America's Cold War strategies would have tragic consequences in the 1960s.

The Cold War greatly affected domestic politics. In their determination to ferret out communist spies, both Democrats and Republicans used loyalty oaths, security investigations, and government hearings. Opportunistic politicians such as Joseph McCarthy and Richard M. Nixon built national reputations based on their zealous anti-communism. As the nation grew increasingly anti-communist, thousands of people found their political beliefs, even those expressed years earlier, subject to question. Liberals, civil rights workers, homosexuals, and labor activists were only a few of those deemed "subversive" in this restrictive political climate. Anti-communist hysteria had a chilling impact on higher education, the entertainment industry, and government.

The Cold War continued under President Dwight D. Eisenhower. Eisenhower modified the containment policy by adopting the "New Look." The policy cut conventional defense spending in favor of relying more heavily on less expensive atomic weapons and expanded covert operations. The United States greatly increased its nuclear arsenal and performed hundreds of atomic tests. To calm civilians terrified by the escalating arms race with the Soviets, the federal government created civil defense programs designed to "prepare" people for a nuclear war. After Stalin died in March 1953, the Cold War reached an impasse in Europe and moved into the developing world. U.S. intelligence operatives worked against leftist governments in Iran, the Philippines, and Guatemala. Working to preserve a bipolar world divided between capitalist and communist nations, the U.S. and the U.S.S.R. avoided direct confrontations. America did not intervene when the Soviets crushed 1953 protests in East Germany and the 1956 Hungarian Revolution. Although the October 1957 launch of *Sputnik* triggered an intense "space race," the United States and the Soviet Union temporarily suspended their atmospheric testing of atomic weapons and began cultural exchanges. However, hopes for improved Soviet-American relations proved short-lived when the 1960 U-2 incident prompted the cancellation of a U.S.-Soviet summit meeting. The Cold War would rage unabated until its sudden end in 1991.

22.1

GEORGE F. KENNAN,
THE LONG TELEGRAM (1946)

In early 1946, relations between the United States and the Soviet Union deteriorated markedly. While militarily occupying most of Eastern Europe, the Soviets were installing communist regimes in several countries. U.S. officials opposed these actions and believed citizens had the right to choose their own governments. If the Soviets were allowed to expand their territory, President Truman and his advisors argued, American political and economic interests would be imperiled and international relations would be destabilized. Empowered by possession of the atomic bomb and the world's strongest economy, the Truman administration started fighting the spread of communism.

George F. Kennan (1904-) was one of the leading architects of U.S. foreign policy in the post-WWII era. After graduating from Princeton in 1925, he entered the Foreign Service and worked in several countries including Switzerland and Germany. From 1929-1931, he took intensive courses in Russian studies at the University of Berlin. In 1933, when the United States formally recognized the Soviet Union, Kennan accompanied U.S. ambassador William C. Bullitt to Moscow. From there, Kennan proceeded to Vienna, Prague, and Berlin before returning to the U.S.S.R. in 1942.

Although Kennan adored the Russian language and culture, he detested Stalinism. In February 1946, when asked to interpret recent Soviet statements and actions, Kennan composed an 8,000-word telegram. This "long telegram" was widely circulated within the Truman administration and became the basis of the containment policy—the guiding principle of U.S. foreign policy during the Cold War. In 1947, Kennan was named director of the State Department's Policy Planning Staff. After leaving the government in 1950, Kennan joined the Institute for Advanced Study at Princeton and became a prize-winning historian and memoirist. He served as the U.S. ambassador to the Soviet Union (1952-1956) and to Yugoslavia (1961-1963).

FOCUS QUESTIONS

1. According to Kennan, what are the origins of Soviet foreign policy?
2. How does Kennan describe the Soviet government? Does he feel that the Soviets pose a threat to the United States? If so, why?

3. What predictions does Kennan make about the Soviets? How and why does he believe that the United States should respond?

Moscow, February 22, 1946

 t the bottom of Kremlin's neurotic view of world affairs is traditional and instinctive Russian sense of insecurity. Originally, this was insecurity of a peaceful agricultural people trying to live on vast exposed plain in neighborhood of fierce nomadic peoples. To this was added, as Russia came into contact with economically advanced West, fear of more competent, more powerful, more highly organized societies in that area. But this latter type of insecurity was one which afflicted rather Russian rulers than Russian people; for Russian rulers have invariably sensed that their rule was relatively archaic in form fragile and artificial in its psychological foundation, unable to stand comparison or contact with political systems of Western countries. For this reason they have always feared foreign penetration, feared direct contact between Western world and their own, feared what would happen if Russians learned truth about world without or if foreigners learned truth about world within. And they have learned to seek security only in patient but deadly struggle for total destruction of rival power, never in compacts and compromises with it.

It was no coincidence that Marxism, which had smoldered ineffectively for half a century in Western Europe, caught hold and blazed for first time in Russia. Only in this land which had never known a friendly neighbor or indeed any tolerant equilibrium of separate powers, either internal or international, could a doctrine thrive which viewed economic conflicts of society as insoluble by peaceful means. After establishment of Bolshevist regime, Marxist dogma, rendered even more truculent and intolerant by Lenin's interpretation, became a perfect vehicle for sense of insecurity with which Bolsheviks, even more than previous Russian rulers, were afflicted. In this dogma, with its basic altruism of purpose, they found justification for their instinctive fear of outside world, for the dictatorship without which they did not know how to rule, for cruelties they did not dare not to inflict, for sacrifice they felt bound to demand. In the name of Marxism they sacrificed every single ethical value in their methods and tactics. Today they cannot dispense with it. It is fig leaf of their moral and intellectual respectability. Without it they would stand before history, at best, as only the last of that long succession of cruel and wasteful Russian rulers who have relentlessly forced country on to ever new heights of military power in order to guarantee external security of their internally weak regimes…. This thesis provides justification for that increase of military and police power of Russian state, for that isolation of Russian population from outside world, and for that fluid and constant pressure to extend limits of Russian police power which are together the natural and instinctive urges of Russian rulers….

In summary, we have here a political force committed fanatically to the belief that with US there can be no permanent *modus vivendi* that it is desirable and necessary that the internal harmony of our society be disrupted, our traditional way of life be destroyed, the international authority of our state be broken, if Soviet power is to be secure. This political force has complete power of disposition over energies of one of world's greatest peoples and resources of world's richest national territory, and is borne along by deep and powerful currents of Russian nationalism. In addition, it has an elaborate and far flung apparatus for exertion of its influence in other countries, an apparatus of amazing flexibility and versatility, managed by people whose experience and skill in underground methods are presumably without parallel in history....

This is admittedly not a pleasant picture. Problem of how to cope with this force [is] undoubtedly greatest task our diplomacy has ever faced and probably greatest it will ever have to face.... I cannot attempt to suggest all answers here. But I would like to record my conviction that problem is within our power to solve—and that without recourse to any general military conflict. And in support of this conviction there are certain observations of a more encouraging nature I should like to make:

(1) Soviet power, unlike that of Hitlerite Germany, is neither schematic nor adventuristic. It does not work by fixed plans. It does not take unnecessary risks. Impervious to logic of reason, it is highly sensitive to logic of force. For this reason it can easily withdraw—and usually does when strong resistance is encountered at any point. Thus, if the adversary has sufficient force and makes clear his readiness to use it, he rarely has to do so. If situations are properly handled there need be no prestige-engaging showdowns.

(2) Gauged against Western World as a whole, Soviets are still by far the weaker force. Thus, their success will really depend on degree of cohesion, firmness and vigor which Western World can muster. And this is factor which it is within our power to influence.

(3) Success of Soviet system, as form of internal power, is not yet finally proven. It has yet to be demonstrated that it can survive supreme test of successive transfer of power from one individual or group to another.... In Russia, party has now become a great and—for the moment—highly successful apparatus of dictatorial administration, but it has ceased to be a source of emotional inspiration. Thus, internal soundness and permanence of movement need not yet be regarded as assured.

(4) All Soviet propaganda beyond Soviet security sphere is basically negative and destructive. It should therefore be relatively easy to combat it by any intelligent and really constructive program.

For those reasons I think we may approach calmly and with good heart problem of how to deal with Russia. As to how this approach should be made, I only wish to advance, by way of conclusion, following comments:

(1) Our first step must be to apprehend, and recognize for what it is, the nature of the movement with which we are dealing. We must study it with same courage, detachment, objectivity, and same determination not to be emotionally provoked or unseated by it, with which doctor studies unruly and unreasonable individual.

(2) We must see that our public is educated to realities of Russian situation. I cannot over-emphasize importance of this. Press cannot do this alone. It must be done mainly by Government, which is necessarily more experienced and better informed on practical problems involved....

(3) Much depends on health and vigor of our own society. World communism is like malignant parasite which feeds only on diseased tissue. This is point at which domestic and foreign policies meet. Every courageous and incisive measure to solve internal problems of our own society, to improve self-confidence, discipline, morale and community spirit of our own people, is a diplomatic victory over Moscow worth a thousand diplomatic notes and joint communiqués....

(4) We must formulate and put forward for other nations a much more positive and constructive picture of sort of world we would like to see than we have put forward in past. It is not enough to urge people to develop political processes similar to our own. Many foreign peoples, in Europe at least, are tired and frightened by experiences of past, and are less interested in abstract freedom than in security. They are seeking guidance rather than responsibilities. We should be better able than Russians to give them this. And unless we do, Russians certainly will.

(5) Finally we must have courage and self-confidence to cling to our own methods and conceptions of human society. After all, the greatest danger that can befall us in coping with this problem of Soviet communism, is that we shall allow ourselves to become like those with whom we are coping.

KENNAN

Department of State, *Foreign Relations of the United States, 1946*, vol. VI: *Eastern Europe, The Soviet Union* (Washington, D.C.: Government Printing Office, 1969), pp. 696-709.

22.2

THE TRUMAN DOCTRINE (1947)

In 1947, the Truman administration made public its new containment policy. On February 21, the British informed U.S. officials that they could no longer afford to aid the Greek and Turkish governments in their efforts to suppress leftist rebels. Determined to prevent communism from penetrating the Mediterranean, President Harry S. Truman agreed to assume Britain's commitment to Greece and Turkey. Truman and his advisors knew that it would be difficult to gain support for such a radical departure from America's tradition of non-interventionist foreign policy. In a February 27 meeting, congressional leaders told Truman that he would have to frighten the American public in order to gain support for aiding Greece and Turkey.

Truman took this advice. On March 12, he addressed a joint session of Congress and emphasized the precarious state of foreign affairs. If the United States failed to act in the Mediterranean, he warned, democratic governments everywhere would face grave dangers. Although Truman did not specifically mention communism, his speech (soon known as the Truman Doctrine) eloquently enunciated the emerging global struggle between democratic and communist nations. His remarks persuaded a Republican-dominated Congress to approve a $400 million aid package to Greece and Turkey and signaled American willingness to combat the spread of communism abroad.

FOCUS QUESTIONS

1. How does Truman describe conditions in Greece and Turkey? Why does he believe that American aid to these nations is so essential?
2. What does Truman argue is at stake if the United States fails to help free countries facing armed insurgencies? Do you think he was right?

The United States has received from the Greek Government an urgent appeal for financial and economic assistance....

I do not believe that the American people and the Congress wish to turn a deaf ear to the appeal of the Greek Government.

Greece is not a rich country. Lack of sufficient natural resources has always forced the Greek people to work hard to make both ends meet. Since 1940, this industrious and peace loving country has suffered invasion, four years of cruel enemy occupation, and bitter internal strife.

When forces of liberation entered Greece, they found that the retreating Germans had destroyed virtually all the railways, roads, port facilities, communications, and merchant marine. More than a thousand villages had been burned. Eighty-five per cent of the children were tubercular. Livestock, poultry, and draft animals had almost disappeared. Inflation had wiped out practically all savings.

As a result of these tragic conditions, a militant minority, exploiting human want and misery, was able to create political chaos which, until now, has made economic recovery impossible.

Greece is today without funds to finance the importation of those goods which are essential to bare subsistence. Under these circumstances the people of Greece cannot make progress in solving their problems of reconstruction. Greece is in desperate need of financial and economic assistance to enable it to resume purchases of food, clothing, fuel and seeds. These are indispensable for the subsistence of its people and are obtainable only from abroad. Greece must have help to import the goods necessary to restore internal order and security, so essential for economic and political recovery.

The Greek Government has also asked for the assistance of experienced American administrators, economists and technicians to insure that the financial and other aid given to Greece shall be used effectively in creating a stable and self-sustaining economy and in improving its public administration.

The very existence of the Greek state is today threatened by the terrorist activities of several thousand armed men, led by Communists, who defy the government's authority at a number of points, particularly along the northern boundaries....

Meanwhile, the Greek Government is unable to cope with the situation. The Greek army is small and poorly equipped. It needs supplies and equipment if it is to restore the authority of the government throughout Greek territory. Greece must have assistance if it is to become a self-supporting and self-respecting democracy.

The United States must supply that assistance. We have already extended to Greece certain types of relief and economic aid but these are inadequate. There is no other country to which democratic Greece can turn. No other nation is willing and able to provide the necessary support for a democratic Greek government.

The British Government, which has been helping Greece, can give no further financial or economic aid after March 31. Great Britain finds itself under the necessity of reducing or liquidating its commitments in several parts of the world, including Greece.

We have considered how the United Nations might assist in this crisis. But the situation is an urgent one requiring immediate action and the United Nations and its related organizations are not in a position to extend help of the kind that is required....

The Greek Government has been operating in an atmosphere of chaos and extremism. It has made mistakes. The extension of aid by this country does not mean that the United States condones everything that the Greek Government has done or will do. We have condemned in the past, and we condemn now, extremist measures of the right or the left. We have in the past advised tolerance, and we advise tolerance now.

Greece's neighbor, Turkey, also deserves our attention.

The future of Turkey as an independent and economically sound state is clearly no less important to the freedom-loving peoples of the world than the future of Greece. The circumstances in which Turkey finds itself today are considerably different from those of Greece. Turkey has been spared the disasters that have beset Greece. And during the war, the United States and Great Britain furnished Turkey with material aid.

Nevertheless, Turkey now needs our support.

Since the war Turkey has sought financial assistance from Great Britain and the United States for the purpose of effecting that modernization necessary for the maintenance of its national integrity. That integrity is essential to the preservation of order in the Middle East.

The British government has informed us that, owing to its own difficulties can no longer extend financial or economic aid to Turkey. As in the case of Greece, if Turkey is to have the assistance it needs, the United States must supply it. We are the only country able to provide that help.

I am fully aware of the broad implications involved if the United States extends assistance to Greece and Turkey, and I shall discuss these implications with you at this time.

One of the primary objectives of the foreign policy of the United States is the creation of conditions in which we and other nations will be able to work out a way of life free from coercion. This was a fundamental issue in the war with Germany and Japan. Our victory was won over countries which sought to impose their will, and their way of life, upon other nations.

To ensure the peaceful development of nations, free from coercion, the United States has taken a leading part in establishing the United Nations. The United Nations is designed to make possible lasting freedom and independence for all its members. We shall not realize our objectives, however, unless we are willing to help free peoples to maintain their free institutions and their national integrity against aggressive movements that seek to impose upon them totalitarian regimes....

At the present moment in world history nearly every nation must choose between alternative ways of life. The choice is too often not a free one.

One way of life is based upon the will of the majority, and is distinguished by free institutions, representative government, free elections, guarantees of individual liberty, freedom of speech and religion, and freedom from political oppression.

The second way of life is based upon the will of a minority forcibly imposed upon the majority. It relies upon terror and oppression, a controlled press and radio, fixed elections, and the suppression of personal freedoms.

I believe that it must be the policy of the United States to support free peoples who are resisting attempted subjugation by armed minorities or by outside pressures.

I believe that we must assist free peoples to work out their own destinies in their own way.

I believe that our help should be primarily through economic and financial aid which is essential to economic stability and orderly political processes.

The world is not static, and the status quo is not sacred. But we cannot allow changes in the status quo in violation of the Charter of the United Nations by such methods as coercion, or by such subterfuges as political infiltration. In helping free and independent nations to maintain their freedom, the United States will be giving effect to the principles of the Charter of the United Nations.

It is necessary only to glance at a map to realize that the survival and integrity of the Greek nation are of grave importance in a much wider situation. If Greece should fall under the control of an armed minority, the effect upon its neighbor, Turkey, would be immediate and serious. Confusion and disorder might well spread throughout the entire Middle East.

Moreover, the disappearance of Greece as an independent state would have a profound effect upon those countries in Europe whose peoples are struggling against great difficulties to maintain their freedoms and their independence while they repair the damages of war.

It would be an unspeakable tragedy if these countries, which have struggled so long against overwhelming odds, should lose that victory for which they sacrificed so much. Collapse of free institutions and loss of independence would be disastrous not only for them but for the world. Discouragement and possibly failure would quickly be the lot of neighboring peoples striving to maintain their freedom and independence.

Should we fail to aid Greece and Turkey in this fateful hour, the effect will be far reaching to the West as well as to the East.

We must take immediate and resolute action.

I therefore ask the Congress to provide authority for assistance to Greece and Turkey in the amount of $400,000,000 for the period ending June 30, 1948....

This is a serious course upon which we embark.

I would not recommend it except that the alternative is much more serious. The United States contributed $341,000,000,000 toward winning World War II. This is an investment in world freedom and world peace. The assistance that I am recommending for Greece and Turkey amounts to little more than 1 tenth of 1 per cent of this investment. It is only common sense that we should safeguard this investment and make sure that it was not in vain.

The seeds of totalitarian regimes are nurtured by misery and want. They spread and grow in the evil soil of poverty and strife. They reach their full growth when the hope of a people for a better life has died. We must keep that hope alive.

The free peoples of the world look to us for support in maintaining their freedoms. If we falter in our leadership, we may endanger the peace of the world—and we shall surely endanger the welfare of our own nation.

Great responsibilities have been placed upon us by the swift movement of events.

I am confident that the Congress will face these responsibilities squarely.

Harry S Truman, Speech, March 12, 1947, *Public Papers of the Presidents, Harry S Truman, 1947* (Washington: Government Printing Office, 1963), pp. 176-180).

22.3

SECRETARY OF STATE GEORGE C. MARSHALL OFFERS AID TO EUROPE (1947)

In June 1947, three months after announcing the Truman Doctrine, the U.S. government offered European nations assistance in rebuilding their economies. The timing was propitious. Many European nations were mired in poverty, starvation, and disease. Recovery efforts had stalled. The brutal winter of 1946-47 made things worse. Capitalizing on these grave conditions, communists were gaining power in France and Italy. Truman and his advisors were alarmed by these developments and proposed bold measures to rehabilitate the European economy.

On June 5, 1947, Secretary of State George C. Marshall announced the European Recovery Plan (also known as the Marshall Plan) during an address at Harvard University. Significantly, the U.S. offered aid to virtually all European nations, even those currently under communist domination. Truman and his aides assumed, correctly, that Stalin would not permit Eastern European participation *because the plan required that U.S. officials supervise and administer aid. Between 1948 and 1951, sixteen West European nations working with the new Economic Cooperation Administration received $13 billion in U.S. economic assistance. Several nations experienced stunning industrial and agricultural recoveries and became new markets for American products. As conditions improved, communism declined. The Marshall Plan is now considered one of the greatest successes in American foreign policy and has inspired other international development programs.*

FOCUS QUESTIONS

1. According to Marshall, what are the political and economic conditions in Europe? How does he propose that the United States respond?
2. Was the Marshall Plan necessary? What did the United States gain from offering economic assistance to Europe?

 need not tell you that the world situation is very serious. That must be apparent to all intelligent people. I think one difficulty is that the problem is one of such enormous complexity that the very mass of facts presented to the public by press and radio make it exceedingly difficult for the man in the street to reach a clear appraisement of the situation. Furthermore, the people of this country are distant from the troubled areas of the earth and it is hard for them to comprehend the plight and consequent reactions of the long-suffering peoples, and the effect of those reactions on their governments in connection with our efforts to promote peace in the world.

In considering the requirements for the rehabilitation of Europe, the physical loss of life, the visible destruction of cities, factories, mines, and railroads was correctly estimated, but it has become obvious during recent months that this visible destruction was probably less serious than the dislocation of the entire fabric of European economy. For the past ten years conditions have been abnormal. The feverish preparation for war and the more feverish maintenance of the war effort engulfed all aspects of national economies. Machinery has fallen into disrepair or is entirely obsolete. Under the arbitrary and destructive Nazi rule, virtually every possible enterprise was geared into the German war machine. Long-standing commercial ties, private institutions, banks, insurance companies, and shipping companies disappeared through loss of capital, absorption through nationalization, or by simple destruction. In many countries, confidence in the local currency has been severely shaken. The breakdown of the business structure of Europe during the war was complete. Recovery has been seriously retarded by the fact that two years after the close of hostilities a peace settlement with Germany and Austria has not been agreed upon. But even given a more prompt solution of these difficult problems, the rehabilitation of the economic structure of Europe quite evidently will require a much longer time and greater effort than has been foreseen.

There is a phase of this matter which is both interesting and serious. The farmer has always produced the foodstuffs to exchange with the city dweller for the other necessities of life. This division of labor is the basis of modern civilization. At the present time it is threatened with breakdown. The town and city industries are not producing adequate goods to exchange with the food-producing farmer. Raw materials and fuel are in short supply. Machinery is lacking or worn out. The farmer or the peasant cannot find the goods for sale which he desires to purchase. So the sale of his farm produce for money which he cannot use seems to him an unprofitable transaction. He, therefore, has withdrawn many fields from crop cultivation and is using them for grazing. He feeds more grain to stock and finds for himself and his family an ample supply of food, however short he may be on clothing and the other ordinary gadgets of civilization. Meanwhile, people in the cities are short of food and fuel, and in some places approaching the starvation levels. So the governments are forced to use their foreign money and credits to procure these necessities abroad. This process exhausts funds which are urgently needed for reconstruction. Thus a very serious situation is rapidly developing which bodes no good for the world. The modern system of the division of labor upon which the exchange of products is based is in danger of breaking down.

The truth of the matter is that Europe's requirements for the next three or four years of foreign food and other essential products—principally from America—are so much greater than her present ability to pay that she must have substantial additional help or face economic, social, and political deterioration of a very grave character.

The remedy lies in breaking the vicious circle and restoring the confidence of the European people in the economic future of their own countries and of Europe as a whole. The manufacturer and the farmer throughout wide areas must be able and willing to exchange their product for currencies, the continuing value of which is not open to question.

Aside from the demoralizing effect on the world at large and the possibilities of disturbances arising as a result of the desperation of the people concerned, the consequences to the economy of the United States should be apparent to all. It is logical that the United States should do whatever it is able to do to assist in the return of normal economic health in the world, without which there can be no political stability and no assured peace. Our policy is directed not against any country or doctrine but against hunger, poverty, desperation, and chaos. Its purpose should be the revival of a working economy in the world so as to permit the emergence of political and social conditions in which free institutions can exist. Such assistance, I am convinced, must not be on a piecemeal basis as various crises develop. Any assistance that this Government may render in the future should provide a cure rather than a mere palliative. Any government that is willing to assist in the task of recovery will find full cooperation, I am sure, on the part of the United States Government. Any government which maneuvers to block the recovery of other countries cannot expect help from us. Furthermore, governments, political parties or groups which seek to perpetuate human misery in order to profit there from politically or otherwise will encounter the opposition of the United States.

It is already evident that, before the United States Government can proceed much further in its efforts to alleviate the situation and help start the European world on its way to recovery, there must be some agreement among the countries of Europe as to the requirements of the situation and the part those countries themselves will take in order to give proper effect to whatever action might be undertaken by this Government. It would be neither fitting nor efficacious for this Government to undertake to draw up unilaterally a program designed to place Europe on its feet economically. This is the business of the Europeans. The initiative, I think, must come from Europe. The role of this country should consist of friendly aid in the drafting of a European program and of later support of such a program so far as it may be practical for us to do so. The program should be a joint one, agreed to by a number, if not all, European nations.

An essential part of any successful action on the part of the United States is an understanding on the part of the people of America of the character of the problem and the remedies to be applied. Political passion and prejudice should have no part. With foresight, and a willingness on the part of our people to face up to the vast responsibility which history has clearly placed upon our country, the difficulties I have outlined can and will be overcome....

Department of State, *Bulletin*, XV1, No. 415 (June 15, 1947), pp. 1159-1160.

22.4

WALTER LIPPMANN QUESTIONS CONTAINMENT (1947)

Some Americans were deeply troubled by the possible implications of the containment policy. Walter Lippmann (1884-1974), a nationally syndicated columnist for the New York Herald Tribune, *was one of the staunchest critics of the policy. In July 1947, Mr. "X," later revealed to be George F. Kennan, published "The Sources of Soviet Conduct" in the influential journal* Foreign Affairs. *Kennan's article reiterated many of the concepts of his "long telegram" (see Document 22.1). Lippmann responded with a series of essays called* The Cold War *(1947)—a term actually coined by financier Bernard Baruch but popularized by Lippmann. Lippmann later opposed McCarthyism, the Korean War, and the Vietnam War. Three excerpted essays from* The Cold War *follow.*

FOCUS QUESTIONS

1. What are Lippmann's views of the Soviets?
2. What are his major criticisms of the containment policy?
3. How do Lippmann's opinions differ from those expressed by George F. Kennan and Harry S. Truman (Documents 22.1 and 22.2)? Whose views do you find most persuasive and why?

r. X's article is…not only an analytical interpretation of the sources of Soviet conduct. It is also a document of primary importance on the sources of American foreign policy—or at least that part of it which is known as the Truman Doctrine.

As such I am venturing to examine it critically in this essay. My criticism, I hasten to say at once, does not arise from any belief or hope that our conflict with the Soviet government is imaginary or that it can be avoided or ignored, or easily disposed of. I agree entirely with Mr. X that the Soviet pressure cannot "be charmed or talked out of existence." I agree entirely that the Soviet power will expand unless it is prevented from expanding because it is confronted with power, primarily American power, that it must respect. But I believe, and shall argue, that the strategical conception and plan which Mr. X recommends is fundamentally unsound, and that it cannot be made to work, and that the attempt to make it work will cause us to squander our substance and our prestige.

We must begin with the disturbing fact…that Mr. X's conclusions depend upon the optimistic prediction that the "Soviet power…bears within itself the seeds of its own decay, and that the sprouting of seeds is well advanced;" that if "anything were ever to occur to disrupt the unity and the efficacy of the Party as a political instrument, Soviet Russia might be changed overnight from one of the strongest to one of the weakest and most pitiable of national societies."…

Of this optimistic prediction Mr. X himself says that it "cannot be proved. And it cannot be disproved." Nevertheless, he concludes that the United States should construct its policy on the assumption that the Soviet power is inherently weak and impermanent, and that this unproved assumption warrants our entering "with reasonable confidence upon a policy of firm containment, designed to confront the Russians with unalterable counterforce at every point where they show signs of encroaching upon the interests of a peaceful and stable world."

I do not find much ground for reasonable confidence in a policy which can be successful only if the most optimistic prediction should prove to be true. Surely a sound policy must be addressed to the worst and hardest that may be judged to be probable, and not to the best and easiest way that may be possible….

In Mr. X's estimates there are no reserves for a rainy day. There is no margin of safety for bad luck, bad management, error, and the unforeseen. He asks us to assume that the Soviet power is already decaying. He exhorts us to believe that our own highest hopes for ourselves will soon have been realized….

Surely it is by no means proved that the way to lead mankind is to spend the next ten or fifteen years, as Mr. X proposes we should, in reacting at "a series of constantly shifting geographical and political points, corresponding to the shifts and maneuvers of Soviet policy." For if history has indeed intended us to bear the responsibility of leadership, then it is not leadership to adapt ourselves to the shifts and maneuvers of Soviet policy at a series of constantly shifting geographical and political points. For that would mean for ten or fifteen years Moscow, not Washington, would define the issues, would make the challenges, would select the ground where the conflict was to be waged, and would choose the weapons. And the best that Mr. X can say for his own proposal is that if for a long period of time we can prevent the Soviet power from winning, the Soviet power will eventually perish or "mellow" because it has been "frustrated."

This is a dismal conclusion. Mr. X has, I believe, become bogged down in it because as he thought more and more about the conduct of the Soviet, he remembered less and less about the conduct of the nations of the world. For while it may be true that the Soviet power would perish of frustration, if it were contained for ten or fifteen years, this conclusion is only half baked until he has answered the crucial question which remains: can the western world operate a policy of containment? Mr. X...does not answer this question....

Now the strength of the western world is great, and we may assume that its resourcefulness is considerable. Nevertheless, there are weighty reasons for thinking that the kind of strength we have and the kind of resourcefulness we are capable of showing are peculiarly unsuited to operating a policy of containment.

How, for example, under the Constitution of the United States is Mr. X going to work out an arrangement by which the Department of State has the money and the military power always available in sufficient amounts to apply "counterforce" at constantly shifting points all over the world? Is he going to ask Congress for a blank check on the Treasury and for a blank authorization to use the armed forces? Not if the American constitutional system is to be maintained. Or is he going to ask for an appropriation and for authority each time the Russians "show signs of encroaching upon the interests of a peaceful and stable world"? If that is his plan for dealing with the maneuvers of a dictatorship, he is going to arrive at the points of encroachment with too little and he is going to arrive too late. The Russians, if they intend to encroach, will have encroached while Congress is getting ready to hold hearings.

A policy of shifts and maneuvers may be suited to the Soviet system of government, which, as Mr. X tells us, is animated by patient persistence. It is not suited to the American system of government.

It even more unsuited to the American economy which is unregimented and uncontrolled, and therefore cannot be administered according to a plan. Yet a policy of containment cannot be operated unless the Department of State can plan and direct exports and imports. For the policy demands that American goods be delivered or withheld at "constantly shifting geographical and political points corresponding to the shifts and maneuvers of Soviet policy."

Thus Mr. X and the planners of policy in the State Department, and not the supply and demand in the world market, must determine continually what portion of the commodities produced here may be sold in the United States, what portion is to be set aside for export, and then sold, lent, or given to this foreign country rather than to that one. The Department of State must be able to allocate the products of American industry and agriculture, to ration the goods allocated for export among the nations which are to contain the Soviet Union, and to discriminate among them, judging correctly and quickly how much each nation must be given, how much each nation can safely be squeezed, so that all shall be held in line to hold the line against the Russians....

I find it hard to understand how Mr. X could have recommended such a strategic monstrosity....

There is...no rational ground for confidence that the United States could muster "unalterable counterforce" at all the individual sectors. The Eurasian continent is a big place, and the military power of the United States, though it is very great, has certain limitations which must be borne in mind if it is to be used effectively. We live on an island continent. We are separated from the theaters of conflict by the great oceans. We have a relatively small population, of which the greater proportion must in time of war be employed in producing, transporting, and servicing the complex weapons and engines which constitute our military power. The United States has, as compared with the Russians, no adequate reserves of infantry. Our navy commands the oceans and we posses the major offensive weapons of war. But on the ground of the interior of the Eurasian continent...there may be many "individual sectors" where only infantry can be used as the "counterforce."...

American military power is peculiarly unsuited to a policy of containment which has to be enforced persistently and patiently for an indefinite period of time. If the Soviet Union were an island like Japan, such a policy could be enforced by American sea and air power. The United States could, without great difficulty, impose a blockade. But the Soviet Union has to be contained on land, and "holding the line" is therefore a form of trench warfare.

Yet the genius of American military power does not lie in holding positions indefinitely. That requires a massive patience by great hordes of docile people. American military power is distinguished by its mobility, its speed, its range, and its offensive striking force. It is therefore, not an efficient instrument for a diplomatic policy of containment. It can only be the instrument of a policy which has as its objective a decision and a settlement. It can and should be used to redress the balance of power which has been upset by the war. But it is not designed for, or adapted to, a strategy of containing, waiting, countering, blocking, with no more specific objective than the eventual "frustration" of the opponent.

The Americans would themselves probably be frustrated by Mr. X's policy long before the Russians were.

PP. 9-20 from *The Cold War: A Study in U.S. Foreign Policy* by Walter Lippman, Copyright 1947 by Walter Lippman. Copyright renewed 1975 by Walter Lippman. Reprinted by permission of HarperCollins Publishers Inc.

22.5

JOHN HOWARD LAWSON TESTIFIES BEFORE HUAC (1947)

When World War II ended, fears of domestic radicalism resurfaced. In 1945, when federal agents found classified documents in the offices of the journal Amerasia, *they discovered that two State Department officials and a naval attaché had passed the materials to the editors. The following year, the Canadian government exposed a large spy network that had penetrated the Manhattan Project and passed atomic secrets to the Soviets.*

Such revelations convinced Democrats and Republicans that the United States needed to ferret out potentially disloyal Americans. As Cold War anxieties deepened, neither party wished to appear "soft on communism." In March 1947, President Harry S. Truman issued an executive order creating a federal loyalty program. Rather than focus only on those employees suspected of disloyalty, investigators evaluated the political beliefs and personal associations of all federal employees. Between 1947 and 1951, the loyalty board forced almost 3,000 employees to resign and dismissed 300 others. Although the investigations revealed no evidence of espionage or conspiracy within the federal government, 39 states instituted similar security measures.

In 1947, responding to public fears of subversion, the House Un-American Activities Committee (HUAC) began investigating communism in U.S. society. Those suspected of disloyalty were called before Congress and not permitted to confront their accusers. If one failed to cooperate or invoked the 5th Amendment protecting a citizen from self-incrimination, he or she could face imprisonment, blacklisting, and/or loss of employment. The House probes first targeted organized labor and the entertainment industry. Terrified unions and studios began firing radicals and suspected radicals in hopes of safeguarding their economic and political interests. Labor leaders and entertainment moguls distanced themselves from liberal and progressive causes for several years thereafter.

Not everyone complied with HUAC's demands. In October 1947, when congressional investigators subpoenaed dozens of Hollywood figures, ten men refused to answer questions about their political views and affiliations. The Hollywood Ten were charged with contempt of Congress and sentenced to six- to twelve-month prison terms. Following his release from jail, director Edward Dmytryk became a "friendly witness" for HUAC. After admitting to being a communist and identifying twenty-six others, Dmytryk was removed from the studios' blacklist and went on to direct several more films. Less cooperative members of the Hollywood Ten remained blacklisted for many years. Some never worked in Hollywood again. Others published scripts using pseudonyms, including Dalton Trumbo who, using the name "Robert Rich," won the 1956 Academy Award for best screenplay for The Brave One. Hollywood abandoned the black-lists in the early 1960s.

In this selection, John Howard Lawson (1894-1977), a member of the Hollywood Ten, faces HUAC. In the 1920s and 1930s, Lawson wrote plays about the working class. In the 1940s, he wrote scripts for the films Action in the North Atlantic (1943) and Sahara (1943). He was also a founder and the first president of the Screen Writers Guild.

FOCUS QUESTIONS

1. Why does Lawson refuse to cooperate with HUAC? How do the committee members respond?
2. Why do you think that HUAC was interested in whether or not communists worked in Hollywood?

3. Were loyalty oaths and blacklists rational responses to the Cold War? Explain your answer.

October 27, 1947

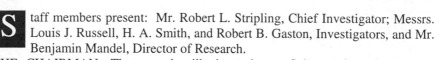taff members present: Mr. Robert L. Stripling, Chief Investigator; Messrs. Louis J. Russell, H. A. Smith, and Robert B. Gaston, Investigators, and Mr. Benjamin Mandel, Director of Research.

THE CHAIRMAN: The record will show that a Subcommittee is present, consisting of Mr. Vail, Mr. McDowell, and Mr. Thomas.

MR. LAWSON: Mr. Chairman, I have a statement here which I wish to make.

THE CHAIRMAN: Well, all right, let me see your statement.

(*Statement handed to the Chairman.*)

THE CHAIRMAN: I don't care to read any more of the statement. The statement will not be read. I read the first line.

MR. LAWSON: You have spent one week vilifying me before the American public—

THE CHAIRMAN: Just a minute.

MR. LAWSON:—and you refuse to allow me to make a statement on my rights as an American citizen.

THE CHAIRMAN: I refuse to let you make the statement because of the first sentence. That statement is not pertinent to the inquiry. Now, this is a Congressional Committee set up by law. We must have orderly procedure, and we are going to have orderly procedure. Mr. Stripling, identify the witness.

MR. LAWSON: The rights of American citizens are important in this room here, and I intend to stand up for those rights, Congressman Thomas.

MR. STRIPLING: Mr. Lawson, will you state your full name, please?

MR. LAWSON: I wish to protest against the unwillingness of this Committee to read a statement, when you permitted Mr. [Jack] Warner, Mr. [Louis B.] Mayer, and others to read statements in this room. My name is John Howard Lawson.

MR. STRIPING: When and where were you born?

MR. LAWSON: New York City.

MR. STRIPLING: What year?

MR. LAWSON: 1894.

MR. STRIPLING: Give us the exact date.

MR. LAWSON: September 25.

MR. STRIPLING: Mr. Lawson, you are here in response to a subpoena which was served upon you on September 19, 1947, is that true?

MR. LAWSON: That is correct.

MR. STRIPLING: What is your occupation, Mr. Lawson?

MR. LAWSON: I am a writer.

MR. STRIPLING: How long have you been a writer?

MR. LAWSON: All my life—at least thirty-five years—my adult life.

MR. STRIPLING: Are you a member of the Screen Writers Guild?

MR. LAWSON: The raising of any question here in regard to membership, political beliefs, or affiliation—

MR. STRIPLING: Mr. Chairman.

MR. LAWSON: —is absolutely beyond the powers of this Committee.

MR. STRIPLING: Mr. Chairman—

MR. LAWSON: But—

(*The Chairman pounding gavel.*)

MR. LAWSON: It is a matter of public record that I am a member of the Screen Writers Guild.

MR. STRIPLING: I repeat the question, Mr. Lawson: Have you ever held any position in the Screen Actors Guild?

MR. LAWSON: I stated that it is outside the purview of the rights of this Committee to inquire into any form of association.

THE CHAIRMAN: The Chair will determine what is in the purview of this committee.

MR. LAWSON: My rights as an American citizen are no less than the responsibilities of this Committee of Congress.

THE CHAIRMAN: Now, you are just making a big scene for yourself and getting all 'het up.' (*Laughter.*) Be responsive to the questioning, just the same as all the witnesses have. You are no different from the rest. Go ahead, Mr. Stripling.

MR. LAWSON: I am being treated differently than the rest.

THE CHAIRMAN: You are not being treated differently.

MR. LAWSON: Other witnesses have made statements, which included quotations from books, references to material which had no connection whatsoever with the interest of this Committee.

THE CHAIRMAN: We will determine whether it has connection. Now you go ahead—MR. LAWSON: It is absolutely beyond the power of this Committee to inquire into my association in any organization.

THE CHAIRMAN: Mr. Lawson, you will have to stop or will leave the witness stand. And you will leave the witness stand because you are in contempt. That is why you will leave the witness stand. And if you are just trying to force me to put you in contempt, you won't have to try much harder. You know what happened to a lot of people that have been in contempt of this Committee, don't you?

MR. LAWSON: I am glad that you have made it perfectly clear that you are going to threaten and intimidate the witnesses, Mr. Chairman.

(*The Chairman pounding the gavel.*)

MR. LAWSON: I am an American and I am not at all easy to intimidate, and don't think I am. (*The Chairman pounding the gavel.*)

MR. STRIPLING: Mr. Lawson, I repeat the question. Have you ever held a position in Screen Writer's Guild?

MR. LAWSON: I have stated that the question is illegal. But it is matter of public record that I have held many offices in the Screen Writers Guild. I was its first president in 1933, and I have held office on the board of directors of the Screen Writers Guild at other times.

MR. STRIPLING: You have been employed in the motion-picture industry, have you not?

MR. LAWSON: I have.

MR. STRIPLING: Would you state some of the studios where you have been employed?

MR. LAWSON: Practically, all of the studios, all the major studios.

MR. STRIPLING: As a screen writer?

MR. LAWSON: That is correct.

MR. STRIPLING: Would you list some of the pictures which you have written the script for?

MR. LAWSON: I must state again that you are now inquiring into the freedom of the press and communications, over which you have no control whatsoever. You don't have to bring me here three thousand miles to find out what pictures I have written. The pictures I have written are very well known. They are such pictures as *Action in the North Atlantic*, *Sahara*....

MR. STRIPLING: Mr. Lawson, are you now or have you ever been a member of the Communist Party of the United States?

MR. LAWSON: In framing my answer to that question I must emphasize the points I have raised before. The question of Communism is in no way related to this inquiry, which is an attempt to get control of the screen and to invade the basic rights of American citizens in all fields.

MR. MCDOWELL: Now, I must object—

MR. STRIPLING: Mr. Chairman—

(*The Chairman pounding gavel.*)

MR. LAWSON: The question here relates not only to the question of my membership in any political organization, but this Committee is attempting to establish the right—

(*The Chairman pounding gavel.*)

MR. LAWSON: —which has been historically denied to any committee of this sort, to invade the rights and privileges and immunity of American citizens, whether they be Protestant, Methodist, Jewish, or Catholic, whether they be Republicans or Democrats or anything else.

THE CHAIRMAN (pounding gavel): Mr. Lawson, just quiet down again. Mr. Lawson, the most pertinent question that we can ask is whether or not you have ever been a member of the Communist Party. Now, do you care to answer that question?

MR. LAWSON: You are using the old technique, which was used in Hitler Germany in order to create a scare here—

THE CHAIRMAN (*pounding gavel*): Oh—

MR. LAWSON: —in order to create an entirely false atmosphere in which this hearing is conducted—

(*The Chairman pounding gavel.*)

MR. LAWSON: —in order that you can smear the motion-picture industry, and you can proceed to the press, to any form of communication in this country.

THE CHAIRMAN: You have learned—

MR. LAWSON: The Bill of Rights was established precisely to prevent the operation of any committee which could invade the basic of Americans. Now, if you want to know—

MR. STRIPLING: Mr. Chairman, the witness is not answering the question.

MR. LAWSON: If you want to know—

(*The Chairman pounding gavel.*)

MR. LAWSON: —about the perjury that has been committed here and the perjury that is planned—

THE CHAIRMAN: Mr. Lawson—

MR. LAWSON: —permit me and my attorneys to bring in here the witnesses that testified last week and permit us to cross-examine these witnesses, and we will show up the whole tissue of lies—

THE CHAIRMAN (*pounding gavel*): We are going to get the answer to that question if we have to stay here for a week. Are you a member of the Communist Party, or have you ever been a member of the Communist Party?

MR. LAWSON: It is unfortunate and tragic that I have to teach this Committee the basic principles of American—

THE CHAIRMAN (*pounding gavel*): That is not the question. That is not the question. The question is: Have you ever been a member of the Communist Party?

MR. LAWSON: I am framing my answer in the only way in which any American citizen can frame his answer to a question which absolutely invades his rights.

THE CHAIRMAN: Then you refuse to answer that question; is that correct?

MR. LAWSON: I have told you that I will offer my beliefs, affiliations, and everything else to the American public, and they will know where I stand.

THE CHAIRMAN (*pounding gavel*): Excuse the witness—

MR. LAWSON: As they do from what I have written.

THE CHAIRMAN (*pounding gavel*): Stand away from the stand.

MR. LAWSON: I have written Americanism for many years, and I shall continue to fight for the Bill or Rights, which you are trying to destroy.

THE CHAIRMAN: Officers, take this man away from the stand....

United States House of Representatives, 80th Congress, 1st Session, Committee on Un-American Activities, *Hearings*, October 27, 1947.

22.6

JOSEPH MCCARTHY ON COMMUNISTS IN THE U.S. GOVERNMENT (1950)

By early 1950, the second Red Scare had pervaded American political culture. Many citizens viewed the Alger Hiss case, the arrests of Julius and Ethyl Rosenberg, the "loss" of China, and the Soviet explosion of an atomic bomb as evidence that American conspirators were undermining the U.S. government. No individual would make such charges more passionately than Senator Joseph R. McCarthy, a Republican senator from Wisconsin. Born in 1908, McCarthy became an attorney and served as a circuit judge until enlisting in the Marines in 1942. In

1946, he won election to the U.S. Senate. He gained little notice until he made the following address to a Republican women's group in Wheeling, West Virginia. In the speech, McCarthy alleged that communists were working in the U.S. State Department. Although he failed to prove his claims, McCarthy gained national attention. For the next four years, he led investigations of several federal agencies and interrogated hundreds of suspected subversives. His ruthless tactics and militant anticommunism won admirers and detractors. In December 1954, the Senate officially censured McCarthy for unbecoming conduct. He died in relative obscurity three years later.

---■---

FOCUS QUESTIONS

1. How does McCarthy describe global affairs?
2. Whom does McCarthy hold responsible for the problems facing the United States?
3. What impact did McCarthy's charges have?
4. Why do you think that McCarthyism gained so much popular support?

ive years after a world war has been won, men's hearts should anticipate a long peace and men's minds should be free from the heavy weight that comes with war. But this is not such a period—for this is not a period of peace. This is a time of the "cold war." This is a time when all the world is split into two vast, increasingly hostile armed camps—a time of a great armaments race.

Today we can almost physically hear the mutterings and rumblings of an invigorated god of war. You can see it, feel it, and hear it all the way from the hills of Indochina, from the shores of Formosa [Taiwan], right over into the very heart of Europe itself.

The one encouraging thing is that the "mad moment" has not yet arrived for the firing of the gun or the exploding of the bomb which will set civilization about the final task of destroying itself. There is still a hope for peace if we finally decide that no longer can we safely blind our eyes and close our ears to those facts which are shaping up more and more dearly. And that is that we are now engaged in a show-down fight—not the usual war between nations for land areas or other material gains, but a war between two diametrically opposed ideologies....

At war's end we were physically the strongest nation on earth and, at least potentially, the most powerfully intellectually and morally. Ours could have been the honor of being a beacon in the desert of destruction, a shining living proof that civilization was not yet ready to destroy itself. Unfortunately, we have failed miserably and tragically to arise to the opportunity.

The reason why we find ourselves in a position of impotency is not because our only powerful potential enemy has sent men to invade our shores, but rather because of the traitorous actions of those who have been treated so well by this Nation. It has not been the less fortunate or members of minority groups who have been selling this Nation out, but rather those who have had all the benefits that the wealthiest nation on earth has had to offer—the finest homes, the finest college education, and the finest jobs in Government we can give.

This is glaringly true in the State Department. There the bright young men who are born with silver spoons in their mouths are the ones who have been the worst.

Now I know it is very easy for anyone to condemn a particular bureau or department in general terms. Therefore, I would like to cite one rather unusual case the case of a man who has done much to shape our foreign policy.

When Chiang Kai-shek was fighting our war, the State Department had in China a young man named John S. Service. His task, obviously, was not to work for the communization of China. Strangely, however, he sent official reports back to the State Department urging that we torpedo our ally Chiang Kai-shek and stating, in effect, that communism was the best hope of China.

Later, this man—John Service—was picked up by the Federal Bureau of Investigation for turning over to the Communists secret State Department information. Strangely, however, he was never prosecuted. However, Joseph Grew, the Under Secretary of State, who insisted on his prosecution, was forced to resign. Two days after Grew's successor, Dean Acheson, took over as Under Secretary of State, this man—John Service—who had been picked up by the FBI and who had previously urged that communism was the best hope of China, was not only reinstated in the State Department but promoted, and finally, under Acheson, placed in charge of all placements and promotions.

Today, ladies and gentlemen, this man Service is on his way to represent the State Department and Acheson in Calcutta—by far and away the most important listening post in the Far East.

Now, let's see what happens when individuals with Communist connections are forced out of the State Department. Gustave Duran, who was labeled as (I quote) "a notorious international Communist" was made assistant to the Assistant Secretary of State in charge of Latin American affairs. He was taken into the State Department from his job as lieutenant colonel in the Communist International Brigade. Finally, after intense congressional pressure and criticism, he resigned in 1946 from the State Department—and, ladies and gentlemen, where do you think he is now? He took over a high-salaried job as Chief of Cultural Activities Section in the office of the Assistant Secretary General of the United Nations....

This, ladies and gentlemen, gives you somewhat of a picture of the type of individuals who have been helping to shape our foreign policy. In my opinion the State Department, which is one of the most important government departments, is thoroughly infested with Communists.

I have in my hand 57 cases of individuals who would appear to be either card carrying members or certainly loyal to the Communist Party, but who nevertheless are still helping to shape our foreign policy....

As you hear this story of high treason, I know what you are saying to yourself, "Well, why doesn't the Congress do something about it?" Actually, ladies and gentlemen, one of the most important reasons for the graft, the corruption, the dishonesty, the disloyalty, the treason in high Government positions—one of the most important reasons why this continues is a lack of moral uprising on the part of the 140,000,000 American people. In the light of history, however, this is not hard to explain.

It is the result of an emotional hang-over and a temporary moral lapse which follows every war. It is the apathy to evil which people who have been subjected to the tremendous evils of war feel. As the people of the world see mass murder, the destruction of defenseless and innocent people, and all of the crime and lack of morals which go with war, they become numb and apathetic. It has always been thus after war.

However, the morals of our people have not been destroyed. They still exist. This cloak of numbness and apathy has only needed a spark to rekindle them. Happily, this spark has finally been supplied....

"Communists in Government Service," *Congressional Record*, 81st Congress, 2nd Session, part 2 (20 February 1950): 1952-1954.

22.7

THE LAVENDER SCARE (1950)

During the early Cold War, deep cultural anxieties about global politics mixed with fears about changing ideas about gender and sexuality. Anyone who deviated from heterosexual norms became suspect. Experts claimed that gay men and lesbians posed an especially grave risk to national security and family life. In 1950, U.S. senators began investigating "homosexuals and other sex perverts" in government. Their findings, excerpted here, resulted in the dismissal of thousands of alleged homosexuals working for the federal government.

FOCUS QUESTIONS

1. What claims does the report make about homosexuals? On what evidence are these allegations based?
2. Why do the authors believe that homosexuals should not be federal employees?
3. What does this reading suggest about American political culture in this era?

 ven among the experts there existed considerable difference of opinion concerning the many facets of homosexuality and other forms of sex perversion.... For the purpose of this report the subcommittee has defined sex perverts as "those who engage in unnatural sexual acts" and homosexuals are perverts who may be broadly defined as "persons of either sex who as adults engage in sexual activities with persons of the same sex." In this inquiry the subcommittee is not concerned with so-called latent sex perverts, namely, those persons who knowingly or unknowingly have tendencies or inclinations toward homosexuality or other types of sex perversion, but who, by the exercise of self-restraint or for other reasons, do not indulge in overt acts of perversion. This investigation is concerned only with those who engage in overt acts of homosexuality or other sex perversion.

The subcommittee found that most authorities agree on certain basic facts concerning sex perversion: ...that sex deviation results from psychological rather than physical causes, and in many cases there are no outward characteristics or physical traits that are positive as identifying marks of sex perversion. Contrary to a common belief, all homosexual males do not have feminine mannerisms, nor do all female homosexuals display masculine characteristics in their dress or actions. The fact is that many male homosexuals are very masculine in their physical appearance and general demeanor, and many female homosexuals have every appearance of femininity in their outward behavior.

Generally speaking, the overt homosexual of both sexes can be divided into two general types: the active, aggressive or male type, and the submissive, passive or female type. The passive type of male homosexual, who is often effeminate in his mannerisms and appearance, is attracted to the masculine type of man and is friendly and congenial with women. On the other hand the active male homosexual often has a dislike for women. He exhibits no traces of femininity in his speech or mannerisms which would disclose his homosexuality This active type is almost exclusively attracted to the passive type of homosexual or to young men or boys who are not necessarily homosexual but who are effeminate in general appearance. The active and passive types of female homosexuals follow the same general patterns as their male counterparts. It is also a known fact that some perverts are bisexual. This type engages in normal heterosexual relationships as well as homosexual activities. These bisexual individuals are often married and have children, and except for their perverted activities they appear to lead normal lives.

Psychiatric physicians generally agree that indulgence in sexually perverted practices indicates a personality which has failed to reach sexual maturity. The authorities agree that most sex deviates respond to psychiatric treatment and can be cured if they have a genuine desire to be cured. However, many overt homosexuals have no real desire to abandon their way of life and in such cases cures are difficult if not impossible. The subcommittee sincerely believes that persons afflicted with sexual desires which result in their engaging in overt acts of perversion should be considered as proper cases for medical and psychiatric treatment. However, sex perverts, like all other persons who by their overt acts violate moral codes and laws and the accepted standards of conduct, must be treated as transgressors and dealt with accordingly....

Those charged with the responsibility of operating the agencies of Government must insist that Government employees meet acceptable standards of personal conduct. In the opinion of this subcommittee homosexuals and other sex perverts are not proper persons to be employed in Government for two reasons: first, they are generally unsuitable, and second, they constitute security risks....

Overt acts of sex perversion, including acts of homosexuality, constitute a crime under our Federal, State, and municipal statutes and persons who commit such acts are law violators. Aside from the criminality and immorality involved in sex perversion such behavior is so contrary to the normal accepted standards of social behavior that persons who engage in such activity are looked upon as outcasts by society generally. The social stigma attached to sex perversion is so great that many perverts go to great lengths to conceal their perverted tendencies. This situation is evidenced by the fact that perverts are frequently victimized by blackmailers who threaten to expose their sexual deviations.

Law enforcement officers have informed the subcommittee that there are gangs of blackmailers who make a regular practice of preying upon the homosexual. The modus operandi in these homosexual blackmail cases usually follow the same general pattern. The victim, who is a homosexual, has managed to conceal his perverted activities and usually enjoys a good reputation in his community. The blackmailers, by one means or another, discover that the victim is addicted to homosexuality and under the threat of disclosure they extort money from him. These blackmailers often impersonate police officers in carrying out their blackmail schemes. Many cases have come to the attention of the police where highly respected individuals have paid out substantial sums of money to blackmailers over a long period of time rather than risk the disclosure of their homosexual activities. The police believe that this type of blackmail racket is much more extensive than is generally known, because they have found that most of the victims are very hesitant to bring the matter to the attention of the authorities.

In further considering the general suitability of perverts as Government employees, it is generally believed that those who engage in overt acts of perversion lack the emotional stability of normal persons. In addition there is an abundance of evidence to sustain the conclusion that indulgence in acts of sex perversion weakens the moral fiber of an individual to a degree that he is not suitable for a position of responsibility.

Most of the authorities agree and our investigation has shown that the presence of a sex pervert in a Government agency tends to have a corrosive influence upon his fellow employees. These perverts will frequently attempt to entice normal individuals to engage in perverted practices. This is particularly true in the case of young and impressionable people who might come under the influence of a pervert. Government officials have the responsibility of keeping this type of corrosive influence out of the agencies under their control. It is particularly important that the thousands of young men and women who are brought into Federal jobs not be subjected to that type of influence while in the service of the Government. One homosexual can pollute a Government office.

Another point to be considered in determining whether a sex pervert is suitable for Government employment is his tendency to gather other perverts about him. Eminent psychiatrists have informed the subcommittee that the homosexual is likely to seek his own kind because the pressures of society are such that he feels uncomfortable unless he is with his own kind. Due to this situation the homosexual tends to surround himself with other homosexuals, not only in his social, but in his business life. Under these circumstances if a homosexual attains a position in

Government where he can influence the hiring of personnel, it is almost inevitable that he will attempt to place other homosexuals in Government jobs....

The lack of emotional stability which is found in most sex perverts and the weakness of their moral fiber, makes them susceptible to the blandishments of the foreign espionage agent. It is the experience of intelligence experts that perverts are vulnerable to interrogation by a skilled questioner and they seldom refuse to talk about themselves. Furthermore, most perverts tend to congregate at the same restaurants, night clubs, and bars, which places can be identified with comparative ease in any community, making it possible for a recruiting agent to develop clandestine relationships which can be used for espionage purposes....

Employment of Homosexuals and Other Sex Perverts in Government, Committee on Expenditures in the Executive Departments, Subcommittee on Investigations, 81st Congress, 2nd Sess., Senate Document No. 241, December 15, 1950.

22.8

A GUIDE FOR SURVIVING NUCLEAR WAR (1950)

After the United States dropped atomic bombs on Japan in August 1945, the Soviets began an intensive effort to build their own nuclear weapons. Tremendous government support and information from spies within the American atomic program enabled them to succeed quickly. In August 1949, the first Soviet atomic bomb was exploded in Kazakhstan.

U.S. officials were determined to maintain the edge in the nuclear arms race. Following detonation of the Soviet bomb, President Harry S. Truman approved the development of a more powerful fusion-based hydrogen bomb. In November 1952, the first American hydrogen bomb was successfully tested on the Pacific island of Eniwetok. Nine months later, the Soviets exploded their own hydrogen weapon. At the same time, the Eisenhower administration adopted the "New Look," a defense strategy based on an expanded nuclear arsenal, additional collective security agreements, and greater use of covert operations. Because nuclear weapons were less expensive than their conventional counterparts, Secretary of Defense Charles Wilson explained, the New Look offered "more bang for the buck."

As the U.S. nuclear arsenal grew, the federal government tried to calm popular anxiety about atomic war. From 1951 until 1965, the Atomic Energy Commission (AEC) conducted civil defense programs all over the United States. Through publications, films, and evacuation drills, the AEC trained citizens to "prepare" for nuclear attack. During the same period, the United States conducted hundreds of atmospheric and underground nuclear tests in the Pacific Ocean and the Nevada desert. The tests usually went unnoticed by the general public and the government made little effort to assess the effects of the fallout released. In response, atomic scientists and peace activists warned that fallout could trigger epidemics of cancer and widespread birth defects. In 1958, fears of fallout prompted the United States and the Soviet Union to suspend atmospheric nuclear tests.

FOCUS QUESTIONS

1. How would you describe the tone of the pamphlet? How does it portray the threat posed by atomic weapons?
2. According to the pamphlet, what measures would increase one's chances of surviving an atomic attack? What is your opinion of these suggestions?
3. Throughout much of the Cold War, U.S. policymakers claimed that America's large nuclear arsenal decreased the chances of war with the Soviet Union. Do you agree? Explain your answer.
4. Since the 9-11 attacks, the government has instituted new civil defense programs that urge citizens to "be prepared" for terrorist attacks. Compare these initiatives to their Cold War predecessors.

ou can survive. You can live through an atomic bomb raid and you won't have to have a Geiger counter, protective clothing, or special training in order to do it. The secrets of survival are:

KNOW THE BOMB'S TRUE DANGERS
KNOW THE STEPS YOU TAKE TO ESCAPE THEM

To begin with, you must realize that atom-splitting is just another way of causing an explosion. While an atomic bomb holds more death and destruction than man has ever before wrapped in a single package, its total power is definitely limited. Not even hydrogen bombs could blow the earth apart or kill us all by mysterious radiation.

Because the power of all bombs is limited, your chances of living through an atomic attack are much better than you may have thought. In the city of Hiroshima, slightly over half the people who were a mile from the bomb lived to tell their experiences. Today, thousands of survivors of these two atomic attacks live in new houses built right where their old ones once stood. The war may have changed their way of life, but they are not riddled with cancer. Their children are normal. Those who were temporarily unable to have children because of the radiation now are having children again....

Just like fire bombs and ordinary high explosives, atomic weapons cause most of their death and damage by blast and heat. So first let's look at a few things you can do to escape these two dangers.

Even if you have only a second's warning, there is one important thing you can do to lessen your chances of injury by blast: Fall flat on your face.

More than half of all wounds are the result of being bodily tossed about or being struck by falling and flying objects. If you lie down flat, you are least likely to be thrown about. If you have time to pick a good spot, there is less chance of your being struck by flying glass and other things.

If you are inside a building, the best place to flatten out is close against the cellar wall. If you haven't time to get down there, lie down along an inside wall, or duck under a bed or table....

If caught out-of-doors, either drop down alongside the base of a good substantial building—avoid flimsy, wooden ones likely to be blown over on top of you—or else jump in any handy ditch or gutter.

When you fall flat to protect yourself from a bombing, don't look up to see what is coming. Even during the daylight hours, the flash from a bursting A-bomb can cause several moments of blindness, if you're facing that way. To prevent it, bury your face in your arms and hold it there for 10 to 12 seconds after the explosion....

To prevent flash burns, try to find a shelter where there is a wall, a high bank or some other object between you and the bursting bomb. You can expect that the bomber will aim for the city's biggest collection of industrial buildings....

If you work in the open, always wear full-length, loose-fitting, light-colored clothes in time of emergency. Never go around with your sleeves rolled up. Always wear a hat—the brim could save you a serious face burn.

In all stories about atomic weapons, there is a great deal about radioactivity.

Radioactivity is the only way—besides size—in which the effects of A or H bombs are different from ordinary bombs. But, with the exception of underwater or ground explosions, the radioactivity from atomic bursts is much less to be feared than blast and heat....

In spite of the huge quantities of lingering radioactivity loosed by atomic explosions, people fortunately are not very likely to be exposed to dangerous amounts of it in most atomic raids....

Regardless of all you may have heard or read concerning the dangers of radioactive clouds, after the first minute and a half there is actually little or nothing to hear from those produced by high-level bursts. While most of the radioactive materials swept up into the sky eventually fall back to earth, they are so widely and so thinly spread that are very unlikely to offer any real dangers to humans. Thousands of bombs would have to be set off in the air before serious ground contamination would be found over really large areas....

To sum up, always remember that blast and heat are the two greatest dangers you face. The things that you do to protect yourself from these dangers usually will go a long way toward providing protection from the explosive radioactivity loosed by atomic explosions.

While the lingering radioactivity that occasionally follows some types of atomic bursts may be dangerous, still it is no more to be feared than typhoid fever or other diseases that sometimes follow major disasters. The only difference is that we can't now ward it off with a shot in the arm; you must simply take steps to avoid it.

If you follow the pointers in this little booklet, you stand far better than an even chance of surviving the bomb's blast, heat, and radioactivity. What's more, you will make a definite contribution to civil defense in your community, because civil defense must start with you. But if you lose your head and blindly attempt to run from the dangers, you may touch off a panic that will cost your life and put tremendous obstacles in the way of your Civil Defense Corps.

Executive Office of the President, National Security Resources Board, Civil Defense Office, NSRB Doc. 130, *Survival under Atomic Attack* (Washington: Government Printing Office, 1950).

SECONDARY SOURCE

JOHN LEWIS GADDIS, "COLD WAR EMPIRES: EUROPE"

Historians have long debated the origins, causes, and ramifications of the Cold War. They disagree, sometimes passionately, on whether the United States or the Soviet Union was primarily responsible for the conflict. John Lewis Gaddis, a diplomatic historian at Yale University, examines some of these issues in this excerpt from We Now Know: Rethinking Cold War History *(1997).*

Go to *Speaking of America* CD-ROM to read "Cold War Empires: Europe."

FOCUS QUESTIONS

1. Why does Gaddis think that the Cold War was an "imperial" struggle?
2. How does he contrast the Soviet and American "empires"?
3. Why does he believe that the West did not resist Soviet expansionism earlier?
4. According to Gaddis, what caused the Cold War? Does he hold either side more responsible? Why or why not?
5. Do you think that the Cold War was inevitable? Did U.S. policymakers respond appropriately to communist expansionism? Explain your answers.

AMERICAN JOURNEY ONLINE

http://ajaccesss.wadsworth.com [†]

About U.S. Foreign Policy
— In The Cold War
   Documents
   •   U.S. State Department, Protocol of the Proceedings of the Crimea Conference (1945)

[†] Enter password, choose the Archive indicated above, click on Contents, choose •Documents, •Images, or •Multimedia, and click on the title of the item.

- U.S. State Department, Declaration on Liberated Europe (1945)
- Franklin D. Roosevelt, Letter to Joseph Stalin on Poland, April 1, 1945
- Charles Bohlen, Briefing of President Truman by W. Averell Harriman on Soviet Actions in Eastern Europe, April 20, 1945
- Winston Churchill, Iron Curtain Speech, March 5, 1946
- Edmund O. Clubb, The Consul General at Peiping to the Secretary of State (1949)
- William Knowland, Excerpt from a Speech to the U.S. Senate (1949)
- Paul H. Nitze, National Security Council No. 68 (1950)
- National Security Council, U.S. Position with Respect to Germany (1953)
- U.S. State Department, SEATO Treaty (1954)
- John Foster Dulles, Evolution of Foreign Policy (1954)
- National Security Council, Memorandum of Discussion at a Special Meeting of the National Security Council (1959)
- Richard J. Barnet, A Balance Sheet: Lippmann, Kennan, and the Cold War (1992)

Images
- Truman and Hiss (1945)
- George F. Kennan
- Image—Berlin Airlift Begins (1948)
- U.S. Diplomats Acheson and McCloy Arrive in Germany (1949)
- Patrick McCarran and the China Hands (undated)
- Early CIA Directors Smith and Dulles (1953)
- Guatemalan Leader Overthrown in CIA Coup (1954)
- Nation's Top Spook (undated)
- Eisenhower and Dulles Confer (1954)
- Fidel Speaks (1959)
- Ike in Taiwan (1960)
— In Vietnam Era
Documents
- George F. Kennan, The Sources of Soviet Conduct (1947)
Images
- Secretary of State Dean Acheson (1949)
- Secretary of State John Foster Dulles, June 24, 1954

About Soviet Foreign Policy
— In The Cold War
Documents
- Joseph Stalin's Interview, March 13, 1946
- Nikolai Novikov, The Novikov Telegram, September 27, 1946
- Yur Zhukov, Excerpt from "Aiding or Undermining the Reconstruction of Europe?" (1947)
- Andrei Vishinsky, Excerpt from A Soviet Criticism of the Truman Doctrine and Marshall Plan (1947)
- Editorial in *Pravda* Regarding President Truman's Speech, December 19, 1950

- Alexander Tchakovsky, Excerpt from *Fiendish Fanatics* (1951)
- Stalin and the SED Leadership (1952)

Images
- Joseph Stalin (1952)
- Khrushchev Meets Mao (1954)
- Nikita S. Khrushchev and Fidel Castro (1960)

About the Korean War
— In The Cold War
Documents
- U.S. State Department, Memorandum of Conversation by the Ambassador at Large, June 26, 1950
- U.S. Department of Defense, U.S. Courses of Action in Korea (1950)
- Discussion between President Harry S. Truman and Douglas MacArthur (1950)
- Harry S. Truman, Radio Broadcast, April 11, 1951
- Document with Audio Commentary—Douglas MacArthur, Farewell Speech to the Joint Houses of the U.S. Congress, April 19, 1951
- Merle Miller, The Korean Decision (1974)

Images
- United States Navy, Landing at Inchon, South Korea (1950)
- United Marine Corps, Bitter Conditions Near the Chosin Reservoir (1950)
- U.S. Marine Corps, Chinese Casualties in Korea (1951)
- Ike Reacts to MacArthur Sacking (1951)
- United States Marine Corps, Captured Enemy Forces in South Korea (1951)

— In Vietnam Era
Images
- The Korean War

About the Origins of the Vietnam War
— In Vietnam Era
Documents
- U.S. State Department, Differing Perspectives on Vietnam (1945)
- Ho Chi Minh, Declaration of Independence of the Democratic Republic of Vietnam, September 2, 1945
- Ho Chi Minh, Cable to President Harry S. Truman, October 17, 1945
- Nguyen Dynasty Kinship Chart
- Ho Chi Minh, Franco-Vietnamese Agreement on the Status of Vietnam, March 6, 1946
- Ho Chi Minh, Appeal to the Entire People to Wage This Resistance War, December 20, 1946
- Ho Chi Minh, Message to the Vietnamese, French, and the Peoples of the Allied Nations, December 21, 1946
- George C. Marshall, Cable to U.S. Embassy in Paris, February 3, 1947

- Dean Acheson and U.S. State Department, Telegram to the U.S. Consulate, Hanoi, May 20, 1949; Memorandum to the French Foreign Office, June 6, 1949
- National Security Council, The Position of the United States with Respect to Indochina (1950)
- Dean Acheson, Ho Chi Minh's True Colors (1950)
- Bernard Fall, Solution in Indochina (1954)
- John Foster Dulles, Discussion with Congressmen, April 5, 1954
- Dwight D. Eisenhower, Presidential Press Conference, April 7, 1954
- National Security Council, Record of NSC Meeting, April 29, 1954
- U.S. Government, Instruction to U.S. Delegation at Geneva, May 12, 1954
- Rob McClintock, Communication to State Department, July 4, 1954
- Ho Chi Minh, Statement on Geneva Accords, July 15, 1954
- Final Declaration of Geneva Conference, July 21, 1954
- U.S. Government, U.S. Response to Geneva Accords (1954)
- Ngo Dinh Diem, Response to Geneva Accords, July 22, 1954
- National Security Council, Record of NSC Meetings, October 22 and 26, 1954
- Dwight D. Eisenhower, Letter to Ngo Dinh Diem (1954)
- Tran Van Giau, The Growing Crisis in the South (1957)
- Bernard Fall, The Last Day (1966)

Images
- Bao Dai in Vietnam Era
- Ho Chi Minh at a Paris Press Conference, June 25, 1946
- Ho Chi Minh and French Officials Review Military Parade in Paris, July 14, 1946
- Mao Tse-tung (1949) in Vietnam Era
- American C-47 Planes Lined Up on Do Son Airstrip, April 19, 1952
- Map of Indochina (1953) in Vietnam Era
- French Patrol Searches the Forest Near Dien Bien Phu (1954)
- Map Shows Viet Minh Advance at Dien Bien Phu (1954)
- Viet Minh Forces Surrender to French, April 12, 1954
- Map of Dien Bien Phu, April 29, 1954
- Van Tien Dung, June 11, 1954
- Recently Abandoned French Military Outpost at Nhai Thuu, July 8, 1954
- Pierre Mendes-France, July 23, 1954
- Map of Vietnam with Division at Seventeenth Parallel (1954)
- Viet Minh Stage Victory Parade in Hanoi, October 22, 1954
- Ngo Dinh Diem and President Dwight D. Eisenhower (1957)
- Ngo Dinh Nhu and President Eisenhower (1957)

— In The Cold War
Documents
- U.S. State Department, Military Aid for Indochina (1950)
- John Foster Dulles, Radio and Television Address to the Nation, May 7, 1954

Images
- Ho Chi Minh (1954)

About the Sputnik Launch
— In The Cold War
Videos
- Eisenhower Publicly Responds to *Sputnik* Launch (1957)
- Satellite Tracking Becomes Part of the Cold War (undated)

About the U-2 Crisis
— In The Cold War
Documents
- Llewellyn E. Thompson, Telegram from Embassy in the Soviet Union to the Department of State, May 9, 1960
- Stepan Chervonenko, Memorandum of Conversation with the General Secretary of the CC CCP, Member of the Politiburo of the CC CCP, Deng Xiaoping, 17 May 1960
Images
- Soviets Trumpet Shooting Down of U-2 Spy Plane (1960)
- Image with Audio Commentary—U-2 Frances Gary Powers at Hearing (1962)

About Nuclear Weapons
— In The Cold War
Documents
- Stalin's Secret Order: Build the Bomb "on a Russian Scale" (1944, 1946)
- George F. Kennan, International Control of Atomic Energy (1950)
- Elie Abel, Dulles Says U.S. Pins Retaliation on Small A-Bomb (1955)
— In Vietnam Era
Images
- U.S. Navy, Atomic Bomb Blast over Bikini, July 25, 1946
— In World War II
Images
- J. Robert Oppenheimer (1947)

About Domestic Anti-Communism
— In The Constitution and Supreme Court
Documents
- Howard W. Smith, The Smith Act (1940)
- Fred M. Vinson, *Dennis v. United States* (1951)
— In The Cold War
Documents
- J. Edgar Hoover, Speech Delivered at the Annual Convention of the American Legion, San Francisco, CA, September 30, 1946
- Henry Steele Commager, Washington Witch Hunt (1947) in The Cold War
- Harry S. Truman, Statement by the President on the Government's Employee Loyalty Program, November 14, 1947

- Millard Tydings, Democratic Rebuttal, July 20, 1950
- Joseph McCarthy, Introduction to *America's Retreat from Victory* (1951)
- U.S. Senate, Hearings, June 9, 1954
- William F. Buckley and L. Brent Bozell, Excerpt from *McCarthy and His Enemies* (1954)
- Paul Robeson, Testimony at HUAC Hearing, June 12, 1956
- Edwin R. Bayley, Versions of the Wheeling Speech (1981)

Images
- The Hollywood Ten (1948)
- Hiss Called to Testify before House Committee (1948)
- Chambers Makes Sensational Charges in Hiss Case (1948)
- Image with Audio Commentary—McCarthy at Map (1950)
- Professor Victimized by McCarthyism (1951)
- Julius Rosenberg Faces Death Penalty for Espionage (1951)
- Ethel Rosenberg Faces Same Fate as Her Husband (1951)
- J. Edgar Hoover Testifies on Red Threat (1953)
- McCarthy and Dulles (undated)
- Films Reflect Cold War Themes (1956)

— In Civil Rights in the United States

Documents
- U.S. Supreme Court, *American Communication Association v. Douds* (1950)

Images
- Harry S. Truman (undated)
- House Un-American Activities Committee (1948)
- Paul Robeson (1949)
- Trial of the Hollywood Ten (1950)
- Trial of Julius and Ethel Rosenberg (1951)
- Rosenbergs' Executions (1953)
- Senator Joseph McCarthy (1954)

Videos
- Alger Hiss and Whittaker Chambers Testify (1948) in Civil Rights in the United States
- Rosenbergs Convicted and Executed (1953)

— In Vietnam Era

Images
- Alger Hiss before the House Un-American Activities Committee (1948)

— In World War II

Documents
- Ronald Reagan, Reds Beaten in Hollywood (1951)

About U.S.-Soviet Cultural Exchanges

— In The Cold War

Documents
- U.S. State Department, United States and U.S.S.R. Sign Agreement on East-West Exchanges (1958)

- U.S. State Department, U.S.-Soviet Exhibits a Successful Exchange (1959)
- U.S. State Department, Memorandum of Conversation, September 15, 1959
- Richard M. Nixon, Nixon-Khrushchev Kitchen Debate, 1959 (1962)

Images
- U.S. Information Agency, U.S. Fair Trumpets Consumerism (1959)
- Khrushchev Visits the United States (1959)

POSTWAR AMERICA

After years of depression and war, Americans welcomed the stability and prosperity of the post-WWII era. They married and had children. They bought homes, cars, and other items. Many moved to new suburban communities. Although millions improved their lives, the era also exposed inequities and anxieties. Cold War tensions and the nuclear arms race dominated U.S. foreign relations. Anti-communism pervaded politics and society. Racial minorities challenged discrimination. While *I Love Lucy*, hula hoops, and 3-D movies reflected the period's innocence, civil defense drills, the Emmett Till lynching, and the Korean War embodied its dangers and complexities.

President Harry S. Truman presided over the nation's transition from war to peace. A Democrat, he faced a highly partisan Republican Party and deep divisions within his own party. When World War II ended in August 1945, Truman acquiesced to popular demands that U.S. troops be brought home quickly. Between 1945 and 1948, the number of American forces dropped from 12 million to 1.5 million.

As the veterans returned, the nation experienced serious economic problems. The closure of war plants created mass unemployment. A housing shortage worsened. In response, the federal government took steps to prevent a depression. The GI Bill financed educations, unemployment benefits, and loans for veterans. The Bretton Woods agreement made the United States the center of international finance among non-communist countries. America's economic position enabled U.S. companies to export and import with very favorable terms. Technological and scientific innovations increased productivity and created new industries. In 1946, the U.S. economy began a period of remarkable growth that lasted until the late 1960s.

A wave of consumerism helped fuel this prosperity. Americans rushed to buy goods that had not been available or affordable in previous years. Sales of homes, cars, appliances, and other products soared as people started families and built comfortable lifestyles.

This climate proved politically inhospitable to New Deal-style liberalism. When Truman tried to institute new social welfare benefits in housing, health care, education, and employment, Congress stonewalled him. When he attempted to control inflation by extending wartime price controls, producers and retailers protested. Employees' frustrations at rising prices and stagnant wages exploded in a wave of strikes. In 1946, major industries including steel, auto, coal, and railroads stalled as 4.5 million workers joined strikes. Truman's hostile response to these protests alienated many voters. The 1946 midterm elections underscored Truman's unpopularity as the Republicans won control of Congress for the first time in eighteen years.

The stinging defeat forced Truman to change his domestic policies. When congressional conservatives cut tax rates for the wealthy and opposed new federal education and housing programs, Truman reestablished good relations with organized labor and courted other traditional Democratic constituencies. In 1947, he vetoed the Taft-Hartley Act barring the closed shop and allowing presidents to delay strikes under certain conditions. Although Congress easily overrode his veto, Truman's pro-labor stand pleased unionists. His support for the new state of Israel and opposition to communism in Eastern Europe won support from Jewish and ethnic voters. Outraged by reports of racial violence in the South, Truman established the President's Committee on Civil Rights. When the group recommended strong civil rights laws, Truman backed many of its suggestions. He also issued executive orders barring racial discrimination in federal employment and integrating the armed services.

When white southern Democrats protested these civil rights measures, Truman backtracked. At the 1948 Democratic convention, his endorsement of a weak civil rights plank in the party platform pleased neither southern conservatives nor liberals. Several southern Democrats broke from the party and established the States' Rights Democratic Party. The "Dixiecrats" tapped Strom Thurmond, the Democratic governor of South Carolina, as their presidential nominee and promised to defend segregation from federal interference. Truman's chances of reelection declined further when Democratic leftists formed another splinter party, the Progressives. Their presidential nominee, former secretary of agriculture Henry Wallace, attacked Truman's policies toward the Soviet Union.

Against all odds, Truman managed to win reelection. His tireless campaigning and attacks on the "do-nothing" Republican Congress won critical support from moderates, African Americans, and organized labor. With his authority renewed, Truman proposed the Fair Deal, a broad agenda of civil rights laws, expanded Social Security benefits, public housing programs, an increased minimum wage, national health insurance, and federal aid to education. Ultimately, few of these measures passed. As fighting communism and ensuring national security consumed national political life, domestic reforms became less of a priority.

As discussed in the previous chapter, U.S. officials responded strongly to the threat of international communism. Through policies such as the Truman Doctrine, the Marshall Plan, and NSC-68, the Truman administration helped to rebuild wartorn Europe and challenged Soviet expansionism. The costs of the new Cold War were high. As anti-communism pervaded American political culture, civil liberties were curtailed. An escalating nuclear arms race made global annihilation a terrifying possibility. Almost 55,000 Americans perished in the $54 billion Korean War.

In 1952, public apprehension about the Cold War and Democratic financial scandals helped the Republicans regain the presidency. Popular war hero Dwight D. Eisenhower easily triumphed over Illinois Governor Adlai Stevenson. Republicans also won control of both houses of Congress.

Eisenhower's affable demeanor and moderate policies were well-suited to 1950s America. He reassured voters and usually steered clear of controversies. With the guidance of cabinet officers drawn from private corporations, Eisenhower slashed government spending and promoted economic development. To the consternation of conservatives, he did not dismantle the New Deal welfare state and worked with organized labor. Indeed, he expanded Social Security benefits, raised the minimum wage, and supported the most expensive public works program in U.S. history, the Interstate Highway Act of 1956. Although Eisenhower avoided public confrontations with Senator Joseph McCarthy, he worked behind the scenes to weaken McCarthy's crusade against alleged subversives in the federal government. In foreign affairs, Eisenhower continued the containment policies of the Truman administration and signed an armistice in Korea. To make national defense more cost-effective, he approved a "New Look" defense strategy built on the expansion of the nuclear arsenal, covert operations, and collective security arrangements. Ike's tactics worked well and he was resoundingly reelected in 1956.

The Eisenhower years were marked by affluence and stability. By 1960, a majority of Americans owned homes, cars, and televisions. From 1950 to 1960, the gross national product (GNP) rose from $318 billion to $488 billion. Much of this economic growth stemmed from a massive increase in federal spending, particularly on national defense. Many workers saw significant increases in their wages. Technological and scientific advances in the chemical, electronics and transportation industries created jobs and increased efficiency. Corporations grew larger and more diversified.

The social costs of these developments were less obvious. Few people paid attention to the wasteful use of energy and the pollution of natural resources. Because unions had already won high wages and generous benefits, they had a difficult time sustaining the militancy of earlier decades. As Americans bought more consumer products, they began borrowing more money and saving less. Millions soon carried credit card debt, mortgages, and car loans.

Many people preferred to focus on the "good life" of the postwar era. People married young and had large families. They flocked to thriving suburban communities. They celebrated medical advances like the Polio vaccine. They spent millions on leisure activities and entertainment. They packed churches in higher numbers. Popular culture glorified consumerism and domesticity.

Such trends masked the complexities in American life. In the so-called "affluent society," 35 million people—one-fifth of the national population—lived in poverty. An energized civil rights movement won important legal victories only to meet brutal opposition from white southerners and indifference from federal officials. Mexican-Americans and American Indians combated poverty and exploitative government policies. Artists and writers rejected the era's conformity and materialism. Millions of young people embraced the sensuality of rock and roll music. These were only a few signs of the discontent that exploded in the social movements and culture of the 1960s.

23.1

DR. BENJAMIN SPOCK ADVISES PARENTS (1946)

Following years of depression and war, Americans welcomed the prosperity and peace of the postwar era. The desire for stability inspired millions to marry and start families. The average age of marriage fell to 22 for men and 20 for women. After decades of declining birth rates, these young couples had record numbers of children. Between 1946 and 1964, 76 million children were born. When the "baby boom" peaked in 1957, the U.S. population was growing at the same rate as that of India. The baby boom generation dominated the nation's demographic, economic, and cultural trends.

Many new parents relied on Dr. Benjamin Spock (1903-1998). After receiving his medical degree from Columbia University, Spock became a pediatrician and professor at Cornell University Medical College. In this era, prevailing doctrines of childrearing stressed rigid feeding schedules and discouraged open displays of affection between parents and children. In Baby and Child Care, *Spock rejected these theories and instead urged parents to be flexible and understanding toward their children. First published in 1945, Spock's book provided guidance and assurance to millions of parents. The book went through several editions and sold 28 million copies. In the 1960s, some social commentators blamed Spock's permissive ideas for the lifestyles of young people in the anti-war movement and the counterculture. Spock himself was a vocal opponent of the Vietnam War.*

This passage is drawn from the 1946 edition of Baby and Child Care.

FOCUS QUESTIONS

1. What advice does Spock offer parents? Why do you think that so many parents took Spock's advice?
2. How do today's notions of childrearing compare with Spock's?
3. Why do you think that critics claimed that Spock's ideas contributed to the permissive attitudes of the 1960s youth culture?

TRUST YOURSELF
You know more than you think you do. Soon you're going to have a baby. Maybe you have him already. You're happy and excited, but if you haven't had much experience, you wonder whether you are going to know how to do a

good job. Lately, you have been listening more carefully to your friends and relatives when they talk about bringing up a child. You've begun to read articles by experts in the magazines and newspapers. After the baby is born, the doctors and nurses will begin to give you instructions too. Sometimes it sounds like a very complicated business. You find out all the vitamins a baby needs and all the immunizations. One mother tells you you must use the black kind of nipples, another says the yellow. You hear that a baby must be handled as little as possible, and that a baby must be cuddled plenty; that spinach is the most valuable vegetable; that spinach is a worthless vegetable. Some say that fairy tales make children nervous, others that fairy tales are a wholesome outlet for children's fears.

Don't take too seriously all that the neighbors say. Don't be overawed by what the experts say. Don't be afraid to trust your own common sense. Bringing up your child won't be a complicated job if you take it easy, trust your own instincts, and follow the directions that your doctor gives you. We know for a fact that the natural loving care that kindly parents give their children is a hundred times more valuable than their knowing how to pin a diaper on just right or making a formula expertly. Every time you pick your baby up, even if you do it a little awkwardly at first, every time you change him, bathe him, feed him, smile at him, he's getting the feeling that he belongs to you and that you belong to him. Nobody else in the world, no matter how skillful, can give that to him.

It may surprise you to hear that the more people have studied different methods of bringing up children, the more they have come to the conclusion that what good mothers and fathers instinctively feel like doing for their babies is usually best after all. Furthermore, all parents do their best job when they have a natural, easy confidence in themselves. Better to make a few mistakes from being natural than to try to do everything letter-perfect out of a feeling of worry....

You'd think from all you hear about babies demanding attention that they come into the world determined to get their parents under their thumbs by hook or by crook. This is not true at all. Your baby is born to be a reasonable, friendly human being. If you treat him nicely, he won't take advantage of you. Don't be afraid to love him or respond to his needs. Every baby needs to be smiled at, talked to, played with, fondled—gently and lovingly—just as much as you he needs vitamins and calories, and the baby who doesn't get any loving will grow up cold and unresponsive. When he cries, it's for a good reason—maybe it's hunger, or wetness, or indigestion, or just because he's on edge and needs soothing. His cry is there to call you. The uneasy feeling you have when you hear him cry, the feeling that you want to comfort him, is meant to be part of your nature, too....

You may hear people say that you have to get your baby strictly regulated in his feeding, sleeping, bowel movements, and other habits—but don't believe this either. In the first place, you can't get a baby regulated beyond a certain point, no matter how hard you try. In the second place, you are more apt, in the long run, to make him balky and disagreeable when you go at his training too hard. Everyone wants his child to turn out to be healthy in his habits and easy to live with. But each child wants, himself, to eat at sensible hours, and later to learn good table manners. His bowels (as long as the movement don't become too hard) will move according to their own healthy pattern, which may or may not be regular; and when he is much older and wiser, you can show him where to sit and move them. He will develop his own pattern of sleep, according to his own needs. In all these habits, he will fit into the family's way of doing things sooner or later without much effort on your part....

Enjoy him as he is—that's how he'll grow up best. Every baby's face is different from every other's. In the same way every baby's pattern of development is different. One may be very advanced in his general bodily strength and coordination, an early sitter, stander, walker—a sort of infant athlete. And yet he may be slow in doing careful, skillful things with his fingers, in talking. Even a baby who is an athlete in rolling over, standing, and creeping may turn out to be slow to learn to walk. A baby who's advanced in his physical activities may be very slow in teething and vice versa. A child who turns out later to be smart in his schoolwork may have been so slow in beginning to talk that his parents were afraid for awhile that he was dull; and a child who has just an ordinary amount of brains is sometimes a very early talker....

Love and enjoy your child for what he is, for what he looks like, for what he does, and forget about the qualities that he doesn't have. I don't give you this advice just for sentimental reasons. There's a very important practical point here. The child who is appreciated for what he is, even if he is homely, or clumsy, or slow, will grow up with confidence in himself, happy. He will have a spirit that will make the best of all the capacities that he has, and of all the opportunities that come his way. He will make light of any handicaps. But the child who has never been quite accepted by his parents, who has always felt that he was not quite right, grow up lacking confidence. He'll never be able to make full use of what brains, what skills, what physical attractiveness he has. If he starts life with a handicap, physical or mental, it will be multiplied tenfold by the time he is grown up.

Benjamin Spock, *The Common Sense Book of Baby and Child Care* (New York: Duell, Sloan and Pearce, 1946), pp. 3-4, 19-22. Courtesy of Mary Morgan.

23.2

A VETERAN ON THE GI BILL

In June 1944, Congress passed the Servicemen's Readjustment Act, better known as the "GI Bill of Rights." The legislation greatly expanded the middle class and changed American society dramatically. The GI Bill stemmed from months of vigorous debate about the best way to reintegrate veterans. Because many economists were predicting terrible economic problems after the war ended, experts pushed for programs to counter the expected rise in unemployment. The American Legion drafted much of the GI Bill. The legislation offered veterans of all races and both sexes educational benefits, loan guarantees, unemployment stipends, job placement aid, and low-interest mortgages. Opponents claimed that the bill would bankrupt the nation and encourage veterans to be lazy. Prestigious colleges like the University of Chicago and Harvard University doubted that veterans had the intellectual capabilities to complete higher education.

Veterans soon quieted their critics, as 2.2 million veterans used the GI Bill to attend college. Universities scrambled to accommodate thousands of new students. Many veterans took heavy course loads and raised families while completing their degrees. Contrary to their initial misgivings about the veterans' readiness for academic life, administrators and professors raved about their dedication and performance. An additional 3.4 million veterans attended vocational or technical schools, while 2 million others received job training. The $14.5 billion that the federal government spent on the GI Bill stimulated extraordinary prosperity as millions of veterans financed new homes and businesses and used their educations for lucrative employment.

In this selection, Don Condren, an Army veteran, recounts how the GI Bill affected him.

———————————■———————————

FOCUS QUESTIONS

1. How did the GI Bill change Don Condren's life?
2. Was the GI Bill a wise investment for the U.S. government? Explain your answer.

I got out of the service in the late fall of 1945 and returned to Amarillo. After I graduated from high school I had gone to junior college for about a year and worked as a drugstore clerk until I was drafted. I had no idea what to study at junior college, though, or what to do for a living.

Being in the service had improved my expectations because all of a sudden I had the GI Bill, and I needed it. I could go to college and it would be paid for.

I read a number of articles in books and magazines that said we were becoming an increasingly technological society, that there was going to be a lot of opportunity for engineers. So I took engineering courses at the junior college in Amarillo, then I transferred to the University of Colorado, where I completed my degree. While at the University of Colorado I married, and after I graduated, my wife and I bought our first home on a GI loan. It cost ten thousand dollars. Sometimes I tell my kids I never even had a room of my own until I was married.

I considered the GI Bill a good piece of fortune, but I didn't consider it charity. World War II was a popular war, so we all came home heroes. The people around us looked upon us with approval. They thought we deserved the GI Bill and were happy for us to have it.

I'm not sure whether I could ever have gone to college without the GI Bill. I doubt if I would have moved away from the Texas Panhandle. The GI Bill had a major impact on the country. It set a whole new standard of improved education for a large number of people, a whole new standard of improved housing. A college graduate has higher expectations, and he finds way to realize these expectations, or tries to. I think the GI Bill gave the whole country an upward boost economically and in every other way—at least in the late forties and early fifties.

Mark Jonathan Harris, Franklin D. Mitchell, and Steven J. Schechter, eds. *The Homefront: America during World War II* (New York: G.P. Putnam's Sons, 1984), pp. 221-222.

23.3

A JOURNALIST DESCRIBES LEVITTOWN (1948)

By the end of World War II, the United States had a severe housing shortage. Many families crowded into tiny apartments or lived in boardinghouses. Couples longed to fulfill the American dream of home ownership. William Levitt (1907-1994) helped millions realize that aspiration. Born in Brooklyn, Levitt dropped out of New York University and took a job in his father's law firm. In 1929, he founded a construction company called Levitt and Sons. In 1941, he won a Navy contract to build housing for defense workers in Norfolk, Virginia. Using mass production techniques pioneered by Henry Ford, his workers quickly erected 2,350 housing units. Cognizant of the nation's housing crisis, Levitt decided to apply these methods to private homes. Buying 1,200 acres of potato farms near Hicksville, Long Island, Levitt supervised the construction of a massive residential community. At a time when the average contractor built only five houses a year, Levitt's men completed 36 houses a day.

When Levittown opened in 1947, it was a smashing success. His 17,000 homes sold quickly. With the aid of the GI Bill, veterans could buy a home for about $55 a month. Strict guidelines governed the appearance of homes and barred African Americans. Levittown was copied across the nation. Levitt's methods, government loans, federal tax deductions for mortgage interest, and automobiles fueled the phenomenal growth of white, middle-class suburbs.

In this reading, Eric Larrabee describes Levittown for readers of Harper's Magazine.

FOCUS QUESTIONS

1. What attracted people to Levittown? Who wanted to live there?
2. What made Levitt so successful in the housing industry?
3. Levitt once said, "No man who owns his own house and lot can be a communist. He has too much to do." Why would Levitt make such a declaration? What do you think he meant?

4. How does Malvina Reynolds's portrayal of suburban life (Document 23.4) differ from the one presented here? Do you think that the suburbs were a positive or negative development in American society? Explain your answer.

The largest private builder of houses in the Eastern United States is the firm of Levitt & Sons, of Manhasset, Long Island, whose president—William J. Levitt—is to the housing industry somewhat as Robert R. Young first was to the railroads. Both men have been successful, both have called attention to the shortcomings of their professions, and both have preached reform, rationalization, and respect for the public....

Before the war dotted defense areas with large developments made up of many small houses, most private housebuilders put up less than two thousand houses a year. Since the war, Levitt & Sons have built over six thousand. The figure is as of the beginning of this month; in April they were finishing 60 houses a week; in May, 100 a week; and in July, 150 a week.

Levitt—Bill Levitt refers to the firm in the third person singular—is now at work on a 1,400-acre, 6,000-house project called "Levittown," near Hicksville, Long Island, where 4 1/2-room "bungalows" are rented, to veterans only, for 65 dollars a month. Each house comes complete with radiant-heating, General Electric range and refrigerator, and Venetian blinds. The grounds will be landscaped, all utilities will be connected, and there will be concrete roads. Levittown will be zoned as a park district, and Levitt will build one swimming pool for each thousand houses—also three shopping centers (with nearly a hundred retail units), five schools (built by county on public contract), and six churches (plots donated by Levitt & Sons). Levittown will be finished by the end of this year. "Anyone who comes to us now," Bill Levitt said last April, "will have a house in October."

As soon as one of the first 1,800 veterans to rent a house in Levittown has been there a year, he is given an option by Levitt to buy the house for $7,990; if he does not buy, Levitt will rent for one year more. "I think they'll buy alright," he has said with a pride anyone might reasonably take in watching well-made plans come to fruition. The veterans will be backed by GI loan and will thus require no cash, they will get back a $100 deposit from Levitt, and the carrying charges on the loan will be less than the rent they are now paying—a combination difficult to resist....The 1947 price on the basic small Levitt House was $7,500....Costs have risen since then and comparisons on the basis of profit per house are deceptive (according to Bill Levitt, they are no longer used in the firm), but it was estimated in 1947 that he undersold his nearest competitor by $1,500 and still made $1,000 profit on each house....

Bill Levitt is becoming a kind of bellwether of the building trades, and he believes that he is setting patterns which the others must eventually adopt. The housing industry, if it can properly be called an industry, has traditionally been based on limited construction by small contractors, consumer financing, and craft unions. Levitt & Sons are substituting mass construction by a single company, production financing, and either industrial unions or no unions at all....

The Levitt small house is a cultural index, a mean between what the money will buy and what people are willing to pay for. The houses might look quite attractive if there weren't so incredibly many of them. Levittown is about ten miles away from the sea on the Long Island flats. From the Wantagh Parkway, the town stretches away to the east as far as the eye can see, house after identical house, a horizon broken only by telegraph poles. The exterior colors are varied and good (among them a strong, dark red), and the houses, which might have been in even lines, are at least slightly staggered. Each house is built on a concrete slab (no cellar) into which copper pipes for radiant heating have been embedded. The floors are of asphalt tile and the walls of composition rock-board (the rooms are designed in multiples of four feet, the standard width of the composition panels). A stairway leads to an unfinished attic; under one side is a scroll trimmed alcove for the Bendix [washing machine]; under the other, bookshelves for the living room. The focal point is the kitchen, at the front of the house to the right of the door, which is full of cabinets and designed with a sharp eye on the magazine-reading, ruffled-chintz housewife.

"A dream house," Levitt wrote for a GE ad, "is a house the buyer and his family will want to live in a long time…an electric kitchen-laundry is the one big item that gives the homeowner all the advantages and conveniences that make his home truly livable." To include a Bendix washer in the sales price may seem frivolous and extravagant, but it is worth every bit of the cost in sales appeal and publicity. "And it will sell faster," Levitt added. His house is the Model-T equivalent of the rose-covered cottage—or Cape Coddage, as some one has called it. It is meant to look like the Little Home of One's Own that was a subsidiary myth of the American Dream long before Charlie Chaplin put it into "Modern Times."…

A house that goes up in Levittown will have been handled by Levitt & Sons from the start to finish. When Bill Levitt uses a favorite phrase, "vertical organization," he is talking about a principle he has applied as rigorously as the housing business will allow. His lumber, for example comes from the Grizzly Park Lumber Company, of Blue Lake, California, which he owns. All of his appliances (a Bendix, say, or a GE refrigerator) are purchased from the North Shore Supply Company, which he owns. He doesn't buy nails and concrete blocks; he makes them himself. Like most builders, he has many contractors working for him (the number varies in the neighborhood of fifty), but here also the vertical principle is retained. All of his contractors work for him and for no one else, and most of them were put in business by Levitt.

The advantages of this top-to-bottom control are considerable. The timber can be cut at the mill in California to the exact size at which it will finally be used in the house. This means not only a saving on freight and handling (the wood can bypass the Levitt factory at Roslyn, Long Island, and go directly to the site), but also an initial cost saving of 30 per cent—the mark-up that Levitt and the consumer, would be paying if he didn't own his source of basic material.

The same applies to a Bendix or GE range. The traditional echelons through which an appliance must pass are from manufacturer to distributor to wholesaler to builder, each adding an additional mark-up as it goes. Levitt, by owning his wholesaler, absorbs at least one of the mark-ups and continues to moan with pain about the others. He buys appliances as a rule, by the carload lot, and they proceed direct from the factory to his railroad siding at Roslyn. He cannot understand why several people who never see the merchandise should be paid merely for handling the bills....

The actual building techniques used by Levitt, of course, are not those of which a carpenter's guild would be likely to approve. He uses time and labor-saving machinery whenever possible, even when such use (as paint sprayers) is specifically forbidden by the union. Beginning with a trenching machine, through transit-mix trucks to haul concrete, to an automatic trowler that smoothes the foundation-slab, Levitt takes advantage of whatever economies mechanization can give him. The site of the houses becomes one vast assembly line, with trucks dropping off at each house the exact materials needed by the crew then moving up. Some parts—plumbing, staircases, window frames, cabinets—are actually prefabricated in the factory at Roslyn and brought to the house ready to install. The process might be called one of semi-prefabrication, in which a great deal of building is actually done on the site, but none that is unnecessary or that could be better done elsewhere—a lot of hammering, as Bill Levitt says, but very little sawing.

Eric Larrabee, "The Six Thousand Houses That Levitt Built," *Harper's Magazine* (September 1948), pp. 79-83.

23.4

MALVINA REYNOLDS, LITTLE BOXES (1962)

During the 1950s, the suburban population almost doubled as 18 million people joined the exodus from the nation's cities. New federally funded highways made it easy for suburbanites to commute to urban centers. Many Americans saw little reason not to flee the cities' crime, pollution, and crowded living conditions.

Not all Americans shared this enthusiasm. Social critic Lewis Mumford called suburbs "a low-grade uniform environment from which escape is impossible." Other commentators criticized restrictive lending and real estate practices that barred African Americans from many suburban communities.

Malvina Reynolds (1900-1978) echoed these sentiments. Born to Jewish socialists in San Francisco, she attended the University of California at Berkeley and received B.A., M.A., and Ph.D. degrees in English. In 1934, she married William Reynolds, a carpenter and labor organizer. They had a daughter a year later. In 1936, after completing her doctorate, she unsuccessfully sought a college professorship. Instead, she became a social worker and columnist for a leftist newspaper. During WWII, she worked in a bomb factory. When her father died, she and her husband ran her parents' tailor shop in Long Beach, California. After meeting Pete Seeger and other folk singers, she began writing songs. Several artists including Harry Belafonte and Joan Baez recorded her music and she performed at dozens of protest rallies. Her 1962 song "Little Boxes" offers a clever critique of suburban life.

———————————◼———————————

FOCUS QUESTIONS

1. How does Reynolds criticize suburbs and suburban lifestyles?
2. How does Malvina Reynolds's portrayal of suburban life differ from the one presented by Eric Larrabee (Document 23.3)? Do you think that the suburbs were a positive or negative development in American society? Explain your answer.

ittle boxes on the hillside,
Little boxes made of ticky tacky
Little boxes on the hillside,
Little boxes all the same,
There's a green one and a pink one
And a blue one and a yellow one
And they're all made out of ticky tacky
And they all look just the same.

And the people in the houses
All went to the university
Where they were put in boxes
And they came out all the same
And there's doctors and lawyers
And business executives
And they're all made out of ticky tacky
And they all look just the same.

And they all play on the golf course
And drink their martinis dry
And they all have pretty children
And the children go to school,
And the children go to summer camp
And then to the university
Where they are put in boxes
And they come out all the same.

And the boys go into business
And marry and raise a family
In boxes made of ticky tacky
And they all look just the same,
There's a green one and a pink one
And a blue one and a yellow one
And they're all made out of ticky tacky
And they all look just the same.

Words and Music by Malvina Reynolds © 1962 Schroder Music, renewed 1990 Nancy Schimmel.

23.5

THE U.S. SUPREME COURT STRIKES DOWN SCHOOL SEGREGATION (1954)

In the 1930s, lawyers at the National Association for the Advancement of Colored People (NAACP) outlined a long-term strategy for challenging segregation. Charles Houston (1895-1950) led these efforts. After graduating from Harvard University Law School, Houston became a professor at Howard University Law School in Washington, D.C. While at Howard, Houston served as the school's vice-dean and trained future civil rights lawyers including Thurgood Marshall, William Bryant, and Oliver Hill. From 1935 to 1940, Houston was the NAACP's first full-time, paid special counsel. When Houston resigned due to health problems, Marshall became the legal director of NAACP.

In the 1940s, the NAACP legal team won several important Supreme Court cases. In Smith v. Allwright *(1944), the Court outlawed white primaries in the South. In* Shelley v. Kramer *(1948), the Court prohibited racially restrictive covenants. In* Sweatt v. Painter *(1950) and* McLaurin v. Oklahoma State Regents *(1950), the Court struck down segregation in graduate schools. Inspired by these precedents, the NAACP filed lawsuits demanding the integration of public schools in Kansas, Delaware, South Carolina, and Virginia. Consolidated as* Brown v. Board of Education of Topeka, *the cases reached the Supreme Court. During oral arguments on December 9, 1952, Marshall attacked the legal premises of* Plessy v. Ferguson *(1896), the Supreme Court decision concluding that "separate but equal" facilities were constitutional. Marshall also presented evidence that segregation psychologically damaged black children even if facilities were equal. In defending segregation laws, attorney John W. Davis claimed that the federal government had no right to interfere with state policies on education. When Earl Warren, an Eisenhower appointee, became chief justice of the Supreme Court shortly thereafter, he demanded that the Court reach a unanimous decision on* Brown. *The national importance of the issues raised in* Brown, *Warren argued, dictated an unequivocal ruling. Unable to agree on the legal basis for outlawing segregation, the Court reheard oral arguments in December 1953. The attorneys were asked to prove that Congress had meant to desegregate schools when it drafted the 14th Amendment in 1868. Although the justices did not reach a definitive decision on the historical interpretation of the 14th Amendment, they issued a unanimous decision in May 1954. While the ruling did not abolish segregation in all public places, it struck down school segregation laws in twenty-one states. The Court did not, however, set a deadline by which public schools were to be integrated. In 1967, Lyndon Johnson appointed Thurgood Marshall to the U.S. Supreme Court.*

FOCUS QUESTIONS

1. What did the Court rule in *Brown*?
2. On what legal bases did the Court make this decision?
3. What were the limitations of the *Brown* ruling? What were the ramifications of these limitations?

MR. CHIEF JUSTICE WARREN delivered the opinion of the Court. These cases come to us from the States of Kansas, South Carolina, Virginia, and Delaware. They are premised on different facts and different local conditions, but a common legal question justifies their consideration together in this consolidated opinion.

In each of the cases, minors of the Negro race, through their legal representatives, seek the aid of the courts in obtaining admission to the public schools of their community on a nonsegregated basis. In each instance, they had been denied admission to schools attended by white children under laws requiring or permitting segregation according to race. This segregation was alleged to deprive the plaintiffs of the equal protection of the laws under the Fourteenth Amendment. In each of the cases other than the Delaware case, a three-judge federal district court denied relief to the plaintiffs on the so-called "separate but equal" doctrine announced by this Court in *Plessy v. Ferguson*, 163 U.S. 537. Under that doctrine, equality of treatment is accorded when the races are provided substantially equal facilities, even though these facilities be separate. In the Delaware case, the Supreme Court of Delaware adhered to that doctrine, but ordered that the plaintiffs be admitted to the white schools because of their superiority to the Negro schools.

The plaintiffs contend that segregated public schools are not "equal" and cannot be made "equal," and that hence they are deprived of the equal protection of the laws. Because of the obvious importance of the question presented, the Court took jurisdiction. Argument was heard in the 1952 Term, and reargument was heard this Term on certain questions propounded by the Court.

Reargument was largely devoted to the circumstances surrounding the adoption of the Fourteenth Amendment in 1868. It covered exhaustively consideration of the Amendment in Congress, ratification by the states, then-existing practices in racial segregation, and the views of proponents and opponents of the Amendment. This discussion and our own investigation convince us that, although these sources cast some light, it is not enough to resolve the problem with which we are faced. At best, they are inconclusive. The most avid proponents of the post-War Amendments undoubtedly intended them to remove all legal distinctions among "all persons born or naturalized in the United States." Their opponents, just as certainly, were antagonistic to both the letter and the spirit of the Amendments and wished them to have the most limited effect. What others in Congress and the state legislatures had in mind cannot be determined with any degree of certainty.

An additional reason for the inconclusive nature of the Amendment's history with respect to segregated schools is the status of public education at that time. In the South, the movement toward free common schools, supported by general taxation, had not yet taken hold. Education of white children was largely in the hands of private groups. Education of Negroes was almost nonexistent, and practically all of the race were illiterate. In fact, any education of Negroes was forbidden by law in some states. Today, in contrast, many Negroes have achieved outstanding success in the arts and sciences, as well as in the business and professional world. It is true that public school education at the time of the Amendment had advanced further in the North, but the effect of the Amendment on Northern States was generally ignored in the congressional debates. Even in the North, the conditions of public education did not approximate those existing today. The curriculum was usually rudimentary; ungraded schools were common in rural areas; the school term was but three months a year in many states, and compulsory school attendance was virtually unknown. As a consequence, it is not surprising that there should be so little in the history of the Fourteenth Amendment relating to its intended effect on public education.

In the first cases in this Court construing the Fourteenth Amendment, decided shortly after its adoption, the Court interpreted it as proscribing all state-imposed discriminations against the Negro race. The doctrine of "separate but equal" did not make its appearance in this Court until 1896 in the case of *Plessy v. Ferguson*, supra, involving not education but transportation. American courts have since labored with the doctrine for over half a century. In this Court, there have been six cases involving the "separate but equal" doctrine in the field of public education. In *Cumming v. County Board of Education*, 175 U.S. 528, and *Gong Lum v. Rice*, 275 U.S. 78, the validity of the doctrine itself was not challenged. In more recent cases, all on the graduate school level, inequality was found in that specific benefits enjoyed by white students were denied to Negro students of the same educational qualifications. *Missouri ex rel. Gaines v. Canada*, 305 U.S. 337; *Sipuel v. Oklahoma*, 332 U.S. 631; *Sweatt v. Painter*, 339 U.S. 629; *McLaurin v. Oklahoma State Regents*, 339 U.S. 637. In none of these cases was it necessary to reexamine the doctrine to grant relief to the Negro plaintiff. And in *Sweatt v.*

Painter, supra, the Court expressly reserved decision on the question whether *Plessy v. Ferguson* should be held inapplicable to public education.

In the instant cases, that question is directly presented. Here, unlike *Sweatt v. Painter*, there are findings below that the Negro and white schools involved have been equalized, or are being equalized, with respect to buildings, curricula, qualifications and salaries of teachers, and other "tangible" factors. Our decision, therefore, cannot turn on merely a comparison of these tangible factors in the Negro and white schools involved in each of the cases. We must look instead to the effect of segregation itself on public education.

In approaching this problem, we cannot turn the clock back to 1868, when the Amendment was adopted, or even to 1896, when *Plessy v. Ferguson* was written. We must consider public education in the light of its full development and its present place in American life throughout the Nation. Only in this way can it be determined if segregation in public schools deprives these plaintiffs of the equal protection of the laws.

Today, education is perhaps the most important function of state and local governments. Compulsory school attendance laws and the great expenditures for education both demonstrate our recognition of the importance of education to our democratic society. It is required in the performance of our most basic public responsibilities, even service in the armed forces. It is the very foundation of good citizenship. Today it is a principal instrument in awakening the child to cultural values, in preparing him for later professional training, and in helping him to adjust normally to his environment. In these days, it is doubtful that any child may reasonably be expected to succeed in life if he is denied the opportunity of an education. Such an opportunity, where the state has undertaken to provide it, is a right which must be made available to all on equal terms.

We come then to the question presented: Does segregation of children in public schools solely on the basis of race, even though the physical facilities and other "tangible" factors may be equal, deprive the children of the minority group of equal educational opportunities? We believe that it does.

In *Sweatt v. Painter*, supra, in finding that a segregated law school for Negroes could not provide them equal educational opportunities, this Court relied in large part on "those qualities which are incapable of objective measurement but which make for greatness in a law school." In *McLaurin v. Oklahoma State Regents*, supra, the Court, in requiring that a Negro admitted to a white graduate school be treated like all other students, again resorted to intangible considerations: "...his ability to study, to engage in discussions and exchange views with other students, and, in general, to learn his profession." Such considerations apply with added force to children in grade and high schools. To separate them from others of similar age and qualifications solely because of their race generates a feeling of inferiority as to their status in the community that may affect their hearts and minds in a way unlikely ever to be undone. The effect of this separation on their educational opportunities was well stated by a finding in the Kansas case by a court which nevertheless felt compelled to rule against the Negro plaintiffs:

Segregation of white and colored children in public schools has a detrimental effect upon the colored children. The impact is greater when it has the sanction of the law, for the policy of separating the races is usually interpreted as denoting the inferiority of the negro group. A sense of inferiority affects the motivation of a child to learn. Segregation with the sanction of law, therefore, has a tendency to [retard] the educational and mental development of negro children and to deprive them of some of the benefits they would receive in a racial[ly] integrated school system.

Whatever may have been the extent of psychological knowledge at the time of *Plessy v. Ferguson*, this finding is amply supported by modern authority. Any language in *Plessy v. Ferguson* contrary to this finding is rejected.

We conclude that, in the field of public education, the doctrine of "separate but equal" has no place. Separate educational facilities are inherently unequal. Therefore, we hold that the plaintiffs and others similarly situated for whom the actions have been brought are, by reason of the segregation complained of, deprived of the equal protection of the laws guaranteed by the Fourteenth Amendment. This disposition makes unnecessary any discussion whether such segregation also violates the Due Process Clause of the Fourteenth Amendment....

Supreme Court of the United States, *Brown v. Board of Education*, 347 U.S. 483 (1954) (USSC+).

23.6

----•----

ANNE MOODY RECALLS THE LYNCHING
OF EMMETT TILL (1968)

The murder of Emmett Till brought international attention to the horrors of racial violence in the segregated South. On August 21, 1955, Till, a fourteen-year-old boy, traveled from Chicago to visit relatives near Money, Mississippi. Unfamiliar with the strict racial order of the Deep South, Till showed some boys a photograph of a white girl whom he claimed was his girlfriend. Calling Till on his boast, the boys dared him to talk to a white woman in Bryant's Grocery. Till went into the store and bought some bubble gum. When he left, the boys later reported, he either whistled at or said "Bye, baby" to Caroline Bryant, wife of the storeowner.

On August 28, Roy Bryant, the storeowner, and J.W. Milam, his half-brother, stormed into the cabin of Mose Wright, Till's great uncle. Bryant and Milam kidnapped Till. They brutally beat him, shot him in the head, tied his body to a cotton gin fan, and threw his corpse in the Tallahatchie River. The following day, local police arrested Bryant and Milam on kidnapping charges. On August 31, Till's bloated body was pulled from the Tallahatchie. Only a signet ring enabled Wright to identify his mutilated nephew.

The Till murder horrified many Americans. Mississippi officials claimed that all "decent" whites wanted Bryant and Milam to be fully prosecuted. Mamie Bradley, Till's mother, asked that his body be returned to Chicago. Declaring she wanted "all the world [to] see what they did to my son," she insisted on an open-casket funeral. 50,000 African Americans attended the service. Millions more saw a Jet *magazine photograph of Till's corpse.*

On September 19, Bryant and Milam's trial began in Sumner, Mississippi. Local laws barred women and blacks from serving on juries. Despite Wright's courageous open-court identification of Bryant and Milam as the men who kidnapped Till, the all-white jury acquitted them in only 67 minutes. In January 1956, Bryant and Milam accepted $4,000 to tell their story to Look *magazine. They graphically described how they murdered Till.*

The Till case was an awakening for millions of African Americans. In this excerpt from her acclaimed autobiography Coming of Age in Mississippi *(1968), Anne Moody describes how the Till lynching inspired her to join the civil rights movement.*

FOCUS QUESTIONS

1. How is Moody affected by news of Emmett Till's lynching?
2. How do other African Americans respond when Moody tries to discuss the Till murder? Give several examples.
3. Describe Moody's relationship with her white employer, Mrs. Burke. What does Mrs. Burke do in response to the Till lynching?
4. Why do you think that the Till case made such a profound impression on Americans like Anne Moody?

ot only did I enter high school with a new name, but also with a completely new insight into the life of Negroes in Mississippi. I was now working for one of the meanest white women in town, and a week before school started Emmett Till was killed.

Up until his death, I had heard of Negroes found floating in a river or dead somewhere with their bodies riddled with bullets. But I didn't know the mystery behind these killings then. I remember once when I was only seven I heard Mama and one of my aunts talking about some Negro who had been beaten to death. "Just like them lowdown skunks killed him they will do the same to us," Mama had said. When I asked her who killed the man and why, she said, "An Evil Spirit killed him. You gotta be a good girl or it will kill you too." So since I was seven, I had lived in fear of that "Evil Spirit." It took me eight years to learn what that spirit was.

I was coming from school the evening I heard about Emmett Till's death. There was a whole group of us, girls and boys, walking down the road headed home. A group of about six high school boys were walking a few paces ahead of me and several other girls. We were laughing and talking about something that had happened in school that day. However, the six boys in front of us weren't talking very loud. Usually they kept up so much noise. But today they were just walking and talking among themselves. All of a sudden they began to shout at each other.

"Man, what in the hell do you mean?"

"What I mean is these goddamned white folks is gonna start some shit here you just watch!"

"That boy wasn't but fourteen years old and they killed him. Now what kin a fourteen-year-old boy do with a white woman? What if he did whistle at her, he might have thought the whore was pretty."

"Look at all these white men here that's fucking over our women. Everybody knows it too and what's done about that? Look how many white babies we got walking around in our neighborhoods. Their mama's ain't white either. That boy was from Chicago, shit, everybody fuck everybody up there. He probably didn't even think of the bitch as white."

What they were saying shocked me. I knew all of those boys and I had never heard them talk like that. We walked on behind them for a while listening. Questions about who was killed, where, and why started running through my mind. I walked up to one of the boys.

"Eddie, what boy was killed?"

"Moody, where've you been?" he asked me. "Everybody talking about that fourteen-year-old boy who was killed in Greenwood by some white men. You don't know nothing that's going on besides what's in them books of yours, huh?"

Standing there before the rest of the girls, I felt so stupid. It was then that I realized I really didn't know what was going on all around me. It wasn't that I was dumb. It was just that ever since I was nine, I'd had to work after school and do my lessons on lunch hour. I never had time to learn anything, to hang around with people my own age. And you never were told anything by adults.

That evening when I stopped off at the house on my way to Mrs. Burke's, Mama was singing. Any other day she would have been yelling at Adline and Junior them to take off their school clothes. I wondered if she knew about Emmett Till. The way she was singing she had something on her mind and it wasn't pleasant either.

> I got a shoe, you got a shoe,
> All of God's chillun got shoes;
> When I get to hebben, I'm gonna put on my shoes,
> And gonna tromp all over God's hebben.
> When I get to hebben I'm gonna put on my shoes,
> And gonna walk all over God's hebben.

Mama was dishing up beans like she didn't know anyone was home. Adline, Junior, and James had just thrown their books down and sat themselves at the table. I didn't usually eat before I went to work. But I wanted to ask Mama about Emmett Till. So I ate and thought of some way of asking her.

"These beans are some good, Mama," I said, trying to sense her mood.

"Why is you eating anyway? You gonna be late for work. You know how Miss Burke is," she said to me.

"I don't have much to do this evening. I kin get it done before I leave work," I said.

The conversation stopped after that. Then Mama started humming that song again.

> When I get to hebben, I'm gonna put on my shoes,
> And gonna tromp all over God's hebben.

She put a plate on the floor for Jennie Ann and Jerry.

"Jennie Ann! you and Jerrry sit down here and eat and don't put beans all over this floor."

Ralph, the baby, started crying, and she went in the bedroom to give him his bottle. I got up and followed her.

"Mama, did you hear about that fourteen-year-old Negro boy who was killed a little over a week ago by some white men?" I asked her.

"Where did you hear that?" she said angrily.

"Boy, everybody really thinks I am dumb or deaf or something. I heard Eddie them talking about it this evening coming from school."

"Eddie them better watch how they go around here talking. These white folks git a hold of it they gonna be in trouble," she said.

"What are they gonna be in trouble about, Mama? People got a right to talk, ain't they?"

"You go on to work before you is late. And don't you let on like you know nothing about that boy being killed before Miss Burke them. Just do your work like you don't know nothing," she said. "That boy's a lot better off in heaven than he is here," she continued and then started singing again.

On my way to Mrs. Burke's that evening, Mama's words kept running through my mind. Just da your work like you don't know nothing." "Why is Mama acting so scared?" I thought. "And what if Mrs. Burke knew we knew? Why must I pretend I don't know? Why these people killing Negroes? What did Emmett Till do besides whistle at that woman?"

By the time I got to work, I had worked my nerves up some. I was shaking as I walked up on the porch. "Do your work like you don't know nothing." But once I got inside, I couldn't have acted normal if Mrs. Burke were paying me to be myself.

I was so nervous, I spent most of the evening avoiding them going about the house dusting and sweeping. Everything went along fairly well until dinner was served.

"Don, Wayne, and Mama, y'all come on to dinner. Essie, you can wash up the pots and dishes in the sink now. Then after dinner you won't have as many," Mrs. Burke called to me.

If I had the power to mysteriously disappear at that moment, I would have. They used the breakfast table in the kitchen for most of their meals. The dining room was only used for Sunday dinner or when they had company. I wished they had company tonight so they could eat in the dining room while I was at the kitchen sink.

"I forgot the bread," Mrs. Burke said when they were all seated. "Essie, will you cut it and put it on the table for me?"

I took the cornbread, cut it in squares, and put it on a small round dish. Just as I was about to set it on the table, Wayne yelled at the cat. I dropped the plate and the bread went all over the floor.

"Never mind, Essie," Mrs. Burke said angrily as she got up and got some white bread from the breadbox.

I didn't say anything. I picked up the cornbread from around the table and went back to the dishes. As soon as I got to the sink, I dropped a saucer on the floor and broke it. Didn't anyone say a word until I had picked up the pieces.

"Essie, I bought some new cleanser today. It's setting on the bathroom shelf. See if it will remove the stains in the tub," Mrs. Burke said.

I went to the bathroom to clean the tub. By the time I got through with it, it was snow white. I spent a whole hour scrubbing it. I had removed the stains in no time but I kept scrubbing until they finished dinner.

When they had finished and gone one into the living room as usual to watch TV, Mrs. Burke called me to eat. I took a clean plate out of the cabinet and sat down. Just as I was putting the first forkful of food in my mouth, Mrs. Burke entered the kitchen.

"Essie, did you hear about that fourteen-year-old boy who was killed in Greenwood?" she asked me, sitting down in one of the chairs opposite me.

"No, I didn't hear that," I answered, almost choking on the food.

"Do you know why he was killed?" she asked and I didn't answer.

"He was killed because he got out of his place with a white woman. A boy from Mississippi would have known better than that. This boy was from Chicago. Negroes up North have no respect for people. They think they can get away with anything. He just came to Mississippi and put a whole lot of notions in the boys' heads here and stirred up a lot of trouble," she said passionately.

"How old are you, Essie?" she asked me after a pause.

"Fourteen. I will soon be fifteen though," I said.

"See, that boy was just fourteen too. It's a shame he had to die so soon." She was so red in the face, she looked as if she was on fire.

When she left the kitchen I sat there with my mouth open and my food untouched. I couldn't have eaten now if I were starving. "Just do your work like you don't know nothing" ran through my mind again and I began washing the dishes.

I went home shaking like a leaf on a tree. For the first time out of all her trying, Mrs. Burke had made me feel like rotten garbage. Many times she had tried to instill fear within me and subdue me and had given up. But when she talked about Emmett Till there was something in her voice that sent chills and fear all over me.

Before Emmett Till's murder, I had known the fear of hunger, hell, and the Devil. But now there was a new fear known to me—the fear of being killed just because I was black. This was the worst of my fears. I knew once I got food, the fear of starving to death would leave. I also was told that if I were a good girl, I wouldn't have to fear the Devil or hell. But I didn't know what one had to do or not do as a Negro not to be killed; probably just being a Negro period was enough, I thought.

A few days later, I went to work and Mrs. Burke had about eight women over for tea. They were all sitting around in the living room when I got there. She told me she was having a "guild meeting," and asked me to help her serve the cookies and tea.

After helping her, I started cleaning the house. I always swept the hallway and porch first. As I was sweeping the hall, I could hear them talking. When I heard the word "nigger," I stopped sweeping and listened. Mrs. Burke must have sensed this, because she suddenly came to the door.

"Essie, finish the hall and clean the bathroom," she said hesitantly. "Then you can go for today. I am not making dinner tonight." Then she went back in the living room with the rest of the ladies.

Before she interrupted my listening, I had picked up the words "NAACP" and "that organization." Because they were talking about niggers, I knew NAACP had something to do with Negroes. All that night I kept wondering what could that NAACP mean?

Later when I was sitting in the kitchen at home doing my lessons, I decided to ask Mama. It was about twelve thirty. Everyone was in bed but me. When Mama came in to put some milk in Ralph's bottle, I said, "Mama, what do NAACP mean?"

"Where did you git that from?" she asked me, spilling milk all over the floor.

"Mrs. Burke had a meeting tonight—"

"What kind of meeting?" she asked, cutting me off.

"I don't know. She had some women over—she said it was a guild meeting," I said.

"A guild meeting," she repeated.

"Yes, they were talking about Negroes and I heard some woman say 'that NAACP' and another 'that organization,' meaning the same thing."

"What else did they say?" she asked me.

"That's all I heard. Mrs. Burke must have thought I was listening, so she told me to clean the bathroom and leave."

"Don't you ever mention that word around Mrs. Burke or no other white person, you hear! Finish your lesson and cut that light out and go to bed," Mama said angrily and left the kitchen.

"With a Mama like that you'll never learn anything," I thought as I got into bed. All night long I thought about Emmet Till and the NAACP. I even got up to look up NAACP in my little concise dictionary. But I didn't find it.

The next day at school, I decided to ask my homeroom teacher Mrs. Rice the meaning of NAACP. When the bell sounded for lunch, I remained in my seat as the other students left the room.

"Are you going to spend your lunch hour studying again today, Moody?" Mrs. Rice asked me.

"Can I ask you a question, Mrs. Rice?" I asked her.

"You *may* ask me a question, yes, but I don't know if you *can* or not," she said.

"What does the word NAACP mean?" I asked.

"Why do you want to know?"

"The lady I worked for had a meeting and I overheard the word mentioned."

"What else did you hear?"

"Nothing. I didn't know what NAACP meant, that's all." I felt like I was on the witness stand or something.

"Well, next time your boss has another meeting you listen more carefully. NAACP is a Negro organization that was established a long time ago to help Negroes gain a few basic rights," she said.

"What's it gotta do with the Emmett Till murder?" I asked.

"They are trying to get a conviction in Emmett Till's case. You see the NAACP is trying to do a lot for the Negroes and get the right to vote for Negroes in the South. I shouldn't be telling you all this. And don't you dare breathe a word of what I said. It could cost me my job if word got out I was teaching my students such. I gotta go to lunch and you should go outside too because it's nice and sunny out today," she said leaving the room. "We'll talk more when I have time."

About a week later, Mrs. Rice had me over for Sunday dinner, and I spent about five hours with her. Within that time, I digested a good meal and accumulated a whole new pool of knowledge about Negroes being butchered and slaughtered by whites in the South. After Mrs. Rice had told me all this, I felt like the lowest animal on earth. At least when other animals (hogs, cows, etc.) were killed by man, they were used as food. But when man was butchered or killed by man, in the case of Negroes by whites, they were left lying on a road or found floating in a river or something.

Mrs. Rice got to be something like a mother to me. She told me anything I wanted to know. And made me promise that I would keep all this information she was passing on to me to myself. She said she couldn't, rather didn't, want to talk about these things to the other teachers, that they would tell Mr. Willis and she would be fired. At the end of that year she was fired. I never found out why. I haven't seen her since then.

Coming of Age in Mississippi, by Anne Moody, copyright © 1968 by Anne Moody. Used by permission of Doubleday, a division of Random House, Inc.

23.7

THE SOUTHERN MANIFESTO (1956)

The Brown *decision outraged many white southerners. In 1955, when the Supreme Court issued a second ruling (known as "Brown II") ordering the South to integrate "with all deliberate speed," the border states complied. But the Deep South, encouraged by President Eisenhower's refusal to endorse the* Brown *decision, adopted a strategy of "massive resistance" to integration. Ku Klux Klan membership surged after decades of decline. Newly formed White Citizens' Councils used social and economic coercion against blacks and white supporters of desegregation. Opportunistic white politicians staunchly defended segregation in order to attract white voters.*

In March 1956, 96 southern members of Congress issued a statement denouncing integration. Their "Southern Manifesto" follows.

FOCUS QUESTIONS

1. Why do these southerners object to the *Brown v. Board of Education* decision?
2. Compare the legal arguments used in the *Brown* decision (Document 23.5) to those expressed in the Southern Manifesto.
3. What were some of the ways that the South resisted integration?

THE DECISION OF THE SUPREME COURT IN THE SCHOOL CASES—DECLARATION OF CONSTITUTIONAL PRINCIPLES

Mr. [Walter F.] GEORGE. Mr. President, the increasing gravity of the situation following the decision of the Supreme Court in the so-called segregation cases, and the peculiar stress in sections of the country where this decision has created many difficulties, unknown and unappreciated, perhaps, by many people residing in other parts of the country, have led some Senators and some Members of the House of Representatives to prepare a statement of the position which they have felt and now feel to be imperative.

I now wish to present to the Senate a statement on behalf of 19 Senators, representing 11 States, and 77 House Members, representing a considerable number of States likewise....

DECLARATION OF CONSTITUTIONAL PRINCIPLES

The unwarranted decision of the Supreme Court in the public school cases is now bearing the fruit always produced when men substitute naked power for established law.

The Founding Fathers gave us a Constitution of checks and balances because they realized the inescapable lesson of history that no man or group of men can be safely entrusted with unlimited power. They framed this Constitution with its provisions for change by amendment in order to secure the fundamentals of government against the dangers of temporary popular passion or the personal predilections of public officeholders.

We regard the decisions of the Supreme Court in the school cases as a clear abuse of judicial power. It climaxes a trend in the Federal Judiciary undertaking to legislate, in derogation of the authority of Congress, and to encroach upon the reserved rights of the States and the people.

The original Constitution does not mention education. Neither does the 14th Amendment nor any other amendment. The debates preceding the submission of the 14th Amendment clearly show that there was no intent that it should affect the system of education maintained by the States.

The very Congress which proposed the amendment subsequently provided for segregated schools in the District of Columbia.

When the amendment was adopted in 1868, there were 37 States of the Union....

Every one of the 26 States that had any substantial racial differences among its people, either approved the operation of segregated schools already in existence or subsequently established such schools by action of the same law-making body which considered the 14th Amendment.

As admitted by the Supreme Court in the public school case (*Brown v. Board of Education*), the doctrine of separate but equal schools "apparently originated in *Roberts v. City of Boston* (1849), upholding school segregation against attack as being violative of a State constitutional guarantee of equality." This constitutional doctrine began in the North, not in the South, and it was followed not only in Massachusetts, but in Connecticut, New York, Illinois, Indiana, Michigan, Minnesota, New Jersey, Ohio, Pennsylvania and other northern states until they, exercising their rights as states through the constitutional processes of local self-government, changed their school systems.

In the case of *Plessy v. Ferguson* in 1896 the Supreme Court expressly declared that under the 14th Amendment no person was denied any of his rights if the States provided separate but equal facilities. This decision has been followed in many other cases. It is notable that the Supreme Court, speaking through Chief Justice Taft, a former President of the United States, unanimously declared in 1927 in *Lum v. Rice* that the "separate but equal" principle is "within the discretion of the State in regulating its public schools and does not conflict with the 14th Amendment."

This interpretation, restated time and again, became a part of the life of the people of many of the States and confirmed their habits, traditions, and way of life. It is founded on elemental humanity and commonsense, for parents should not be deprived by Government of the right to direct the lives and education of their own children.

Though there has been no constitutional amendment or act of Congress changing this established legal principle almost a century old, the Supreme Court of the United States, with no legal basis for such action, undertook to exercise their naked judicial power and substituted their personal political and social ideas for the established law of the land.

This unwarranted exercise of power by the Court, contrary to the Constitution, is creating chaos and confusion in the States principally affected. It is destroying the amicable relations between the white and Negro races that have been created through 90 years of patient effort by the good people of both races. It has planted hatred and suspicion where there has been heretofore friendship and understanding.

Without regard to the consent of the governed, outside mediators are threatening immediate and revolutionary changes in our public schools systems. If done, this is certain to destroy the system of public education in some of the States.

With the gravest concern for the explosive and dangerous condition created by this decision and inflamed by outside meddlers:

We reaffirm our reliance on the Constitution as the fundamental law of the land.

We decry the Supreme Court's encroachment on the rights reserved to the States and to the people, contrary to established law, and to the Constitution.

We commend the motives of those States which have declared the intention to resist forced integration by any lawful means.

We appeal to the States and people who are not directly affected by these decisions to consider the constitutional principles involved against the time when they too, on issues vital to them may be the victims of judicial encroachment.

Even though we constitute a minority in the present Congress, we have full faith that a majority of the American people believe in the dual system of government which has enabled us to achieve our greatness and will in time demand that the reserved rights of the States and of the people be made secure against judicial usurpation.

We pledge ourselves to use all lawful means to bring about a reversal of this decision which is contrary to the Constitution and to prevent the use of force in its implementation.

In this trying period, as we all seek to right this wrong, we appeal to our people not to be provoked by the agitators and troublemakers invading our States and to scrupulously refrain from disorder and lawless acts.

Congressional Record, 84th Congress, Second Session, Vol. 102, part 4 (March 12, 1956). Washington, D.C.: Governmental Printing Office, 1956: 4459-4460.

23.8

DWIGHT D. EISENHOWER ON DESEGREGATION IN LITTLE ROCK (1957)

The South's "massive resistance" reached new levels in September 1957, when Arkansas Governor Orval Faubus blocked the federally mandated integration of Little Rock's Central High School. On May 24, 1954, only seven days after the Supreme Court issued its Brown v. Board of Education of Topeka *decision, the Little Rock School Board had unanimously adopted a plan to begin gradually integrating high schools. In the spring of 1957, the board interviewed black students who wished to attend the all-white Central High School. They selected seventeen students, eight of whom elected to remain at all-black Horace Mann High School. In the weeks preceding the 1957-1958 school year, local opponents of integration organized the Capital Citizens Council and the Mothers' League of Central High School. The groups were unsuccessful in winning a federal injunction halting desegregation.*

On September 2, 1957, Governor Faubus ordered the Arkansas National Guard to surround Central High School. Faubus claimed that such action was necessary to prevent outside agitators from inciting violence. Two days later, when the black students ("The Little Rock Nine") attempted to enter Central High, the Guardsmen turned them away. On September 20, Federal District Judge Ronald Davies ruled that Faubus was using the Guard to prevent integration, not to preserve order. In response, Faubus removed the Guardsmen. Three days later, a small group of Little Rock policemen confronted hundreds of protestors seeking to bar the Little Rock Nine from entering Central High. Afraid that the children would be harmed, police transported them off school property. Little Rock Mayor Woodrow Mann sent President Eisenhower a telegram asking for federal assistance in ensuring a peaceful integration process. Outraged by Faubus's violation of federal law and sensitive to international criticisms of the Little Rock crisis, Eisenhower made the statement included below.

On September 25, Army troops escorted the nine black students into Central High School. The soldiers remained on campus for the duration of the school year. The following year, Little Rock closed its public high schools rather than continue desegregation. The city's public schools were not fully integrated until 1972.

FOCUS QUESTIONS

1. How does Eisenhower describe the situation in Little Rock?
2. What actions does Eisenhower take? Why does he believe these measures are necessary?

3. Did Eisenhower respond appropriately to the crisis in Little Rock? Explain your answer.

September 24, 1957, 9 p.m.

Good Evening, My Fellow Citizens:

For a few minutes this evening I want to speak to you about the serious situation that has arisen in Little Rock. To make this talk I have come to the President's office in the White House. I could have spoken from Rhode Island, where I have been staying recently, but I felt that, in speaking from the house of Lincoln, of Jackson and of Wilson, my words would better convey both the sadness I feel in the action I was compelled today to take and the firmness with which I intend to pursue this course until the orders of the Federal Court at Little Rock can be executed without unlawful interference.

In that city, under the leadership of demagogic extremists, disorderly mobs have deliberately prevented the carrying out of proper orders from a Federal Court. Local authorities have not eliminated that violent opposition and, under the law, I yesterday issued a Proclamation calling upon the mob to disperse.

This morning the mob again gathered in front of the Central High School of Little Rock, obviously for the purpose of again preventing the carrying out of the Court's order relating to the admission of Negro children to that school.

Whenever normal agencies prove inadequate to the task and it becomes necessary for the Executive Branch of the Federal Government to use its powers and authority to uphold Federal Courts, the President's responsibility is inescapable.

In accordance with that responsibility, I have today issued an Executive Order directing the use of troops under Federal authority to aid in the execution of Federal law at Little Rock, Arkansas. This became necessary when my Proclamation of yesterday was not observed, and the obstruction of justice still continues.

It is important that the reasons for my action be understood by all our citizens.

As you know, the Supreme Court of the United States has decided that separate public educational facilities for the races are inherently unequal and therefore compulsory school segregation laws are unconstitutional.

Our personal opinions about the decision have no bearing on the matter of enforcement; the responsibility and authority of the Supreme Court to interpret the Constitution are very clear. Local Federal Courts were instructed by the Supreme Court to issue such orders and decrees as might be necessary to achieve admission to public schools without regard to race—and with all deliberate speed.

During the past several years, many communities in our Southern States have instituted public school plans for gradual progress in the enrollment and attendance of school children of all races in order to bring themselves into compliance with the law of the land.

They thus demonstrated to the world that we are a nation in which laws, not men, are supreme.

I regret to say that this truth—the cornerstone of our liberties—was not observed in this instance.

It was my hope that this localized situation would be brought under control by city and State authorities. If the use of local police powers had been sufficient, our traditional method of leaving the problems in those hands would have been pursued. But when large gatherings of obstructionists made it impossible for the decrees of the Court to be carried out, both the law and the national interest demanded that the President take action.

Here is the sequence of events in the development of the Little Rock school case.

In May of 1955, the Little Rock School Board approved a moderate plan for the gradual desegregation of the public schools in that city. It provided that a start toward integration would be made at the present term in the high school, and that the plan would be in full operation by 1963. Here I might say that in a number of communities in Arkansas integration in the schools has already started and without violence of any kind. Now this Little Rock plan was challenged in the courts by some who believed that the period of time as proposed in the plan was too long.

The United States Court at Little Rock, which has supervisory responsibility under the law for the plan of desegregation in the public schools, dismissed the challenge, thus approving a gradual rather than an abrupt change from the existing system. The court found that the school board had acted in good faith in planning for a public school system free from racial discrimination.

Since that time, the court has on three separate occasions issued orders directing that the plan be carried out. All persons were instructed to refrain from interfering with the efforts of the school board to comply with the law.

Proper and sensible observance of the law then demanded the respectful obedience which the nation has a right to expect from all its people. This, unfortunately, has not been the case at Little Rock. Certain misguided persons, many of them imported into Little Rock by agitators, have insisted upon defying the law and have sought to bring it into disrepute. The orders of the court have thus been frustrated.

The very basis of our individual fights and freedoms rests upon the certainty that the President and the Executive Branch of Government will support and insure the carrying out of the decisions of the Federal Courts, even, when necessary with all the means at the President's command.

Unless the President did so, anarchy would result.

There would be no security for any except that which each one of us could provide for himself.

The interest of the nation in the proper fulfillment of the law's requirements cannot yield to opposition and demonstrations by some few persons.

Mob rule cannot be allowed to override the decisions of our courts.

Now, let me make it very clear that Federal troops are not being used to relieve local and state authorities of their primary duty to preserve the peace and order of the community. Nor are the troops there for the purpose of taking over the responsibility of the School Board and the other responsible local officials in running Central High School. The running of our school system and the maintenance of peace and order in each of our States are strictly local affairs and the

Federal Government does not interfere except in a very few special cases and when requested by one of the several States. In the present case the troops are there, pursuant to law, solely for the purpose of preventing interference with the orders of the Court.

The proper use of the powers of the Executive Branch to enforce the orders of a Federal Court is limited to extraordinary and compelling circumstances. Manifestly, such an extreme situation has been created in Little Rock. This challenge must be met and with such measures as will preserve to the people as a whole their lawfully protected rights in a climate permitting their free and fair exercise.

The overwhelming majority of our people in every section of the country are united in their respect for observance of the law—even in those cases where they may disagree with that law.

They deplore the call of extremists to violence.

The decision of the Supreme Court concerning school integration, of course, affects the South more seriously than it does other sections of the country. In that region I have many warm friends, some of them in the city of Little Rock. I have deemed it a great personal privilege to spend in our Southland tours of duty while in the military service and enjoyable recreational periods since that time.

So from intimate personal knowledge, I know that the overwhelming majority of the people in the South—including those of Arkansas and of Little Rock—are of good will, united in their efforts to preserve and respect the law even when they disagree with it.

They do not sympathize with mob rule. They, like the rest of our nation, have proved in two great wars their readiness to sacrifice for America.

A foundation of our American way of life is our national respect for law.

In the South, as elsewhere, citizens are keenly aware of the tremendous disservice that has been done to the people of Arkansas in the eyes of the nation, and that has been done to the nation in the eyes of the world.

At a time when we face grave situations abroad because of the hatred that Communism bears toward a system of government based on human rights, it would be difficult to exaggerate the harm that is being done to the prestige and influence, and indeed to the safety, of our nation and the world.

Our enemies are gloating over this incident and using it everywhere to misrepresent our whole nation. We are portrayed as a violator of those standards of conduct which the peoples of the world united to proclaim in the Charter of the United Nations. There they affirmed "faith in fundamental human rights" and "in the dignity and worth of the human person" and they did so "without distinction as to race, sex, language or religion."

And so, with deep confidence, I call upon the citizens of the State of Arkansas to assist in bringing to an immediate end all interference with the law and its processes. If resistance to the Federal Court orders ceases at once, the further presence of Federal troops will be unnecessary and the City of Little Rock will return to its normal habits of peace and order and a blot upon the fair name and high honor of our nation in the world will be removed.

Thus will be restored the image of America and of all its parts as one nation, indivisible, with liberty and justice for all.

Good night, and thank you very much.

New York Times, September 25, 1957.

23.9

JOHN KENNETH GALBRAITH, *THE AFFLUENT SOCIETY* (1958)

Perhaps the most striking element of the postwar era was its extraordinary economic growth. After a short downturn in the immediate aftermath of World War II, a wave of economic expansion began and continued with only brief pauses until the late 1960s. Between 1945 and 1960, the gross national product increased over 250 percent, from $200 billion to almost $500 billion. Unemployment dropped from Depression-era highs of 20 percent to five percent or lower. Inflation remained steady at three percent or less. This remarkable growth stemmed from many sources including federal spending, population expansion, suburbanization, and consumerism. The average worker saw his or her purchasing power rise by over 20 percent. The American people enjoyed the highest standard of living in the world. Prosperity, advertising, and credit fed consumerism. By 1955, with only six percent of the global population, the United States purchased one-third of the world's products.

Although popular culture offered few clues about economic inequalities, not all Americans were thriving financially. The decline of the coal industry took a great toll on many Southern communities. Throughout much of Appalachia, people lacked adequate schools, health care, and social services. The nation's farmers struggled as agricultural prices fell. Millions of blacks who had fled the South and Hispanic immigrants languished in inner-city ghettoes. In isolated rural areas, living conditions resembled those of the developing world.

America's uneven economic development disturbed economist John Kenneth Galbraith (1908-present). Born in Ontario, Canada, Galbraith moved to the United States to attend the University of California-Berkeley. After completing his doctorate, Galbraith taught first at Princeton and then at Harvard. He became noted for incisive commentaries on public affairs. In The Affluent Society *(1958), he challenged government economic policies and Americans' consumerism. He later served as an advisor to President John F. Kennedy and was U.S. ambassador to India from 1961 to 1963. He has written several books including* The Great Crash, 1929 *(1955),* The Anatomy of Power *(1983), and* The Culture of Contentment *(1992).*

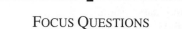

FOCUS QUESTIONS

1. What does Galbraith find troubling about the state of the U.S. political economy? Give several examples.
2. Does Galbraith propose any solutions to economic problems? If so, what?
3. Compare today's America to Galbraith's "affluent society."

T he final problem of the productive society is what it produces. This manifests itself in an implacable tendency to provide an opulent supply of some things and a niggardly yield of others. This disparity carries to the point where it is a cause of social discomfort and social unhealth. The line which divides our area of wealth from our area of poverty is roughly that which divides privately produced and marketed goods and services from publicly rendered services. Our wealth in the first is not only in startling contrast with the meagerness of the latter, but our wealth in privately produced good is, to a marked degree, the cause of crisis in the supply of public services. For we have failed to see the importance, indeed the urgent need, of maintaining a balance between the two....

In the years following World War II, the papers of any major city—those of New York were an excellent example—told daily of the shortages and shortcomings in the elementary municipal and metropolitan services. The schools were old and overcrowded. The police force was under strength and underpaid. The parks and playgrounds were insufficient. Streets and empty lots were filthy, and the sanitation staff was underequipped and in need of men. Access to the city by those who work there was uncertain and painful and becoming more so. Internal transportation was overcrowded, unhealthful and dirty. So was the air....

The discussion of this public poverty competed, on the whole successfully, with the stories of ever-increasing opulence in privately produced goods. The Gross National Product was rising. So were retail sales. So was personal income. Labor productivity had also advanced. The automobiles that could not be parked were being produced at an expended rate. The children, though without schools, subject in the playgrounds to the affectionate interest of adults with odd tastes, and disposed to increasingly imaginative forms of delinquency, were admirably equipped with television sets. We had difficulty finding storage space for the great surpluses of food despite a national disposition to obesity. Food was grown and packaged under private auspices. The care and refreshment of the mind, in contrast with the stomach, was principally in the public domain. Our colleges and universities were severely overcrowded and underprovided, and the same was true of mental hospitals.

The contrast was and remains evident not alone to those who read. The family which takes its mauve and cerise, air-conditioned, power steered and power-braked automobile out for a tour passes through cities that are badly paved, made hideous by litter, blighted buildings, billboards, and posts for wires that should long since have been put underground. They pass on into a countryside that has been rendered largely invisible by commercial art. (The goods which the latter advertise have an absolute priority in our value system. Such aesthetic considerations as a view of the countryside accordingly come second. On such maters we are consistent.) They picnic on exquisitely packaged food from a portable icebox by a polluted stream and go on to spend the night at a park which is a menace to public health and morals. Just before dozing off on an air mattress, beneath a nylon tent, amid the stench of decaying refuse, they may reflect vaguely on the curious unevenness of their blessings. Is this, indeed, the American genius?...

These circumstances have caused a profoundly interesting although little recognized change in what may be termed the political economy of poverty. With the transition of the very poor from a majority to a comparative minority position, they ceased to be automatically an object of interest to the politician. Political identification with those of the lowest estate has anciently brought the reproaches of the well-to-do, but it has had the compensating advantage of alignment with a large majority. Now any politician who speaks for the very poor is speaking for a small and also inarticulate minority. As a result the modern liberal politician aligns himself not with the poverty-ridden members of the community but with the far more numerous people who enjoy the far more affluent income of (say) the modern trade union member....

The poverty-stricken are further forgotten because it is assumed that with increasing output poverty must disappear. Increased output eliminated the general poverty of all who worked. Accordingly, it must, sooner or later, eliminate the special poverty that still remains. As we have just seen, this is not to be expected or, in any case, it will be an infinitely time-consuming and unreliable remedy. Yet just as the arithmetic of modern politics makes it tempting to overlook the very poor, so the supposition that increasing output will remedy their case has made it easy to do so too.

To put the problem another way, the concern for inequality had vitality only so long as the many suffered privation while a few had much. It did not survive as a burning issue in a time when the many had much even though others had much more. It is our misfortune that when inequality declined as an issue, the slate was not left clean. A residual and in some ways rather more hopeless problem remained.

An affluent society, that is also both compassionate and rational, would not doubt, secure to all who needed it the minimum income essential for decency and comfort. The corrupting effect on the human spirit of a small amount of unearned revenue has unquestionably been exaggerated as, indeed, have the character-building values of hunger and privation. To secure to each family a minimum standard, as a normal function of the society, would help insure that the misfortunes of parents, deserved or otherwise, were not visited on their children. It would help insure that poverty was not self-perpetuating...

To eliminate poverty efficiently we should invest more than proportionately in the children of the poor community. It is there that high quality schools, strong health services, special provision for nutrition and recreation are most needed to compensate for the very low investment which families are able to make in their own offspring....

Much can be done to treat those characteristics which cause people to reject or be rejected by the modern industrial society. Educational deficiencies can be overcome. Mental deficiencies can be treated. Physical handicaps can be remedied. The limiting factor is not knowledge of what can be done. Overwhelmingly it is our failure to invest in people....

Poverty—grim, degrading, and ineluctable—is not remarkable in India. For few the fate is otherwise. But in the United States the survival of poverty is remarkable. We ignore it because we share with all societies at all times the capacity for not seeing what we do not wish to see. Anciently this has enabled the nobleman to enjoy his dinner while remaining oblivious to the beggars around his door. In our own day it enables us to travel in comfort through south Chicago and the South. But while our failure to notice can be explained, it cannot be excused. "Poverty," [British prime minister William] Pitt exclaimed, "is no disgrace but it is damned annoying." In the contemporary United States it is not annoying but it is a disgrace.

From THE AFFLUENT SOCIETY by John Kenneth Galbraith. Copyright © 1958, renewed 1986 by John Kenneth Galbraith. Reprinted by permission of Houghton Mifflin Company. All rights reserved.

23.10

JACKSON POLLOCK, *LAVENDAR MIST: NUMBER 1, 1950* (1950)

In the late 1940s, a group of artists known as Abstract Expressionists made New York City the world's leading center of modern painting. Their ranks included Willem de Koonig, Robert Motherwell, Helen Frankenthaler, and Mark Rothko. Although the school encompasses a variety of techniques, Abstract Expressionism is characterized by freedom from conventional forms and dynamic depictions of emotion.

Jackson Pollock (1912-1956) was one of the leading exponents of Abstract Expressionism. After growing up in Arizona and California, Pollock moved to New York City in 1930. He enrolled at Arts Students League where he studied with the Regionalist painter Thomas Hart Benton. From 1935 to 1943, he worked for the Federal Art Project, a New Deal program. For much of this period, Pollock received psychiatric treatment for alcoholism and a nervous breakdown that he suffered in 1938. In 1943, Peggy Guggenheim contracted him for a one-man show at her Art of This Century Gallery in Manhattan. In 1945, Pollock married Lee Krasner, a highly accomplished artist who became a tireless champion of Pollock's work. They moved to a farmhouse in East Hampton, Long Island.

In 1947, Pollock perfected "drip" painting technique that became his artistic hallmark. Abandoning the traditional easel, Pollock placed a canvas on the floor or a wall and then poured or dripped paint directly from the can. He manipulated the paint with knives or sticks instead of brushes. Often applying several layers of paint and occasionally mixing in sand or other foreign objects, Pollock usually took weeks to finish a painting. Rejecting the notion that art should have political or social meaning, Pollock saw painting as a personal expression of one's unconscious. Art critic Howard Rosenberg called the technique "action painting." By the time of his death in a car accident in 1956, Pollock had won widespread recognition and publicity. His work had a profound influence on artists in the United States and Western Europe.

FOCUS QUESTIONS

1. What do you think Pollock was feeling when he painted *Lavender Mist: Number 1, 1950*?
2. Pollock was one of the few painters to earn acclaim during his lifetime. What you think attracted people to Pollock's work?
3. Compare Pollock's *Lavender Mist: Number 1, 1950* to Grant Wood's *American Gothic* (Document 20.9). How do the styles of the Regionalists and the Abstract Expressionists differ? Which painting do you prefer and why?

1976.37.1 (2697)/PA: Pollock, Jackson. *Number 1, 1950, (Lavender Mist)*, Alisa Mellon Bruce Fund, Image © 2003 Board of Trustees, National Gallery of Art, Washington, 1950, oil, enamel, and aluminum on canvas; 2.210 x 2.997 (87 x 118); framed: 2.235 x 3.023 x .038 (88 x 119 x 1-1/2).

23.11

Two Versions of "Shake, Rattle, and Roll" (1954)

In the 1950s, the emergence of rock and roll changed the face of American music. Melding country and rhythm and blues, black bands and artists began producing songs with suggestive themes and strong beats. Disc jockeys such as Alan Freed of Cleveland, Ohio and Dewey Philips of Memphis, Tennessee publicized the music. The eroticism and energy of rock and roll, itself a euphemism for sexual intercourse, thrilled millions of white teenagers. To the dismay of segregationists, parents, and ministers, these teens rushed to buy the records and see the performances of African-American artists and Elvis Presley, a white singer whose sexualized movements and "black" sound transgressed racial and sexual boundaries. This merger of black and white culture was enormously popular and influential. Artists such as Presley, Little Richard, Fats Domino, Buddy Holly, and Jerry Lee Lewis became international stars.

Music industry executives found rock's seedy reputation troubling. In response, some record companies hired white performers to record tepid versions of bawdy songs. This reading features two versions of the song, "Shake, Rattle, and Roll" illustrating this trend. The first is the original as performed by Big Joe Turner, a black artist. The second is a remake by Bill Haley and His Comets, a white band.

Focus Questions

1. Compare the two versions of the song. In what ways, did Bill Haley and the Comets change it? Why do you think they made these adjustments?
2. Do music industry executives still use these tactics? Why or why not? Give examples.
3. Why do you think that segregationists, religious leaders, and others objected to rock and roll? Does popular music generate similar criticism today? Explain your answers.

SHAKE RATTLE & ROLL
As performed by Joe Turner, written by Charles Calhoun.

Get outta that bed, wash your face and hands
Get outta that bed, wash your face and hands
Well, you get in that kitchen, make some noise with the pots and pans

Well, you wear low dresses, the sun comes shining through
Well, you wear low dresses, the sun comes shining through
I can't believe my eyes all that mess belongs to you

I believe to my soul you're a devil in nylon hose
I believe to my soul you're a devil in nylon hose
Well, the harder I work, the faster my money goes

I said, shake, rattle and roll, shake, rattle and roll
Shake, rattle and roll, shake, rattle and roll
Well, you won't do right to save your doggone soul

I'm like a one-eyed cat peeping in a seafood store
I'm like a one-eyed cat peeping in a seafood store
Well, I can look at you and tell you ain't no child no more

Ah, shake, rattle and roll, shake, rattle and roll
Shake, rattle and roll, shake, rattle and roll
Well, you won't do right to save your doggone soul

I said, over the hill and way down underneath
I said, over the hill and way down underneath
You make me roll my eyes, Baby, make me grit my teeth

I said, shake, rattle and roll, shake, rattle and roll
Shake, rattle and roll, shake, rattle and roll
Well, you won't do right to save your doggone soul

SHAKE RATTLE & ROLL
As performed by Bill Haley and His Comets, written by Charles Calhoun

et out from that kitchen
and rattle those pots and pans,
Get out from that kitchen
and rattle those pots and pans.
Well, roll my breakfast,
'cause I'm a hungry man.

I said Shake rattle and roll,
I said Shake rattle and roll,
I said Shake rattle and roll,
I said Shake rattle and roll;
Well you never do nothin'
to save your doggone soul.

Wearin' those dresses,
your hair done up so right
Wearin' those dresses,
your hair done up so right;
You look so warm,
but your heart is cold as ice.

I said Shake rattle and roll,
I said Shake rattle and roll,
I said Shake rattle and roll,
I said Shake rattle and roll,
Well you never do nothin'
to save your doggone soul.

I'm like a one-eyed cat,
peepin' in a sea-food store,
I'm like a one-eyed cat,
peepin' in a sea-food store;
I can look at you,
till you don't love me no more.

I believe you're doin' me wrong
and now I know,
I believe you're doin' me wrong
and now I know;
The more I work,
the faster my money goes.

I said Shake rattle and roll,
I said Shake rattle and roll,
I said Shake rattle and roll,
I said Shake rattle and roll,
Well you never do nothin'
to save your doggone soul.
Shake rattle and rollllllllllllllllllllll

Published at The History of Rock and Roll, http://www.history-of-rock.com/shake_rattle_and_roll.htm.

23.12

ALLEN GINSBERG, "HOWL" (1956)

In the aftermath of World War II, a new literary and social movement called Beat emerged in San Francisco's North Beach, Los Angeles's Venice West, and New York's Greenwich Village. "Beat" had many meanings including physical exhaustion, musicality, and spiritual peace. Beats, derided as "beatniks" by their critics, revolted against the middle-class norms of "square" America. They attacked materialism and advocated freedom of expression. In their quest for immediacy and fulfillment, they experimented sexually, used drugs, and explored

Eastern religions. Beat poets hoped to liberate poetry from stodgy academic settings. They read poems, often with jazz music accompaniment, in unconventional settings like bookstores and coffeehouses. Much of the verse and prose in Beat literature is free-flowing and devoid of traditional dramatic structure.

Most literary scholars consider Allen Ginsberg (1926-1997) the most significant Beat poet. While at Columbia University, Ginsberg befriended Jack Kerouac and William Burroughs, both of whom became important Beat novelists. After leaving Columbia, Ginsberg traveled and held a variety of jobs including janitor and market researcher.

Ginsberg's published book, Howl and Other Poems *(1956), became the subject of a famous obscenity trial. First printed by Villiers in England and then reprinted by Lawrence Ferlinghetti, owner of the San Francisco bookstore City Lights, "Howl" is a blistering attack on conformity in postwar America. Its profanity and references to homosexuality and narcotics prompted U.S. Customs officials to seize the book. With the assistance of the American Civil Liberties Union, Ferlinghetti contested the confiscation and arranged the publication of a new American edition of "Howl," one not subject to Customs inspection. Local police eventually arrested Ferlinghetti for publishing and selling obscene material. Ginsberg, living in Tangier at the time, was not charged or arrested. During Ferlinghtetti's trial during the summer of 1957, several literary critics, editors, and scholars attested to "Howl's" artistic merit and protested censorship. Judge Clayton Moore ruled that the book was not obscene or without "redeeming social importance." The ruling set a legal precedent which led to the eventual repeal of obscenity laws and the U.S. publication of many formerly banned works of literature including D.H. Lawrence's* Lady Chatterly's Lover *and Henry Miller's* Tropic of Cancer. *"Howl" is excerpted below.*

FOCUS QUESTIONS

1. What are the major themes of this section of "Howl"?
2. Is the poem obscene? Should it have been banned? Why or why not?
3. In what ways were Jackson Pollock's *Lavender Mist: Number 1, 1950* (Document 23.10), the original version of "Shake, Rattle, and Roll" (Document 23.11), and "Howl" rejections of mainstream culture in the postwar era? Why do you think these works are culturally significant?

HOWL
For Carl Solomon

 saw the best minds of my generation destroyed by madness,
starving hysterical naked,
dragging themselves through the negro streets at dawn
looking for an angry fix,

angelheaded hipsters burning for the ancient heavenly
connection to the starry dynamo in the machinery of night,
who poverty and tatters and hollow-eyed and high sat
up smoking in the supernatural darkness of
cold-water flats floating across the tops of cities contemplating jazz,
who bared their brains to Heaven under the El and
saw Mohammedan angels staggering on tenement roofs illuminated,
who passed through universities with radiant cool eyes
hallucinating Arkansas and Blake-light tragedy
among the scholars of war,
who were expelled from the academies for crazy &
publishing obscene odes on the windows of the skull,
who cowered in unshaven rooms in underwear, burning their money in
wastebaskets and listening
to the Terror through the wall,
who got busted in their pubic beards returning through
Laredo with a belt of marijuana for New York,
who ate fire in paint hotels or drank turpentine in
Paradise Alley, death, or purgatoried their torsos night after night
with dreams, with drugs, with waking nightmares, alcohol and cock and
endless balls,
incomparable blind; streets of shuddering cloud and
lightning in the mind leaping toward poles of Canada & Paterson,
illuminating all the motionless world of Time between,
Peyote solidities of halls, backyard green tree cemetery
dawns, wine drunkenness over the rooftops,
storefront boroughs of teahead joyride neon
blinking traffic light, sun and moon and tree
vibrations in the roaring winter dusks of Brooklyn,
ashcan rantings and kind king light of mind,
who chained themselves to subways for the endless
ride from Battery to holy Bronx on benzedrine
until the noise of wheels and children brought
them down shuddering mouth-wracked and
battered bleak of brain all drained of brilliance
in the drear light of Zoo,...
who talked continuously seventy hours from park to
pad to bar to Bellevue to museum to the Brooklyn Bridge,
a lost battalion of platonic conversationalists jumping
down the stoops off fire escapes off windowsills
off Empire State out of the moon,
yacketayakking screaming vomiting whispering facts
and memories and anecdotes and eyeball kicks
and shocks of hospitals and jails and wars,
whole intellects disgorged in total recall for seven days

and nights with brilliant eyes, meat for the
Synagogue cast on the pavement,
who vanished into nowhere Zen New Jersey leaving a
trail of ambiguous picture postcards of Atlantic City Hall,
suffering Eastern sweats and Tangerian bone-grindings
and migraines of China under junk-withdrawal in Newark's bleak furnished room,
who wandered around and around at midnight in the
railroad yard wondering where to go, and went,
leaving no broken hearts,
who lit cigarettes in boxcars boxcars boxcars racketing
through snow toward lonesome farms in grandfather night....
who reappeared on the West Coast investigating the
F.B.I. in beards and shorts with big pacifist eyes sexy in their dark skin
passing out incomprehensible leaflets,
who burned cigarette holes in their arms protesting
the narcotic tobacco haze of Capitalism,
who distributed Supercommunist pamphlets in Union
Square weeping and undressing while the sirens
of Los Alamos wailed them down, and wailed
down Wall, and the Staten Island ferry also wailed,...
who bit detectives in the neck and shrieked with delight
in police cars for committing no crime but their
own wild cooking pederasty and intoxication,...
who let themselves be fucked in the ass by saintly
motorcyclists, and screamed with joy,
who blew and were blown by those human seraphim,
the sailors, caresses of Atlantic and Caribbean love,...
who copulated ecstatic and insatiate with a bottle of
beer a sweetheart a package of cigarettes a candle and fell off the bed,
and continued along
the floor and down the hall and ended fainting
on the wall with a vision of ultimate cunt and
come eluding the last gyzym of consciousness,...
who went out whoring through Colorado in myriad
stolen night-cars, N.C., secret hero of these
poems, cocksman and Adonis of Denver—joy
to the memory of his innumerable lays of girls
in empty lots & diner backyards, moviehouses'
rickety rows, on mountaintops in caves or with
gaunt waitresses in familiar roadside lonely petticoat upliftings
& especially secret gas-station solipsisms of johns,
& hometown alleys too,

who faded out in vast sordid movies, were shifted in
dreams, woke on a sudden Manhattan, and
picked themselves up out of basements hung
over with heartless Tokay and horrors of Third
Avenue iron dreams & stumbled to unemployment offices,
who walked all night with their shoes full of blood on
the snowbank docks waiting for a door in the
East River to open to a room full of steamheat and opium,
who created great suicidal dramas on the apartment
cliff-banks of the Hudson under the wartime
blue floodlight of the moon & their heads shall
be crowned with laurel in oblivion,...
who threw their watches off the roof to cast their ballot
for Eternity outside of Time, & alarm clocks
fell on their heads every day for the next decade,
who cut their wrists three times successively unsuccessfully, gave up and
were forced to open antique
stores where they thought they were growing old and cried,
who were burned alive in their innocent flannel suits
on Madison Avenue amid blasts of leaden verse
& the tanked-up clatter of the iron regiments
of fashion & the nitroglycerine shrieks of the
fairies of advertising & the mustard gas of sinister intelligent editors, or
were run down by the
drunken taxicabs of Absolute Reality,...
who sang out of their windows in despair, fell out of
the subway window, jumped in the filthy Passaic, leaped on negroes,
cried all over the street,
danced on broken wineglasses barefoot smashed
phonograph records of nostalgic European
1930s German jazz finished the whiskey and
threw up groaning into the bloody toilet, moans
in their ears and the blast of colossal steam whistles,...
ah, Carl, while you are not safe I am not safe, and
now you're really in the total animal soup of time...
to recreate the syntax and measure of poor human
prose and stand before you speechless and intelligent and shaking with
shame, rejected yet confessing out the soul to conform to the rhythm
of thought in his naked and endless head,
the madman bum and angel beat in Time, unknown,
yet putting down here what might be left to say
in time come after death,

and rose reincarnate in the ghostly clothes of jazz in
the goldhorn shadow of the band and blew the
suffering of America's naked mind for love into
an eli eli lamma lamma sabacthani saxophone
cry that shivered the cities down to the last radio
with the absolute heart of the poem of life butchered
out of their own bodies good to eat a thousand years.

Allen Ginsberg, "Howl," from *Howl and Other Selected Poems* (San Francisco: City Lights Books, 1956), pt. I.

SECONDARY SOURCE

■

STEPHANIE COONTZ, "AMERICAN FAMILIES IN THE 1950S"

Few Americans would dispute the claim that popular culture shapes our views of the past. This is certainly the case about the 1950s. Many people associate the era with images from popular television programs. In this excerpt from The Way We Never Were: American Families and the Nostalgia Trap *(1992; revised edition, 2000), Stephanie Coontz, professor of history and family studies at Evergreen State College, explains how the realities of 1950s family life were more complicated than shows like "Father Knows Best" and "Happy Days" suggest.*

 Go to your *Speaking of America* CD-ROM to read "American Families in the 1950s."

■

FOCUS QUESTIONS

1. Contrast the ways in which today's liberals and conservatives use idealized visions of 1950s families to advance their political agendas.
2. According to Coontz, what were some ways in which the 1950s was a "profamily" era?
3. Why does Coontz believe that 1950s families are the exception, not the rule, in the social history of modern America?
4. How was family life in the 1950s more complicated than the sit-coms of the era suggest? Provide several examples.
5. Were the 1950s an age of "traditional" sexual morality? Why or why not?
6. Do you think that American families were better-off in the 1950s than today? Explain your answer.

AMERICAN JOURNEY ONLINE

———————■———————

http://ajaccesss.wadsworth.com [†]

About Civil Rights
— In <u>Civil Rights in the United States</u>
  Documents
  • U.S. Supreme Court, *Shelley v. Kraemer* (1948)
  • Harry S. Truman, Desegregation of the U.S. Armed Forces (1948)
  • Alexander Meiklejohn, The Meaning of the First Amendment (1955)
  • U.S. Supreme Court, *National Association for the Advancement of Colored People v. Alabama* (1958)
  Images
  • Charles Hamilton Houston
  • Harry Truman
  • Earl Warren Appointed to Supreme Court
  • Thurgood Marshall (1955)
  • Rosa Parks Fingerprinted (1955)
  • Segregated Bus (1956)
  • Dwight D. Eisenhower
  Videos
  • Integration of Central High School, Little Rock (1957)
— In <u>The African-American Experience</u>
  Documents
  • Harry S. Truman, Executive Order 9808 (1946)
  • Philip Randolph, Testimony before the Senate Armed Services Committee (1948)
  • *Bolling et al v. Sharpe et al* (1954)
  • *Brown et al v. Board of Education et al* (1955)
  • School Desegregation March (circa 1955)
  • Daisy Bates, Excerpt from *The Long Shadow of Little Rock* (1962)
— In <u>The Constitution and Supreme Court</u>
  Images
  • Thurgood Marshall (1954)
  • W.D. Lawson, A Letter Critical of Desegregation (1956)
  • The Little Rock Nine (1957)

[†] Enter password, choose the Archive indicated above, click on Contents, choose
•Documents, •Images, or •Multimedia, and click on the title of the item.

About Law
— In <u>Civil Rights in the United States</u>
  Documents
  • U.S. Supreme Court, *Everson v. Board of Education of Ewing Township, New Jersey* (1947)
  • U.S. Supreme Court, *Roth v. United States* (1957)
  Images
  • Fred Vinson (1946)
— In <u>The Constitution and Supreme Court</u>
  Documents
U.S. Congress, The Twenty-sS
  • Felix Frankfurter (1957)

About Domestic Politics
— In <u>The Great Depression and the New Deal</u>
  Images
  • Tom Connally, Sam Rayburn, and John McCormack (1949)

About U.S. Foreign Policy
— In <u>World War II</u>
  Images
  • Harry S. Truman, U.S. Recognition of the State of Israel (1948)

About Immigration
— In <u>The Immigrant Experience</u>
  Documents
  • United Nations, Refugee Definition (1951, 1957)
  • U.S. Congress, Excerpt of the McCarran-Walter Act (1952)
  • Immigration and Naturalization Service, Report of the Immigration and Naturalization Service (1955)
  Images
  • Refugee Children Arrive in Brooklyn (1957) in The Immigrant Experience
— In <u>The Asian-American Experience</u>
  Documents
  • U.S. Congress, Excerpt of the Immigration and Naturalization Act (1952)

About Women
— In <u>Women in America</u>
  Images
  • Clare Booth Luce (circa 1950)

About American Indians
— In <u>The Native American Experience</u>
  Documents

- U.S. Congress, Indian Claims Commission Act (1946)
- U.S. Congress, House Concurrent Resolution 108 (1953)
- U.S. Congress, Public Law 280 (1953)
- Sophie D. Aberle, Menominee Termination

Images
- The Swearing in of the Indian Claims Commission (1947)
- Bureau of Indian Affairs, Relocation Poster (circa 1950)
- Ira Hamilton Hayes
- The Menominee Regain Recognition (1973)

About Culture
— In The African-American Experience
  Images
  - Richard Wright (1948)
  - Jackie Robinson (1949)
  - Duke Ellington (1950)
  - Mahalia Jackson (1951)
— In The Asian-American Experience
  Images
  - Sammy Lee (1948)
— In Civil Rights in the United States
  Images
  - Jackie Robinson (1948)

THE TUMULTUOUS SIXTIES

Few decades in American history have been as turbulent as the 1960s. Civil rights protests, urban riots, anti-war activism, and the counterculture were only a few of the forces that rocked U.S. society. The decade witnessed moments of great hope and tragic loss. On both the right and the left, sweeping political changes occurred. Young people, people of color, and women mobilized for social and economic equality. But the optimism inspired by the Kennedy presidency was short-lived. By 1968, racial unrest, the Vietnam War, the Great Society, and assassinations polarized the nation. The country's mood shifted from buoyancy to cynicism. The United States emerged from the 1960s a changed nation, but Americans remain divided in their assessments of the era.

John F. Kennedy's victory in the 1960 presidential race set the tone for the decade. Although Kennedy's opponent, Vice-President Richard M. Nixon, had more political experience, he lacked Kennedy's charisma—a fact that did not escape viewers when Kennedy and Nixon met in the first televised presidential debates. While trying to deflect concerns about his Catholicism, Kennedy pointed to a lagging economy, the U-2 incident, and the "missile gap" as evidence of Republican failure. In the end, he won one of the narrowest margins of victory in U.S. history. His youth and style signaled a new era in American politics.

Kennedy's charm did, however, did not impress Congress. Widely considered a lightweight among his former colleagues on Capitol Hill, Kennedy had a difficult time gaining support for his domestic reform initiatives. His proposals for economic growth met more success. At Kennedy's urging, Congress expanded defense spending and financed a $25 billion effort to land men on the Moon by 1970. He also won passage of lower corporate taxes. By the time of Kennedy's assassination in November 1963, economic growth had doubled, unemployment had fallen, and inflation was a mere 1.3% percent a year.

Kennedy's record on civil rights was less notable. Unwilling to alienate conservative Democrats, Kennedy initially tried to avoid racial issues. The tactic failed as civil rights activists organized sit-ins, freedom rides, and mass protests that drew violent white resistance throughout the Deep South. Such incidents forced Kennedy to dispatch law enforcement officials and troops to restore order. In June 1963, America's deteriorating image abroad and escalating racial tensions at home compelled Kennedy to declare civil rights "a moral issue" and to introduce comprehensive civil rights legislation.

To pressure Congress to pass Kennedy's bill and to demonstrate their movement's non-violent nature, civil rights activists organized the March on Washington for Jobs and Freedom. On August 28, 1963, nearly 250,000 people converged on the nation's capital for the historic rally. Martin Luther King, Jr.'s "I Have a Dream" speech inspired millions. But the demonstration did not persuade Congress to enact Kennedy's legislation, nor did it halt white resistance in the South. Just days after the March, four black girls perished in a Birmingham, Alabama church bombing.

Throughout his presidency, Kennedy was a staunch Cold Warrior. Adopting a "flexible response" strategy, he called for greater nuclear capabilities, increased defense expenditures, and the establishment of counterinsurgency forces. He instituted programs to "modernize" and aid the developing world such as the Alliance for Progress, the Peace Corps, and the Agency for International Development.

Like Truman and Eisenhower, Kennedy supported the containment policy and was willing to use military power to defend U.S interests. In April 1961, the failure of the Bay of Pigs invasion, a CIA plan to oust Cuban leader Fidel Castro, handed Kennedy an embarrassing setback. Although Eisenhower had originally approved the mission, Kennedy took responsibility for its collapse. Several additional U.S. attempts to remove Castro also failed.

Kennedy was more successful in confronting Soviet Premier Nikita Khrushchev. In July 1961, when Khrushchev threatened West Berlin, Kennedy deployed 150,000 troops to defend the city. Although Khrushchev retreated, he was determined to stop East Germans from fleeing to the West. In August, he ordered the construction of a wall to seal off East Berlin. The Berlin Wall became the most visible symbol of the communists' willingness to use repression in order to maintain power.

Cold War tensions almost caused a nuclear catastrophe in October 1962. Upon discovering that the Soviets were installing nuclear missiles on Cuba, Kennedy publicly demanded that the Soviets remove them. To enforce this ultimatum, Kennedy imposed a naval blockade to prevent the Soviets from delivering additional missiles. For several days, the United States and the Soviet Union veered perilously close to nuclear war. The crisis ended when Khrushchev agreed to remove the missiles in exchange for a U.S. promise not to invade Cuba. In the wake of the affair, Kennedy and Khrushchev worked to improve U.S.-Soviet relations. In August 1963, they signed the Limited Test Ban Treaty outlawing the atmospheric and undersea testing of nuclear weapons. Yet, in subsequent years, both superpowers dramatically expanded their stores of Inter-Continental Ballistic Missiles (ICBMs) and nuclear submarines. Although the Americans and the Soviets backed away from direct confrontations, they transferred their rivalry to proxies in the developing world.

Nowhere was this more evident than in Southeast Asia. Kennedy continued Eisenhower's policy of sending financial and military aid to South Vietnam (see the introduction to Chapter 23). Between 1961 and 1963, the number of U.S. "advisors" in South Vietnam rose from 700 to over 16,000. These measures proved inadequate as Ngo Dinh Diem's failure to institute social improvements and brutal treatment of political opponents generated intense popular discontent. In May 1963, the world watched Buddhists monks set themselves aflame in protest of Diem's repression. Convinced that Diem was losing control, U.S. leaders secretly backed a military coup. On November 1, a group of South Vietnamese generals seized Diem and his brother Nhu and murdered them. The United States quickly announced support for the new military regime. Three weeks later, Kennedy was assassinated. Historians disagree about the course of action he might have taken in Vietnam.

Kennedy's assassination stunned the country. On November 23, 1963, during a trip in support of Texas Democrats, Kennedy was fatally shot as he rode in an open car through downtown Dallas. For the next four days, grieving citizens were riveted to their televisions as they absorbed the loss of their young president; watched night club owner Jack Ruby kill Lee Harvey Oswald, Kennedy's alleged assassin; and observed the president's solemn funeral. Although the Warren Commission concluded that Oswald acted alone in murdering Kennedy, experts continue to offer alternative explanations of Kennedy's assassination.

Lyndon Baines Johnson, Kennedy's unlikely successor, inherited the dreams and problems of the fallen president's administration. Where Kennedy exuded class and eloquence, Johnson was crude and manipulating. But Johnson was also a legislative genius. Formerly one of the most effective Majority Leaders in Senate history, Johnson used his political skills to implement the most sweeping domestic agenda since the New Deal.

Invoking Kennedy's memory, Johnson persuaded Congress to pass a $10 billion tax cut and the long-stalled Civil Rights Act of 1964. The latter outlawed segregation, created the Equal Employment Opportunity Commission (EEOC), and prohibited job discrimination on basis of race, religion, national origin, or sex. Boldly declaring his desire for a "Great Society," Johnson then proposed a host of measures including job training, federally funded health care for the poor and elderly, federal aid to education, Head Start programs for impoverished preschoolers, consumer protection and conservation laws, urban renewal, and national endowments for the arts and humanities. The scope of Johnson's vision was breathtaking, though its effects remain disputed.

In 1964, Johnson won a landslide victory over Barry Goldwater, a Republican Senator from Arizona. Goldwater's nomination marked a historic realignment in the Republican Party and the birth of a conservative movement called the New Right. Although Goldwater lost decisively, his staunch anticommunism, opposition to welfare programs and civil rights legislation, and call for fiscally responsible government heralded a new GOP agenda. In the aftermath of Goldwater's defeat, conservatives pioneered campaign tactics and fundraising strategies that greatly expanded their ranks. By the mid-1970s, the New Right was poised to alter the American political landscape.

In the early 1960s, the civil rights movement achieved remarkable successes. Civil rights laws ended *de jure* segregation and created new economic and educational opportunities for people of color. By 1968, ratification of the Twenty-Third Amendment abolishing poll taxes and passage of the Voting Rights Act of 1965 allowed 2.1 million southern blacks to join the one million already registered to vote.

But these victories did not remedy the poverty, crime, and dissolution that gripped many black communities. In response, some blacks embraced the philosophies of Malcolm X or the Black Panthers. Others vented their rage in riots that engulfed dozens of American cities between 1964 and 1968. Authorities claimed the unrest stemmed from poverty, police brutality, and poor housing and education. But politicians differed in their proposed solutions. Conservatives demanded more "law and order." Liberals called for more jobs, public housing, and social spending. While officials argued, a white backlash against civil rights and the Great Society intensified.

Throughout the 1960s, unprecedented numbers of young people asserted themselves politically and culturally. The baby boom had an incalculable impact on American society. In the 1960s, eight million Americans were enrolled in colleges and universities, a 50 percent increase from the previous decade. More than half of Americans were younger than age 30. Most either pursued higher education or went to work after completing high school. Their life goals were similar to those of their parents. Given the media images of the 1960s, it is easy to forget that the majority of the baby boomers did not become political activists or join the counterculture. But the minority who did challenge the status quo sent shockwaves through the nation.

Political organizing was an essential component of many young activists' lives. On the right, conservative students formed groups like Young Americans for Freedom (YAF) and campaigned for Barry Goldwater and Richard Nixon. They called for a strong national defense, hated communism, and detested campus radicalism. On the left, liberal students founded Students for a Democratic Society (SDS). They supported the civil rights movement and the Great Society and opposed the Vietnam War.

While the media paid little attention to the New Right, New Left actions such as the Free Speech Movement and anti-war protests received wide exposure. When demonstrators at the 1968 Democratic National Convention in Chicago chanted, "the whole world is watching," they were not exaggerating. But visibility could not prevent—and probably contributed to—the New Left's implosion in the late 1960s.

Native Americans, Chicanos, and women were also mobilizing during this era. With the worst poverty and lowest life expectancy of all Americans, Indians created multi-tribe organizations to draw attention to their plight. Their efforts convinced the Johnson administration to form the National Council on Indian Opportunity and to request greater federal assistance for native peoples. Echoing the cultural pride of the "Black Power" movement, young Indian activists espoused "Red Power." They fought job discrimination, called for the creation of

Native American studies programs, and sought legal redress for lost tribal lands and fishing rights.

Mexican Americans also challenged discrimination and poverty. Cesar Chávez of the National Farm Workers Association protested working and living conditions among agricultural laborers. In 1965, Chávez organized a strike by California grape pickers as well as a national consumer boycott of grapes. Like their African-American and American Indian counterparts, young Latinos rejected assimilation and celebrated their ethnic identity. "Brown Power" found voice in new political organizations like Alianza, the Crusade for Justice, and La Raza. They pushed for bilingual education, economic opportunities, and political inclusion.

After decades of inaction following ratification of the Nineteenth Amendment in 1920, a "second wave" of women's activists profoundly changed American society and politics. Making good on a campaign pledge, Kennedy established the Presidential Commission on the Status of Women in 1961. Two years later, the group released a report documenting substantial pay differentials between men and women and barriers to the educational and professional advancement of women. In response, Congress passed the Equal Pay Act of 1963 mandating that men and women performing the same jobs receive equal wages. The same year, Betty Friedan published *The Feminine Mystique*, a landmark text describing the dissatisfaction many women felt in lives exclusively defined by marriage and motherhood. In 1964, Congress barred job discrimination on the basis of sex as well as on racial and religious grounds. Almost immediately, however, it became clear that federal officials and the media did not take sexism seriously.

Alarmed by these dismissive attitudes, Friedan and 300 others founded the National Organization for Women (NOW) to lobby for gender equality. At the same time, younger female activists working in the anti-war and civil rights movements began to protest the chauvinism of their male colleagues. When their complaints met derision, these women formed the women's liberation movement. Through consciousness-raising groups and flamboyant demonstrations, they demanded that women receive social status equal to men. Declaring "the personal is political," they brought attention to formerly taboo subjects such as breast cancer, rape, sexual harassment, and domestic violence. By the 1970s, the women's movement was growing rapidly.

The Vietnam War coexisted—and at times, overshadowed—the extraordinary changes occurring in American life. Following the collapse of the Diem regime, the United States faced a stark choice between abandoning South Vietnam or expanding U.S. efforts to defeat Ho Chi Minh. A fervent believer in the domino theory and fearful of the political ramifications of withdrawal from Vietnam, Johnson chose escalation. In May 1964, his aides drafted a resolution authorizing the president to "take all necessary measures" to defeat communists in Southeast Asia. In August, after North Vietnamese patrol boats allegedly attacked two U.S. destroyers in the Gulf of Tonkin, Johnson asked Congress to approve the resolution. Congress complied with only two dissenting votes and virtually no discussion. Johnson now possessed broad power to conduct war without an official declaration of war. In February 1965, following a communist attack on U.S. Marines in Pleiku, Johnson ordered an enormous "Rolling Thunder" bombing campaign in North Vietnam. By 1968, although the United States had dropped more tonnage on North Vietnam than was used in all of the theaters of World War II, the bombing only stiffened North Vietnamese resistance. In March 1965, Johnson sent two battalions of Marines to South Vietnam. He abandoned the fiction that U.S. troops were only "advising" the South Vietnamese government. Within three years, the number of U.S. soldiers in Vietnam reached 500,000.

As the United States escalated its involvement in Vietnam, an anti-war movement emerged. As early as March 1965, college faculty and students were publicly questioning American strategy in Southeast Asia. By 1967, people of all ages and professions were participating in enormous anti-war marches. As the Johnson administration spent $2 billion a month in Vietnam, the economy stalled. Johnson watched in horror as "that bitch of a war" polarized the country and derailed his Great Society.

Some of the biggest changes in American society were entirely apolitical. Some young people eschewed conventional expectations and sought self-realization through drugs, music, sexual experimentation, and fashion. The "live free" philosophy of the "hippies" attracted thousands. But the counterculture's impact went far beyond those who actually joined communes and abandoned traditional lifestyles.

The sexual revolution had a similar ripple effect. While the sexual revolution did not hit with full force until the 1970s, it stemmed from technological, legal, and social changes in the 1960s. In 1960, the introduction of the birth control pill greatly diminished fears of unwanted pregnancy. By 1970, 12 million women were "on the pill." Court decisions expanding access to contraception and striking down obscenity laws also contributed to freer sexual attitudes. In 1967, Governor Ronald Reagan signed legislation making California the first state to legalize abortion. While the sexual revolution thrilled many Americans, it repulsed others.

The year 1968 highlighted the bitter divisions in the nation and culminated in a major political realignment. In late January, the North Vietnamese launched the Tet Offensive. Within hours, they seized control of several cities including the South Vietnam capital, Saigon. Although U.S. forces quickly regained lost territory and exacted devastating losses on the North Vietnamese, Tet convinced many Americans that the war was unwinnable.

In February, foreign policy experts persuaded Johnson not to send an additional 206,000 troops to Vietnam. At the same time, Senator Eugene McCarthy (D-MN), a strong opponent of the war, was challenging LBJ for the Democratic nomination for president. McCarthy's impressive performance in the New Hampshire primary inspired Senator Robert F. Kennedy (D-NY), another critic of Vietnam, to declare his candidacy. Kennedy's name recognition and appeal to the poor, the working-class, and minorities made him a real threat to Johnson. Shattered by Tet and unwilling to risk losing his party's nomination, Johnson announced on March 31 that he would not run for reelection. Instead, he promised to devote himself to negotiating peace in Vietnam.

Johnson's pronouncement was just the first in a series of shocking political developments. On April 4, James Earl Ray assassinated Martin Luther King, Jr. in Memphis, Tennessee. The news sparked riots in 125 cities. On June 5, Robert F. Kennedy was killed by Sirhan Sirhan, a Palestinian enraged by RFK's pro-Israeli views. Kennedy's death created despair among Democrats hoping to end the war and to continue federal efforts to aid the poor and disfranchised.

In August, supporters of Vice-President Hubert Humphrey and Eugene McCarthy battled at the Democratic National Convention in Chicago. Anti-war protestors descended on the city, eager to persuade the delegates to adopt an anti-war platform. Chicago police, acting on orders from Mayor Richard Daley, clubbed and arrested the mostly peaceful demonstrators. After rancorous debates, the Democrats nominated Humphrey and decided to continue the war until a negotiated settlement could be reached. They left the convention shaken and divided.

Rejoicing at the Democrats' travails, Republicans nominated Richard Nixon. Cognizant that many Americans were terrified and enraged by the violence and tumult plaguing the nation, Nixon promised to restore "law and order" and to honor "the forgotten Americans" who were not engaging in social protests. He accused the Warren Court of expanding the rights of criminals at the expense of law-abiding citizens. He claimed to have a "secret plan" to bring "peace with honor" in Vietnam. At the same time, Nixon adopted ideas from third-party candidate George Wallace, an opponent of civil rights, the counterculture, and the anti-war movement.

Although Humphrey gained momentum in the final weeks of the campaign, Nixon won 43.4 percent of the vote to Humphrey's 42.7 percent, while 13.5 percent of the electorate chose Wallace. Republicans assembled a new coalition of white southerners, opponents of "wasteful" federal spending, and critics of forced busing. Although many social movements continued into the 1970s, Nixon's victory reflected a growing political conservatism. As Americans grappled with the continuing war in Vietnam, economic problems, and Watergate, disillusionment replaced the optimism of the Kennedy years.

24.1

---•---

JOHN F. KENNEDY, INAUGURAL ADDRESS (1961)

The presidential election of 1960 was a turning point in American political history. Democrat John F. Kennedy (1917-1963) faced Republican Richard M. Nixon (1913-1994). Both candidates were in their forties and WWII veterans. But Nixon, who served two terms as vice president under Eisenhower, had more political experience than Kennedy, a U.S. Senator from Massachusetts. Pundits predicted a Nixon landslide.

Kennedy ignored these gloomy forecasts. Born the second of nine children in an Irish Catholic family, he grew up in a privileged, competitive environment. His father, Joseph P. Kennedy, had made a fortune as a banker, bootlegger, and film producer. In the 1930s, he headed the Securities and Exchange Commission and then served as U.S. ambassador to Great Britain. John accompanied his father to Europe and examined Britain's belated response to the Nazis in his Harvard senior thesis. In 1940, when John published the essay as Why England Slept, *his father secretly bought 40,000 copies to ensure that the book became a bestseller. In 1943, while Kennedy was serving in the U.S. Navy, a Japanese destroyer rammed and sank his patrol torpedo (PT) boat in the Solomon Islands. His heroic efforts in saving his crew were recognized with the U.S. Navy and Marine Corps Medal. The incident aggravated an old back injury that left Kennedy in constant pain despite three surgeries. He also suffered from Addison's disease, a rare endocrine disorder characterized by weight loss, muscle weakness, fatigue, and low blood pressure. Throughout his career, Kennedy concealed this ailment as well as his use of several prescription drugs.*

These impediments did not thwart Kennedy's ambition. After his older brother died in combat, John deferred to his father's wish that he enter politics. In 1946, at age 29, he won the House of Representatives seat for the Massachusetts 11th district. In 1952, he ran successfully for the U.S. Senate and became known for his anti-communism and New Deal liberalism. In 1953, Kennedy married the elegant Jacqueline Lee Bouvier. Three years later, he published the Pulitzer Prize-winning Profiles in Courage, *later revealed to be mainly the work of Ted Sorenson, a Kennedy aide. When the Democrats almost selected him as Adlai Stevenson's 1956 running mate, Kennedy became a national sensation. During his 1960 campaign for the presidency, Kennedy assured Protestant voters that his Catholicism would not interfere with his political judgment. After winning the Democratic nomination, he defeated Nixon by only 118,500 popular votes and a 303-219 vote in the Electoral College. Many observers claimed that voter fraud had determined the close election.*

Dismissing such allegations, Kennedy supporters adored the eloquent and stylish president. On January 20, 1961, Kennedy withstood frigid weather and gave his inaugural address outside the U.S. Capital.

FOCUS QUESTIONS

1. What tone does Kennedy try to establish for his presidency and the nation as a whole?
2. What are Kennedy's foreign policy goals? Did he realize these objectives? Support your answer with examples.
3. Why do you think that Kennedy's remarks inspired so many Americans?
4. How should we weigh recent revelations about Kennedy's private life in assessing his presidency? What is your evaluation of his presidency?

W e observe today not a victory of party but a celebration of freedom— symbolizing an end as well as a beginning—signifying renewal as well as change. For I have sworn before you and Almighty God the same solemn oath our forbears prescribed nearly a century and three quarters ago.

The world is very different now. For man holds the power to abolish all forms of human poverty and all forms of human life. And yet the same revolutionary beliefs for which our forebears fought are still at issue around the globe—the belief that the rights of man come not from the generosity of state but from the hand of God.

We dare not forget today that we are the heirs of that first revolution. Let the word go forth from this time and place, to friend and foe alike, that the torch has been passed to a new generation of Americans—born in this century, tempered by war, disciplined by a hard and bitter peace, proud of our ancient heritage—and unwilling to witness or permit the slow undoing of those human rights to which this nation has always been committed, and to which we are committed today at home and around the world. Let every nation know, whether it wishes us well or ill, that we shall pay any price, bear any burden, meet any hardship, support any friend, oppose any foe to assure the survival and the success of liberty.

This much we pledge—and more.

To those old allies whose cultural and spiritual origins we share, we pledge the loyalty of faithful friends. United, there is little we cannot do in a host of cooperative ventures. Divided, there is little we can do—for we dare not meet a powerful challenge at odds and split asunder.

To those new States whom we welcome to the ranks of the free, we pledge our word that one form of colonial control shall not have passed away merely to be replaced by a far more iron tyranny. We shall not always expect to find them supporting our view. But we shall always hope to find them strongly supporting their own freedom—and to remember that, in the past, those who foolishly sought power by riding the back of the tiger ended up inside.

To those peoples in the huts and villages of half the globe struggling to break the bonds of mass misery, we pledge our best efforts to help them help themselves, for whatever period is required—not because the communists may be doing it, not because we seek their votes, but because it is right. If a free society cannot help the many who are poor, it cannot save the few who are rich.

To our sister republics south of our border, we offer a special pledge to convert our good words into good deeds—in a new alliance for progress—to assist free men and free governments in casting off the chains of poverty. But this peaceful revolution of hope cannot become the prey of hostile powers. Let all our neighbors know that we shall join with them to oppose aggression or subversion anywhere in the Americas. And let every other power know that this Hemisphere intends to remain the master of its own house....

Finally, to those nations who would make themselves our adversary, we offer not a pledge but a request: that both sides begin anew the quest for peace, before the dark powers of destruction unleashed by science engulf all humanity in planned or accidental self-destruction.

We dare not tempt them with weakness. For only when our arms are sufficient beyond doubt can we be certain beyond doubt that they will never be employed.

But neither can two great and powerful groups of nations take comfort from our present course—both sides overburdened by the cost of modern weapons, both rightly alarmed by the steady spread of the deadly atom, yet both racing to alter that uncertain balance of terror that stays the hand of mankind's final war.

So let us begin anew—remembering on both sides that civility is not a sign of weakness, and sincerity is always subject to proof. Let us never negotiate out of fear. But let us never fear to negotiate.

Let both sides explore what problems unite us instead of belaboring those problems which divide us.

Let both sides, for the first time, formulate serious and precise proposals for the inspection and control of arms—and bring the absolute power to destroy other nations under the absolute power to control all nations.

Let both sides seek to invoke the wonders of science instead of its terrors. Together let us explore the stars, conquer the deserts, eradicate disease, tap the ocean depths and encourage the arts and commerce....

And if a beach-head of cooperation may push back the jungle of suspicion, let both sides join in creating a new endeavor, not a new balance of power, but a world of law, where the strong are just and the weak secure and the peace preserved.

All this will not be finished in the first one hundred days. Nor will it be finished in the first one thousand days, nor in the life of this Administration, nor perhaps in our lifetime on this planet. But let us begin.

In your hands, my fellow citizens, more than mine, will rest the final success or failure of our course. Since this country was founded, each generation of Americans has been summoned to give testimony to its national loyalty. The graves of young Americans who answered the call to service surround the globe.

Now the trumpet summons us again—not as a call to bear arms, though arms we need—not as a call to battle, though embattled we are—but a call to bear the burden of a long twilight struggle, year in and year out, "rejoicing in hope, patient in tribulation"—a struggle against the common enemies of man: tyranny, poverty, disease and war itself.

Can we forge against these enemies a grand and global alliance, North and South, East and West, that can assure a more fruitful life for all mankind? Will you join in that historic effort?

In the long history of the world, only a few generations have been granted the role of defending freedom in its hour of maximum danger. I do not shrink from this responsibility—I welcome it. I do not believe that any of us would exchange places with any other people or any other generation. The energy, the faith, the devotion which we bring to this endeavor will light our country and all who serve it—and the glow from that fire can truly light the world.

And so, my fellow Americans: ask not what your country can do for you— ask what you can do for your country.

My fellow citizens of the world: ask not what America will do for you, but what together we can do for the freedom of man.

Finally, whether you are citizens of America or citizens of the world, ask of us here the same high standards of strength and sacrifice which we ask of you. With a good conscience our only sure reward, with history the final judge of our deeds, let us go forth to lead the land we love, asking His blessing and His help, but knowing that here on earth God's work must truly be our own.

"Inaugural Address," *Public Papers of the Presidents of the United States: John F. Kennedy, 1961* (Washington DC, 1962), 1-3.

24.2

YOUNG AMERICANS FOR FREEDOM, THE SHARON STATEMENT (1960)

In the 1940s and 1950s, a number of intellectuals revitalized American conservatism. Books like Friedrich Hayek's The Road to Serfdom *(1944), Richard Weaver's* Ideas Have Consequences *(1948) and Russell Kirk's* The Conservative Mind *(1953) denounced communism, celebrated individual freedom and private enterprise, and called for a return to "traditional" religious and moral values. These ideas inspired a new generation of conservative activists, many of whom avidly supported Barry M. Goldwater (R-AZ) in his quest to win the 1960 Republican presidential nomination. When Republicans chose the more moderate Richard Nixon as their candidate, conservative leaders regrouped. In September 1960, they held a meeting of young conservatives at the Sharon, Connecticut estate of William F. Buckley, Jr., publisher of* The National Review. *The ninety delegates founded Young Americans for Freedom (YAF) and adopted the Sharon Statement. In subsequent years, YAF spearheaded Goldwater's 1964 presidential campaign, attacked left-wing groups like Students for a Democratic Society, and supported U.S. efforts in Vietnam. YAF remains an active presence at many colleges and universities.*

FOCUS QUESTIONS

1. What are the major principles of the Sharon Statement? At whom do you think the statement is directed?
2. How do the framers of the Sharon Statement propose to solve the problems facing the country?

3. Compare the Sharon Statement to the Port Huron Statement (Document 24.3). Which most closely resembles your own political views? Why? Which statement would attract more support at your college? Why?

Adopted in conference at Sharon, Connecticut, on 11 September 1960.

n this time of moral and political crises, it is the responsibility of the youth of America to affirm certain eternal truths.

We, as young conservatives, believe:

That foremost among the transcendent values is the individual's use of his God-given free will, whence derives his right to be free from the restrictions of arbitrary force;

That liberty is indivisible, and that political freedom cannot long exist without economic freedom;

That the purpose of government is to protect those freedoms through the preservation of internal order, the provision of national defense, and the administration of justice;

That when government ventures beyond these rightful functions, it accumulates power, which tends to diminish order and liberty;

That the Constitution of the United States is the best arrangement yet devised for empowering government to fulfill its proper role, while restraining it from the concentration and abuse of power;

That the genius of the Constitution—the division of powers—is summed up in the clause that reserves primacy to the several states, or to the people, in those spheres not specifically delegated to the Federal government;

That the market economy, allocating resources by the free play of supply and demand, is the single economic system compatible with the requirements of personal freedom and constitutional government, and that it is at the same time the most productive supplier of human needs;

That when government interferes with the work of the market economy, it tends to reduce the moral and physical strength of the nation; that when it takes from one man to bestow on another, it diminishes the incentive of the first, the integrity of the second, and the moral autonomy of both;

That we will be free only so long as the national sovereignty of the United States is secure; that history shows periods of freedom are rare, and can exist only when free citizens concertedly defend their rights against all enemies;

That the forces of international Communism are, at present, the greatest single threat to these liberties;

That the United States should stress victory over, rather than coexistence with, this menace; and

That American foreign policy must be judged by this criterion: does it serve the just interests of the United States?

Young Americans for Freedom, http://www.yaf.com/sharon.shtml.

24.3

STUDENTS FOR A DEMOCRATIC SOCIETY, THE PORT HURON STATEMENT (1962)

The civil rights movement and the Kennedy presidency inspired many young liberals to become politically active. Some were "red diaper" babies whose parents were socialists or communists in the 1930s and 1940s. Sharing their parents' political idealism, these students led a resurgence of campus radicalism called the New Left. The most significant New Left organization was Students for a Democratic Society (SDS), founded in 1959 as an offshoot of the socialist League for Industrial Democracy. SDS chapters across the nation participated in civil rights demonstrations. In 1962, several SDS members gathered in Port Huron, Michigan and adopted a manifesto written primarily by Tom Hayden, a recent graduate of the University of Michigan. The statement stirred thousands of people who were dissatisfied with mainstream liberalism and the political status quo.

When the United States escalated its involvement in the Vietnam War, SDS membership skyrocketed. Between 1965 and 1969, SDS was the leading anti-war organization among college students. The group organized dozens of anti-war protests and marches. But SDS was plagued by internal divisions and splintered by 1969. The most radical SDS faction, the Weathermen, advocated violence against "the Establishment." Although no more than 300 people belonged to the Weathermen, their terrorist tactics tarnished the reputation of SDS as a whole. In the mid-1970s, as the Vietnam War ended and activists burned out, SDS disbanded.

FOCUS QUESTIONS

1. How does SDS describe the state of the nation?
2. What do they believe are the biggest national problems? What solutions do they propose?
3. Compare the Port Huron Statement to the Sharon Statement (Document 24.2). Which most closely resembles your own political views? Why? Which statement would attract more support at your college? Why?

 NTRODUCTION: AGENDA FOR A GENERATION

We are people of this generation, bred in at least modest comfort, housed now in universities, looking uncomfortably to the world we inherit.

When we were kids the United States was the wealthiest and strongest country in the world: the only one with the atom bomb, the least scarred by modern war, an initiator of the United Nations that we thought would distribute Western influence throughout the world. Freedom and equality for each individual, government of, by, and for the people—these American values we found good, principles by which we could live as men. Many of us began maturing in complacency.

As we grew, however, our comfort was penetrated by events too troubling to dismiss. First, the permeating and victimizing fact of human degradation, symbolized by the Southern struggle against racial bigotry, compelled most of us from silence to activism. Second, the enclosing fact of the Cold War, symbolized by the presence of the Bomb, brought awareness that we ourselves, and our friends, and millions of abstract "others" we knew more directly because of our common peril, might die at any time. We might deliberately ignore, or avoid, or fail to feel all other human problems, but not these two, for these were too immediate and crushing in their impact, too challenging in the demand that we as individuals take the responsibility for encounter and resolution.

While these and other problems either directly oppressed us or rankled our consciences and became our own subjective concerns, we began to see complicated and disturbing paradoxes in our surrounding America. The declaration "all men are created equal…" rang hollow before the facts of Negro life in the South and the big cities of the North. The proclaimed peaceful intentions of the United States contradicted its economic and military investments in the Cold War status quo.

We witnessed, and continue to witness, other paradoxes. With nuclear energy whole cities can easily be powered, yet the dominant nation-states seem more likely to unleash destruction greater than that incurred in all wars of human history. Although our own technology is destroying old and creating new forms of social organization, men still tolerate meaningless work and idleness. While two-thirds of mankind suffers undernourishment, our own upper classes revel amidst superfluous abundance. Although world population is expected to double in forty years, the nations still tolerate anarchy as a major principle of international conduct and uncontrolled exploitation governs the sapping of the earth's physical resources. Although mankind desperately needs revolutionary leadership, America rests in national stalemate, its goals ambiguous and tradition-bound instead of informed and clear, its democratic system apathetic and manipulated rather than "of, by, and for the people."…

Some would have us believe that Americans feel contentment amidst prosperity—but might it not better be called a glaze above deeply felt anxieties about their role in the new world? And if these anxieties produce a developed indifference to human affairs, do they not as well produce a yearning to believe there is an alternative to the present, that something can be done to change circumstances in the school, the workplaces, the bureaucracies, the government? It is to this latter yearning, at once the spark and engine of change, that we direct our present appeal….

TOWARDS AMERICAN DEMOCRACY

Every effort to end the Cold War and expand the process of world industrialization is an effort hostile to people and institutions whose interests lie in perpetuation of the East-West military threat and the postponement of change in the "have not" nations of the world. Every such effort, too, is bound to establish greater democracy in America. The major goals of a domestic effort would be:

1. America must abolish its political party stalemate. Two genuine parties, centered around issues and essential values, demanding allegiance to party principles shall supplant the current system of organized stalemate which is seriously inadequate to a world in flux....
2. Mechanisms of voluntary association must be created through which political information can be imparted and political participation encouraged.... These do not exist in America in quantity today. If they did exist, they would be a significant politicizing and educative force bringing people into touch with public life and affording them means of expression and action. Today, giant lobby representatives of business interests are dominant, but not educative. The Federal government itself should counter the latter forces whose intent is often public deceit for private gain, by subsidizing the preparation and decentralized distribution of objective materials on all public issues facing government.
3. Institutions and practices which stifle dissent should be abolished, and the promotion of peaceful dissent should be actively promoted. The first Amendment freedoms of speech, assembly, thought, religion and press should be seen as guarantees, not threats, to national security. While society has the right to prevent active subversion of its laws and institutions, it has the duty as well to promote open discussion of all issues—otherwise it will be in fact promoting real subversion as the only means to implementing ideas. To eliminate the fears and apathy from national life it is necessary that the institutions bred by fear and apathy be rooted out: the House Un-American Activities Committee, the Senate Internal Security Committee, the loyalty oaths on Federal loans, the Attorney General's list of subversive organizations, the Smith and McCarran Acts. The process of eliminating these blighting institutions is the process of restoring democratic participation. Their existence is a sign of the decomposition and atrophy of the participation.
4. Corporations must be made publicly responsible. It is not possible to believe that true democracy can exist where a minority utterly controls enormous wealth and power....
5. The allocation of resources must be based on social needs. A truly "public sector" must be established, and its nature debated and planned....

All these tendencies suggest that not only solutions to our present social needs but our future expansion rests upon our willingness to enlarge the "public sector" greatly. Unless we choose war as an economic solvent, future public spending will be of a non-military nature—a major intervention into civilian production by the government. The issues posed by this development are enormous:...

5. America should concentrate on its genuine social priorities: abolish squalor, terminate neglect, and establish an environment for people to live in with dignity and creativeness.

6. A program against poverty must be just as sweeping as the nature of poverty itself. It must not be just palliative, but directed to the abolition of the structural circumstances of poverty. At a bare minimum it should include a housing act far larger than the one supported by the Kennedy Administration, but one that is geared more to low- and middle-income needs than to the windfall aspirations of small and large private entrepreneurs, one that is more sympathetic to the quality of communal life than to the efficiency of city-split highways. Second, medical care must become recognized as a lifetime human right just as vital as food, shelter and clothing—the Federal government should guarantee health insurance as a basic social service turning medical treatment into a social habit, not just an occasion of crisis, fighting sickness among the aged, not just by making medical care financially feasible but by reducing sickness among children and younger people. Third, existing institutions should be expanded so the Welfare State cares for everyone's welfare.... Social Security payments should be extended to everyone and should be proportionately greater for the poorest. A minimum wage of at least $1.50 should be extended to all workers (including the 16 million currently not covered at all). Equal educational opportunity is an important part of the battle against poverty.

7. A full-scale public initiative for civil rights should be undertaken despite the clamor among conservatives (and liberals) about gradualism, property rights, and law and order. The executive and legislative branches of the Federal government should work by enforcement and enactment against any form of exploitation of minority groups. No Federal cooperation with racism is tolerable—from financing of schools, to the development of Federally supported industry, to the social gatherings of the President. Laws ensuring school desegregation, voting rights, and economic protection for Negroes are needed right now....

8. The promise and problems of long-range Federal economic development should be studied more constructively.... given teeth, and pursued rigorously by Federal authorities.

We must meet the growing complex of "city" problems; over 90% of Americans will live in urban areas in the next two decades. Juvenile delinquency, untended mental illness, crime increase, slums, urban tenantry and uncontrolled housing, the isolation of the individual in the city—all are problems of the city and are major symptoms of the present system of economic priorities and lack of public planning....

ALTERNATIVES TO HELPLESSNESS

The goals we have set are not realizable next month, or even next election—but that fact justifies neither giving up altogether nor a determination to work only on immediate, direct, tangible problems. Both responses are a sign of helplessness, fearfulness of visions, refusal to hope, and tend to bring on the very conditions to be avoided. Fearing vision, we justify rhetoric or myopia. Fearing hope, we reinforce despair....

The bridge to political power, though, will be built through genuine cooperation, locally, nationally, and internationally, between a new left of young people, and an awakening community of allies. In each community we must look within the university and act with confidence that we can be powerful, but we must look outwards to the less exotic but more lasting struggles for justice.

To turn these possibilities into realities will involve national efforts at university reform by an alliance of students and faculty. They must wrest control of the educational process from the administrative bureaucracy. They must make fraternal and functional contact with allies in labor, civil rights, and other liberal forces outside the campus. They must import major public issues into the curriculum—research and teaching on problems of war and peace is an outstanding example. They must make debate and controversy, not dull pedantic cant, the common style for educational life. They must consciously build a base for their assault upon the loci of power.

As students for a democratic society, we are committed to stimulating this kind of social movement, this kind of vision and program is campus and community across the country. If we appear to seek the unattainable, it has been said, then let it be known that we do so to avoid the unimaginable.

Civics Online, http://www.civics-online.org/library/formatted/texts/port_huron.html.

24.4

RACHEL CARSON, *SILENT SPRING* (1962)

The 1960s were a pivotal time in the history of the modern environmental movement. In many communities, it became impossible to ignore the environmental damage resulting from industry, agriculture, and automobiles. In Cleveland, Ohio, for example, the Cuyahoga River periodically burst into flames when factories dumped petroleum byproducts into it. Such events prompted scientists, lawyers, and lobbyists to advocate federal environmental protection laws. Ecologists played a critical role in alerting the public to environmental hazards. Ecology, the study of the interrelationship between organisms and the environment, grew rapidly in the post-WWII years. Ecological concepts such as biodiversity, ecosystems, and endangered species gained wide acceptance.

The biologist Rachel Carson (1907-1964) was greatly influenced by ecology. After completing graduate study at Johns Hopkins University (M.A., 1932) and the Woods Hole Marine Biology Laboratory, Carson became an aquatic biologist for the U.S. Fish and Wildlife Service. Combining scientific knowledge and an approachable writing style, she wrote about the ocean in mainstream publications. Her second book, The Sea Around Us *(1951) was an international bestseller and won a National Book Award. In the late 1950s, Carson grew increasingly concerned about the impact of DDT (short for dichlorodiphenyltrichloroethane) and other pesticides. First used during World War II to combat insect-borne tropical diseases, DDT was thought harmless to humans and widely applied by farmers and gardeners. In 1962, Carson published her findings in* Silent Spring. *Within six months, the book sold 500,000 copies and generated worldwide awareness of the dangers posed by chemicals. Chemical industry executives unsuccessfully tried to suppress its publication and to discredit Carson. Due in large part to her research, the federal government established the Environmental Protection Agency in 1970 and outlawed the use of DDT in 1972. Sadly, Carson died of breast cancer before she could see the extraordinary impact of her work.*

■

FOCUS QUESTIONS

1. Why is Carson so alarmed by pesticides and other chemicals?
2. Why do you think that chemical industry reacted so negatively to *Silent Spring*?
3. How have attitudes toward the environment changed since Carson published *Silent Spring*?

T he contamination of our world is not alone a matter of mass spraying. Indeed, for most of us this is of less importance than the innumerable small-scale exposures to which we are subjected day by day, year by year. Like the constant dripping of water that tears away the hardest stone, this birth-to-death contact with dangerous chemicals may in the end prove disastrous. Each of these recurrent exposures, no matter how slight, contributes to the progressive build-up of chemicals in our bodies and so to cumulative poisoning. Probably no person is immune to contact with this spreading contamination unless he lives in the most isolated situation imaginable. Lulled by the soft sell and the hidden persuader, the average citizen is seldom aware of the deadly materials with which he is surrounding himself; indeed, he may not realize he is using them at all.

So thoroughly has the age of poisons become established that anyone may walk into a store and, without questions being asked, buy substances of far greater death-dealing power than the medicinal drug for which he may be required to sign a "poison book" in the pharmacy next door. A few minutes' research in any supermarket is enough to alarm the most stouthearted customer—provided, that is, that he has even a rudimentary knowledge of the chemicals presented for his choice.

If a huge skull and crossbones were suspended above the insecticide department the customer might at least enter it with the respect normally accorded death-dealing materials. But instead the display is homey and cheerful, and, with the pickles and olives across the aisle and the bath and laundry soaps adjoining, the rows upon rows of insecticides are displayed. Within easy reach of a child's exploring hand are chemicals in *glass* containers. If dropped to the floor by a child or careless adult everybody nearby could be splashed with the same chemical that has sent spraymen using it into convulsions. These hazards of course follow the purchaser right into his home. A can of a mothproofing material containing DDD [a close relative of DDT], for example, carries in very fine print the warning that its contents are under pressure and that it may burst if exposed to heat or open flame. A common insecticide for household use, including assorted uses in the kitchen, is chlordane. Yet the Food and Drug Administration's chief pharmacologist has declared the hazard of living in a house sprayed with chlordane to be "very great." Other household preparations contain the even more toxic dieldrin.

Use of poisons in the kitchen is made both attractive and easy. Kitchen shelf paper, white or tinted to match one's color scheme, may be impregnated with insecticide, not merely on one but on both sides. Manufacturers offer us do-it-yourself booklets on how to kill bugs. With push-button ease, one may send a fog of dieldrin into the most inaccessible nooks and crannies of cabinets, corners, and baseboards.

If we are troubled by mosquitoes, chiggers, or other insect pests on our persons we have a choice of innumerable lotions, creams, and sprays for application to clothing or skin. Although we are warned that some of these will dissolve varnish, paint, and synthetic fabrics, we are presumably to infer that the human skin is impervious to chemicals. To make certain that we shall at all times be prepared to repel insects, an exclusive New York store advertises a pocket-sized insecticide dispenser, suitable for the purse or for beach, golf or fishing gear.

We can polish our floors with a wax guaranteed to kill any insect that walks over it. We can hang strips impregnated with the chemical lindane in our closets and garment bags or place in our bureau drawers for a half year's freedom from worry over moth damage. The advertisements contain no suggestion that lindane is dangerous. Neither do the ads for an electronic device that dispenses lindane fumes—we are told that it is safe and odorless. Yet the truth of the matter is that the American Medical Association considers lindane vaporizers so dangerous that it conducted an extensive campaign against them in its *Journal*.

The Department of Agriculture, in a *Home and Garden Bulletin*, advises us to spray our clothing with oil solutions of DDT, dieldrin, chlordane, or any of several other moth killers. If excessive spraying results in a white deposit of insecticide on the fabric, this may be removed by brushing, the Department says, omitting to caution us to be careful where and how the brushing is done. All these matters attended to, we may round out our day with insecticides by going to sleep under a mothproof blanket impregnated with dieldrin.

Gardening is now firmly linked with the super poisons. Every hardware store, garden-supply shop, and supermarket has rows of insecticides for every conceivable horticultural situation. Those who fail to make wide use of this array of lethal sprays and dusts are by implication remiss, for almost every newspaper's garden page and the majority of the gardening magazines take their use for granted.

So extensively are even the rapidly lethal organic phosphorous insecticides applied to lawns and ornamental plants that in 1960 the Florida State Board of Health found it necessary to forbid the commercial use of pesticides in residential areas by anyone who had not first obtained a permit and met certain requirements.

A number of deaths from parathion had occurred in Florida before this regulation was adopted.

Little is done, however, to warn the gardener or homeowner that he is handling extremely dangerous materials. On the contrary, a constant stream of new gadgets make it easier to use poisons on lawn and garden—and increase the gardener's contact with them. One may get a jar-type attachment for the garden hose, for example, by which such extremely dangerous chemicals as chlordane or dieldrin are applied as one waters the lawn. Such a device is not only a hazard to the person using the hose; it is also a public menace. The *New York Times* found it necessary to issue a warning on its garden page to the effect that unless special protective devices were installed poisons might get into the water supply by back siphonage. Considering the number of such devices that are in use, and the scarcity of warnings such as this, do we need to wonder why our public waters are contaminated?

As an example of what may happen to the gardener himself, we might look at the case of a physician—an enthusiastic sparetime gardener—who began using DDT and then malathion on his shrubs and lawn, making regular weekly applications. Sometimes he applied the chemicals with a hand spray, sometimes with an attachment to his hose. In doing so, his skin and clothing were often soaked with spray. After about a year of this sort of thing, he suddenly collapsed and was hospitalized. Examinations of a biopsy specimen of fat showed an accumulation of 23 parts per million of DDT. There was extensive nerve damage, which his physicians regarded as permanent. As time went on he lost weight, suffered extreme fatigue, and experienced a peculiar muscular weakness, a characteristic effect of malathion. All of these persisting effects were severe enough to make it difficult for the physician to carry on his practice.

Besides the once-innocuous garden hose, power mowers also have been fitted with devices for the dissemination of pesticides, attachments that will dispense a cloud of vapor as the homeowner goes about the task of mowing his lawn. So to the potentially dangerous fumes from gasoline are added the finely divided particles of whatever insecticide the probably unsuspecting suburbanite has chosen to distribute, raising the level of air pollution above his own grounds to something few cities could equal.

Yet little is said about the hazards of the fad of gardening by poisons, or of insecticides used in the home; warnings on labels are printed so inconspicuously in small type that few take the trouble to read or follow them. An industrial firm recently undertook to find out just *how* few. Its survey indicated that fewer than fifteen people out of a hundred of those using insecticide aerosols and sprays are even aware of the warnings on the containers.

The mores of suburbia now dictate that crabgrass must go at whatever cost. Sacks containing chemicals designed to rid the lawn of such despised vegetation have become almost a status symbol. These weed-killing chemicals are sold under brand names that never suggest their identity or nature. To learn that they contain chlordane or dieldrin one must read exceedingly fine print placed on the least conspicuous part of the sack. The descriptive literature that may be picked up in any hardware- or garden-supply store seldom if ever reveals the true hazard involved in handling or applying the material. Instead, the typical illustration portrays a happy family scene, father and son smilingly preparing to apply the chemical to the lawn, small children tumbling over the grass with a dog.

Rachel Carson, *Silent Spring* (Boston: Houghton Mifflin Company, 1962), pp. 173-178.

24.5

BETTY FRIEDAN, *THE FEMININE MYSTIQUE* (1963)

During the early 1960s, several events exposed the disjuncture between the images and realities of American women's lives. As popular culture enthusiastically celebrated marriage and motherhood, women who expressed dissatisfaction with childrearing or homemaking were often dismissed as neurotic. Nonetheless, increasing numbers of women were working outside the home and attaining college degrees. Many of these women encountered job discrimination. The airlines, for example, routinely fired women who were older than thirty-two or who got married. In most industries, wage disparities between men and women were commonplace. The few feminist organizations that remained active were weak.

Women's issues gained renewed visibility with the election of John F. Kennedy. In 1961, he formed the Presidential Commission on the Status of Women. After the committee documented widespread pay inequities between the sexes, Congress passed the Equal Pay Act of 1963, which required equal wages for men and women in the same jobs. But the law's effect was limited since few women held such "male" jobs.

Betty Friedan's The Feminine Mystique *(1963) had a much larger impact. Born in Peoria, Illinois in 1921, Betty Goldstein graduated with a psychology degree from Smith College in 1942. After spending a year at the University of California-Berkeley, she moved to New York City. In 1947, she married Carl Friedan (they divorced in 1969). While working as a free-lance magazine writer, Friedan raised three children and lived as a suburban housewife. When she attended her college reunion in 1957, she circulated a questionnaire to her former classmates. Their answers revealed deep frustration and unhappiness. Struck by these results, Friedan interviewed dozens of women, psychologists, and other experts. She published her conclusions in* The Feminine Mystique. *The book became an immediate and controversial bestseller. Friedan received thousands of letters from grateful women. In 1966, she helped to found the National Organization for Women (NOW). She remains an active writer and women's activist.*

FOCUS QUESTIONS

1. According to Friedan, what is the "problem that has no name?" Why are so many women dissatisfied?
2. What solutions does Friedan propose?
3. Describe the social and political impact of *The Feminine Mystique*. Who do you think found Friedan's message most compelling? Who do you think found it most objectionable?

The problem lay buried, unspoken, for many years in the minds of American women. It was a strange stirring, a sense of dissatisfaction, a yearning that women suffered in the middle of the twentieth century in the United States. Each suburban wife struggled with it alone. As she made the beds, shopped for groceries, matched slipcover material, ate peanut butter sandwiches with her children, chauffeured Cub Scouts and Brownies, lay beside her husband at night— she was afraid to ask even of herself the silent question—"Is this all?"

For over fifteen years there was no word of this yearning in the millions of words written about women, for women, in all the columns, books and articles by experts telling women their role was to seek fulfillment as wives and mothers Over and over women heard in voices of tradition and of Freudian sophistication that they could desire no greater destiny than to glory in their own femininity. Experts told them how to catch a man and keep him, how to breastfeed children and handle their toilet training, how to cope with sibling rivalry and adolescent rebellion; how to buy a dishwasher, bake bread, cook gourmet snails, and build a swimming pool with their own hands, how to dress, look, and act more feminine and make marriage more exciting; how to keep their husbands from dying young and their sons from growing into delinquents. They were taught to pity the neurotic, unfeminine, unhappy women who wanted to be poets or physicists or presidents. They learned that truly feminine women do not want career, higher education, political rights—the independence and the opportunities that the old-fashioned feminists fought for. Some women, in their forties and fifties, still remembered painfully giving up those dreams, but most of the younger women no longer even thought about them. A thousand expert voices applauded their femininity, their adjustment, their new maturity. All they had to do was devote their lives from earliest girlhood to finding a husband and bearing children

In the fifteen years after World War II, this mystique of feminine fulfillment became the cherished and self-perpetuating core of contemporary American culture. Millions of women lived their lives in the image of those pretty pictures of the American suburban housewife, kissing their husbands goodbye in front of the picture window, depositing their stationwagonsful of children at school, and smiling as they ran the new electric waxer over the spotless kitchen floor. They baked their own bread, sewed their own and their children's clothes, kept their new washing machines and dryers running all day. They changed the sheets on the beds twice a week instead of once, took the rug-hooking class in adult education, and pitied their poor frustrated mother, who had dreamed of having a career. Their only dream was to be perfect wives and mothers; their highest ambition to have five children and a beautiful house, their only fight to get and keep their husbands. They had no thought for the unfeminine problems of the world outside the home; they wanted the men to make the major decisions. They gloried in their role as women, and wrote proudly on the census blank "Occupation: housewife."...

If a woman had a problem in the 1950's and 1960's, she knew that something must be wrong with her marriage, or with herself. Other women were satisfied with their lives, she thought. What kind of a woman was she if she did not feel this mysterious fulfillment waxing the kitchen floor? She was so ashamed to admit her dissatisfaction that she never knew how many other women shared it. If she tried to tell her husband, he didn't understand what she was talking about. She did not understand it herself. For over fifteen years women in America found it harder to talk about the problem than about sex. Even the psychoanalysts had no name for it. When a woman did, she would say, "I am so ashamed," or "I must be hopelessly neurotic."...

Gradually I came to realize that the problem that has no name was shared by countless women in America.... The groping words I heard from other women, on quiet afternoons when children were at school or on quiet evenings when husbands worked late, I think I understood first as a woman long before I understood their larger social and psychological implications.

Just what was this problem that has no name? What were the words women used when they tried to express it? Sometimes a woman would say "I feel empty somehow...incomplete." Or she would say, "I feel as if I don't exist." Sometimes she blotted out the feeling with a tranquilizer. Sometimes she thought the problem was with her husband, or her children, or that what she really needed was to redecorate her house, or move to a better neighborhood, or have an affair, or another baby. Sometimes, she went to a doctor with symptoms she could hardly describe: "A tired feeling...I get so angry with the children it scares me...I feel like crying without any reason." (A Cleveland doctor called it "the housewife's syndrome.")...

It is no longer possible to ignore that voice, to dismiss the desperation of so many American women. This is not what being a woman means, no matter what the experts say. For human suffering there is a reason; perhaps the reason has not been found because the right questions have not been asked, or pressed far enough. I do not accept the answer that there is no problem because American women have luxuries that women in other times and lands never dreamed of; part of the strange newness of the problem is that it cannot be understood it terms of the age-old material problems of man: poverty, sickness, hunger, cold....

It is no longer possible today to blame the problem on loss of femininity: to say that education and independence and equality with men have made American women unfeminine. I have heard so many women try to deny this dissatisfied voice within themselves because it does not fit the pretty-picture of femininity the experts have given them. I think, in fact, that this is the first clue to the mystery: the problem cannot be understood in the generally accepted terms by which scientists have studied women, doctors have treated them, counselors have advised them, and writers have written them. Women who suffer this problem in whom this voice is tiring, have lived their whole lives in the pursuit of feminine fulfillment. They are not career women (although career women may have other problems); they are women whose greatest ambition has been marriage and children. For the oldest of these women, these daughters of the American middle class, no other dream was possible. The ones in their forties and fifties who once had other dreams gave them up and threw themselves joyously into life as housewives. For the youngest, the new wives and mothers, this was the only dream. They are the ones who quit high school and college to marry, or marked time in some job in which they had no real interest until they married. These women are very "feminine" in the usual sense, and yet they still suffer the problem....

If I am right, the problem that has no name stirring in the midst of so many American women today is not a matter of loss of femininity or too much education, or demands of domesticity. It is far more important than anyone recognizes. It is the key to women and their husbands and children, and puzzling their doctors and educators for years. It may well be the key to our future as a nation and a culture. We can no longer ignore that voice within women that says: "I want something more than my husband and my children and my home."

The Feminine Mystique by Betty Friedan. Copyright © 1983, 1974, 1973, 1963 by Betty Friedan. Used with permission of W.W. Norton & Company, Inc.

24.6

MARTIN LUTHER KING, JR., LETTER FROM A BIRMINGHAM JAIL (1963)

In the spring of 1963, Martin Luther King, Jr. and the Southern Christian Leadership Conference (SCLC) joined Reverend Fred Shuttleworth's Alabama Christian Movement for Human Rights in an attempt to integrate Birmingham, Alabama. Known as one of the most segregated cities in America, Birmingham was a formidable target. When civil rights demonstrators organized sit-ins and marches, police arrested and imprisoned them. When black children joined the protests, Police Commissioner Eugene "Bull" Connor directed his men to attack them with dogs, cattle prods, and firehouses. Media coverage of the assaults generated an international uproar.

Martin Luther King, Jr. (1929-1968) was among those arrested in Birmingham. While completing a doctorate in theology at Boston University, King had become pastor of the Dexter Avenue Baptist Church in Montgomery, Alabama. In December 1955, after Rosa Parks's arrest for refusing to yield her seat to a white passenger triggered a citywide bus boycott, activists chose King to lead the newly formed Montgomery Improvement Association. King's eloquent advocacy of non-violent social protest gained national attention. After a 444-day boycott in Montgomery, a federal court ordered the desegregation of the city's buses. Hoping to build on this success, King organized the SCLC. He lectured about the civil rights movement to dozens of audiences in the United States and abroad. In 1960, he moved to Atlanta with his wife Coretta Scott King and their four children to become co-pastor of the Ebenezer Baptist Church. In October, he and 33 students were arrested during a sit-in at a local department store. Although the charges against King were dropped, he was sent to a prison farm for an earlier traffic violation. His incarceration and Dwight Eisenhower's failure to intervene triggered a national outcry. In response, presidential candidate John F. Kennedy secured King's release. The move inspired thousands of African Americans to vote for JFK. Kennedy, however, was not initially a forceful advocate for racial equality. By the time that King reached Birmingham, he was very concerned about the state of the civil rights movement. In 1961-1962, SCLC had suffered several setbacks including the failure to integrate Albany, Georgia. King desperately needed a victory to prove that non-violence worked.

While King sat in a Birmingham jail, a group of eight white ministers implored him to cancel the demonstrations. Denied writing paper by the prison guards, King composed his reply in the margins of a copy of the New York Times *and on pieces of scrap paper. After passage of the Civil Rights Act of 1964, King won the Nobel Peace Prize.*

Focus Questions

1. Why is King responding to these ministers? How does he refute their arguments?
2. What are the principles of non-violent direct action? How does King justify violating segregation laws?
3. Why does King reject gradualism?
4. Why is King so dissatisfied with white moderates?
5. What does King predict will happen if his non-violent strategies fail?
6. Compare King's arguments to those of Malcolm X (Document 24.7). Whose vision for improving the lives of African Americans do you find more compelling? Why?

April 16, 1963

Y DEAR FELLOW CLERGYMEN:
While confined here in the Birmingham City Jail, I came across your recent statement calling our present activities "unwise and untimely." Seldom, if ever, do I pause to answer criticism of my work and ideas.... But since I feel that you are men of genuine goodwill and your criticisms are sincerely set

forth, I would like to answer your statement in what I hope will be patient and reasonable terms.

I think I should give the reason for my being in Birmingham, since you have been influenced by the argument of "outsiders coming in."... I am here...because I have basic organizational ties here. Beyond this, I am in Birmingham because injustice is here....

Moreover, I am cognizant of the interrelatedness of all communities and states. I cannot sit idly by in Atlanta and not be concerned about what happens in Birmingham. Injustice anywhere is a threat to justice everywhere....

You deplore the demonstrations that are presently taking place in Birmingham. But I am sorry that your statement did not express a similar concern for the conditions that brought the demonstrations into being....

There can be no gainsaying of the fact that racial injustice engulfs this community. Birmingham is probably the most thoroughly segregated city in the United States. Its ugly record of police brutality is known in every section of this country. Its unjust treatment of Negroes in the courts is a notorious reality. There have been more unsolved bombings of Negro homes and churches in Birmingham than any city in this nation. These are the hard, brutal and unbelievable facts.

On the basis of these conditions, Negro leaders sought to negotiate with the city fathers. But the political leaders consistently refused to engage in good faith negotiation. Then came the opportunity last September to talk with some of the leaders of the economic community. In these negotiating sessions certain promises were made by the merchants—such as the promise to remove the humiliating racial signs from the stores.

On the basis of these promises Rev. Shuttlesworth and the leaders of the Alabama Christian Movement for Human Rights agreed to call a moratorium on any type of demonstrations. As the weeks and months unfolded we realized that we were the victims of a broken promise. The signs remained.

As in so many experiences of the past we were confronted with blasted hopes, and the dark shadow of a deep disappointment settled upon us. So we had no alternative except that of preparing for direct action, whereby we would present our very bodies as a means of laying our case before the conscience of the local and national community.

We were not unmindful of the difficulties involved. So we decided to go through a process of self-purification. We started having workshops on nonviolence and repeatedly asked ourselves the questions: "Are you able to accept blows without retaliating?" "Are you able to endure the ordeals of jail?"...

You may well ask: "Why direct action? Why sit-ins, marches, etc.? Isn't negotiation a better path?" You are exactly right in your call for negotiation. Indeed, this is the purpose of direct action. Nonviolent direct action seeks to create such a crisis and establish such creative tension that a community that has constantly refused to negotiate is forced to confront the issue. It seeks so to dramatize the issue that it can no longer be ignored....

One of the basic points in your statement is that our acts are untimely. Some have asked, "Why didn't you give the new administration time to act?" The only answer that I can give to this inquiry is that the new Birmingham administration must be prodded about as much as the outgoing one before it acts....

My friends, I must say to you that we have not made a single gain in civil rights without determined legal and nonviolent pressure.... We know through painful experience that freedom is never voluntarily given by the oppressor; it must be demanded by the oppressed. Frankly, I have never yet engaged in a direct action movement that was "well timed," according to the timetable of those who have not suffered unduly from the disease of segregation.

For years now I have heard the words [sic] "Wait!" It rings in the ear of every Negro with a piercing familiarity. This "Wait" has almost always meant "Never." We must come to see with the distinguished jurist of yesterday that "justice too long delayed is justice denied."

We have waited for more than three hundred and forty years for our constitutional and God-given rights. The nations of Asia and Africa are moving with jet-like speed toward the goal of political independence, and we still creep at horse and buggy pace toward the gaining of a cup of coffee at a lunch counter. I guess it is easy for those who have never felt the stinging darts of segregation to say, "Wait."

But when you have seen vicious mobs lynch your mothers and fathers at will and drown your sisters and brothers at whim;

when you have seen hate filled policemen curse, kick, brutalize and even kill your black brothers and sisters with impunity;

when you see the vast majority of your twenty million Negro brothers smothering in an airtight cage of poverty in the midst of an affluent society;

when you suddenly find your tongue twisted and your speech stammering as you seek to explain to your six-year-old daughter why she can't go to the public amusement park that has just been advertised on television, and see tears welling up in her eyes when she is told that Funtown is closed to colored children, and see the depressing clouds of inferiority begin to form in her little mental sky, and see her begin to distort her little personality by unconsciously developing a bitterness toward white people;

when you have to concoct an answer for a five-year-old son asking in agonizing pathos: "Daddy, why do white people treat colored people so mean?";

when you take a cross-country drive and find it necessary to sleep night after night in the uncomfortable corners of your automobile because no motel will accept you;

when you are humiliated day in and day out by nagging signs reading "white" and "colored";

when your first name becomes "nigger," your middle name becomes "boy" (however old you are) and your last name becomes "John," and your wife and mother are never given the respected title "Mrs.";

when you are harried by day and haunted by night by the fact that you are a Negro, living constantly at tip-toe stance never quite knowing what to expect next, and plagued with inner fears and outer resentments;

when you are forever fighting a degenerating sense of "nobodiness"—then you will understand why we find it difficult to wait.

There comes a time when the cup of endurance runs over, and men are no longer willing to be plunged into an abyss of despair. I hope, sirs, you can understand our legitimate and unavoidable impatience.

You express a great deal of anxiety over our willingness to break laws. This is certainly a legitimate concern. Since we so diligently urge people to obey the Supreme Court's decision of 1954 outlawing segregation in the public schools, it is rather strange and paradoxical to find us consciously breaking laws.

One may well ask: "How can you advocate breaking some laws and obeying others?" The answer is found in the fact that there are two types of laws: There are just and there are unjust laws. I would agree with Saint Augustine that "An unjust law is no law at all."

Now, what is the difference between the two? How does one determine when a law is just or unjust? A just law is a man-made code that squares with the moral law or the law of God. An unjust law is a code that is out of harmony with the moral law.

To put it in the terms of Saint Thomas Aquinas, an unjust law is a human law that is not rooted in eternal and natural law. Any law that uplifts human personality is just. Any law that degrades human personality is unjust.

All segregation statutes are unjust because segregation distorts the soul and damages the personality. It gives the segregator a false sense of superiority, and the segregated a false sense of inferiority....

Let me give another explanation. An unjust law is a code inflicted upon a minority which that minority had no part in enacting or creating because they did not have the unhampered right to vote. Who can say that the legislature of Alabama which set up the segregation laws was democratically elected?

Throughout the state of Alabama all types of conniving methods are used to prevent Negroes from becoming registered voters and there are some counties without a single Negro registered to vote despite the fact that the Negro constitutes a majority of the population. Can any law set up in such a state be considered democratically structured?...

I hope you can see the distinction I am trying to point out. In no sense do I advocate evading or defying the law as the rabid segregationist would do. This would lead to anarchy.

One who breaks an unjust law must do it openly, lovingly,...and with a willingness to accept the penalty. I submit that an individual who breaks a law that conscience tells him is unjust, and willingly accepts the penalty by staying in jail to arouse the conscience of the community over its injustice, is in reality expressing the very highest respect for law....

I must confess that over the last few years I have been gravely disappointed with the white moderate. I have almost reached the regrettable conclusion that the Negro's great stumbling block in the stride toward freedom is not the White Citizen's Council-er or the Ku Klux Klanner, but the white moderate who is more devoted to "order" than to justice; who prefers a negative peace which is the absence of tension to a positive peace which is the presence of justice; who constantly says "I agree with you in the goal you seek, but I can't agree with your methods of direct action;" who paternalistically feels he can set the timetable for another man's freedom; who lives by the myth of time and who constantly advises the Negro to wait until a "more convenient season."

Shallow understanding from people of goodwill is more frustrating than absolute misunderstanding from people of ill will. Lukewarm acceptance is much more bewildering than outright rejection....

In your statement you asserted that our actions, even though peaceful, must be condemned because they precipitate violence. But can this assertion be logically made? Isn't this like condemning the robbed man because his possession of money precipitated the evil act of robbery?...

We must come to see, as the federal courts have consistently affirmed, that it is immoral to urge an individual to withdraw his efforts to gain his basic constitutional rights because the quest precipitates violence. Society must protect the robbed and punish the robber.

I had also hoped that the white moderate would reject the myth of time.... Actually time is neutral. It can be used either destructively or constructively. I am coming to feel that the people of ill-will have used time much more effectively than the people of good will. We will have to repent in this generation not merely for the vitriolic words and actions of the bad people, but for the appalling silence of the good people....

You spoke of our activity in Birmingham as extreme. At first I was rather disappointed that fellow clergymen would see my nonviolent efforts as those of the extremist. I started thinking about the fact that I stand in the middle of two opposing forces in the Negro community.

One is a force of complacency made up of Negroes who, as a result of long years of oppression, have been so completely drained of self-respect and a sense of "somebodiness" that they have adjusted to segregation, and, of a few Negroes in the middle class who, because of a degree of academic and economic security, and because at points they profit by segregation, have unconsciously become insensitive to the problems of the masses.

The other force is one of bitterness, and hatred comes perilously close to advocating violence. It is expressed in the various black nationalist groups that are springing up over the nation, the largest and best-known being Elijah Muhammad's Muslim movement. This movement is nourished by the contemporary frustration over the continued existence of racial discrimination. It is made up of people who have lost faith in America, who have absolutely repudiated Christianity, and who have concluded that the white man is an incurable "devil."

I have tried to stand between these two forces saying that we need not follow the "do-nothingism" of the complacent or the hatred and despair of the black nationalist. There is the more excellent way of love and nonviolent protest. I'm grateful to God that, through the Negro church, the dimension of nonviolence entered our struggle.

If this philosophy had not emerged, I am convinced that by now many streets of the South would be flowing with floods of blood. And I am further convinced that if our white brothers dismiss as "rabble rousers" and "outside agitators" those of us who are working through the channels of nonviolent direct action and refuse to support our nonviolent efforts, millions of Negroes, out of frustration and despair, will seek solace and security in black-nationalist ideologies, a development that will lead inevitably to a frightening racial nightmare.

Oppressed people cannot remain oppressed forever. The urge for freedom will eventually come. This is what happened to the American Negro. Something within has reminded him of his birthright of freedom; something without has reminded him that he can gain it…. Recognizing this vital urge that has engulfed the Negro community, one should readily understand public demonstrations. The Negro has many pent up resentments and latent frustrations. He has to get them out. So let him march sometime; let him have his prayer pilgrimages to the city hall; understand why he must have sit-ins and freedom rides.

If his repressed emotions do not come out in these nonviolent ways, they will come out in ominous expressions of violence. This is not a threat; it is a fact of history….

I had hoped that the white moderate would see this. Maybe I was too optimistic. Maybe I expected too much. I guess I should have realized that few members of a race that has oppressed another race can understand or appreciate the deep groans and passionate yearnings of those that have been oppressed and still fewer have the vision to see that injustice must be rooted out by strong, persistent and determined action.

I am thankful, however, that some of our white brothers have grasped the meaning of this social revolution and committed themselves to it. They are still all too small in quantity, but they are big in quality. Some like Ralph McGill, Lillian Smith, Harry Golden and James Dabbs have written about our struggle in eloquent, prophetic and understanding terms.

Others have marched with us down nameless streets of the South. They have languished in filthy roach-infested jails, suffering the abuse and brutality of angry policemen who see them as "dirty nigger lovers." They, unlike so many of their moderate brothers and sisters, have recognized the urgency of the moment and sensed the need for powerful "action" antidotes to combat the disease of segregation….

I must close now. But before closing I am impelled to mention one other point in your statement that troubled me profoundly. You warmly commended the Birmingham police force for keeping "order" and "preventing violence." I don't believe you would have so warmly commended the police force if you had seen its angry violent dogs literally biting six unarmed, nonviolent Negroes. I don't believe you would so quickly commend the policemen if you would observe their ugly and inhuman treatment of Negroes here in the city jail; if you would watch them push and curse old Negro women and young Negro girls; if you would see them slap and kick old Negro men and young boys; if you will observe them, as they did on two occasions, refuse to give us food because we wanted to sing our grace together. I'm sorry that I can't join you in your praise for the police department....

I wish you had commended the Negro sit-inners and demonstrators of Birmingham for their sublime courage, their willingness to suffer and their amazing discipline in the midst of the most inhuman provocation. One day the South will recognize its real heroes. They will be the James Merediths, courageously and with a majestic sense of purpose, facing jeering and hostile mobs and with the agonizing loneliness that characterizes the life of the pioneer. They will be old oppressed, battered Negro women, symbolized in a seventy-two year old woman of Montgomery, Alabama, who rose up with a sense of dignity and with her people decided not to ride the segregated buses, and responded to one who inquired about her tiredness with ungrammatical profundity; "my feet is tired, but my soul is rested."

They will be the young high school and college students, young ministers of the gospel and a host of their elders courageously and nonviolently sitting-in at lunch counters and willingly going to jail for conscience's sake. One day the South will know that when these disinherited children of God sat down at lunch counters they were in reality standing up for the best in the American dream and the most sacred values in our Judeo-Christian heritage, and thusly, carrying our whole nation back to those great wells of democracy which were dug deep by the founding fathers in the formulation of the Constitution and the Declaration of Independence.

Never before have I written a letter this long, (or should I say a book?). I'm afraid it is much too long to take your precious time. I can assure you that it would have been much shorter if I had been writing from a comfortable desk, but what else is there to do when you are alone for days in the dull monotony of a narrow jail cell other than write long letters, think strange thoughts, and pray long prayers?...

Yours for the cause of Peace and Brotherhood,
Martin Luther King, Jr.

Martin Luther King, Jr., *Why We Can't Wait* (1963). Reprinted by arrangement with the Estate of Martin Luther King, Jr. c/o Writers House as agent for the proprietor New York, NY. Copyright 1963 Dr. Martin Luther King, Jr., copyright renewed 1991, Coretta Scott King.

24.7

MALCOLM X, "THE BALLOT OR THE BULLET" (1964)

Not all African Americans believed that integration would bring racial equality. Some found inspiration in the separatist teachings of Malcolm X (1925-1965). Born Malcolm Little, Malcolm's boyhood was seared by racial violence.

Earl Little, his father, was an outspoken Baptist minister and supporter of Marcus Garvey's United Negro Improvement Association. In 1929, the KKK burned down the Littles' Michigan home. Two years later, Earl's mutilated corpse was found lying across East Lansing's streetcar tracks—it was widely rumored that white supremacists had murdered him. After their mother had a nervous breakdown and was committed to a mental hospital, Malcolm and his seven siblings were placed in foster care and orphanages. Though a bright student, Malcolm lost interest in school and drifted into crime. By 1942, he was living in Harlem and involved in drugs, prostitution, and gambling. In 1946, he received a seven-year sentence for burglary.

While in jail, Malcolm joined the Nation of Islam, a black religious sect. Upon his release in 1952, he moved to Chicago to work with Elijah Muhammad, leader of the Nation of Islam. Abandoning his "slave" name Little, Malcolm adopted the surname "X" as a symbol of his lost family lineage. A riveting speaker, Malcolm traveled the country preaching the Nation of Islam's philosophy of racial separation, black superiority, and self-sufficiency. He founded several new mosques and was largely responsible for a significant increase in the Nation's membership. His characterization of whites as "devils," rejection of integration, and advocacy of violence if used in self-defense contrasted sharply with the views of Martin Luther King, Jr. His inflammatory rhetoric terrified many whites and prompted the Federal Bureau of Investigation (FBI) to infiltrate the Nation of Islam.

In March 1964, after months of feuding with Elijah Muhammad, Malcolm broke with the Nation. The following month, he made the customary Muslim pilgrimage to Mecca, Saudi Arabia. He returned to the United States profoundly changed. He abandoned his view that whites were inherently evil and began working with civil rights activists. He converted to traditional Islam and changed his name to el-Hajj Malik el-Shabazz. In February 1965, after escaping several previous attempts on his life, Malcolm was assassinated by members of the Nation of Islam.

Malcolm's influence grew tremendously upon publication of The Autobiography of Malcolm X *(1965). Written with Alex Haley before his death, the book became an instant classic. Malcolm is now considered one of the most significant figures in African-American history. He made the following speech on April 3, 1964 at a Congress of Racial Equality (CORE) symposium in Cleveland, Ohio. The U.S. Congress was then locked in a months-long filibuster on John F. Kennedy's proposed civil rights law. Two weeks after giving this address, Malcolm made his life-changing trip to Mecca.*

———————■———————

FOCUS QUESTIONS

1. How would you describe Malcolm's tone? What are the main themes of his speech?
2. How does Malcolm characterize white America? What is his opinion of the American political process?

3. What solutions does Malcolm propose? How does he define black nationalism?
4. Compare Malcolm's speech to Martin Luther King, Jr.'s "Letter from a Birmingham Jail"? (Document 24.6) Whose vision for improving the lives of African Americans do you find more compelling? Why?

...B rothers and sisters, friends and enemies: I just can't believe everyone in here is a friend and I don't want to leave anybody out. The question tonight, as I understand it, is "The Negro Revolt, and Where Do We Go from Here?" or "What Next?" In my little humble way of understanding it, it points toward either the ballot or the bullet....

Although I'm still a Muslim, I'm not here tonight to discuss my religion. I'm not here to try and change your religion. I'm not here to argue or discuss anything that we differ about, because it's time for us to submerge our differences and realize that it is best for us to first see that we have the same problem, a common problem, a problem that will make you catch hell whether you're a Baptist, or a Methodist, or a Muslim, or a nationalist. Whether you're educated or illiterate, whether you live on the boulevard or in the alley, you're going to catch hell just like I am. We're all in the same boat and we all are going to catch the same hell from the same man. He just happens to be a white man. All of us have suffered here, in this country, political oppression at the hands of the white man, economic exploitation at the hands of the white man, and social degradation at the hands of the white man.

Now in speaking like this, it doesn't mean that we're anti-white, but it does mean we're anti-exploitation, we're anti-degradation, we're anti-oppression. And if the white man doesn't want us to be anti-him, let him stop oppressing and exploiting and degrading us. Whether we are Christians or Muslims or nationalists or agnostics or atheists, we must first learn to forget our differences. If we have differences, let us differ in the closet; when we come out in front, let us not have anything to argue about until we get finished arguing with the man....

If we don't do something real soon, I think you'll have to agree that we're going to be forced either to use the ballot or the bullet. It's one or the other in 1964. It isn't that time is running out—time has run out! 1964 threatens to be the most explosive year America has ever witnessed. The most explosive year. Why? It's also a political year. It's the year when all of the white politicians will be back in the so-called Negro community jiving you and me for some votes. The year when all of the white political crooks will be right back in your and my community with their false promises, building up our hopes for a letdown, with their trickery and their treachery, with their false promises which they don't intend to keep. As they nourish these dissatisfactions, it can only lead to one thing, an explosion; and now we have the type of black man on the scene in America today...who just doesn't intend to turn the other cheek any longer....

I'm not a politician, not even a student of politics; in fact, I'm not a student of much of anything. I'm not a Democrat, I'm not a Republican, and I don't even consider myself an American. If you and I were Americans, there'd be no problem. Those Hunkies that just got off the boat, they're already Americans;

Polacks are already Americans; the Italian refugees are already Americans. Everything that came out of Europe, every blue-eyed thing, is already an American. And as long as you and I have been over here, we aren't Americans yet.

Well, I am one who doesn't believe in deluding myself. I'm not going to sit at your table and watch you eat, with nothing on my plate, and call myself a diner. Sitting at the table doesn't make you a diner, unless you eat some of what's on that plate. Being here in America doesn't make you an American. Being born here in America doesn't make you an American. Why, if birth made you American, you wouldn't need any legislation, you wouldn't need any amendments to the Constitution, you wouldn't be faced with civil-rights filibustering in Washington, D.C., right now. They don't have to pass civil-rights legislation to make a Polack an American.

No, I'm not an American. I'm one of the 22 million black people who are the victims of Americanism. One of the 22 million black people who are the victims of democracy, nothing but disguised hypocrisy....

These 22 million victims are waking up. Their eyes are coming open. They're beginning to see what they used to only look at. They're becoming politically mature. They are realizing that there are new political trends from coast to coast. As they see these new political trends, it's possible for them to see that every time there's an election the races are so close that they have to have a recount.... Well, what does this mean? It means that when white people are evenly divided, and black people have a bloc of votes of their own, it is left up to them to determine who's going to sit in the White House and who's going to be in the dog house.

It was the black man's vote that put the present administration in Washington, D.C. Your vote, your dumb vote, your ignorant vote, your wasted vote put in an administration in Washington, D.C., that has seen fit to pass every kind of legislation imaginable, saving you until last, then filibustering on top of that. And your and my leaders have the audacity to run around clapping their hands and talk about how much progress we're making. And what a good president we have. If he wasn't good in Texas, he sure can't be good in Washington, D.C. Because Texas is a lynch state. It is in the same breath as Mississippi, no different; only they lynch you in Texas with a Texas accent and lynch you in Mississippi with a Mississippi accent. And these Negro leaders have the audacity to go and have some coffee in the White House with a Texan [Kennedy's successor, Lyndon B. Johnson], a Southern cracker—that's all he is—and then come out and tell you and me that he's going to be better for us because, since he's from the South, he knows how to deal with the Southerners....

So it's time in 1964 to wake up.... It's got to be the ballot or the bullet. The ballot or the bullet. If you're afraid to use an expression like that, you should get on out of the country, you should get back in the cotton patch, you should get back in the alley. They get all the Negro vote, and after they get it, the Negro gets nothing in return....

I was in Washington, D.C., a week ago Thursday, when they were debating whether or not they should let the bill come onto the floor. And in the back of the room where the Senate meets, there's a huge map of the United States, and on that map it shows the location of Negroes throughout the country. And it shows that the Southern section of the country, the states that are most heavily concentrated with Negroes, are the ones that have senators and congressmen standing up filibustering and doing all other kinds of trickery to keep the Negro from being able to vote. This is pitiful. But it's not pitiful for us any longer; it's actually pitiful for the white man, because soon now, as the Negro awakens a little more and sees the vise that he's in, sees the bag that he's in, sees the real game that he's in, then the Negro's going to develop a new tactic.

These senators and congressmen actually violate the constitutional amendments that guarantee the people of that particular state or county the right to vote. And the Constitution itself has within it the machinery to expel any representative from a state where the voting rights of the people are violated. You don't even need new legislation....

If the black man in these Southern states had his full voting rights, the key Dixiecrats in Washington, D. C., which means the key Democrats in Washington, D.C., would lose their seats. The Democratic Party itself would lose its power. It would cease to be powerful as a party....

In the North, they do it a different way. They have a system that's known as gerrymandering, whatever that means. It means when Negroes become too heavily concentrated in a certain area, and begin to gain too much political power, the white man comes along and changes the district lines. You may say, "Why do you keep saying white man?" Because it's the white man who does it. I haven't ever seen any Negro changing any lines. They don't let him get near the line....

So, what I'm trying to impress upon you, in essence, is this: You and I in America are faced not with a segregationist conspiracy, we're faced with a government conspiracy. Everyone who's filibustering is a senator—that's the government. Everyone who's finagling in Washington, D.C., is a congressman— that's the government. You don't have anybody putting blocks in your path but people who are a part of the government. The same government that you go abroad to fight for and die for is the government that is in a conspiracy to deprive you of your voting rights, deprive you of your economic opportunities, deprive you of decent housing, deprive you of decent education. You don't need to go to the employer alone, it is the government itself, the government of America, that is responsible for the oppression and exploitation and degradation of black people in this country. And you should drop it in their lap. This government has failed the Negro. This so-called democracy has failed the Negro. And all these white liberals have definitely failed the Negro....

Whenever you're going after something that belongs to you, anyone who's depriving you of the right to have it is a criminal. Understand that. Whenever you are going after something that is yours, you are within your legal rights to lay claim to it. And anyone who puts forth any effort to deprive you of that which is yours, is breaking the law, is a criminal. And this was pointed out by the Supreme Court decision. It outlawed segregation. Which means segregation is against the law. Which means a segregationist is breaking the law. A segregationist is a criminal.

You can't label him as anything other than that. And when you demonstrate against segregation, the law is on your side. The Supreme Court is on your side.

Now, who is it that opposes you in carrying out the law? The police department itself. With police dogs and clubs. Whenever you demonstrate against segregation, whether it is segregated education, segregated housing, or anything else, the law is on your side, and anyone who stands in the way is not the law any longer. They are breaking the law, they are not representatives of the law. Any time you demonstrate against segregation and a man has the audacity to put a police dog on you, kill that dog, kill him, I'm telling you, kill that dog....

If you don't take this kind of stand, your little children will grow up and look at you and think "shame." If you don't take an uncompromising stand—I don't mean go out and get violent; but at the same time you should never be nonviolent unless you run into some nonviolence. I'm nonviolent with those who are nonviolent with me. But when you drop that violence on me, then you've made me go insane, and I'm not responsible for what I do. And that's the way every Negro should get. Any time you know you're within the law, within your legal rights, within your moral rights, in accord with justice, then die for what you believe in. But don't die alone. Let your dying be reciprocal. This is what is meant by equality....

When we begin to get in this area, we need new fiends, we need new allies. We need to expand the civil-rights struggle to a higher level—to the level of human rights. Whenever you are in a civil-rights struggle, whether you know it or not, you are confining yourself to the jurisdiction of Uncle Sam. No one from the outside world can speak out in your behalf as long as your struggle is a civil-rights struggle. Civil rights comes within the domestic affairs of this country....

When you expand the civil-rights struggle to the level of human rights, you can then take the case of the black man in this country before the nations in the UN. You can take it before the General Assembly. You can take Uncle Sam before a world court.... Uncle Sam's hands are dripping with blood, dripping with the blood of the black man in this country. He's the earth's number-one hypocrite. He has the audacity—yes, he has—imagine him posing as the leader of the free world. The free world! And you over here singing "We Shall Overcome." Expand the civil-rights struggle to the level of human rights, take it into the United Nations, where our African brothers can throw their weight on our side, where our Asian brothers can throw their weight on our side, where our Latin-American brothers can throw their weight on our side, and where 800 million Chinamen are sitting there waiting to throw their weight on our side....

The political philosophy of black nationalism means that the black man should control the politics and the politicians in his own community....

The economic philosophy of black nationalism is pure and simple. It only means that we should control the economy of our community. Why should white people be running all the stores in our community? Why should white people be running the banks of our community? Why should the economy of our community be in the hands of the white man?...Our people have to be made to see that any time you take your dollar out of your community and spend it in a community where you don't live, the community where you live will get poorer and poorer, and the community where you spend your money will get richer and richer.... If we own the stores, if we operate the businesses, if we try and establish some industry in our own community, then we're developing to the position where we are creating employment for our own kind. Once you gain control of the economy of your own community, then you don't have to picket and boycott and beg some cracker downtown for a job in his business.

The social philosophy of black nationalism only means that we have to get together and remove the evils, the vices, alcoholism, drug addiction, and other evils that are destroying the moral fiber of our community. We our selves have to lift the level of our community, the standard of our community to a higher level, make our own society beautiful....

So I say, in spreading a gospel such as black nationalism, it is not designed to make the black man re-evaluate the white man—you know him already—but to make the black man re-evaluate himself. Don't change the white man's mind— you can't change his mind, and that whole thing about appealing to the moral conscience of America—America's conscience is bankrupt....

We want to hear new ideas and new solutions and new answers. And at that time, if we see fit then to form a black nationalist party, we'll form a black nationalist party. If it's necessary to form a black nationalist army, we'll form a black nationalist army. It'll be the ballot or the bullet. It'll be liberty or it'll be death....

George Breitman, ed. *Malcolm X Speaks: Selected Speeches and Statements* (New York: Grove Weidenfeld, 1965, reprint 1990), pp. 23-44.

24.8

LYNDON JOHNSON PROPOSES THE "GREAT SOCIETY" (1964)

Raised in an impoverished part of southwest Texas, Lyndon B. Johnson (1908-1973) succeeded through sheer force of will. While attending Southwest Texas State Teachers College, he taught at a predominately Mexican-American school and was deeply affected by his students' poverty. Upon graduating, he began working in Washington, D.C. as a legislative assistant to a Texas congressman. In 1934, he married Claudia "Lady Bird" Taylor. In 1937, he won election to the U.S. House of Representatives. Twelve years later, he won a seat in the U.S. Senate. He quickly ascended through the Democratic ranks and in 1955, became the youngest Senate majority leader ever. Johnson possessed an extraordinary talent for effecting compromises and built a powerful Democratic coalition.

Although he was disappointed when he lost the 1960 presidential nomination to John F. Kennedy, he agreed to be Kennedy's running mate. He found the vice-presidency frustrating and disliked many of Kennedy's aides. Nonetheless, when

Kennedy was assassinated, he retained many Kennedy advisors and pushed the fallen president's policies. Using his formidable political skills, he secured passage of a federal civil rights law significantly stronger than the one that Kennedy originally proposed.

In May 1964, in a commencement address at the University of Michigan, Johnson outlined his own domestic agenda. His "Great Society" was the most ambitious legislative program since the New Deal. It included job training, preschool for poor children, anti-poverty initiatives, additional civil rights laws, federally funded health benefits for the elderly and poor, public housing, urban renewal, conservation, public broadcasting, consumer protection, federal aid for education, and new immigration policies. It contributed to a substantial decline in poverty. Between 1959 and 1969, the percentage of Americans living below the poverty line fell from 21 percent to 12 percent.

At the same time, the Great Society expanded government spending and the federal bureaucracy. At first, a thriving economy enabled the nation to absorb its costs. But, as the Vietnam War escalated, the Great Society foundered and Johnson's reform consensus disintegrated. The economy stalled. Some programs failed. Poor Americans grew disillusioned. Black radicalism and urban riots alienated many whites. In the years to come, Americans would hotly debate the impact of the Great Society and the proper role of the federal government in addressing social problems.

───────────■───────────

FOCUS QUESTIONS

1. How does Johnson define the "Great Society"?
2. What programs does he propose?
3. Was the Great Society a success? What role should the federal government play in addressing social problems? Explain your answers.

 I have come today from the turmoil of your Capital to the tranquility of your campus to speak about the future of your country.

The purpose of protecting the life of our Nation and preserving the liberty of our citizens is to pursue the happiness of our people. Our success in that pursuit is the test of our success as a Nation.

For a century we labored to settle and to subdue a continent. For half a century we called upon unbounded invention and untiring industry to create an order of plenty for all of our people.

The challenge of the next half century is whether we have the wisdom to use that wealth to enrich and elevate our national life, and to advance the quality of our American civilization.

Your imagination, your initiative, and your indignation will determine whether we build a society where progress is the servant of our needs, or a society where old values and new visions are buried under unbridled growth. For in your time we have the opportunity to move not only toward the rich society and the powerful society, but upward to the Great Society.

The Great Society rests on abundance and liberty for all. It demands an end to poverty and racial injustice, to which we are totally committed in our time. But that is just the beginning.

The Great Society is a place where every child can find knowledge to enrich his mind and to enlarge his talents. It is a place where leisure is a welcome chance to build and reflect, not a feared cause of boredom and restlessness. It is a place where the city of man serves not only the needs of the body and the demands of commerce but the desire for beauty and the hunger for community.

It is a place where man can renew contact with nature. It is a place which honors creation for its own sake and for what is adds to the understanding of the race. It is a place where men are more concerned with the quality of their goals than the quantity of their goods.

But most of all, the Great Society is not a safe harbor, a resting place, a final objective, a finished work. It is a challenge constantly renewed, beckoning us toward a destiny where the meaning of our lives matches the marvelous products of our labor.

So I want to talk to you today about three places where we begin to build the Great Society—in our cities, in our countryside, and in our classrooms.

Many of you will live to see the day, perhaps 50 years from now, when there will be 400 million Americans—four-fifths of them in urban areas. In the remainder of this century urban population will double, city land will double, and we will have to build homes, highways, and facilities equal to all those built since this country was first settled. So in the next 40 years we must re-build the entire urban United States.

Aristotle said: "Men come together in cities in order to live, but they remain together in order to live the good life." It is harder and harder to live the good life in American cities today. The catalog of ills is long: there is the decay of the centers and the despoiling of the suburbs. There is not enough housing for our people or transportation for our traffic. Open land is vanishing and old landmarks are violated.

Worst of all expansion is eroding the precious and time-honored values of community with neighbors and communion with nature. The loss of these values breeds loneliness and boredom and indifference.

Our society will never be great until our cities are great. Today the frontier of imagination and innovation is inside those cities and not beyond their borders. New experiments are already going on. It will be the task of your generation to make the American city a place where future generations will come, not only to live but to live the good life.

I understand that if I stayed here tonight I would see that Michigan students are really doing their best to live the good life.

This is the place where the Peace Corps was started. It is inspiring to see how all of you, while you are in this country, are trying so hard to live at the level of the people.

A second place where we begin to build the Great Society is in our country-side. We have always prided ourselves on being not only America the strong and America the free, but America the beautiful. Today that beauty is in danger. The water we drink, the food we eat, the very air that we breathe, are threatened with pollution. Our parks are overcrowded, our seashores overburdened. Green fields and dense forests are disappearing.

A few years ago we were greatly concerned about the "Ugly American." Today we must act to prevent an ugly America.

For once the battle is lost, once our natural splendor is destroyed, it can never be recaptured. And once man can no longer walk with beauty or wonder at nature his spirit will wither and his sustenance be wasted.

A third place to build the Great Society is in the classrooms of America. There your children's lives will be shaped. Our society will not be great until every young mind is set free to scan the farthest reaches of thought and imagination. We are still far from that goal.

Today, 8 million adult Americans, more than the entire population of Michigan, have not finished 5 years of school. Nearly 20 million have not finished 8 years of school. Nearly 54 million—more than one-quarter of all America—have not even finished high school.

Each year more than 100,000 high school graduates, with proved ability, do not enter college because they cannot afford it. And if we cannot educate today's youth, what will we do in 1970 when elementary school enrollment will be 5 million greater than 1960? And high school enrollment will rise by 5 million. College enrollment will increase by more than 3 million.

In many places, classrooms are overcrowded and curricula are outdated. Most of our qualified teachers are underpaid, and many of our paid teachers are unqualified. So we must give every child a place to sit and a teacher to learn from. Poverty must not be a bar to learning, and learning must offer an escape from poverty.

But more classrooms and more teachers are not enough. We must seek an educational system which grows in excellence as it grows in size. This means better training for our teachers. It means preparing youth to enjoy their hours of leisure as well as their hours of labor. It means exploring new techniques of teaching, to find new ways to stimulate the love of learning and the capacity for creation.

These are three of the central issues of the Great Society. While our Government has many programs directed at those issues, I do not pretend that we have the full answer to those problems.

But I do promise this: We are going to assemble the best thought and the broadest knowledge from all over the world to find those answers for America. I intend to establish working groups to prepare a series of White House conferences and meetings—on the cities, on natural beauty, on the quality of education, and on other emerging challenges. And from these meetings and from this inspiration and from these studies we will begin to set our course toward the Great Society.

The solution to these problems does not rest on a massive program in Washington, nor can it rely solely on the strained resources of local authority. They require us to create new concepts of cooperation, a creative federalism, between the National Capital and the leaders of local communities.

Woodrow Wilson once wrote: "Every man sent out from his university should be a man of his Nation as well as a man of his time."

Within your lifetime powerful forces, already loosed, will take us toward a way of life beyond the realm of our experience, almost beyond the bounds of our imagination.

For better or for worse, your generation has been appointed by history to deal with those problems and to lead America toward a new age. You have the chance never before afforded to any people in any age. You can help build a society where the demands of morality, and the needs of the spirit, can be realized in the life of the Nation.

So, will you join in the battle to give every citizen the full equality which God enjoins and the law requires, whatever his belief, or race, or the color of his skin?

Will you join in the battle to give every citizen an escape from the crushing weight of poverty?

Will you join in the battle to make it possible for all nations to live in enduring peace—as neighbors and not as mortal enemies?

Will you join in the battle to build the Great Society, to prove that our material progress is only the foundation on which we will build a richer life of mind and spirit?

There are those timid souls who say this battle cannot be won; that we are condemned to a soulless wealth. I do not agree. We have the power to shape the civilization that we want. But we need your will, your labor, your hearts, if we are to build that kind of society.

Those who came to this land sought to build more than just a new country. They sought a new world. So I have come here today to your campus to say that you can make their vision our reality. So let us from this moment begin our work so that in the future men will look back and say: It was then, after a long and weary way, that man turned the exploits of his genius to the full enrichment of his life.

Thank you. Good-bye.

Public Papers of the Presidents of the United States, Lyndon Johnson, 1963-1964 (Washington, 1965), 704-707.

24.9

GEORGE BALL AND ROBERT MCNAMARA ON U.S. POLICY IN VIETNAM (1965)

In the months following the Diem and Kennedy assassinations, the situation in South Vietnam deteriorated. Convinced that the collapse of the anti-communist government was imminent, U.S. officials urged Lyndon Johnson to escalate

American military involvement in Vietnam. At first, Johnson acted cautiously and approved only the dispatch of an additional 5,000 military advisors. Focused on defeating Barry Goldwater in the 1964 presidential race, Johnson avoided public discussions on the American role in Vietnam. "If you've got an ugly mother-in-law, and she's got one eye in the middle of her forehead, you don't put her in the living room." he explained in his inimitable fashion.

Privately, however, Johnson's aides were drafting a resolution that would dramatically expand the president's ability to fight communism in Southeast Asia. On August 2, 1964, North Vietnamese torpedo boats fired on the U.S. destroyer Maddox *during an espionage mission in the Gulf of Tonkin. Two days later, sailors on a second U.S. destroyer mistakenly reported a second attack. Johnson purposefully misconstrued the incidents in order to win authorization to "take all necessary measures" in Vietnam. Congress complied by passing the Gulf of Tonkin Resolution 416-0 in the House and 88-2 in the Senate.*

In February 1965, after Viet Cong guerillas killed U.S. Marines at Pleiku, Johnson approved Operation Rolling Thunder, a bombing campaign on North Vietnam that continued with periodic suspensions until 1968. A month after the Pleiku attack, Johnson sent two Marine battalions to Da Nang. In late July 1965, after weeks of careful deliberations with his advisors, Johnson announced plans to increase the number of U.S. troops in Vietnam from 75,000 to 125,000. By the end of 1967, the figure swelled to 485,000. In these memos from July 1965, Under Secretary of State George Ball and Secretary of Defense Robert S. McNamara give the president conflicting advice on U.S. strategy in Vietnam.

■

FOCUS QUESTIONS

1. How do George Ball and Robert McNamara differ in their appraisals of the situation in Vietnam?
2. What course of action does each man recommend? On what bases do they make these suggestions?
3. Whose advice did Lyndon Johnson accept? Why do you think he made this choice?
4. Was U.S. military intervention in Vietnam justified? Why or why not?

Paper by Under Secretary of State (Ball),
July 1, 1965

 COMPROMISE SOLUTION FOR SOUTH VIET-NAM

1. A Losing War: The South Vietnamese are losing the war to the Viet Cong. No one can assure you that we can beat the Viet Cong or even force them to the conference table on our terms, no matter how many hundred thousand *white, foreign* (U.S.) troops we deploy.

No one has demonstrated that a white ground force of whatever size can win a guerrilla war—which is at the same time a civil war between Asians—in jungle terrain in the midst of a population that refuses cooperation to the white forces (and the South Vietnamese) and thus provides a great intelligence advantage to the other side. Three recent incidents vividly illustrate this point: (a) the sneak attack on the Da Nang Air Base which involved penetration of a defense perimeter guarded by 9,000 Marines. (b) the B-52 raid that failed to hit the Viet Cong who had obviously been tipped off; (c) the search and destroy mission of the 173rd Air Borne Brigade which spent three days looking for the Viet Cong, suffered 23 casualties, and never made contact with the enemy who had obviously gotten advance word of their assignment.

2. *The Question to Decide:* Should we limit our liabilities in South Vietnam and try to find a way out with minimal long-term costs?

The alternative—no matter what we may wish it to be—is almost certainly a protracted war involving an open-ended commitment of U.S. forces, mounting U.S. casualties, no assurance of a satisfactory solution, and a serious danger of escalation at the end of the road.

3. *Need for a Decision Now:* So long as our forces are restricted to advising and assisting the South Vietnamese, the struggle will remain a civil war between Asian peoples. Once we deploy substantial numbers of troops in combat it will become a war between the U.S. and a large part of the population of South Vietnam, organized and directed from North Vietnam and backed by the resources of both Moscow and Peiping.

The decision you face now, therefore, is crucial. Once large numbers of U.S. troops are committed to direct combat, they will begin to take heavy casualties in a war they are ill-equipped to fight in a non-cooperative if not downright hostile countryside.

Once we suffer large casualties, we will have started a well-nigh irreversible process. Our involvement will be so great that we cannot—without national humiliation—stop short of achieving our complete objectives. *Of the two possibilities I think humiliation would be more likely than the achievement of our objectives—even after we have paid terrible costs.*

4. *A Compromise Solution:* Should we commit US manpower and prestige to a terrain so unfavorable as to give a very large advantage to the enemy—or should we seek a compromise settlement which achieves less than our stated objectives and thus cut our losses while we still have the freedom of maneuver to do so?

5. *Costs of Compromise Solution:* The answer involves a judgment as to the costs to the United States of such a compromise settlement in terms of our relations with the countries in the area of South Viet-Nam, the credibility of our commitments and our prestige around the world. In my judgment, if we act before we commit substantial US forces to combat in South Viet-Nam we can, by accepting some short-term costs, avoid what may well be a long-term catastrophe. I believe we have tended greatly to exaggerate the costs involved in a compromise settlement....

6. With these considerations in mind, I strongly urge the following program:
    A. *Military Program*
        1. Complete all deployments already announced (15 battalions) but decide not to go beyond the total of 72,000 men represented by this figure.
        2. Restrict the combat role of American forces to the June 9 announcement, making it clear to General Westmoreland that this announcement is to be strictly construed.
        3. Continue bombing in the North but avoid the Hanoi-Haiphong area and any targets nearer to the Chinese border than those already struck.
    B. *Political Program*
        1. In any political approaches so far, we have been the prisoners of whatever South Vietnamese Government was momentarily in power. If we are ever to move toward a settlement it will probably be because the South Vietnamese Government pulls the rug out from under us and makes its own deal or because we go forward quietly without advance pre-arrangement with Saigon....
        2. So far we have not given the other side a reason to believe that there is *any* flexibility in our negotiating approach. And the other side has been unwilling to accept what *in their terms* is complete capitulation.
        3. Now is the time to start some serious diplomatic feelers, looking towards a solution based on some application of the self-determination principle.
        4. I would recommend approaching Hanoi rather than any of the other probable parties (the National Liberation Front, Moscow or Peiping). Hanoi is the only one that has given any signs of interest in discussion. Peiping has been rigidly opposed. Moscow has recommended that we negotiate with Hanoi. The National Liberation Front has been silent....
        6. If the initial feelers lead to further secret exploratory talks we can inject the concept of self-determination that would permit the Viet Cong some hope of achieving some of their political objectives through local elections or some other device.
        7. The contact on our side should be handled through a non-governmental cutout (possibly a reliable newspaperman who can be repudiated.)
        8. If progress can be made at this level the basis can be laid for a multinational conference. At some point obviously the government of South Viet-Nam will have to be brought on board but I would postpone this step until after a substantial feeling out of Hanoi.
        9. Before moving to any formal conference we should be prepared to agree that once the conference is started (a) the United States will stand down its bombing of the North, (b) the South Vietnamese will

initiate no offensive operations in the South, and (c) the DRV will stop terrorism and other aggressive acts in the South.

10. Negotiations at the conference should aim at incorporating our understanding with Hanoi in the form of a multi-national agreement guaranteed by the United States, the Soviet Union and possibly other parties, and providing for an international mechanism to supervise its execution.

George W. Ball

Paper by Under Secretary of State (Ball), July 1, 1965, *Foreign Relations of the United States*, 1964-1968, Volume III, *Vietnam, June-December 1965*, http://www.state.gov/www/about_state/history/vol_iii/040.html.

Memorandum From Secretary of Defense McNamara to President Johnson
Washington, July 1, 1965.

S UBJECT: Program of expanded military and political moves with respect to Vietnam

Introduction. Our objective is to create conditions for a favorable settlement by demonstrating to the VC/DRV [Viet Cong/Democratic Republic of (North) Vietnam] that the odds are against their winning. Under present conditions, however, the chances of achieving this objective are small—and the VC are winning now—largely because the ratio of guerrilla to anti-guerrilla forces is unfavorable to the government. With this in mind, we must choose among three courses of action with respect to South Vietnam: (1) Cut our losses and withdraw under the best conditions that can be arranged; (2) continue at about the present level, with US forces limited to, say, 75,000, holding on and playing for the breaks while recognizing that our position will probably grow weaker; or (3) expand substantially the US military pressure against the Viet Cong in the South and the North Vietnamese in the North and at the same time launch a vigorous effort on the political side to get negotiations started. An outline of the third of these approaches follows.

I. *Expanded military moves.*

The following military moves should be taken together with the political initiatives in Part II below.

A. Inside South Vietnam. Increase US/GVN [United States/Government of (South) Vietnam] military strength in SVN [South Vietnam] enough to prove to the VC that they cannot win and thus to turn the tide of the war.

1. Increase combined US/GVN ground strength to the level required effectively to counter the current and likely VC ground strength....

2. Deploy 13 additional US helicopter companies and 5 additional Chinook platoons to increase effectiveness of US/GVN forces.

3. Deploy additional US artillery batteries and engineers to reinforce ARVN [Army of Republic of (South) Vietnam] divisions and corps.

    4.   Carry out 800 B-52 sorties a month in strikes against VC havens (followed promptly by entry of ground-forces into the struck areas).

B. Against North Vietnam. While avoiding striking population and industrial targets not closely related to the DRV's supply of war material to the VC, we should announce to Hanoi and carry out actions to destroy such supplies and to interdict their flow into and out of North Vietnam.

    1.   Quarantine the movement of war supplies into North Vietnam—by sea, rail and road....

    2.   Destroy the war-making supplies and facilities of North Vietnam wherever they may be located....

    3.   Interdict movement of war supplies within and out of North Vietnam by an expanded strike and armed reconnaissance program against LOCs west and south of Hanoi....

    4.   Be prepared to destroy airfields and SAM [surface-to-air missile] sites....

C. In the United States. Even if US deployments to Vietnam are no more than 100,000 men, we should:

    1.   Call up selected reserve forces (approximately 100,000 men).

    2.   Extend tours of duty in all Services.

II. *Expanded political moves.*

Together with the above military moves, we should take the following political initiatives in order (a) to open a dialogue with Hanoi, Peking, and the VC looking toward a settlement in Vietnam, (b) to keep the Soviet Union from deepening its military involvement and support of North Vietnam until the time when settlement can be achieved, and (c) to cement the support for US policy by the US public, allies and friends, and to keep international opposition at a manageable level. While our approaches may be rebuffed until the tide begins to turn, they nevertheless should be made....

C. Estimate of success.

    1.   Militarily. The success of the above program from a military point of view turns on whether the increased effort stems the tide in the South; that in turn depends on two things—on whether the South Vietnamese hold their own in terms of numbers and fighting spirit, and on whether the US forces can be effective in a quick-reaction reserve role, a role in which they have not been tested. The number of US troops is too small to make a significant difference in the traditional 10-1 government-guerrilla formula, but it is not too small to make a significant difference in the kind of war which seems to be evolving in Vietnam—a "Third Stage" or conventional war in which it is easier to identify, locate and attack the enemy....

    2.   Politically. It is frequently alleged that such a large expansion of US military personnel, their expanded military role (which would put them in close contact and offer some degree of control over South Vietnamese citizens), and the inevitable expansion of US voice in the operation of the GVN economy and facilities, command and

government services will be unpopular; it is said that they could lead to the rejection of the government which supported this American presence, to an irresistible pressure for expulsion of the Americans, and to the greatly increased saleability of Communist propaganda. Whether these allegations are true, we do not know.

The political initiatives are likely to be successful in the early stages only to demonstrate US good faith; they will pay off toward an actual settlement only after the tide begins to turn (unless we lower our sights substantially). The tide almost certainly cannot begin to turn in less than a few months, and may not for a year or more; the war is one of attrition and will be a long one. Since troops once committed as a practical matter cannot be removed, since US casualties will rise, since we should take call-up actions to support the additional forces in Vietnam, the test of endurance may be as much in the United States as in Vietnam.

3. Generally (CIA estimate). Over the longer term we doubt if the Communists are likely to change their basic strategy in Vietnam (i.e., aggressive and steadily mounting insurgency) unless and until two conditions prevail: (1) they are forced to accept a situation in the war in the South which offers them no prospect of an early victory and no grounds for hope that they can simply outlast the US and (2) North Vietnam itself is under continuing and increasingly damaging punitive attack. So long as the Communists think they scent the possibility of an early victory (which is probably now the case), we believe that they will persevere and accept extremely severe damage to the North....

Robert S. McNamara

Memorandum from Secretary of Defense McNamara to President Johnson, July 1, 1965, *Foreign Relations of the United States*, 1964-1968, Volume III, *Vietnam, June-December 1965*, http://www.state.gov/www/about_state/history/vol_iii/030.html.

24.10

PAUL POTTER, "THE INCREDIBLE WAR" (1965)

In the initial stages of the U.S. military build-up in Vietnam, a large majority of Americans supported the Johnson administration's actions. But as the war dragged on and casualties mounted, popular opposition surged. By 1967, tens of thousands of Americans from all walks of life were joining antiwar demonstrations.

College professors and students were among the first to protest. In March 1965, the University of Michigan hosted a teach-in to foster awareness of U.S.

policies. Others colleges held similar events. The following month, 25,000 people, mostly students, gathered for the March on Washington to End the War in Vietnam, an event organized by Students for a Democratic Society (SDS). Paul Potter, SDS president, gave the following speech at the rally. SDS became the leading anti-war group among leftists and college students. In 1966, as the government called up more draftees, resistance escalated. Opponents of the draft criticized the system's impact on the poor and minorities as well as loopholes that enabled the affluent to escape military service. As the war's costs reached $20 billion a year, many Americans were outraged when Congress instituted new taxes and cut Great Society programs. Liberal intellectuals, pacifists, clergy, business leaders, and politicians joined those criticizing the war. By 1969, Americans were polarized in their views on Vietnam.

FOCUS QUESTIONS

1. Why is Potter so opposed to the Vietnam War?
2. How does Potter claim that the war is affecting American society?
3. What does Potter believe is necessary to stop the war? Are his recommendations practical?
4. What impact did anti-war demonstrations have on U.S. policies in Vietnam? Would you have joined the anti-war movement? Explain your answers.

Most of us grew up thinking that the United States was a strong but humble nation, that involved itself in world affairs only reluctantly, that respected the integrity of other nations and other systems, and that engaged in wars only as a last resort. This was a nation with no large standing army, with no design for external conquest, that sought primarily the opportunity to develop its own resources and its own mode of living. If at some point we began to hear vague and disturbing things about what this country had done in Latin America, China, Spain and other places, we somehow remained confident about the basic integrity of this nation's foreign policy. The Cold War with all of its neat categories and black and white descriptions did much to assure us that what we had been taught to believe was true.

But in recent years, the withdrawal from the hysteria of the Cold War era and the development of a more aggressive, activist foreign policy have done much to force many of us to rethink attitudes that were deep and basic sentiments about our country. The incredible war in Vietnam has provided the razor, the terrifying sharp cutting edge that has finally severed the last vestige of illusion that morality and democracy are the guiding principles of American foreign policy. The saccharine self-righteous moralism that promises the Vietnamese a billion dollars of economic aid at the very moment we are delivering billions for economic and social destruction and political repression is rapidly losing what power it might ever have had to reassure us about the decency of our foreign policy. The further we explore the reality of what this country is doing and planning in Vietnam the more we are driven toward the conclusion of Senator [Wayne] Morse that the United States may well be the greatest threat to peace in the world today. That is a terrible and bitter insight for people who grew up as we did—and our revulsion at that insight, our refusal to accept it as inevitable or necessary, is one of the reasons that so many people have come here today.

The President says that we are defending freedom in Vietnam. Whose freedom? Not the freedom of the Vietnamese. The first act of the first dictator, Diem, the United States installed in Vietnam, was to systematically begin the persecution of all political opposition, non-Communist as well as Communist. The first American military supplies were not used to fight Communist insurgents; they were used to control, imprison or kill any who sought something better for Vietnam than the personal aggrandizement, political corruption and the profiteering of the Diem regime. The elite of the forces that we have trained and equipped are still used to control political unrest in Saigon and defend the latest dictator from the people....

The pattern of repression and destruction that we have developed and justified in the war is so thorough that it can only be called cultural genocide. I am not simply talking about napalm or gas or crop destruction or torture, hurled indiscriminately on women and children, insurgent and neutral, upon the first suspicion of rebel activity. That in itself is horrendous and incredible beyond belief. But it is only part of a larger pattern of destruction to the very fabric of the country. We have uprooted the people from the land and imprisoned them in concentration camps called "sunrise villages." Through conscription and direct political intervention and control, we have destroyed local customs and traditions, trampled upon those things of value which give dignity and purpose to life....

Not even the President can say that this is a war to defend the freedom of the Vietnamese people. Perhaps what the President means when he speaks of freedom is the freedom of the American people.

What in fact has the war done for freedom in America? It has led to even more vigorous governmental efforts to control information, manipulate the press and pressure and persuade the public through distorted or downright dishonest documents such as the White Paper on Vietnam. It has led to the confiscation of films and other anti-war material and the vigorous harassment by the FBI of some of the people who have been most outspokenly active in their criticism of the war.... How much more of Mr. Johnson's freedom can we stand? How much freedom will be left in this country if there is a major war in Asia? By what weird logic can it be said that the freedom of one people can only be maintained by crushing another?

In many ways this is an unusual march because the large majority of people here are not involved in a peace movement as their primary basis of concern. What is exciting about the participants in this march is that so many of us view ourselves consciously as participants as well in a movement to build a more decent society. There are students here who have been involved in protests over the quality and kind of education they are receiving in growingly bureaucratized, depersonalized institutions called universities; there are Negroes from Mississippi and Alabama who are struggling against the tyranny and repression of those states; there are poor people here—Negro and white—from Northern urban areas who are attempting to build movements that abolish poverty and secure democracy; there are faculty who are beginning to question the relevance of their institutions to the critical problems facing the society. Where will these people and the movements they are a part of be if the President is allowed to expand the war in Asia? What happens to the hopeful beginnings of expressed discontent that are trying to shift American attention to long-neglected internal priorities of shared abundance, democracy and decency at home when those priorities have to compete with the all-consuming priorities and psychology of a war against an enemy thousands of miles away?

The President mocks freedom if he insists that the war in Vietnam is a defense of American freedom. Perhaps the only freedom that this war protects is the freedom of the warhawks in the Pentagon and the State Department to experiment with counter-insurgency and guerilla warfare in Vietnam.

Vietnam, we may say, is a laboratory run by a new breed of gamesmen who approach war as a kind of rational exercise in international power politics. It is the testing ground and staging area for a new American response to the social revolution that is sweeping through the impoverished downtrodden areas of the world. It is the beginning of the American counter-revolution, and so far no one— none of us, not the N.Y. Times, nor 17 Neutral Nations, nor dozens of worried allies, nor the United States Congress have been able to interfere with the freedom of the President and the Pentagon to carry out that experiment.

Thus far the war in Vietnam has only dramatized the demand of ordinary people to have some opportunity to make their own lives, and of their unwillingness, even under incredible odds, to give up the struggle against external domination. We are told, however, that the struggle can be legitimately suppressed since it might lead to the development of a Communist system, and before that ultimate menace all criticism is supposed to melt.

This is a critical point and there are several things that must be said here—not by way of celebration, but because I think they are the truth. First, if this country were serious about giving the people of Vietnam some alternative to a Communist social revolution, that opportunity was sacrificed in 1954 when we helped to install Diem and his repression of non-Communist movements.... Second, those people who insist now that Vietnam can be neutralized are for the most part looking for a sugar coating to cover the bitter pill. We must accept the consequence that calling for an end of the war in Vietnam is in fact allowing for the likelihood that a Vietnam without war will be a self-styled Communist Vietnam. Third, this country must come to understand that creation of a Communist country in the world today is not an ultimate defeat. If people are given the opportunity to choose their own lives it is likely that some of them will choose what we have called "Communist systems." We are not powerless in that situation.... And yet the war that we are creating and escalating in Southeast Asia is rapidly eroding the base of independence of North Vietnam as it is forced to turn to China and the Soviet Union, involving them in the war and involving itself in the compromises that that implies. Fourth, I must say to you that I would rather see Vietnam Communist than see it under continuous subjugation of the ruin that American domination has brought.

But the war goes on; the freedom to conduct that war depends on the dehumanization not only of Vietnamese people but of Americans as well; it depends on the construction of a system of premises and thinking that insulates the President and his advisors thoroughly and completely from the human consequences of the decisions they make. I do not believe that the President or Mr. Rusk or Mr. McNamara or even McGeorge Bundy are particularly evil men. If asked to throw napalm on the back of a ten-year-old child they would shrink in horror—but their decisions have led to mutilation and death of thousands and thousands of people....

If the people of this country are to end the war in Vietnam, and to change the institutions which create it, then the people of this country must create a massive social movement....

By a social movement I mean more than petitions or letters of protest, or tacit support of dissident Congressmen; I mean people who are willing to change their lives, who are willing to challenge the system, to take the problem of change seriously. By a social movement I mean an effort that is powerful enough to make the country understand that our problems are not in Vietnam, or China or Brazil or outer space or at the bottom of the ocean, but are here in the United States. What we must do is begin to build a democratic and humane society in which Vietnams are unthinkable, in which human life and initiative are precious. The reason there are twenty thousand people here today and not a hundred or none at all is because five years ago in the South students began to build a social movement to change the system. The reason there are poor people, Negro and white, housewives, faculty members, and many others here in Washington is because that movement has grown and spread and changed and reached out as an expression of the broad concerns of people throughout the society. The reason the war and the system it represents will be stopped, if it is stopped before it destroys all of us, will be because the movement has become strong enough to exact change in the society....

But that means that we build a movement that works not simply in Washington but in communities and with the problems that face people throughout the society. That means that we build a movement that understands Vietnam in all its horror as but a symptom of a deeper malaise, that we build a movement that makes possible the implementation of the values that would have prevented Vietnam, a movement based on the integrity of man and a belief in man's capacity to tolerate all the weird formulations of society that men may choose to strive for; a movement that will build on the new and creative forms of protest that are beginning to emerge, such as the teach-in, and extend their efforts and intensify them; that we will build a movement that will find ways to support the increasing numbers of young men who are unwilling to and will not fight in Vietnam; a movement that will not tolerate the escalation or prolongation of this war but will, if necessary, respond to the administration war effort with massive civil disobedience all over the country, that will wrench the country into a confrontation with the issues of the war; a movement that must of necessity reach out to all these people in Vietnam or elsewhere who are struggling to find decency and control for their lives.

For in a strange way the people of Vietnam and the people on this demonstration are united in much more than a common concern that the war be ended. In both countries there are people struggling to build a movement that has the power to change their condition. The system that frustrates these movements is the same. All our lives, our destinies, our very hopes to live, depend on our ability to overcome that system.

Rebels With a Cause, http://www.sdsrebels.com/potter.htm.

24.11

SOLDIERS WRITE HOME FROM VIETNAM (1967-1970)

Between 1962 and 1975, 2.5 million American soldiers served in Vietnam. They faced numerous obstacles including a tropical climate, jungle terrain, and an elusive enemy. In the war's early stages, those who fought in Vietnam were optimistic and committed. They believed that the war was a noble cause and that saving South Vietnam from communism was a worthy goal. The guerilla nature of the conflict challenged these attitudes. It was very difficult for soldiers to distinguish enemies from civilians. Atrocities perpetrated by all sides created moral ambiguity. In contrast to conventional battles with defined front lines, troops went on "search and destroy" missions where hours of boredom were punctuated by moments of terror. Driving rains, searing heat, leeches, mosquitoes, booby traps, and mines added to the rigors of combat.

As the war continued, soldiers' confidence gave way to cynicism. Many resented the fact that 80 percent of those serving were from working-class or poor backgrounds and had been unable to use college deferments or family connections to avoid the draft. Most were infuriated by the disjuncture between official pronouncements that victory was imminent and the less decisive realities in the field. At the same time, most soldiers felt fierce loyalty toward their comrades in arms.

As the United States began withdrawing its forces from Vietnam, soldiers' morale plummeted. In the early 1970s, reports of insubordination, desertion, drug use, and racial conflict significantly increased. In extreme cases, soldiers shot or killed officers rather than fight. Between 1969 and 1971, the Pentagon reported 730 such "fraggings" resulting in the deaths of 83 officers.

Veterans returned to a country polarized by the war. Where the 12 million men and women who served in World War II were almost universally hailed as heroes, Vietnam veterans were often ignored or even harassed. Some joined the anti-war movement. Others suffered severe post-traumatic stress disorder, physical disabilities, or drug or alcohol addiction. Not until 1982, when the nation dedicated the Vietnam Veterans Memorial in Washington, D.C., did many veterans feel that their countrymen recognized their sacrifices in America's most divisive war.

——————————■——————————

FOCUS QUESTIONS

1. How do these soldiers describe their experiences in Vietnam? What are their attitudes toward their fellow soldiers?
2. What are their views toward the Vietnamese?
3. What are their attitudes toward the war? How do these views change over time?

[June 1967]

D ear Editor:

I'm writing this letter to you to help clarify some of the objectives of the United States' participation in the Vietnam War as I see them.

I was with the 9th Infantry Division in the Mekong Delta and we had many missions to accomplish. Search-and-destroy missions were carefully planned to avoid any loss of life to innocent Vietnamese.

Pamphlets were dropped by air in advance to warn the people of our attack....

Every soldier in Vietnam is much more than a fighting man, for on many missions we passed among the villages information concerning the Chieu Hoi ("Open Arms") program which is set up for VC defectors. Defectors that turn themselves in are given the opportunity of starting a new life with the help of the United States and South Vietnam governments.

Many of us were engaged in our own civic action programs on our own time. It might be giving undernourished children C-rations, teaching a teenage boy a little English or helping an old man tie a bag of rice on his bicycle. Wherever we were, we had to win over the people if we wanted to accomplish our assigned mission. The Vietnamese are naturally wary of our presence for they have been taken advantage of before (by the French) and they don't want it to happen again.

The spirit of the men in Vietnam is overwhelming, for most every man believes that he is doing an important job and believe me, he is.

To see your buddy step on a VC antipersonnel mine is a hard thing to take, but the real scare is when you go back to your base camp and see the smiling villagers all around you and then start to wonder if one of them set it there.

Here also our job is twofold, for we must protect the farmers from the VC terrorism, taxation and pillaging of the hard-earned crops. Also, after doing this we have to gain the confidence of the people and make them understand that we don't intend to take over where the VC left off.

The men we have in the Republic of South Vietnam know why they are there and are willing to fight in this country where the people have really never known what a free society is like.

It is a weird feeling to prop yourself against a dike at night in a dry rice paddy and think about the Golden Gate and Telegraph Avenue and wonder if you'll ever see them again. Your short periods of sleep are uneasy, for you are constantly scared of the possibility of the deadly mortars that may come silently on your position at any time. Every sound is a potential danger, and a good night's sleep is an unreality for the American in South Vietnam. You wonder if the South Vietnamese ever sleep well....

I am writing this letter from a hospital bed in Yokohama, Japan. I was wounded about six weeks ago by a Russian pineapple grenade which was booby-trapped by a VC who was most likely just a brainwashed farmer.

There are about 800 soldiers here at this hospital, and this is one of several in the country. Most every guy here realizes that he was wounded while doing an important job in South Vietnam. Most of the wounded here are, or were, in pretty bad shape. It's a hard sight to see an 18-year-old soldier with one leg shot off struggling with his first pair of crutches. The morale here is surprisingly high, and there are more laughs than tears, thank goodness.

Myself, with God's help, I'll be able to walk in 8 to 12 months.

In closing, I'd just like to say that every American should know by now that the war we're fighting in South Vietnam is a war against communist aggression, which is an ever-present threat to the free world today.

Take a minute now and think about the guys in South Vietnam and the guys that are going home on stretchers and in pine boxes. They are your countrymen, and, believe it or not, they have been fighting for you.

Sp/4 Rodney D. Baldra

Rodney Baldra had been in country 42 days, serving with the 5th Battalion, 60th Infantry (Mechanized), 9th Infantry Division, out of Bear Cat, when he was wounded by a booby trap on 1 April 1967. He lives in Walnut Creek, California, and is a self-employed restaurant consultant. He wrote this letter to the Berkeley (California) Gazette.

5th or 6th Oct. 67

H i Honey,
     I had a hell of a day yesterday. I'll explain it from the time I started out on patrol with my platoon until yesterday evening....

We were going up this valley, and I got a report that approximately 60 VC were spotted on the ridgeline next to my location. I told my point man to change direction towards that position. We came to a river that was deep and wide due to all of the rain we've been getting. We were looking for a way across when six VC took off out of a hut across the river.

We immediately opened fire, and my front element jumped into the river to try and head them off. I went across the river and told my platoon sergeant to take control of the rear element and to provide cover fire. After I was across, the dinks divided into two groups and took off up the mountain to our front.

My platoon sergeant crossed with his element and gave chase on the right flank. I took control of the left flank, and we took them under fire. We hit one, but he dropped into a tunnel and we lost sight of him.

Meanwhile, on the right flank, a VC popped out of a hole and threw a grenade. My M-79 man stood his ground and fired at the dink [at] the same time he threw the grenade. My M-79 got hit in the leg with shrapnel from the grenade, and the dink that threw it got knocked down with the blast from the M-79. My man crawled into the bushes. His helmet, wallet, pictures and letters were scattered all over, not to mention his weapon. He started yelling "medic," so I ran over to him with the medic and called in the dust-off.

My right element chased the dinks up into the brush and wounded two more. They left two big blood trails in the brush as we tracked them down, but they got in their tunnels and we could not get them. I told the men to throw grenades into those tunnels, which they did.

Meanwhile, the track unit that we are attached to came up in their APCs [armored personnel carriers], and I had them rake the hill with their 50s.

At about the same time, I was comforting the man who had been hit. It was raining, and his blood was mixing with the water in the puddle he was lying in. He wanted to hold my hand because it was hurting him so bad. I held his hands and told him he had a million-dollar wound. He was in pain so bad he was clenching his teeth, but he tried to smile at that. Everyone in the field wants the million-dollar wound so they can be sent back to the States.

The dust-off came in at that time, and I "popped" smoke so he would know where we were located. The chopper landed about 15 feet way, and one of the men in [it] jumped out with a collapsible stretcher. When we picked the man up, he cried out in agony and passed out. We put him on the chopper, and they took off.

I took my left element up the left side and sent the right element up the right side of our hill. We found tunnels, spiderholes, [and] straw mats where [the VC] had been sleeping, and food cans. We found medical supplies in a hut at the bottom of the hill plus canteens, propaganda and—get this—at one of the tables, six hands of cards. One hand was thrown all over the floor but otherwise they had been so surprised they had left all six hands on the table.

All of the tracks got stuck in the damn rice paddies, and we had to pull back and guard them, so the rest of the dinks got away. When the tracks finally got loose from the mud, it was getting dark, so we had to pull back to our bridge.

On the way back we searched this hut and found a VC gas mask and a clip of ammo for a carbine rifle. We took [four women] prisoners and brought them in. They will have some explaining to do about that equipment they had.

I told my men that the first squad to kill a dink with a weapon, I would buy them a bottle of whisky. They can't wait to kill one of them now.

I just heard an explosion down the road. From the radio I hear that an Army vehicle hit a mine and the dust-off has been called. The mine demolished the truck and blew a three-foot hole in the road. This is some war. A man can't feel safe anywhere in this whole country.

I'll never forget the look on that man's face when I was holding his hand.

Well, my love, one of these days, I'll get some mail and I'll read those sweet words "I Love You."

With All My Love,
Fred

2 Lt. Fred Downs, platoon leader, Co. C, 1/14th inf., 4th Inf. Div., Pleiku province, 1967-1968, WIA 11 January 1968.

4 June 1969
Wednesday

Dear Mom & Dad,
Got your letter of 28th, Mom, yesterday, 3 June. Today I got Dad's of 26th April. Never know what is going on with the mall. Haven't gotten the package yet. Heaven only knows when they will arrive and in what condition.

Worked in ICU [Intensive Care Unit] again today. Was lucky, got to 102° today, and ICU is air-conditioned. They have a lot of really sick patients. Had three die yesterday. They still have four on respirators. None too good, either.

One of the GI's who died yesterday was from Ward 8, medical. Had malaria. During the previous night he had been nauseated and kept getting up to the latrine to vomit. Got up at 2 A.M. and was running to the latrine. Fell really hard and cracked his head on the cement floor. The nurse who was on duty said you could hear his skull fracture. He immediately started bleeding from ears and nose and stopped breathing. Then had cardiac arrest. They got him going again and transferred him to ICU but he died anyway yesterday. Had severe brain damage. Other death was [a] GI with multiple fragment wounds from a mine explosion. He was there two weeks ago when I worked that other day in ICU. Also a Vietnamese died. Don't know what was wrong with him.

Census hit the 10,000 mark yesterday. This unit, the 312th [Evacuation Hospital], has treated 10,000 patients since [we] arrived last September. Unbelievable. Registrar office had a poll going as to what time and what date the 10,000th patient would be admitted. Was yesterday morning. Haven't heard who won the money yet.

They put plastic or rubber floor tile down in the mess hall the evening before last. Looked real nice until yesterday noon when it got hot. The tar came up between the tile and it got tracked all over the place. Couldn't move your chair at all. It was stuck to the floor.

How did the home-made ice cream turn out? Start "nights" tomorrow so don't have to get up early tomorrow. Nice thought.

Still very quiet around here. Haven't gotten mortared for couple of weeks now. We are getting some new nurses this week. They are from the unit who will over when the 312th goes home in September. Their hospital is farther south somewhere. They are handling 80% Vietnamese casualties now so are turning their hospital over to the Viets and coming here to take over. Supposed to get the new chief nurse tomorrow. So the unit will change names in September. However, they are supposed to be an RA [Regular Army] group. Not a reserve unit like the

312th is. Things are supposed to get a lot more "strict Army style." No one is looking forward to it.

Read a book last night and missed a good Lee Marvin movie at the mess hall. Had a movie star visit here the second or third week I was here. Named Ricardo Montalban? Ever hear of him? Forgot to mention it previously. Some of the older people here remembered him. Said he was in movies with Esther Williams.

Will stop for now. Getting sleepy.

See you sooner.
Shar

2 Lt. Sharon A. Lane, a nurse from Canton, Ohio, arrived at the 312th Evacuation Hospital, Chu Lai, in April 1969. Two months later, on 8 June, she was killed by shrapnel during a rocket attack. She was one month short of her 26th birthday.

July 15, 1969

Dear Mom,
We went out again with the 17th Armored Cavalry. We drove all over this area. We went to some villages and searched the hooches for VC or weapons. All we found were some tools. We took them from the dinks.

I still can't believe how these people live. They're just like animals. They live way out in the middle of nowhere. There isn't even a road for miles. It's all just unused rice paddies. Their homes are made of grass and mud. They crouch down to eat their little bowl of rice and I don't know what else but it smells like dead dog. They don't mind the flies all over their food.

When they go to the bathroom they just do it wherever they may be. They don't do it in the house.

When we come roaring in on our armored personal carriers, the men take off (probably VC). The women and kids stay behind and beg stuff off the GIs.

They have holes in the ground that are amazing. Some of them run for miles and some are big enough to stand up in. Some are very large living quarters and usually run into the smaller ones. We just throw a few grenades in or blast the hole with a large charge of TNT. These people are like moles. They can dig miles of tunnel but there is no dirt to be found anywhere. They must eat it.

Some of these people are treacherous. They say "GI number one" when we're in their village, but at night the dirty little rats are VC. Well, we haven't seen anything exciting lately, just routine patrolling. It is boring.

I'll keep you informed.

Tell Francis and George to write once in a while. Patricia and you write a lot.

Love,
Paul

Paul Kelly was a sergeant with the 1st Battalion, 52nd Infantry, 198th Light Infantry Brigade, Americal Division, operating in I Corps, from March 1969 through March 1970. He is a grade-school science teacher in Garden City, New York.

20 July 1969

Dear Mom,
    I've become involved recently in a situation that I had heard about but was never fully aware of before. I thought, as a child, that growing up in a single-parent family was rough. Now I know that I was very well off compared to those with no parents at all, no home life to build a healthy young life on. I think of something in the Bible, "I cried because I had no shoes, and then I saw a man who had no feet."

Let me start from the beginning. When I first arrived in Vietnam, and was assigned here in Ban Me Thuot, I was astonished at the poor, seemingly unimprovable conditions that the majority of Vietnamese live under. True, over the last three decades new conveniences [and] new ideas have been introduced by us and the French before us. [But] I had to talk with the people before I realized that the sole hope of this nation lies in its youth. The elders, the parents, are tired. They've lived with war, and the hardships involved, for too long. They no longer believe another kind of life is possible. The children do, though. They want to learn. They want to do things the way we do, have things like we have. They have hope for their future.

One day when I wasn't scheduled to fly, my platoon leader, Capt. Roy Ferguson, asked me if I wanted to go to the orphanage in town with him. We picked up some things some friends had sent him and went down to the Vinh-Son Orphanage and School, run by eight sisters of the Daughters of Charity of St. Vincent de Paul.

Sister Beatrice, in charge of the school, greeted us at the gate. As we walked through the grounds, we were followed by scores of children who wanted to touch us, talk to us, or just smile at us. We left the books and pencils we had brought with Sister Beatrice and walked to the building which is the orphanage itself.

We were welcomed by Sister Helen and a group of kids that had been playing in front of the building. They just went wild when they saw us. And no wonder—for the past five months, Capt. Ferguson, who comes from Wyalusing, Pennsylvania, has been practically their only link with the life of clothing, toys and personal American friendship. They've adopted him, in their own way, as a sort of godfather.

I was at once ashamed and proud. Proud because we in America have so much, and ashamed because we take our good fortune for granted, wasting so much that these people, especially the children in this orphanage, so desperately need. Things like blankets and sheets, clothes for little boys and girls, even shoes. How many times have you or I made a rag out of something because it had a little hole in it? Mom, these children need those things desperately. Capt. Ferguson will be leaving soon, and I will sort of assume the privilege of being the go-between for these children and the assistance that comes in from their friends in the United States.... The most beneficial thing we can do is donate our time by going down to the school to teach English to the more than 1,200 students that receive an education there.

I'm amazed that eight nuns can oversee so large an effort. In addition to the orphanage and school, they run a dispensary, giving aid to the local Vietnamese and Montagnard families in the area. They have so little for themselves, and yet they give away what they do have.

The shame of it all is that these children had nothing to do with bringing all this on themselves. It's hard to sympathize with someone who causes his own misfortune. These children, though, are the victims not of their generation, but of yours and mine. Many are orphans because their parents have been killed. They haven't died of old age or heart attacks...they've been killed by terrorism while defending their homes, their country, their freedom. Others are orphans as a result of the assistance we have given to their country. We have fathered many children, unable to take them home, their mothers unable to care for them. You and I must do something for these children, for this orphanage, [so it] can expand its work and care for children who now walk the streets with no one, no one at all.

The children need things that are part of our everyday lives. Toothpaste, soap, a pencil, a pen, a notebook to write in as they go through school. A picture book that says, "See the dog. His name is Spot. Watch the dog run. Run, Spot, run." These kids aren't underprivileged—they're nonprivileged, and they're running. Running towards a way of life where they can better themselves on their own. But they're so young, we have to help them to walk before we let them run.

Plates on which to put their food, silverware to eat it with, even the food itself—they need it all. They raise chickens and pigs, and all of their vegetables. The only way they can buy even rice is to sell one of their pigs.

[The children] are taught by a staff of 30 teachers who work for nothing or are paid in produce. There's no law here requiring children to attend school. They go because they are hungry for knowledge and because their stomachs are hungry. An education can change that, and we must help them get that education.

I could write a book about these children, about the look of fear in their eyes, their cries of joy upon seeing an American, someone who can help them change their circumstances. Some are too young to fully realize what it's like to have nothing. You and I and our friends must prevent them from finding out. We speak different languages, but we're all the same kind of people. They need, and we have. We must help them.

I'll stop here, because the sooner this letter gets to you, the sooner our friends at the orphanage will get some help. Send anything that might be useful to Vinh-Son Orphanage care of myself. I'll see that it gets there. And don't be surprised if the next piece of mail you get from Vietnam is a thank-you note from some very, very grateful Vietnamese youngster.

Run, Spot, run.

With love and thanks,
Your Son

Bruce McInnes was a chief warrant officer with the 155th Assault Helicopter Company 10th Combat Assault Battalion, 1st Aviation Brigade, from May 1969 to December 1970, based at Ban Me Thuot. He works as a tree doctor in New York City.

Sept. 23, '69

R ed,
    I never made it down to Nha Trang for extra recondo training. A rear-echelon sergeant took me off the list and put his name there, so he went in my place and I went into the field for a three-day recon in the monsoons. Someday climb into the shower with all your clothes on, stay there three days under the water, shutting it off every now and then, but always turning the water back on before your clothes can dry out, and you'll have a reasonably good idea of what it's like in the boonies during the seasonal rains. I looked like a prune by the time we came back.

    For two days we staggered over ridgeline after ridgeline trying to get to our AO (area of operations) since our chopper pilot became slightly confused and inserted us two miles south of the area we were to recon. On the last day we stopped for a break when two NVA walked by making enough noise for a platoon. I've read statements from NVA POWs claiming the American soldier is too clumsy and noisy in the jungles, but 12 of us followed both of them for over a half mile and they never knew we were there until it didn't matter—for them. They led us right into a platoon-sized base camp, and we made the biggest haul ever for Chu Lai Rangers.

    The platoon was having a siesta-fiesta break, and we crawled within six feet of one group and then charged, and all hell broke loose. It had to be a tremendous shock. I've never seen such panic and pandemonium. NVA tumbled out of hammocks, hit the ground running, and took off leaving all their equipment. One man went down fighting, shot our point man in the ankle at fistfighting range, and then was blown apart by the sergeant leading us. I won't go into detail, but it is unbelievable what an M-16 will do to a man—particularly at close range. The only conceivable comparison is swatting a bug with a chain-mail glove. Enough said—too much perhaps. The whole thing lasted less than 30 seconds, then we were alone, standing among piles of food and equipment, blood trails and corpses. We brought back weapons ranging from a mortar to AK-47s, clothes, medical kits and documents and were mentioned on radio and TV over here for that day's work.

    It was a very successful patrol, and everyone seemed happy with it—everyone but the point man, that is. His wound, of itself, wasn't serious, but the power and shock of a modern rifle bullet is absolutely unbelievable and within two minutes of being hit he was fighting for his life in shock. There was a foulup in the extraction, and for half an hour we were stuck in a wide-open rice paddy, in a valley, with helicopters trying to find us but not having our radio frequency, while the hills all around [were crawling] with communists who, if they had come back, could have wiped us out. The wounded man stopped breathing three times on the LZ but was revived via mouth-to-mouth resuscitation and a few punches on the chest. He is now on his way home by way of Japan, where his ankle will be taken care of, so maybe, in a way, he was the luckiest one out there. He's going home to his wife in one piece, with his eyes and all his limbs, and will probably not even have a limp, while we'll be going back out until either our time or luck runs out. He'll never take to the field again. He's home safe—we're not. In that distinction lies the difference between those who have luck, and those who aren't yet sure [if] they have it or not.

George

Sp/4 George Olsen, Co. G, 75th Inf. (Ranger), Americal Div., Chu Lai, 1969-1970, KIA 3 March 1970.

July 1970

ear Editor:]
This letter I am writing is not only from me but quite a few of my friends. I just thought you might like it.

This letter is from the men who daily risk their lives in the air over the war-wrought land of Vietnam. It is the combined thoughts and beliefs of 1st and 2nd flight platoons, B Company, 159th Aviation Battalion, 101st Airborne Division, and you can believe me that a lot of our descriptive phrases are being omitted due to the grossness and obscenities of them.

The outburst of raw violence and malice spontaneously occurred when the following quotation was read aloud to them from a letter: "We've had some memorial services for them at school and there's a movement for a strike." The quotation was in regards to the recent killings at Kent [State University] in Ohio. We are sorrowful and mourn the dead, but it grieves us no end and shoots pain into our hearts that the "biggest upset is over the kids who got killed at Kent [State]."

So why don't your hearts cry out and shed a tear for the 40-plus thousand red-blooded Americans and brave, fearless, loyal men who have given their lives so a bunch of bloody bastard radicals can protest, dissent and generally bitch about our private and personal war in Vietnam and now Cambodia?

During my past 18 months in hell I've seen and held my friends during their last gasping seconds before they succumbed to death. And not once, I repeat, and not one goddamn time did they chastise our country's involvement in Vietnam. Christ, we cheered when Nixon sent troops to Cambodia—we are praying we'll also see Laos.

And how in the hell do you think that we in Vietnam feel when we read of the dissension and unrest in our country caused by young, worthless radicals and the foremost runner of them all: the vile and disease ridden SDS. This is what we feel like: We have an acute hatred, an unfathomable lust to maim, yes, even kill. You ask, "Is this towards the NVA and VC?" We answer, "Hell, no, it's for all of you back in the World who are striving to make us feel like a piece of shit for fighting and dying for what we believe in—freedom."."

Last month my company lost 12 good men and five more were torn up so bad that they have been sent back to the States. We shed true tears for these men. What did you do? Protest. In your feeble and deteriorating and filthy degenerate minds you have forced and caused these men to die for nothing. Do you place such a low value on our heads? We are trying to end the war so that our loved ones will never have to face the harsh realities of death in our own country.

Do not judge us wrongly. We are not pleading for your praise. All we ask is for our great nation to unite and stand behind President Nixon. Support us, help us end the war, damn it, save our lives....

I am coming home soon. Don't shout and preach your nothingness to me. I am ashamed to be fighting to keep you safe, the rest of the loyal Americans. I am proud to give my life for you members of the SDS and your followers. I am returning to educate you on what it feels like to be in Nam. Yes, I am bringing the war home. We'll see if you're as good in fighting as you are in protesting.

Prepare yourselves—the makers are returning. May your children honor and respect our dead and chastise your actions.

We personally challenge you to come to Vietnam and talk with the VC and NVA in the A Shau Valley. Let us know what they say, if you live.

We the undersigned are in full [agreement] with the forth-put statements....

With love,
Greg Lusco
Phu Bai
South Vietnam

Sp/4 Gregory Lusco, who served in Vietnam between November 1968 and August 1970, and 19 other soldiers from Company B. 159th Aviation Battalion, 101st Airborne Division, wrote this letter, which was published in the Greenfield (Massachusetts) Recorder on 23 July 1970 He is now in the Navy, stationed in Japan aboard the U.S.S. Midway.

6 September '70

Dear John,
...Saigon [is] completely different from I Corps—almost luxurious. The MACV [Military Assistance Command/Vietnam] complex, where so many of my friends work, has a golf course, Olympic-size swimming pool, etc. But with all the surface glitter and bustle of Saigon, I came away with a very gloomy feeling. The people are frantically trying to make every last cent they can from the Americans before [the soldiers] leave. The war has brought out all the venality imaginable in these people....

My friends are somewhat depressed. It now seems they have to rewrite all their reports because the truth they are putting out is too pessimistic. The higher echelons, for their career's sake and the plans of Nixon's Vietnamization, will not allow a bad situation to exist—no matter how true it may be! I saw myself some of the different drafts of some reports that were to go to [General Creighton] Abrams [commander of American forces in Vietnam]—and how they had to be changed to get to him. What a disgrace—and still people are dying every day!

To top this all off, we got hit again last week—twice in one night. The second phase was while we were all watching a Korean floor show. It was mass hysteria when those rockets started coming in! Chairs flying, people running to bunkers! Boy, do I hate those things. I'm going to be a nervous wreck when I get out of here! Then, there has begun a witch hunt for pot smokers. We have a group of self-appointed vigilantes (most of whom are Southern beer-drinking, obnoxious alcoholics! You can see my prejudices in that statement!) who go around spreading untrue rumors about those they do not like. It's at such a point that open warfare might break out in the company. I'm so worked up now because one of the vigilantes is my own boss. It just makes me sick! My own impressions are that the supposed "pot heads" are much easier to work with, more pleasant, never bothersome, and more intelligent than the redneck faction of boozers! Yet that counts for nothing in the Army....

John, Peace—my warmest regards and thanks for letting me ramble on and take out my frustrations.

Tom

Sp/5 Thomas Pellaton, 101st Avn. Gp., 101st Abn. Div., Phu Bai, 1970-1971.

Dear America: Letters Home from Vietnam edited by Bernard Edelman for The New York Vietnam Veterans Memorial Commission, originally published by W.W. Norton & Company in 1985 and reissued in 2002, pp. 207-209, 68-70, 285-286, 109-113, 64-65, 226-227, 149-150.

24.12

GUY STRAIT, "WHAT IS A HIPPIE?"

While some young people gravitated to the political movements of the sixties, others were attracted to the counterculture. Like their predecessors the Beats, the "hippies" or "flower children" challenged traditional views of sexuality and capitalism. Seeking self-realization through the abandonment of inhibitions and the pursuit of pleasure, hippies were heterosexually adventurous. Hoping to broaden their perspectives, they smoked marijuana and took hallucinogens like LSD. Adopting a "live free" philosophy, they wore clothing from thrift stores, avoided conventional jobs, and, in some cases, moved to rural communes. Their public use of obscene language flouted decorum.

Rock music was an integral element of the counterculture. Some artists, like Bob Dylan and Phil Ochs, used music as a tool of social protest. Others, like The Beatles, The Doors, and The Grateful Dead celebrated sensuality and mysticism. In August 1969, almost 400,000 people attended Woodstock, a music festival in upstate New York. The peaceful crowd spent three days frolicking in the rain, having sex, and taking drugs. Since most of the attendees were not true hippies, Woodstock demonstrated how deeply the counterculture had pervaded mainstream culture. By 1969, many young Americans had adopted long hair, flamboyant fashions, and freer attitudes toward sex and drugs.

Many Americans loathed the counterculture and viewed the hippies as parasitic and immoral. Indeed, there were negative elements of the lifestyle. Some hippies abused the welfare system or resorted to theft. Reports of venereal disease and rape complicated notions of "free love." Jimi Hendrix, Janis Joplin, Jim Morrison, and hundreds of others died of drug overdoses. The Altamont music festival, held on December 6, 1969 in Livermore, California, was as violent as Woodstock had been peaceful. Hired as security guards, Hell's Angels motorcycle gang members fought with concertgoers and killed a man as the Rolling Stones sang "Sympathy for the Devil" on stage. By the time the concert ended, four people were dead. Depending on one's perspective, either Woodstock or Altamont exemplified the counterculture.

In this 1967 essay, Guy Strait, a San Francisco-based journalist, explains the counterculture.

FOCUS QUESTIONS

1. According to Strait, how and why are the hippies challenging middle-class norms? Is he sympathetic to the hippies' cause?
2. How does Strait explain the "straight" community's objections to the hippies?
3. Would you have wanted to be a hippie? Why or why not?

It is strange and disturbing to watch the straight [i.e., mainstream] community's angry, sometimes violent reaction to the hippies. There are many reasons for this. The principal one is appearance. The hippies dress strangely. They dress this way because they have thrown a lot of middle-class notions out the window and with them the most sensitive middle-class dogma: the neutral appearance.

The straight world is a jungle of taboos, fears, and personality games. People in that jungle prey on each other mercilessly. Therefore to survive in any jungle requires good protective coloring: the camouflage of respectable appearance. The anonymity of middle-class dress is like a flag of truce. It means (whether true or not): "I'm not one of the predators." It is in the nature of an assurance of harmlessness. Unusual or bright-colored clothing then becomes an alarm, a danger signal to the fearful and their armed truce with the rest of mankind. They see it as a challenge. They are fearful, unsure of themselves, and fear sours into anger. It is but a step to thinking that the anger is "good." The oldest fallacy in the world is that anything that makes you angry must be bad.

The sin of the hippies is that they will not play the straight game of camouflage. Their non-participation, in effect, exposes them as another tribe, whose disregard of straight taboos of dress makes them seem to be capable of anything, and therefore a danger. That danger moreover is felt clear up to city hall, that shrine of Squaredom. Why else, I submit, does the Health Department of this city have such a tender solicitude about the living conditions of human beings at the Haight when they have ignored the conditions at Hunter's Point, the Mission and the Fillmore?

Many people cannot understand the hippies' rejection of everything that is commonly expected of the individual in regard to employment and life goals: steady lucrative employment, and the accumulation through the years of possessions and money, building (always building) security for the future. It is precisely this security hypochondria, *this checking of bank book rather than pulses*, this worrying over budgets instead of medicine cabinets, that drives the youth of today away. It is this frantic concern with money that also drives the young into the Haight-Ashbury. They have seen their parents slave for years, wasting away a lifetime to make sure that the house was paid off, that the kids got through school in order to get "good" jobs so that they could join the frantic scramble, later on. The parents' reward for this struggle is that they wind up old and tired, alienated from their children, and just as often each parent from the other. They have thought so long in terms of money and possessions, that they have forgotten how to think in terms of people. So they think of "my son," and "my daughter," and talk to their children as one would speak from a great distance to a check book.

"But you've got to build a future for yourself. If you don't support yourself, no one else is going to!" The tired, lined face argues to the young. "It's a hard world." And pray tell who makes it hard, participating in the scramble for material "security?" Who makes it difficult by insisting that everyone must participate in that scramble or suffer social censure? Listen to the tone of those who lecture about the "economic realities" of life. Are they presenting impartial facts? Or do they sound like someone expounding church doctrine? It is the latter. The conventional folk of our society, the "normal" people, so called, believe in the rat race. Competition is holy. Keeping up with the Joneses a mandate from God. The requirement of keeping up a respectable front is the principal article of faith.

It has been demonstrated over and over again throughout history by the best possible people that very little is required for happiness. It is the fight for money and possessions and the prestige they bring that sets people at odds, and that is what makes the world hard. We are the richest nation in the world, with the highest living standard. By our own fond illusions about prosperity we should also be the happiest. Are we? Suicides, racial violence, and the exodus of the young from comfortable homes suggest otherwise. The terrible truth is that our prosperity is the bringer of misery. We have been brainwashed by the advertising industry into being the most dissatisfied people in the world. We are told we must all be handsome or beautiful, sexually devastating, and owners of a staggering amount of recreational gadgetry or doomed to frustration. The result is that most of us are frustrated. It is exactly this that the hippie avoids like poison. He wants no part of self-defeating goals.

It is very likely that the hippie will go hungry and suffer exposure, and perhaps freak out. But he considers these far less dangerous than the kind of dehumanization society tried to wreak on him before his rebellion. He has escaped from a culture where the machine is god, and men judge each other by mechanical standards of efficiency and usefulness. He sees a madness in the constant fight to sell more washing machines, cars, toilet paper, girdles, and gadgets than the other fellow. He is equally horrified at the grim ruthlessness of the men who participate in that fight.

Alexander Bloom and Wini Breines, eds., *Takin It To The Streets: A Sixties Reader* (New York: Oxford University Press, 1997), pp. 310-312.

24.13

THE KERNER COMMISSION EXPLAINS URBAN RIOTS (1968)

In the mid-1960s, poor blacks vented their frustration at the slow pace of civil rights reforms and disappointment with Lyndon Johnson's Great Society by inciting violence in several cities. After a few minor incidents in the summer of 1964, the first major riot erupted on August 11, 1965 in the Watts section of Los Angeles—just five days after Johnson signed the Voting Rights Act. Watts exploded after a white police officer clubbed a black bystander during a traffic arrest. For the next six days, as many as 10,000 people looted, committed arson, and attacked policemen. National Guardsmen finally quelled the unrest. Watts was only the beginning. By the summer of 1968, urban riots had resulted in 200 deaths, 7,000 injuries, 40,000 arrests, and $200 million in property damage.

In July 1967, Johnson selected Illinois governor Otto Kerner to chair a federal commission on "civil disorders." The commission's final report identified several causes of urban unrest and made sweeping recommendations for solving the problems of the inner cities. In April 1968, one month after the report's release, riots erupted in over 100 cities following the assassination of Martin Luther King, Jr.

FOCUS QUESTIONS

1. How does the Kerner commission describe life in the inner cities? Do similar conditions exist today?
2. According to the commissioners, what are the causes of the riots? Who is rioting?
3. What are the commissioners' suggestions for resolving the urban crisis?
4. Lyndon Johnson ignored the Kerner commission's recommendations. Consider the state of the nation in mid-1968 and explain why Johnson may have made this decision.

T he record before this Commission reveals that the causes of recent racial disorders are imbedded in a massive tangle of issues and circumstances— social, economic, political, and psychological—which arise out of the historical pattern of Negro-white relations in America....

Despite these complexities, certain fundamental matters are clear. Of these, the most fundamental is the racial attitude and behavior of white Americans toward black Americans.... At the base of this mixture are three of the most bitter fruits of white racial attitudes:

Pervasive discrimination and segregation. The first is surely the continuing exclusion of great numbers of Negroes from the benefits of economic progress through discrimination in employment and education, and their enforced confinement in segregated housing and schools. The corrosive and degrading effects of this condition and the attitudes that underlie it are the source of the deepest bitterness and at the center of the problem of racial disorder.

Black migration and white exodus. The second is the massive and growing concentration of impoverished Negroes in our major cities resulting from Negro migration from the rural South, rapid population growth and the continuing movement of the white middle-class to the suburbs. The consequence is a greatly increased burden on the already depleted resources of cities, creating a growing crisis of deteriorating facilities and services and unmet human needs.

Black ghettos. Third, in the teeming racial ghettos, segregation and poverty have intersected to destroy opportunity and hope and to enforce failure. The ghettos too often mean men and women without jobs, families without men, and schools where children are processed instead of educated, until the return to the street—to crime, to narcotics, to dependency on welfare, and to bitterness and resentment against society in general and white society in particular.

These three forces have converged on the inner city in recent years and on the people who inhabit it. At the same time, most whites and many Negroes outside the ghetto have prospered to a degree unparalleled in the history of civilization. Through television—the universal appliance in the ghetto—and the other media of mass communications, this affluence has been endlessly flaunted before the eyes of the Negro poor and the jobless ghetto youth....

Yet these facts alone—fundamental as they are—cannot be said to have caused the disorders. Other and more immediate factors help explain why these events happened now....

Frustrated hopes. The expectations aroused by the great judicial and legislative victories of the civil rights movement have led to frustration, hostility and cynicism in the face of the persistent gap between promise and fulfillment. The dramatic struggle for equal rights in the South has sensitized Northern Negroes to the economic inequalities reflected in the deprivations of ghetto life.

Legitimation of violence. A climate that tends toward the approval and encouragement of violence as a form of protest has been created by white terrorism directed against nonviolent protest, including instances of abuse and even murder of some civil rights workers in the South but the open defiance of law and federal authority by state and local officials resisting desegregation; and by some protest groups engaging in civil disobedience who turn their backs on nonviolence, go beyond the Constitutionally protected rights of petition and free assembly, and resort to violence to attempt to compel alteration of laws and policies with which they disagree....

Powerlessness. Finally, many Negroes have come to believe that they are being exploited politically and economically by the white "power structure."...The frustrations of powerlessness have led some to the conviction that there is no effective alternative to violence as a means of expression and redress, as a way of "moving the system." More generally, the result is alienation and the white society which controls them. This is reflected in the reach toward racial consciousness and solidarity reflected in the slogan "Black Power."...

Incitement and encouragement of violence. These conditions have created a volatile mixture of attitudes and beliefs which needs only a spark to ignite mass violence. Strident appeals to violence, first heard from white racists, were echoed and reinforced last summer in the inflammatory rhetoric of black racists and militants. Throughout the year, extremists crisscrossed the country preaching a doctrine of black power and violence. Their rhetoric was widely reported in the mass media; it was echoed by local "militants" and organizations; it became the ugly background noise of the violent summer....

The Police. It is the convergence of all these factors that makes the role of the police so difficult and so significant. Almost invariably the incident that ignites disorder arises from police action. Harlem, Watts, Newark and Detroit—all the major outbursts of recent years—were precipitated by routine arrests of Negroes for minor offenses by white police.

But the police are not merely the spark. In discharge of their obligation to maintain order and insure public safety in the disruptive conditions of ghetto life, they are inevitably involved in sharper and more frequent conflicts with ghetto residents than with the residents of other areas. Thus, to many Negroes police have come to symbolize white power, white racism and white repression. And the fact is that many police do reflect and express these white attitudes. The atmosphere of hostility and cynicism is reinforced by a widespread perception among Negroes of the existence of police brutality and corruption, and of a "double standard" of justice and protection—one for Negroes and one for whites....

The future of these cities, and of their burgeoning Negro populations, is grim. Most new employment opportunities are being created in suburbs and outlying areas. This trend will continue unless important changes in public policy are made....

RECOMMENDATIONS FOR NATIONAL ACTION

Employment

Pervasive unemployment and underemployment are the most persistent and serious grievances in minority areas. They are inextricably linked to the problem of civil disorder....

The Commission recommends that the federal government:

Undertake joint efforts with cities and states to consolidate existing manpower programs to avoid fragmentation and duplication.

Take immediate action to create 2,000,000 new jobs over the next three years...

Provide on-the-job training by both public and private employers with reimbursement to private employers for the extra costs of training the hard-core unemployed, by contract or by tax credits.

Provide tax and other incentives to investment in rural as well as urban poverty areas in order to offer to the rural poor an alternative to migration to urban centers.

Take new and vigorous action to remove artificial barriers to employment and promotion, including not only racial discrimination but, in certain cases, arrest records or lack of a high school diploma. Strengthen those agencies such as the Equal Employment Opportunity Commission, charged with eliminating discriminatory practices, and provide full support for Title VI of the 1964 Civil Rights Act allowing federal grant-in-aid funds to be withheld from activities which discriminate on grounds of color or race....

Education

Education in a democratic society must equip children to develop their potential and to participate fully in American life. For the community at large, the schools have discharged this responsibility well. But for many minorities, and particularly for the children of the ghetto, the schools have failed to provide the educational experience which could overcome the effects of discrimination and deprivation....

[T]he Commission recommends:

Sharply increased efforts to eliminate de facto segregation in our schools through substantial federal aid to school systems seeking to desegregate either within the system or in cooperation with neighboring school systems....

Extension of quality early childhood education to every disadvantaged child in the country.

Efforts to improve dramatically schools serving disadvantaged children through substantial federal funding of year-round compensatory education programs, improved teaching, and expanded experimentation and research.

Elimination of illiteracy through greater federal support for adult basic education.

Enlarged opportunities for parent and community participation in the public schools.

Reoriented vocational education emphasizing work-experience training and the involvement of business and industry.

Expanded opportunities for higher education through increased federal assistance to disadvantaged students.

Revision of state aid formulas to assure more per student aid to districts having a high proportion of disadvantaged school-age children.

The Welfare System

Our present system of public welfare is designed to save money instead of people, and tragically ends up doing neither. This system has two critical deficiencies:

First, it excludes large numbers of persons who are in great need, and who, if provided a decent level of support, might be able to become more productive and self-sufficient. No federal funds are available for millions of men and women who are needy but neither aged, handicapped nor the parents of minor children.

Second, for those included, the system provides assistance well below the minimum necessary for a decent level of existence, and imposes restrictions that encourage continued dependency on welfare and undermine self-respect.

A welter of statutory requirements and administrative practices and regulations operate to remind recipients that they are considered untrustworthy, promiscuous and lazy. Residence requirements prevent assistance to people in need who are newly arrived in the state. Regular searches of recipients' homes violate privacy. Inadequate social services compound the problems.

The Commission recommends that the federal government, acting with state and local governments where necessary, reform the existing welfare system to:

Establish uniform national standards of assistance at least as high as the annual "poverty level" of income, now set by the Social Security Administration at $3,335 per year for an urban family of four.

Require that all states receiving federal welfare contributions participate in the Aid to Families with Dependent Children—Unemployed Parents program (AFDC-UP) that permits assistance to families with both father and mother in the home, thus aiding the family while it is still intact.

Bear a substantially greater portion of all welfare costs—at least 90 percent of total payments.

Increase incentives for seeking employment and job training, but remove restrictions recently enacted by the Congress that would compel mothers of young children to work.

Provide more adequate social services through neighborhood centers and family-planning programs....

As a long-range goal, the Commission recommends that the federal government seek to develop a national system of income supplementation based strictly on need with two broad and basic purposes:

To provide, for those who can work or who do work, any necessary supplements in such a way as to develop incentives for fuller employment;

To provide, for those who cannot work and for mothers who decide to remain with their children, a minimum standard of decent living, and to aid in the saving of children from the prison of poverty that has held their parents....

Housing

After more than three decades of fragmented and grossly underfunded federal housing programs, nearly six million substandard housing units remain occupied in the United States.

The housing problem is particularly acute in the minority ghettos. Nearly two-thirds of all non-white families living in the central cities today live in neighborhoods marked with substandard housing and general urban blight....

Two points are fundamental to the Commission's recommendations:

First: Federal housing programs must be given a new thrust aimed at over-coming the prevailing patterns of racial segregation....

Second: The private sector must be brought into the production and financing of low and moderate rental housing to supply the capabilities and capital necessary to meet the housing needs of the nation.

The Commission recommends that the federal government:

Enact a comprehensive and enforceable federal open housing law to cover the sale or rental of all housing, including single family homes.

Reorient federal housing programs to place more low and moderate income housing outside of ghetto areas.

Bring within the reach of low and moderate income families within the next five years six million new and existing units of decent housing....

United States. Kerner Commission, *Report of the National Advisory Commission on Civil Disorders* (Washington: U.S. Government Printing Office, 1968).

24.14

No More Miss America (1968)

As Betty Friedan and the National Organization for Women worked within the political systems to challenge sex discrimination, many younger women adopted a more radical feminism. Mostly white, affluent, and educated, these women drew inspiration from the New Left and the counterculture. While working as anti-war or civil rights activists, some drew parallels between their demeaning treatment by male colleagues and the subordinate status of racial minorities. They coined the term "sexism" to describe their plight and began organizing a women's liberation movement. Thousands of women gathered in small "consciousness-raising" groups to discuss their frustrations and aspirations. These powerful forums inspired many participants to join larger protests.

In one of the earliest women's liberation events, demonstrators picketed the 1968 Miss America Pageant in Atlantic City. Protestors tossed girdles, steno pads, false eyelashes, stiletto heels, and other items into a "Freedom Trash Can." They did not, however, burn any bras because city officials denied them a fire permit. Nonetheless, journalists called the activists "bra burners" and the name stuck. In this pamphlet, organizers invite women to join the Miss America rally.

Focus Questions

1. Why do these women find Miss America Pageant objectionable? How would you characterize their tone?
2. Are men urged to join the protests? Why or why not?

3. Explain how organizers are using the Miss America Pageant to critique American society as a whole.

4. Compare "No More Miss America" to Betty Friedan's *The Feminine Mystique* (Document 24.5). Which reading do you find more effective? Why?

On September 7th in Atlantic City, the Annual Miss America Pageant will again crown "your ideal." But this year, reality will liberate the contest auction-block in the guise of "genyooine" de-plasticized, breathing women. Women's Liberation Groups, black women, high-school and college women, women's peace groups, women's welfare and social-work groups, women's job-equality groups, pro-birth control and pro-abortion groups—women of every political persuasion—all are invited to join us in a day-long boardwalk-theater event, starting at 1:00 p.m. on the Boardwalk in front of Atlantic City's Convention Hall. We will protest the image of Miss America, an image that oppresses women in every area in which it purports to represent us.

There will be: Picket Lines; Guerrilla Theater; Leafleting; Lobbying Visits to the contestants urging our sisters to reject the Pageant Farce and join us; a huge Freedom Trash Can (into which we will throw bras, girdles, curlers, false eyelashes, wigs, and representative issues of *Cosmopolitan, Ladies' Home Journal, Family Circle,* etc.—bring any such woman-garbage you have around the house); we will also announce a Boycott of all those commercial products related to the Pageant, and the day will end with a Women's Liberation rally at midnight when Miss America is crowned on live television. Lots of other surprises are being planned (come and add your own!) but we do not plan heavy disruptive tactics and so do not expect a bad police scene. It should be a groovy day on the Boardwalk in the sun with our sisters. In case of arrests, however, we plan to reject all male authority and demand to be busted by policewomen only. (In Atlantic City, women cops are not permitted to make arrests—dig that!)

Male chauvinist-reactionaries on this issue had best stay away, nor are male liberals welcome in the demonstrations. But sympathetic men can donate money as well as cars and drivers.

Male reporters will be refused interviews. We reject patronizing reportage. *Only newswomen will be recognized.*

THE TEN POINTS

We Protest:

1. *The Degrading Mindless-Boob-Girlie Symbol.* The Pageant contestants epitomize the roles we are all forced to play as women. The parade down the runway blares the metaphor of the 4-H Club county fair, where the nervous animals are judged for teeth, fleece, etc., and where the best "Specimen" gets the blue ribbon. So are women in our society forced daily to compete for male approval, enslaved by ludicrous "beauty" standards we ourselves are conditioned to take seriously.

2. *Racism with Roses.* Since its inception in 1921, the Pageant has not had one Black finalist, and this has not been for a lack of test-case contestants. There

has never been a Puerto Rican, Alaskan, Hawaiian, or Mexican-American winner. Nor has there ever been a *true* Miss America—an American Indian.

3. *Miss America as Military Death Mascot.* The highlight of her reign each year is a cheerleader-tour of American troops abroad—last year she went to Vietnam to pep-talk our husbands, fathers, sons and boyfriends into dying and killing with a better spirit. She personifies the "unstained patriotic American womanhood our boys are fighting for." The Living Bra and the Dead Soldier. We refuse to be used as Mascots for Murder.

4. *The Consumer Con-Game.* Miss America is a walking commercial for the Pageant's sponsors. Wind her up and she plugs your product on promotion tours and TV-all in an "honest, objective" endorsement. What a shill.

5. *Competition Rigged and Unrigged.* We deplore the encouragement of an American myth that oppresses men as well as women: the win-or-you're-worthless competitive disease. The "beauty contest" creates only one winner to be *"used"* and forty-nine losers who are "useless."

6. *The Woman as Pop Culture Obsolescent Theme.* Spindle, mutilate, and then discard tomorrow. What is so ignored as last year's Miss America? This only reflects the gospel of our Society, according to Saint Male: women must be young, juicy, malleable—hence age discrimination and the cult of youth. And we women are brainwashed into believing this ourselves!

7. *The Unbeatable Madonna-Whore Combination.* Miss America and Playboy's centerfold are sisters over the skin. To win approval, we must be both sexy and wholesome, delicate but able to cope, demure yet titillatingly bitchy. Deviation of any sort brings, we are told, disaster: "You won't get a man!!"

8. *The Irrelevant Crown on the Throne of Mediocrity.* Miss America represents what women are supposed to be: inoffensive, bland, apolitical. If you are tall, short, over or under what weight The Man prescribes you should be, forget it. Personality, articulateness, intelligence, and commitment—unwise. Conformity is the key to the crown—and, by extension, to success in our Society.

9. *Miss America as Dream Equivalent to—?* In this reputedly democratic society, where every little boy supposedly can grow up to be President, what can every little girl hope to grow to be? Miss America. That's where it's at. Real power to control our own lives is restricted to men, while women get patronizing pseudo-power, an ermine clock and a bunch of flowers; men are judged by their actions, women by appearance.

10. *Miss America as Big Sister Watching You.* The pageant exercises Thought Control, attempts to sear the Image onto our minds, to further make women oppressed and men oppressors; to enslave us all the more in high-heeled, low-status roles; to inculcate false values in young girls; women as beasts of buying; to seduce us to our selves before our own oppression.

NO MORE MISS AMERICA

The Chicago Women's Liberation Union Herstory Archive, Classic Feminist Writings, http://www.cwluherstory.com/CWLUArchive/miss.html.

24.15

●

RICHARD NIXON ACCEPTS THE REPUBLICAN NOMINATION FOR PRESIDENT (1968)

By 1968, most Americans longed for stability. Some politicians sensed the nation's mood and began appealing to people weary of social protests and urban unrest. After a failed attempt to win the 1964 Democratic presidential nomination, George Wallace made an impressive showing as a third-party in the 1968 presidential race. As governor of Alabama, Wallace had established himself as one of the nation's leading segregationists. His attacks on court-ordered busing, the expansion of the federal bureaucracy and government spending, and urban riots tapped into rising white discontent with liberalism and the Democratic Party. Wallace's supporters took particular delight at his disdain for anti-war protestors and the counterculture.

Republican candidate Richard Nixon (1913-1994) stressed similar themes in his 1968 campaign for the presidency. Born in Yorba Linda, California, Nixon was the second of five children. His father, Frank, operated a grocery store and gas station. His mother, Hannah, was a devout Quaker who greatly influenced her son. Nixon's youth was scarred by the deaths of two of his brothers. After graduating from Whittier College and Duke University Law School, Nixon returned to California to practice law. In 1940, he married Thelma "Pat" Ryan. In 1942, he joined the navy and was stationed as an aviation ground officer in the Pacific. Upon returning home in 1946, he ran for the U.S. House of Representatives against Jerry Voorhis, a five-term incumbent. Nixon won after repeatedly insinuating that Voorhis was a communist. Such smear tactics became a staple in Nixon's political arsenal.

Nixon gained national prominence while serving as a member of the House Un-American Activities Committee (HUAC). His dogged pursuit of Alger Hiss, a former State Department official accused of being a Soviet spy by journalist and former communist Whittaker Chambers, sealed Nixon's reputation as a stalwart anti-communist. In 1950, he successfully ran for the U.S. Senate against Helen Gahagan Douglas. He again resorted to innuendoes and accused Douglas of being "pink right down to her underwear."

Looking for someone who would satisfy the GOP right wing and who could attract voters in the West, Dwight Eisenhower chose Nixon as his running mate in the 1952 presidential race. Ike almost dropped Nixon from the ticket when the New York Post *revealed that Nixon had a secret "slush fund" financed by wealthy businessmen from southern California. The fund was not illegal, but was considered unseemly. To demonstrate his integrity, Nixon made a televised appeal that became known as the "Checkers Speech." In minute detail, he listed his family's assets and debts while his wife Pat looked on with discomfort. Nixon was defiant about his receipt of one political gift—a black and white cocker spaniel puppy whom his six-year-old daughter named Checkers. Nixon's performance persuaded Eisenhower not to drop him, but also widened the gulf between his supporters and detractors.*

After serving two terms as Eisenhower's vice-president, Nixon won the Republican nomination for president in 1960. Although viewed as the front-runner, Nixon lost to John F. Kennedy by a razor-thin margin of 112,000 popular votes. Amid charges of voter fraud in Illinois and Texas, Republican leaders encouraged Nixon to contest the election, but Nixon refused to do so for fear of tarnishing the nation's international image. His patriotic and selfless gesture won wide acclaim. Two years later, he lost a race for governor of California. In this instance, Nixon handled defeat less graciously. In a post-election press conference, he announced his retirement from politics and blasted the press for distorting his record. "You won't have Dick Nixon to kick around anymore." he vowed. He moved his family to New York City and became a successful attorney and respected expert on foreign affairs.

The polarizing events of the mid-1960s changed Nixon's political fortunes. Republican leaders persuaded Nixon that he could win the presidency in 1968. Declaring himself a "new Nixon," he built a broad coalition. Fending off a last-minute surge by Democrat Hubert Humphrey, Nixon won 43.4 percent of the popular vote to Humphrey's 42.7 percent, a margin of only 500,000 votes. Nixon won the electoral vote by 301-191. George Wallace won 13.5 percent of the popular vote and carried five southern states.

In accepting the 1968 Republican nomination for president, Nixon explained his vision for the nation.

FOCUS QUESTIONS

1. What are Nixon's major themes?
2. What does Nixon identify as the biggest problems facing the country? How does he propose to resolve them?
3. Why is Nixon's appeal to the "forgotten Americans" significant? Is Nixon's message a unifying or divisive one? Explain your answers.

August 8, 1968

 r. Chairman, delegates to this convention, my fellow Americans: Sixteen years ago I stood before this convention to accept your nomination as the running mate of one of the greatest Americans of our time or any time— Dwight D. Eisenhower. Eight years ago I had the highest honor of accepting your nomination for President of the United States. Tonight I again proudly accept that nomination for President of the United States.

But I have news for you. This time there's a difference—this time we're going to win....

We're going to win because this great convention has demonstrated to the nation that the Republican Party has the leadership, the platform and the purpose that America needs.

We're going to win because you have nominated as my running mate a statesman of the first rank who will be a great campaigner, and one who is fully qualified to undertake the new responsibilities that I shall give to the next Vice President of the United States [Maryland governor Spiro Agnew].

And he is a man who fully shares my conviction and yours that after a period of 40 years when power has gone from the cities and the states to the Government in Washington, D.C., it's time to have power go back from Washington to the states and to the cities of this country all over America.

We're going to win because at a time that America cries out for the unity that this Administration has destroyed, the Republican party, after a spirited contest for its nomination for President and Vice President, stands united before the nation tonight....

And a party that can unite itself will unite America....

As we look at America, we see cities enveloped in smoke and flame. We hear sirens in the night. We see Americans dying on distant battlefields abroad. We see Americans hating each other; fighting each other; killing each other at home.

And as we see and hear these things, millions of Americans cry out in anguish: Did we come all this way for this? Did American boys die in Normandy and Korea and in Valley Forge for this?

Listen to the answers to those questions.

It is another voice, it is a quiet voice in the tumult of the shouting. It is the voice of the great majority of Americans, the forgotten Americans, the non shouters, the non demonstrators. They're not racists or sick; they're not guilty of the crime that plagues the land; they are black, they are white; they're native born and foreign born; they're young and they're old.

They work in American factories, they run American businesses. They serve in government; they provide most of the soldiers who die to keep it free. They give drive to the spirit of America. They give lift to the American dream. They give steel to the backbone of America.

They're good people. They're decent people; they work and they save and they pay their taxes and they care.

Like Theodore Roosevelt, they know that this country will not be a good place for any of us to live in unless it's a good place for all of us to live in.

And this I say, this I say to you tonight, is the real voice of America. In this year 1968, this is the message it will broadcast to America and to the world.

Let's never forget that despite her faults, America is a great nation. And America is great because her people are great....

America's in trouble today not her people have failed but because her leaders have failed. And what America wants are leaders to match the greatness of her people.

And this great group of Americans—the forgotten Americans and others— know that the great question Americans must answer by their votes in November is this: Whether we will continue for four more years the policies of the last five years.

And this is their answer, and this is my answer to that question: When the strongest nation in the world can be tied up for four years in a war in Vietnam with no end in sight, when the richest nation in the world can't manage its own economy, when the nation with the greatest tradition of the rule of law is plagued by unprecedented lawlessness, when a nation that has been known for a century for equality of opportunity is torn by unprecedented racial violence, and when the President of the United States cannot travel abroad or to any major city at home without fear of a hostile demonstration—then it's time for new leadership for the United States of America.

Thank you. My fellow Americans, tonight I accept the challenge and the commitment to provide that new leadership for America and I ask you to accept it with me....

We've had enough of big promises and little action. The time has come for an honest government in the United States of America.

And so tonight I do not promise the millennium in the morning. I don't promise that we can eradicate poverty and end discrimination and eliminate all danger of wars in the space of four or even eight years. But I do promise action. A new policy for peace abroad, a new policy for peace and progress at home....

And I pledge to you tonight that the first priority foreign policy objective of our next Administration will be to bring an honorable end to the war in Vietnam. We shall not stop there. We need a policy to prevent more Vietnams. All of America's peacekeeping institutions and all of America's foreign commitments must be reappraised....

It's ironic to note, when we were a small nation, weak militarily and poor economically, America was respected. And the reason was that America stood for something more powerful than military strength or economic wealth.

The American Revolution was a shining example of freedom in action which caught the imagination of the world, and today, too often, America is an example to be avoided and not followed.

A nation that can't keep the peace at home won't be trusted to keep the peace abroad. A President who isn't treated with respect at home will not be treated with respect abroad. A nation which can't manage its own economy can't tell others how to manage theirs....

The American Revolution was and is dedicated to progress. But our founders recognized that the first requisite of progress is order.

Now there is no quarrel between progress and order because neither can exist without the other.

So let us have order in America, not the order that suppresses dissent and discourages change but the order which guarantees the right to dissent and provides the basis for peaceful change.

And tonight it's time for some honest talk about the problem of order in the United States. Let us always respect, as I do, our courts and those who serve on them, but let us also recognize that some of our courts in their decisions have gone too far in weakening the peace forces as against the criminal forces in this country.

Let those who have the responsibility to enforce our laws, and our judges who have the responsibility to interpret them, be dedicated to the great principles of civil rights. But let them also recognize that the first civil right of every American is to be free from domestic violence. And that right must be guaranteed in this country....

And if we are to restore order and respect for law in this country, there's one place we're going to begin: We're going to have a new Attorney General of the United States of America.

I pledge to you that our new Attorney General will be directed by the President of the United States to launch a war against organized crime in this country.

I pledge to you that the new Attorney General of the United States will be an active belligerent against the loan sharks and the numbers racketeers that rob the urban poor in our cities.

I pledge to you that the new Attorney General will open a new front against the pill peddlers and the narcotics peddlers who are corrupting the lives of the children of this country....

And to those who say that law and order is the code word for racism, here is a reply: Our goal is justice—justice for every American. If we are to have respect for law in America, we must have laws that deserve respect. Just as we cannot have progress without order, we cannot have order without progress....

And this brings me to the clearest choice among the great issues of this campaign.

For the past five years we have been deluged by Government programs for the unemployed, programs for the cities, programs for the poor, and we have reaped from these programs an ugly harvest of frustrations, violence and failure across the land. And now our opponents will be offering more of the same—more billions for Government jobs, Government housing, Government welfare. I say it's time to quit pouring billions of dollars into programs that have failed in the United States of America....

Instead of Government jobs and Government housing and Government welfare, let Government use its tax and credit policies to enlist in this battle the greatest engine of progress ever developed in the history of man—American private enterprise.

Let us enlist in this great cause the millions of Americans in volunteer organizations who will bring a dedication to this task that no amount of money can ever buy.

And let us build bridges, my friends, build bridges to human dignity across that gulf that separates black America from white America.

Black Americans—no more than white Americans—do not want more Government programs which perpetuate dependency. They don't want to be a colony in a nation. They want the pride and the self-respect and the dignity that can only come if they have an equal chance to own their own homes, to own their own businesses, to be managers and executives as well as workers, to have a piece of the action in the exciting ventures of private enterprise.

I pledge to you tonight that we shall have new programs which will provide that equal chance....

And that great light shining out from America will again become a beacon of hope for all those in the world who seek freedom and opportunity....

The Texas A&M Department of Communication Presidential Speech Archive, http://www.tamu.edu/scom/pres/speeches/rmnaccept.html.

SECONDARY SOURCE

MAURICE ISSERMAN AND MICHAEL KASIN, "THE FAILURE AND SUCCESS OF THE NEW RADICALISM"

Americans remain divided in their assessments of the Sixties. Some consider the era a time of idealism and achievement; others a time of moral decline and anarchy. It is, however, indisputable that the 1960s reshaped American politics and society. In this essay written at the end of the Reagan years, Maurice Isserman and Michael Kazin, both noted political historians, examine the contested legacy of the New Left.

 Go to your *Speaking of America* CD-ROM to read "The Failure and Success of the New Radicalism."

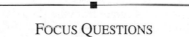

FOCUS QUESTIONS

1. What were the origins of the New Left? What were the original goals of SDS? How and why did SDS change over time?
2. What were some of the factors that made many young people receptive to political radicalism in the 1960s?
3. In their conclusion, Isserman and Kazin write, "The contradictory legacy of the sixties...provides evidence of both the failures and successes of the new radicalism—'failures' that were sometimes unavoidable, and sometimes self-inflicted, and 'successes' that were usually unrecognized and were often the opposite of what was intended." What do they mean?
4. What are some ways that liberals and conservatives have continued to debate the legacies of the sixties since this article was written in 1989?
5. Prior to completing this chapter, what were your views of the sixties? Explain how these readings have modified those views. Do you think that the sixties changed America for better or worse? Why?

AMERICAN JOURNEY ONLINE

——————■——————

http://ajaccesss.wadsworth.com [†]

About the Cold War
— In The Hispanic-American Experience
Images
- Ernesto "Che" Guevara (1960)
- Soldiers Departing for the Dominican Republic (1965)
— In The Cold War
Documents
- John F. Kennedy, Statement by President John F. Kennedy on the Berlin Wall, August 24, 1961
- Central Intelligence Agency, Guidelines for Operation Mongoose (1962)
- John F. Kennedy, et al, Transcript of a Meeting at the White House, October 16, 1962
- Osvaldo Dorticos Torrado, Excerpt from Cuban Protests against U.S. Aggression (1962)
- Nikita S. Khrushchev, Telegram from the Embassy in the Soviet Union to the Department of State, October 26, 1962
- Excerpt from Soviet and American Officials at the Havana Conference (undated)
- John F. Kennedy, Excerpt from Speech by President John F. Kennedy at the United Nations General Assembly, New York, NY, September 20, 1963
- UN Security Council, Resolution 242 (1967)
- U.S. State Department, Airgram from the Embassy in Czech., 11/29/68
- National Security Council, NSC Paper: The United States, Europe, and the Czechoslovakia Crisis (1968)
Images
- Bay of Pigs Disaster (1961)
- Ike and Kennedy Mull Bay of Pigs Disaster (1961)
- Kennedy and Khrushchev Meet (1961)
- John F. Kennedy, Television Address of John F. Kennedy, June 6, 1961
- Berlin Wall Goes Up (1961)
- The Berlin Wall (1961)
- American Spymaster (undated)
- Adlai Stevenson at the United Nations (1962)
- ExComm (1962)

[†] Enter password, choose the Archive indicated above, click on Contents, choose
•Documents, •Images, or •Multimedia, and click on the title of the item.

- Civil Defense Preparedness Agency, A Sheltered Existence (undated)
- Missile Sites in Cuba Abandoned (1962)
- Rusk, Fulbright Debate the Cold War (1962)
- Kennedy Adored in West Berlin (1963)
- NSC-68, Paul H. Nitze (1967) in The Cold War

About the Vietnam War
— In <u>Vietnam Era</u>
  Documents
- National Liberation Front, Let's Liberate the South (undated)
- Le Duan, Third National Congress Endorses Creation of National Liberation Front, September 1960
- Elbridge Durbrow, Report to the State Department, September 16, 1960
- Vo Nguyen Giap, "People's War, People's Army" (1961)
- Lyndon B. Johnson, Report to John F. Kennedy, May 23, 1961
- Pham Van Bach, Ngo Dinh Diem's Anti-Communist Law (1961)
- U.S. State Department, *A Threat to Peace: North Vietnam's Effort to Conquer South Vietnam* (1961)
- Dean Rusk, Cable 1006 (1962)
- Joseph Alsop, Homer Brigart, and Robert Trumbull, Reporters' Frustrations (1962)
- Communist Party (Vietnam), Needs of the Revolution (circa 1962)
- Henry D. Felt, Memorandum to Arthur Sylvester, November 26, 1962
- John Mecklin, Memorandum to Frederick Nolting, November 27, 1962
- Joint Chiefs of Staff, Roswell Gilpatric and Department of Defense, Cables, Reports Regarding Battle of Ap Bac, January 2, 1963
- Joint Chiefs of Staff, Excerpt of a Report of Visit of the Joint Chiefs of Staff, January 1963
- Charles Mohr and Merton Perry, The View from Saigon (1963)
- John E. Moss, et al, United States Information Policy in Vietnam (1963)
- Henry Cabot Lodge, Jr., cable Urges Support for Coup, October 30, 1963
- McGeorge Bundy, Cable to Henry Cabot Lodge, Jr. (1963)
- Henry Cabot Lodge, Jr., Last Conversation with Diem, November 1, 1963
- National Security Council, NSAM 273, November 26, 1963
- Communist Party (Vietnam), Decision to Send Support to the South (1963)
- Robert S. McNamara, Bleak Prospects in Vietnam (1963)
- Peter Grose, Letter to Emmanuel Freedman, February 29, 1964
- Robert S. McNamara, McNamara Report, March 16, 1964 (NSAM 288)
- National Security Agency, Reprisal Strikes Against North Vietnam (1965)
- Ho Chi Minh, Excerpt from Against U.S. Aggression for National Salvation (1965)
- Vo Nguyen Giap, Excerpt from Dien Bien Phu (1964)

- A Gulf of Tonkin Chronology, August 4, 1964
- James L. Greenfield, Memorandum for Discussion, December 8, 1964
- Central Intelligence Agency, Communist Reaction to BARREL ROLL Missions, December 29, 1964
- John MacNaughton, U.S. Interests in Vietnam (1965)
- George Ball, A Dissenting Voice (1965)
- Le Duan, We Will Certainly Win, the Enemy Will Certainly Lose (1965)
- Robert S. McNamara, Proposals for War, July 20, 1965
- Lyndon B. Johnson et al., A Council for War (1965)
- National Security Council, LBJ's Decisions for War (1965)
- Frank Sieverts, et al., Memorandums on the Maximum-Candor Policy (1965)
- Central Intelligence Agency and Defense Intelligence Agency, An Appraisal of the Bombing of North Vietnam, October 27, 1965
- Le Duan, Excerpt from Thu Vao Nam (1965)
- Communist Party (North Vietnam), Excerpt from The Anti-U.S. Resistance War for National Salvation, 1954-1975 (1965)
- Central Intelligence Agency and Defense Intelligence Agency, An Appraisal of the Bombing of North Vietnam: Effects on the DRV Economy (1965)
- David Halberstam, Excerpt from *The Making of a Quagmire* (1965)
- Special National Intelligence Estimate, Possible Effects of Proposed U.S. Courses of Action on DRV Capability to Support the Insurgency in South Vietnam (1966)
- Central Intelligence Agency, The Current Status of PAVN Infiltration to South Vietnam (1966)
- U.S. Government, Jason Study, September 13, 1966; Effectiveness of B-52 Operations, January 10, 1967; Effectiveness of the Present Bombing Campaign, December 16, 1967
- Nguyen Bao Tri, Barry Zorthian, and Rodger R. Bankson, Memorandum for Correspondents: Rules Governing Public Release of Military Information in Vietnam (1966)
- Central Intelligence Agency and Defense Intelligence Agency, An Appraisal of the Bombing of North Vietnam (1966)
- Harrison Salisbury, Hanson Baldwin, and Clifton Daniel, Memorandums at the *New York Times* (1966)
- Central Intelligence Agency, North Vietnam's Military Position in the Southern DRV (1967)
- Winant Sidle, Briefing Summary Presented by Brigadier General Sidle at Commanders Conference, Nha Trang, September 24, 1967
- William C. Westmoreland, Speech to National Press Club, November 22, 1967
- Earle Wheeler, Report to Lyndon B, Johnson on Tet Offensive, February 27, 1968

- Lyndon B. Johnson, et al., Conversation with Generals Wheeler and Abrams, March 26, 1968
- Lyndon B. Johnson, et al., Meeting with Wise Men, March 26, 1968
- Lyndon B. Johnson, Speech, March 31, 1968
- Earle Wheeler, Memorandum for the President, April 30, 1968
- Willard Pearson, Memorandum: Post Mortem on Vietnam Strategy, September 6, 1968

Images
- John F. Kennedy at the State Department with Map of Communist Rebel Areas, March 22, 1961
- U.S. Army, General Paul D. Harkins Inspects South Vietnamese Training Camp (1963)
- Malcolm Browne, Self-Immolation of Buddhist Monk, June 11, 1963
- The Assassination of Ngo Dinh Diem (1963)
- General Nguyen Khanh (undated)
- Secretary of Defense Robert S. McNamara in South Vietnam (1964)
- U.S. Navy, *U.S.S. Maddox* (1964)
- General William C. Westmoreland Inspects South Vietnamese Troops, October 1964
- U.S. Marines Land at Da Nang, March 1965
- Henry Cabot Lodge, Jr. is Greeted by Nguyen Van Thieu (1965)
- U.S. Air Force, Bombing Along the DMZ (1965)
- Ho Chi Minh (1966)
- Lyndon B. Johnson Confers with South Vietnamese in Honolulu, February 1966
- U.S. Infantry in Paddy with Villagers (undated)
- U.S. Infantry and National Liberation Front Tunnels (undated)
- Sean Flynn in South Vietnam, April 26, 1966
- Nguyen Cao Ky Inspects Captured Enemy Weapons, August 1966
- Lyndon B. Johnson, William C. Westmoreland, Nguyen Van Thieu (1966)
- U.S. Department of Defense, Bombing of Hanoi (1966)
- Family in Bombed Home (undated)
- National Liberation Front Guerillas with Primitive Rocket Launcher (undated)
- U.S. Infantry with Dead National Liberation Front Cadres (undated)
- U.S. Soldier in Vietnam (1966)
- New Marine Recruits Arrive on the USS General John Pope in Da Nang Harbor, August 15, 1967
- 173rd Airborne Brigade in Captured North Vietnamese Bunkers on Hill 875, November 22, 1967
- Lyndon B. Johnson at His Desk (1967)
- National Liberation Front Guerillas Set Trap (undated)
- North Vietnamese Soldiers Stand Near a Soviet-Made SAM near Haiphong, January 10, 1968

- Destructive War (1968)
- GI Wounded during Tet Offensive (1968)
- Street Execution Scene, Saigon (1968)
- Saigon Burning (1968)
- *USS Manley* Fires on Hue during the Tet Offensive (1968)
- Military Police, Kneeling Behind Wall, and 101st Airborne Division Fight Viet Cong at U.S. Embassy, Saigon, January 31, 1968
- Buddha Statute in Saigon during Tet Offensive (1968)
- Clark Clifford with President Johnson (1968)
- Walter Cronkite at Hue (1968)
- Mass Graves at Hue (1968)
- Two Unidentified Bodies at Roadside, My Lai (1968)
- Lyndon B. Johnson and Ambassador Ellsworth Bunker at Camp David, April 9, 1968
- *The Green Berets* (1968)
- General Creighton Abrams (1968)
- Nguyen Van Thieu (1968)
- South Vietnamese President Nguyen Van Thieu (1968)
- Maps of the Ho Chi Minh Trail (1984)
- Two Soldiers Confront an Old Man at My Lai (1968)

Videos
- U.S. Department of Defense, South Vietnam's Independence Day Celebrations (1962)
- (4 Parts)—United States Information Agency, Guardian at the Gate
- United States Information Agency, Lyndon B. Johnson Speaks to American Students (1965)
- Saigon during the Tet Offensive (1968)
— In The Cold War

Documents
- U.S. Department of Defense, Buddhist Crisis of 1963
- U.S. Congress, Gulf of Tonkin Resolution, August 7, 1964
- U.S. Senate Foreign Relations Committee, Excerpt from Debate between Secretary of State Dean Rusk and Senator J. William Fulbright, January 28, February 4,8,10,17,18, 1966
- George F. Kennan Criticizes the American Military Commitment (1966)
- J. William Fulbright, Statement by Senator J. William Fulbright on the "Arrogance of Power" (1966)

Images
- U.S. Escalates War after Gulf of Tonkin Incident (1964)
- United States Air Force, Heavy U.S. Bombing of Indochina (1965)
- Key U.S. Senators during the Vietnam War (undated)
- Cold War Insider Clark Clifford (1968)
- Atrocities in the Vietnam War: My Lai Massacre (1968)

— In <u>The Constitution and Supreme Court</u>
Images
- GIs Burning a Vietnamese Hut (1967)

About the Civil Rights Movement
— In <u>Civil Rights in the United States</u>
Documents
- Martin Luther King, Jr., I Have a Dream (1963)
- Document with Audio Commentary—U.S. Congress, Civil Rights Act of 1964
- U.S. Congress, Civil Rights Act of 1964, Title VII
- Document with Audio Commentary—Lyndon B. Johnson, Address to Congress (1965)
Images
- Image with Audio Commentary—Martin Luther King, Jr.
- Martin Luther King, Jr. (1963)
- King Receives Nobel Peace Prize (1964)
- Voting Machines
- Assassination of Dr. Martin Luther King, Jr. (1968)
- Ralph Abernathy (1968)
Videos
- James Meredith Enters the University of Mississippi (1962)
- Lyndon Johnson Signs Civil Rights Act (1964)
— In <u>The Great Depression and the New Deal</u>
Images
- Philip Randolph (1963)
— In <u>The African-American Experience</u>
Documents
- Fannie Lou Hamer and J.H. O'Dell, An Interview with Fannie Lou Hamer (1965)
Images
- Images with Audio Commentary—The March on Washington, August 28, 1963
- Civil Rights Leaders at the Lincoln Memorial (1963)
- Open Housing (1963)

About the Free Speech Movement
— In <u>Vietnam Era</u>
Documents
- Evolution of the Student Movement (1964)
Images
- Mario Savio of the Free Speech Movement Addresses the Crowd in Berkeley, CA, December 4, 1964

— In <u>Civil Rights in the United States</u>
Images
- Free Speech Movement at the University of California (1964)

About the Anti-War Movement
— In <u>Vietnam Era</u>
Documents
- Student Nonviolent Coordinating Committee (SNCC) and Dr. Martin Luther King, Jr., African-American Protests against the War (1967)
- Eugene McCarthy and Robert F. Kennedy, Antiwar Movement Enters the Political Mainstream (1967)
- Dr. Benjamin Spock, A Call to Resist Illegitimate Authority (1967)
- Dr. Benjamin Spock et al, American Deserters Committee, Resisting Military Service (1968)
Images
- Vietnam War Protestors Picket in Front of the White House, April 17, 1965
- Freedom Draft Card (undated)
- U.S. Marshals Pushing Back Demonstrators (1967)
- LBJ Depicted as a War Criminal (1967)
- Antiwar Protestors in Chicago Riots (1968)

About Urban Unrest
— In <u>Civil Rights in the United States</u>
Documents
- Lyndon B. Johnson, On the 1965 Watts Riots (1965)
Images
- Race Riots in Watts (1965)

About Domestic Politics
— In <u>Civil Rights in the United States</u>
Images
- John F. Kennedy (undated)
- Lyndon B. Johnson (undated)
- Robert Weaver (1966)
— In <u>The Cold War</u>
Images
- Staunch Conservative Barry Goldwater (1964)
- LBJ Pulls Out of the 1968 Campaign (1968)
— In <u>Vietnam Era</u>
Images
- Robert F. Kennedy on the Campaign Trail, June 1968

About Law/Law Enforcement
— In <u>The Constitution and Supreme Court</u>
   Documents
   • U.S. Congress, The Twenty-Third Amendment (1961)
   • Tom C. Clark, *Mapp v. Ohio* (1961)
   • William J. Brennan, Jr., *Baker v. Carr* (1962)
   • Tom C. Clark, *Katzenbach v. McClung* (1964)
   • U.S. Congress, The Twenty-Fourth Amendment (1964)
   • William J. Brennan, Jr., *New York Times v. Sullivan* (1964)
   • William O. Douglas, *Griswold v. Connecticut* (1965)
   • Earl Warren, *Miranda v. Arizona* (1966)
   • U.S. Congress, The Twenty-Fifth Amendment (1967)
   • Sam J. Ervin, Ervin on the Fortas Nomination (1968)
   Images
   • Clarence Gideon, Clarence Gideon's In Forma Pauperis Petition (1963)
   • The Miranda Warning (circa 1966)
   • Miranda Rights (undated)
— In <u>Civil Rights in the United States</u>
   Documents
   • U.S. Supreme Court, *Robinson v. California* (1962)
   • U.S. Supreme Court, *Engel v. Vitale* (1962)
   • U.S. Supreme Court, *Gideon v. Wainwright* (1963)
   • U.S. Supreme Court, *Gibson v. Florida Legislative Commission* (1963)
   • U.S. Congress, Civil Rights Act of 1964, Title VII (1964)
   • U.S. Supreme Court, *In re Gault* (1967)
   • U.S. Supreme Court, *United States v. O'Brien* (1968)
   Images
   • Sunday Closing Signs (1961)
   • Police Lineup (1962)
   • Police Arrest (undated)
   • Right to Counsel (1966)
   • Police Violence (1968)
— In <u>The African-American Experience</u>
   Documents
   • Patricia Roberts, The Law and Moral Issues (1963)

About Religion
— In <u>Civil Rights in the United States</u>
   Documents
   • Southern Baptist Convention, Religious Liberty (1963)

About Immigration
— In <u>Civil Rights in the United States</u>
   Images
   • Cuban Refugees (1965)

— In <u>The Immigrant Experience</u>
   Documents
   - U.S. Congress, Immigration Act of 1965

About the Environment
— In <u>Civil Rights in the United States</u>
   Images
   - Rachel Carson (1963)

About Culture
— In <u>Civil Rights in the United States</u>
   Images
   - Lenny Bruce (1964)
— In <u>The African-American Experience</u>
   Images
   - Playwright Leroi Jones (1965)

About Women
— In <u>Women in America</u>
   Documents
   - National Organization for Women (NOW), NOW Statement of Purpose (1966)
   - National Organization for Women (NOW), NOW's First Election Ballot (1966)

About Hispanic Americans
— In <u>The Hispanic-American Experience</u>
   Images
   - Braceros (1963)
   - Cesar Chavez (undated)

About Asian Americans
— In <u>The Asian-American Experience</u>
   Images
   - Hayakawa Is Not Our Leader (circa 1968)

About American Indians
— In <u>Civil Rights in the United States</u>
   Documents
   - U.S. Congress, Indian Civil Rights Act (1968)

CONSERVATIVE RESURGENCE

When Richard Nixon assumed the presidency in 1969, he vowed to reunify the nation and to end the Vietnam War. Just five years later, Nixon resigned from office. His conduct during the Watergate affair left Americans disillusioned and bitterly divided. Although the women's and gay rights movements made strides during the 1970s, they met increasing opposition from conservatives. Most Americans avoided social activism altogether as they struggled with the decade's severe economic problems. Presidents Ford and Carter searched in vain for solutions to rising inflation, energy shortages, and increasing international economic competition. As Soviet expansionism in the developing world destroyed Nixon's détente policy, conservatives like Ronald Reagan called for a restoration of U.S. prestige and military superiority. In the wake of an Islamic revolution in Iran, the United States faced new dangers in the Middle East. Reagan's victory in the 1980 presidential election marked the political triumph of the New Right. Reagan's economic policies, anti-Soviet rhetoric, massive defense build-up, and emphatic patriotism thrilled many Americans—and terrified others.

Nixon devoted much of his presidency to foreign policy. He and Henry Kissinger, his national security advisor, were strong believers in *realpolitik*—the view that power, not idealism, should determine international relations. They shared a penchant for secrecy and a desire to keep foreign-policymaking within the Executive Branch. Hoping to lessen Cold War tensions, Nixon and Kissinger pursued a "triangular diplomacy" exploiting the rivalry between Communist China and the Soviet Union.

Nixon's plans for ending the Vietnam War were multi-faceted. His Vietnamization strategy combined negotiations, troop withdrawals, and attacks on North Vietnamese supply lines. As the United States removed its forces, the South Vietnamese army played a larger role in the continuing war against the communists. In March 1969, Nixon secretly ordered the bombing of Cambodia, Vietnam's neutral neighbor. On April 30, 1970, Nixon announced that U.S. and South Vietnamese ground forces were invading Cambodia.

The incursion incited explosive anti-war demonstrations. After months of relative inaction, anti-war protestors shut down over 400 colleges and universities. At Kent State University and Jackson State University, students died in altercations with law enforcement officials. The incidents accelerated the fragmentation of the anti-war movement. Some activists abandoned organizing in favor of pursuits like farming, religious worship, and raising families. Others joined the women's, environmental, or gay rights movements or worked in social services, education, or public-interest law. A few radical factions began an "underground" war against "The Establishment." Their violent tactics drew intense government surveillance.

While the anti-war movement wound down, Nixon continued his efforts in Vietnam. In 1971, South Vietnamese troops invaded Laos, but were soundly defeated. Convinced that victory was within reach, North Vietnam mounted a major offensive in the spring of 1972. Nixon responded by ordering the mining of major North Vietnamese ports and the bombing of Hanoi and other cities. At the same time, Kissinger and Le Duc Tho, North Vietnam's Foreign Minister, tried to hammer out an armistice. On October 26, 1972, just days before Nixon won reelection, Kissinger announced that peace was imminent. South Vietnamese President Nguyen Thieu, however, refused to accept any agreement that permitted North Vietnam to leave its troops in the South. Negotiations stalled again. In December, Nixon approved the massive "Christmas bombing" of North Vietnam in order to break the impasse. Shortly thereafter, the warring nations signed accords that were virtually identical to the agreement announced weeks earlier.

The Vietnam War exacted tremendous costs for all of its participants. Fifty-eight thousand Americans and more than two million Vietnamese died. The United States spent over $150 billion on the conflict. Vast portions of Vietnam, Laos, and Cambodia were littered with toxic chemicals and unexploded ordinance. In April 1975, North Vietnam finally defeated South Vietnam. In Cambodia, Chinese-backed Khmer Rouge guerillas seized control and murdered as many as three million people in their quest to build a Marxist utopia.

While extricating the United States from Vietnam, Nixon pursued a détente strategy designed to lessen Cold War tensions. In February 1972, he visited China—a major step toward the resumption of official diplomatic relations between the nations. Three months later, Nixon went to Moscow. He and Soviet Premier Leonid Brezhnev signed trade agreements and a Strategic Arms Limitation Treaty (SALT I) limiting the nuclear arsenals of the United States and the Soviet Union.

Détente had little effect in the Middle East. In the Six-Day War of 1967, Israel occupied Egypt's Sinai Peninsula and Gaza Strip, Jordan's West Bank and East Jerusalem, and Syria's Golan Heights. Although Israel promised to return the territories if its neighbors acknowledged its right to exist, the Arab nations refused to negotiate. Extremists in the Palestinian Liberation Organization (PLO) attacked Israelis and Israel retaliated. In 1973, Syria and Egypt attempted to recoup their losses in the Six-Day War by launching a surprise attack on the Jewish holy day, Yom Kippur. Bolstered with U.S. military equipment, Israel fended off the assault. In response, the Organization of Petroleum Exporting Countries (OPEC) punished the United States and its allies by imposing an embargo. Between October 1973 and March 1974, crude oil prices rose from $3 a barrel to $12. Alarmed by the energy crisis and Soviet influence in the Arab world, Kissinger began "shuttle" diplomatic missions between Middle East capitals. His efforts resulted in marginally improved relations in the region and ended the OPEC embargo.

At the same time, the United States increased its support of authoritarian regimes in Iran, Brazil, South Korea, South Africa and elsewhere. In Chile, the CIA facilitated a 1973 coup in which Augusto Pinochet ousted leftist Salvador Allende. Such policies thwarted Soviet expansionism, but also increased anti-Americanism.

At home, Nixon's domestic record was mixed. He expanded social security, job training, and housing programs. He signed laws limiting pesticides, establishing the Environmental Protection Agency, and regulating pollution. He enacted affirmative action guidelines for federal contractors. He was, however, unsuccessful in his efforts to reform welfare by guaranteeing all Americans an annual income. His plans to foster economic growth, curb inflation, and create jobs also faltered.

Ironically, Nixon's biggest failures stemmed from his illegal methods of ensuring "law and order." Determined to undermine black militants and New Left activists, he directed the IRS, the FBI, the CIA, and the Department of Justice to harass dissidents. Nixon and his aides used campaign funds to finance "dirty tricks" against political opponents and compiled an "enemies' list" of public figures deemed hostile to the administration.

These tactics led to the downfall of the Nixon administration. Although Nixon was expected to win reelection easily, members of the Committee to Reelect the President (CREEP) decided to wiretap the Democratic National Committee headquarters at the Watergate Hotel. In June 1972, five men were arrested during the operation. In order to conceal White House involvement in the affair, Nixon ordered his aides to pay "hush money" and to obstruct an FBI investigation. The cover-up did not come to public attention for several months. In November, Nixon crushed Democrat George McGovern in the 1972 presidential election. McGovern had endorsed the redistribution of income, the legalization of marijuana, an immediate pullout from Vietnam, and pardons for draft evaders—positions that many Americans found too liberal.

Nixon's victory proved short-lived. Facing long prison sentences, the Watergate burglars began revealing their ties to the Nixon administration. At the same time Carl Bernstein and Bob Woodward, two reporters for the *Washington Post*, uncovered evidence of the cover-up. In February 1973, the Senate convened the Special Committee on Presidential Campaign Activities. By May, Nixon had fired his legal counsel and two top advisors. That summer, millions watched televised hearings on the Watergate affair. For several months, Nixon attempted to withhold evidence that documented his role in the scandal. In July 1974, the Supreme Court ordered Nixon to surrender tapes of his conversations in the Oval Office. On August 9, 1974, facing three articles of impeachment, Nixon resigned.

Watergate and the Vietnam War dramatically changed American political culture. Millions of Americans became suspicious of politicians and the government. Some withdrew from social activism and devoted themselves to personal improvement. Critics denounced the materialism and self-absorption of the "Me Generation."

Nonetheless, many social movements remained vibrant in the 1970s. Between 1970 and 1975, the women's movement made remarkable gains. Hundreds of thousands of women participated in marches and demonstrations. Women successfully challenged discriminatory practices by banks and other financial establishments; persuaded advertisers and journalists to portray women more positively; and established scores of women's institutions such as bookstores, record companies, health care centers, and domestic violence shelters. Feminists secured passage of laws barring sex discrimination in higher education and legalizing abortion. In 1972, Congress approved the Equal Rights Amendment and sent the measure to the states for ratification.

The 1970s also witnessed the emergence of the modern gay rights movement. Inspired by the New Left and the counterculture, gay men and lesbians proudly declared "gay is good" and fought laws that criminalized gay sex and barred gays from congregating in public places. By 1973, almost 800 gay organizations were active across the United States. In 1974, gay activists convinced the American Psychological Association to remove homosexuality from its list of mental disorders. Dozens of cities passed laws barring discrimination on the basis of sexual orientation.

American Indians also mobilized for political change. Like Hispanics and African Americans, Indians celebrated their distinct racial identity and history. Indian militants organized large protests at Alcatraz Island, the Bureau of Indian Affairs, and Wounded Knee, South Dakota. In 1970, President Nixon ended the federal termination policy and thus allowed tribes greater autonomy. In 1974, the Indian Self-Determination Act gave tribes more control over federal funds used on reservations. These changes enabled many tribes to develop successful businesses such as casinos, factories, and mines. In several cases, tribes won substantial legal settlements for lost lands and natural resources. Although high rates of unemployment, alcoholism, and poverty persist among Native Americans, conditions for some have improved markedly.

During the 1970s, the sexual revolution hit mainstream America. More couples lived together without getting married. Use of birth control increased among women of all class and racial backgrounds. After the Supreme Court legalized abortion in *Roe v. Wade* (1973), the average number of abortions performed annually hit 1.5 million. Straight and gay people alike flocked to sexually charged bars and nightclubs. More college and high school students reported having premarital sex. The pornography industry exploded with the introduction of home videocassette recorders.

These changes drew organized opposition. Anti-pornography activists called for laws banning X-rated theaters and bookstores in their towns. The *Roe* v. *Wade* decision triggered a pro-life movement. An anti-gay movement emerged. Parents challenged public school sex education curricula. Religious leaders denounced rising divorce rates, homosexuality, feminism, unmarried cohabitation, and premarital sex.

Throughout the 1970s, there was a wave of renewed interest in religion. Some Americans embraced Eastern religions, but the most significant growth occurred among evangelical Protestant sects like the Assemblies of God and the Southern Baptists. These evangelicals believed in the literal interpretation of the Bible and the ability to be "born-again"—the cleansing of one's past sins and subsequent adherence to a life devoted to Jesus Christ. Christian bookstores, radio stations, and music companies spread quickly. Televangelists like Oral Roberts, Jimmy Swaggert, and Jim and Tammy Bakker drew huge audiences. Some evangelicals became politically active. In 1976, Jimmy Carter, a self-identified "born-again Christian" became president. In 1979, Jerry Falwell established the Moral Majority. By 1984, the group had two million members. Following the success of his 1988 presidential campaign, Pat Robertson founded the Christian Coalition, a political action committee. From the 1980s onward, the "religious right" wielded great influence in American political life.

In the wake of Watergate, Gerald Ford confronted serious domestic and foreign crises. Unemployment, inflation, and energy shortages paralyzed the nation's economy. Critics of détente pointed to communist gains in the developing world as evidence of the policy's failure.

In 1977, Jimmy Carter took office vowing to change the culture of Washington, but lacking an overall political vision. Carter's proposals for national health insurance, reform of the welfare system, and revision of the tax code won little support from Congress. He was more successful in efforts to deregulate private industry. Although he placed human rights at the center of his foreign policy agenda, his administration applied the policy inconsistently. While denouncing the autocratic regimes of South Africa and Chile, his aides continued supporting dictators in South Korea and the Philippines. But Carter also scored notable successes. He won passage of a treaty surrendering U.S. control of the Panama Canal; officially opened diplomatic relations with Communist China; and brokered an historic agreement between Israel and Egypt.

In the late 1970s, the contradictions in U.S. foreign policy became glaringly apparent. In Iran, where the United States had supported the repressive Shah since the 1950s, a powerful Islamic resistance arose. Millions of Muslims began opposing the Shah's oppression and attempts to westernize Iran. In January 1979, the Shah fled the country. Ayatollah Ruhollah Khomeini, a Muslim cleric exiled by the Shah years earlier, returned to lead the world's first Islamic revolution. U.S. officials tried to maintain relations with the increasingly militant Iranian government. But, in October 1979, when Carter allowed the Shah to receive cancer treatment at a New York hospital, all hell broke loose. On November 4, a mob entered the American embassy in Tehran and seized dozens of hostages. Fifty-three Americans remained prisoners for 444 days. To many Americans, the hostages symbolized Carter's failed presidency.

On December 27, 1979, Carter received another crushing blow when Soviet troops invaded Afghanistan. Carter strongly condemned the move with severe economic sanctions, cancellation of U.S. participation in the 1980 Summer Olympics in Moscow, and withdrawal of the SALT II treaty from Senate consideration. Carter ordered a build-up of the U.S. military and dispatched military and financial aid to Afghan rebels fighting the Soviets. Carter's efforts did little to improve his standing in public opinion polls.

Ronald Reagan capitalized on these events in the 1980 presidential race. His unapologetic patriotism and staunch anti-communism inspired many voters. They welcomed his promise to cut taxes in order to stimulate the economy and balance the federal budget. His opposition to abortion won support from the religious right. His call to revitalize private industry drew millions of blue-collar workers who usually voted Democratic. In the end, Reagan carried 51 percent of the popular vote to Carter's 41 percent. Independent candidate John Anderson won the remainder of the vote.

In his first term, Reagan focused on his economic program and national security issues. In May 1981, Congress demonstrated its support of supply-side economics (also called Reaganomics) by reducing federal taxes by 25 percent. To offset lost tax revenues, the Reagan administration proposed deep cuts in social programs. They also attempted to foster economic growth by deregulating the banking, savings and loan, transportation, and communication sectors. At first, Reaganomics did not result in lower inflation or unemployment. A widening trade deficit, high interest rates, and increasing budget deficits also impeded economic recovery. But in early 1983, the economy rebounded. The stock market boomed. Inflation, interest rates, and unemployment fell.

Reagan proved equally bold in his foreign policy. His harsh anti-communist rhetoric evoked the early Cold War. Determined to thwart the spread of communism in Latin America, the Reagan administration supported the government of El Salvador's effort to suppress leftist insurgents backed by Cuba and Nicaragua. U.S. officials financed the Contras in their attempt to unseat the communist Sandinista government of Nicaragua. In October 1983, Reagan sent 2,000 marines to Grenada to overthrow a leftist government.

Although the Iranian hostage crisis ended as Reagan was sworn-in, the Middle East continued to bedevil U.S. policymakers. After the PLO and Israel signed a 1981 cease-fire agreement, many PLO members sought sanctuary in Lebanon, a nation locked in a civil war between Muslims and Christians. When the PLO assassinated Israel's ambassador to Great Britain, the Israeli army forcibly ejected the PLO from Lebanon. Lebanese Christian militias then attacked Palestinian refugee camps. To defuse the increasingly volatile situation, the United States sent 2,000 marines to Beirut as peacekeepers. Lebanese Muslims viewed the marines as pro-Israeli and pro-Christian and began attacking them. In October 1983, an Islamic terrorist drove a truck loaded with explosives into the marine compound, killing 239 U.S. soldiers. After briefly shelling the Lebanese coast, the United States withdrew from Lebanon. The departure inspired Islamic terrorists to escalate their campaign against the West. While confronting the threat of terrorism, the Reagan administration proved unable to restart peace negotiations among Middle Eastern nations.

Reagan presided over the most massive buildup of the armed forces in U.S. history. Between 1981 and 1985, defense spending soared from $171 billion annually to $300 billion. Reagan greatly expanded the U.S. nuclear arsenal and approved a deployment of 572 additional nuclear missiles to Western Europe. In March 1983, he called for the development of the Strategic Defense Initiative (SDI or "Star Wars"), a system of lasers and satellites designed to protect the United States from a nuclear attack. Reagan ignored criticism of the project's technological flaws and enormous costs.

Reagan's policies generated widespread protests. Activists denounced the impact of budget cuts on children, the mentally ill, the elderly, and the poor. Economists decried the huge budget deficits created by Reaganomics. Millions of Americans joined anti-nuclear rallies and nine states adopted nuclear freeze resolutions. Others assailed the resurgence of Cold War tensions.

This opposition did not prevent Reagan from winning a landslide reelection in 1984. Claiming responsibility for the thriving economy and renewed sense of national pride, Reagan handily defeated Walter Mondale, his Democratic challenger. Reagan's second term would be marred by the Iran-Contra scandal and social crises such as AIDS, drugs, and homelessness. But Reagan also signed sweeping agreements with the Soviet Union and helped to end the Cold War.

25.1

RICHARD NIXON, ADDRESS TO THE NATION
ON THE WAR IN VIETNAM (1969)

Richard Nixon was determined to reestablish America's international prestige and to restore domestic stability. He considered extricating the United States from Vietnam essential to achieving those objectives. By 1969, 30,000 American soldiers had died in the war. The conflict was weakening the economy and dividing the public.

Sidestepping the State Department and the Pentagon, Nixon and Henry Kissinger, his national security advisor, formulated a multi-faceted strategy to bring "peace with honor" in Vietnam. At home, they took steps to neutralize the anti-war movement. Because the Johnson administration had gradually abolished many draft deferments (such as fatherhood, marriage, and enrollment in graduate school), the draft became a key anti-war issue. Demonstrators burned their draft cards, refused induction into the armed forces, or fled to other countries. In response, the Nixon administration instituted a lottery system in which only a limited number of nineteen-year-old men were drafted. Nixon then called for the creation of an all-volunteer military. Congress complied by suspending the Selective Service Act in 1973. Following the Soviet invasion of Afghanistan in late 1979, Congress reinstated draft registration.

While revising the draft system, Nixon and Kissinger crafted the Vietnamization policy. The plan included gradual withdrawal of U.S. forces in Vietnam, escalation and expansion of bombing campaigns, and diplomatic negotiations. In March 1969, Nixon secretly ordered the bombing of Cambodia in order to destroy

North Vietnamese supply lines. Without informing the South Vietnamese, Kissinger began peace talks with Le Duc Tho, foreign minister of North Vietnam. In July, Nixon announced that the United States would maintain its treaty obligations and provide financial aid and military equipment to Asian nations fighting communism, but these countries would have to use their own forces to defend themselves. The policy became known as the Nixon Doctrine.

Nixon's failure to end the war immediately inflamed the anti-war movement. In October 1969, anti-war demonstrations drew hundreds of thousands of people. On November 3, Nixon explained Vietnamization to the American people. He received thousands of supportive telegrams. Although more than 500,000 people participated in the Vietnam Moratorium on November 15, the anti-war movement waned as Nixon expedited troop withdrawals from Vietnam.

FOCUS QUESTIONS

1. How does Nixon describe the situation in Vietnam? Whom does he hold responsible for the continuing war?
2. Why does he refuse to withdraw U.S. troops immediately?
3. What steps is Nixon taking to end the war?
4. How does he characterize anti-war protestors? What is the significance of his appeal to "the great silent majority"?
5. Did Vietnamization work? Why or why not?

ood evening, my fellow Americans:
    Tonight I want to talk to you on a subject of deep concern to all Americans and to many people in all parts of the world—the war in Vietnam.

I believe that one of the reasons for the deep division about Vietnam is that many Americans have lost confidence in what their Government has told them about our policy. The American people cannot and should not be asked to support a policy which involves the overriding issues of war and peace unless they know the truth about that policy....

Now, let me begin by describing the situation I found when I was inaugurated on January 20.

— The war had been going on for 4 years.
— 31,000 Americans had been killed in action.
— The training program for the South Vietnamese was behind schedule.
— 540,000 Americans were in Vietnam with no plans to reduce the number.
— No progress had been made at the negotiations in Paris and the United States had not put forth a comprehensive peace proposal.
— The war was causing deep division at home and criticism from many of our friends as well as our enemies abroad.

In view of these circumstances there were some who urged that I end the war at once by ordering the immediate withdrawal of all American forces.

From a political standpoint this would have been a popular and easy course to follow. After all, we became involved in the war while my predecessor was in office. I could blame the defeat which would be the result of my action on him and come out as the Peacemaker.... But I had a greater obligation than to think only of the years of my administration and of the next election. I had to think of the effect of my decision on the next generation and on the future of peace and freedom in America and in the world.

Let us all understand that the question before us is not whether some Americans are for peace and some Americans are against peace....

The great question is: How can we win America's peace?...

For the South Vietnamese, our precipitate withdrawal would inevitably allow the Communists to repeat the massacres which followed their takeover in the North 15 years before.

— They then murdered more than 50,000 people and hundreds of thousands more died in slave labor camps.

— We saw a prelude of what would happen in South Vietnam when the Communists entered the city of Hue last year. During their brief rule there, there was a bloody reign of terror in which 3,000 civilians were clubbed, shot to death, and buried in mass graves.

— With the sudden collapse of our support, these atrocities of Hue would become the nightmare of the entire nation—and particularly for the million and a half Catholic refugees who fled to South Vietnam when the Communists took over in the North.

For the United States, this first defeat in our Nation's history would result in a collapse of confidence in American leadership, not only in Asia but throughout the world....

For the future of peace, precipitate withdrawal would thus be a disaster of immense magnitude.

— A nation cannot remain great if it betrays its allies and lets down its friends.

— Our defeat and humiliation in South Vietnam without question would promote recklessness in the councils of those great powers who have not yet abandoned their goals of world conquest.

— This would spark violence wherever our commitments help maintain the peace in the Middle East, in Berlin, eventually even in the Western Hemisphere.

Ultimately, this would cost more lives.

It would not bring peace; it would bring more war.

For these reasons, I rejected the recommendation that I should end the war by immediately withdrawing all of our forces. I chose instead to change American policy on both the negotiating front and battlefront.

In order to end a war fought on many fronts, I initiated a pursuit for peace on many fronts. In a television speech on May 14, in a speech before the United Nations, and on a number of other occasions I set forth our peace proposals in great detail.

— We have offered the complete withdrawal of all outside forces within one year.

— We have proposed a cease-fire under international supervision.

— We have offered free elections under international supervision with the Communists participating in the organization and conduct of the elections as an organized political force. And the Saigon Government has pledged to accept the result of the elections.

We have not put forth our proposals on a take-it-or-leave-it basis. We have indicated that we are willing to discuss the proposals that have been put forth by the other side. We have declared that anything is negotiable except the right of the people of South Vietnam to determine their own future....

Hanoi has refused even to discuss our proposals. They demand our unconditional acceptance of their terms, which are that we withdraw all American forces immediately and unconditionally and that we overthrow the Government of South Vietnam as we leave....

It has become clear that the obstacle in negotiating an end to the war is not the President of the United States. It is not the South Vietnamese Government.

The obstacle is the other side's absolute refusal to show the least willingness to join us in seeking a just peace. And it will not do so while it is convinced that all it has to do is to wait for our next concession, and our next concession after that one, until it gets everything it wants....

Now let me turn, however, to a more encouraging report on another front.

At the time we launched our search for peace I recognized we might not succeed in bringing an end to the war through negotiation. I, therefore, put into effect another plan to bring peace—a plan which will bring the war to an end regardless of what happens on the negotiating front....

In the previous administration, we Americanized the war in Vietnam. In this administration, we are Vietnamizing the search for peace.

The policy of the previous administration not only resulted in our assuming the primary responsibility for fighting the war, but even more significantly did not adequately stress the goal of strengthening the South Vietnamese so that they could defend themselves when we left.

The Vietnamization plan was launched following Secretary [of Defense Melvin] Laird's visit to Vietnam in March. Under the plan, I ordered first a substantial increase in the training and equipment of South Vietnamese forces....

And now we have begun to see the results of this long overdue change in American policy in Vietnam.

— After 5 years of Americans going into Vietnam, we are finally bringing American men home. By December 15, over 60,000 men will have been withdrawn from South Vietnam—including 20 percent of all of our combat forces.

— The South Vietnamese have continued to gain in strength. As a result they have been able to take over combat responsibilities from our American troops.

Two other significant developments have occurred since this administration took office.

— Enemy infiltration, infiltration which is essential if they are to launch a major attack, over the last 3 months is less than 20 percent of what it was over the same period last year.

— Most important — United States casualties have declined during the last 2 months to the lowest point in 3 years.

Let me now turn to our program for the future.

We have adopted a plan which we have worked out in cooperation with the South Vietnamese for the complete withdrawal of all U.S. combat ground forces, and their replacement by South Vietnamese forces on an orderly scheduled timetable. This withdrawal will be made from strength and not from weakness. As South Vietnamese forces become stronger, the rate of American withdrawal can become greater.

I have not and do not intend to announce the timetable for our program. And there are obvious reasons for this decision which I am sure you will understand. As I have indicated on several occasions, the rate of withdrawal will depend on developments on three fronts.

One of these is the progress which can be or might be made in the Paris talks. An announcement of a fixed timetable for our withdrawal would completely remove any incentive for the enemy to negotiate an agreement. They would simply wait until our forces had withdrawn and then move in.

The other two factors on which we will base our withdrawal decisions are the level of enemy activity and the progress of the training programs of the South Vietnamese forces. And I am glad to be able to report tonight progress on both of these fronts has been greater than we anticipated when we started the program in June for withdrawal. As a result, our timetable for withdrawal is more optimistic now than when we made our first estimates in June. Now, this clearly demonstrates why it is not wise to be frozen in on a fixed timetable....

Hanoi could make no greater mistake than to assume that an increase in violence will be to its advantage. If I conclude that increased enemy action jeopardizes our remaining forces in Vietnam, I shall not hesitate to take strong and effective measures to deal with that situation....

I recognize that some of my fellow citizens disagree with the plan for peace I have chosen. Honest and patriotic Americans have reached different conclusions as to how peace should be achieved.

In San Francisco a few weeks ago, I saw demonstrators carrying signs reading: "Lose in Vietnam, bring the boys home."

Well, one of the strengths of our free society is that any American has a right to reach that conclusion and to advocate that point of view. But as President of the United States, I would be untrue to my oath of office if I allowed the policy of this Nation to be dictated by the minority who hold that point of view and who try to impose it on the Nation by mounting demonstrations in the street.

For almost 200 years, the policy of this Nation has been made under our Constitution by those leaders in the Congress and the White House elected by all of the people. If a vocal minority, however fervent its cause, prevails over reason and the will of the majority, this Nation has no future as a free society.

And now I would like to address a word, if I may, to the young people of this Nation who are particularly concerned, and I understand why they are concerned, about this war.

I respect your idealism.

I share your concern for peace.

I want peace as much as you do.

There are powerful personal reasons I want to end this war. This week I will have to sign 83 letters to mothers, fathers, wives, and loved ones of men who have given their lives for America in Vietnam. It is very little satisfaction to me that this is only one-third as many letters as I signed the first week in office. There is nothing I want more than to see the day come when I do not have to write any of those letters.

— I want to end the war to save the lives of those brave young men in Vietnam.

— But I want to end it in a way which will increase the chance that their younger brothers and their sons will not have to fight in some future Vietnam someplace in the world.

— And I want to end the war for another reason. I want to end it so that the energy and dedication of you, our young people, now too often directed into bitter hatred against those responsible for the war, can be turned to the great challenges of peace, a better life for all Americans, a better life for all people on this earth.

I have chosen a plan for peace. I believe it will succeed....

I know it may not be fashionable to speak of patriotism or national destiny these days. But I feel it is appropriate to do so on this occasion

Two hundred years ago this Nation was weak and poor. But even then, America was the hope of millions in the world. Today we have become the strongest and richest nation in the world. And the wheel of destiny has turned so that any hope the world has for the survival of peace and freedom will be determined by whether the American people have the moral stamina and the courage to meet the challenge of free world leadership.

Let historians not record that when America was the most powerful nation in the world we passed on the other side of the road and allowed the last hopes for peace and freedom of millions of people to be suffocated by the forces of totalitarianism.

And so tonight—to you, the great silent majority of my fellow Americans—I ask for your support. I pledged in my campaign for the Presidency to end the war in a way that we could win the peace. I have initiated a plan of action which will enable me to keep that pledge.

The more support I can have from the American people, the sooner that pledge can be redeemed; for the more divided we are at home, the less likely, the enemy is to negotiate at Paris.

Let us be united for peace. Let us also be united against defeat. Because let us understand: North Vietnam cannot defeat or humiliate the United States. Only Americans can do that....

Published at http://www.nixonlibrary.org/TheNixons/archive/silent.pdf.

25.2

MARY CROW DOG RECALLS THE SIEGE OF WOUNDED KNEE (1973)

In 1968, a group of young Indians founded the American Indian Movement (AIM). Their initial goal was to assist Indians living in urban areas. Over time, AIM supported other objectives including economic empowerment, decreased government involvement in Indian affairs, renewal of traditional cultural practices, and restoration of illegally seized Indian lands and natural resources. Although Congress had passed the Indian Civil Rights Act in 1968, AIM activists remained dissatisfied and began organizing highly publicized protests. From 1969 to 1971, AIM was one of several organizations that occupied Alcatraz Island in San Francisco Bay. In response to Indian demands, Richard Nixon appointed a Mohawk-Sioux commissioner of Indian Affairs and promised increased federal aid and greater tribal autonomy. But the demonstrations continued. In 1972, about 1,000 Indians seized and ransacked the Bureau of Indian Affairs (BIA) in Washington, D.C.

In February 1973, AIM took over Wounded Knee, South Dakota—the site of the 1890 massacre of 200 Sioux by U.S. troops. Led by Dennis Banks and Russell Means, activists declared an "Independent Oglala Sioux Nation" and called for new tribal leadership and the enforcement of federal Indian treaties. After U.S. marshals surrounded the town, a 71-day siege ensued. Two Indians died and a marshal was seriously wounded in altercations. On May 8, the protestors surrendered their arms and left Wounded Knee in exchange for government promises to address their concerns.

In this excerpt from her autobiography Lakota Woman (1990), Mary Crow Dog, (1953-present) describes the Wounded Knee occupation.

FOCUS QUESTIONS

1. How does Mary Crow Dog portray conditions at Wounded Knee?
2. Was occupying Wounded Knee an effective way to convey Indian grievances? Why or why not?

Wounded Knee lasted seventy-one long days. These days were not all passed performing heroic deeds or putting up media shows for reporters. Most of the time was spent in boredom, just trying to keep warm and finding something to eat. Wounded Knee was a place one got scared in occasionally, a place in which people made love, got married Indian style, gave birth, and died. The oldest occupants were over eighty, the youngest under eight....

We organized ourselves. The biggest room in the store became the community hall. A white man's home, the only house with heat and tap water, became the hospital, and women were running it. The museum became the security office. We all took turns doing the cooking, sewing shirts, and making sleeping bags for the men in the bunkers. We embroidered the words "Wounded Knee" on rainbow-colored strips of cloth. Everybody got one of those as a badge of honor, "to show your grandchildren sometime," as Dennis [Banks] said. We shared. We did things for each other. At one time a white volunteer nurse berated us for doing the slave work while the men got all the glory. We were betraying the cause of womankind, was the way she put it. We told her that her kind of women's lib was a white, middle-class thing, and that at this critical stage we had other priorities. Once our men had gotten their rights and their balls back, we might start arguing with them about who should do the dishes. But not before.

Actually, our women played a major part at Wounded Knee. We had two or three pistol-packing mamas swaggering around with six-shooters dangling at their hips, taking their turns on the firing line, swapping lead with the feds. The Indian nurses bringing in the wounded under a hail of fire were braver than many warriors. The men also did their share of the dirty work. Bob Free, our first chief of engineers, had a crew which built twelve fortified bunkers, made an apartment house out of the trading post, dug latrines and constructed wooden privies, kept the juice going, repaired cars, operated the forklift and an earth-moving bulldozer. The men also formed a sanitary squad, picking up garbage and digging trenches to bury all that crap. One day Bob laid down the law: "Okay, that's it. The only electricity we keep is for the freezers to store the meat, for the gas pumps and three lights. That's all!" And he enforced it.

For a while I stayed at the trading post. But it was too much for me. Too many people and too little privacy. I figured that I would have my baby within two weeks. I moved into a trailer house at the edge of Wounded Knee. The then daily exchanges of fire had become commonplace. The bullets were flying as I got bigger and bigger. One day the government declared a cease-fire so that the women and children could leave. One of the AIM leaders came up to me: "You're leaving. You're pregnant, so you've got to go." I told him, "No, I won't. If I'm going to die, I'm going to die here. All that means anything to me is right here. I have nothing to live for out there."

But we were not going. I stayed, all the older women stayed, most of the young mothers with children stayed, the sweethearts of the warriors stayed. Only a handful took advantage of the cease-fire and left. The deadline passed. The firing started again. Heavy MGs, automatic rifles, tripwire flares, single shots from the government sniper experts....

The three hundred feds, the goons, and the BIA police were never able to seal us off completely.... So there was a lot of sneaking through the perimeter, a lot of coming and going. Indians from Denver, New Mexico, and L.A. trickled in, a dozen or half-dozen at a time. A group of Iroquois from New York joined us for a while, Most of them were guided by some of our local Sioux who knew every bush and every little hillock around us and could find their way blindfolded.

Usually people started walking in from the Porcupine area about eight or nine miles away. Some carried heavy packs of food. The government had their APCs [armored personnel carriers] out and illuminated the nights with their flares. They also kept the whole area under steady fire, shooting blindly…. It never stopped the brothers and sisters from coming….

Lakota Woman by Mary Crow Dog with Richard Erdoes. Copyright © 1990 by Mary Crow Dog and Richard Erdoes. Used by permission of Grove/Atlantic, Inc.

25.3

ROE V. WADE (1973)

Few Supreme Court decisions have provoked more controversy than Roe v. Wade. *In 1973, the Court delivered a 7-2 ruling granting women the right to choose abortion during the first three months of pregnancy. Justice Harry Blackmun wrote the majority opinion; Justices Byron White and William Rehnquist issued separate dissents. The case began when an unmarried pregnant woman (called Jane Roe to protect her identity) challenged a Texas law allowing abortion only when the mother's life was in jeopardy. Roe filed suit against Henry Wade, the district attorney of Dallas County. Citing recent decisions asserting a constitutional right to privacy, the Court agreed to hear Roe's case. But, by the time the Court ruled, Roe (later revealed to be Norma McCorvey) had given birth and placed her baby up for adoption.*

Roe v. Wade *remains a flashpoint in American life. Where pro-choice advocates see abortion as an essential civil right, pro-life supporters view it as state-sanctioned murder. Although the Court has consistently upheld* Roe v. Wade, *it has allowed restrictions such as imposing waiting periods before women can terminate a pregnancy, barring public funding of abortions, and requiring minors to obtain consent from a parent, guardian, or judge. Ironically, Norma McCorvey, after working at an abortion clinic for many years, became a pro-life activist in the mid-1990s.*

FOCUS QUESTIONS

1. What did the Supreme Court rule in *Roe v. Wade*? On what legal bases, did it make this decision?
2. Do you agree or disagree with the *Roe v. Wade* decision? Why?

MR. JUSTICE BLACKMUN delivered the opinion of the Court.
…We forthwith acknowledge our awareness of the sensitive and emotional nature of the abortion controversy, of the vigorous opposing views, even among physicians, and of the deep and seemingly absolute convictions

that the subject inspires. One's philosophy, one's experiences, one's exposure to the raw edges of human existence, one's religious training, one's attitudes toward life and family and their values, and the moral standards one establishes and seeks to observe, are all likely to influence and to color one's thinking and conclusions about abortion.

In addition, population growth, pollution, poverty, and racial overtones tend to complicate and not to simplify the problem.

Our task, of course, is to resolve the issue by constitutional measurement, free of emotion and of predilection. We seek earnestly to do this, and, because we do, we have inquired into, and in this opinion place some emphasis upon, medical and medical-legal history and what that history reveals about man's attitudes toward the abortion procedure over the centuries....

The Texas statutes that concern us here are Arts. 1191-1194 and 1196 of the State's Penal Code. These make it a crime to "procure an abortion," as therein defined, or to attempt one, except with respect to "an abortion procured or attempted by medical advice for the purpose of saving the life of the mother." Similar statutes are in existence in a majority of the States....

Jane Roe, a single woman who was residing in Dallas County, Texas, instituted this federal action in March 1970 against the District Attorney of the county. She sought a declaratory judgment that the Texas criminal abortion statutes were unconstitutional on their face, and an injunction restraining the defendant from enforcing the statutes.

Roe alleged that she was unmarried and pregnant; that she wished to terminate her pregnancy by an abortion "performed by a competent, licensed physician, under safe clinical conditions"; that she was unable to get a "legal" abortion in Texas because her life did not appear to be threatened by the continuation of her pregnancy; and that she could not afford to travel to another jurisdiction in order to secure a legal abortion under safe conditions. She claimed that the Texas statutes were unconstitutionally vague and that they abridged her right of personal privacy, protected by the First, Fourth, Fifth, Ninth, and Fourteenth Amendments. By an amendment to her complaint Roe purported to sue "on behalf of herself and all other women" similarly situated....

The principal thrust of appellant's attack on the Texas statutes is that they improperly invade a right, said to be possessed by the pregnant woman, to choose to terminate her pregnancy. Appellant would discover this right in the concept of personal "liberty" embodied in the Fourteenth Amendment's Due Process Clause; or in personal, marital, familial, and sexual privacy said to be protected by the Bill of Rights...or among those rights reserved to the people by the Ninth Amendment....

It perhaps is not generally appreciated that the restrictive criminal abortion laws in effect in a majority of States today are of relatively recent vintage. Those laws, generally proscribing abortion or its attempt at any time during pregnancy except when necessary to preserve the pregnant woman's life, are not of ancient or even of common-law origin. Instead, they derive from statutory changes effected, for the most part, in the latter half of the 19th century....

It is undisputed that at common law, abortion performed before "quickening"—the first recognizable movement of the fetus *in utero*, appearing usually from the 16th to the 18th week of pregnancy—was not an indictable offense.... In this country, the law in effect in all but a few States until mid-19th century was the pre-existing English common law....

Gradually, in the middle and late 19th century the quickening distinction disappeared from the statutory law of most States and the degree of the offense and the penalties were increased. By the end of the 1950's, a large majority of the jurisdictions banned abortion, however and whenever performed, unless done to save or preserve the life of the mother....

It is thus apparent that at common law, at the time of the adoption of our Constitution, and throughout the major portion of the 19th century, abortion was viewed with less disfavor than under most American statutes currently in effect. Phrasing it another way, a woman enjoyed a substantially broader right to terminate a pregnancy than she does in most States today....

The Constitution does not explicitly mention any right of privacy. In a line of decisions, however,...the Court has recognized that a right of personal privacy, or a guarantee of certain areas or zones of privacy, does exist under the Constitution.... This right of privacy, whether it be founded in the Fourteenth Amendment's concept of personal liberty and restrictions upon state action, as we feel it is, or, as the District Court determined, in the Ninth Amendment's reservation of rights to the people, is broad enough to encompass a woman's decision whether or not to terminate her pregnancy. The detriment that the State would impose upon the pregnant woman by denying this choice altogether is apparent. Specific and direct harm medically diagnosable even in early pregnancy may be involved. Maternity, or additional offspring, may force upon the woman a distressful life and future. Psychological harm may be imminent. Mental and physical health may be taxed by child care. There is also the distress, for all concerned, associated with the unwanted child, and there is the problem of bringing a child into a family already unable, psychologically and otherwise, to care for it. In other cases, as in this one, the additional difficulties and continuing stigma of unwed motherhood may be involved. All these are factors the woman and her responsible physician necessarily will consider in consultation.

On the basis of elements such as these, appellant and some amici argue that the woman's right is absolute and that she is entitled to terminate her pregnancy at whatever time, in whatever way, and for whatever reason she alone chooses. With this we do not agree.... The Court's decisions recognizing a right of privacy also acknowledge that some state regulation in areas protected by that right is appropriate. As noted above, a State may properly assert important interests in safeguarding health, in maintaining medical standards, and in protecting potential life. At some point in pregnancy, these respective interests become sufficiently compelling to sustain regulation of the factors that govern the abortion decision. The privacy right involved, therefore, cannot be said to be absolute....

In view of all this, we do not agree that, by adopting one theory of life, Texas may override the rights of the pregnant woman that are at stake. We repeat, however, that the State does have an important and legitimate interest in preserving and protecting the health of the pregnant woman, whether she be a resident of the State or a nonresident who seeks medical consultation and treatment there, and that it has still another important and legitimate interest in protecting the potentiality of human life. These interests are separate and distinct. Each grows in substantiality as the woman approaches term and, at a point during pregnancy, each becomes "compelling."

With respect to the State's important and legitimate interest in the health of the mother, the "compelling" point, in the light of present medical knowledge, is at approximately the end of the first trimester. This is so because of the now-established medical fact...that until the end of the first trimester mortality in abortion may be less than mortality in normal childbirth. It follows that, from and after this point, a State may regulate the abortion procedure to the extent that the regulation reasonably relates to the preservation and protection of maternal health. Examples of permissible state regulation in this area are requirements as to the qualifications of the person who is to perform the abortion; as to the licensure of that person; as to the facility in which the procedure is to be performed, that is, whether it must be a hospital or may be a clinic or some other place of less-than-hospital status; as to the licensing of the facility; and the like.

This means, on the other hand, that, for the period of pregnancy prior to this "compelling" point, the attending physician, in consultation with his patient, is free to determine, without regulation by the State, that, in his medical judgment, the patient's pregnancy should be terminated. If that decision is reached, the judgment may be effectuated by an abortion free of interference by the State.

With respect to the State's important and legitimate interest in potential life, the "compelling" point is at viability. This is so because the fetus then presumably has the capability of meaningful life outside the mother's womb. State regulation protective of fetal life after viability thus has both logical and biological justifications. If the State is interested in protecting fetal life after viability, it may go so far as to proscribe abortion during that period, except when it is necessary to preserve the life or health of the mother.

Measured against these standards, Art. 1196 of the Texas Penal Code, in restricting legal abortions to those "procured or attempted by medical advice for the purpose of saving the life of the mother," sweeps too broadly. The statute makes no distinction between abortions performed early in pregnancy and those performed later, and it limits to a single reason, "saving" the mother's life, the legal justification for the procedure. The statute, therefore, cannot survive the constitutional attack made upon it here....

Roe v. Wade, 410 *U.S. Reports* 113 (1973).

25.4

■

RICHARD NIXON, RESIGNATION SPEECH (1974)

On June 17, 1972, five men were arrested during a break-in at the headquarters of the Democratic National Committee at the Watergate, a Washington D.C. office and hotel complex. The men were carrying surveillance equipment and were charged with burglary and wiretapping. Charges were also levied against E. Howard Hunt, a former CIA operative, and G. Gordon Liddy, general counsel for the Committee to Reelect the President (CREEP). Although CREEP hired the burglars, there is no evidence that Richard Nixon ordered the break-in. He was, however, deeply involved in efforts to conceal the White House's involvement in the affair. He ordered his aides to thwart an FBI investigation and secretly pay-off the burglars.

While the cover-up proceeded, Carl Bernstein and Bob Woodward, two reporters at the Washington Post, investigated the Watergate incident. With the assistance of an unnamed White House source called "Deep Throat," they traced the money trail leading from CREEP to the burglars. They also uncovered evidence that Nixon campaign aides used harassment, espionage, and sabotage to discredit their political opponents. Despite these allegations, Nixon was overwhelmingly reelected in the 1972 presidential election.

In 1973, public interest in Watergate soared when the Senate convened a special committee to look into presidential campaign activities. At the same time, James McCord and Jeb Magruder, now facing long jail sentences for their participation in the Watergate break-in, exposed the Nixon administration's involvement in the burglary and the subsequent cover-up. In April, Nixon attempted to clear himself by accepting the resignations of several of his advisors including H.R. Halderman, John Ehrlichman, John Dean, and Attorney General Richard Kleindiest. Nixon denied any personal connection to political espionage or the cover-up.

Elliot Richardson, the new attorney general, named Archibald Cox as special Watergate prosecutor.

In May 1973, the Senate Watergate committee began televised hearings in which Dean and others exposed the Nixon administration's illegal activities. Dean's testimony was especially crucial since he was the first person to implicate Nixon in the cover-up. When Alexander Butterfield, a former presidential secretary, revealed the existence of a White House taping system, Cox and the Senate committee subpoenaed the tapes. For several weeks, Nixon refused to surrender the tapes, but offered to release written transcripts instead. When Cox rejected the proposal, Nixon ordered Richardson to fire Cox, but Richardson resigned rather than comply. By the time the so-called Saturday Night Massacre ended, Nixon had fired Richardson's assistant and coerced Solicitor General Robert Bork into firing Cox. After a federal district court ruled that Cox's dismissal violated the law, Nixon was forced to appoint another special prosecutor amid calls for his *impeachment. In December, after assuring the public "I'm not a crook," Nixon released seven of the nine requested tapes. One tape contained a mysterious eighteen and half minute gap.*

By the beginning of 1974, several former Nixon aides had been indicted for or pleaded guilty to crimes related to Watergate. On July 24, the Supreme Court ordered Nixon to turn over sixty-four tapes of White House conversations, rejecting his claims of executive privilege. By July 30, the Senate Judiciary Committee passed three articles of impeachment: obstruction of justice, abuse of power, and defiance of congressional subpoenas. On August 5, Nixon submitted transcripts from three tapes proving his involvement in cover-up. Facing near-certain conviction by the Senate, Nixon announced his resignation three days later. On September 8, Gerald Ford, Nixon's successor, pardoned him for any crimes he may have committed while president.

FOCUS QUESTIONS

1. How does Nixon appear to regard Watergate? Why does he resign?
2. Why does he stress the highlights of his presidency?
3. What was the long-range importance of Watergate?
4. Compare Watergate to the impeachment of Bill Clinton. Was impeachment warranted in both instances? Why or why not?

ood evening. This is the 37th time I have spoken to you from this office in which so many decisions have been made that shape the history of this nation. Each time I have done so to discuss with you some matters that I believe affected the national interest. And all the decisions I have made in my public life I have always tried to do what was best for the nation.

Throughout the long and difficult period of Watergate, I have felt it was my duty to persevere; to make every possible effort to complete the term of office to which you elected me.

In the past few days, however, it has become evident to me that I no longer have a strong enough political base in the Congress to justify continuing that effort. As long as there was such a base, I felt strongly that it was necessary to see the constitutional process through to its conclusion; that to do otherwise would be unfaithful to the spirit of that deliberately difficult process, and a dangerously destabilizing precedent for the future.

But with the disappearance of that base, I now believe that the constitutional purpose has been served. And there is no longer a need for the process to be prolonged.

I would have preferred to carry through to the finish whatever the personal agony it would have involved, and my family unanimously urged me to do so. But the interests of the nation must always come before any personal considerations. From the discussions I have had with Congressional and other leaders I have concluded that because of the Watergate matter I might not have the support of the Congress that I would consider necessary to back the very difficult decisions and carry out the duties of this office in the way the interests of the nation will require.

I have never been a quitter.

To leave office before my term is completed is opposed to every instinct in my body. But as President I must put the interests of America first.

America needs a full-time President and a full-time Congress, particularly at this time with problems we face at home and abroad.

To continue to fight through the months ahead for my personal vindication would almost totally absorb the time and attention of both the President and the Congress in a period when our entire focus should be on the great issues of peace abroad and prosperity without inflation at home.

Therefore, I shall resign the Presidency effective at noon tomorrow.

Vice President Ford will be sworn in as President at that hour in this office....

As he assumes that responsibility he will deserve the help and the support of all of us. As we look to the future, the first essential is to begin healing the wounds of this nation. To put the bitterness and divisions of the recent past behind us and to rediscover those shared ideals that lie at the heart of our strength and unity as a great and as a free people.

By taking this action, I hope that I will have hastened the start of that process of healing which is so desperately needed in America.

I regret deeply any injuries that may have been done in the course of the events that led to this decision. I would say only that if some of my judgments were wrong—and some were wrong—they were made in what I believed at the time to be the best interests of the nation.

To those who have stood with me during these past difficult months, to my family, my friends, the many others who joined in supporting my cause because they believed it was right, I will be eternally grateful for your support.

And to those who have not felt able to give me your support, let me say I leave with no bitterness toward those who have opposed me, because all of us in the final analysis have been concerned with the good of the country however our judgments might differ.

So let us all now join together in firming that common commitment and in helping our new President succeed for the benefit of all Americans.

I shall leave this office with regret at not completing my term but with gratitude for the privilege of serving as your President for the past five and a half years. These years have been a momentous time in the history of our nation and the world. They have been a time of achievement in which we can all be proud achievements that represent the shared efforts of the administration, the Congress and the people. But the challenges ahead are equally great.

And they, too, will require the support and the efforts of a Congress and the people, working in cooperation with the new Administration.

We have ended America's longest war. But in the work of securing a lasting peace in the world, the goals ahead are even more far-reaching and more difficult. We must complete a structure of peace, so that it will be said of this generation—

our generation of Americans—by the people of all nations, not only that we ended one war but that we prevented future wars.

We have unlocked the doors that for a quarter of a century stood between the United States and the People's Republic of China. We must now insure that the one-quarter of the world's people who live in the People's Republic of China will be and remain, not our enemies, but our friends.

In the Middle East, 100 million people in the Arab countries, many of whom have considered us their enemies for nearly 20 years, now look on us as their friends. We must continue to build on that friendship so that peace can settle at last over the Middle East and so that the cradle of civilization will not become its grave. Together with the Soviet Union we have made the crucial breakthroughs that have begun the process of limiting nuclear arms. But, we must set as our goal, not just limiting, but reducing and finally destroying these terrible weapons so that they cannot destroy civilization.

And so that the threat of nuclear war will no longer hang over the world and the people, we have opened a new relation with the Soviet Union. We must continue to develop and expand that new relationship so that the two strongest nations of the world will live together in cooperation rather than confrontation. Around the world—in Asia, in Africa, in Latin America, in the Middle East—there are millions of people who live in terrible poverty, even starvation. We must keep as our goal turning away from production for war and expanding production for peace so that people everywhere on this earth can at last look forward, in their children's time if not in our time, to having the necessities for a decent life. Here in America we are fortunate that most of our people have not only the blessings of liberty but also the means to live full and good, and by the world's standards even abundant lives.

We must press on, however, toward a goal not only of more and better jobs but of full opportunity for every man, and of what we are striving so hard right now to achieve—prosperity without inflation.

For more than a quarter of a century in public life, I have shared in the turbulent history of this evening.

I have fought for what I believe in. I have tried, to the best of my ability, to discharge those duties and meet those responsibilities that were entrusted to me. Sometimes I have succeeded. And sometimes I have failed. But always I have taken heart from what Theodore Roosevelt said about the man in the arena whose face is marred by dust and sweat and blood, who strives valiantly, who errs and comes short again and again because there is not effort without error and short-coming, but who does actually strive to do the deed, who knows the great devotion, who spends himself in a worthy cause, who at the best knows in the end the triumphs of high achievements and with the worst if he fails, at least fails while daring greatly.

I pledge to you tonight that as long as I have a breath of life in my body I shall continue in that spirit. I shall continue to work for the great causes to which I have been dedicated throughout my years as a Congressman, a Senator, Vice President and President, the cause of peace—not just for America but among all nations—prosperity, justice and opportunity for all of our people.

There is one cause above all to which I have been devoted and to which I shall always be devoted for as long as I live.

When I first took the oath of office as President five and a half years ago, I made this sacred commitment; to consecrate my office, my energies and all the wisdom I can summon to the cause of peace among nations.

As a result of these efforts, I am confident that the world is a safer place today, not only for the people of America but for the people of all nations, and that all of our children have a better chance than before of living in peace rather than dying in war.

This, more than anything, is what I hoped to achieve when I sought the Presidency. This, more than anything, is what I hope will be my legacy to you, to our country, as I leave the Presidency.

To have served in this office is to have felt a very personal sense of kinship with each and every American. In leaving it, I do so with this prayer: May God's grace be with you in all the days ahead.

Texas A&M University Presidential Speech Archive, http://www.tamu.edu/scom/pres/speeches/rmnresign.html.

25.5

PHYLLIS SCHLAFLY ATTACKS THE EQUAL RIGHTS AMENDMENT (1977)

In the early 1970s, feminists urged Congress to pass the Equal Rights Amendment (ERA) to the U.S. Constitution. First introduced in 1923, ERA states "Equality of rights under the law shall not be denied or abridged by the United States or by any state on account of sex." In 1972, Congress passed the ERA and sent it to the states for ratification.

As the women's movement achieved successes, a backlash against feminism emerged. Conservatives organized a movement to defeat the Equal Rights Amendment. Their arguments resonated with many Americans and the ERA ratification process stalled. In 1982, the amendment died, falling three states short of the thirty-eight needed for ratification.

Phyllis Schlafly (1924-present) was instrumental in the defeat of ERA. After graduating from Washington University, Schlafly earned a Master's degree in Government from Harvard and a law degree from Washington University. While caring for her husband and six children, she became very active in the Republican Party. In 1972, she founded the Eagle Forum, a leading pro-family organization. The author or editor of twenty books, Schlafly publishes a monthly newsletter, writes a syndicated newspaper column, and hosts a talk radio show. She is a frequent guest on public affairs and news programs.

In this excerpt from The Power of the Positive Woman *(1977), Schlafly criticizes the Equal Rights Amendment.*

FOCUS QUESTIONS

1. Why does Schlafly reject the Equal Rights Amendment? How does she believe that its ratification would change America? Do you find her arguments convincing? Why or why not?
2. What does the defeat of the ERA suggest about American society in this era?

The fundamental error of the Equal Rights Amendment, or ERA, is that it will mandate the gender-free, rigid, absolute equality of treatment of men and women under every federal and state law, bureaucratic regulation, and court decision, and in every aspect of our lives that is touched directly or indirectly by public funding. This is what the militant women's liberationists want and are working for with passionate and persistent determination....

Pro-ERA speakers go up and down the country reciting a tiresome litany of obsolete complaints about women, not being able to serve on juries, and not being admitted to law or medical schools. All those past discriminations were remedied years ago, or decades ago, or even generations ago. They have no relevance to present-day America. Pro-ERA speakers paint a picture of American women in "serfdom," treated like "chattel" and trampled on as "second-class citizens," and then offer the Equal Rights Amendment as the remedy for an alleged oppression that exists only in their distorted minds.

Some pro-ERA speakers even claim that the United States Constitution does not treat women as "persons." The facts are clear that the United States Supreme Court back in 1875 in the case of *Minor v. Happersett* specifically declared that women are "persons" as well as "citizens" under the Constitution, including the Fourteenth Amendment, entitled to all the rights and privileges of persons and citizens except the right to vote—and women received that right in 1920 under the Nineteenth Amendment.

In July, 1976, thirty-five women's magazines—including those with respectable reputations, women's liberationist journals such as *Ms.*, those that feature the "true confession" type of sensationalism, and pornographic publications—published articles on ERA. Most were blatantly pro-ERA.

Redbook, the magazine that instigated the pro-ERA consortium, featured an article by Cathleen Douglas, fourth wife of three-times-divorced former Supreme Court Justice William O. Douglas. Her article contained a lot of nonsense about a wife's being "considered the 'chattel,' or property, of her husband, with the same legal rights as a goat, a hog or a piece of land."

It is too bad that some women believe such falsehoods. This is the way the women's liberation movement deliberately degrades the homemaker and hacks away at her sense of self-worth and pride and pleasure in being female. The best cure for women who are limited in their own self-esteem is to stop reading women's magazines!

Many people have supported the Equal Rights Amendment in the mistaken belief that it means "equal pay for equal work." The fact is that ERA will add no new employment rights whatsoever. Federal employment laws are already completely sex-neutral. ERA will not add any new rights to those spelled out in the Equal Employment Opportunity Act of 1972, which prohibits all sex discrimination in hiring, pay, and promotion.

If any woman thinks she has been discriminated against, she can file her claim with the Equal Employment Opportunity Commission, and the government will pay the costs. Under this law, women have already won multi-million-dollar settlements against some of the largest companies in the country including $38 million against AT&T and $30 million against the big steel companies. There is nothing more that ERA can do....

Americans have the immense good fortune to live in a civilization that respects the family as the basic unit of society. This respect is not merely a matter of social custom. We have a great fabric of federal and state laws designed to protect the institution of the family. These laws are not for the purpose of giving one sex a preference over the other. They were not born of oppression or discrimination, but of vision and enlightened judgment. They are designed to keep the family together and to assure the child a home in which to grow up.

The results of these laws are highly beneficial to the wife. Based on the fundamental fact of life that women have babies and men don't—which no legislation or agitation can erase—these laws make it the obligation of the husband to support his wife financially and provide her with a home. Since God ordained that women have babies, our laws properly and realistically establish that men must provide financial support for their wives and children. The women's liberation movement has positioned itself in total opposition to the entire concept of "roles," but in so doing, they are opposing Mother Nature herself....

The Equal Rights Amendment would invalidate all the state laws that require the husband to support his wife and family and provide them with a home, because the Constitution would then prohibit any law that imposes an obligation on one sex that it does not impose equally on the other. Thus, if ERA ever becomes part of the United States Constitution, all laws that say the *husband* must support his *wife* would immediately become unconstitutional. In the liberationist jargon, such laws are "sexist." ERA would impose a constitutionally mandated legal equality in all matter, including family support. This would be grossly unfair to a woman because it would impose on her the double burden of financial obligation plus motherhood and homemaking. The law cannot address itself to who has the baby, changes the diapers, or washes the dishes....

There are at least two legal theories according to which abortion may be established as constitutional right under ERA: (1) any restriction of abortion would be "sexist" or discriminatory because it impacts on one sex only.... (2) Since the mandate of ERA is for sex equality, abortion is essential to relieve women of their unequal burden of being forced to bear an unwanted baby....

Another prong of the attack on the family is the drive to legalize homosexuality. Although usually blanketed in such euphemisms as "the right to be different" or "the right to sexual orientation" or "sexual preference," it is clear that homosexuals and lesbians are seeking not merely the right of consenting adults to act in private. They want the right to "marry" and thereby qualify for joint income tax and homestead benefits enjoyed by husbands and wives. They want the right to adopt children. They want the right to teach in schools.

To extend such rights to homosexuals would be a grave interference with the rights of the rest of our citizens, especially children. It would be an assault on our right to have a country in which the family is recognized, protected, and encouraged as the basic unit in society. It would interfere with the right of an adoptable child to be placed in a home with a mother and a father. It would negate the right of a father to secure custody of his own child from its mother who had become a lesbian. It would interfere with the right of parents to have their children taught by teachers who respect moral law....

These are some of the reasons why the various proposed homosexual and lesbian bills are usually rejected by state and local units of government. What homosexuals and lesbians have failed to achieve at the federal, state, and local levels, however, they are planning on accomplishing through the Equal Rights Amendment. While no one can predict with absolute certainty how the United States Supreme Court will rule on any issue, leading legal authorities are convinced that ERA will legalize homosexual "marriages" and grant them the special rights and benefits given by law to husbands and wives....

ERA has sometimes been called a men's lib amendment. It is true that it will provide some liberation for the offbeat and the deadbeat male—that is, to the homosexual who wants the same rights as husbands, to the husband who wants to escape supporting his wife and children, and to the coward who wants to get out of military service by giving his place to a woman.

But ERA will be tremendously hurtful to the overwhelming majority of men who are decent, law-abiding, moral, and family oriented. It will cost them higher taxes, loss of jobs for which they are qualified, loss of personal fulfillment as providers and protectors of their families, and loss of the essential rights of husbands to establish homes and name their children....

...Man's role as family provider gives him the incentive to curb his primitive nature. Everyone needs to be needed. The male satisfies his sense of need through his role as provider; otherwise he tends to drop out of the family and revert to the primitive masculine role of hunter and fighter.

The women's liberation movement to the contrary, there *are* male and female roles. It is just as hurtful to a man to be deprived of his role as provider and protector as it to a woman to be deprived of her maternal role. It is just as hurtful to a husband to be deprived of his right to have a wife who is a mother to children as it is to a wife to be deprived of her right to be a full-time homemaker.

Phyllis Schlafly. *The Power of the Positive Woman* (New Rochelle, NY: Arlington House Publishers, 1977), pp. 68-73, 89-90, 95-96.

25.6

---■---

JIMMY CARTER ON THE NATION'S "CRISIS OF CONFIDENCE" (1979)

James Earl "Jimmy" Carter (1924-present) served as president during a time of severe domestic and international problems. Born in Plains, Georgia, Carter was the son of a peanut grower and a registered nurse. After graduating from the U.S. Naval Academy in 1946, he married Rosalyn Smith and they had three children. Carter spent seven years working on nuclear submarines. When his father died in 1953, he left the navy to assume control of the family business. Carter began his political career on the Plains school board. In 1962, he won a seat in the Georgia State Senate. Dispirited by a failed bid for the Georgia governorship in 1966, Carter became a "born-again" Christian. Four years later, he won the governor's race. He distinguished himself by appointing women and minorities to government positions, reorganizing the state bureaucracy, and imposing fiscal discipline.

In 1974, Carter announced his candidacy for the Democratic presidential nomination. Although he lacked national name recognition and major donors, his tireless campaigning enabled him to win political and financial support. Carter's outsider status and integrity appealed to Americans disillusioned by Watergate and Vietnam. Upon winning the Democratic nomination, he chose Senator Walter Mondale (D-MN) as his running mate. In November 1976, Carter defeated Gerald Ford with 51 percent of the popular vote.

Carter tried to set a new tone in Washington. His inaugural walk down Pennsylvania Avenue, casual dress and speech, and frequent press conferences demonstrated his desire to make the presidency less imperial. His domestic achievements included civil service reform, expanded Social Security benefits, deregulation of the trucking and airline industries, and the creation of the departments of education and energy. But clashes with Congress and scandals within his administration weakened his political capital. Carter's record on foreign policy was more impressive. His advocacy of international human rights, facilitation of the Camp David Accords between Egypt and Israel, completion of SALT II negotiations with the Soviet Union, and establishment of full diplomatic relations with China were among his greatest accomplishments.

But a stagnant economy and international crises soon poisoned Carter's presidency. With inflation and interest rates at near-record highs, he struggled in vain to jumpstart the economy. High energy prices and gas shortages proved equally insoluble. Searching for ideas, Carter invited dozens of prominent Americans to the Camp David presidential retreat. For a week, Carter listened to criticisms of his leadership. On July 15, 1979, Carter gave a nationally televised speech, featured below, responding to the Camp David proceedings and offering solutions for the crises facing the nation.

The speech did little to improve Carter's dismal approval ratings. Although some commentators praised the speech, many others accused Carter of blaming the American people for the country's problems. Carter's decision to reorganize his Cabinet just two days after the speech drew additional criticism. In late 1979, the seizure of 53 Americans by Iranians and the Soviet invasion of Afghanistan added to Carter's already considerable problems. In the 1980 presidential race, Ronald Reagan easily defeated him.

Since leaving the White House, Carter's reputation has improved markedly. He has earned wide acclaim for his diplomatic skills and his leadership in Habitat for Humanity, an international organization that builds homes for the needy. He received the 2002 Nobel Peace Prize.

———————■———————

FOCUS QUESTIONS

1. How does Carter describe his meetings at Camp David?
2. Why does he believe American is suffering "a crisis of confidence"? How does he propose to resolve the nation's problems?
3. Compare Carter's remarks to Ronald Reagan's inaugural address (Document 25.8). Whose speech do you prefer? Why?

Good evening. This is a special night for me. Exactly three years ago, on July 15, 1976, I accepted the nomination of my party to run for president of the United States.

I promised you a president who is not isolated from the people, who feels your pain, and who shares your dreams and who draws his strength and his wisdom from you.

During the past three years I've spoken to you on many occasions about national concerns, the energy crisis, reorganizing the government, our nation's economy, and issues of war and especially peace. But over those years the subjects of the speeches, the talks, and the press conferences have become increasingly narrow, focused more and more on what the isolated world of Washington thinks is important. Gradually, you've heard more and more about what the government thinks or what the government should be doing and less and less about our nation's hopes, our dreams, and our vision of the future.

Ten days ago I had planned to speak to you again about a very important subject—energy. For the fifth time I would have described the urgency of the problem and laid out a series of legislative recommendations to the Congress. But as I was preparing to speak, I began to ask myself the same question that I now know has been troubling many of you. Why have we not been able to get together as a nation to resolve our serious energy problem?

It's clear that the true problems of our Nation are much deeper—deeper than gasoline lines or energy shortages, deeper even than inflation or recession. And I realize more than ever that as president I need your help. So I decided to reach out and listen to the voices of America.

I invited to Camp David people from almost every segment of our society—business and labor, teachers and preachers, governors, mayors, and private citizens. And then I left Camp David to listen to other Americans, men and women like you.

It has been an extraordinary ten days, and I want to share with you what I've heard. First of all, I got a lot of personal advice. Let me quote a few of the typical comments that I wrote down.

This from a southern governor [Arkansas governor Bill Clinton] "Mr. President, you are not leading this nation—you're just managing the government."

"You don't see the people enough any more."

"Some of your Cabinet members don't seem loyal. There is not enough discipline among your disciples."

"Don't talk to us about politics or the mechanics of government, but about an understanding of our common good."

"Mr. President, we're in trouble. Talk to us about blood and sweat and tears."

"If you lead, Mr. President, we will follow."

Many people talked about themselves and about the condition of our nation.

This from a young woman in Pennsylvania: "I feel so far from government. I feel like ordinary people are excluded from political power."

And this from a young Chicano: "Some of us have suffered from recession all our lives."

"Some people have wasted energy, but others haven't had anything to waste."

And this from a religious leader: "No material shortage can touch the important things like God's love for us or our love for one another."

And I like this one particularly from a black woman who happens to be the mayor of a small Mississippi town: "The big-shots are not the only ones who are important. Remember, you can't sell anything on Wall Street unless someone digs it up somewhere else first."

This kind of summarized a lot of other statements: "Mr. President, we are confronted with a moral and a spiritual crisis."...

These ten days confirmed my belief in the decency and the strength and the wisdom of the American people, but it also bore out some of my long-standing concerns about our nation's underlying problems.

I know, of course, being president, that government actions and legislation can be very important. That's why I've worked hard to put my campaign promises into law—and I have to admit, with just mixed success. But after listening to the American people I have been reminded again that all the legislation in the world can't fix what's wrong with America. So, I want to speak to you first tonight about a subject even more serious than energy or inflation. I want to talk to you right now about a fundamental threat to American democracy.

I do not mean our political and civil liberties. They will endure. And I do not refer to the outward strength of America, a nation that is at peace tonight everywhere in the world, with unmatched economic power and military might.

The threat is nearly invisible in ordinary ways. It is a crisis of confidence. It is a crisis that strikes at the very heart and soul and spirit of our national will. We can see this crisis in the growing doubt about the meaning of our own lives and in the loss of a unity of purpose for our nation.

The erosion of our confidence in the future is threatening to destroy the social and the political fabric of America....

In a nation that was proud of hard work, strong families, close-knit communities, and our faith in God, too many of us now tend to worship self-indulgence and consumption. Human identity is no longer defined by what one does, but by what one owns. But we've discovered that owning things and consuming things does not satisfy our longing for meaning. We've learned that piling up material goods cannot fill the emptiness of lives which have no confidence or purpose.

The symptoms of this crisis of the American spirit are all around us. For the first time in the history of our country a majority of our people believe that the next five years will be worse than the past five years. Two-thirds of our people do not even vote. The productivity of American workers is actually dropping, and the willingness of Americans to save for the future has fallen below that of all other people in the Western world.

As you know, there is a growing disrespect for government and for churches and for schools, the news media, and other institutions. This is not a message of happiness or reassurance, but it is the truth and it is a warning.

These changes did not happen overnight. They've come upon us gradually over the last generation, years that were filled with shocks and tragedy.

We were sure that ours was a nation of the ballot, not the bullet, until the murders of John Kennedy and Robert Kennedy and Martin Luther King, Jr. We were taught that our armies were always invincible and our causes were always just, only to suffer the agony of Vietnam. We respected the presidency as a place of honor until the shock of Watergate.

We remember when the phrase "sound as a dollar" was an expression of absolute dependability, until ten years of inflation began to shrink our dollar and our savings. We believed that our nation's resources were limitless until 1973, when we had to face a growing dependence on foreign oil.

These wounds are still very deep. They have never been healed. Looking for a way out of this crisis, our people have turned to the Federal government and found it isolated from the mainstream of our nation's life....

What you see too often in Washington and elsewhere around the country is a system of government that seems incapable of action. You see a Congress twisted and pulled in every direction by hundreds of well-financed and powerful special interests. You see every extreme position defended to the last vote, almost to the last breath by one unyielding group or another. You often see a balanced and a fair approach that demands sacrifice, a little sacrifice from everyone, abandoned like an orphan without support and without friends.

Often you see paralysis and stagnation and drift. You don't like it, and neither do I. What can we do?

First of all, we must face the truth, and then we can change our course. We simply must have faith in each other, faith in our ability to govern ourselves, and faith in the future of this nation. Restoring that faith and that confidence to

America is now the most important task we face. It is a true challenge of this generation of Americans....

We are at a turning point in our history. There are two paths to choose. One is a path I've warned about tonight, the path that leads to fragmentation and self-interest. Down that road lies a mistaken idea of freedom, the right to grasp for ourselves some advantage over others. That path would be one of constant conflict between narrow interests ending in chaos and immobility. It is a certain route to failure.

All the traditions of our past, all the lessons of our heritage, all the promises of our future point to another path, the path of common purpose and the restoration of American values. That path leads to true freedom for our nation and ourselves. We can take the first steps down that path as we begin to solve our energy problem.

Energy will be the immediate test of our ability to unite this nation, and it can also be the standard around which we rally. On the battlefield of energy we can win for our nation a new confidence, and we can seize control again of our common destiny.

In little more than two decades we've gone from a position of energy independence to one in which almost half the oil we use comes from foreign countries, at prices that are going through the roof. Our excessive dependence on OPEC has already taken a tremendous toll on our economy and our people. This is the direct cause of the long lines which have made millions of you spend aggravating hours waiting for gasoline. It's a cause of the increased inflation and unemployment that we now face. This intolerable dependence on foreign oil threatens our economic independence and the very security of our nation. The energy crisis is real. It is worldwide. It is a clear and present danger to our nation. These are facts and we simply must face them.

What I have to say to you now about energy is simple and vitally important.

Point one: I am tonight setting a clear goal for the energy policy of the United States. Beginning this moment, this nation will never use more foreign oil than we did in 1977—never. From now on, every new addition to our demand for energy will be met from our own production and our own conservation....

Point two: To ensure that we meet these targets, I will use my presidential authority to set import quotas....

Point three: To give us energy security, I am asking for the most massive peacetime commitment of funds and resources in our nation's history to develop America's own alternative sources of fuel—from coal, from oil shale, from plant products for gasohol, from unconventional gas, from the sun....

Point four: I'm asking Congress to mandate, to require as a matter of law, that our nation's utility companies cut their massive use of oil by 50 percent within the next decade and switch to other fuels, especially coal, our most abundant energy source.

Point five: To make absolutely certain that nothing stands in the way of achieving these goals, I will urge Congress to create an energy mobilization board which, like the War Production Board in World War II, will have the responsibility and authority to cut through the red tape, the delays, and the endless roadblocks to completing key energy projects.

We will protect our environment. But when this nation critically needs a refinery or a pipeline, we will build it.

Point six: I'm proposing a bold conservation program to involve every state, county, and city and every average American in our energy battle. This effort will permit you to build conservation into your homes and your lives at a cost you can afford.

I ask Congress to give me authority for mandatory conservation and for standby gasoline rationing. To further conserve energy, I'm proposing tonight an extra $10 billion over the next decade to strengthen our public transportation systems. And I'm asking you for your good and for your nation's security to take no unnecessary trips, to use carpools or public transportation whenever you can, to park your car one extra day per week, to obey the speed limit, and to set your thermostats to save fuel. Every act of energy conservation like this is more than just common sense—I tell you it is an act of patriotism....

So, the solution of our energy crisis can also help us to conquer the crisis of the spirit in our country. It can rekindle our sense of unity, our confidence in the future, and give our nation and all of us individually a new sense of purpose.

You know we can do it. We have the natural resources. We have more oil in our shale alone than several Saudi Arabias. We have more coal than any nation on Earth. We have the world's highest level of technology. We have the most skilled work force, with innovative genius, and I firmly believe that we have the national will to win this war.

I do not promise you that this struggle for freedom will be easy. I do not promise a quick way out of our nation's problems, when the truth is that the only way out is an all-out effort. What I do promise you is that I will lead our fight, and I will enforce fairness in our struggle, and I will ensure honesty. And above all, I will act. We can manage the short-term shortages more effectively and we will, but there are no short-term solutions to our long-range problems. There is simply no way to avoid sacrifice....

Little by little we can and we must rebuild our confidence. We can spend until we empty our treasuries, and we may summon all the wonders of science. But we can succeed only if we tap our greatest resources—America's people, America's values, and America's confidence.

I have seen the strength of America in the inexhaustible resources of our people. In the days to come, let us renew that strength in the struggle for an energy secure nation.

In closing, let me say this: I will do my best, but I will not do it alone. Let your voice be heard. Whenever you have a chance, say something good about our country. With God's help and for the sake of our nation, it is time for us to join hands in America. Let us commit ourselves together to a rebirth of the American spirit. Working together with our common faith we cannot fail.

Thank you and good night.

"Energy and National Goals," *Public Papers of the Presidents of the United States: Jimmy Carter, 1979* (Washington, DC, 1980), 1235-1241.

25.7

JERRY FALWELL ON THE MORAL MAJORITY (1981)

In the 1970s, the United States experienced one of the most powerful religious revivals in its history. The most remarkable changes occurred among evangelical Christians. Comprised of several faiths, evangelicals share a belief in personal conversion through direct interaction with God. By the early 1980s, more than 70 million Americans identified as "born-again" Christians. Christian radio and television stations, publishing companies, and schools and universities were established across the nation. The media largely ignored these trends until Jimmy Carter, a self-proclaimed "born-again" Christian, won the 1976 Democratic presidential nomination and drew widespread support among evangelicals. After Carter became president, his family policies, endorsement of ERA, and support of abortion rights alienated some evangelicals. Forming an alliance with fiscal conservatives, many religious conservatives began urging evangelicals to register to vote and to back candidates who shared their beliefs.

Reverend Jerry Falwell (1933-present) is one of the most influential leaders of the religious right. While leading the Thomas Road Baptist Church in Lynchburg, Virginia, Falwell hosts the Old Time Gospel Hour, a popular radio and television show. In 1971, he founded Liberty Baptist College (now Liberty University). In 1979, Falwell established the Moral Majority, a political organization that played a critical role in the election of Ronald Reagan. In 1980 alone, the group claimed to have registered four million voters. In 1989, following a series of scandals involving televangelists, Falwell disbanded Moral Majority.

FOCUS QUESTIONS

1. What motivated religious conservatives to form Moral Majority? What were the group's major political objectives?
2. Why is the emergence of the religious right historically significant?
3. Has the religious right been a positive or negative influence in American political life? Explain your answer.

F acing the desperate need in the impending crisis of the hour, several concerned pastors began to urge me to put together a political organization that could provide a vehicle to address these crucial issues. Men like James Kennedy (Fort Lauderdale, Florida), Charles Stanley (Atlanta, Georgia), Tim La Haye (San Diego, California), and Greg Dixon (Indianapolis, Indiana) began to share with me a common concern. They urged that we formulate a nonpartisan political organization to promote morality in public life and to combat legislation that favored the legalization of immorality. Together we formulated the Moral Majority, Inc. Today Moral Majority, Inc., is made up of millions of Americans, including 72,000 ministers, priests, and rabbis, who are deeply concerned about the moral decline of our nation, the traditional family, and the moral values on which our nation was built. We are Catholics, Jews, Protestants, Mormons, Fundamentalists—blacks and whites—farmers, housewives, businessmen, and businesswomen. We are Americans from all walks of life united by one central concern: to serve as a special-interest group providing a voice for a return to moral sanity in these United States of America. Moral Majority is a political organization and is not based on theological considerations. We are Americans who share similar moral convictions. We are opposed to abortion, pornography, the drug epidemic, the breakdown of the traditional family, the establishment of homosexuality as an accepted alternate life-style, and other moral cancers that are causing our society to rot from within. Moral Majority strongly supports a pluralistic America....

Here is how Moral Majority stands on today's vital issues:

1. *We believe in the separation of Church and State.* Moral Majority, Inc., is a political organization providing a platform for religious and nonreligious Americans who share moral values to address their concerns in these areas. Members of Moral Majority, Inc. have no common theological premise. We are Americans who are proud to be conservative in our approach to moral, social, and political concerns.

2. *We are pro-life.* We believe that life begins at fertilization. We strongly oppose the massive "biological holocaust" that is resulting in the abortion of one and a half million babies each year in America. We are providing a voice and a defense for the human and civil rights of millions of unborn babies.

3. *We are pro-traditional family.* We believe that the only acceptable family form begins with a legal marriage of a man and woman. We feel that homo-sexual marriages and common law marriages should not be accepted as tradi-tional families. We oppose legislation that favors these kinds of "diverse fam-ily form," thereby penalizing the traditional family. We do not oppose civil rights for homosexuals. We do oppose "special rights" for homosexuals who have chosen a perverted life-style rather than a traditional life-style.

4. *We oppose the illegal drug traffic in America.* The youth in America are presently in the midst of a drug epidemic. Through education, legislation, and other means we want to do our part to save our young people from death on the installment plan through illegal drug addiction.

5. *We oppose pornography.* While we do not advocate censorship, we do believe that education and legislation can help stem the tide of pornography and ob-scenity that is poisoning the American spirit today. Economic boycotts are a proper way in America's free-enterprise system to help persuade the media to move back to a sensible moral stand. We most certainly believe in the First Amendment for everyone. We are not willing to sit back, however, while many television programs create cesspools of obscenity and vulgarity in our nation's living rooms.

6. *We support the state of Israel and Jewish people everywhere.* It is impossible to separate the state of Israel from the Jewish family internationally. Many Moral Majority members, because of their theological convictions, are committed to the Jewish people. Others stand upon human and civil rights of all persons as a premise of support of the state of Israel. Support of Israel is one of the essential commitments of the Moral Majority. No anti-Semitic influence is allowed in Moral Majority, Inc.

7. *We believe that a strong national defense is the best deterrent to war.* We believe that liberty is the basic moral issue of all moral issues. The only way America can remain free is to remain strong....

8. *We support equal rights for women.* We agree with President Reagan's commitment to help every governor and every state legislature to move quickly to ensure that during the 1980s every American woman will earn as much money and enjoy the same opportunities for advancement as her male counterpart in the same vocation.

9. *We believe ERA is the wrong vehicle to obtain equal rights for women.* We feel that the ambiguous and simplistic language of the Amendment could lead to court interpretations that might put women in combat, sanction homosexual marriages, and financially penalize widows and deserted wives.

10. *We encourage our Moral Majority state organizations to be autonomous and indigenous.* Moral Majority state organizations may, from time to time, hold positions that are not held by the Moral Majority, Inc., national organization.

Jerry Falwell *et al.*, eds., *The Fundamentalist Phenomenon: The Resurgence of Conservative Christianity* (Garden City: Doubleday & Company, Inc., 1981), pp. 188-190.

25.8

■

RONALD REAGAN, INAUGURAL ADDRESS (1981)

The religious right was part of a larger conservative movement called the New Right. In the wake of Barry Goldwater's crushing defeat in 1964, conservative activist Richard Viguerie used pioneering direct-mail strategies to build a database of 4 million donors and 15 million supporters. Conservatives founded think tanks, lobbying and consulting firms, and academic networks to rival the formidable liberal political establishment.

The New Right's success also stemmed from the emergence of new conservative leaders such as Ronald Reagan (1911-present). Born in Illinois, Reagan had a difficult home life. His father was an alcoholic and the family moved often. After graduating from Eureka College in 1932, Reagan became a radio sportscaster. Five years later, he took a screen test and won a contract at Warner

Brothers studio. He was cast in a series of films including Knute Rockne, All-American *(1940). In 1940, he married actress Jane Wyman. They had a daughter, Maureen, and a son, Michael. In 1948, the couple divorced. During World War II, Reagan received an officer's commission, but he did not go overseas or fight in combat. Instead, he appeared in over 400 army training films. In later years, Reagan occasionally described his wartime experiences in ways that suggested he had actually done things depicted in his films.*

Reagan was initially a New Deal Democrat, but his political views changed dramatically during the early Cold War. From 1947 to 1953, Reagan served as president of the Screen Actors Guild, a film industry union. To the chagrin of many members, Reagan testified as a friendly witness before the House Un-American Activities Committee (HUAC) and helped to blacklist suspected subversives working in Hollywood. In the 1950s, Reagan campaigned actively for Richard Nixon and Dwight D. Eisenhower. In 1962, he officially joined the Republican Party.

In 1949, Reagan met actress Nancy Davis and the couple married three years later. They had two children, Patricia and Ronald. During the 1950s, as Reagan's acting career slowed, he became the host of the TV show General Electric Theater *and served as a GE spokesman. Reagan toured dozens of GE facilities giving pro-business speeches. In 1962, GE fired Reagan after his speeches grew overtly political.*

Two years later, while serving as co-chairman of California Republicans for Goldwater, Reagan gave a nationally televised speech called "A Time to Choose." The thirty-minute address generated one million dollars in campaign contributions and made Reagan a hero to conservatives nationwide. In 1966, he was elected governor of California. During his two terms (1967-1974), Reagan's fiscal policies, reform of the state welfare system, and criticism of the New Left and counterculture won many admirers.

In 1976, Reagan nearly stole the Republican presidential nomination from President Gerald Ford. Reagan launched blistering attacks on Ford's support of détente and appointment of liberal Republican Nelson Rockefeller as vice-president. Ford won renomination only after replacing Rockefeller with Robert Dole (R-KS) and agreeing to support a platform largely written by Senator Jesse Helms (R-NC), a Reagan ally. The changes signaled the declining power of the liberal and moderate wings of the Republican Party.

In 1980, Reagan easily won the Republican presidential nomination. He called for large tax cuts, increased defense spending, a balanced budget, and a constitutional amendment outlawing abortion. Without directly discussing the Iranian hostage crisis, he subtly attacked Jimmy Carter's foreign policy. To millions of Americans, Reagan's proposals and personality were refreshing and inspiring. Reagan defeated Carter with 51 percent of the popular vote.

FOCUS QUESTIONS

1. According to Reagan, what are the major problems facing the nation? How does he propose to solve them?
2. Compare Reagan's address to Jimmy Carter's remarks (Document 25.6). Whose speech do you prefer? Why?

o a few of us here today, this is a solemn and most momentous occasion; and yet, in the history of our Nation, it is a commonplace occurrence. The orderly transfer of authority as called for in the Constitution routinely takes place as it has for almost two centuries and few of us stop to think how unique we really are. In the eyes of many in the world, this every-4-year ceremony we accept as normal is nothing less than a miracle.

Mr. President, I want our fellow citizens to know how much you did to carry on this tradition. By your gracious cooperation in the transition process, you have shown a watching world that we are a united people pledged to maintaining a political system which guarantees individual liberty to a greater degree than any other, and I thank you and your people for all your help in maintaining the continuity which is the bulwark of our Republic.

The business of our nation goes forward. These United States are confronted with an economic affliction of great proportions. We suffer from the longest and one of the worst sustained inflations in our national history. It distorts our economic decisions, penalizes thrift, and crushes the struggling young and the fixed-income elderly alike. It threatens to shatter the lives of millions of our people.

Idle industries have cast workers into unemployment, causing human misery and personal indignity. Those who do work are denied a fair return for their labor by a tax system which penalizes successful achievement and keeps us from maintaining full productivity.

But great as our tax burden is, it has not kept pace with public spending. For decades, we have piled deficit upon deficit, mortgaging our future and our children's future for the temporary convenience of the present. To continue this long trend is to guarantee tremendous social, cultural, political, and economic upheavals.

You and I, as individuals, can, by borrowing, live beyond our means, but for only a limited period of time. Why, then, should we think that collectively, as a nation, we are not bound by that same limitation? We must act today in order to preserve tomorrow. And let there be no misunderstanding—we are going to begin to act, beginning today....

In this present crisis, government is not the solution to our problem; government is the problem.

From time to time, we have been tempted to believe that society has become too complex to be managed by self-rule, that government by an elite group is superior to government for, by, and of the people. But if no one among us is capable of governing himself, then who among us has the capacity to govern someone else? All of us together, in and out of government, must bear the burden. The solutions we seek must be equitable, with no one group singled out to pay a higher price.

We hear much of special interest groups. Our concern must be for a special interest group that has been too long neglected. It knows no sectional boundaries or ethnic and racial divisions, and it crosses political party lines. It is made up of men and women who raise our food, patrol our streets, man our mines and our factories, teach our children, keep our homes, and heal us when we are sick—professionals, industrialists, shopkeepers, clerks, cabbies, and truck drivers. They are, in short, "We the people," this breed called Americans.

Well, this administration's objective will be a healthy, vigorous, growing economy that provides equal opportunity for all Americans, with no barriers born of bigotry or discrimination. Putting America back to work means putting all Americans back to work. Ending inflation means freeing all Americans from the terror of runaway living costs. All must share in the productive work of this "new beginning" and all must share in the bounty of a revived economy. With the idealism and fair play which are the core of our system and our strength, we can have a strong and prosperous America at peace with itself and the world.

So, as we begin, let us take inventory. We are a nation that has a government—not the other way around. And this makes us special among the nations of the Earth. Our Government has no power except that granted it by the people. It is time to check and reverse the growth of government which shows signs of having grown beyond the consent of the governed.

It is my intention to curb the size and influence of the Federal establishment and to demand recognition of the distinction between the powers granted to the Federal Government and those reserved to the States or to the people. All of us need to be reminded that the Federal Government did not create the States; the States created the Federal Government.

Now, so there will be no misunderstanding, it is not my intention to do away with government. It is, rather, to make it work—work with us, not over us; to stand by our side, not ride on our back. Government can and must provide opportunity, not smother it; foster productivity, not stifle it.

If we look to the answer as to why, for so many years, we achieved so much, prospered as no other people on Earth, it was because here, in this land, we unleashed the energy and individual genius of man to a greater extent than has ever been done before. Freedom and the dignity of the individual have been more available and assured here than in any other place on Earth. The price for this freedom at times has been high, but we have never been unwilling to pay that price.

It is no coincidence that our present troubles parallel and are proportionate to the intervention and intrusion in our lives that result from unnecessary and excessive growth of government. It is time for us to realize that we are too great a nation to limit ourselves to small dreams. We are not, as some would have us believe, doomed to an inevitable decline. I do not believe in a fate that will fall on us no matter what we do. I do believe in a fate that will fall on us if we do nothing. So, with all the creative energy at our command, let us begin an era of national renewal. Let us renew our determination, our courage, and our strength. And let us renew; our faith and our hope.

We have every right to dream heroic dreams. Those who say that we are in a time when there are no heroes just don't know where to look. You can see heroes every day going in and out of factory gates. Others, a handful in number, produce enough food to feed all of us and then the world beyond. You meet heroes across a counter—and they are on both sides of that counter. There are entrepreneurs with faith in themselves and faith in an idea who create new jobs, new wealth and opportunity. They are individuals and families whose taxes support the Government and whose voluntary gifts support church, charity, culture, art, and education. Their patriotism is quiet but deep. Their values sustain our national life....

In the days ahead I will propose removing the roadblocks that have slowed our economy and reduced productivity. Steps will be taken aimed at restoring the balance between the various levels of government. Progress may be slow—measured in inches and feet, not miles—but we will progress. Is it time to reawaken this industrial giant, to get government back within its means, and to lighten our punitive tax burden. And these will be our first priorities, and on these principles, there will be no compromise....

And as we renew ourselves here in our own land, we will be seen as having greater strength throughout the world. We will again be the exemplar of freedom and a beacon of hope for those who do not now have freedom.

To those neighbors and allies who share our freedom, we will strengthen our historic ties and assure them of our support and firm commitment. We will match loyalty with loyalty. We will strive for mutually beneficial relations. We will not use our friendship to impose on their sovereignty, for our own sovereignty is not for sale.

As for the enemies of freedom, those who are potential adversaries, they will be reminded that peace is the highest aspiration of the American people. We will negotiate for it, sacrifice for it; we will not surrender for it—now or ever.

Our forbearance should never be misunderstood. Our reluctance for conflict should not be misjudged as a failure of will. When action is required to preserve our national security, we will act. We will maintain sufficient strength to prevail if need be, knowing that if we do so we have the best chance of never having to use that strength.

Above all, we must realize that no arsenal, or no weapon in the arsenals of the world, is so formidable as the will and moral courage of free men and women. It is a weapon our adversaries in today's world do not have. It is a weapon that we as

Americans do have. Let that be understood by those who practice terrorism and prey upon their neighbors.

I am told that tens of thousands of prayer meetings are being held on this day, and for that I am deeply grateful. We are a nation under God, and I believe God intended for us to be free. It would be fitting and good, I think, if on each Inauguration Day in future years it should be declared a day of prayer....

This is the first time in history that this ceremony has been held, as you have been told, on this West Front of the Capitol. Standing here, one faces a magnificent vista, opening up on this city's special beauty and history. At the end of this open mall are those shrines to the giants on whose shoulders we stand.

Directly in front of me, the monument to a monumental man: George Washington, Father of our country. A man of humility who came to greatness reluctantly. He led America out of revolutionary victory into infant nationhood. Off to one side, the stately memorial to Thomas Jefferson. The Declaration of Independence flames with his eloquence.

And then beyond the Reflecting Pool the dignified columns of the Lincoln Memorial. Whoever would understand in his heart the meaning of America will find it in the life of Abraham Lincoln.

Beyond those monuments to heroism is the Potomac River, and on the far shore the sloping hills of Arlington National Cemetery with its row on row of simple white markers bearing crosses or Stars of David. They add up to only a tiny fraction of the price that has been paid for our freedom.

Each one of those markers is a monument to the kinds of hero I spoke of earlier. Their lives ended in places called Belleau Wood, The Argonne, Omaha Beach, Salerno and halfway around the world on Guadalcanal, Tarawa, Pork Chop Hill, the Chosin Reservoir, and in a hundred rice paddies and jungles of a place called Vietnam.

Under one such marker lies a young man—Martin Treptow—who left his job in a small town barber shop in 1917 to go to France with the famed Rainbow Division. There, on the western front, he was killed trying to carry a message between battalions under heavy artillery fire.

We are told that on his body was found a diary. On the flyleaf under the heading, "My Pledge," he had written these words: "America must win this war. Therefore, I will work, I will save, I will sacrifice, I will endure, I will fight cheerfully and do my utmost, as if the issue of the whole struggle depended on me alone."

The crisis we are facing today does not require of us the kind of sacrifice that Martin Treptow and so many thousands of others were called upon to make. It does require, however, our best effort, and our willingness to believe in ourselves and to believe in our capacity to perform great deeds; to believe that together, with God's help, we can and will resolve the problems which now confront us.

And, after all, why shouldn't we believe that? We are Americans. God bless you, and thank you.

"Inaugural Address," *Public Papers of the Presidents of the United States: Ronald Reagan, 1981* (Washington, DC, 1982), pp. 1-4.

25.9

■

RONALD REAGAN, THE "EVIL EMPIRE" SPEECH (1983)

Convinced that détente and the Vietnam War had eroded American military strength and international prestige, Ronald Reagan took office determined to reverse these trends. He called for huge increases in defense spending and aggressively combated communism. Under a policy eventually known as the Reagan Doctrine, the United States began challenging communist insurgencies throughout the developing world, regardless of whether or not the Soviets were directly aiding these leftists. The policy led to a significant expansion of U.S. activism abroad, especially in Latin America. In the 1980s, the United States supported anti-communists in El Salvador and Nicaragua and deployed troops to oust the leftist government of Grenada.

During Reagan's first term, his militant anticommunism and Soviet aggression markedly increased Cold War tensions. In December 1981, the Soviets forced the communist government of Poland to impose martial law in order to quash the independent labor movement Solidarity. In September 1983, the Soviets destroyed a Korean airliner that strayed over Sakhalin Island. All 269 passengers, including 61 Americans, perished. At the same time, the Reagan administration began the most massive peacetime military build-up in history. Armed with secret intelligence showing grave weaknesses in the Soviet economy, U.S. officials concluded that the Soviets could not afford a renewed arms race.

Reagan's strategy terrified and enraged his opponents. Critics howled when defense spending reached $40 million an hour at its peak. A massive anti-nuclear movement arose in Europe and the United States. In 1982, approximately one million protestors gathered for a "nuclear freeze" rally in New York's Central Park, perhaps the largest demonstration ever.

Soviet-American relations were particularly bleak in March 1983. On March 8, Reagan gave a harshly anti-communist speech, included below, before the National Association of Evangelicals. His uncompromising rhetoric received worldwide attention. Three weeks later, Reagan called for the development of the Strategic Defense Initiative (SDI or "Star Wars"), a system of lasers and satellites designed to prevent a nuclear missile strike. Although critics denounced the costs and technological flaws of Reagan's proposal, the Soviets later identified SDI as a key factor in the eventual collapse of the Soviet Union. SDI, they explained, highlighted their economical and technological limitations.

During Reagan's second term, Soviet-American relations dramatically improved. In 1985, Mikhail Gorbachev became Soviet premier and ushered in a remarkable array of political and economic reforms. Tempering their initial suspicions of one another, Gorbachev and Reagan came extremely close to abolishing half of their nuclear arsenals at a 1986 summit in Reykjavik, Iceland. Although Reagan's refusal to abandon SDI ended those discussions, they signed a sweeping arms agreement the following year. The Intermediate-Range Nuclear

Forces (INF) Treaty removed all intermediate-range nuclear missiles from Europe. By late 1991, the Iron Curtin fell and the Soviet Union ceased to exist. While experts continue to debate Reagan's role in ending the Cold War, his foreign policy was undoubtedly bold.

FOCUS QUESTIONS

1. How does Reagan characterize the Soviet Union? What does he believe is the proper response to communism?
2. What are Reagan's opinions of the nuclear arms race and the nuclear freeze movement?
3. This speech drew heated criticism from some U.S. commentators. Anthony Lewis of the *New York Times* called it "primitive." The renowned historian Henry Steele Commager declared, "It was the worst presidential speech in American history, and I've read them all." Do you agree or disagree with these remarks? Why?

During my first press conference as President, in answer to a direct question, I pointed out that, as good Marxist-Leninists, the Soviet leaders have openly and publicly declared that the only morality they recognize is that which will further their cause, which is world revolution. I think I should point out I was only quoting Lenin, their guiding spirit, who said in 1920 that they repudiate all morality that proceeds from supernatural ideas—that's their name for religion—or ideas that are outside class conceptions. Morality is entirely subordinate to the interests of class war. And everything is moral that is necessary for the annihilation of the old, exploiting social order and for uniting the proletariat.

Well, I think the refusal of many influential people to accept this elementary fact of Soviet doctrine illustrates an historical reluctance to see totalitarian powers for what they are. We saw this phenomenon in the 1930's. We see it too often today.

This doesn't mean we should isolate ourselves and refuse to seek an understanding with them. I intend to do everything I can to persuade them of our peaceful intent, to remind them that it was the West that refused to use its nuclear monopoly in the forties and fifties for territorial gain and which now proposes 50-percent cut in strategic ballistic missiles and the elimination of an entire class of land-based, intermediate-range nuclear missiles.

At the same time, however, they must be made to understand we will never compromise our principles and standards. We will never give away our freedom. We will never abandon our belief in God. And we will never stop searching for a genuine peace. But we can assure none of these things America stands for through the so-called nuclear freeze solutions proposed by some.

The truth is that a freeze now would be a very dangerous fraud, for that is merely the illusion of peace. The reality is that we must find peace through strength.

I would agree to a freeze if only we could freeze the Soviets' global desires. A freeze at current levels of weapons would remove any incentive for the Soviets to negotiate seriously in Geneva and virtually end our chances to achieve the major arms reductions which we have proposed. Instead, they would achieve their objectives through the freeze.

A freeze would reward the Soviet Union for its enormous and unparalleled military buildup. It would prevent the essential and long overdue modernization of United States and allied defenses and would leave our aging forces increasingly vulnerable. And an honest freeze would require extensive prior negotiations on the systems and numbers to be limited and on the measures to ensure effective verification and compliance. And the kind of a freeze that has been suggested would be virtually impossible to verify. Such a major effort would divert us completely from our current negotiations on achieving substantial reductions.

A number of years ago, I heard a young father, a very prominent young man in the entertainment world, addressing a tremendous gathering in California. It was during the time of the cold war, and communism and our own way of life were very much on people's minds. And he was speaking to that subject. And suddenly, though, I heard him saying, "I love my little girls more than anything—"And I said to myself, "Oh, no, don't. You can't—don't say that." But I had underestimated him. He went on: "I would rather see my little girls die now, still believing in God, than have them grow up under communism and one day die no longer believing in God."

There were thousands of young people in that audience. They came to their feet with shouts of joy. They had instantly recognized the profound truth in what he had said, with regard to the physical and the soul and what was truly important.

Yes, let us pray for the salvation of all of those who live in that totalitarian darkness—pray they will discover the joy of knowing God. But until they do, let us be aware that while they preach the supremacy of the state, declare its omnipotence over individual man, and predict its eventual domination of all peoples on the Earth, they are the focus of evil in the modern world....

So, I urge you to speak out against those who would place the United States in a position of military and moral inferiority.... So, in your discussions of the nuclear freeze proposals, I urge you to beware the temptation of pride—the temptation of blithely declaring yourselves above it all and label both sides equally at fault, to ignore the facts of history and the aggressive impulses of an evil empire, to simply call the arms race a giant misunderstanding and thereby remove yourself from the struggle between right and wrong and good and evil.

I ask you to resist the attempts of those who would have you withhold your support for our efforts, this administration's efforts, to keep America strong and free, while we negotiate real and verifiable reductions in the world's nuclear arsenals and one day, with God's help, their total elimination.

I believe that communism is another sad, bizarre chapter in human history whose last pages even now are being written. I believe this because the source of our strength in the quest for human freedom is not material, but spiritual. And because it knows no limitation, it must terrify and ultimately triumph over those who would enslave their fellow man. For in the words of Isaiah: "He giveth power to the faint; and to them that have no might He increased strength.... But they that wait upon the Lord shall renew their strength; they shall mount up with wings as eagles; they shall run, and not be weary...."

Yes, change your world. One of our Founding Fathers, Thomas Paine, said, "We have it within our power to begin the world over again." We can do it, doing together what no one church could do by itself.

God bless you, and thank you very much.

"Remarks at the Annual Convention of the National Association of Evangelicals in Orlando, Florida," *Public Papers of the Presidents of the United States: Ronald Reagan, 1983: Book I-January 1983 to July 1, 1983* (Washington, D.C.: Government Printing Office, 1984), pp. 362-364.

25.10

MARIO CUOMO, "A TALE OF TWO CITIES" (1984)

"Supply-side" economics (also called "Reaganomics") was the centerpiece of Ronald Reagan's domestic program. Based on the idea that high taxes stunted economic growth, supply-side economics called for large tax reductions for the wealthy and corporations in order to free up capital that could then be plowed into new investments. As the economy revived, supply-siders claimed, Americans of all classes would benefit. To offset lost tax revenue, government expenditures would be slashed. In 1981, Reagan proposed 30 percent decrease in corporate and individual taxes over a three-year period and $40 billion in budget cuts. Although Congress lowered the tax reduction to 25 percent, it approved most of Reagan's suggested cuts.

Deregulation was another critical element of Reagan's domestic agenda. Reagan and his advisors believed that stringent government rules impeded economic growth. Accordingly, they slashed the budgets of many federal agencies and relaxed or ignored the enforcement of laws and regulations in several areas including the environment, civil rights, and the savings and loan industry.

Reagan's policies had mixed effects. In early 1982, the country plunged into the worst recession since the 1930s. Unemployment hit 11 percent. Bankruptcies and foreclosures skyrocketed. The U.S. trade deficit soared from $25 billion in 1980 to $111 billion in 1984. Because the budget cuts that Reagan instituted were much smaller than the costs of his massive defense build-up, enormous deficits accrued. Between 1981 and 1988, the national debt tripled to $2.5 trillion. The deficit forced Reagan to back away from supply-side economics and to accept a $98.3 billion tax increase in 1982. He also instituted additional budget cuts in "discretionary" spending on education, Medicaid and Medicare, low-income housing subsidies, food stamps, school lunches for poor children, and Aid to Families with Dependent Children (AFDC).

Despite these events, the economy quickly recovered in 1983. Unemployment, inflation, and energy costs fell. The Federal Reserve lowered interest rates. The stock market started a boom that lasted for most of the decade. Consumer spending and business investment significantly increased. While Reagan's supporters claimed his policies produced the thriving economy, his critics accused him of creating only the illusion of prosperity and of ignoring a widening gap between the rich and poor.

This contrast was evident in the presidential election of 1984. Reagan's campaign emphasized his vibrant personality and the nation's economic vitality and international leadership. At their national convention in San Francisco, the Democrats chose Senator Walter Mondale (D-MN) as their nominee. In the keynote address, New York governor Mario Cuomo (1932-present) blasted Reagan's policies. The speech, featured here, catapulted Cuomo to national political prominence. In November, Reagan crushed Mondale with 59 percent of the popular vote, carrying every state except for Minnesota and the District of Columbia.

FOCUS QUESTIONS

1. Why is Cuomo so critical of the Reagan administration? How does he contrast the political objectives of Democrats and Republicans?
2. How does Cuomo's portrait of American society and the role of government differ from that presented by Ronald Reagan (Document 25.11)?

July 16, 1984

T en days ago, President Reagan admitted that although some people in this country seemed to be doing well nowadays, others were unhappy, even worried, about themselves, their families and their futures. The president said that he didn't understand that fear. He said, "Why, this country is a shining city on a hill." And the president is right. In many ways we are a shining city on a hill.

But the hard truth is that not everyone is sharing in this city's splendor and glory. A shining city is perhaps all the president sees from the portico of the White House and the veranda of his ranch, where everyone seems to be doing well. But there's another city; there's another part to the shining the city; the part where some people can't pay their mortgages, and most young people can't afford one, where students can't afford the education they need, and middle-class parents watch the dreams they hold for their children evaporate.

In this part of the city there are more poor than ever, more families in trouble, more and more people who need help but can't find it. Even worse: There are elderly people who tremble in the basements of the houses there. And there are people who sleep in the city streets, in the gutter, where the glitter doesn't show. There are ghettos where thousands of young people, without a job or an education, give their lives away to drug dealers every day. There is despair, Mr. President, in the faces that you don't see, in the places that you don't visit in your shining city.

In fact, Mr. President, this is a nation is more a "Tale of Two Cities" than it is a "shining city on a hill."

Maybe if you visited more places, Mr. President, you'd understand.

Maybe if you went to Appalachia where some people still live in sheds, maybe if you went to Lackawanna where thousands of unemployed steel workers wonder why we subsidized foreign steel while we surrender their dignity to unemployment and to welfare checks; maybe, if you stepped in at a shelter in Chicago and spoke to the homeless there; maybe, Mr. President, if you asked a woman who had been denied the help she needed to feed her children because you said you needed the money for a tax break for a millionaire or for a missile we couldn't afford to use; maybe then you'd understand.

Maybe, Mr. President. But I'm afraid not.

Because, the truth is, ladies and gentlemen, that this is how we were warned it would be. President Reagan told us from very the beginning that he believed in a kind of social Darwinism. Survival of the fittest. "Government can't do everything," we were told. "So it should settle for taking care of the strong and hope that economic ambition and charity will do the rest. Make the rich richer—and what falls from their table will be enough for the middle class and those who are trying desperately to work their way into the middle class."

You know, the Republicans called it trickle-down when Hoover tried it. Now they call it supply side. But it's the same shining city for those relative few who are lucky enough to live in its good neighborhoods. But for the people who are excluded—for the people who are locked out—all they can do is to stare from a distance at that city's glimmering towers....

Today our great Democratic Party, which has saved this nation from depression, from fascism, from racism, from corruption, is called upon to do it again—this time to save the nation from confusion and division, from the threat of eventual fiscal disaster and most of all from the fear of a nuclear holocaust.

In order to succeed, we must answer our opponent's polished and appealing rhetoric with a more telling reasonableness and rationality....

We Democrats must unite so that the entire nation can unite because surely the Republicans won't bring this country together. Their policies divide the nation—into the lucky and the left-out, into the royalty and the rabble. The Republicans are willing to treat that division as victory. They would cut this nation in half, into those temporarily better off and those worse off than before, and they would call that division recovery.

We should not, we should not be embarrassed or dismayed or chagrined if the process of unifying is difficult, even wrenching at times. Remember that, unlike any other party, we embrace men and women of every color, every creed, every orientation, every economic class. In our family are gathered everyone from the abject poor of Essex County in New York, to the enlightened affluent of the gold coasts at both ends of the nation. And in between is the heart of our constituency. The middle class—the people not rich enough to be worry-free, but not poor enough to be on welfare. The middle class, those people who work for a living because they have to, not because some psychiatrist told them it was a convenient way to fill the interval between birth and eternity. White collar and blue collar. Young professionals. Men and women in small business desperate for the capital and contracts that they need to prove their worth.

We speak for the minorities who have not yet entered the mainstream. We speak for ethnics who want to add their culture to the magnificent mosaic that is America. We speak, we speak for women who are indignant that this nation refuses to etch into its governmental commandments the simple rule "thou shalt not sin against equality," a rule so obvious it can be spelled in three letters: E.R.A.!

We speak for young people demanding an education and a future. We speak for senior citizens who are terrorized by the idea that their only security—their *Social* Security—is being threatened.

We speak for millions of reasoning people fighting to preserve our environment from greed and from stupidity. And we speak for reasonable people who are fighting to preserve our very existence from a macho intransigence that refuses to make intelligent attempts to discuss the possibility of nuclear holocaust with our enemy. Refusing because they believe we can pile missiles so high that they will pierce the clouds and the sight of them will frighten our enemies into submission....

We're proud of this diversity as Democrats.... But we pay a price for it.

The different people that we represent have different points of view. And sometimes they compete and even debate, and even argue.... If you need any more inspiration to put some small part of your own differences aside to create this consensus, all you need to do is to reflect on what the Republican policy of divide and cajole has done to this land since 1980.

The president has asked us to judge him on whether or not he's fulfilled the promise he made four years ago. I accept that. Just consider what he has said and what he's done.

Inflation is down since 1980. But not because of the supply-side miracle promised to us by the president. Inflation was reduced the old-fashioned way, with a recession, the worst since 1932. We could have brought inflation down that way. How did he do it? Fifty-five thousand bankruptcies. Two years of massive unemployment. Two hundred thousand farmers and ranchers forced off the land. More homeless than at any time since the Great Depression in 1932. More hungry, in this nation of enormous affluence, the United States of America, more hungry. More poor—most of them women—and he paid one more thing, a nearly $200 billion deficit threatening our future.

The president's deficit is a direct and dramatic repudiation of his promise to balance our budget by 1983. The deficit is the largest in the history of this universe.... It is a debt so large that as much as one-half of our revenue from the income tax goes just to pay the interest. It is a mortgage on our children's future that can be paid only in pain and that could bring this nation to its knees....

How important is this question of the deficit?

Think about it practically: What chance would the Republican candidate have had in 1980 if he had told the American people that he intended to pay for his so-called economic recovery with bankruptcies, unemployment, more homeless, more hungry and the largest government debt known to humankind? Would American voters have signed the loan certificate for him on Election Day? Of course not! That was an election won with smoke and mirrors...and illusions. And that's the kind of recovery we have now as well....

That is the Republican record.

That its disastrous quality is not more fully understood by the American people is attributable, I think, to the president's amiability and the failure by some to separate the salesman from the product....

It's now up to us to make the case to America. And to remind Americans that if they are not happy with all the president has done so far, they should consider how much worse it will be if he is left to his radical proclivities for another four years unrestrained by the need once again to come before the American people....

Where would another four years take us? Where would four years more take us? How much larger will the deficit be?

How much deeper the cuts in programs for the struggling middle class and the poor to limit that deficit? How high will the interest rates be? How much more acid rain killing our forests and fouling our lakes?

What kind of Supreme Court will we have? What kind of court and country will be fashioned by the man who believes in having government mandate people's religion and morality?

The man who believes that trees pollute the environment, the man that believes that the laws against discrimination against people go too far. The man who threatens Social Security and Medicaid and help for the disabled.

How high will we pile the missiles? How much deeper will the gulf be between us and our enemies?...

This election will measure the record of the past four years. But more than that, it will answer the question of what kind of people we want to be.

We Democrats *still* have a dream. We still believe in this nation's future.

And this is *our* answer to the question, this is *our* credo:

We believe in *only* the government we need but we insist on all the government we need....

We believe, as Democrats, that a society as blessed as ours, the most affluent democracy in the world's history, one that can spend trillions on instruments of destruction, ought to be able to help the middle class in its struggle, ought to be able to find work for all who can do it, room at the table, shelter for the homeless, care for the elderly and infirm, and hope for the destitute. And we proclaim as loudly as we can the utter insanity of nuclear proliferation and the need for a nuclear freeze, if only to affirm the simple truth that peace is better than war because life is better than death.

We believe in firm but fair law and order. We believe proudly in the union movement. We believe in privacy for people, openness by government, civil rights, and human rights.

We believe in a single fundamental idea that describes better than most textbooks and any speech that I could write what a proper government should be. The idea of family. Mutuality. The sharing of benefits and burdens for the good of all. Feeling one another's pain. Sharing one another's blessings. Reasonably, honestly, fairly—without respect to race, or sex, or geography or political affiliation....

That struggle to live with dignity is the real story of the shining city. And it's a story, ladies and gentlemen, that I didn't read in a book, or learn in a classroom. I saw it, and lived it. Like many of you. I watched a small man with thick calluses on both hands work 15 and 16 hours a day. I saw him once literally bleed from the bottoms of his feet, a man who came here uneducated, alone, unable to speak the language, who taught me all I needed to know about faith and hard work by the simple eloquence of his example. I learned about our kind of democracy from my father. And, I learned about our obligation to each other from him and from my mother. They asked only for a chance to work and to make the world better for their children and they asked to be protected in those moments when they would not be able to protect themselves. This nation and this nation's government did that for them.

And that they were able to build a family and live in dignity and see one of their children go from behind their little grocery store in South Jamaica on the other side of the tracks where he was born, to occupy the highest seat in the greatest state of the greatest nation in the only world we know, is an ineffably beautiful tribute to the democratic process....

I ask you—ladies and gentlemen, brothers and sisters—for the good of all of us, for the love of this great nation, for the family of America, for the love of God. Please, make this nation remember how futures are built.

Copyright © 1993 by Mario Cuomo. *More than Words: The Speeches of Mario Cuomo*. Reprinted by permission of St. Martin's Press, LLC.

SECONDARY SOURCE

LAURA A. BELMONTE, "GO WEST, YOUNG MEN: HARVEY MILK, SAN FRANCISCO, AND THE GAY MIGRATION"

Many of the political and cultural trends of the 1970s converged in the gay rights movement. As gay men and lesbians mobilized for political equality and became more visible in American society, they encountered ferocious opposition. In this essay, Laura A. Belmonte, a history professor at Oklahoma State University, examines the development of the San Francisco gay community and the unlikely political career of Harvey Milk, the first openly gay man elected to a significant public office.

 Go to your *Speaking of America* CD-ROM to read "Go West Young Men: Harvey Milk, San Francisco, and the Gay Migration."

FOCUS QUESTIONS

1. What were the origins of the gay community in San Francisco?
2. Describe Harvey Milk's background.
3. Why did Harvey Milk decide to run for public office? What were his major political ideas? Who voted for him?
4. How did the influx of gays change the Eureka Valley neighborhood? Why did Harvey Milk become a neighborhood leader?
5. How and why did anti-gay activists respond to the gay rights movement in the 1970s? What impact did anti-gay politics have in California? How did Harvey Milk respond?
6. Describe Dan White's background. Contrast he and Milk's experiences while serving on the San Francisco Board of Supervisors.
7. Why did White kill George Moscone and Harvey Milk? What happened at his trial? How did gays react?
8. If Harvey Milk were alive today, would you vote for him? Why or why not?

AMERICAN JOURNEY ONLINE

http://ajaccesss.wadsworth.com [†]

About the Vietnam War
— In <u>Vietnam Era</u>
  Documents
  • Document with Audio Commentary—Find, Fix, and Fight (1969)
  • Document with Audio Commentary—Officer Problems (1969)
  • *New York Times*, Excerpt from Interview with Private Paul Meadlo, November 25, 1969
  • Richard M. Nixon, Speech on the Cambodian Incursion, April 30, 1970
  • Le Duc Tho, Democratic Republic of Vietnam Nine-Point Plan (1971)
  • Ronald J. Glasser, The Shaping-Up of Macabe (1971)
  • Robert D. Heinl, Jr., The Collapse of the Armed Forces (1971)
  • Document with Audio Commentary—Harold G. Moore, Joseph L. Galloway, Edward F. Murphy, and Ronald J. Glasser, Excerpts from *We Were Soldiers Once...and Young* (1971, 1992, 1993)
  • U.S. Government, Policy Debate in November (1971)
  • Henry A. Kissinger, Statement of U.S. Position, January 26, 1972

[†] Enter password, choose the Archive indicated above, click on Contents, choose •Documents, •Images, or •Multimedia, and click on the title of the item.

- Richard M. Nixon, Response to North Vietnamese Easter Offensive, April 26, 1972
- Nguyen Van Thieu, South Vietnamese Opposition to Kissinger-Tho Agreement (1972)
- Henry A. Kissinger, Peace Is at Hand (1972)
- Richard M. Nixon, Letter to Nguyen Van Thieu, December 17, 1972
- Henry A. Kissinger and Le Duc Tho, The Paris Peace Accords, January 27, 1973
- Document—Henry A. Kissinger, The Christmas Bombing of Hanoi Was Justified (1973) in Vietnam Era
- Protest Note from the Government of the Republic of Vietnam [South Vietnam] to the Government of the Democratic Republic of Vietnam [North Vietnam], September 10, 1973
- U.S. Congress, Debate Between Sen. William Proxmire (D-Wisc.) and Sen. Barry Goldwater (R-Ariz). Over Aid to South Vietnam (1974)
- Kissinger Appears before Congress with Emergency Aid Request for South Vietnam (1975)
- Bui Diem with David Chanoff, Excerpt of *In the Jaws of History* (1975)
- Van Tien Dung, Directive from the Political Bureau, Vietnam Worker's Party, April 29, 1975
- James Webb, The Invisible Vietnam Veteran (1976)
- Gloria Emerson, Michael Bilton, and Kevin Sim, Excerpts of *Winners and Losers: Four Hours at My Lai* (1976)
- Richard M. Nixon, Letter to Democratic Republic of Vietnam Prime Minister Pham Van Dong, February 1, 1973 (1977)
- Philip Caputo, Excerpts from *A Rumor of War* (1977), 2 parts
- Department of Veterans Affairs, Two Documents on Agent Orange, Veterans Administration (1978, 1983, 1997)
- Michael Herr, Excerpt from *Dispatches* (1978)
- Tran Van Don, Excerpt from *Our Endless War Inside Vietnam* (1978)
- Vietnam, Ministry of Foreign Affairs, Excerpt from The Truth about Vietnam-China Relations over the Last Thirty Years (1979)
- Communist Party (Vietnam), The Ho Chi Minh Campaign to Liberate South Vietnam (1980)
- Tran Van Tra, Excerpt from *History of the Bulwark B-2 Theatre* (1982)
- Ronald Reagan, Remarks on Presenting the Presidential Citizens Medal of Freedom to Raymond Weeks at a Veterans Day Ceremony, November 11, 1982
- John McAuliff, Speech before Congress on Normalization, May 1, 1989
- George Bush, Remarks on Signing the National POW/MIA Recognition Day Proclamation (1989)
- John Balaban, Excerpt from *Remembering Heaven's Face* (1991)
- Hoang Van Thai, Excerpt from How South Vietnam Was Liberated (1992)

- Marlin Fitzwater, Statement by Press Secretary Fitzwater on Relations with Vietnam (1992)
- Jade Ngoc Quang Huynh, Excerpt from South Wind Changing (1994)
- Document with Audio Commentary-Patience Mason and Jonathan Shay, Excerpt on Post-Traumatic Stress Disorder (1994, 1995)
- Walt Rostow, The Case for the Vietnam War (1995)
- Lady Borton, Excerpt from *After Sorrow: An American among the Vietnamese* (1995)
- Document with Audio Commentary—Bennett Lovett-Graff, Rehabilitation and Fitting In (1998)

Images
- Paris Peace Talks, Opening Session, January 25, 1969
- Nixon Visits Troops, July 1969
- Governor Louis Nunn of Kentucky and S.W. (Phil) Matlock Carry Floral Wreath to Vietnam Memorial, Louisville (undated)
- U.S. Marines Board Transport Plane for Okinawa, July 10, 1969
- Vietnamization (undated)
- U.S. Troops Press Deeper into Cambodia (1970)
- Map of Cambodian Incursion, May 1970
- Dana Stone (1970)
- Nixon Press Conference on Cambodia, April 1970
- Truck Convoy on Bombed-Out Section of Ho Chi Minh Trail in Laos, January 16, 1970
- Bomb Shelters on Streets of Hanoi (undated)
- Camouflaged North Vietnamese Supply Truck in Laos, August 30, 1970
- Convoy of Trucks Travel on the Sturdy Roads of the Ho Chi Minh Trail (1970)
- Liberation Army's Victory Smashes Scheme to Cut Off Ho Chi Minh Trail (1971)
- U.S. Soldier Smoking from a Hookah Made out of Wine Bottle and .45-Caliber Shell Casing, Quang Tri, July 13, 1971
- Map of Easter Offensive, March 30, 1972
- Children Fleeing after Napalm Attack (1972)
- U.S. Marine Corps, Prisoner of War in His Cell (undated)
- U.S. Air Force, The Christmas Bombing (1972)
- Rubble Surrounding Cuban Embassy in Hanoi after Christmas Bombing, January 3, 1973
- Henry Kissinger in Plane (1973)
- Henry A. Kissinger Signs Paris Peace Accords, January 1973
- Henry A. Kissinger and Le Duc Tho in Paris, January 24, 1973
- Air Force Captain Ronald Bliss Greets His Wife at San Antonio Airport, March 6, 1973
- Children Welcoming POWs Home (1973)
- Richard M. Nixon and Henry A. Kissinger (1974)
- Liberation Army Marches Toward Saigon, March 29, 1975

- Map of the Ho Chi Minh Campaign, March-April 1975
- Nguyen Van Thieu's Farewell Address on Television, April 21, 1975
- Evacuation from Saigon, April 29, 1975
- U.S. Marine Corps, Sea Evacuation of Da Nang (1975)
- North Vietnam Takes Over (1975)
- U.S. Marine Corps, Tan Son Nhut Air Base, April 29, 1975
- The Hon Gai Depot Near Saigon, with 30 Million Dollars' Worth of Material Left Behind (1975)
- Front Page of *Stars and Stripes* Issue on Fall of Saigon (1975)
- U.S. Embassy Grounds in Saigon, April 29, 1975
- The Deer Hunter (1978)
- Freighter Hai Hong Crowded with Vietnamese Refugees, Anchored off Port Kelang, Malaysia, November 22, 1978
- Color Guard Reflected at Vietnam Veterans Memorial Wall, Washington, D.C. (1982)
- Frederick Hart, Three Grunts (undated)
- T-Shirt, Kentuckiana Chapter of the Vietnam Veterans of America (undated)
- T-Shirt, Circle of Sisters, Circle of Friends—Civilian Women in Service in Vietnam (undated)
- Letter Left at the Vietnam Veterans Memorial (1983)
- Boots and Hat Left at Vietnam Veterans Memorial in Washington, DC (undated)
- China Beach (1987)
- POW/MIA Flag Being Waved by Marine Corps Vietnam Veteran Louis Ortega Amid Combat Boots Representing Men Missing in Action, November 6, 1987
- Amerasian Child Reunited with Her Father (1987)
- *Born on the Fourth of July* (1991)
- Senator Robert Kerry, Marcy 25, 1993
- Pete Peterson, U.S. Ambassador to Vietnam (undated)
- Senator John McCain, Former POW (1998)
— In The Cold War
Documents
- Nixon's Plan for Vietnam (1969)
Images
- Vietnam War Critic Ellsberg Leaks Pentagon Papers (1971)
- General Giap (1972)
- Kissinger, Pham Van Dong Sign Paris Peace Accords (1973)
— In Civil Rights in the United States
Images
- Pentagon Papers Trial (1973)

About the Anti-war Movement
— In <u>Civil Rights in the United States</u>
Images
- Protests at Columbia University (1969)
- Sit-ins at Harvard University (1969)
- Benjamin Spock (1971)
— In <u>Vietnam Era</u>
Documents
- Karen Ashley, et al., Excerpt from The Weathermen Manifesto (1969)
- William Crandell and John Kerry, Statements by Vietnam Veterans against War (1971)

Images
- Weathermen March Across Chicago River during Days of Rage, October 11, 1969
- Defendants Known as Chicago Eight, November 2, 1969
- Moratorium on the War, November 15, 1969
- Students Aiding Fellow Student Wounded by National Guardsmen at Kent State University, May 4, 1970
- Antiwar Protest (1971)
- Veterans and Reservists Protest Vietnam War (undated)
- Antiwar Demonstrators Burn Draft Cards on the Steps of the Pentagon, May 22, 1972
- Image with Audio Commentary—Robert Louis Posner, Self-Portrait in Medicine Chest Mirror (1973)

About the Cold War
— In <u>The Cold War</u>
Documents
- U.S. Congress, U.S. Covert Action in Chile, 1963-1973 (1975)
- E.I. Afanasenko, et al., Soviet Documents on Angola and Southern Africa, 1975-1979 (1979)
- U.S. Senate, CIA Assassination Plots against Castro (1975)
- U.S. Senate, Summary of U.S. Senate Interim Report (1975) in The Cold War
- Anatoly Dobrynin, The Path to Disagreement: U.S.-Soviet Communications Leading to Vance's March 1977 Trip to Moscow (1976)
- Fidel Castro, Excerpt from Transcript of Honecker-Castro, April 3, 1977
- Jimmy Carter, President Jimmy Carter's Speech to the Nation, October 1, 1979
- President Ronald Reagan's Address to the Nation on Defense and National Security, March 23, 1983
- George F. Kennan, On Nuclear War (1983)
- George F. Kennan, Is Détente Worth Saving? (1983)
- Union of Concerned Scientists, The Evolution of Space Weapons (1984)

Images
- Kissinger and Zhou Enlai in China (1971)
- Nixon and Brezhnev Toast Détente (1972)
- Nixon in China (1972)
- Nixon and Kissinger at the Moscow Summit (1972)
- Dennis Renault, Realpolitik and Support for Dictatorships (1974)
- Scott Long, Military Spending (1974)
- Cold Warriors Nitze and Rostow Back Reagan (1974)
- Ken Alexander, Souring of Détente (1975)
- Bush and Mao Meet (1975)
- Bob Artley, Soviets Seen as Duping the United States (1976)
- Jim Knudsen, Soviet Occupation of Eastern Europe (1976)
- Karl Hubenthal, Controversial Helsinki Accords (1976)
- Tom Darcy, Nuclear Peril (1977)
- High-Flying U-2 (1978)
- Carter All Smiles (1978)
- "Death to Carter!' (1979)
- Afghan Rebels (1979)
- John R. Thornton, Olympic Politics (1980)
- Lech Walesa and Solidarity Ride High (1981)
- Gene Basset, Castro Releases Families—and Criminals (1981)
- Nuclear Weapons and Their Destructiveness (undated)
- Kennan as Elder Statesman (undated)

— In <u>Women in America</u>
   Documents
   - Jeane Kirkpatrick, Speech Attacking Democrats (1984)

About Watergate
— In <u>Civil Rights in the United States</u>
   Images
   - Richard M. Nixon (undated)
— In <u>The Constitution and Supreme Court</u>
   Images
   - Katharine Graham (circa 1973)
   - Warren E. Burger, *United States v. Nixon* (1974)
   - Richard M. Nixon's Letter of Resignation (1974)
— In <u>The Cold War</u>
   Images
   - Watergate Scandal (undated)
   - Watergate-Period Meeting of Nixon Advisors (1974)

About Law/Law Enforcement
— In <u>Civil Rights in the United States</u>
   Documents
   - U.S. Supreme Court, *Tinker v. Des Moines School District* (1969)

About Women
— In <u>Civil Rights in the United States</u>
Images
  • Demonstration for the Equal Rights Amendment (1970)
  • U.S. Congress, Proposed Equal Rights Amendment (1972)
  • Betty Friedan (1981)
— In <u>Women in America</u>
Documents
  • Wilma Heide, NOW Statement on the Equal Rights Amendment (1970)
  • Shirley Chisholm, Statement on the Equal Rights Amendment by Rep. Shirley Chisholm (1970)
  • Gloria Steinem, Testimony on the Equal Rights Amendment (1970)
  • Images
  • Planned Parenthood Ad Supporting Right of Abortion (1973)

About American Indians
— In <u>Civil Rights in the United States</u>
Documents
  • Richard M. Nixon, Message to Congress on Indian Affairs (1970)
Images
  • Occupation of Alcatraz Island (1969)
  • Occupation of Bureau of Indian Affairs (1972)
  • American Indian Movement at Wounded Knee (1973)
  • American Indian Movement Barbara Anne Richards (1978)

About Asian Americans
— In <u>The Asian-American Experience</u>
Documents
  • Willie Barientos, Some Are Bought, Some Fight (1976)
Images
  • Bruce Lee (1973)

About Hispanic Americans
— In <u>The Hispanic-American Experience</u>
Documents
  • Reies Lopez Tijerina, Excerpt from A Letter from the Santa Fe Jail (1969)
  • Alurista (?) and Rodolfo Gonzáles, El Plan Espiritual de Aztlán (1969)
  • Rodolfo "Corky" Gonzáles, Excerpt from "Chicano Nationalism: The Key to Unity for La Raza" (1970)
Images
  • Rodolfo "Corky" Gonzáles (1971)
  • Cubans Leaving from the Port of Mariel (1980)

About Gay Rights
— In <u>Civil Rights in the United States</u>
Documents
• Harvey Milk, Note about Assassination (1977) in Civil Rights
Images
• Harvey Milk (1977)

About the Environment
— In <u>Civil Rights in the United States</u>
Images
• Water Pollution (undated)

STATE OF THE UNION

In the late 1980s, the Cold War ended with remarkable speed and peacefulness. The Reagan administration veered from stunning triumphs to damaging scandals. Reagan's successor, George H.W. Bush, led the transition to a post-Cold War world and assembled a multinational force to combat Iraq's 1990 invasion of Kuwait. But Bush's approval ratings fell in the wake of the Persian Gulf War. As voters focused on an economic recession and domestic problems, they grew dissatisfied. After a bruising campaign, Arkansas governor Bill Clinton narrowly won the 1992 presidential race. Clinton was undoubtedly the most colorful president in modern memory. An extraordinarily gifted politician though a rather careless individual, Clinton energized—and polarized—the country. In recent years, anxieties about terrorism, war, and economic security have pervaded American political culture. Partisanship and ideological differences often paralyze the democratic process. Americans struggle to reconcile themselves with changing demographic realities. Globalization is fraught with promise and perils. However formidable these obstacles, Americans demonstrate ingenuity, spirit, and courage— traits abundantly displayed in the aftermath of the 9-11 terrorist attacks. While the path for the nation's future is uncertain, history attests to the ability of the American people to use the tools of democracy to meet the challenges along the way.

During his second term, Ronald Reagan confronted serious domestic problems. The budget deficit and trade gap continued to expand. Deregulation of the savings and loan industry proved disastrous. Increasing numbers of undocumented aliens entered the country. Drugs, violence, and poverty gripped the inner cities. AIDS exacted a devastating toll on gay men, hemophiliacs, and IV drug users. Battles over multiculturalism, abortion, feminism, and censorship divided Americans. Scandals at the Pentagon, the Department of Justice, the Department of Labor, the Central Intelligence Agency, the Environmental Protection Agency, the Department of Interior, and the Department of Housing and Urban Development revealed illegalities among Reagan's subordinates.

At the same time, Reagan faced new dangers in the Middle East. In December 1987, Palestinians in the Gaza Strip and the West Bank began the *intifada*, an uprising against Israel. Secretary of State George Schultz was unable to negotiate a settlement between the Palestinians and Israelis. Encouraged by the U.S. withdrawal from Lebanon in 1984, Islamic terrorists targeted Westerners with kidnappings, airplane hijackings, and bombings. In 1986, after a bombing on a Berlin nightclub frequented by American soldiers, Reagan ordered a retaliatory air strike on Libya, a sponsor of terrorist activity. In December 1988, terrorists blew up Pan Am 103 in the skies over Lockerbie, Scotland, and 269 people died. In 1991, the United States and Britain charged two Libyans with conspiracy and murder for their roles in the incident. By early 2002, a Dutch court had sentenced one suspect to life and acquitted the other.

The most damaging scandal of the Reagan presidency also originated in the Middle East. In the aftermath of the Iranian Revolution, the United States severed diplomatic relations with the regime of Ayatollah Ruhollah Khomeini. In 1980, when an eight-year war erupted between Iran and Iraq, U.S. officials sent military equipment and financial assistance to Iraqi dictator Saddam Hussein. In 1985, despite their continuing support of Iraq, Reagan aides attempted to secure the release of American hostages being held by pro-Iranian radicals in Lebanon by selling 508 anti-tank missiles to Iran. U.S. officials illegally diverted the proceeds from the arms sales to the Contras in Nicaragua. Although Reagan was never directly implicated in the Iran-Contra Affair, several of his assistants were later convicted of crimes related to the matter.

Reagan's relationship with Soviet premier Mikhail Gorbachev was much more successful. As Gorbachev instituted *glasnost* (openness) and *perestroika* (restructuring) in the USSR, he began decreasing the Soviet role in Eastern Europe and forming a close partnership with Reagan. In December 1987, they signed the Intermediate Nuclear Forces (INF) Treaty, a landmark arms agreement that removed 2,500 Soviet and American nuclear missiles from Europe and eliminated *all* intermediate-range nuclear missiles. During a May 1988 visit to Moscow, Reagan averred that the Soviet "evil empire" no longer existed and Gorbachev announced Soviet withdrawal from Afghanistan. Just months later, the Cold War would end.

In 1988, Democrats hoped to recapture the presidency. They chose little-known Massachusetts governor Michael Dukakis as their nominee. The Republicans selected Vice-President George H.W. Bush. The contest marked the emergence of political consultants, "sound bites," and "photo ops." Although Bush promised a "kinder, gentler America," he ran one of the nastiest campaigns in U.S. history. A Bush ad attacked Dukakis's record on crime by featuring Willie Horton, an African-American man who raped a white woman during a prison furlough in Massachusetts. Critics blasted the commercial's racist overtones and its failure to mention that Dukakis had not created the prison program. Simultaneously, Bush operatives made *liberal* an epithet by assaulting Dukakis's membership in the American Civil Liberties Union (ACLU), a political organization committed to defending the Bill of Rights. Dukakis refused to engage in mudslinging, but ran a dull, uninspired campaign. In November, Bush carried 54 percent of the popular vote and won forty states. The Democrats, however, retained control of both houses of Congress.

As president, Bush skillfully handled foreign policy crises. After Gorbachev refused to send troops to quash independence movements in Eastern Europe, the

Cold War rapidly ended. By 1990, Poland, Hungary, Czechoslovakia, Bulgaria, Romania, East Germany, Yugoslavia, and Albania overthrew or transformed their communist governments. All established democracies. In 1990, East and West Germany reunified and Latvia, Estonia, and Lithuania declared independence from the Soviet Union. In 1991, Bush and Gorbachev agreed to a twenty-five percent reduction in their nuclear arsenals. After a failed coup by communist hard-liners in August 1991, Gorbachev lost political credibility. By early 1992, he resigned and the Soviet Union broke into several independent republics. Boris Yeltsin controlled Russia, the largest of the former Soviet regions.

Following the disintegration of the USSR, Bush adjusted U.S. foreign policy to meet post-Cold War realities. In the former Soviet Union, where the collapse of communism generated economic chaos, crime, and ethnic conflicts, Bush encouraged the International Monetary Fund (IMF) and private investors to support its transition to a free-market economy. Bush cut the U.S. nuclear arsenal and ended American involvement in Cold War-related conflicts in Nicaragua and El Salvador.

While the end of Cold War defused some international tensions, it highlighted others. In 1989, the Chinese government crushed pro-democracy demonstrations in Beijing. Although appalled by China's human rights abuses, Bush and his successors did not sever economic ties with the modernizing Chinese state. The same year, Bush ordered the invasion of Panama in order to capture dictator Manuel Noriega. Although the CIA funded Noriega during the Cold War, the United States chose not to ignore his involvement in the Latin American drug trade. Noreiga is currently serving a life sentence in a U.S. prison. In South Africa, where the United States and other nations had imposed economic sanctions to protest apartheid, President F.W. de Klerk released Nelson Mandela after twenty-seven years of incarceration. By 1995, apartheid ended and Mandela became the first black president of South Africa.

Bush's biggest triumph was his response to Iraq's invasion of Kuwait in August 1990. Assembling a multinational coalition that included the Soviet Union and several Arab countries, the Bush administration persuaded the United Nations to impose economic sanctions on Iraq and to establish a January 15, 1991 deadline for Iraq to leave Kuwait. The deployment of 690,000 troops to the Persian Gulf included 425,000 American soldiers. On January 12, 1991, after a spirited debate, Congress voted to authorize the use of military force in Iraq. Four days later, when the UN deadline passed, U.S. planes began a massive bombing campaign in Iraq. After six weeks, 200,000 UN ground troops entered Iraq and met little resistance. Within three days, the Iraqis surrendered. The short war left approximately 23,000 Iraqis and 148 Americans dead.

Although Bush's approval ratings soared to 90 percent in the days following the Gulf War, a troubled economy soon diminished his popularity. Bush had inherited grievous economic problems from the Reagan administration. Reagan's deregulation of the savings and loan industry spawned risky practices that led to the failure of nearly 600 financial institutions. Millions lost their life savings. Bound to honor federal insurance on individual deposits, the federal government spent $500 *billion* on the savings and loan bailout. Violating his "no new taxes" campaign pledge, Bush agreed to a substantial tax increase in 1990. Nonetheless, the deficit rose to $269 billion in 1991 and to $290 billion the following year. By 1992, the savings and loan crisis, the Gulf War, and rising health care costs contributed to a recession. Retail and housing sales plummeted. Unemployment hit 7 percent. States cut social welfare spending in response to budget shortfalls.

Bush's record on other domestic issues was mixed. In 1991, after vetoing two previous versions of the bill, Bush signed legislation broadening federal protections against job discrimination. Amidst outcry over the 1989 *Exxon Valdez* oil spill on the Alaskan coast, warnings about global warming, and increased rates of air pollution, Bush backed the Federal Clean Act of 1990, but continued supporting offshore drilling and demands for petroleum exploration in the Arctic National Wildlife Refuge. In 1991, Bush's appointment of Clarence Thomas to the Supreme Court enraged feminists and some African Americans. Pro-choice advocates decried the rightward shift of the Court and denounced violent extremists in the pro-life movement. In April 1992, the Los Angeles riot exposed desperation and rage in the nation's inner cities.

These factors significantly harmed Bush's chance for reelection. In early 1992, Bush proposed an economic plan to foster recovery, but few voters paid attention. Instead, they drifted to Democratic nominee Bill Clinton, the five-term governor of Arkansas, or H. Ross Perot, an eccentric billionaire running as a third-party candidate. Clinton's program of economic growth and job creation attracted some voters even as allegations of draft-dodging, marijuana use, and adultery repelled others. In November, Clinton won with 43 percent of the popular vote to Bush's 38 percent and Perot's 19 percent. The Democrats controlled both houses of Congress and record numbers of women and minorities won congressional seats.

When Clinton took office in 1993, he proposed the most ambitious legislative agenda since the Great Society. Clinton wanted to focus on economic recovery and health care reform, but missteps and scandals jeopardized his political goals. Controversies forced him to withdraw appointees and to accept the "don't ask, don't tell" compromise on gays in the military. The president's troubles mounted when Paula Jones, a former Arkansas state employee, filed a sexual harassment lawsuit against him and an independent counsel began investigating Whitewater, an Arkansas real estate development. In September 1994, after intense lobbying by the insurance and pharmaceutical industries, Congress abandoned Clinton's sweeping health care proposal.

Despite these difficulties, Clinton achieved some successes. Congress passed his plan to reduce the budget deficit by $496 billion over five years. Passage of the Family Medical Leave Act granted workers up to twelve weeks of unpaid leave to tend a newborn or adopted child or to care for an ailing relative. Gun control advocates cheered his signing of the Brady Bill, a federal law mandating a five-day waiting period and criminal background checks for handgun purchases. In 1994, Congress approved his $30.2 billion crime prevention program. In April 1996, following the 1993 bombing at the World Trade Center and the 1995 destruction of the Alfred P. Murrah Federal Building in Oklahoma City, Clinton signed a one billion dollar anti-terrorism bill permitting deportation of non-citizens suspected of terrorism and barring fund-raising by terrorist groups. The legislation omitted Clinton's request to expand FBI wiretapping operations.

Throughout the 1990s, U.S. officials searched for a coherent post-Cold War foreign policy. Clinton's approach included containment and mediation as well as humanitarian and "nation-building" initiatives. In 1993, he launched an air strike on Baghdad in retaliation for an Iraqi plot to assassinate President George H.W. Bush. Clinton presided over the historic Oslo Peace Accords between Israel and the Palestinians. In Somalia, he deployed 15,000 U.S reinforcements after local warlords attacked American soldiers during a UN humanitarian mission. In October 1994, after months of failed negotiations and sanctions, Clinton sent U.S. forces to Haiti to restore ousted President Jean-Bertrand Aristide to power. The same year, U.S. officials ended a long-standing trade embargo on Vietnam. In 1995, the United States and Vietnam established diplomatic relations. As the former Yugoslavia disintegrated into civil war and "ethnic cleansing," U.S. officials and NATO troops pressured the Serbs to end their campaign against the Croats and Bosnians. Clinton and Secretary of State Warren Christopher facilitated a peace settlement. Shortly thereafter, NATO peacekeepers backed with 20,000 U.S. troops arrived in Bosnia-Herzegovina to enforce the cease-fire agreement.

Trade was an integral element of Clinton's international agenda. Eager to compete with the European Union and to decrease the $150 billion trade deficit, Clinton tore down trade barriers. In 1993, he signed the North American Free Trade Agreement (NAFTA) creating a single free-trade zone in the United States, Canada, and Mexico. In 1994, the Senate ratified the General Agreement on Tariffs and Trade (GATT), the most significant restructuring of international trade regulations since the 1944 Bretton Woods Agreement. Designed to gradually eliminate obstacles to global free trade, GATT established the World Trade Organization (WTO) to enforce its provisions.

Clinton's mixed record enabled the Republicans to win a landslide victory in the 1994 elections. For the first time in forty years, the GOP controlled both houses of Congress. In the House, Newt Gingrich (R-GA) became Speaker of the House and vowed to enact the "Contract with America," a conservative plan for balancing the federal budget, reforming the welfare system, reducing government regulations, and cutting taxes. With notable discipline, House Republicans passed most of the Contract, but met staunch opposition in the Senate.

Rather than be cowed by the Gingrich juggernaut, Clinton moved to the right politically. In late 1995, the federal government shut down twice after Clinton and the House failed to reach agreement on the budget. Voters blamed Gingrich and the Speaker's popularity tumbled. In August 1996, after vetoing two previous versions, Clinton signed a welfare reform bill, thus depriving the Republicans of a powerful campaign issue.

Clinton's strategy enabled him to win reelection in 1996. He faced Senator Robert Dole (R-KS), who ran on a platform combining supply-side economics with social conservatism. While deflecting charges of fund-raising improprieties,

Clinton emphasized the nation's booming economy. On Election Day, Clinton won with 49 percent of the popular vote to Dole's 41 percent and Ross Perot's 8 percent.

During his second term, Clinton pursued a modest agenda aimed at helping the middle-class. In 1997, he signed legislation to balance the federal budget by 2002 and providing $152 billion in tax cuts. In 1998, he announced that the United States had a budget surplus for the first time since 1969 and he urged Congress to use the funds to bolster the faltering Social Security system. In foreign policy, Clinton brokered the Good Friday Peace Accords between Catholics and Protestants in Northern Ireland. He also mediated the Wye River agreement calling for an Israeli troop withdrawal from the West Bank and other measures to defuse tensions in the region. In December 1998, Clinton ordered a four-day bombing raid on Iraq after Saddam Hussein refused entry to UN weapons inspectors. In January 1999, NATO and U.S. forces began a bombing campaign against Serbia in response to aggression in Kosovo. After seventy-nine days, Serbian leader Slobodan Milosevic capitulated. UN peacekeepers were dispatched to enforce the peace settlement. Local protestors forced Milosevic to flee Belgrade in October 2000.

Accusations of sexual indiscretion overshadowed much of Clinton's second term. In January 1998, attorneys representing Paula Jones announced plans to depose Monica Lewinsky, a former White House intern, about her alleged affair with the president. Although a judge dismissed Jones's lawsuit three months later, Kenneth Starr, the independent counsel examining the Whitewater real estate scandal, broadened his investigation to assess whether Clinton and his aides had encouraged Lewinsky to lie. Using slippery language and dramatic apologies, Clinton at first denied and then acknowledged having an "inappropriate relationship" with Lewinsky. In September 1998, Starr released a report documenting, in lurid detail, Clinton's involvement with Lewinsky and his efforts to conceal the affair. In December, the House of Representatives narrowly approved two articles of impeachment against Clinton, one for perjuring himself in grand jury testimony about Lewinsky and another for obstruction of justice. Congressional Democrats and a majority of the public opposed impeachment. In February 1999, the Senate acquitted Clinton of both charges. In September 2000, Robert Ray, Starr's successor as independent counsel, closed the $50 million Whitewater investigation after finding insufficient evidence to merit criminal charges against the president or Hillary Clinton, the first lady.

Although the Lewinsky scandal irreparably harmed Clinton's reputation, it also hurt the Republicans. In the 1998 elections, the Democrats gained five congressional seats—a testament to voters' satisfaction with a thriving economy and disdain for the partisanship driving the impeachment process. Ironically, two Republicans, not Clinton, were pushed from office. First, Gingrich resigned as Speaker of the House after the disappointing election returns. Then, Bob Livingston (R-MS), Gingrich's designated successor, resigned when reporters exposed his own marital infidelity. Clinton, meanwhile, retained a 59 percent approval rating.

No one could have predicted the drama of the 2000 presidential elections. The Democrats chose Vice-President Al Gore as their nominee. The Republicans picked George W. Bush, the two-term governor of Texas. Both candidates ran as centrists. Gore and Bush differed in their views on the best uses for projected federal budget surpluses and the proper role of the federal government. Bush advocated large tax cuts, partial privatization of Social Security, and government-funded vouchers for private education. Gore supported putting the surpluses into Social Security and Medicare. Bush was pro-life; Gore was pro-choice. Although Pat Buchanan ran as the Reform Party nominee and Ralph Nader represented the Green Party, neither won significant national support.

The election itself was a forty-two day roller coaster ride. Senate elections resulted in a 50-50 Democratic-Republican split. Early on election night, commentators declared Gore winner of Florida. Later, they claimed Bush had won. Then, they said that the race was too close to call. Returns from the rest of the nation gave Gore a 337,000 lead in the popular vote and 267 electoral votes. Carrying the South and much of the Midwest, Bush had 246 electoral votes. Because neither had the 270 electoral votes to win, the outcome of the election hinged on Florida's 25 electoral votes.

In Florida, mandatory recounts began. Voters protested unclear "butterfly ballots," "under votes," antiquated voting machines, and unhelpful poll officials. With the nation's attention riveted on his state, Governor Jeb Bush, brother of George W. Bush, tried to keep order amidst the chaos. Baffled officials tried to interpret ballots with pregnant, dimpled, and hanging chads (the pieces of cardboard removed when punching a ballot). On November 27, Florida Secretary of State Katherine Harris, a leader in the state Bush campaign organization, ended the recounts and certified Bush the winner by 537 votes. After Gore won an appeal to the Florida Supreme Court demanding a statewide hand recount, the Bush cam-paign appealed to the U.S. Supreme Court insisting that the recounts be stopped. On the evening of December 12, the U.S. Supreme Court issued a 5-4 decision ordering the completion of all recounts by December 13—a deadline that was obviously impossible to meet. The four opposing justices issued blistering dis-sents. Despite winning the popular vote by a 540,000 margin, Gore lost the electoral vote, 267-271. Bush became the nation's forty-third president.

Although he lacked a mandate, Bush pursued a vigorous conservative agenda. In April 2001, Republicans lost control of the Senate when James Jeffords of Vermont left the GOP to become an Independent. Because Vice-President Richard Cheney would no longer cast the deciding vote in the tied Senate, the Democrats became the majority party. Undaunted by Jeffords' defection, Bush won passage of a $1.35 trillion tax cut, the largest in American history. But the tax rebate checks ($600 for couples, $300 for individuals) that Americans began receiving in August did little to shore up the sagging economy.

During his first seven months in office, Bush made several foreign policy decisions widely perceived as unilateralist. Abrogating the 1972 Anti-Ballistic Missile Treaty, Bush pushed for the development of a missile defense system to thwart a nuclear attack on the United States. At the United Nations, Bush refused to support an international criminal court. Claiming that its inspections would harm U.S. biotechnology firms, he rejected an international convention against germ warfare. Most controversially, Bush abandoned the Kyoto Treaty on global warming, an agreement signed by 178 nations. Although the United States produces a quarter of the world's greenhouse gases, Bush claimed the accord would damage the American economy. The president withdrew from efforts to resolve the Israeli-Palestinian conflict and ended negotiations with North Korea.

On September 11, 2001, terrorist attacks on the World Trade Center and the Pentagon permanently changed American life. Armed with box cutters, Islamic radicals hijacked two commercial airliners flying from Boston to Los Angeles. They rerouted the planes and flew them directly into the north and south towers of the World Trade Center in New York City. Both towers soon collapsed. At the same time, a third plane, en route from Washington, DC to Los Angeles, struck the Pentagon. Passengers on a fourth hijacked plane headed from Newark to San Francisco, learned of the other attacks and rushed their hijackers. The plane crashed into a field in Shanksville, Pennsylvania instead of its likely target, either the White House or the U.S. Capitol. All 269 passengers on the planes died and over 3,000 perished in the World Trade Center and Pentagon attacks—the largest single-day loss of life in U.S. history.

As Americans and the world absorbed the tragedies, the nineteen Saudi hijackers were linked to Osama bin Laden, leader of the *al-Qaeda* terrorist network. Enraged by the stationing of U.S. troops in Saudi Arabia during and after the Gulf War, bin Laden began using his substantial fortune to fund terrorist assaults on the West. By 2001, U.S. intelligence agents linked *al-Qaeda* to bombings of the U.S. embassies in Kenya and Tanzania and the *U.S.S. Cole*.

The events of 9-11 inspired a strong wave of patriotism in the United States. Americans rushed to buy flags, give blood, and volunteer. Charities received $1 billion in donations. Commentators hailed the courage of police officers and fire fighters helping with rescue efforts. New York Mayor Rudolph Giuliani won wide praise for his decisive, eloquent response to the crisis.

The Bush administration also reacted strongly and the president's approval ratings soared to 90 percent. Bush announced that he would capture bin Laden "dead or alive" and warned nations of dire consequences if they assisted terrorists. He and his aides quickly mobilized an international coalition against terrorism. In October 2001, U.S. and British forces began bombing Afghanistan. Ruled by the despotic Taliban regime since 1996, Afghanistan had harbored bin Laden and his *al Qaeda* training camps. With the assistance of Taliban rival factions, U.S. ground troops gained control of Afghan cities. In early December, the Taliban collapsed and abandoned its final stronghold in Kandahar. By 2003, more than 2,700 suspected terrorists in 98 countries had been abducted or killed. Bin Laden, however, remained at large and *al-Qaeda* renewed its terrorist activities with bombings in Bali, Tunisia, Yemen, and Saudi Arabia.

At home, the "war on terrorism" produced tremendous changes. After anthrax-tainted letters arrived in several locations in the fall of 2001, the U.S. postal service instituted new screening practices. Expanded security procedures transformed air travel. Congressional passage of the USA Patriot Act granted law enforcement officials sweeping new powers to detain and deport suspected terrorists, to use wiretapping and other surveillance tools, and to conduct searches without warrants. Within months, more than 1,200 people were secretly detained and denied access to attorneys. Courts are only beginning to assess the constitutionality of these measures. In late 2002, Congress approved the Department of Homeland Security, a consolidation of twenty-two federal agencies. Government officials issued color-coded "terrorist alerts" and urged Americans to prepare for terrorist attacks.

In the aftermath of 9-11, the Bush administration began fundamentally reshaping U.S. foreign policy. Abandoning containment, President Bush and his aides offered a doctrine of preemption in which the United States uses its power and influence to remove regimes that threaten American interests and security. In early 2002, Bush declared that Iran, Iraq, and North Korea formed an "axis of evil." Denouncing Iraqi dictator Saddam Hussein's possession of "weapons of mass destruction" and alleged links to *al-Qaeda*, the administration advocated a preemptive strike in Iraq. When these declarations generated heated opposition, U.S. officials made the case against Iraq at the United Nations. In March 2003, amidst enormous anti-war demonstrations and bitter diplomatic quarrels at the UN and NATO, 240,000 U.S. and U.K. forces invaded Iraq. Within a month, the Saddam regime collapsed and the American-British coalition began a costly and difficult process of rebuilding Iraqi society.

While reacting cautiously to the dangers posed by terrorism, Americans confronted new economic realities. Through much of the 1990s, digital technologies, mergers, and cost-saving measures generated incredible prosperity. In 2000, the Gross National Product (GNP) reached $9.8 trillion, almost quadrupling its 1980 value. Fueled by high-priced technology stocks, the Dow Jones index hit 11,000, up from 1,000 in 1980. Inflation dipped below three percent and unemployment remained low.

Things changed dramatically in 2001. In April 2001, technology stocks plummeted. As the market collapsed, other industries got caught in the maelstrom. Between 2000 and 2002, the Dow lost 27.5 percent of its value. Corporate lay-offs and cost-cutting measures escalated. After 9-11, the economy went into recession. Many businesses, especially tourism and the airlines, sustained great losses. States and cities faced huge budget shortfalls as tax revenues declined. A wave of business scandals triggered bankruptcies and demands for closer scrutiny of corporate practices.

Despite the faltering economy, Bush defied historic trends and led the Republicans to significant gains in the mid-term elections. The GOP regained the Senate and increased their strength in the House. In May 2003, Bush won passage of a $350 billion tax reduction package. Undaunted by Bush's high approval ratings, several Democrats entered the 2004 presidential race.

Only time will tell how and when Americans will emerge from these anxious times. Hopefully, generosity and unity will triumph over self-interest and division. Undoubtedly, the wondrous, complex chorus of voices that comprise the American nation will continue to speak.

26.1

LARRY KRAMER, "1,112 AND COUNTING" (1983)

In early 1981, the Centers for Disease Control (CDC) noted an unusually high number of cases of Pneumocystis carinii *pneumonia (PCP) and Karposi's sarcoma (KS) among gay men in New York and Los Angeles. Within months, scientists documented a collection of symptoms, originally called GRID (Gay-Related Immune Disorder), in which the body's immune system ceased to function. When the syndrome began appearing in heterosexual drug users, hemophiliacs, and Haitian refugees, it was renamed AIDS (Acquired Immune Deficiency Syndrome). Virtually all of those who contracted AIDS soon died. As AIDS rapidly spread, doctors raced to identify its causative agent and to understand its transmission.*

The Reagan administration responded very slowly to the AIDS epidemic. Because the disease initially struck marginalized populations like gay men and drug users, officials were reluctant to provide research funding or information. President Reagan did not publicly acknowledge the AIDS crisis until more than 30,000 Americans had died. Erroneous reports that AIDS could be spread through casual contact generated widespread panic. In 1983, French and American doctors identified HIV, the virus that causes AIDS and is passed through blood, saliva, or semen. Enraged by the government's indifference to the devastating impact of AIDS on their community, gay men and lesbians began raising public awareness about the disease and providing services for people with AIDS.

Larry Kramer (1935-present) was one of the earliest and most provocative AIDS activists. Born in Connecticut, Kramer graduated from Yale University and worked in the British film industry. His screenplay for Women in Love *(1969) received an Academy Award nomination. Kramer later became a successful novelist and playwright. In 1981, he and five friends founded the Gay Men's Health Crisis (GMHC), the world's largest AIDS service organization. Six years later, he founded the AIDS Coalition to Unleash Power (ACT UP), a group whose flamboyant, controversial protests revolutionized health care advocacy. In this article from the March 1983 edition of* New York Native, *a now-defunct gay newspaper, Kramer implores gays to respond to the AIDS crisis. Widely reprinted and distributed, the essay inspired AIDS activism across the country.*

———————————————■———————————————

FOCUS QUESTIONS

1. How would you characterize Kramer's tone? Why does he write in this manner?
2. According to Kramer, what impact is AIDS having on its victims and the medical establishment? How is the epidemic progressing? How are public officials and insurance companies responding?
3. What does Kramer urge gays to do in response to AIDS? Were his suggestions appropriate? Why or why not?
4. How and why did AIDS change public opinion about gays and lesbians?
5. How have attitudes toward AIDS and treatments for it changed since Kramer wrote this article?

I f this article doesn't scare the shit out of you, we're in real trouble. If this article doesn't rouse you to anger, fury, rage, and action, gay men may have no future on this earth. Our continued existence depends on how angry you can get.

I am writing this as Larry Kramer, and I am speaking for myself, and my views are not to be attributed to Gay Men's Health Crisis.

I repeat: Our continued existence as gay men upon the face of this earth is at stake. Unless we fight for our lives, we shall die. In all the history of homosexuality we have never before been so close to death and extinction. Many of us are dying or already dead.

Before I tell you what we must do, let me tell you what is happening to us.

There are now 1,112 cases of serious Acquired Immune Deficiency Syndrome. When we first became worried, there were only 41. In only twenty-eight days, from January 13th to February 9th, there were 164 new cases—and 73 more dead. The total death tally is now 418. Twenty percent of all cases were registered this January alone. There have been 195 dead in New York City from among 526 victims. Of all serious AIDS cases, 47.3 percent are in the New York metropolitan area.

These are the serious cases of AIDS, which means Karposi's sarcoma, *Pneumocystis carinii* pneumonia, and other deadly infections. These numbers do not include the thousands of us walking around with what is also being called AIDS: various forms of swollen lymph glands and fatigues that doctors don't know what to label or what they might portend.

The rise in these numbers is terrifying. Whatever is spreading is now spreading faster as more and more people come down with AIDS.

And, for the first time in this epidemic, leading doctors and researchers are finally admitting they don't know what's going on. I find this terrifying too—as terrifying as the alarming rise in numbers. For the first time, doctors are saying out loud and up front, "I don't know."

For two years they weren't talking like this. For two years we've heard a different theory every few weeks. We grasped at straws of possible cause: promiscuity, poppers [amyl nitrate inhalers], back rooms, the baths, rimming, fisting, anal intercourse, urine, semen, shit, saliva, sweat, blood, blacks, a single virus, a new virus, repeated exposure to a virus, amoebas carrying a virus, drugs, Haiti, voodoo, Flagyl [an antibiotic], constant bouts of amebiasis, hepatitis A and B, syphilis, gonorrhea.

I have talked with the leading doctors treating us. One said to me, "If I knew in 1981 what I know now, I would never have become involved with this disease." Another said, "The thing that upsets me the most in all of this is that at any given moment one of my patients is in the hospital and something is going on with him that I don't understand. And it's destroying me because there's some craziness going on in him that destroying him." A third said to me, "I'm very depressed. A doctor's job is to make patients well. And I can't. Too many of my patients die."

After almost two years of an epidemic, there are still no answers. After almost two years of an epidemic, the cause of AIDS remains unknown. After almost two years of an epidemic, there is no cure.

Hospitals are so filled with AIDS patients that there is often a waiting period of up to a month before admission, no matter how sick you are. And, once in, patients are now more and more being treated like lepers as hospital staffs become increasingly worried that AIDS is infectious.

Suicides are now being reported of men who rather die than face such medical uncertainty, such uncertain therapies, such hospital treatment, and the appalling statistics that 86 percent of all serious AIDS cases die after three years' time.

If all of this had been happening to any other community for two long years, there would have been, long ago, such an outcry from that community and all its members that the government of this city and this country would not know what had hit them.

Why isn't every gay man in this city so scared shitless that he is screaming for action? Does every gay man in New York *want* to die?

Let's talk about a few things specifically.

• *Let's talk about which gay men get AIDS.*

No matter what you've heard, there is no single profile for all AIDS victims. There are drug users and non-drug users. There are the truly promiscuous and the almost monogamous. There are reported cases of single-contact infection.

All it seems to take is the one wrong fuck. That's not promiscuity—that's bad luck.

• *Let's talk about AIDS happening in straight people.*

We've been hearing from the beginning of this epidemic that it was only a question of time before the straight community came down with AIDS, and that when that happened AIDS would suddenly be high on all agendas for funding and research and then we would finally be looked after and all would be well.

I myself thought, when AIDS occurred in the first baby, that would be the breakthrough point. It was. For one day the media paid an enormous amount of attention. And that was it, kids.

There have been no confirmed cases of AIDS in straight, white, non-intravenous-drug-using, middle-class Americans. The only confirmed straights struck down by AIDS are members of groups just as disenfranchised as gay men: intravenous drug users, Haitians, eleven hemophiliacs (up from eight), black and Hispanic babies, and wives or partners of IV drug users and bisexual men.

If there have been—and there may have been—any cases in straight, white, non-intravenous-drug-using, middle-class Americans, the Centers for Disease Control [CDC] isn't telling anyone about them. When pressed, the CDC says there are "a number of cases that don't fall into any of the other categories." The CDC says it's impossible to fully investigate most of these "other category" cases; most of them are dead. The CDC also tends not believe living, white, middle class male victims when they say they're straight, or female victims when they say their husbands are straight and don't take drugs.

Why isn't AIDS happening to more straights? Maybe it's because gay men don't have sex with them.

Of all serious AIDS cases, 72.4 percent are in gay and bisexual men.

• *Let's talk about "surveillance."*

The Centers for Disease Control is charged by our government to fully monitor all epidemics and unusual diseases.

To learn something from an epidemic, you have to keep records and statistics. Statistics come from interviewing victims and getting as much information from them as you can. Before they die. To get the best information, you have to ask the right questions.

There have been so many AIDS victims that the CDC is no longer able to get to them fast enough. It has given up. (The CDC also had been using a questionnaire that was fairly insensitive to the lives of gay men, and thus the data collected from its early study of us have been disputed by gay epidemiologists. The National Institutes of Health [NIH] is also fielding a very naïve questionnaire.)

Important, vital case histories are now being lost because of this cessation of CDC interviewing. This is a woeful waste with as terrifying implications for us as the alarming rise in case numbers and doctors finally admitting they don't know what is going on. As each man dies, as one or both sets of men who had interacted with each other come down with AIDS, yet more information that might reveal patterns of transmissibility is not being monitored and collected and studied. We are being denied perhaps the easiest and fastest research tool available at this moment.

It will require at least $200,000 to prepare a new questionnaire to study the next important question that must be answered: *How* is AIDS being transmitted? (In which bodily fluids, by which sexual behaviors, in what social environments?)

For months, the CDC has been asked to begin such preparations for continued surveillance. The CDC is stretched to its limits and is dreadfully underfunded for what it's being asked, in all areas, to do.

• *Let's talk about various forms of treatment.*

It is very difficult for a patient to find out which hospital to go to or which doctor to go to or which mode of treatment to attempt.

Hospitals and doctors are reluctant to reveal how well they're doing with each type of treatment. They may, if you press them, give you a general idea. Most will not show you their precise number of how many patients are doing well on what and how many have failed to respond adequately.

Because of the ludicrous requirements of the medical journals, doctors are prohibited from revealing publicly the specific data they are gathering from their treatments of our bodies. Doctors and hospitals need money for research, and this money (from the National Institutes of Health, from cancer research funding organizations, from rich patrons) comes based on the performance of their work (i.e., their tabulations of their results of their treatment of our bodies); this performance is written up as "papers" that must be submitted to and accepted by such "distinguished' medical publications as the *New England Journal of Medicine*. Most of these "distinguished" publications, however, will not publish anything that has been spoken of, leaked, announced, or intimated publicly in advance. Even after acceptance, the doctors must hold their tongues until the article is actually published. Dr. Bijan Safai of Sloan-Kettering has been waiting over six months for the *New England Journal*, which has accepted his interferon study, to publish it. Until that happens, he is only permitted to speak in the most general terms of how interferon is or is not working.

Priorities in this area appear to be peculiarly out of kilter at this moment of life or death.

• *Let's talk about hospitals.*

Everybody's full up, fellows. No room in the inn.

Part of this is simply overcrowding. Part of this is cruel. Sloan-Kettering still enforces a regulation from pre-AIDS days that only one dermatology patient per week can be admitted to that hospital. (Karposi's sarcoma fails under dermatology at Sloan-Kettering.) But Sloan-Kettering is also the second largest treatment center for AIDS patients in New York. You can be near death and still not get into Sloan-Kettering.

Additionally, Sloan-Kettering (and the Food and Drug Administration) require patients to receive their initial shots of interferon while they are hospitalized. A lot of men want to try interferon at Sloan-Kettering before they try chemotherapy elsewhere.

It's not hard to see why there is such a waiting list to get into Sloan-Kettering.

Most hospital staffs are still so badly educated about AIDS that they don't know much about it, except they've heard it's infectious. (There still have been no cases in hospital staff or among the very doctors who have been treating AIDS victims for two years.) Hence, as I said earlier, AIDS patients are being treated like lepers.

For various reasons, I would not like to be a patient at the Veterans Administration Hospital on East 24th Street or at New York Hospital. (Incidents involving AIDS patients at these two hospitals have been reported in news stories in the *Native*.)

I believe it falls to this city's Department of Health, under Commissioner David Spencer, and the Health and Hospitals Corporation, under Commission Stanley Brezenoff, to educate this city, its citizens, and its hospital workers about all areas of a public health emergency. Well, they have done an appalling job of educating our citizens, our hospital workers, and even, in some instances, our doctors. Almost everything this city knows about AIDS has come to it, in one or another, through Gay Men's Health Crisis, and that includes television programs, magazine articles, radio commercials, newsletters, health-recommendation brochures, open forums, and sending speakers everywhere including—when asked—into hospitals. If three out of four AIDS cases were occurring in straight men instead of gay men, you can bet all hospitals and staff would know what was happening. And it would be this city's Health and Hospitals Corporation who would be telling them.

- *Let's talk about what gay tax dollars are buying for gay men.*

Now we're arriving at the truly scandalous.

For over a year and a half, the National Institutes of Health has been "reviewing" which from among some $55 million worth of grant applications for AIDS research money it will eventually fund.

It's not even a question of NIH having to ask Congress for money. It's already there. Waiting. NIH has almost $8 million already appropriated that it has yet to release into usefulness.

There is no question that if this epidemic was happening to the straight, white, non-intravenous-drug-using middle-class, that money would have been put into use almost two years ago, when the first alarming signs of this epidemic were noticed by Dr. Alvin Friedman-Kien and Dr. Linda Laubenstein at New York University Hospital.

During the first *two weeks* of the Tylenol scare, the United States government spent $10 million to find out what was happening.[1]

Every hospital in New York that's involved in AIDS research has used up every bit of the money it could find for researching AIDS while waiting for NIH

---

[1] In 1982, seven people in the Chicago area died after consuming Tylenol capsules that had been injected with cyanide. It was the first case of product tampering in the United States and inspired many companies to adopt tamper-proof packaging. The case remains unsolved.

grants to come through. These hospitals have been working on AIDS for up to two years and are now desperate for replenishing funds. Important studies that began last year, such as Dr. Michael Lange's at St. Luke's-Roosevelt, are now going under for lack of money. Important leads that were and are developing cannot be pursued. (For instance, few hospitals can afford plasmapheresis machines, and few patients can afford this experimental treatment either, since few insurance policies will cover the $16,600 bill.) New York University Hospital, the largest treatment center for AIDS patients in the world, has had its grant application pending at NIH for a year and a half. Even if the application is successful, the earliest time that NYU could receive any money would be late summer.

The NIH would probably reply that it's foolish just to throw money away, that that hasn't worked before. And, NIH would say, if nobody knows what's happening, what's to study?

Any good administrator with half a brain could survey the entire AIDS mess and come up with twenty leads that merit further investigation. I could do so myself. In any research, in any investigation, you have to start somewhere. You can't just not start anywhere at all.

But then, AIDS is happening mostly to gay men, isn't it?

All of this is indeed ironic. For within AIDS, as most researchers have been trying to convey to the NIH, perhaps may reside the answer to the question of what it is that causes cancer itself. If straights had more brains, or were less bigoted against gays, they would see that, as with hepatitis B, gay men are again doing their suffering for them, revealing this disease to them. They can use us as guinea pigs to discover the cure for AIDS before it hits them, which most medical authorities are still convinced will be happening shortly in increasing numbers.

(As if it had not been malevolent enough, the NIH is now, for unspecified reasons, also turning away AIDS patients from its hospital in Bethesda, Maryland. The hospital, which had been treating anyone and everyone with AIDS free of charge, now will only take AIDS patients if they fit into their current investigating protocol. Whatever that is. The NIH publishes "papers," too.)

Gay men pay taxes just like everyone else. NIH money should be paying for our research just like everyone else's. We desperately need something from our government to save our lives, and we're not getting it.

• *Let's talk about health insurance and welfare problems.*

Many of the ways of treating AIDS are experimental, and many health insurance policies do not cover most of them. Blue Cross is particularly bad about accepting anything unusual.

Many serious victims of AIDS have been unable to work and unable to qualify for welfare because AIDS is not on the list of qualifying disability illnesses. (Immune deficiency is an acceptable determining factor for welfare among children, but not adults. Figure that one out.) There are also increasing number of men unable to pay their rent, men thrown out on the street with nowhere to live and no money to live with, and men who have been asked by roommates to leave because of their illnesses. And men with serious AIDS are being fired from certain jobs.

The horror stories in this area, of those suddenly found destitute, of those facing this illness with insufficient insurance, continue to mount. (One man who'd had no success on other therapies was forced to beg from his friends the $16,600 he needed to try, as a last resort, plasmapheresis.)

- *Finally, let's talk about our mayor, Ed Koch.*

Our mayor, Ed Koch, appears to have chosen, for whatever reason, not to allow himself to be perceived by the non-gay world as visibly helping us in this emergency.

Repeated requests to meet with him have been denied us. Repeated attempts to have him make a very necessary public announcement about this crisis and public health emergency have been refused by his staff.

On October 28th, 1982, Mayor Koch was implored to make a public announcement about our emergency. If he done so then, and if he was only to do so now, the following would be put into action:

1. The community at large would be alerted (you would be amazed at how many people, including gay men, still don't know enough about the AIDS danger).
2. Hospital staffs and public assistance offices would also be alerted and their education commenced.
3. The country, President Reagan, and the National Institutes of Health, as well Congress would be alerted, and these constitute the most important ears of all.

If the mayor doesn't think it's important enough to talk up AIDS, none of these people is going to, either.

The Mayor of New York has an enormous amount of power—when he wants to use it. When he wants to help his people. With the failure yet again of our civil rights bill, I'd guess our mayor doesn't want his power to help us.

With his silence on AIDS, the Mayor of New York is helping to kill us.

I am sick of our electing officials who in no way represent us. I am sick of our stupidity in believing in candidates who promise us everything for our support and promptly forget us and insult us after we have given them our votes. Koch is the prime example, but not the only one. [U.S. Senator] Daniel Patrick Moynihan isn't looking very good at this moment, either. Moynihan was requested by gay leaders to publicly ask Margaret Heckler, at her confirmation hearing for Secretary of Health and Human Services, if she could be fair to gays in view of her voting record of definite anti-gay bias. (Among other horrors, she voted to retain the sodomy law in Washington, D.C., at Jerry Falwell's request.) Moynihan refused to ask this question, as he has refused to meet with us about AIDS, despite our repeated requests. Margaret Heckler will have important jurisdiction over the CDC, over the NIH, over the Public Health Service, over the Food and Drug Administration—indeed, over all areas of AIDS concerns. Thank you, Daniel Patrick Moynihan. I am sick of our not realizing we have enough votes to defeat these people, and I am sick of our not electing our own openly gay officials in the first place. Moynihan doesn't even have an openly gay person on his staff, and he represents the city with the largest gay population in America.

I am sick of closeted gay doctors who won't come out to help us fight to rectify any of what I'm writing about. Doctors—the very letters "M.D."—have enormous clout, particularly when they fight in groups. Can you imagine what gay doctors could accomplish, banding together in a network, petitioning local and federal governments, straight colleagues, and the American Medical Association. I am sick of the passivity or nonparticipation or half-hearted protestation of all the gay medical associations. (American Physicians for Human Rights, Bay Area Physicians for Human Rights, Gay Psychiatrists of New York, etc., etc.), and particularly of our own New York Physicians for Human Rights, a group of 175 of our gay doctors who have, as a group, done *nothing*. You can count on one hand the number of our doctors who have really worked for us.

I am sick of the *Advocate*, one of this country's largest gay publications, which has yet to quite acknowledge that there's anything going on. The newspaper's recent AIDS issue was so innocuous you'd have thought all we were going through was little worse than a rage of the latest designer flu. And their own associate editor, Brent Harris, died from AIDS. Figure that one out.

With the exception of the *New York Native* and a few, very few, other gay publications, the gay press has been useless. If we can't get our own papers and magazines to tell us what's really happening to us, and this negligence is added to the negligent non-interest of the straight press. (*The New York Times* took a leisurely year and a half between its major pieces, and the *Village Voice* took a year and a half to write anything at all), how are we going to get the word around that we're dying? Gay men in smaller towns and cities everywhere must be educated, too. Has the *Times* or the *Advocate* told you that twenty-nine cases have been reported from Paris?

I am sick of gay men who won't support gay charities. Go give your bucks to straight charities, fellows, while we die. Gay Men's Health Crisis is going crazy trying to accomplish everything it does—printing and distributing hundreds of thousands of educational items, taking care of several hundred AIDS victims (some of them straight) in and out of hospitals, arranging community forums and speakers all over this country, getting media attention, fighting bad hospital care, on and on and on, fighting for you in two thousand ways, *and* trying to sell 17,600 circus tickets, too. Is the Red Cross doing this for you? Is the American Cancer Society? Your college alumni fund? The United Jewish Appeal? Catholic Charities? The United Way? The Lenox Hill Neighborhood Association, or any of the other fancy straight charities for which faggots put on black ties and dance at the Plaza? The National Gay Task Force—our only hope for national leadership, with its new and splendid leader, Virginia Apuzzo—which is spending more and more time fighting for the AIDS issue, is broke. Senior Action in a Gay Environment [SAGE] and Gay Men's Health Crisis are, within a few months, going to be without office space they can afford, and thus will be out on the street. The St. Mark's Clinic, held together by some of the few devoted gay doctors in this city who aren't interested in becoming rich, lives in constant terror of even higher rent and eviction. This community is desperate for the services these organizations are providing for it. And these organizations are desperate for money, which is certainly not coming from straight people or President Reagan or Mayor Koch. (If every gay man within a 250-mile radius of Manhattan isn't in Madison Square Garden on the night of April 30th to help Gay Men's Health Crisis make enough money to get through the next horrible year of fighting against AIDS, I shall lose all hope that we have any future whatsoever.)

I am sick of closeted gays. It's 1983 already, guys, when are you going to come out? By 1984 you could be dead. Every gay man who is unable to come forward now and fight to save his own life is truly helping to kill the rest of us. There is only one thing that's going to save some of us, and this is *numbers* and pressure and our being perceived as united and a threat. As more and more of my friends die, I have less and less sympathy for men who are afraid their mommies will find out or afraid their bosses will out or afraid their fellow doctors or professional associates will find out. Unless we can generate visibility, numbers, masses, we are going to die.

I am sick of everyone in this community who tells me to stop creating a panic. How many of us have to die before *you* get scared off your ass and into action? Aren't 195 dead New Yorkers enough? Every straight person who is knowledgeable about the AIDS epidemic can't understand why gay men aren't marching on the White House. Over and over again I hear from them, "Why aren't you guys doing anything?" Every politician I have spoken to has said to me confidentially, "You guys aren't making enough noise. Bureaucracy only responds to pressure."

I am sick of people who say "it's no worse than statistics for smokers and lung cancer" or "considering how many homosexuals there are in the United States, AIDS is really statistically affecting only a very few." That would wash if there weren't 164 cases in twenty-eight days. That would wash if the numbers hadn't jumped from 41 to 1,112 in eighteen months. That would wash if cases in one city—New York—hadn't jumped to cases in fifteen countries and thirty-five states (up from thirty-four last week). That would wash if cases weren't coming in at more than four a day nationally and over two a day locally. That would wash if the mortality rate didn't start at 38 percent the first year of diagnosis and climb to a grotesque 86 percent after three years. Get your stupid heads out of the sand, you turkeys!

I am sick of guys who moan that giving up careless sex until this blows over is worse than death. How can they value life so little and cocks and asses so much? Come with me, guys, while I visit a few of our friends in Intensive Care at NYU. Notice the looks in their eyes, guys. They'd give up sex forever if you could promise them life.

I am sick of guys who think that all being gay means is sex in the first place. I am sick of guys who can only think with their cocks.

I am sick of "men" who say, "We've got to keep quiet or *they* will do such and such." *They* usually mean the straight majority, the "Moral" Majority, or similarly perceived representations of *them*. Okay, you "men"—be my guests. You can march off now to the gas chambers; just get right in line.

We shall always have enemies. Nothing we can ever do will remove them. Southern newspapers and Jerry Falwell's publications are already printing editorials proclaiming AIDS as God's deserved punishments on homosexuals. So what? Nasty words make poor little sissy pansy wilt and die?

And I am very sick and saddened by every gay man who does not get behind this issue totally and with commitment—to fight for his life.

I don't want to die. I can only assume you don't want to die. Can we fight together?

For the past few weeks, about fifty community leaders and organization representatives have been meeting at Beth Simchat Torah, the gay synagogue, to prepare action. We call ourselves the AIDS Network. We come from all areas of health concern: doctors, social workers, psychologists, psychiatrists, nurses; we come from Gay Men's Health Crisis, from the National Gay Health Education Foundation, from New York Physicians for Human Rights, the St. Mark's Clinic, the Gay Men's Health Project; we come from the gay synagogue, the Gay Men's Chorus, from the Greater Gotham Business Council, SAGE, Lambda Legal Defense, Gay Fathers, the Christopher Street Festival Community, Dignity, Integrity; we are lawyers, actors, dancers, architects, writers, citizens; we come from many component organizations of the Gay and Lesbian Community Council.

We have a leader. Indeed, for the first time our community appears to have a true leader. Her name is Virginia Apuzzo, she is head of the National Gay Task Force, and, as I have said, so far she has proved to be magnificent.

The AIDS Network has sent a letter to Mayor Koch. It contains twelve points that are urged for his consideration and action.

The letter to Mayor Koch also contains the following paragraph:

> *It must be stated at the outset that the gay community is growing increasing aroused and concerned and angry. Should our avenues to the mayor of our city and the members of the Board of Estimate not be available, it is our feeling that the level of frustration is such that it will manifest itself in a manner heretofore not associated with this community and the gay population at large. It should be stated, too, at the outset, that as of February 25th, there were 526 cases of serious AIDS in New York's metropolitan area and 195 deaths (and 1,112 cases nationally and 418 deaths) and it is the sad and sorry fact that most gay men in our city now have close friends and lovers who have either been stricken with or died from this disease. It is against this background that this letter is addressed. It is this issue that has, ironically, united our community in a way not heretofore thought possible.*

Further, a number of AIDS Network members have been studying civil disobedience with one of the experts from Dr. Martin Luther King's old team. We are learning how. Gay men are the strongest, toughest people I know. We are perhaps shortly to get an opportunity to show it.

I'm sick of hearing that Mayor Koch doesn't respond to pressures and threats from the disenfranchised, that he walks away from confrontation. Maybe he does. But we have *tried* to make contact with him, we are *dying*, so what other choice but confrontation has he left us?

I hope we don't have to conduct sit-ins or tie up traffic or get arrested. I hope our city and our country will start to do something to help start saving us. But it is time for us to be perceived for what we truly are: an angry community and a strong community, and therefore *a threat*. Such as the realities of politics. Nationally, we are 24 million strong, which more than there are Jews or blacks or Hispanics in this country.

I want to make a point about what happens if we *don't* get angry about AIDS. There are the obvious losses, of course: Little of what I've written about here is likely to be rectified with the speed necessary to help the growing number of victims. But something worse will happen, and is already happening. Increasingly, we are being *blamed* for AIDS, for this epidemic; we are being called its perpetrators, through our blood, through our "promiscuity," through just being the gay men so much of the rest of the world has learned to hate. We can point out until we are blue in the face that we are not the cause of AIDS but its victims; that AIDS has landed among us first, as it could have landed among them first. But other frightened populations are going to drown out these truths, by playing on the worst bigoted fears of the straight world, and send the status of gays right back to the Dark Ages. Not all Jews are blamed for Meyer Lansky, Rabbis Bergman and Kehane, or for money-lending. All Chinese aren't blamed for the recent Seattle slaughters. But all gays are blamed for John Gacy, the North American Man/Boy Love Association, and AIDS.

Enough. I am told this is one of the longest articles the *Native* has ever run. I hope I have not been guilty of saying ineffectively in five thousand words what I could have said in five: we must fight to live.

I am angry and frustrated almost beyond the bound of my skin and bones and body and brain can encompass. My sleep is tormented by nightmares and visions of lost friends, and my days are flooded by the tears of funerals and memorial services and seeing my sick friends. How many of us must die before *all* of us living fight back?

I know that unless I fight with every ounce of my energy I will hate myself. I hope, I pray, I implore you to feel the same.

I am going to close by doing what Dr. Ron Grossman did at GMHC's second Open Forum last November at Julia Richman High School. He listed the names of the patients he had lost to AIDS. Here is a list of twenty dead men I knew:

Nick Rock, Rick Wellikoff, Jack Nau, Shelly, Donald Krintzman, Jerry Green, Michael Maletta, Paul Graham, Toby, Harry Blumenthal, Stephen Sperry, Brian O'Hara, Barry, David, Jeffrey Croland, Z., David Jackson, Tony Rappa, Robert Christian, Ron Doud. And one more, who will be dead by the time these words appear in print. If we don't act immediately, then we face our approaching doom.

New York Native (March 1983), reprinted in Larry Kramer, *Reports from the holocaust: the making of an AIDS activist* (New York: St. Martin's Press, 1989), pp. 33-51. Reprinted by permission of the author.

26.2

THE IRAN-CONTRA AFFAIR (1987)

Two years after winning reelection, Ronald Reagan became embroiled in a scandal that threatened to destroy his presidency. The Iran-Contra Affair began in late 1985, when Robert McFarlane, the head of the National Security Council (NSC), approved a secret plan to sell anti-tank and anti-aircraft missiles to Iran in exchange for Iran's assistance in arranging the release of Americans being held by Islamic terrorists in Lebanon. The sale contradicted the administration's publicly stated policies of refusing to negotiate with terrorists or to aid Iran, a sponsor of terrorism, in its war against Iraq. The trade also violated an arms embargo placed on Iran following its seizure of America hostages in 1979. In November 1986, a Beirut newspaper exposed the arms-for-hostages deal. Shortly thereafter, Attorney General Edwin Meese announced that some of the $48 million from the missile sale had been diverted to the anti-communist Contras in Nicaragua—an act that directly violated the Boland Amendment, a federal law barring U.S. military aid to any group working to overthrow the government of Nicaragua. Lieutenant Colonel Oliver North, an aide at the NSC, arranged the money transfer with the approval of his boss, Rear Admiral John Poindexter, McFarlane's successor.

The Iran-Contra Affair outraged many Americans. Reagan fired North and Poindexter and appointed former senator John Tower to lead a special committee to investigate the matter. Reagan also named Lawrence Walsh as an independent counsel. In the summer of 1987, North's televised testimony to a joint congressional committee made him a hero to conservatives nationwide. Although he admitted orchestrating the diversion of funds to the Contras as well as shredding government documents, North denied that Reagan had knowledge of his actions. Poindexter acknowledged authorizing the funds transfer without the president's approval. Portions of the congressional committee's report follow.

The Iran-Contra Affair led to several criminal convictions. In 1988, McFarlane pled guilty to obstructing Congress and later received a $20,000 fine and two years of probation. As a result of Walsh's findings, North and Poindexter were indicted on several charges including conspiracy to defraud the U.S. government. In 1989, North was found guilty and given a $150,000 fine and *a three-year suspended sentence. The following year, Poindexter was convicted and sentenced to six months in prison. Both men, however, won appeals on the basis that their convictions stemmed from statements given under limited immunity protection. While Reagan took responsibility for the Iran-Contra affair, no evidence of his or Vice-President George H.W. Bush's involvement in the matter has ever surfaced. Despite the damaging scandal, Reagan left office with high approval ratings.*

Focus Questions

1. How does the report describe the Iran-Contra affair?
2. Whom does the committee hold most responsible for Iran-Contra? How does the committee characterize President Reagan's role in the matter?
3. Compare the Iran-Contra Affair to Watergate (Document 25.4). Which incident do you think was more serious? Why?

F INDINGS AND CONCLUSIONS

The common ingredients of the Iran and Contra policies were secrecy, deception and distain for the law. A small group of senior officials believed that they alone knew what was right. They viewed knowledge of their actions by others in the Government as a threat to their objectives. They told neither the Secretary of State, the Congress nor the American people of their actions. When disclosure was threatened, they destroyed official documents and lied to Cabinet officials, to the public, and to elected representatives in Congress. They testified that they even withheld key facts from the President....

POLICY CONTRADICTIONS AND FAILURES

The Administration's departure from democratic processes created the conditions for policy failure, and led to contradictions which undermined the credibility of the United States.

The United States simultaneously pursued two contradictory foreign policies—a public one and a secret one:

—The public policy was not to make any concessions for the release of hostages lest such concessions encourage more hostage-taking. At the same time, the United States was secretly trading weapons to get the hostages back.

—The public policy was to ban arms shipments to Iran and to exhort other Governments to observe this embargo. At the same time, the United States was secretly selling sophisticated missiles to Iran and promising more.

—The public policy was to improve relations with Iraq. At the same time, the United States secretly shared military intelligence on Iraq with Iran and North told the Iranians in contradiction to United States policy that the United States would help promote the overthrow of the Iraqi government....

—The public policy was to observe the 'letter and spirit' of the Boland Amendment's prescriptions against military or paramilitary assistance to the

Contras. At the same time, the NSC staff was secretly assuming direction and funding of the Contras' military effort....

—The public policy, embodied in Executive Order 12333, was to conduct covert operations solely through the CIA or other organs of the intelligence community specifically authorized by the President. At the same time, although the NSC was not authorized, the NSC staff secretly became operational and used private, non-accountable agents to engage in covert activities.

These contradictions in policy inevitably resulted in policy failure:

—The United States armed Iran, including its most radical elements, but attained neither a new relationship with that hostile regime nor a reduction in the number of American hostages.

—The arms sales did not lead to a moderation of Iranian policies. Moderates did not come forward, and Iran to this day sponsors actions directed against the United States in the Persian Gulf and elsewhere.

—The United States opened itself to blackmail by adversaries who might reveal the secret arms sales and who, according to North, threatened to kill the hostages if the sales stopped.

—The United States undermined its credibility with friends and allies, including moderate Arab states, by its public stance of opposing arms sales to Iran while undertaking such arms sales in secret....

—The United States sought to illicit funding for the Contras through profits from the secret arms sales, but a substantial portion of those profits ended up in the personal bank accounts of the private individuals executing the sales—while the exorbitant amounts charged for the weapons inflamed the Iranians with whom the United States was seeking a new relationship....

DISHONESTY AND SECRECY

The Iran-Contra Affair was characterized by pervasive dishonesty and inordinate secrecy.

North admitted that he and other officials lied repeatedly to Congress and the American people about the Contra covert action and Iran arms sales, and that he altered and destroyed official documents. North's testimony demonstrates that he also lied to members of the Executive branch, including the Attorney General, and officials of the State Department, CIA and NSC.

Secrecy became an obsession. Congress was never informed of the Iran or Contra covert actions, not withstanding the requirement in the law that Congress be notified of all covert actions in a "timely fashion."...

It was not operational security that motivated such conduct—not when our own Government was the victim. Rather, the NSC staff feared, correctly, that any disclosure to Congress or the Cabinet of the arms-for-hostages and arms-for-profit activities would produce a storm of outrage....

LACK OF ACCOUNTABILITY

The confusion, deception, and privatization which marked the Iran-Contra Affair were the inevitable products of an attempt to avoid accountability. Congress, the Cabinet, and the Joint Chiefs of Staffs were denied information and excluded from the decision-making process. Democratic procedures were disregarded....

Officials who make public policy must be accountable to the public. But the public cannot hold officials accountable for policies of which the public is unaware.... Policies that are secret become the private preserve of the few, mistakes are inevitably perpetuated, and the public loses control over the Government. That is what happened in the Iran-Contra Affair:

—The President's NSC staff carried out a covert action in furtherance of his policy to sustain the Contras, but the President said he did not know about it.

—The President's NSC staff secretly diverted millions of dollars in profits from the Iran arms sales to the Contras, but the President said he did not know about it and Poindexter claimed he did not tell him.

—The Chairman of the Joint Chief of Staff was not informed of the Iran arms sales, nor was he ever consulted regarding the impact of such sales on the Iran-Iraq war or on U.S. military readiness.

—The Secretary of State was not informed of the millions of dollars in Contra contributions solicited by the NSC staff from foreign governments with which the State Departments deals each day.

—The Congress was told almost nothing—and what it was told was false....

DISDAIN FOR LAW

In the Iran-Contra Affair, officials viewed the law not as setting boundaries for their actions, but raising impediments to their goals. When the goals and the law collided the law gave way:

—The covert program of support for the Contras evaded the Constitution's most significant check on Executive power: the President can spend funds on a program only if he can convince Congress to appropriate the money.

—When Congress enacted the Boland Amendment, cutting off funds for the war in Nicaragua, Administration officials raised funds for the Contras from other sources—foreign Governments, the Iran arms sales, and private individuals; and the NSC staff controlled the expenditures of these funds....

—In addition, the covert program of support for the Contras was an evasion of the letter and spirit of the Boland Amendment. The President made it clear that while he opposed restrictions on military or paramilitary assistance to the Contras, he recognized that compliance with the law was not optional. "(W)hat I might personally wish or what our Government might wish still would not justify us violating the law of the land," he said in 1983....

The Committees make no determination as to whether any particular individual involved in the Iran-Contra Affair acted with criminal intent or was guilty of any crime. That is a matter for the Independent Counsel and the Courts. But the Committees reject any notion that worthy ends justify violations of law by Government officials; and the Committees condemn without reservation the making of false statements to Congress and the withholding, shredding, and alteration of documents relevant to a pending inquiry.

Administration officials have, if anything, an even greater responsibility than private citizens to comply with the law. There is no place in Government for law breakers....

WHO WAS RESPONSIBLE

Who was responsible for the Iran-Contra Affair? Part of our mandate was to answer that question, not in a legal sense (which is the responsibility of the Independent Counsel), but in order to reaffirm that those who serve the Government are accountable for their actions. Based on our investigation, we reach the following conclusions.

At the operational level, the central figure in the Iran-Contra Affair was Lt. Col. North, who coordinated all of the activities and was involved in all aspects of the secret operations. North, however did not act alone.

North's conduct had the express approval of Admiral John Poindexter, first as Deputy National Security Adviser, and then as National Security Adviser. North also had at least the tacit support of Robert McFarlane, who served as National Security Adviser until December 1985.

In addition, for reasons cited earlier, we believe that the late Director of Central Intelligence, William Casey, encouraged North, gave him direction, and promoted the concept of an extra-legal covert organization. Casey, for the most part, insulated the CIA career employees from knowledge of what he and the NSC staff were doing....

There is no evidence that the Vice President [George H.W. Bush] was aware of the diversion. The Vice President attended several meetings on the Iran initiative, but none of the participants could recall his views....

The central remaining question is the role of the President in the Iran-Contra Affair. On this critical point, the shredding of documents by Poindexter, North, and others, and the death of Casey, leave the record complete.

As it stands, the President has publicly stated that he did not know of the diversion. North said that he never told President, but assumed that the President knew. Poindexter told North on November 21, 1986 that he had not informed the President of the diversion....

Nevertheless, the ultimate responsibility for the events in the Iran-Contra Affair must rest with the President. It the President did not know what his National Security Advisers were doing, he should have. It is his responsibility to communicate unambiguously to his subordinates that they must keep him advised of important actions they take for the Administration....

Members of the NSC staff appeared to believe that their actions were consistent with the President's desires. It was the President's policy—not an isolated decision by North or Poindexter—to sell arms secretly to Iran and to maintain the Contras 'body and soul', the Boland Amendment notwithstanding. To the NSC staff, implementation of these policies became the overriding concern.

Several of the President's advisers pursued a covert action to support the Contras in disregard of the Boland Amendment and of several statutes and Executive orders requiring Congressional notification. Several of the same advisers lied, shredded documents, and covered up their actions.... The actions of those individuals do not comport with the notion of a country guided by the rule of law....

Thus, the question whether the President knew of the diversion is not conclusive on the issue of his responsibility. The President created or at least tolerated an environment where those who did not know of the diversion believed with certainty that they were carrying out the President's policies....

U.S. Congress, *Report of the Congressional Committees Investigating the Iran-Contra Affair*, 100th Cong., 1st sess. (Washington, D.C.: Government Printing Office, 1987), pp. 11-22.

26.3

ROSA AND JOSÉ URBINA ON LIVING AS UNDOCUMENTED ALIENS (1988)

Since 1970, the United States has experienced one of the biggest waves of immigration in its history. Approximately 45 percent of these immigrants come from countries in the Western Hemisphere. This figures does not include millions of people who enter the United States illegally. In 1986, Congress passed the Immigration Reform Control Act, a law that prohibits hiring undocumented workers and strengthened border patrols between the United States and Mexico. The legislation also granted amnesty to all undocumented aliens who entered the United States prior to 1982. Nonetheless, many immigrants still enter the U.S. illegally in pursuit of economic opportunities or to join relatives. In this 1988 interview, Rosa María and José Luis Urbina explain why they fled Mexico and entered the United States illegally.

FOCUS QUESTIONS

1. How do Rosa and José describe their life in El Paso? Why did they come to the United States? What is their attitude toward America?
2. What obstacles did they encounter along the U.S.-Mexican border?
3. What types of jobs do Rosa and José have? Do you think they are competing with native-born Americans for these positions? Why or why not?
4. In recent years, there have been heated political debates in several states over whether undocumented aliens should continue to have access to public education and emergency health care. Since 1996, federal law has prohibited legal as well as illegal immigrants from receiving welfare benefits. What is your opinion on these issues? How should the challenge of illegal immigration be resolved?

J OSÉ: My hometown is Juárez [Mexican town across the border from El Paso, Texas]. Since I was nine years old, I've been coming to El Paso to work. At first I did gardening in people's yards, but I have stayed in El Paso constantly since 1981, going out to the fields to do farm work. I used to go to Juárez to visit my relatives at least one day each month. But in the last year, I haven't gone, because of the new immigration law. To visit Juárez I have to swim across the river. I can't cross the bridge or the *migra* [Border Patrol officers] can catch me right there.

During the past few months, the river has been very high and fast. That's one reason why not so many people have been crossing lately. I am not working now, because it isn't the growing or harvesting season on the big farms. On February 15, we usually begin to plant onions. That is when the main agricultural season begins. But during a three-month period between planting and harvesting, there is no work.

We haven't paid our rent since December. If we're lucky, I can find some part-time work to pay for food. Our baby, José Luis, is two months old. Because he was born in El Paso, he is an American citizen. We can only get food assistance for him. Once in a while, I find a job as a construction laborer, house painter, whatever is available. We use the money to buy food for the baby and the other three children first.

ROSA: I haven't been able to work lately, because the baby is so small. My other children are all in school. Lorenzo is twelve years old. José Rubén is ten, and Miriam is seven. From the time I came to El Paso, I have worked as a housekeeper and minding homes for people. I am not used to staying in the apartment every day, but I have no other choice, because of my small baby.

I have known many changes in my life. I moved to Juárez from a farm in Zacatecas when I was seven years old. My mother and father were split up. After mother remarried, my stepfather took us to Juárez. We lived in an adobe house in the *colonias* [ramshackle housing projects] up in the hills.

When I was a teenager, I worked as a hairdresser in a beauty salon, cutting hair. My first husband was a mechanic, fixing cars. We made a good living. But my husband spent the money he made drinking in the *cantinas*. And after a while, he wouldn't let me work, because I had young children to take care of. When he died in 1984, he left me nothing at all. He drank too much and died from cirrhosis of his liver. I had no money...nothing. My children were nine, seven, and three years old. I had to find a way to pay rent and feed them.

At that time, the economy in Mexico had become horrible. Inflation was going crazy. The peso jumped to 500 per dollar. Today it is still climbing at 1,000 per dollar. I found a job working on an assembly line at a factory. We produced rubber gloves for hospitals and medical supplies like little caps for syringes. I would go into work at 4:30 in the afternoon and stay until 2:00 A.M. I was paid only 7,000 pesos [$14] each week. That was not enough to feed my kids. And I didn't have any relatives or friends to watch the kids while I worked. So I had no other choice but to put them in a special institution, like an orphanage, for children without parents. This upset me very much. But with my husband dead, and no other form of support, there was nothing I could do.

My only hope was to cross the river to the United States. If I could find a job that paid enough money, my children could join me. I wanted them to have an education and a proper life...to be some one.

After I made up my mind to cross the river, I met José Luis. It was like fate—we just found each other. You could say it was love at first sight. [Laughs]. I had two young boys who needed a good man to learn from. When he asked me to live with him, I said yes.

JOSÉ: Before I met Rosa, I lived with my grandmother in Juárez. I would go back and forth across the river to work in El Paso or on the farms in New Mexico. After Rosa and I fell in love, we decided to rent this apartment in El Paso and live together.

ROSA: Before I met José Luis, I crossed back and forth across the river five days each week to my housekeeping jobs in El Paso. On weekends, I took my children out of the orphanage. Then I had to reluctantly return them to the orphanage on Sunday evenings and prepare to go back across the river.

For a while I traveled alone, which can be dangerous. But after I met José, we crossed together. There are men who carry people across the river on their shoulders. The water is kind of rough, but that's what these men do to make a living. They charge passengers 1,500 to 2,000 pesos [$1.50 to $2.50]. The water is up to their chests, but they manage to hold us up on their shoulders so we can get to work dry.

JOSÉ: Crossing the river can be very dangerous, especially if you cross alone. There are fast water currents, and sometimes the water is quite high. If you don't know how to swim, the undercurrents can pull you right down. And in places the bottom of the river is like quicksand that can trap you. The water turns into kind of a funnel that can drag you down. Some friends of mine have died.

ROSA: I don't know how to swim. I relied on José Luis, who is good swimmer. We were both very lucky. I can clearly remember an incident where we almost drowned. It began on a Sunday evening which is a customary time for crossing. At the time, a man was running loose who was raping and killing women who crossed alone. So there were a lot of American border patrolmen and Mexican police along both banks.

After the sun went down and it became quite dark, José and I waited for a while near the riverbank, but it seemed hopeless to try to cross the river undetected. We waited until the next morning to try again.

When the sun came up, we saw that the men who carried people across on their shoulders weren't working, because of all the police. When we noticed that the border patrolmen had left the area, we decided to try to cross by ourselves. That was a big mistake. The current was very fast that day. In the middle of the river, we lost our balance and began to be dragged downstream. I felt helpless and began to panic. Fortunately, another man who was a strong swimmer came to our rescue. He pulled us to the shore.

After José and I began living together in El Paso, I decided to bring my children across the river. The water was too high and swift to risk men carrying them on their shoulders. So I had the children taxied across on a rubber raft.

JOSÉ: Another danger for people who cross the river is crime. Packs of men hang around the riverbank like wolves. They try to steal people's knapsacks or purses. Sometimes they demand that you give your wallet or wristwatch. If you don't obey them, they will knife you.

Were we ever caught by the *migra* when we crossed the river together? Oh, yes. [Laughs] Lots of times. But the patrolmen are really okay people. They arrest you, ask the usual questions. If you get rough, they will get rough, too. Otherwise they are fine. It all depends on the person who arrests you. If he has a mean personality, he will treat you rudely, whether you are impolite or not. But most of the time, it is a routine procedure.

When the *migra* catch us, they just put us in their truck and take us to their station. They ask our name, address, where we were born. They keep us in a cell maybe three or four hours. Then they put us in a bus and drive us kick to Juárez. They drop the women off very near the main bridge. The men are taken a little further away from town.

Our favorite place to cross the river is close to the Black Bridge, which is not far from downtown El Paso. Many of us would stand on the Juárez riverbank and wait for the change of Border Patrol shifts. Each morning, the shift changes between seven-thirty and eight-thirty, sometimes nine-thirty. We learn by observing over long periods of time. And all of our friends have been held in the immigration station. We observed certain patrolmen coming in to work and others checking out after their shifts.

Experienced river crossers pass this information to new people who are just learning the daily routines. Over a period of time, we learn the shift changes by recognizing different officers' faces. Some Mexican people even know the *migra* by name.

ROSA: Suppose I am caught by the patrolmen at seven-thirty in the morning. They will take me to the station and hold me for a few hours, then bus me back to Juárez. I would walk back to a crossing point and try once again. It is like a game. I think the most times I was ever caught by the *migra* was six times in one day. No matter how many times they catch me, I keep coming back.

The majority of the people in the *colonia* where I lived in Juárez worked in El Paso, mostly as housekeepers, construction workers, or helpers in the fields. In the United States there is a lot of work, but in Mexico we have nothing.

JOSÉ: The men, like myself, who work in the fields come across the river at around 2:30 A.M. to meet the buses that take us to the fields from El Paso. The transportation is owned by the *padrone* of the farms, or by the labor-crew chiefs who hire and pay the workers. In the evenings, we ride the buses back to the river. Sometimes I work twelve hours in a day and earn $20. I've learned to check around to see which farms pay the best. Some pay up to $35 a day.

Farm-labor jobs are not very steady. We just grab whatever is open at the moment. I accept anything, any time, as long as it is work. But suppose I take a job that only pays me $12 a day. It would only be enough to cover my transportation and meals in the field. I must find jobs that pay enough to feed my family.

In order to make $25, I must pick seventy-two buckets of chili peppers. That could take me four or five hours, it depends on how fast my hands are. The total amount of buckets we pick depends upon the amount contracted by the big companies in California. For a big contract, we work as long as necessary to complete the order. But the most I can earn in one day is $35.

During the summer, it gets very hot in the fields, up to 110 degrees. We work for eight hours with a half-hour break for lunch. To save money, I bring my lunch from home. The companies usually provide us with a thermo bottle of cold water. The farthest we travel from El Paso is to Lordsburg, New Mexico. That is around three and a half hours by bus. We leave El Paso at 3:00 A.M. For Las Cruces we leave at 5:00 or 5:30 A.M.

ROSA: To my housekeeping jobs I can take a regular El Paso city bus at 7:00 A.M. or 8:00 A.M. I usually come home around 3:30 or 4:00 P.M. each day. For a long while, I worked at one house—a Mexican-American family. They started me at $20 a day. Eventually they increased my wages to $25. They live near a large shopping center in the eastern part of town. The job was a little bit easier than working in the factory in Juárez, and paid much better.

In the factory, a whistle blows to let us know when to start, when to stop, when to eat dinner, and when to resume work. Doing housecleaning, I can rest a little when I need to take a short break.

To compare our apartment in El Paso with where I lived in Juárez , I prefer it a little better over there, because in the *colonia* I had a place to hang my clothes after I washed them. The bathroom was outside the house. But we don't have a bathroom in our apartment here, either. All of the apartments in this part of the building share a toilet on the back stairwell. But in this apartment, we have electric appliances, which makes life better than my previous home.

JOSÉ: The landlord who owns this building is very generous. He lets us owe him rent for the months that I am not working. He understands how tough our life is. We pay whatever we can, even if it's only $50. And he knows that, if the day comes where we are raided by immigration officers, we will run.

The rent for this apartment is $125 a month plus electricity. We all live and sleep in this one room. The two boys sleep on the couch. Our daughter, Miriam, sleeps with us on the bed. And the baby sleeps in a crib next to our bed. Fortunately, we have a kitchen, and a closet in this room. Living conditions in Juárez were better, but there was no work at all.

If it is possible, Rosa and I would like to become American citizens. I would have my documents, and the government wouldn't be after us. All we want is to be able to work in peace.

Our dream is to be able to give the children the best of everything. We know that, for them to have a better future and purpose in life, they need a good education. Of the three children in school now, Miriam is the fastest learner. She received an award for being an honor student, the best in her classroom.

We hope the children can finish high school and have the career of their choice. We are going to sacrifice for them, so that they can have the profession that they desire.

I was only allowed to finish grammar school. I am the oldest in my family, of five sisters and two boys. I had to stop going to school when I was twelve, to work with my father to support the family. I would have liked to finish school, but my parents needed me to work. They chose my sisters to study. So I gave up my studies to support my sisters.

At first, I liked working better than going to school. But after a while, I wanted to attend junior high school. But my mother told me that the family couldn't afford to let me go, and she said my sisters seemed to like the books better than I did. So I continued working. My father had a fruit-and-vegetable business. We sold from a pushcart in downtown Juárez, and I came across the river to do some gardening.

Even though I've come to work in Texas and New Mexico for many years, I've never learned to speak much English. I would like to learn, but I've never had the chance to study. I have a lot of responsibility now to provide for the children. It is more important that they have school, so I must work.

The dreams that Rosa Maria and I had of living in the U.S. and reality are not the same. We hoped to find a job and live comfortably. Now that we are here, our main purpose is to survive.

I worry about our status under the new immigration law. In the previous place where I lived, I paid the rent all the time, but the landlord threw away all of the receipts. So we have no proof that we have been living here enough years to qualify for amnesty.

On the farms where I worked, my employers or crew bosses didn't keep any pay records, because I only worked temporarily at each place. And, besides, I was illegal. So what was the use? If the police showed up, we would be in trouble whether or not the employer had a record. And the employers wanted to protect themselves. They didn't pay us with checks, it was always cash.

Fortunately, the last farmer I worked for took taxes and Social Security out of our wages. He is sending me a W-2 form as proof. I am waiting for it now. But things are getting worse, because the immigration police are putting pressure on people who hire undocumented workers. If the police catch illegals on a job site, the boss can be arrested under the new law. So most places have stopped hiring illegals. For example, my last job in El Paso, I was fired because the *migra* would raid the construction site every day. We would have to stop working and run.

When the planting season begins on the farms, I hope the immigration police don't show up. They raid a farm with a truck and four or five police cars. They position themselves outside the entrance to the farm and wait for us to walk by. They ask us for identification. If we cannot show proof that we are legal, we've had it. They'll take us away.

On the farms where I work, some people are legal and others aren't. If you drive your own car, the police usually won't question. But if you come to work in the employer's bus, they'll take you away.

ROSA: In town, we don't feel comfortable walking on the street. If the immigration officers see us, they will grab us. We are not afraid for ourselves, because we are accustomed to it. But I worry about the children. They have just begun studying in school here in El Paso. They like it very much. My sons are in the sixth and fifth grades, and Miriam is in second grade. They are learning English very quickly. My oldest boy, Lorenzo, likes social studies and mathematics, he would like to be a doctor. My other son likes the army a lot. He could probably be a good soldier.

JOSÉ: If we become citizens and the United States government asks them to spend time in the army, we would be honored if they are chosen to serve. We would be very proud of our children for doing their duty for their country.

"Mojados (Wetbacks)" from *New Americans: An Oral History* by Al Santoli, copyright © 1988 by Al Santoli. Used by permission of Viking Penguin, a division of Penguin Group (USA) Inc.

26.4

GEORGE H.W. BUSH CALLS FOR "A NEW WORLD OF FREEDOM" (1989)

Upon becoming Soviet premier in 1985, Mikhail Gorbachev rapidly transformed the USSR. His glasnost (openness) policy abolished many of the totalitarian elements of Soviet society. With perestroika (reform), he introduced elements of capitalism, such as private ownership and competition, in an attempt to revive the decrepit Soviet economy. His nation's serious economic problems prompted Gorbachev to curtail Soviet involvement in Eastern Europe. When several East Bloc nations began exerting independence, he did not intervene. By 1990, every communist regime in Eastern Europe had been transformed into more democratic forms of government.

In May 1989, these remarkable events inspired students in Beijing to hold massive pro-democracy rallies. But, in early June, the Chinese government crushed the protests, killing a still-undisclosed number of people in Tiananmen

Square. China retained its communist political system while westernizing its economy, but it was an exception to a worldwide movement toward democratization in the early 1990s.

On November 9, 1989, millions of people rejoiced when the East German government opened the country's borders. Thousands of East and West Germans gathered at the Berlin Wall, a global symbol of Cold War divisions. Erected in August 1961 to stop East Germans from fleeing to the West (2.5 million had done so between 1949 and 1961), the Wall evolved from barbed wire to concrete walls guarded by armed soldiers and landmines. Although about 5,000 East Germans managed to escape in subsequent years, 5,000 others were captured and 191 were killed. In 1990, East and West Germany reunited. Most of the Wall has been destroyed. In late 1991, after Gorbachev's reforms weakened the Communist Party, the Soviet Union broke into fifteen newly independent nations.

In this Thanksgiving message to the American people, President George H.W. Bush assesses the implications of the Cold War's end.

————————■————————

Focus Questions

1. According to Bush, what has changed in global politics? What role does he envision for the United States in the post-Cold War era?
2. Why did the Cold War end? Did the United States win? Explain your answers.
3. Is the world safer in the post-Cold War era? Why or why not?

November 22, 1989

Good evening. Like many of you, I'm spending tomorrow with family. And we'll say grace and carve the turkey and thank God for our many blessings and for our great country....

And this will be a very special Thanksgiving. It marks an extraordinary year. But before our families sit down tomorrow, we will give thanks for yet another reason: Around the world tonight, new pilgrims are on a voyage to freedom, and for many, it's not a trip to some place faraway but to a world of their own making.

On other Thanksgivings, the world was haunted by the images of watchtowers, guard dogs, and machineguns. In fact, many of you had not even been born when the Berlin Wall was erected in 1961. But now the world has a new image, reflecting a new reality: that of Germans, East and West, pulling each other to the top of the wall, a human bridge between nations; entire peoples all across Eastern Europe bravely taking to the streets, demanding liberty, pursuing democracy. This is not the end of the book of history, but it's a joyful end to one of history's saddest chapters.

Not long after the wall began to open, West German Chancellor [Helmut] phoned, and he asked me to give you, the American people, a message of thanks. He said that the remarkable change in Eastern Europe would not be taking place without the steadfast support of the United States—fitting praise from a good friend. For 40 years, we have not wavered in our commitment to freedom. We are grateful to our American men and women in uniform, and we should also be grateful to our postwar leaders. You see, we helped rebuild a continent through the Marshall plan; and we built a shield, NATO, behind which Americans, Europeans could forge a future in freedom.

For so many of these 40 years, the test of Western resolve, the contest between the free and the unfree, has been symbolized by an island of hope behind the Iron Curtain: Berlin. In the 1940's, West Berlin remained free because Harry Truman said: Hands off! In the 1950's, Ike backed America's words with muscle. In the 1960's, West Berliners took heart when John F. Kennedy said: "I am a Berliner." In the 1970's, Presidents Nixon, Ford, and Carter stood with Berlin by standing with NATO. And in the 1980's, Ronald Reagan went to Berlin to say: "Tear down this wall!" And now we are at the threshold of the 1990's. And as we begin the new decade, I am reaching out to President Gorbachev, asking him to work with me to bring down the last barriers to a new world of freedom. Let us move beyond containment and once and for all end the cold war.

We can make such a bold bid because America is strong and 40 years of perseverance and patience are finally paying off. More recently, quiet diplomacy, working behind the scenes, has achieved results. We can now dare to imagine a new world, with a new Europe, rising on the foundations of democracy. This new world was taking shape when my Presidency began with these words: "The day of the dictator is over." And during the spring and summer we told the people of the world what America believes and what America wants for the future. America believes that "liberty is an idea whose time has come in Eastern Europe." America wants President Gorbachev's reforms, known as perestroika, to succeed. And America wants the Soviets to join us in moving beyond containment to a new partnership. Some wondered if all this was realistic. And now, though we are still on the course set last spring, events are moving faster than anyone imagined or predicted.

Look around the world. In the developing nations, the people are demanding freedom. Poland and Hungary are now fledgling democracies—a non-Communist government in Poland and free elections coming soon in Hungary. And in the Soviet Union itself, the forces of reform under Mikhail Gorbachev are bringing unprecedented openness and change.

But nowhere in the world today, or even in the history of man, have the warm hearts of men and women triumphed so swiftly, so certainly, over cold stone as in Berlin, indeed, in all of East Germany. If I may paraphrase the words of a great poet, Robert Frost: There is certainly something in us that doesn't love a wall.

When I spoke to the German people in Mainz last May, I applauded the removal of the barriers between Hungary and Austria, saying: "Let Berlin be next." And the West German people joined us in a call for a Europe whole and free.

Just yesterday, the West German Foreign Minister gave me a piece of the Berlin Wall, and it's on my desk as a reminder of the power of freedom to bring down the walls between people....

Change is coming swiftly, and with this change the dramatic vindication of free Europe's economic and political institutions. The new Europe that is coming is being built—must be built—on the foundation of democratic values. But the faster the pace, the smoother our path must be. After all, this is serious business. The peace we are building must be different than the hard, joyless peace between two armed camps we've known so long. The scars of the conflict that began a half a century ago still divide a continent. So, the historic task before us now is to begin the healing of this old wound.

Thanksgiving Address to the Nation, November 22, 1989, *Public Papers of the Presidents of the United States, George Bush 1989, Book II.* (Washington, D.C.: Government Printing Office, 1990), pp. 1581-1582.

26.5

MAJOR RHONDA CORNUM ON THE PERSIAN GULF WAR (1991)

On August 2, 1990, Iraq's invasion of neighboring Kuwait triggered international protests. Iraqi dictator Saddam Hussein annexed Kuwait in hopes of acquiring its large oil reserves. Within a week, the UN Security Council demanded that Iraq withdraw from Kuwait and imposed a trade embargo on Iraq. On August 7, President George H.W. Bush deployed U.S. troops to Saudi Arabia to guard Saudi oil fields. Bush then spent several weeks building a multinational coalition to resist Iraq. On November 29, the UN Security Council authorized the use of force to eject Iraq from Kuwait if Iraq did not withdraw by January 15, 1991. Under Operation Desert Shield, approximately 700,000 soldiers, including 540,000 Americans, gathered on the border between Kuwait and Saudi Arabia. On January 12, 1991, the U.S. Congress approved military action in Iraq.

When the UN deadline passed three days later, the allies began a massive bombing campaign called Operation Desert Storm. For six weeks, air attacks destroyed Iraq's military bases, munitions factories, communications and transportation facilities, and government buildings. In mid-February, allied ground troops moved into southern Iraq and Kuwait. On February 28, with Iraqi forces in shambles, Bush declared a cease-fire. An estimated 300 allies and 20,000 Iraqis died in the brief conflict. Iraq and Kuwait sustained enormous property damage. While Kuwait regained its independence, Saddam Hussein remained in power. In the aftermath of the war, he brutally suppressed internal Shiite and Kurdish revolts. From 1991 on, he repeatedly flouted the terms of the UN peace agreement. In 1993 and 1998, U.S. and British forces launched missile strikes on Iraq. In early 2003, the UN was poised for another war against Saddam.

The U.S. mobilization for the Gulf War included unprecedented numbers of women. Women comprised 7 percent of active forces and 17 percent of Reserve and National Guard troops. Over 40,000 female soldiers served in combat-support positions. Major Rhonda Cornum (1955-present), a U.S. Army flight surgeon, was among the women stationed in the Persian Gulf. On February 27, 1991, the last day of the war, the helicopter carrying Cornum and her crew was shot down during a search-and-rescue mission. Five members of the eight-person crew died. Cornum was captured and held as a POW for eight days. Despite serous injuries and a sexual assault, Cornum refused to divulge classified information. Her courage helped reshape women's roles the military. After she testified about her experience in 1992, Congress opened several combat positions to women. In this passage from her memoirs, Cornum describes the helicopter crash and her subsequent capture.

---■---

FOCUS QUESTIONS

1. What happened during Cornum's mission?
2. How do Cornum's captors treat her? What is her response?
3. What is your opinion of women fighting in combat? Should women be excluded from any positions in the armed forces? Explain your answers.

e were flying fast and low…. I was sitting on the floor in the back of the Black Hawk, leaning against my medical gear and a stretcher…. I could see endless columns of American tanks and trucks, full of water, ammo, and fuel driving across the hard-packed, rocky sand….

About forty-five seconds after we passed over the last American vehicle, and without any warning, green tracers began streaking up at us from the ground, while I heard the crack-crack of weapons firing. The empty desert below us erupted with fire and white flashes of light…. Sergeant Ortiz, the lead Pathfinder [an infantryman trained for helicopter missions], took my head and slammed it to the floor, and in a second all three Pathfinders instinctively were half lying on me with their weapons ready. I almost laughed at their reaction: it would have been a good way to cover me in a foxhole, but we were in a helicopter. I'm sure their hearts were in the right place, but the rounds were coming up at us from the ground, so I was actually shielding them. The Pathfinders were very protective of me because that was their mission: protect the doctor and the patient. We didn't have the patient yet, so they worried about protecting me.

The two door gunners—SSgt. Daniel Stamaris and Sfc. William Butts—were fighting back and spraying machine-gun fire at the ground. I heard the sharp pop-pop-pop and clank of metal, and smelled acrid burning gunpowder inside the helicopter….

We heard the rattling Iraqi antiaircraft guns following us across the sky, and the rounds began tearing through the metal tail boom and the fuselage and rocking the aircraft. I clutched the floor in front of me, not knowing if a bullet would come ripping up through the helicopter and into my body…. The pilots tried to get away by breaking sharply to the left….

I felt something big hit the aircraft and I knew it wasn't doing well. The engine strained and the fuselage shook and shimmied. Then Garvey yelled, "We're going in!"...I remember having time to hold on, knowing we were going to crash.... We were still banked to the left when the left nose hit the sand, flattening, and then twenty thousand pounds of aircraft went end over end in a ball of flying metal and gear and spinning rotors. Everything went black....

I had to get out by myself, but I couldn't move my arms, presumably because they were pinned. I took stock of what I could use to escape from under the fuselage. The only part of my body that still worked reasonably well was my left leg. I pulled the good leg toward me and straightened it again to push the sand away. I pushed and pushed to clear the sand away from my right leg.... I dug and scraped at the sand until there was a shallow hole underneath me that freed my legs from the fuselage. With my body in the slight hole, I could move my right leg a little, but my knee hurt badly. I didn't mind, though, because if it hurt, I figured it was still connected, and it was another sign that I was alive.

The flames flicked in the corner of my eyes. Keep digging. All I could think about was, I have to get out from under the helicopter. I dug the heel of my left boot deeper into the ground and pushed away more sand. When I was clear enough to move, I tried to turn over and crawl out, but I couldn't turn or crawl. My arms were no longer stuck under the fuselage, but they wouldn't respond. I'm hurt worse than I thought, I realized. Things are broken. Still, there was no pain, just numbness as the shock of the crash froze the nerves.

I was wiggling around on my left side trying to get out and away from the helicopter when I looked up and saw four or five Iraqi soldiers standing over me. They were wearing good uniforms and helmets and carrying AK-47s, the Soviet-made assault rifle. They had a professional way about them, and I recognized them as members of the Republican Guard [elite corps in the Iraqi army]. One of them, without saying anything, reached down and grabbed my right arm. He pulled me hard to get up, and the pain shot through me and came out of my mouth in a piercing scream.... My arm was broken between the shoulder and the elbow, but it wasn't a displaced fracture. At least not until the Iraqi pulled apart the pieces of bones.

The men were taking among themselves in Arabic. I couldn't understand the words, but it seemed they were trying to decide what to do with me. A couple of them swarmed over me like ants, taking off my pistol, my survival vest with the radio, my flak jacket, and my helmet. I stood still, looking at the ground. When they took off my green helmet, my hair came tumbling down. That's when they realized I was female. There was a flurry of comment about it, and they talked louder and faster for a moment, but I couldn't understand them. I stared straight ahead, standing with my weight on my left leg since my right leg hurt when I tried to stand out it. I was just a few feet from the wreckage. The helicopter disintegrated and pieces were thrown everywhere, but I didn't see any fire...

One of the Iraqis grabbed my arm again and tried to drag me forward. I yelled sharply in pain, and he dropped my arm. The arm flopped in front of me like a piece of meat, completely out of my control. Then he grabbed a bunch of my hair, and pulled me along with him across the sand. I had no choice but to follow.... I realized that not one arm, but both of them, were broken between the elbows and the shoulders, and they were swinging uselessly beside me....

The sky was growing darker. The Iraqis didn't have flashlights, but they obviously knew where we were going....

I wasn't afraid at that point....

I'd talked about dying in my final letters to my family, just before February 24, when we launched the air assault north and west of Kuwait to cut off the Republican Guard. We only half-jokingly called the mission the "Air Assault to Hell," and we knew it was dangerous. I wanted my family to know that I went to war because the battalion wanted me to go, and I wanted to be with them. I wrote my grandparents that I was proud of what I was doing, and that if anything happened to me, they should remember that I chose to be here. I told my sister that if something bad happened, she should make sure my parents didn't do anything embarrassing. My worst fear was that they would shame me or the army; that they would be hysterical, try to sue the government, or say I shouldn't have been in combat because I was a doctor or a woman or just because I was their daughter. All I hoped was that my parents would take their folded American flag gracefully after the funeral, say "Thank you," and quietly hang it on the wall....

The Iraqis led me toward a hole that opened in the earth like the shadowed entrance to a coal mine. In the fading light of the darkening evening I could see sandbag stairs leading down into an underground bunker. This network of bunkers was the reason we had not seen any Iraqi soldiers from the helicopter. The passageway was fairly wide, but there were soldiers lining both sides of the stairs. Two guards went ahead of me and two followed behind, pushing me step by step through the gauntlet of soldiers. They jeered and shouted at me, but no one tried to touch me as I slowly negotiated the stairs with a bad leg and two broken arms....

At the bottom of the stairs, there was a junior Iraqi officer, probably a lieutenant, sitting at a wooden table, staring at me and the procession of jeering soldiers. He questioned one of my guards and then said to me in heavily accented English, "Who are you?"

"Major Rhonda Cornum."

I was not going to keep my name a secret, since it was printed on the name tag on my flight suit. I noticed my dog tag chain was partially out of my flight suit, and I remembered my wedding ring threaded on the chain...

It was then that I saw Sergeant Dunlap...He was in the center of a circle of Iraqi soldiers, kneeling down in the sand, looking at the ground in front of him. His hands were tied behind his back. My hands were tied in front...

The guard put his hand heavily on my shoulder and tried to shove me to the ground. I resisted for a moment because I was afraid I would fall on my bad knee, but then I carefully went down on my left knee and balanced precariously. Dunlap glanced over at me and gave me a little smile. I nudged him, as much I could nudge him with my arms broken, and I said something stupid, something motherly: "It's going to be okay." He smiled weakly. Dunlap was almost young enough to be my son. He was twenty; I was thirty-six. I was a doctor and an officer; he was an enlisted man. I couldn't really do much for him, but I felt responsible and I wanted to make him feel better. "No talking!" one of the Iraqis yelled in English.

There were two soldiers standing behind us, both with rifles pointed at our uncovered heads. I could feel the cold metal barrel poking me in the back of the neck. The Iraqis were having an animated discussion, and it seemed they were trying to decide what to do with us. This was the first time I was truly afraid. It was then that I realized we would be killed....

Without warning, a strong hold grabbed me by the hair and jerked me to my feet. Another soldier roughly picked up Dunlap. The ring of shouting Iraqis parted, and they marched Dunlap across the sand to a small civilian pickup truck, with me following. What are they doing? Maybe we're not going to be killed. At least for now. It seemed the Iraqis couldn't decide what to do with us, and there was nothing else to do. We were prisoners, but maybe we were being allowed to live.

I was badly injured, but I knew I'd heal eventually. The crash had been so devastating that I should have died then, and I regarded every minute I was alive as a gift. The Iraqis could have killed us easily when they found us at the crash site, but they chose not to. Then in the circle of men, a slight pressure on a single trigger would have been enough to kill us, but we had been spared. It was just enough good luck for me to grab on to and hold. I vowed to survive.

Rhonda Cornum as told to Peter Copeland, *She Went to War: The Rhonda Cornum Story* (Novato, CA: Presidio Press, 1992), pp. 9-18.

26.6

THE HILL-THOMAS HEARINGS (1991)

In 1986, in Meritor Savings Bank v. Vinson, *the U.S. Supreme Court recognized sexual harassment as a violation of Title VII of the Civil Rights Act of 1964. But the issue of sexual harassment did not capture the public's attention until 1991, when President George H.W. Bush nominated Clarence Thomas [1948-present] to fill the seat of retiring Supreme Court justice Thurgood Marshall. Born in Georgia, Thomas graduated from Holy Cross College and Yale Law School. From 1974 to 1981, he worked as an attorney and legislative aide in Missouri. In 1981, he became assistant secretary for civil rights at the U.S. Department of Education. The following year, he was appointed chairman of the Equal Employment Opportunity Commission (EEOC). Thomas left the EEOC in 1990 to serve as a justice at the U.S. Court of Appeals for the District of Columbia. In September 1991, the Senate Judiciary Committee began confirmation hearings on Thomas's nomination for the U.S. Supreme Court. Senators and journalists pressed Thomas to clarify his views on abortion, but he refused. Some witnesses claimed that he* was not qualified for the nation's highest court. On September 27, the Judiciary Committee voted 7-7 to submit Thomas's nomination for a full Senate vote.

Thomas's confirmation seemed assured—until Anita Hill's allegations of sexual harassment surfaced. Anita Hill [1956-present] was a law professor at the University of Oklahoma who worked with Thomas at the Department of Education and the EEOC. In an FBI report, Hill accused Thomas of making repeated sexual advances and discussing pornography. Hill reiterated her assertions in a personal statement sent to the Senate Judiciary Committee. But not all of the senators read her statement or the FBI report before their vote on September 27th.

After Hill's accusations were leaked to National Public Radio and Newsday, a firestorm of national debate ensued. In response, the Judiciary Committee reopened Thomas's confirmation hearings on October 11. In three days of televised testimony, Hill, Thomas, and several witness for both addressed Hill's claims. Members of the all-white male Judiciary Committee vigorously challenged Hill, an African-American woman. Thomas, an African-American man, fiercely defended himself. The hearings became a lightning rod for national attitudes about racism and sexism. On October 15, the Senate confirmed Thomas with a 52-48 vote.

The Hill-Thomas hearings permanently changed American society. In their aftermath, employers implemented anti-harassment codes and diversity training for employees. Hill's harsh treatment by the all-male Judiciary Committee inspired dozens of women to run for public office. In 1992, a record twenty-nine women were elected to Congress. After Hill returned to the University of Oklahoma, several state politicians called for her resignation. She eventually joined the faculty at Brandeis University. In 1997, she published Speaking Truth to Power, a memoir. Thomas remains an associate justice on the Supreme Court.

In this reading, Anita Hill and Clarence Thomas give their opening statements to the Senate Judiciary Committee.

FOCUS QUESTIONS

1. What accusations does Anita Hill make against Clarence Thomas? How does he respond?
2. Whom do you believe? Why? Should Clarence Thomas have been appointed to the Supreme Court?
3. What does the furor surrounding the Hill-Thomas hearings suggest about American political culture in the early 1990s?

ANITA HILL: My name is Anita F. Hill, and I am a professor of law at the University of Oklahoma. I was born on a farm in Okmulgee County, Oklahoma, in 1956. I am the youngest of thirteen children....

For my undergraduate work, I went to Oklahoma State University and graduated from there in 1977. I am attaching to this statement a copy of my resume for further details of my education....

I graduated from the university with academic honors, and proceeded to the Yale Law School, where I received my J.D. degree in 1980.

Upon graduation from law school, I became a practicing lawyer with the Washington, D.C., firm of Wald, Wakrader & Ross. In 1981, I was introduced to now Judge Thomas by a mutual friend. Judge Thomas told me that he was anticipating a political appointment, and asked if I would be interested in working with him. He was, in fact, appointed as assistant secretary of education for civil rights. After he had taken that post, he asked if I would become his assistant, and I accepted that position.

In my early period there, I had two major projects. First was an article I wrote for Judge Thomas's signature on the education of minority students. The second was the organization of a seminar on high-risk students, which was abandoned because Judge Thomas transferred to the EEOC, where he became the chairman of that office.

During this period at the Department of Education my working relationship with Judge Thomas was positive. I had a good deal of responsibility and independence. I thought he respected my work, and that he trusted my judgment.

After approximately three months of working there, he asked me to go out socially with him. What happened next, and telling the world about it, are the two most difficult things, experiences of my life. It is only after a great deal of agonizing consideration, and a number of sleepless nights, that I am able to talk of these unpleasant matters to anyone but my closest friends.

I declined the invitation to go out socially with him, and explained to him that I thought it would jeopardize what at the time I considered to be a very good working relationship. I had a normal social life with men outside of the office. I believed then, as now, that having a social relationship with a person who was supervising my work would be ill-advised. I was very uncomfortable with the idea and told him so.

I thought that by saying "no" and explaining my reasons, my employer would abandon his social suggestions. However, to my regret, in the following few weeks, he continued to ask me out on several occasions. He pressed me to justify reasons for saying no to him. These incidents took place in his office, or mine. They were in the form of private conversation which would not have been overheard by anyone else.

My working relationship became even more strained when Judge Thomas began to use work situations to discuss sex. On these occasions he would call me info his office for reports on education issues and projects, or he might suggest that because of the time pressures of his schedule, we go to lunch to a government cafeteria. After a brief discussion of work, he would turn the conversation to a discussion of sexual matters. His conversations were very vivid.

He spoke about acts that he had seen in pornographic films involving such matters as women having sex with animals, and films showing group sex or rape scenes. He talked about pornographic materials depicting individuals with large penises or large breasts, in various sex acts.

On several occasions, Thomas told me graphically of his own sexual prowess. Because I was extremely uncomfortable talking about sex with him at all, and particularly in such a graphic way, I told him that I did not want to talk about these subjects. I would also try to change the subject to education matters or to nonsexual personal matters, such as his background or his beliefs. My efforts to change subject were rarely successful.

Throughout the period of these conversations, he also from time to time asked me for social engagements. My reaction to these conversations was to avoid them by limiting opportunities for us to engage in extended conversations. This was difficult because, at the time, I was his only assistant at the office of education—or the office for civil rights.

During the latter part of my time at the Department of Education, the social pressures, and any conversation of his offensive behavior, ended. I began both to believe and hope that our relationship could be a proper, cordial, and professional one.

When Judge Thomas was made chair of the EEOC, I needed to face the question of whether to go with him. I was asked to do so, and I did. The work itself was interesting, and at the time it appeared that the sexual overtures which had so troubled me had ended.

I also faced the realistic fact that I had no alternative job. While I might have gone back to private practice, perhaps in my old firm or another, I was dedicated to civil rights work and my first choice was to be in that field. Moreover, at that time, the Department of Education itself was a dubious venture. President Reagan was seeking to abolish the entire department.

For my first months at the EEOC, where I continued to be an assistant to Judge Thomas, there were no sexual conversations or overtures. However, during the fall and winter of 1982, these began again. The comments were random and ranged from pressing me about why I didn't go out with him, to remarks about my personal appearance. I remember his saying that some day I would have to tell him the real reason that I wouldn't go out with him.

He began to show displeasure in his tone and voice, and his demeanor and his continued pressure for an explanation. He commented on what I was wearing in terms of whether it made me more or less sexually attractive. The incidents occurred in his inner office at the EEOC.

One of the oddest episodes I remember was an occasion in which Thomas was drinking a Coke in his office. He got up from the table at which we were working, went over to his desk, looked at the can, and asked, "Who has put pubic hair on my Coke?"

On other occasions, he referred to the size of his own penis as being larger than normal, and he also spoke on some occasions of the pleasures he had given to women with oral sex. At this point, late in 1982, I began to feel severe stress on the job. I began to be concerned that Clarence Thomas might take out his anger with me by degrading me, or not giving me important assignments. I also thought that he might find an excuse for dismissing me.

In January of 1983, I began looking for another job. I was handicapped because I feared that if he found out, he might make it difficult for me to find other employment and I might be dismissed from the job I had. Another factor that made my search more difficult was that this was during a period of a hiring freeze in the government....

On, as I recall, the last day of my employment at the EEOC in the summer of 1983, I did have dinner with Clarence Thomas. We went directly from work to a restaurant near the office. We talked about the work I had done, both at Education and at the EEOC. He told me that he was pleased with all of it, except for an article and speech that I had done for him while we were at the Office for Civil Rights. Finally he made a comment that I will vividly remember. He said that if I ever told anyone of his behavior, it would ruin his career. This was not an apology; nor was it an explanation. That was his last remark about the possibility of our going out or reference to his behavior.

In July of 1983 I left the Washington, D.C., area and have had minimal contacts with Judge Clarence Thomas since....

I may have used poor judgment early on in my relationship with this issue. I was aware, however, that telling at any point in my career could adversely affect my future career....

It would have been more comfortable to remain silent. I took no initiative to inform anyone. But when I was asked by a representative of this committee to report my experience, I felt that I had to tell the truth. I could not keep silent.

JUDGE THOMAS: As excruciatingly difficult as the last two weeks have been, I welcome the opportunity to clear my name today. No one other than my wife and Senator Danforth, to whom I read this statement at 6:30 a.m., has seen or heard the statement, no handlers, no advisors.

The first I learned of the allegations by Professor Anita Hill was on September 25, 1991, when the FBI came to my home to investigate her allegations. When informed by the FBI agent of the nature of the allegations and the person making them, I was shocked, surprised, hurt and enormously saddened.

I have not been the same since that day. For almost a decade my responsibilities included enforcing the rights of victims of sexual harassment. As a boss, as a friend, and as a human being I was proud that I have never had such an allegation leveled against me, even as I sought to promote women, and minorities into nontraditional jobs.

In addition, several of my friends, who are women, have confided in me about the horror of harassment on the job, or elsewhere. I thought I really understood the anguish, the fears, the doubts, the seriousness of the matter. But since September 25th, I have suffered immensely as these very serious charges were leveled against me.

I have been wracking my brains, and eating my insides out trying to think of what I could have said or done to Anita Hill to lead her to allege that I was interested in her in more than a professional way, and that I talked with her about pornographic or X-rated films.

Contrary to some press reports, I categorically denied all of the allegations and denied that I ever attempted to date Anita Hill, when first interviewed by the FBI. I strongly reaffirm that denial. Let me describe my relationship with Anita Hill....

During my tenure at the Department of Education, Anita Hill was an attorney-advisor who worked directly with me. She worked on special projects, as well as day-to-day matters. As I recall, she was one of two professionals working directly with me at the time. As a result, we worked closely on numerous matters.

I recall being pleased with her work product and the professional, but cordial relationship which we enjoyed at work. I also recall engaging in discussions about politics and current events.

Upon my nomination to become Chairman of the Equal Employment Opportunity Commission, Anita Hill, to the best of my recollection, assisted me in the nomination and confirmation process. After my confirmation, she and Diane Holt, then my secretary, joined me at EEOC. I do not recall that there was any question or doubts that she would become a special assistant to me at EEOC, although as a career employee she retained the option of remaining at the Department of Education.

At EEOC our relationship was more distant. And our contacts less frequent, as a result of the increased size of my personal staff and the dramatic increase and diversity of my day-to-day responsibilities.

Upon reflection, I recall that she seemed to have had some difficulty adjusting to this change in her role. In any case, our relationship remained both cordial and professional. At no time did I become aware, either directly or indirectly that she felt I had said, or done anything to change the cordial nature of our relationship....

Throughout the time that Anita Hill worked with me I treated her as I treated my other special assistants. I tried to treat them all cordially, professionally, and respectfully. And I tried to support them in their endeavors, and be interested in and supportive of their success.

I had no reason or basis to believe my relationship with Anita Hill was any thing but this way until the FBI visited me a little more than two weeks ago. I find it particularly troubling that she never raised any hint that she was uncomfortable with me. She did not raise or mention it when considering moving with me to EEOC from the Department of Education. And she never raised it with me when she left EEOC and was moving on in her life.

And to my fullest knowledge, she did not speak to any other women working with or around me, who would feel comfortable enough to raise it with me, especially Diane Holt, to whom she seemed closest on my personal staff. Nor did she raise it with mutual friends, such as Linda Jackson, and Gil Hardy.

This is a person I have helped at every turn in the road, since we met. She seemed to appreciate the continued cordial relationship we had since day one. She sought my advice and counsel, as did virtually all of the members of my personal staff.

During my tenure in the executive branch as a manager, as a policy maker and as a person, I have adamantly condemned sex harassment. There is no member of this committee or this Senate who feels stronger about sex harassment than I do.

As a manager, I made every effort to take swift and decisive action when sex harassment raised or reared its ugly head.

The fact that I feel so very strongly about sex harassment and spoke loudly about it at EEOC has made these allegations doubly hard on me. I cannot imagine anything that I said or did to Anita Hill that could have been mistaken for sexual harassment.

But with that said, if there is anything that I have said that has been misconstrued by Anita Hill or anyone else, to be sexually harassment, then I can say that I am so very sorry and I wish I had known. If I did know I would have stopped immediately and I would not, as I have done over the past two weeks, had to tear away at myself trying to think of what I could possibly have done. But I have not said or done the things that Anita Hill has alleged. God has gotten me through the days since September 25th and he is my judge....

Though I am, by no means, a perfect person, no means, I have not done what she has alleged, and I still do not know what I could possibly have done to cause her to make these allegations.

When I stood next to the President in Kennebunkport, being nominated to the Supreme Court of the United States, that was a high honor. But as I sit here, before you, 103 days later, that honor has been crushed. From the very beginning charges were leveled against me from the shadows—charges of drug abuse, anti-Semitism, wife-beating, drug use by family members, that I was a quota appointment, confirmation conversion and much, much more, and now, this.

I have complied with the rules. I responded to a document request that produced over 30,000 pages of documents. And I have testified for five full days, under oath. I have endured this ordeal for 103 days. Reporters sneaking into my garage to examine books I read. Reporters and interest groups swarming over divorce papers, looking for dirt. Unnamed people starting preposterous and damaging rumors. Calls all over the country specifically requesting dirt. This is not American. This is Kafka-esque. It has got to stop. It must stop for the benefit of future nominees, and our country. Enough is enough.

I am not going to allow myself to be further humiliated in order to be confirmed. I am here specifically to respond to allegations of sex harassment in the workplace. I am not here to be further humiliated by this committee, or anyone else, or to put my private life on display for a prurient interest or other reasons. I will not allow this committee or anyone else to probe into my private life. This is not what America is all about....

Mr. Chairman, in my 43 years on this earth, I have been able, with the help of others and with the help of God, to defy poverty, avoid prison, overcome segregation, bigotry, racism, and obtain one of the finest educations available in this country. But I have not been able to overcome this process. This is worse than any obstacle or anything that I have ever faced....

Mr. Chairman, I am proud of my life, proud of what I have done, and what I have accomplished, proud of my family, and this process, this process is trying to destroy it all. No job is worth what I have been through, no job. No horror in my life has been so debilitating. Confirm me if you want, don't confirm me if you are so led, but let this process end. Let me and my family regain our lives. I never asked to be nominated. It was an honor. Little did I know the price, but it is too high....

Mr. Chairman, I am a victim of this process and my name has been harmed, my integrity has been harmed, my character has been harmed, my family has been harmed, my friends have been harmed. There is nothing this committee, this body or this country can do to give me my good name back, nothing.

I will not provide the rope for my own lynching or for further humiliation. I am not going to engage in discussions, nor will I submit to roving questions of what goes on in the most intimate parts of my private live or the sanctity of my bedroom. These are the most intimate parts of my privacy, and they will remain just that, private.

Hearings before the Committee on the Judiciary, United States Senate, 102nd Congress, 1st Session; on the Nomination of Judge Clarence Thomas to be Associate Justice of the Supreme Court of the United States (Washington, D.C.: U.S. Government Printing Office, 1991), part 4, pp. 5-10, 36-40.

26.7

Asian Refugees Describe Life in America (1991)

The Immigration Act of 1965 is one of the most significant laws of the past four decades. Abandoning the quota system of the 1920s, the legislation allowed 170,000 immigrants to enter the United States each year. It maintained restrictions on some Latin American countries, but permitted Europeans, Africans, and Asians to enter the country on equal terms. The policy dramatically changed the nature of U.S. immigration. In 1965, 90 percent of immigrants were from Europe. In 1990, 80 percent of immigrants came from non-European nations. The change is particularly striking among Asians. Beginning in the late 1970s, new communities of Laotians, Cambodians, Vietnamese, Thai, Koreans, Filipinos, and Asian Indians developed all over the country, especially in the West. While some of these immigrants were fleeing poverty and political unrest in the wake of the Vietnam War, most were well-educated and joining relatives already living in the United States. According to the 2000 U.S. Census, there are now 11.9 million Asian Americans, 4.2 percent of the total U.S. population of 281.4 million.

In these accounts, Asian refugees describe their experiences in the United States.

Focus Questions

1. How do these refugees portray their lives in America? Why have they immigrated to the United States?

2. Compare their experiences to Rosa and José Urbina (Document 26.3). Are these immigrants a positive or negative influence on American society? Explain your answer.

H O XUAN TAM—Dreams of Stanford

He is wearing a three-piece blue business suit. There is a great deal of self-confidence in the way he presents himself.

I would like to study math at Stanford University when I finish high school next year. I have been in the United States seven years this fall. Sometimes, I wish I could just skip my senior year and go to Stanford; I've learned enough—I'm bored and I've learned all I am going to learn from high school.

My mother and father were very educated people from Saigon, and there was always pressure to study. I can remember my father helping me with my studies when I was first in this country; he had difficulty with the language, but somehow he always understood my assignments. It was always a big ritual after dinner to study with him; I know he looked forward to it. The higher math I had was difficult for him, but he kept at it until trig, and then he said I could complete that assignment without his assistance. My mother played hardly any place in this homework help.

My father was a famous lawyer in Vietnam; he had a great love for books. He always told me that a book was like a beautiful bird—the more you read of it the more beautiful it becomes. He was very, very proud when my older sister got a scholarship to study premed last year at Stanford. It was as if he got the scholarship. So this is pretty much what I'm going to do—go to Stanford.

We have always lived in the Tenderloin section in San Francisco, and I go to Galileo High School—which isn't so bad. Most of the students are okay, but your friends are always from your people—your own nationality.

Tell me about your friends.

I have two Vietnamese friends. It is difficult to break into any new group, people stick to themselves. My one Vietnamese friend knows a few Chinese, but it's more that they are polite to her rather than they are friends.

Scholastically, Galileo is not the best high school in San Francisco. Most Asians do pretty well in school, and there is always some jealousy by the black and Spanish students, but I don't care. If they are jealous, I can't do anything about it. I work hard, they can too. Besides, the Vietnamese are supposed to raise the math and science scores in all of the San Francisco schools, so we help improve the system for everybody.

I think one of the big problems in the school is all this wasted time in lunch and study halls, and most of the teachers are not so good. They just keep repeating what they've already said. Me, I'd change the whole system and speed it up—let you get out of there earlier.

To get a full scholarship to Stanford is very difficult. They want to see somebody with everything going for them. I don't think my guidance counselor at Galileo understands how important this is to me. All he talks about are the second and third choices of schools. I want the best and he doesn't know my father. In some ways, I'm following in my sister's shadow. So everyone thinks I will do the same. I wish my parents could see that.

Do you attend school sports events?

No, and I don't go to school dances; there are more important things to do. I want to be able to get a higher SAT score than my sister had. It's not impossible, but it's not very realistic because I'm still weak in my verbal scores. I need to practice more. For me, math is the purest of all sciences. It is the most powerful language, and you can learn to speak it even if your English is not perfect.

HENG MUI—Citizenship
She has very expressive eyes, and has brought me a collection of photographs of herself, mostly from her life in this country.

I became a citizen last year; I am now an American. I do not especially feel like an American, but I don't know if there is any special way I should feel. There are lots of stereotypes about how Americans look and how they act; I don't fall into any of those categories.

For some refugees, becoming an American is not an easy thing to do. It means you give up that final thing that is yours, your nationality. To take away your nationality is to deprive you of an important piece of your identity. We have lost so much, so many of us arrived with nothing. To give up our nationality is just too much to ask. I know people who are not ready to do this; it's too painful, too embarrassing.

I remember when my sister suddenly died in France, and I went to the immigration office and applied for a travel document. When the woman at the desk asked me to write my nationality, which was question three, I wrote South Vietnam. When she saw the application, she took a pencil and put two lines through the word Vietnam and wrote "stateless." Those two pencil lines scratched through my heart. In a few minutes she took away my nationality. There was nothing I could do.

When I took my oath [for U.S. citizenship], I thought, "Oh, my God! Everything is gone!" But after it happened, I never thought about it. The most painful part was just thinking about it. There is something exciting about holding my new blue passport and knowing that I will vote next year for the president.

MONG PANG—A Soldier without a Country
He is wearing green, institutional work clothes, probably from Sears; a red checked bandana is tied around his neck. He is graying at the temples, bespectacled, probably five feet tall. We sit on a bench, talking in English, and drink coffee.

I am a janitor for the Baptist church in Atlanta near Ponce de Leon. This is the job that I have had since I came to the U.S. and to Atlanta in December 1980. I don't think about this fact too much. It is a job for us and we do not live on welfare.

Sometimes when the work gets too much because they have a wedding or some celebration, my wife Duong helps. She never worked for another person before she came here, and she does not mind too much. I have four children. The oldest has just finished high school and wants to study computers. We all live in the same house that was given to us by the church here. The rent is good and it is close so I can walk to work. It is a simple house and often many of our friends are there. You see, Laotians do not mind many people in a house. The Americans do not like this. Here, everyone has his own room; this is not so with Laotian culture.

When I was in Laos I was in the army. I was a colonel in the north and worked for some years with the Americans. I never got to know the Americans but I worked with them and some seemed nice. They drank too much beer....

It was a good life in Laos and I miss my country very much. I want to go back if the Communists get out. I look to that day all of the time. We left so quickly. We just locked the door and left. We don't know about our possessions or our house. I hope it is still there. I think about relatives and friends. Every times the news talks about the war and the Thai/Laos border problems, I worry about my brother left there. I am sure others do the same. I fought very hard for my country, and now all of that is gone and it will not come back. It is very sad.

There is nothing I wish to do here. Why should I? I do not have my heart here. My family soon will become U.S. citizens and they have new lives here. All of that is good and they start new lives. I will be happy for them.

When I first started this work, the tears went into the toilet, I was so sad. There is not much else I can do here in America. What do they do with a soldier who has no country? What could they educate me to be? I don't know. All of these years that I clean the church, I just do it. No one bothers me—I am my own boss. They are good to me, these Christian people. They gave me my first station wagon and they always invited me to church, but I just went to hear the music. I like the organ. Every Christmas they give us food and money.

Voices from Southeast Asia: The Refugee Experience in the United States by John Tenhula (New York: Holmes & Meier, 1991). Copyright © 1991 by Holmes & Meier Publishers, Inc. Reproduced with the permission of the publisher.

26.8

BILL CLINTON OUTLINES HIS AGENDA (1993)

Bill Clinton was one of the more lively presidents in U.S. history. Despite a childhood rocked by the unstable marriage of his mother and stepfather, he graduated from Georgetown University and won a Rhodes scholarship to study at Oxford University. Like many Americans of the era, Clinton opposed the Vietnam War. In 1968, he attempted to extend his draft deferment by applying to the Reserve Officers' Training Corps (ROTC) program at the University of Arkansas

Law School. Clinton later changed his plans and made himself eligible for the draft, but he was not asked to serve. While at Oxford, he wrote the director of the Arkansas ROTC program and thanked him for "saving" him from the draft. In early 1992, the Wall Street Journal *printed the letter and accused Clinton of manipulating the draft system—a charge Clinton denied.*

After finishing his studies at Oxford and graduating from Yale University Law School, Clinton taught at the University of Arkansas School of Law. In 1974, he ran unsuccessfully for the U.S. House of Representatives. The following year, he married Hillary Rodham, a fellow Yale Law graduate. In 1976, he was elected attorney general of Arkansas. Two years later, at age 32, Clinton won the state's governorship, but lost a bid for reelection in 1980. Displaying the determination that became a hallmark of his presidency, Clinton regained the governorship in 1982 and held the post for three successive terms. As a leading member of the Democratic Leadership Council, Clinton advocated centrist positions instead of the party's traditional liberalism.

In January 1992, only weeks after Clinton declared his candidacy for president, allegations of marital infidelity nearly ended his campaign. In response, Clinton and his wife appeared on the television news program 60 Minutes *and admitted past difficulties in their relationship. Shortly thereafter, Clinton revealed that he had experimented with marijuana in college but "didn't inhale." While such tortured explanations alienated some voters, others focused on Clinton's economic stimulus plan and ability to reach ordinary people. In November, Clinton narrowly defeated President George H.W. Bush and independent candidate H. Ross Perot.*

The Clinton administration had an inauspicious beginning. In late January 1993, Clinton drew heated criticism for his nominees for attorney general, his attempt to lift the ban on gays and lesbians in the military, and his decision to appoint Hillary Clinton to head a national task force on health care reform. On February 17, Clinton tried to regain his political focus and presented his economic program to Congress.

FOCUS QUESTIONS

1. How does Clinton describe the current state of the U.S. economy?
2. What are Clinton's major economic goals? Which of these objectives did Clinton achieve? Which did he fail to accomplish?
3. How does today's economy compare to that of the Clinton era?

 ur nation needs a new direction. Tonight, I present to you our comprehensive plan to set our nation on that new course.

I believe we will find our new direction in the basic values that brought us here: opportunity, individual responsibility, community, work, family, and faith. We need to break the old habits of both political parties in Washington. We must say that there can be no more something for nothing, and we are all in this together.

The conditions which brought us to this point are well known. Two decades of low productivity and stagnant wages; persistent unemployment and underemployment; years of huge government deficits and declining investment in our future; exploding health care costs, and lack of coverage; legions of poor children; educational and job training opportunities inadequate to the demands of a high wage, high growth economy. For too long we drifted without a strong sense of purpose, responsibility or community, and our political system too often was paralyzed by special interest groups, partisan bickering and the sheer complexity of our problems....

I tell you this not to assign blame for this problem. There is plenty of blame to go around—in both branches of the government and both parties. The time for blame has come to an end. I came here to accept responsibility; I want you to accept responsibility for the future of this country, and if we do it right, I don't care who gets the credit for it.

Our plan has four fundamental components: First, it reverses our economic decline, by jump-starting the economy in the short term and investing in our people, their jobs and their incomes in the long term.

Second, it changes the rhetoric of the past into the actions of the present, by honoring work and families in every part of our lives.

Third, it substantially reduces the federal deficit, honestly and credibly.

Finally, it earns the trust of the American people by paying for these plans first with cuts in government waste and inefficiency—cuts, not gimmicks, in government spending—and by fairness, for a change, in the way the burden is borne.

Tonight, I want to talk about what government can do, because I believe our government must do more for the hard-working people who pay its way. But let me say first: government cannot do this alone. The private sector is the engine of economic growth in America. And every one of us can be an engine of change in our own lives. We've got to give people more opportunity, but we must also demand more responsibility in return.

Our immediate priority is to create jobs, now. Some say we're in a recovery. Well, we all hope so. But we're simply not creating jobs. And there is no recovery worth its salt that does not begin with new jobs.

To create jobs and guarantee a strong recovery, I call on Congress to enact an immediate jobs package of over 30 billion dollars. We will put people to work right now and create half a million jobs: jobs that will rebuild our highways and airports, renovate housing, bring new life to our rural towns, and spread hope and opportunity among our nation's youth with almost 700,000 jobs for them this summer alone....

Second, our plan looks beyond today's business cycle, because our aspirations extend into the next century. The heart of our plan deals with the long term. It has an investment program designed to increase public and private investment in areas critical to our economic future. And it has a deficit reduction program that will increase savings available for private sector investment, lower interest rates, decrease the percentage of the federal budget claimed by interest payments, and decrease the risk of financial market disruptions that could adversely affect the economy....

In order to accomplish public investment and deficit reduction, government spending is being cut and taxes are being increased. Our spending cuts were carefully thought through to try to minimize any economic impact, to capture the peace dividend for investment purposes, and to switch the balance in the budget from consumption to investment. The tax increases and spending cuts were both designed to assure that the cost of this historic program to face and deal with our problems is borne by those who could most readily afford that cost.

Our plan is designed to improve the health of American business through lower interest rates, improved infrastructure, better-trained workers, and a stronger middle class. Because small businesses generate most of our nation's jobs, our plan includes the boldest targeted incentives for small business in history. We propose a permanent investment tax credit for small business, and new rewards for entrepreneurs who take risks. We will give small business access to the brilliant technologies of our time and to the credit they need to prosper and flourish.

With a new network of community development banks, and one billion dollars to make the dream of enterprise zones real, we will begin to bring new hope and new jobs to storefronts and factories from South Boston to South Texas to south-central Los Angeles.

Our plan invests in our roads, bridges, transit facilities; in high-speed railways and high-tech information systems; and in the most ambitious environmental clean-up of our time.

On the edge of the new century, economic growth depends as never before on opening up new markets overseas. And so we will insist on fair trade rules in international markets.

A part of our national economic strategy must be to expand trade on fair terms, including successful completion of the latest round of world trade talks. A North American Free Trade Agreement with appropriate safeguards for workers and the environment. At the same time, we need an aggressive attempt to create the hi-tech jobs of the future; special attention to troubled industries like aerospace and airlines, and special assistance to displaced workers like those in our defense industry.

I pledge that business, government and labor will work together in a partnership to strengthen America for a change.

But all of our efforts to strengthen the economy will fail unless we take bold steps to reform our health care system. America's businesses will never be strong; America's families will never be secure; and America's government will never be solvent until we tackle our health care crisis.

The rising costs and the lack of care are endangering both our economy and our lives. Reducing health care costs will liberate hundreds of billions of dollars for investment and growth and new jobs. Over the long run, reforming health care is essential to reducing our deficit and expanding investment.

Later this spring, I will deliver to Congress a comprehensive plan for health care reform that will finally get costs under control. We will provide security to all our families, so that no one will be denied the coverage they need. We will root out fraud and outrageous charges, and make sure that paperwork no longer chokes you or your doctor. And we will maintain American standards—the highest quality medical care in the world and the choices we demand and deserve. The American people expect us to deal with health care. And we must deal with it now....

America must ask more of our students, our teachers, and our schools. And we must give them the resources they need to meet high standards.

We will bring together business and schools to establish new apprenticeships, and give young people the skills they need today to find productive jobs tomorrow.

Lifelong learning will benefit workers throughout their careers. We must create a new unified worker training system, so that workers receive training regardless of why they lost their jobs....

Later this year, we will offer a plan to end welfare as we know it. No one wants to change the welfare system as much as those who are trapped by the welfare system.

We will offer people on welfare the education, training, child care and health care they need to get back on their feet. Then, after two years, they must get back to work—in private business if possible; in public service, if necessary. It's time to end welfare as a way of life....

We must reinvent government to make it work again. We'll push innovative education reform to improve learning, not just spend more money. We'll use the Superfund to clean up pollution, not just increase lawyers' incomes. We'll use federal banking regulators, not just to protect the security and safety of our financial institutions, but to break the credit crunch. And we'll change the whole focus of our poverty programs from entitlement to empowerment.

For years, there has been a lot of talk about the deficit, but very few credible efforts to deal with it. This plan does. Our plan tackles the budget deficit—seriously and over the long term. We will put in place one of the biggest deficit reductions and the biggest change of federal priorities in our history at the same time.

We are not cutting the deficit because the experts tell us to do so. We are cutting the deficit so that your family can afford a college education for your children. We are cutting the deficit so that your children will someday be able to buy a home of their own. We are cutting the deficit so that your company can invest in retraining its workers and retooling its factories. We are cutting the deficit so that government can make the investments that help us become stronger and smarter and safer.

If we do not act now, we will not recognize this country ten years from now. Ten years from now, the deficit will have grown to 635 billion dollars a year; the national debt will be almost 80 percent of our gross domestic product. Paying the interest on that debt will be the costliest government program of all, and we will continue to be the world's largest debtor, depending on foreign funds for a large part of our nation's investments....

Our economic plan is ambitious, but it is necessary for the continued greatness of our country. And it will be paid for fairly—by cutting government, by asking the most of those who benefited most in the past—by asking more Americans to contribute today so that all Americans can do better tomorrow.

For the wealthiest—those earning more than 180,000 dollars per year, I ask you to raise the top rate for federal income taxes from 31 percent to 36 percent. Our plan recommends a ten percent surtax on incomes over 250,000 dollars a year. And we will close the loopholes that let some get away without paying any tax at all.

For businesses with taxable incomes over ten million dollars, we will raise the corporate tax rate to 36 percent. And we will cut the deduction for business entertainment.

Our plan attacks tax subsidies that reward companies that ship jobs overseas. And we will ensure that, through effective tax enforcement, foreign corporations who make money in America pay the taxes they owe to America.

Middle-class Americans should know: You're not going alone any more; you're not going first; and you're no longer going to pay more and get less. Ninety-eight point eight percent of America's families will have no increase in their income tax rates. Only the wealthiest one point two percent will see their rates rise....

Our plan includes a tax on energy as the best way to provide us with new revenue to lower the deficit and invest in our people. Moreover, unlike other taxes, this one reduces pollution, increases energy efficiency, and eases our dependence on oil from unstable regions of the world.

Taken together, these measures will cost an American family earning 40 thousand dollars a year less than 17 dollars a month. And because of other programs we will propose, families earning less than 30,000 dollars a year will pay virtually no additional tax at all. Because of our publicly stated determination to reduce the deficit, interest rates have fallen since the election. That means that, for the middle class, the increases in energy costs will be more than offset by lower interest costs for mortgages, consumer loans and credit cards. This is a wise investment for you and for your country.

I ask all Americans to consider the cost of not changing, of not choosing a new direction. Unless we have the courage to start building our future and stop borrowing from it, we are condemning ourselves to years of stagnation, interrupted only by recession, to slow growth in jobs, no growth in incomes, and more debt and disappointment.

Worse yet—unless we change, unless we reduce the deficit, increase investment, and raise productivity so we can generate jobs—we will condemn our children and our children's children to a lesser life and a diminished destiny....

This economic plan cannot please everybody. If this package is picked apart, there will be something that will anger each of us. But, if it is taken as a whole, it will help all of us.

Resist the temptation to focus only on a spending cut you don't like or some investment not made. And nobody likes tax increases. But let's face facts: For 20 years incomes have stalled. For years, debt has exploded. We can no longer afford to deny reality. We must play the hand we were dealt.

The test of our program cannot simply be: "What's in it for me?" The question must be: "What's in it for us?"

If we work hard—and work together—if we rededicate ourselves to strengthening families, creating jobs, rewarding work, and reinventing government, we can lift America's fortunes once again.

Address Before a Joint Session of Congress on Administration Goals, February 17, 1993, *Public Papers of the Presidents of the United States: William J. Clinton 1996: Book I—January 1 to June 30, 1993* (Washington, D.C.: Government Printing Office, 1994), pp. 114-121.

26.9

THE REPUBLICAN CONTRACT WITH AMERICA (1994)

Bill Clinton's first year in office was marked by impressive successes and crushing failures. His victories included passage of the North American Free Trade Agreement (NAFTA), the Family and Medical Leave Act, a $496 billion deficit reduction package, and the Brady Handgun Violence Prevention Act. But Clinton also suffered setbacks like the defeat of his plan to reform the national health care system, the appointment of an independent counsel to investigate Whitewater, and a sexual harassment lawsuit filed by Paula Jones.

Republicans capitalized on Clinton's mixed record. In November 1994, the GOP won fifty-four seats and gained control of the House of Representatives for the first time in forty years. The 104th Congress elected Newt Gingrich (R-GA) as Speaker of the House. Hailed as the architect of the Republican's historic victory, Gingrich (1943-present) vowed to reduce the size and power of the federal government. He quickly emerged as Clinton's biggest political rival. Born in Pennsylvania, Gingrich graduated from Emory University and then earned a doctorate in modern European history from Tulane University. He taught for several years at West Georgia College. In 1978, after two previous defeats, Gingrich won election to the U.S. House and became known for his confrontational style and staunch conservatism. In September 1994, he helped draft the "Contract with America," a legislative agenda for House Republicans. Upon becoming Speaker, Gingrich led the Republican majority in passing most of the plan. Clinton, however, surprised the GOP by embracing some of their ideas and refusing to back down during protracted budget negotiations in late 1995. When the stalemate resulted in two closures of the federal government, voters blamed Gingrich, not Clinton. In 1997, Gingrich paid a $300,000 fine for fund-raising illegalities. In late 1998, after the Republicans lost ten seats in the House (cutting their majority to five seats), he retired from Congress.

FOCUS QUESTIONS

1. What are the major elements of the "Contract with America"?
2. Why was the "Contract with America" historically significant? How did it change the role of the federal government?

s Republican Members of the House of Representatives and as citizens seeking to join that body we propose not just to change its policies, but even more important, to restore the bonds of trust between the people and their elected representatives.

That is why, in this era of official evasion and posturing, we offer instead a detailed agenda for national renewal, a written commitment with no fine print.

This year's election offers the chance, after four decades of one-party control, to bring to the House a new majority that will transform the way Congress works. That historic change would be the end of government that is too big, too intrusive, and too easy with the public's money. It can be the beginning of a Congress that respects the values and shares the faith of the American family.

Like Lincoln, our first Republican president, we intend to act "with firmness in the right, as God gives us to see the right." To restore accountability to Congress. To end its cycle of scandal and disgrace. To make us all proud again of the way free people govern themselves.

On the first day of the 104th Congress, the new Republican majority will immediately pass the following major reforms, aimed at restoring the faith and trust of the American people in their government:

FIRST, require all laws that apply to the rest of the country also apply equally to the Congress;

SECOND, select a major, independent auditing firm to conduct a comprehensive audit of Congress for waste, fraud or abuse;

THIRD, cut the number of House committees, and cut committee staff by one-third;

FOURTH, limit the terms of all committee chairs;

FIFTH, ban the casting of proxy votes in committee;

SIXTH, require committee meetings to be open to the public;

SEVENTH, require a three-fifths majority vote to pass a tax increase;

EIGHTH, guarantee an honest accounting of our Federal Budget by implementing zero base-line budgeting.

Thereafter, within the first 100 days of the 104th Congress, we shall bring to the House Floor the following bills, each to be given full and open debate, each to be given a clear and fair vote and each to be immediately available this day for public inspection and scrutiny.

1. THE FISCAL RESPONSIBILITY ACT: A balanced budget/tax limitation amendment and a legislative line-item veto to restore fiscal responsibility to an out-of-control Congress, requiring them to live under the same budget constraints as families and businesses.

CHAPTER 26

1030

2. THE TAKING BACK OUR STREETS ACT: An anti-crime package including stronger truth-in-sentencing, "good faith" exclusionary rule exemptions, effective death penalty provisions, and cuts in social spending from this summer's "crime" bill to fund prison construction and additional law enforcement to keep people secure in their neighborhoods and kids safe in their schools.

3. THE PERSONAL RESPONSIBILITY ACT: Discourage illegitimacy and teen pregnancy by prohibiting welfare to minor mothers and denying increased AFDC for additional children while on welfare, cut spending for welfare programs, and enact a tough two-years-and-out provision with work requirements to promote individual responsibility.

4. THE FAMILY REINFORCEMENT ACT: Child support enforcement, tax incentives for adoption, strengthening rights of parents in their children's education, stronger child pornography laws, and an elderly dependent care tax credit to reinforce the central role of families in American society.

5. THE AMERICAN DREAM RESTORATION ACT: A S500 per child tax credit, begin repeal of the marriage tax penalty, and creation of American Dream Savings Accounts to provide middle class tax relief.

6. THE NATIONAL SECURITY RESTORATION ACT: No U.S. troops under U.N. command and restoration of the essential parts of our national security funding to strengthen our national defense and maintain our credibility around the world.

7. THE SENIOR CITIZENS FAIRNESS ACT: Raise the Social Security earnings limit which currently forces seniors out of the work force, repeal the 1993 tax hikes on Social Security benefits and provide tax incentives for private long-term care insurance to let Older Americans keep more of what they have earned over the years.

8. THE JOB CREATION AND WAGE ENHANCEMENT ACT: Small business incentives, capital gains cut and indexation, neutral cost recovery, risk assessment/cost-benefit analysis, strengthening the Regulatory Flexibility Act and unfunded mandate reform to create jobs and raise worker wages.

9. THE COMMON SENSE LEGAL REFORM ACT: "Loser pays" laws, reasonable limits on punitive damages and reform of product liability laws to stem the endless tide of litigation.

10. THE CITIZEN LEGISLATURE ACT: A first-ever vote on term limits to replace career politicians with citizen legislators.

Further, we will instruct the House Budget Committee to report to the floor and we will work to enact additional budget savings, beyond the budget cuts specifically included in the legislation described above, to ensure that the Federal budget deficit will be less than it would have been without the enactment of these bills.

Respecting the judgment of our fellow citizens as we seek their mandate for reform, we hereby pledge our names to this Contract with America.

http://www.house.gov/house/Contract/CONTRACT.html.

26.10

THE STARR REPORT (1998)

Allegations of scandal were common throughout the Clinton presidency. During the 1992 campaign, there were rumors that Bill and Hillary Clinton were involved in questionable land deals in a Whitewater, Arkansas housing development in the early 1980s. In July 1993, Vince Foster, the president's deputy counsel, committed suicide. Foster had handled Hillary Clinton's legal matters including Whitewater. Suspicions arose after White House aides prevented investigators from entering Foster's office. In January 1994, following months of Republican criticism, Attorney General Janet Reno, at Clinton's request, appointed Robert Fiske as an independent counsel charged with investigating Whitewater. Six months later, Fiske deposed Bill and Hillary Clinton, the first time a sitting president and first lady were forced to comply with such legal proceedings. Conservatives, however, claimed that Fiske was not being aggressive enough and persuaded a three-judge panel to replace him with Kenneth S. Starr.

Starr (1946-present) was born in Vernon, Texas, the son of a Church of Christ minister. After graduating from George Washington University, Starr earned a Master's degree from Brown University and a law degree from Duke University. Starr served as a clerk for Supreme Court Chief Justice Warren Burger. From 1981 to 1983, he worked in the Department of Justice under the Reagan administration. Upon receiving an appointment to the U.S. Court of Appeals in 1983, Starr opposed affirmative action, flag burning, and abortion. In 1989, he resigned from the bench to become George H.W. Bush's solicitor general. In 1994, Starr left private practice to take over the Whitewater investigation. Starr vigorously pursued several issues not directly related to the Clintons' real estate dealings including Foster's suicide, Hillary Clinton's stock transactions, the dismissal of employees in the White House travel office, and Bill Clinton's alleged sexual relationship with a White House intern named Monica Lewinsky. At one point, Starr persuaded White House staff member Linda Tripp to secretly record her conversations with Lewinsky. As a result of Starr's investigation, eleven people including former Arkansas governor Jim Guy Tucker and Susan and James McDougal, Hillary Clinton's business partners, were convicted of fraud and other crimes. Critics blasted Starr's tactics and close ties to the Republican Party.

In January 1998, news of Clinton's alleged affair with Lewinsky became public. Clinton denied the claim, memorably declaring, "I did not have sexual relations with that woman, Miss Lewinsky." In August 1998, after Clinton was forced to testify to a grand jury, he gave a nationally televised speech admitting having had an inappropriate relationship with Lewinsky. The following month,

*Starr submitted a 445-page report to Congress. The document included sala-
cious details about Clinton and Lewinsky's sexual encounters and accused
Clinton of perjury, obstruction of justice, witness tampering, and abuse of
power. On October 8, 1998, the House of Representatives voted 258-176 to
conduct impeachment hearings. Two months later, the House approved two
articles of impeachment for perjury and obstruction of justice. In February
1999, the Senate acquitted Clinton.*

*This reading features portions of the Starr Report as well as the White
House's response to Starr's findings.*

FOCUS QUESTIONS

1. What accusations does Starr levy against Clinton?
2. How does the Clinton administration respond to Starr's allegations?
3. Did Clinton's actions merit impeachment? Why or why not?
4. Compare Clinton's impeachment to Watergate (Document 25.4). Which
   incident do you find more troubling? Why?

 eferral to the United States House of Representatives pursuant to Title 28,
United States Code, § 595(c)
SUBMITTED BY THE OFFICE OF THE INDEPENDENT COUNSEL
September 9, 1998

INTRODUCTION

As required by Section 595(c) of Title 28 of the United States Code, the Office of the Independent Counsel ("OIC" or "Office") hereby submits substantial
and credible information that President William Jefferson Clinton committed acts
that may constitute grounds for an impeachment.

The information reveals that President Clinton:

lied under oath at a civil deposition while he was a defendant in a sexual
harassment lawsuit; lied under oath to a grand jury; attempted to obstruct justice
by facilitating a witness's plan to refuse to comply with a subpoena; attempted to
obstruct justice by encouraging a witness to file an affidavit that the President
knew would be false, and then by making use of that false affidavit at his own
deposition; lied to potential grand jury witnesses, knowing that they would repeat
those lies before the grand jury; and engaged in a pattern of conduct that was
inconsistent with his constitutional duty to faithfully execute the laws.

The evidence shows that these acts, and others, were part of a pattern that began as an effort to prevent the disclosure of information about the President's
relationship with a former White House intern and employee, Monica S. Lewinsky, and continued as an effort to prevent the information from being disclosed in
an ongoing criminal investigation.

FACTUAL BACKGROUND

In May 1994, Paula Corbin Jones filed a lawsuit against William Jefferson Clinton in the United States District Court for the Eastern District of Arkansas. Ms. Jones alleged that while he was the Governor of Arkansas, President Clinton sexually harassed her during an incident in a Little Rock hotel room....

One sharply disputed issue in the Jones litigation was the extent to which the President would be required to disclose information about sexual relationships he may have had with "other women." Ms. Jones's attorneys sought disclosure of this information, arguing that it was relevant to proving that the President had propositioned Ms. Jones. The President resisted the discovery requests, arguing that evidence of relationships with other women (if any) was irrelevant.

In late 1997, the issue was presented to United States District Judge Susan Webber Wright for resolution. Judge Wright's decision was unambiguous. For purposes of pretrial discovery, President Clinton was required to provide certain information about his alleged relationships with other women....

In mid-December 1997, the President answered one of the written discovery questions posed by Ms. Jones on this issue. When asked to identify all women who were state or federal employees and with whom he had had "sexual relations" since 1986, the President answered under oath: "None." For purposes of this interrogatory, the term "sexual relations" was not defined.

On January 17, 1998, President Clinton was questioned under oath about his relationships with other women in the workplace, this time at a deposition. Judge Wright presided over the deposition. The President was asked numerous questions about his relationship with Monica Lewinsky, by then a 24-year-old former White House intern, White House employee, and Pentagon employee. Under oath and in the presence of Judge Wright, the President denied that he had engaged in a "sexual affair," a "sexual relationship," or "sexual relations" with Ms. Lewinsky. The President also stated that he had no specific memory of having been alone with Ms. Lewinsky, that he remembered few details of any gifts they might have exchanged, and indicated that no one except his attorneys had kept him informed of Ms. Lewinsky's status as a potential witness in the Jones case....

THE SIGNIFICANCE OF THE EVIDENCE OF WRONGDOING

It is not the role of this Office to determine whether the President's actions warrant impeachment by the House and removal by the Senate; those judgments are, of course, constitutionally entrusted to the legislative branch. This Office is authorized, rather, to conduct criminal investigations and to seek criminal prosecutions for matters within its jurisdiction. In carrying out its investigation, however, this Office also has a statutory duty to disclose to Congress information that "may constitute grounds for an impeachment," a task that inevitably requires judgment about the seriousness of the acts revealed by the evidence.

From the beginning, this phase of the OIC's [Office of Independent Counsel] investigation has been criticized as an improper inquiry into the President's personal behavior; indeed, the President himself suggested that specific inquiries into his conduct were part of an effort to "criminalize my private life." The regrettable fact that the investigation has often required witnesses to discuss sensitive personal matters has fueled this perception.

All Americans, including the President, are entitled to enjoy a private family life, free from public or governmental scrutiny. But the privacy concerns raised in this case are subject to limits, three of which we briefly set forth here.

First. The first limit was imposed when the President was sued in federal court for alleged sexual harassment. The evidence in such litigation is often personal. At times, that evidence is highly embarrassing for both plaintiff and defendant....

Third. The third limit is unique to the President. "The Presidency is more than an executive responsibility. It is the inspiring symbol of all that is highest in American purpose and ideals." When he took the Oath of Office in 1993 and again in 1997, President Clinton swore that he would "faithfully execute the Office of President." As the head of the Executive Branch, the President has the constitutional duty to "take Care that the Laws be faithfully executed." The President gave his testimony in the Jones case under oath and in the presence of a federal judge, a member of a co-equal branch of government; he then testified before a federal grand jury, a body of citizens who had themselves taken an oath to seek the truth. In view of the enormous trust and responsibility attendant to his high Office, the President has a manifest duty to ensure that his conduct at all times complies with the law of the land.

In sum, perjury and acts that obstruct justice by any citizen—whether in a criminal case, a grand jury investigation, a congressional hearing, a civil trial, or civil discovery—are profoundly serious matters. When such acts are committed by the President of the United States, we believe those acts "may constitute grounds for an impeachment...."

http://thomas.loc.gov/icreport/.

 RELIMINARY MEMORANDUM CONCERNING REFERRAL OF OFFICE OF INDEPENDENT COUNSEL
September 11, 1998

EXECUTIVE SUMMARY

Summary of Key Points of the President's Case in Anticipation of the Starr Report:

1. The President has acknowledged a serious mistake—an inappropriate relationship with Monica Lewinsky. He has taken responsibility for his actions, and he has apologized to the country, to his friends, leaders of his party, the cabinet and most importantly, his family.

2. This private mistake does not amount to an impeachable action. A relationship outside one's marriage is wrong—and the President admits that. It is not a high crime or misdemeanor. The Constitution specifically states that Congress shall impeach only for "treason, bribery or other high crimes and misdemean-

ors." These words in the Constitution were chosen with great care, and after extensive deliberations.

3. "High crimes and misdemeanors" had a fixed meaning to the Framers of our Constitution—it meant wrongs committed against our system of government. The impeachment clause was designed to protect our country against a President who was using his official powers against the nation, against the American people, against our society. It was never designed to allow a political body to force a President from office for a very personal mistake.

4. Remember—this report is based entirely on allegations obtained by a grand jury—reams and reams of allegations and purported "evidence" that would never be admitted in court, that has never been seen by the President or his lawyers, and that was not subject to cross-examination or any other traditional safeguards to ensure its credibility.

5. Grand juries are not designed to search for truth. They do not and are not intended to ensure credibility, reliability, or simple fairness. They only exist to accuse. Yet this is the process that the Independent Counsel has chosen to provide the "evidence" to write his report.

6. The law defines perjury very clearly. Perjury requires proof that an individual knowingly made a false statement while under oath. Answers to questions that are literally true are not perjury. Even if an answer doesn't directly answer the question asked, it is not perjury if it is true—no accused has an obligation to help his accuser. Answers to fundamentally ambiguous questions also can never be perjury. And nobody can be convicted of perjury based on only one other person's testimony.

7. The President did not commit perjury. Most of the illegal leaks suggesting his testimony was perjurious falsely describe his testimony. First of all, the President never testified in the Jones deposition that he was not alone with Ms. Lewinsky. The President never testified that his relationship with Ms. Lewinsky was the same as with any other intern. To the contrary, he admitted exchanging gifts with her, knowing about her job search, receiving cards and notes from her, and knowing other details of her personal life that made it plain he had a special relationship with her.

8. The President has admitted he had an improper sexual relationship with Ms. Lewinsky. In a civil deposition, he gave narrow answers to ambiguous questions. As a matter of law, those answers could not give rise to a criminal charge of perjury. In the face of the President's admission of his relationship, the disclosure of lurid and salacious allegations can only be intended to humiliate the President and force him from office.

9. There was no obstruction of justice. We believe Betty Currie [Clinton's secretary] testified that Ms. Lewinsky asked her to hold the gifts and that the President never talked to her about the gifts. The President admitted giving and receiving gifts from Ms. Lewinsky when he was asked about it. The

President never asked Ms. Lewinsky to get rid of the gifts and he never asked Ms. Currie to get them. We believe that Ms. Currie's testimony supports the President's.

10. The President never tried to get Ms. Lewinsky a job after she left the White House in order to influence her testimony in the Paula Jones case. The President knew Ms. Lewinsky was unhappy in her Pentagon job after she left the White House and did ask the White House personnel office to treat her fairly in her job search. He never instructed anyone to hire her, or even indicated that he very much wanted it to happen. Ms. Lewinsky was never offered a job at the White House after she left—and it's pretty apparent that if the President had ordered it, she would have been....

12. There was no witness tampering. Betty Currie was not supposed to be a witness in the Paula Jones case. If she was not called or going to be called, it was impossible for any conversations the President had with her to be witness tampering. The President testified that he did not in any way attempt to influence her recollection....

14. Invocation of privileges was not an abuse of power. The President's lawful assertion of privileges in a court of law was only made on the advice of his Counsel, and was in significant measure validated by the courts. The legal claims were advanced sparingly and as a last resort after all attempts at compromise by the White House Counsel's office were rejected to protect the core constitutional and institutional interests of this and future presidencies....

16. The President did not abuse his power by permitting White House staff to comment on the investigation. The President has acknowledged misleading his family, staff and the country about the nature of his relationship with Ms. Lewinsky, and he has apologized and asked for forgiveness. However, this personal failing does not constitute a criminal abuse of power. If allowing aides to repeat misleading statements is a crime, then any number of public officials are guilty of misusing their office for as long as they fail to admit wrong doing in response to any allegation about their activities....

This means that the OIC report is left with nothing but the details of a private sexual relationship, told in graphic details with the intent to embarrass. Given the flimsy and unsubstantiated basis for the accusations, there is a complete lack of any credible evidence to initiate an impeachment inquiry concerning the President. And the principal purpose of this investigation, and the OIC's report, is to embarrass the President and titillate the public by producing a document that is little more than an unreliable, one-sided account of sexual behavior.

Where's Whitewater? The OIC's allegations reportedly include no suggestion of wrongdoing by the President in any of the areas which Mr. Starr spend four years investigating: Whitewater, the FBI files and the White House travel office. What began as an inquiry into a 24-year-old land deal in Arkansas has ended as an inquest into brief, improper personal encounters between the President and Monica

Lewinsky. Despite the exhaustive nature of the OIC's investigation into the Whitewater, FBI files and travel office matters, and a constant stream of suggestions of misconduct in the media over a period of years, to this day the OIC has never exonerated the President or the First Lady of wrongdoing.

White House Publications (http://www.pub.whitehouse.gov/uri-res/I2R?urn:pdi://oma.eop.gov.us/1998/9/11/8.text.1

26.11

THE HIGH-TECH BOOM (1999)

For much of the 1990s, the American economy grew at an astonishing pace. Corporations maximized profits through mergers, reduction of labor costs, and restructuring. The rise of digital technology spawned thousands of new products such as cellular phones, digital cameras, and computers. The "New Economy" created thousands of jobs. Many entrepreneurs gravitated toward the Internet and national interest in "dot-coms" and "e-commerce" appeared boundless. Enthusiasm for technology stocks lifted the Dow Jones Industrial Average over 11,000, its highest rate ever, and spawned the NASDAQ, a stock exchange exclusively for technology shares. Productivity and incomes soared as unemployment and inflation remained low. Between 1994 and 2000, the economy experienced the biggest peacetime expansion in U.S. history. The economy then started to slump and tech stocks collapsed in April 2001. By the fall of 2001, the country was in a recession. A series of scandals at major companies including Enron and World Com further eroded investor confidence. Although the economy began to revive in early 2002, the pace of recovery was slow.

This article from Time *magazine reflects the popular fascination with high-tech endemic in the late 1990s.*

FOCUS QUESTIONS

1. How do the Internet entrepreneurs compare to the first wave of Silicon Valley businessmen such as Bill Gates of Microsoft?
2. Describe the culture and business practices at start-up companies like Maverick Online (later TheMan.com).
3. TheMan.com ceased operations in November 2000. Why do you think the company failed so quickly?
4. How has digital technology changed American life? Are these changes positive or negative? Explain your answers.
5. What does the economic downturn of the early 2000s suggest about the New Economy?

"**H**ave you ever heard of a guy going to a spa on a date?" Calvin Lui, the 27-year-old CEO of Maverick Online, is surveying the company brain trust. Lui has 35 days before the launch of his Internet start-up, a consumer and lifestyle website for men, and he's got another big decision to make.

"I've never done that," says Maverick co-founder Steve Lombardi, "but I'd take it as long as a hot chick was around."

"I wouldn't go to a spa," says Rich Schwerin, the website's editor. "Not unless there was a Japanese woman walking on my back."

Andrew Sugerman, the company's business-development director, admits that he has been to a spa with his wife. "But I would never get a dude to give me a massage. I'm a 100% woman-massage guy," he says.

It takes several more minutes of such debate before Lui makes an executive decision. "All right, getting a massage together is definitely a date," he says. Another testosterone conundrum is solved. The massage date has made the list of 80 assignations that visitors will be able to plan and purchase from Maverick's website—along with the frosty make-your-own-ice-cream date and the steamy strip-poker date.

Unlike their predecessors, Silicon Valley's new entrepreneurs don't spend their time talking about operating systems or Java applications or HTML code. They talk about capturing eyeballs, forging strategic partnerships and "making the dogs eat the dog food." In the '80s they would have been financing junk-bond takeovers. Today these lapsed consultants and investment bankers are fleeing six-figure job offers from Wall Street for the opportunity to build their own empires.

The amazing truth is that in Silicon Valley today they can do it cheaper and faster than anyone has ever done it before. The old fortunes—amassed by Bill Gates, Larry Ellison, David Packard—took years, sometimes more than 10 of them. Now we're talking months. Maverick Online is all of 90 days old. Almost all the ideas involve selling stuff over the Internet and require little more inspiration than walking through a mall and adding to the end of every store's name. But the potential payoff is huge, so everyone is in a rush to get the FMA (first-mover advantage), to do it FBC (faster, bigger, cheaper) and to GBF (get big fast). The goal, of course, is the IPO, initial public offering, in which a hot company converts from private ownership to public, selling shares on the stock market and in the process making its founders Maserati rich.

In the second quarter of this year, venture-capital funding in the U.S. increased 77%, to a record $7.6 billion. More than half went to Internet start-ups. In the wake of the massive IPOs of Web businesses like Amazon.com ($561 million) and eBay ($1.9 billion), venture capitalists (VCs) are eager to take a first-round, $2 million risk on any two guys with a business plan.

Or at least two guys from Stanford's Graduate School of Business, which has become a hothouse for aspiring Internet entrepreneurs. Forty-five students out of this June's graduating class of 360 have already started their own Internet business, more than double the number in 1998. The reason is simple. Stanford M.B.A.s spend two years schmoozing A-list Valley executives and VCs—and other people don't. Garth Saloner, a professor at Stanford, says it works like this:

"You're 27 years old, you are sitting in an auditorium, there's a billionaire in front of you, and you are thinking 'Gee, why not me?'"

And why not Lui and Lombardi, who hatched their business as a class project with two other Stanford students? Last January, while waiting for take-out rotisserie chicken, Lui, who worked as an investment banker after college, had this epiphany: "It would be good if there were just one Man Store," he told Lombardi. "One aisle with stuff for the first date, and a flower aisle for when you screw up with the girl." Lombardi, a former consultant who played football at Cal Poly, instantly saw Lui's vision and volunteered his own embarrassment. On his first anniversary, he bought stacks of fancy stationery for his wife, who doesn't write letters. Only later did he find out that for their paper anniversary, theater tickets would have been appropriate, not to mention more fun. Why wasn't there a website to tell him that? Lui and Lombardi formed Maverick Online a week later.

They considered keeping the Man Store idea to themselves and submitting an inferior project for the class, but decided to trust their classmates with its broad outlines. Over the next six months, Lui and Lombardi worked out of Lombardi's Palo Alto apartment, fitting classes in between meetings with VCs, designers and prospective employees. Commuting the 35 miles between Stanford and San Francisco, they logged more than 2,800 miles and countless uses of the word passion (typical usage: "At the end of the day, this isn't about money. It comes down to passion"). In May they took their business plan to Information Technology Ventures, a small venture-capital firm, and secured $2 million in seed money, some of which they used to pay off the $40,000 tab Lui had amassed on six credit cards.

Two weeks before graduation, they opened an office in San Francisco, rented from Lui's former employer, Lycos. By August, they had 15 employees and a home page. Even by the Valley's standards of secrecy, which make Langley [the headquarters of the CIA] seem gossipy, the founders were notably paranoid, concealing the company behind the stealth name Maverick and insisting that everyone but their parents (probably) sign a three-page nondisclosure agreement before hearing what the company was all about. Last Friday, as its website went live, the company revealed its URL and new name:...

Near the front door to the office, Lui and Lombardi have posted a DAYS TO LAUNCH! countdown and have promised their staff they will both get TheMan.com tattoos if the company meets its deadlines. Lui, a slicked-hair tornado of optimism and new-economy management techniques, is scarily aggressive when he's not overbearing. Roughly four minutes into every conversation, he uncaps a Magic Marker and starts scrawling on the nearest whiteboard. He has decorated the otherwise spartan office with motivational quotes from Steve Young, Jerry Garcia and Hannibal ("We must either find a way or make one"). The newest hire is affectionately referred to as the FNG (f_____ new guy) and is forced to carry a Rugrats doll and order take-out Chinese food, the nightly company meal. "How do you indoctrinate people into your culture? You baptize them," Lui says. "We want everybody to drink out of the same vat of Kool-Aid." Before leaving on Fridays, employees have to rate themselves publicly, from one to four stars, on the week's performance. Lui says the foldout desks and below-average salaries keep his employees "hungry" for the eventual IPO. "We say, 'If you're willing to take a pay cut now so that your equity is worth more later, that's great.' If people don't jump at that, they don't fit." Lui, who keeps a case of caffeinated peppermints near his desk, ends meetings by barking "All right, dudes, let's rock and roll!" and has no shortage of self-assurance, already drawing analogies between TheMan.com and one of his former employers, the Walt Disney Co. "This could be a major, major public company," he says.

But right now TheMan.com is still just another e-commerce start-up trying to urge investors, corporate partners and new recruits to buy in. On one afternoon before the site launched, Lui set up a conference call with an executive from Starwood Hotels, hoping to persuade him to sell getaways through TheMan.com. For the first 10 minutes, Lui refuses to "open the kimono" and reveal details about the company. He rattles off the names of TheMan.com's board members—from Lycos CEO Bob Davis to Eric Weider of *Muscle & Fitness* magazine—to gain more credibility. "You're a smart guy, you worked at Disney, you went to Stanford business school. I believe you," the executive says. But when he suggests waiting six months before cementing a partnership, Lui's kimono winds up in a crumpled ball, as he gives away the entire business plan. Even so, the Starwood exec wraps up the call. Lui slumps a little. "I understand that right now we're a zit compared to everybody else," he says. "But in a year, we're not going to be a zit."

It's impossible to suppress Lui's bravado. While several employees romp through the office trailing Sugerman's dog, Lui spends Friday afternoon cajoling Erin Kelley, a 28-year-old accountant, to join the company as a financial manager. "Where are you right now?" he asks. Kelley says the hours at her current job allow her to play soccer every night; working 80 hours a week would probably put an end to that. "How long is a soccer game?" Lui asks. "Forty-five minutes," Kelley says. "Well," Lui declares, "you can come back here afterwards."

"I want you to make me a promise," he says, leaning in and sounding like Lyndon Johnson. "If there are any concerns, I want you to let me know. I want you to be open with me." Kelley says, "I'm a woman. My gut's going to tell me what to do." Her gut says, No way.

The labor market in the Valley is so tight that start-up CEOs spend most of their time recruiting. New entrepreneurs speak in religious tones about the importance of bringing in "the A people," of getting the right "office mix," about assembling "the team." (Typical usage: "At the end of the day, it's not the business plan that matters. It's all about the team.") That job is slightly easier for pre-IPO firms, which can lure young bodies with fat equity packages, than it is for larger Valley companies, which can offer more security but less potential reward. Radio stations are jammed with spots from companies such as Oracle that beg for employees.

Companies operating in stealth mode have a perverse advantage in recruiting. Kris Hagerman, founder of a start-up called Affinia, which helps people sell stuff on their personal websites, uncovered this phenomenon last spring when he set up a table at a career fair at Stanford's business school. He called his company "Trade Routes Inc., a hush-hush Valley start-up." That was it for details. "You're in for a really tough night," a recruiter for an established software company told him, figuring Hagerman would get no takers. Within five minutes, a line started snaking around the table. By the end of the event, Affinia had 150 resumes; the Compaq recruiter left 45 minutes early.

Never before have the unemployed been so cocky. At a job fair at San Francisco's Exploratorium hosted by a headhunting software company called BridgePath, 2,400, applicants approach potential employers from various start-ups. "I'm Danny. What's the two-minute overview?" an applicant with a mouthful of nachos says by way of introduction to Jeff Reed and Pratap Mukherjee, ex-consultants who are launching an online used-car site. Their company, like most of the start-ups at the job fair, is still in stealth mode. Reed and Mukherjee err by being the only company not to hand out free stuff. They should also have hired a deejay, as did Topica; a clown, a juggler and a woman on stilts, as did Trapezo; or simply have run up to everyone the second they walk in and ask, "Are you an engineer?," as Entera is doing. At the fair, Mukherjee runs into job seeker Dave Morris, who interviewed the day before. "I'm being careful about who I'm handing my resume to. I don't have the bandwidth to meet with everyone," he says.

Mukherjee and Reed's company was born as an entry in an entrepreneurship contest at Stanford. Mukherjee had heard a radio commercial for the auction site eBay, followed by another ad for a used-car center, and thought, What about an auction site for used cars? Reed and Mukherjee pulled the idea out of the competition after reaching the semifinals, opting for secrecy over the paltry $25,000 prize. Good choice. By the time the winner was announced, Reed and Mukherjee had secured $2 million from the venture-capital firm Draper Fisher Jurvetson. Their Stanford connections helped. As an undergraduate, Mukherjee lived in a dorm with partner Steve Jurvetson; Reed played Ultimate Frisbee with director Warren Packard. Without those personal ties, their odds of securing funding would have been slimmer. Out of the 10,000 business plans the firm receives annually, Draper backs 15. "Our first meeting lasted, like, an hour," says Reed, "and we never even talked about the website."

Like a growing number of new Web entrepreneurs, Reed and Mukherjee opened their office in San Francisco's edgy South of Market (SoMa) district—two blocks from Maverick Online—an area that's long been popular with Web designers and multimedia firms. In contrast to most start-ups, people at BestOffer work in offices with doors rather than at makeshift desks. That's about their only perk. As of September, the employee health plan was to be married to someone who has a health plan.

On the basis of the conversation at one staff meeting, it seems that the company's fortunes will rely not on a killer app but on something called the Fluke, a portable diagnostic tool the company's mechanics can use to analyze a seller's car before it is put up for auction on the BestOffer site. "Why don't more people use the Fluke?" Reed asks BestOffer's seven employees, none of whom know much about computers or cars. "A lot of people are using the Fluke," says an employee,

Chris Miller. "Five out of 10 mechanics have a Fluke in their toolbox." This gets everyone excited. "We can get a ton of Flukes tomorrow," Ed Diffendal says. There is much celebration.

Armed with that good news, Reed and Mukherjee feel confident about a meeting with Packard, their VC. They show Packard their just-completed home page ("Great! I think we can go public now," he jokes), then get reprimanded for offering a prospective marketing hire too much money. Packard suggests they offer $20,000 less. "You've got to set the trend for everyone else coming in," he says. "You've got to be careful." Mukherjee nods, but looks as if he's been told he's not getting dessert. "People think that entrepreneurs don't have bosses, but that's not really the case," says Mukherjee.

Though you wouldn't guess it from their business-casual demeanor, Reed and Mukherjee have a feverish launch schedule ahead of them, planning to go live early next month. They are rushing to enter a crowded space. eBay has started selling cars, and Mukherjee is doing opposition research on two other auto-related start-ups, iMobile and CarsDirect.

Other Stanford classmates have been overrun by faster movers. While at Stanford last December, Matt Hobart, 28, began writing a business plan for an online pet-supply company. Bad call. In April, after he had sealed commitments from investors and future employees, several other pet sites—including Pets.com, Petstore.com, Petsmart.com, and Petopia.com—announced that they were preparing to launch. Hobart had no choice but to return the money he had raised and pack it in. "There's no such concept as sitting in a garage and starting a company anymore," he says. "If you have an idea, it's safe to assume that four or five people have the same idea. But it's not the person with the best idea who wins. It's the person who can execute quickly." Hobart is now launching an educational website, TheScience.com, and plans to rent office space in San Francisco from Petopia.com, one of the companies that put him out of business the first time.

E-commerce niches are getting claimed so quickly that there might not be time for business school anymore. Aaron Ross, 27, was an undergraduate at Stanford but turned down a spot in this fall's class at the B school to start his own company, EquipmentLeasing.com. Unable to afford any advertising more expensive than free beer, Ross threw a happy hour last month on the roof of the Potrero Brewing Co. in San Francisco. He sent out invitations to 30 friends via the party-planning website Evite. Two hundred people showed up. "It's all about the buzz," Ross said, basking in the early-evening sun and in his sudden celebrity. "I can't explain it. It's like magic."

This is why people come to the Bay Area, when they could just as easily launch a dog-food site from Wichita, Kans. Internet entrepreneurs network tirelessly, going to happy hours and barbecues to glad-hand investors and glean tips about how to find law firms, Web designers, and publicists. Entrepreneurs from this year's Stanford business-school class gather for a monthly working barbecue that is perhaps the most exclusive ticket in Silicon Valley—so exclusive that the organizers had to take a vote on whether to invite entrepreneurs from the class of 1998.

It's impossible at these gatherings to find anyone talking about anything but one another's Internet start-ups. The new entrepreneurs are oddly proud of knowing nothing about politics, sports or pop culture. And they don't mind admitting that they have no social lives. "Dates bore me," says Ross. "Especially dates with women who aren't in the tech industry. That's my life. If they can't relate to that, then what do we have?"

Perhaps Ross is another potential customer for TheMan.com. So is Lui, for that matter. By the time his site launched last Friday, Lui was in his fourth month of self-imposed exile from the real world. Working 17-hour days, he's gone on one date all summer. And that was for work. "I need to stay in touch with the social world, given our topic area," he says. "I'm married to this now."

Soon, thanks to his site, he will be able to create endless numbers of dates in seconds. His company's research has categorized women into seven archetypes, including "the princess," "the career/professional" and "the trendy/wild." The company's team of engineers has figured out a way to make dating as predictable as an episode of *Providence*. "Once we knew what a princess finds romantic," says Lombardi, "then it was number crunching. It's based on a least-squares algorithm, and it tells you what date is the best match." In the future, apparently, no one will have sex.

On one Thursday afternoon 29 days before the launch, TheMan.com's programmers are hammering out the code that will run the website. One of them lets out a whoop, and everyone rushes to huddle around a computer screen. Mouths agape, they look as if they're witnessing a birth, even though most of them have no idea what they're watching. "We have stuff coming in for the first time," yelps Pravin Kumar, the company's 36-year-old chief engineer. "Stuff is coming from and going to the database!" He turns to Lui and gives him a high five. "You're getting that tattoo!"

That tattoo may prove to be the only thing of permanence for Lui and Lombardi. If TheMan.com hits IPO pay dirt in two years, the pair will probably collect their stock options and step aside to let a gray-haired manager run the company. Of course, the chances are high that the company will go under before that. Only 1 in 30 companies that receive venture-capital funding ultimately goes public. But none of the Valley's new entrepreneurs are paying attention to that—in part because many are congenitally optimistic but also because in Silicon Valley there's no such thing as risk. Should people choose not to buy strip-poker date packages over the Internet, Lui and Lombardi can go back to their VC in two years, wiser from their experience, and get even more money for their next idea. Nor is the tattoo a risk. If the entire Internet economy boom goes bust, they can return to their consulting jobs wearing their failed-start-up tattoos like designer labels. Even Kumar, the engineer, embraces the illogic of the system. "No other place rewards failure like Silicon Valley," he says. "If this is the company that makes it big, then great. If not, I'll do it on my own."

Romesh Ratnesar and Joel Stein, "This Week's Model," *Time* (September 27, 1999), pp. 70-77.

26.12

THE BATTLE IN SEATTLE (1999)

In recent decades, globalization has transformed economic and cultural interactions worldwide. While critics view globalization as an attack on traditional values, local cultures, national sovereignty, workers' rights, and the environment, supporters applaud it for fostering democracy, market economics, and individualism. Whatever one's opinion, globalization is an escapable part of daily life. The Internet, cellular phones, Nike, McDonald's, CNN, Disney, satellite television, and cheap air travel are only a few symbols of the globalized world. While it seems unlikely that globalization will supplant nation-states or create a homogenized world culture, it is clear that it raises important questions about international business practices, labor relations, environmental protection, and technology.

In November 1999, anti-globalization protests at the World Trade Organization (WTO) meeting in Seattle, Washington drew international attention. Established by the 1994 General Agreement on Tariffs and Trade (GATT), the WTO is an international organization charged with supervising and liberalizing global trade. Because many opponents of globalization criticize it on economic grounds, protestors target the WTO, as well as the International Monetary Fund (IMF) and World Bank. Ironically, anti-globalization groups use the Internet, itself a tool of globalization, to mobilize demonstrations. Approximately 50,000 people gathered in Seattle to stage a variety of mostly peaceful protests. But violent factions clashed with police who responded with tear gas and rubber bullets. By the time the WTO meeting ended, Seattle sustained more than three million dollars in property damage. Similar demonstrations engulfed meetings of the World Bank and IMF held in Washington, D.C. and Genoa, Italy. When IMF and World Bank delegates met in 2002, they congregated in an isolated Canadian resort in order to avoid additional protests.

In this feature story from Salon.com, David Moberg examines the WTO protests in Seattle.

FOCUS QUESTIONS

1. How does Moberg describe the atmosphere in Seattle?
2. Who is demonstrating? What are their major criticisms of globalization?
3. What is your opinion of globalization? How do you think that it will change the world during your lifetime?

U nited Steelworkers of America secretary-treasurer Leo Girard was busy explaining to a group of foreign delegates to the World Trade Organization why they couldn't get through the human blockade of protesters sitting in and milling about the streets of Seattle. "We're starting the revolution in America here today," he explained matter-of-factly, a big smile beneath his moustache.

It was easy to understand the hyperbole as the protests unfolded Tuesday morning, preventing the opening of formal WTO activities. Ten years ago, who would have thought that Teamsters and kids in dreadlocks would be marching together, let alone under the banner of "fair trade"? The WTO has united labor and the radical, countercultural left in a way the anti-war movement never could.

Things turned uglier Tuesday night, when police charged protesters who refused to disperse after Mayor Paul Schell declared a 7 p.m. to dawn curfew in the city. Many of the trained non-violent protesters and labor activists who'd descended on Seattle had left for dinner, or a well-attended WTO debate featuring Ralph Nader.

That left behind a harder-core direct-action contingent, some of whom had been spoiling for confrontation. Police fired tear gas, and Gov. Gary Locke called in the National Guard, expected to arrive Wednesday—the same day as President Clinton.

But the day started more peacefully, at a park near the city's famous Pike Place Market, where thousands of protesters gathered in the pre-dawn dark as a chilly rain fell. Singers, rappers and speakers talked about the giant, labor-organized rally coming up later in the day, and the stop-work action taken that same morning by longshoremen up and down the West Coast. They displayed their varied causes with costumes and street theater.

Placards proclaimed, "Secrets are not democracy" and "No Globalization Without Representation," while others declared support for rebels in Chiapas, human rights in Burma and the ethical treatment of animals. People dressed up as dolphins and sea turtles, both of which are endangered by WTO decisions rejecting U.S. laws as trade barriers. Then there was Genetically Modified Man, a costumed character in street theater, one of many objectors to bioengineered food.

The early morning protesters snaked their way through the streets near the Paramount Theater where the opening session was scheduled. Police, carrying clubs and tear gas, wearing riot helmets and gas masks, lined up across the street. Protesters linked hands or sat down in the streets, blocking access to the theater. A few groups—mainly masked young people dressed all in black—tried and occasionally succeeded in breaking windows in a McDonald's, a Nordstrom and other downtown stores. But plenty of others gave the whole affair a joyous flavor by juggling, dancing, playing music and wheeling kids in strollers.

The vast majority were peaceful. When police pulled up in an armored vehicle and began using tear gas, most began chanting, "No violence, peaceful protest." Eventually police made a dozen arrests in the morning, mainly of people who had consciously decided to be arrested as an act of civil disobedience. Police shot some rubber bullets and sprayed a form of tear gas at demonstrators during the morning.

But as the morning blockades slowed down, the action picked up in the stadium north of downtown. There were speeches by labor leaders from the United States and around the world as well as environmentalists and other allies, such as Students Against Sweatshops.

Then the labor delegations began their march downtown. The odd juxtapositions continued. Greenpeace sponsored a green condom made of about 30 foods (the message: "WTO—Practice Safe Trade"), and a contingent of young women with bared breasts chanted for justice with slogans like "No BGH"—the artificial hormone used to stimulate cow milk production—as a giant Steelworkers dirigible floated over their heads.

At the head of the march as it headed toward Seattle's convention center, John Goodman, a Steelworker locked out by Kaiser Aluminum in a contract dispute, carried a banner linking two of the crucial themes of the protests—the threat of the kind of trading regime enforced by the WTO to labor rights and the environment. Kaiser's owner also controls Pacific Lumber, which has been attacked for clear-cutting Northern California forests.

"What brought me here is concern for humanity and our environment that's being destroyed through the world and about the third-world countries that are being exploited," Goodman said. "These people are our brothers and sisters."

The labor movement provided most of the bodies, from a wide variety of unions—Steelworkers, Teamsters, longshoremen, public workers, building trades workers, farm workers. But unlike the labor movement of old, unions embraced a wide coalition of groups whose message they did not control. On WTO issues, organized labor gives primary emphasis to finding ways to enforce core, internationally recognized labor rights —the right to organize and the prohibition of child labor, forced labor and discrimination. But it has also endorsed the goals of environmentalists and advocates of consumer health.

Some unionists supported the militant action by the early morning protesters, who succeeded in disrupting the beginning of the WTO meeting. "It's not enough to get a seat at the table," argued Vic Thorpe, the retiring general secretary of the International Chemical, Energy and Mine Workers, as he watched the street protests. "This is a better protest than to be conferring inside the hall, and in a real sense it's more democratic."

The overwhelming sense of the march was of a magically coherent protest by a staggering range of people —guys in union windbreakers and punks with pierced cheeks, high school students and the elderly—brought together by opposition to the WTO and what they see as a corporate world order that rolls over the needs of young women in sweatshops, sea turtles, displaced American factory hands and anybody who eats food, drinks water or breathes the air.

Despite the diversity of causes, there was a remarkable unity in the message: The WTO and its free-trade rules are the tools of corporate interests, and the losers are the majority of people in the world and the environment. "The WTO gives rights and powers to corporations and takes power away from people," argued 19-year-old Adam Fargason, a University of Alabama student who credits his political awakening to linguist-writer Noam Chomsky and Dead Kennedys rocker Jello Biafra. "It violates democracy."

As the labor rally broke up and marchers headed back to their buses, there were some continued skirmishes, as police fired more gas and the contents of a dumpster burned in the middle of an intersection.

The WTO did accomplish something remarkable: It brought together strains of protest that rarely even talk to each other, let alone act together. "Everything is so divided, but with one spark, everything comes together," Fargason said. "I think that's what's going on here, and it will keep going."

David Moberg, "Bare Breasts, Green Condoms, and Rubber Bullets," Salon.com, News, December 1, 1999, http://www.salon.com/news/feature/1999/12/01/wtoprotest/print.html.

26.13

GEORGE W. BUSH ADDRESSES THE NATION (2001)

On September 11, 2001, the world witnessed the deadliest terrorist attack in its history. That morning, nineteen Islamic extremists hijacked four commercial airplanes, flying two into the World Trade Center in New York City and one into the Pentagon in Washington, D.C. Two towers of the World Trade Center soon collapsed. After passengers tackled their hijackers, the fourth plane crashed in a field southeast of Pittsburgh, Pennsylvania instead of reaching its intended target, either the U.S. Capitol or the White House. The incidents left more than 3,000 people dead.

Within days of the 9-11 attacks, the nineteen Saudi hijackers were identified and linked to Osama bin Laden, leader of the al-Qaeda *terrorist network. A millionaire and fundamentalist Muslim, bin Laden pledged to destroy the United States and the Saudi monarchy. Using his fortune and a wide network of associates, bin Laden orchestrated several attacks on Americans including bombings of the U.S. embassies in Kenya and Tanzania and the* U.S.S. Cole.

The Bush administration responded immediately to the 9-11 incidents. Backed by a multinational coalition against terrorism, U.S. soldiers and intelligence operatives began a global hunt for members of al-Qaeda. *In October 2001, American and British forces launched air strikes on Afghanistan, whose Taliban regime harbored bin Laden and his terrorist training camps. By year's end, the Taliban collapsed, but bin Laden escaped. In the United States, Attorney General John Ashcroft issued several directives limiting access to government information and authorizing the secret detention and deportation of suspected terrorists. Congress passed the USA Patriot Act granting the FBI and other law enforcement agencies broad access to medical, financial, and academic records. The law also significantly expanded the government's ability to conduct surveillance. At the same time, the U.S. Postal Service, airlines, office complexes, stadiums, and many other institutions implemented new security procedures. Although it will take years to assess fully the implications of the "war on terrorism," it is difficult to overstate its immediate impact on American society.*

In this speech, President George W. Bush addresses a joint session of Congress and prepares the nation for the "war on terrorism."

———————■———————

FOCUS QUESTIONS

1. How does Bush describe the domestic and international responses to 9-11? How did you respond to news of the 9-11 attacks?
2. How does Bush depict *al-Queda* and the Taliban?
3. Why and how does Bush appeal to Muslims?
4. According to Bush, what will winning the "war on terror" require? What has changed about American life since 9-11? Do you approve of the way that the government is conducting the "war on terrorism"? Why or why not?

September 20, 2001

In the normal course of events, Presidents come to this chamber to report on the state of the Union. Tonight, no such report is needed. It has already been delivered by the American people.

We have seen it in the courage of passengers, who rushed terrorists to save others on the ground—passengers like an exceptional man named Todd Beamer....

We have seen the state of our Union in the endurance of rescuers, working past exhaustion. We have seen the unfurling of flags, the lighting of candles, the giving of blood, the saying of prayers—in English, Hebrew, and Arabic. We have seen the decency of a loving and giving people who have made the grief of strangers their own.

My fellow citizens, for the last nine days, the entire world has seen for itself the state of our Union—and it is strong.

Tonight we are a country awakened to danger and called to defend freedom. Our grief has turned to anger, and anger to resolution. Whether we bring our enemies to justice, or bring justice to our enemies, justice will be done.

I thank the Congress for its leadership at such an important time. All of America was touched on the evening of the tragedy to see Republicans and Democrats joined together on the steps of this Capitol, singing "God Bless America." And you did more than sing; you acted, by delivering $40 billion to rebuild our communities and meet the needs of our military....

And on behalf of the American people, I thank the world for its outpouring of support. America will never forget the sounds of our National Anthem playing at

Buckingham Palace, on the streets of Paris, and at Berlin's Brandenburg Gate. We will not forget South Korean children gathering to pray outside our embassy in Seoul, or the prayers of sympathy offered at a mosque in Cairo.We will not forget moments of silence and days of mourning in Australia and Africa and Latin America.

Nor will we forget the citizens of 80 other nations who died with our own: dozens of Pakistanis; more than 130 Israelis; more than 250 citizens of India; men and women from El Salvador, Iran, Mexico and Japan; and hundreds of British citizens. America has no truer friend than Great Britain. Once again, we are joined together in a great cause—so honored the British Prime Minister [Tony Blair] has crossed an ocean to show his unity of purpose with America. Thank you for coming, friend.

On September the 11th, enemies of freedom committed an act of war against our country. Americans have known wars—but for the past 136 years, they have been wars on foreign soil, except for one Sunday in 1941. Americans have known the casualties of war—but not at the center of a great city on a peaceful morning. Americans have known surprise attacks—but never before on thousands of civilians. All of this was brought upon us in a single day—and night fell on a different world, a world where freedom itself is under attack.

Americans have many questions tonight. Americans are asking: Who attacked our country? The evidence we have gathered all points to a collection of loosely affiliated terrorist organizations known as *al Qaeda*.They are the same murderers indicted for bombing American embassies in Tanzania and Kenya, and responsible for bombing the *USS Cole*.

Al Qaeda is to terror what the mafia is to crime. But its goal is not making money; its goal is remaking the world—and imposing its radical beliefs on people everywhere.

The terrorists practice a fringe form of Islamic extremism that has been rejected by Muslim scholars and the vast majority of Muslim clerics—a fringe movement that perverts the peaceful teachings of Islam. The terrorists' directive commands them to kill Christians and Jews, to kill all Americans, and make no distinction among military and civilians, including women and children.

This group and its leader—a person named Osama bin Laden—are linked to many other organizations in different countries, including the Egyptian Islamic Jihad and the Islamic Movement of Uzbekistan. There are thousands of these terrorists in more than 60 countries. They are recruited from their own nations and neighborhoods and brought to camps in places like Afghanistan, where they are trained in the tactics of terror. They are sent back to their homes or sent to hide in countries around the world to plot evil and destruction.

The leadership of *al Qaeda* has great influence in Afghanistan and supports the Taliban regime in controlling most of that country. In Afghanistan, we see *al Qaeda*'s vision for the world.

Afghanistan's people have been brutalized—many are starving and many have fled. Women are not allowed to attend school. You can be jailed for owning a television. Religion can be practiced only as their leaders dictate. A man can be jailed in Afghanistan if his beard is not long enough.

The United States respects the people of Afghanistan—after all, we are currently its largest source of humanitarian aid—but we condemn the Taliban regime. It is not only repressing its own people, it is threatening people everywhere by sponsoring and sheltering and supplying terrorists. By aiding and abetting murder, the Taliban regime is committing murder.

And tonight, the United States of America makes the following demands on the Taliban: Deliver to United States authorities all the leaders of *al Qaeda* who hide in your land. Release all foreign nationals, including American citizens, you have unjustly imprisoned. Protect foreign journalists, diplomats and aid workers in your country. Close immediately and permanently every terrorist training camp in Afghanistan, and hand over every terrorist, and every person in their support structure, to appropriate authorities. Give the United States full access to terrorist training camps, so we can make sure they are no longer operating.

These demands are not open to negotiation or discussion. The Taliban must act, and act immediately. They will hand over the terrorists, or they will share in their fate.

I also want to speak tonight directly to Muslims throughout the world. We respect your faith. It's practiced freely by many millions of Americans, and by millions more in countries that America counts as friends. Its teachings are good and peaceful, and those who commit evil in the name of Allah blaspheme the name of Allah. The terrorists are traitors to their own faith, trying, in effect, to hijack Islam itself. The enemy of America is not our many Muslim friends; it is not our many Arab friends. Our enemy is a radical network of terrorists, and every government that supports them.

Our war on terror begins with *al Qaeda*, but it does not end there. It will not end until every terrorist group of global reach has been found, stopped and defeated.

Americans are asking, why do they hate us? They hate what we see right here in this chamber—a democratically elected government. Their leaders are self-appointed. They hate our freedoms—our freedom of religion, our freedom of speech, our freedom to vote and assemble and disagree with each other.

They want to overthrow existing governments in many Muslim countries, such as Egypt, Saudi Arabia, and Jordan. They want to drive Israel out of the Middle East. They want to drive Christians and Jews out of vast regions of Asia and Africa.

These terrorists kill not merely to end lives, but to disrupt and end a way of life. With every atrocity, they hope that America grows fearful, retreating from the world and forsaking our friends. They stand against us, because we stand in their way.

We are not deceived by their pretenses to piety. We have seen their kind before. They are the heirs of all the murderous ideologies of the 20th century. By sacrificing human life to serve their radical visions—by abandoning every value except the will to power—they follow in the path of fascism, and Nazism, and totalitarianism. And they will follow that path all the way, to where it ends: in history's unmarked grave of discarded lies.

Americans are asking: How will we fight and win this war? We will direct every resource at our command—every means of diplomacy, every tool of intelligence, every instrument of law enforcement, every financial influence, and every necessary weapon of war—to the disruption and to the defeat of the global terror network.

This war will not be like the war against Iraq a decade ago, with a decisive liberation of territory and a swift conclusion. It will not look like the air war above Kosovo two years ago, where no ground troops were used and not a single American was lost in combat.

Our response involves far more than instant retaliation and isolated strikes. Americans should not expect one battle, but a lengthy campaign, unlike any other we have ever seen. It may include dramatic strikes, visible on TV, and covert operations, secret even in success. We will starve terrorists of funding, turn them one against another, drive them from place to place, until there is no refuge or no rest. And we will pursue nations that provide aid or safe haven to terrorism. Every nation, in every region, now has a decision to make. Either you are with us, or you are with the terrorists. From this day forward, any nation that continues to harbor or support terrorism will be regarded by the United States as a hostile regime.

Our nation has been put on notice: We are not immune from attack. We will take defensive measures against terrorism to protect Americans. Today, dozens of federal departments and agencies, as well as state and local governments, have responsibilities affecting homeland security. These efforts must be coordinated at the highest level. So tonight I announce the creation of a Cabinet-level position reporting directly to me—the Office of Homeland Security.

And tonight I also announce a distinguished American to lead this effort, to strengthen American security: a military veteran, an effective governor, a true patriot, a trusted friend—Pennsylvania's Tom Ridge. He will lead, oversee and coordinate a comprehensive national strategy to safeguard our country against terrorism, and respond to any attacks that may come.

These measures are essential. But the only way to defeat terrorism as a threat to our way of life is to stop it, eliminate it, and destroy it where it grows.

Many will be involved in this effort, from FBI agents to intelligence operatives to the reservists we have called to active duty. All deserve our thanks, and all have our prayers. And tonight, a few miles from the damaged Pentagon, I have a message for our military: Be ready. I've called the Armed Forces to alert, and there is a reason. The hour is coming when America will act, and you will make us proud.

This is not, however, just America's fight. And what is at stake is not just America's freedom. This is the world's fight. This is civilization's fight. This is the fight of all who believe in progress and pluralism, tolerance and freedom.

We ask every nation to join us. We will ask, and we will need, the help of police forces, intelligence services, and banking systems around the world. The

United States is grateful that many nations and many international organizations have already responded—with sympathy and with support. Nations from Latin America, to Asia, to Africa, to Europe, to the Islamic world. Perhaps the NATO Charter reflects best the attitude of the world: An attack on one is an attack on all.

The civilized world is rallying to America's side. They understand that if this terror goes unpunished, their own cities, their own citizens may be next. Terror, unanswered, can not only bring down buildings, it can threaten the stability of legitimate governments. And you know what—we're not going to allow it.

Americans are asking: What is expected of us? I ask you to live your lives, and hug your children. I know many citizens have fears tonight, and I ask you to be calm and resolute, even in the face of a continuing threat.

I ask you to uphold the values of America, and remember why so many have come here. We are in a fight for our principles, and our first responsibility is to live by them. No one should be singled out for unfair treatment or unkind words because of their ethnic background or religious faith.

I ask you to continue to support the victims of this tragedy with your contributions. Those who want to give can go to a central source of information, libertyunites.org, to find the names of groups providing direct help in New York, Pennsylvania, and Virginia.

The thousands of FBI agents who are now at work in this investigation may need your cooperation, and I ask you to give it.

I ask for your patience, with the delays and inconveniences that may accompany tighter security; and for your patience in what will be a long struggle.

I ask your continued participation and confidence in the American economy. Terrorists attacked a symbol of American prosperity. They did not touch its source. America is successful because of the hard work, and creativity, and enterprise of our people. These were the true strengths of our economy before September 11th, and they are our strengths today.

And, finally, please continue praying for the victims of terror and their families, for those in uniform, and for our great country. Prayer has comforted us in sorrow, and will help strengthen us for the journey ahead.

Tonight I thank my fellow Americans for what you have already done and for what you will do. And ladies and gentlemen of the Congress, I thank you, their representatives, for what you have already done and for what we will do together.

Tonight, we face new and sudden national challenges. We will come together to improve air safety, to dramatically expand the number of air marshals on domestic flights, and take new measures to prevent hijacking. We will come together to promote stability and keep our airlines flying, with direct assistance during this emergency.

We will come together to give law enforcement the additional tools it needs to track down terror here at home. We will come together to strengthen our intelligence capabilities to know the plans of terrorists before they act, and find them before they strike.

We will come together to take active steps that strengthen America's economy, and put our people back to work.

Tonight we welcome two leaders who embody the extraordinary spirit of all New Yorkers: Governor George Pataki, and Mayor Rudolph Giuliani. As a symbol of America's resolve, my administration will work with Congress, and these two leaders, to show the world that we will rebuild New York City.

After all that has just passed—all the lives taken, and all the possibilities and hopes that died with them—it is natural to wonder if America's future is one of fear. Some speak of an age of terror. I know there are struggles ahead, and dangers to face. But this country will define our times, not be defined by them. As long as the United States of America is determined and strong, this will not be an age of terror; this will be an age of liberty, here and across the world.

Great harm has been done to us. We have suffered great loss. And in our grief and anger we have found our mission and our moment. Freedom and fear are at war. The advance of human freedom—the great achievement of our time, and the great hope of every time—now depends on us. Our nation—this generation—will lift a dark threat of violence from our people and our future. We will rally the world to this cause by our efforts, by our courage. We will not tire, we will not falter, and we will not fail....

http://www.whitehouse.gov/news/releases/2001/09/20010920-8.ht.

SECONDARY SOURCE

━━━━━━━━━━━━━ ■ ━━━━━━━━━━━━━

DAVID BROOKS, "ONE NATION, SLIGHTLY DIVISIBLE"

In the early twenty-first century, Americans confront new anxieties and an increasingly complex nation. While the 2000 election reflected profound differences among U.S. citizens, the wave of patriotism following 9-11 displayed great unity. In this article, David Brooks, senior editor at The Weekly Standard *and a contributing editor at* Newsweek *and the* Atlantic Monthly, *contemplates the issues dividing the country and what these differences suggest about American national identity.*

Go to your *Speaking of America* CD-ROM to read "One Nation, Slightly Divisible."

---∎---

FOCUS QUESTIONS

1. According to Brooks, what distinguishes "Red America" and "Blue America"? Which description most accurately defines where you live? Why?
2. What does Brooks believe that these differences suggest about class and culture in the United States? Do you agree or disagree with his claims? Why?
3. In the aftermath of the 2000 Election and 9-11, does Brooks think that Americans are divided or unified? Why? Do you agree or disagree? Why?

AMERICAN JOURNEY ONLINE

---∎---

http://ajaccesss.wadsworth.com [†]

About the Cold War
— In <u>The Cold War</u>
Documents
- Ronald Reagan, Address to the Nation, October 13, 1986
- Lev Semeyko, *Izvestia* Article, August 13, 1987
- John Simpson, Death in the Square (1990)
- John Simpson, Tumbling Down (1990)
- John Lewis Gaddis, The Cold War, The Long Peace, and The Future (1992)
- Walter LaFeber, An End to Which Cold War? (1992)
- Raymond Garthoff, Why Did the Cold War Arise, and Why Did It End? (1992)

Images
- Reykjavik Summit (1986)
- Reagan and Gorbachev Sign Arms Accord (1987)
- Pope and Reagan Share Perspectives (1987)
- Mr. Gorbachev, Tear Down This Wall (1987)
- German Hammers at Berlin Wall (1989)
- Romanian Coup (1989)
- Man Versus the State (1989)
- Dan Adams, Soviet Invasion of Afghanistan (1990)

[†] Enter password, choose the Archive indicated above, click on Contents, choose
•Documents, •Images, or •Multimedia, and click on the title of the item.

About the Iran-Contra Affair
— In The Cold War
  Document
  - U.S. Congress, Executive Summary to Report of the Special Committees Investigating the Iran-Contra Affair (1988)
  Images
  - Reagan Aide Resigns (1985)
  - Contra Rebels (undated)
  - North Testifies (1987)
  - Trial of Oliver North (1987)

About the Persian Gulf War/The Middle East
— In The Cold War
  Images
  - Popular General Colin Powell (1989)
  - Clinton Hosts Middle East Summit (1993)

About Domestic Politics
— In Civil Rights in the United States
  Images
  - Bill Clinton (undated)
— In The Constitution and Supreme Court
  Images
  - Bill and Hillary Clinton (1994)

About Law and Law Enforcement
— In Civil Rights in the United States
  Documents
  - U.S. Congress, Freedom of Information Act Request Letter (1990)
  - U.S. Congress, Hate Crimes Statistics Act (1990)
  - U.S. Supreme Court, *R.A.V. v. City of St. Paul* (1992)
  - U.S. Supreme Court, *Lee v. Weisman* (1992)
  - U.S. Congress, Hate Crime Sentencing Enhancement Act (1994)
  - State of New Jersey, Megan's Law (1994)
  - U.S. Congress, Church Arson Prevention Act (1996)
  - U.S. Supreme Court, *United States v. Virginia* (1996)
  - U.S. Congress, Electronic Communications Privacy Act (1996)
  - Deval Patrick Interview (1997)
  - Libertarian Party, Do Bigots Have First Amendment Rights? (1997)
  - Bill Clinton, On the Central Intelligence Agency (1997)
  - Isabelle Katz Pinzler, Remarks to National Conference of State Legislatures (1997)
  - Alden Munson, Testimony on Classified Information (1997)

- James Ahearn, Voting as a Participant Sport
- John Podesta, Remarks on Classification of Government Documents (1998)
- National Rifle Association, The Instant Check System (1998)
- City of Concord, California, Panhandling Ordinance (1998)
- City of Rolla, Missouri, Parade Permit Ordinance (1998)
- Bill Morlin, Nazi March Through Coeur d'Alene (1998)
- State of New Jersey, Megan's Law: Community Guide (1998)
- National Education Association, Resolution on English as the Official Language (1998)
- American Civil Liberties Union of South Carolina, Objection to Political Sign Laws (1998)
- Bureau of Alcohol, Tobacco, and Firearms, Implementation of the Brady Handgun Violence Prevention Act (1998)
- Ingrid Becker, Breaking Through the Glass Ceiling (1998)
- U.S. Equal Employment Opportunity, Facts about Pregnancy Discrimination (1998)
- U.S. Equal Employment Opportunity, Facts about Sexual Harassment (1998)
- National Coalition Against Censorship, Statement Opposing a Flag Desecration Amendment (1998)
- Privacy Rights Clearinghouse, Your Social Security Number (1999)
- University of Miami, Rules for Compliance with Buckley Amendments (1999)
- U.S. Equal Employment Opportunity Commission, Press Release on Pay Equity for Women (1999)
- American Civil Liberties Union (ACLU), Creating a National Data Bank (1999)
- U.S. Department of Labor, Facts about Family and Medical Leave Act (1999)
- People for the American Way, Public Funds for Public Schools (1999)

Images
- Sandra Day O'Connor (undated)
- Police Search (1986) in Civil Rights in the United States
- Haitians Detained at Guantanamo Bay (1995)
- Bugging Devices (1995)
- Shannon Faulkner at the Citadel (1995)
- Drug Testing (1996)
- Wiretapping (1996) in Civil Rights
- Drunken Driving Tests (1997)

— In The Constitution and Supreme Court
Documents
- Edwin Messe, Meese's Speech before the American Bar Association (1985)

- John Paul Stevens, *Wallace v. Jaffee* (1985)
- Harry A. Blackmun, *Garcia v. San Antonio Metropolitan Transit Authority* (1985)
- Byron White, *Bowers v. Hardwick* (1986)
- U.S. Congress, Judiciary Committee Report on the Bork Nomination (1987)
- U.S. Congress, The Twenty-Seventh Amendment (1992

Images
- Harry A. Blackmun (circa 1985)
- Thurgood Marshall (circa 1985)
— In Women in America
Documents
- U.S. Supreme Court, *Meritor Savings Bank v. Michelle Vinson* (1986)

About Prisons and Prisoner' Rights
— In Civil Rights in the United States
Documents
- U.S. Department of Justice, Report of Incarceration (1997)
- Barbara Spratt, My Letters to the Warden (1998)
- National Conference on Wrongful Convictions and the Death Penalty, The Wrongly Convicted (1998)
- John Vasconcellos, Closing Statements on Corcoran Prison (1998)
- Custodial Officer's Decalogue (undated)
Images
- Seth Perlman, Maximum-Security Prison (1994)
- Prison Visitation (undated)
- Electrocution (undated)

About Immigration
— In The Immigration Experience
Documents
- U.S. Congress, An Act to Revise and Reform Immigration Laws (1986)
— In Civil Rights in the United States
Documents
- U.S. Congress, Immigration Act (1990)
- Leadership Conference on Civil Rights, Statement on Pending Immigration Reform Statute (1996)
- William Branigin, America's Racial and Ethnic Divides: The Melting Pot Myth (1998)
- State of California, English-Language Education for Immigrant Children (1998)
- Immigration News Briefs, Human Rights Watch Blast INS Detention (1998)

- Immigration and Naturalization Service, Naturalization Requirements (1999)

Images
- Vietnamese Immigrants (1995)
- Mexican Migrant Workers (1997)

About Religion
— In <u>Civil Rights in the United States</u>
Documents
- U.S. Supreme Court, *Wallace v. Jaffee* (1985)
- B'nai B'rith, B'nai B'rith Supports Religious Liberty (1995)
- U.S. Government, Federal Guidelines on Religious Exercise (1997)
- Christian Coalition, Pro-Family Accomplishments of the 105th Congress (1998)
- People for the American Way, The Religious Right and American Public Schools (1998)

Images
- Public School Prayer (1984)
- Religious Display on Public Grounds (1984)

About the Welfare Reform
— In <u>Civil Rights in the United States</u>
Documents
- Leadership Conference on Civil Rights, Statement on Welfare Reform (1997)

Images
- Welfare Rights and Welfare Reform (1995)

About Censorship and Obscenity
— In <u>Civil Rights in the United States</u>
Documents
- Jim Exon, Communications Decency Act Remarks (1995)
- American Library Association, Top Ten Banned Books (1997)
- Morality in Media, Letter-Writing Campaign on Obscenity (1998)
- Associated Press, Federal Appeals Court Allows Huck Finn to Remain on School's Reading List (1998)

Images
- Adult Bookstore and Protestors (1995)
- Robert Mapplethorpe Photos Deemed Obscene (1996)

About Affirmative Action
— In <u>The Constitution and Supreme Court</u>
Documents
- Sandra Day O'Connor, *Adarand Constructors, Inc. v. Pena* (1995)

— In <u>Civil Rights in the United States</u>
Documents
- Presidential Commission, Presidential Report on Affirmative Action (1995)
- Bruce Herschensohn, On Affirmative Action (1998)

About Children's Rights
— In <u>Civil Rights in the United States</u>
Documents
- National Committee for Prevention of Child Abuse, Letter to President Clinton about Children's Civil Rights (1995)
- Children's Defense Fund, Stand for Children (1998)
- Child Advocates, Inc., Fifteen Years of Advocacy (1998)
Images
- Marian Wright Edelman (undated)
- Child Abuse (1996)

About the Right-to-Die Movement
— In <u>Civil Rights in the United States</u>
Documents
- Kirk Johnson, Letter to Attorney General of Michigan (1995) in Civil Rights in the United States
- WGBH, Interview with Dr. Timothy Quill (1996) in Civil Rights in the United States
Images
- Assisted Suicide (1991)
- Jack Kevorkian (1998)

About Abortion
— In <u>Civil Rights in the United States</u>
Documents
- U.S. Congress, Freedom of Access to Clinic Entrances Act (1994)
- Presbyterian Church (USA), Statement of Purpose: Presbyterians Pro-Life (1995)
- Planned Parenthood Federation of America, Fact Sheet on Health Benefits to American Society Since Abortion was Legalized (1997)
- American Civil Liberties Union (ACLU), Policy on Picketing Abortion Clinics (1998)
Images
- Pro-Choice Demonstrations (1989)
- Right-to-Life Demonstrations (undated)
- Two Policemen Guard an Abortion Clinic (1994)
- Randall Terry (1996)

— In <u>The Constitution and Supreme Court</u>
  Documents
  - Sandra Day O'Connor, *Planned Parenthood v. Casey* (1992)

About Gay Rights
— In <u>Civil Rights in the United States</u>
  Documents
  - U.S. Supreme Court, *Bowers v. Hardwick* (1986)
  - U.S. Supreme Court, *Romer v. Evans* (1996)
  Images
  - Gay Rights March (1993)

About Animal Rights
— In <u>Civil Rights in the United States</u>
  Documents
  - U.S. Congress, Federal Laboratory Animal Welfare Act (1985)
  - State of New York, Anti-Cruelty (1993)
  - Animal Defense League, Policy Statement on Animal Research (undated)
  - Gary Francione, Animal Rights: The Future (1996)

About Women
— In <u>Civil Rights in the United States</u>
  Documents
  - Interview with Betty Friedan (1994)
  - U.S. Department of Justice, College Board Revises Test to Improve Chances for Girls to Win Scholarships (1997)

American Indians
— In <u>Civil Rights in the United States</u>
  Documents
  - U.S. Supreme Court, *Lyng v. Northwest Indian Cemetery Protective Association* (1988)
  - U.S. Congress, Civil Liberties Act of 1988
  - U.S. Supreme Court, *Employment Division v. Smith* (1990)
  - U.S. Congress, Religious Freedom Restoration Act of 1993
  - U.S. Department of Justice, Policy of Indian Sovereignty (1995)
  - Bill Clinton, Executive Order on Indian Sacred Sites (1996)

About Asian Americans
— In <u>The Immigrant Experience</u>
  Documents
  - John J. McCloy, Letter from John J. McCloy to Jane B. Kaihatsu (1984)
  - Ronald Reagan, Remarks on Internment of Japanese-American Civilians (1988)

— In <u>The Asian-American Experience</u>
Documents
- • U.S. Congress, Civil Liberties Act of 1988
- • Sara Suleri, Excerpt of *Meatless Days* (1989)
- • Jessica Hagedorn, Excerpt of *Dogeaters* (1990)
- • Garrett Hongo, Kubota (1990)
- • Mary Paik Lee, Excerpt of *Quiet Odyssey: A Pioneer Korean Woman in America* (1990)
- • Len Kath, Pol Pot (1991)
- • Ge Lor, Learning American Farming (1991)
- • Chitra Divakaruni, The Founding of Yuba City (1995)
- • Nguyen Qui-Duc, A Taste of Home (1995)
- • Michael Chang (1996)
- • Christian Langworthy, Mango (1996)
- • Document with Audio Commentary—Mary Sit, Kiyo Morimoto (1996)
Images
- • Portrait of Leroy Chiao (circa 1990)

About Hispanic Americans
— In <u>The Hispanic-American Experience</u>
Documents
- • Norberto James, First Person Singular? (1991)
- • Ernesto Reina, Seven Days (1994)
- • Marcio Veloz Maggiolo, The Path to the Ministry (1995)
Images
- • Eduardo Aparicio, Fragments from Cuban Narratives (1993)

About the Environment
— In <u>Westward Expansion</u>
Documents
- • Donald Worster, Excerpt from *Beyond the Agrarian Myth* (1989)
— In <u>Civil Rights in the United States</u>
Documents
- • People of Color Environmental Leadership Council, Principles of Environmental Justice (1991)
- • Sierra Club, Environmental Bill of Rights (1994)
Images
- • Nuclear Waste Facility (1992)
- • Environmental Rights (1996)